The Handbook of Creative Writing

Second edition

Edited by
Steven Earnshaw

EDINBURGH
University Press

First edition © Edinburgh University Press 2007. Copyright in the individual
contributions retained by the authors.

Second edition © editorial matter and organisation Steven Earnshaw, 2014
© the chapters their several authors, 2014

First published by Edinburgh University Press in 2007.

Edinburgh University Press Ltd
The Tun – Holyrood Road
12 (2f) Jackson's Entry
Edinburgh EH8 8PJ

www.euppublishing.com

Typeset in 10/12pt Adobe Goudy by
Servis Filmsetting Ltd, Stockport Cheshire,
and printed and bound in Great Britain by
CPI Group (UK) Ltd, Croydon CR0 4YY

A CIP record for this book is available from the British Library

ISBN 978 0 7486 8939 2 (paperback)
ISBN 978 0 7486 8977 4 (webready PDF)
ISBN 978 0 7486 8978 1 (epub)

The right of Steven Earnshaw to be identified as Editor of this work has been asserted in
accordance with the Copyright, Designs and Patents Act 1988, and the Copyright and
Related Rights Regulations 2003 (SI No. 2498).

The Handbook of Creative Writing

Contents

Acknowledgements

I would like to thank Sean O'Brien, Jane Rogers and Mike Harris for their help in constructing the sections on poetry, prose and script. Lauri Ramey has been an invaluable bridge across the Atlantic throughout, answering my queries on American matters. I would also like to thank the contributors, many of whom I know only through the marvellous if precarious medium of email. I have found generosity everywhere, and it has made the book a pleasure to edit. Finally, I would like to thank Jackie Jones at EUP, whose idea this book was.

Preface to Second Edition

After *The Handbook* was first published I presumed my role in it, other than a brief flurry of publicity at the start, was ended, and I was content with the idea that nothing more could be added to improve the book, because advice on how to write well was good for a very long time, if not forever. However, in the intervening period there have been significant changes in the world of publishing and social media which affect the world of the writer, and at least two new genres have been spotted. In addition, some people quite rightly felt that there were gaps in the original book. This Second Edition has therefore taken stock of a new world and new genres, and remedied previous omissions.

The Craft section has been augmented with chapters on 'Song Lyrics', 'Creative–Critical Hybrids', 'Flash Fiction' and 'Collaboration'. Pat Pattison's 'Song Lyrics and Poetry' takes the reader through a rigorous critique of the popular assertion that a 'lyric' is the same entity as a 'poem'. 'Really?' he responds, and takes off from there, pursuing the profound differences in musicality, rhythm, sound versus sight, and density of meaning. Hazel Smith is one of the foremost commentators and exponents of creative–critical hybrid writing, a genre which fuses two types of writing traditionally regarded as distinct, and she explains the theory and practice of such fusion before setting out exercises for the aspiring hybridist to attempt. Tony Williams grapples with another 'new' genre – 'flash fiction' – a genre that is not just 'shorter short stories', but a prose offering which has its own particular demands and outlets. Here is a chance to extend your repertoire, he urges, with the added benefit that it may improve your longer narratives. Timothy Braun elaborates on the role that collaboration has in theatre for the playwright, the kinds of negotiation that such a process demands, and provides guidelines for keeping your voice in an environment where you will always at some point have to hand your work over to others.

The most noticeable sea-change has been the expansion of digital media into social networks and the world of publishing. Two new chapters cover the possibilities and pitfalls: Jane Rowland looks at 'Self-Publishing and the Rise of the Indie Author', and shows just how 'liberating' self-publishing can be for writers; Lou Treleaven illuminates the ways in which you can 'Meet Your Public' through the (careful) embrace of social media, demonstrating how 'a creative use of social networking can turn the general public into your public'. These chapters are, of course, complementary, since they both register the idea that modern writers are expected to closely engage in the promotion of themselves and their writing. I suggest reading these alongside Alison Baverstock's updated chapter on 'How to Present Yourself as a Writer', a clear, thorough and direct guide to the kind of self-awareness and professionalism writers are best advised to adopt when dealing with the contemporary publishing world. James Sheard's 'Writing for the Web', there in the First Edition, has been updated to take into account those aspects of writing which belong specifically to the virtual ether. The legal side of author's rights and publishing regulations is brought up to the present in the chapter on 'Copyright' (Shay Humphrey, with Lee Penhaligan), including predictions of what may happen in the future.

While the business end of writing may be the most noticeable aspect of the author's life to have been affected, students of writing will be receiving tuition which likewise makes the most of the new technology, and the first chapter, 'Theories of Creativity and Creative Writing Pedagogy' (Anna Leahy, Mary Cantrell and Mary Swander), updated for this edition, incorporates fresh observations in this area, as well as reflecting on some of the other changes already noted.

In the final chapter, 'Making a Living as a Writer', Livi Michael observes that writers are increasingly pulled in opposing directions, one where there is greater opportunity for getting the writing out there, the other a greater difficulty in making a living solely out of writing. At the heart of Livi's chapter – and the book as a whole – is the belief that good writing in all its manifestations matters, and that being a writer – being dedicated to writing – matters. This continues to be the spirit of *The Handbook*.

Introduction

Steven Earnshaw

As a handbook this guide is intended not just to help and inform, but also to provoke and inspire. The contributors are professionals within their fields of expertise and apart from being asked to cover the necessary topic have been free to deal with their subject how they see fit – there has been no attempt to produce regulation and uniform chapters. The book is aimed primarily at the student embarking on a creative writing programme in Higher Education, with many of the writers here also teaching on creative writing MAs or MFAs, and to that end many of the chapters reflect the different teaching styles on offer. This book, therefore, is also intended for tutors. The aim throughout has been to have within the pages of a single book all that you might need as a writer or tutor to further your writing and teaching, and to further your writing career. It explores a number of different contexts within which the student-writer and teacher of creative writing work: literary tradition and genre, the postgraduate degree, the academy, literary culture, literary theory, the world of publishing and production, the world of being a writer and writing.

How to read this book

I don't for a second imagine that anybody will read this book from cover to cover; it is not that type of book. Rather, it is the virtue of a handbook that readers can jump immediately to what they need to know: I want to write a novel (Rogers); teach creative writing in the community (Sargent); introduce literary theory into my workshops (Ramey); publish poetry (Twichell; O'Brien); get an agent (Smith; Friedmann; Brodie), choose a degree (Newman; Vanderslice) and so on. Conversely, if you have no interest in cultural, academic or theoretical contexts you will quickly see that you should avoid Section One, and if you have no interest in knowing how to get your writing out into the 'real' world and make a splash as a writer, you will turn a blind eye to Section Three (although I gather that this is rather unlikely). But if you were, indeed, to be the 'ideal reader' and read the book from one end to the other, you might make a number of surprising connections.

For instance, Brian Kiteley's 'Reading and Writing Historical Fiction' and David Rain's 'Literary Genres' include digressions into different aspects of the history of the novel, and might be read in conjunction with Jane Rogers's 'Introduction to the Novel'. Aaron Kunin's 'New Poetries' is packed full of references to experiments with writing and concepts and takes the reader well beyond the realms of poetry. It could be read alongside

Thalia Field's chapter on 'Experimental Writing', after which there would be the surprise of a different kind of experimental writing to be found in Linda Sargent's 'Writing in the Community'. You certainly might expect to find mention of the experimental French group of writers known as Oulipo in 'New Poetries', but you will also find an Oulipo exercise in the chapter on historical fiction. Both Alan Brown's 'Writing for Children' and Linda Newbery's 'Writing for Teenagers' might open your eyes to ways of thinking about writing which draw on creative processes you might not otherwise encounter, even if you only intend to write for 'grown-ups'. The chapter on 'Writing as "Therapy"' might be a long way down the list of chapters to read if your first interest is 'Form in Poetry', but in Fiona Sampson's piece you will find a section on how text affects audience, spurred on by the poet John Kinsella, and discussing Keats, Kathleen Jamie, Celan, Pound, Eliot, amongst others, along the way. In passing you would note that there are some common reference points: Aristotle's *Poetics* recurs time and again; T. S. Eliot's 'Tradition and the Individual Talent' is surprisingly popular, and William Goldman's dictum, 'get in late, get out early' is commandeered by novel, short story and script.

Also remember that many of the contributors are both writers and teachers. All the pieces have a great enthusiasm. You have only to read Lauri Ramey's piece on 'Creative Writing and Critical Theory' to know that to be involved in her class would treat you to a full-on immersion in both criticism and creativity, alongside the broadest of historical sweeps, and would instil a sense of just how exciting and potent these activities can be for your own writing. And Gareth Creer's plea for the teaching of writing as something that is much, much more than a means of supplementing an income that is always widely variable shows that creative writing teaching, in and out of the academy, can be a necessary part of the writer's *writing* life. You will frequently encounter ideas you will want to introduce into your own practice.

The different approaches offer different models of teaching and reflect the success, or otherwise, of different kinds of writing within contemporary culture. Lee Gutkind's chapter is a replication of teaching 'creative nonfiction' via seminars and workshops, as is E. A. Markham's chapter on the short story. Sean O'Brien's 'Introduction to Poetry' gives practical advice on the use of a workshop, and what should constitute a good one. Some chapters stand as polemic and some as defences for types of writing regarded as 'lesser' in the context of creative writing (for example, Susan Bassnett's chapter on 'Translation' and also James Sheard's 'Writing for the Web'), or little considered ('Writing for Radio' in Mike Harris's chapter, and also in Alan Brodie's 'The Literary Agent: Television, Radio and Theatre'). Sean O'Brien's attack on the dominance of prose over poetry in his essay on 'Verse Drama' has a corollary in Susan Bassnett's note on the 1940s Penguin Classics translations of Homer's *Iliad* and *Odyssey* into prose form rather than a poetic equivalent. O'Brien's chapter highlights verse drama's current near-invisibility and decline and amounts to a virtual 'recovery' of its possibilities and models. Similarly, George Szirtes' chapter champions other poetic art forms that struggle for a good hearing, the long poem and the sequence, and Alan Brodie makes a heartfelt plea for Radio Drama as the purest medium for the scriptwriter. But a book such as this also gives you the opportunity to think about trying out writing you might not normally have considered. Judith Barrington's chapter on 'Writing the Memoir' begins by dispelling the belief that it is a form available only to 'the famous'. Any prose writer would benefit from this chapter as it works through the shaping of narrative. I hope that one of the joys of this book is that, in addition to its primary functions, it has chapters that will reward those curious about all aspects of literary culture and writing.

The book also includes insights into areas of writing and writing contexts that will hopefully be new or unusual. For instance, a continuing assumption by some is that the activities of literary criticism and creative writing make unhappy bedfellows within the academy, with criticism the established forum for literature and creative writing an unwelcome johnny-come-lately. Lauri Ramey's chapter here not only demonstrates the shared heritage for both but the ways in which critical studies from Longinus onwards can be used to engage with creativity, the role of the writer and writing. Similarly, thinking about 'genre' may not immediately spring to mind as a way in to creativity, but its importance is here shown in David Rain's chapter as another feature of contemporary literary culture which has its roots in the Classical age and which can inform the practice of writing and our reflection upon it. But genre isn't just about what we are writing, it is about how we are reading and what we are expecting when we do pick up a poem or novel, or sit down to watch a film or play. And, with the history of the novel as a model, Rain shows how new genres and new literature come into being. Genre is one of the broadest contexts within which a writer can work, yet the student writer is rarely called upon to explore it unless perhaps asked to define the difference between 'literary' and 'genre' fiction (also discussed in Rain's chapter; and you will find an exercise to understand genre in Mike Harris's 'Introduction to Scriptwriting' and discussion of 'genre' in 'Science Fiction and Fantasy' by Crawford Kilian and 'Writing Crime Fiction' by John Dale). Exploration of genre inevitably takes us into questions of originality and levels of artistic ambition (also addressed by Lauri Ramey in the context of literary criticism, and in my chapter on 'The Role of the Artist'), what kind of writing 'enables' others to write, and what can only be admired as one-off performances. Thus Rain asserts: 'Genre is the most important decision a writer makes'. It is a rare starting point for creative writing, but a fruitful one.

As Swander, Leahy and Cantrell point out in their chapter on 'Theories of Creativity and Creative Writing Pedagogy', creative writing within the academy has had a rather difficult time compared to other arts. Artists and composers predated the arrival of writers into academe, where it was not until the 1920s that writing started to lay down roots at the University of Iowa, the institution usually credited with being the first university to embrace creative writing. Elsewhere in the chapter the authors note that the writing programme there has to good effect been underpinned by the Romantic myth that writers are born, not created in the workshop, and that the academy can at best provide an environment for talent to develop. Nevertheless, the danger of this approach for the academy is clear: 'To state openly and confidently that creative writing cannot be taught, however, puts the field at risk as a serious *academic* pursuit'. Its staple method of teaching, the workshop, is 'non-traditional', and, it is often argued, creative writing cannot be assessed and evaluated in the same manner as other academic subjects. At the same time as creative writing is firmly within the academy in the US, the UK and elsewhere, some of these issues remain (see Jenny Newman's essay on 'Evaluation and Assessment'). The tension is not always generated by the literary critics either: it is not unusual for writers themselves to have mixed feelings about their place within the academy, especially those who have not gone through a creative writing programme. The growth of creative writing within the academy, its emphasis on process rather than product through the workshop event and its ways of assessment, has meant that it has developed what Swander, Leahy and Cantrell here identify as a 'signature pedagogy': a way of teaching, learning and assessment specific to creative writing. As Paul Dawson points out, creative writing programmes cannot just claim to be about the passing down of craft, since they 'exist in an intellectual environment of interdisciplinarity, critical self-reflection and oppositional politics on the one hand, and in an institutional envi-ronment of learning outcomes, transferable skills and competitive research funding on the other' ('The Future of Creative Writing'). In America, creative writing has often been seen in opposition to theory, whereas in Australia and the UK it emerged in the last two decades alongside theory to challenge what was regarded as a literary studies *status quo*. Dawson warns that to continue to begin discussions with the opposition between literary theory and creative writing will lead to a stasis. After all, he claims, Creative Writing in the academy is hardly a subject in crisis; instead it flourishes in a 'post-theory' environment. To nail an old problem in relation to creative writing in academia, he states: 'If the question which once dominated discussions of Creative Writing was, "Can or should writing be taught?", it is now, "*What* should we be teach-ing students?"' This book shows just what is being taught, and also, I think, what might be taught.

The one thing needful: reading

What may come as a surprise to some is that time and again authors in this book recom-mend reading first and foremost. I remember a student presenting to the class a scene from a novel he was working on which concerned two children on holiday. One of the chil-dren becomes trapped as the sea is coming in while the other looks on helplessly, and the description of the drowning was cool and unnerving, capped by a very affecting finale. The writer later told me that some of his fellow students would ask him how he had achieved such an accomplished piece of writing, such an effect. This puzzled (and annoyed) him: you simply read how others did it and moved on from there. How else would you go about it? It was obvious.

The fact that this was something of a revelation to other students no doubt gives some credence to the charge from tutors that students don't read enough, and John Milne in 'How to be a Writer' couldn't state it more clearly: 'To write you need to read'. Tutors will also say that the best readers make the best writers. This book is full of references to other works of literature, film, and criticism, and thus gives a generous and exciting reading list. It is not uncommon for courses to begin by asking each student to suggest one or two books that everybody might read, and in that way create a common fund of reading which is specific to that group. E. A. Markham's chapter here begins by setting out what he expects the student to read if he or she is to grasp the complexities of the short story form and gain an understanding of its history; Brighde Mullins' piece on writing for theatre advises: 'It is important that you are able to locate the sources of your connection to the theatre, and to read and see as many plays as you can before you start writing for the stage'; and Susan Hubbard writes 'There's no better way to learn to write humour than to read it'. John Milne gives a host of other reasons why reading will help you as a writer, and Mary Mount puts it just as clearly from the editor's point of view: '*Do* read, read, read'. Being a better writer is also about becoming a better reader, as John Dale says: 'Reading good fiction is not passive like watching bad TV, it requires engagement, concentration to enter the fictional world'.

Writing and re-writing

Authors have also been generous in giving away their exercises. In his essay on 'Form' in poetry, W. N. Herbert remarks: 'In the same way as a musician or dancer must repeat an action enough times for the neural pathways to be established, for the body to learn what is required of it, so too rhythmic awareness needs time to accommodate itself to verbal dexterity'. The same could be said of writing in general – the necessity to keep on writing is rather like exercises in other art forms. I had one tutor who used to start each workshop with a writing task as a means of 'warming up'. Although I am used to this when playing a musical instrument, it never occurred to me that you would do the same for writing, since, no doubt like many others on the course, I always thought that writing 'just happened' – more or less – if you wanted it to happen. You will see throughout this book exercises for you to try out, for easing into writing, or as a means of getting out of a writing rut. The poet Ian Duhig once gave a Masterclass at which he read a number of poems that had started out as exercises. He noted that other poets were often quite sniffy about such pieces, but couldn't see how the objection could be sustained when it produced such results: hang on to your exercises.

I have already intimated that there may be a belief that writing just 'happens', that writers are simply inspired one way or another and that's the end of it. Such a view does have the tendency to elide the graft that is everywhere evident and necessary. Bonnie O'Neill in her chapter on 'Writing for Film' declares: 'Re-write, re-write, re-write', and E. A. Markham *begins* with revision. Any practising writer will tell you that re-writing or redrafting is the hardest thing. After all, inspiration is easy: you just have to be there. John Dale serves up the following advice: 'Thomas Mann said that a writer is somebody for whom writing is more difficult than it is for other people. And it's true. Good writing is hard work and looks easy. It has energy yet never appears rushed'. So just as you will be urged to read, you will be urged to re-write, to revise, to redraft. Be your 'inner editor', as Crawford Kilian puts it.

The Masters experience

There's nothing quite like taking a creative-writing postgraduate degree, nor, for that matter, teaching on one. Here is an absolute community of writers whose whole activity is to talk about writing, share writing, and see how it might be improved. Although degrees may be structured differently from country to country, the sense of excitement, ambition and challenge is familiar across countries and continents (for comparisons of degree structures see Jenny Newman's chapter [UK] and Stephanie Vanderslice's [US], and look at Graeme Harper's, which compares different formats for creative-writing higher degrees in the US, UK, Australia and Canada). A number of the chapters touch on the tension that creative writing within the academy creates and undergoes, including modules where creative-writing students are expected to engage with academic, theoretical and critical work (Lauri Ramey; Scott McCracken). As McCracken notes: 'Ideas such as the "death of the author", which can seem fresh and exciting in a third year undergraduate seminar on a traditional English degree, can appear absurd in a room full of struggling novelists; and their derision is hardly likely to be contradicted by a creative writing tutor who writes to live'. Nevertheless, the experience of doing a creative-writing Masters is something quite unique, as Sean O'Brien states in his 'Introduction to Poetry': 'The poet studying on a Writing course should feel free – no, should feel obliged – to be imaginatively and intellectually gluttonous. You may never have a better opportunity. Enjoy it!' The input from tutors and other writers is a constant incentive to read more and to improve your writing. It is very difficult to discover the same week-by-week intensity and sense of belonging to the writing community outside of this environment, and it can take some students a while to adjust to the essentially 'lonely' occupation that writing is once the class has been left behind, although it is not unusual for a group to continue to meet after formal sessions have ended. I have even seen one group which rotated the 'role of tutor' so that it replicated the workshop situation the students had been used to. As Jenny Newman points out, you should make the most of all the feedback that you get while it is there. It is not so easy to come by once the degree is over.

The writer's life

For most students (not all), one of the reasons for taking a creative-writing Masters is that it is a route to publication. Not only will you be improving your writing and be immersed in a hot-bed of intellectual endeavour, you will expect to see a procession of famous writers, top agents and classy publishers throw themselves at your feet. Undoubtedly MA/MFA programmes are important in giving the opportunities for student-writers to come into contact with the 'business end' of writing. One of the advantages of such contacts is that the world of publishing and production and agenting is seen to consist of people who have as much interest in providing good literature as you have. Agents often get a bad press, somehow stuck in the middle between publishers and writers, harder to get than a publisher if you're not already known and simply creaming off unearned percentages of those who probably don't need an agent. The chapters on publishers and agents in this book should deliver quite a different message, with both practical advice and a wider sense of the contexts within which they are working.

Equally, if you are looking at what life as a writer might be, you will no doubt be drawn to John Milne's 'How to be a Writer', Livi Michael's 'Making a Living as a Writer' and Tom Shapcott's chapter on 'Literary Life: Prizes, Anthologies, Festivals, Reviewing, Grants'. In addition, you should look at Gareth Creer's 'The Writer as Teacher', which shows the benefits of expanding your repertoire as writer and teacher, and the mutually beneficial rewards of both activities. The latter piece also takes in life as a student of creative writing, and in Sean O'Brien's 'Introduction to Poetry' you will find advice on the pressures of combining a commitment to writing with life elsewhere. The word here is 'vocation', and although aimed specifically at poets it could be taken as referring to all those serious about writing. Mary Mount's 'The World of Publishing' will give you insights into how the world looks like from that end of fiction, and Alison Baverstock's 'How to Get Published' will give you a measure of how professional you need to be beyond the writing (as will Livi Michael's chapter). Students often believe that things will take care of themselves based on the merit of their writing, but as all these pieces will indicate, this is very far from the truth, even for those writers who gain a relatively easy path to publishing. Writers require robustness and a thick skin. Mary Mount warns: '*Don't* expect fame and money! There are easier and quicker ways to get rich and famous', and Sean O'Brien suggests that anyone wanting to be a poet who expects to make money is either a fool or a charlatan. 'Don't despair!' is thus another theme running through the book. Writing is hard work, and sometimes the writing has to be its own reward: 'Most published writers have experienced the torturous path that got us to where we wanted to be . . . And what probably kept us motivated throughout this was our sense of ourselves as writers' (Alison Baverstock); or John Dale: 'Above all, a writer needs persistence'. But of course some writers have 'excess' energy, a desire to be active in the culture of writing and publication beyond their own immediate writing: for these I would suggest taking a look at Rebecca Wolff's chapter 'How to Start a Literary Magazine' (a chapter which includes a fair amount of advice on being an editor, and through which I winced in agreement).

National differences

The contributors to this book come from the UK, America, Canada and Australia, and naturally are drawn to examples from the cultures they are more familiar with, although when it comes to literary references these show an international understanding. On a couple of occasions it was felt that the differences warranted separate chapters: the systems of evaluation (if not necessarily delivery) of creative-writing Masters in the UK and America are quite different, and publishing poetry in the UK and publishing in the US are treated separately. There are also differences in relation to the creative-writing PhD, but these are dealt with specifically in Graeme Harper's essay on that topic, and the reader will also find useful comments on Masters and Doctoral degrees across all four countries in Paul Dawson's chapter. The chapter on 'Copyright' takes into account copyright law in all four countries mentioned. Stephen V. Duncan's chapter on 'Writing for Television' is geared towards the American system, but most of the points made apply equally to such writing elsewhere, and any writer would always be advised to research the policies of television companies and agents in their own country before attempting approaches, even if not specifically covered in this part. The differences between the UK and US are dealt with in John Milne's following piece, written as a complement to Duncan's. Fiona Sampson's chapter on 'Writing as "Therapy"' and Linda Sargent's on 'Writing in the Community' are drawn very much from local experience, as you might expect, but have general application, both theoretically and practically.

Enjoy the book

These chapters open up worlds of writing and worlds of imagination, ways of thinking about form, structure, plot, language, character, genre, creativity, reading, teaching, audience . . . and being a writer. I hope you enjoy it.

Steven Earnshaw

Section One

Writing: Theories and Contexts

1

Theories of Creativity and Creative Writing Pedagogy

Anna Leahy, Mary Cantrell and Mary Swander

Creative writing as a distinct academic field – one with dedicated courses and programmes, with professors whose scholarship is entirely or primarily original creative work, and with professional journals and books devoted to reflections upon the field – is relatively new but has been rapidly expanding in the US, the UK, and elsewhere. As such, we are just beginning to amass articulated theories about the creative process and how we might best teach creative writing as an academic discipline. Joseph Moxley (1989), Wendy Bishop and Hans Ostrom (1994), and D. G. Meyers (1996) documented the emergence of creative writing as an academic pursuit in the US. To grasp the current state of the field, it is important to consider its overall and recent history, the dominant approaches to creativity and to creative writing pedagogy, and the application of theories and approaches to classrooms.

The history of creative writing as an academic pursuit

Today, in virtually every college and university across the US, students busily workshop, as we say, each other's poems and short stories. These students roam the hallways with stacks of copied poems, stories, and essays or with files looming on their laptops or devices. They enter their creative writing classrooms, pull out or up their marginal notes, and prepare to discuss and offer formative criticism of each other's work. Creative writing is now an established part of the curriculum in higher education, and most English departments have a poet, fiction writer, creative nonfiction writer, or playwright on their rosters. According to Gradschools.com, a comprehensive site on graduate programmes worldwide, the UK, Australia, Ireland, and Canada all have universities offering university and graduate programmes leading to degrees with an emphasis in creative writing. Korea, Mexico, Spain, Norway, and the Philippines also support such programmes. Even high school students in both the US and the UK are often offered the opportunity for creative writing as part of their English studies.

Yet the inclusion of creative writing in academe in the US is a relatively recent phenomenon. As late as 1965, few four-year colleges had resident writers, much less an emphasis in creative writing. While it had become more common for writers to accept university teaching positions, most writers supported their early efforts as they always had: as cabdrivers and carpenters, as postmasters (William Faulkner), journalists (Willa Cather), librarians

(Marianne Moore), insurance executives (Wallace Stevens), and doctors (William Carlos Williams). Visual artists and composers had long before found a home in academe, but writers were still viewed with suspicion. Writing was a craft that one was supposed to pick up by osmosis through a study of literature. If a young writer wanted a mentor, he or she could move to either coast or, better yet, to Paris, buy a cigarette holder and beret, hang out in the coffeehouses and bars, and hope for the best.

The University of Iowa changed the literary landscape in the US. During the 1920s, along the banks of the Iowa River where the summer heat and humidity create a natural greenhouse for the surrounding agricultural fields of corn and beans, the fine arts flourished. When F. Scott Fitzgerald and Zelda were dancing and drinking their way through Europe, when Gertrude Stein and Alice B. Toklas were entertaining Pablo Picasso and Ernest Hemingway with marijuana-laced brownies in Paris, when Ezra Pound was immersing himself in the study of Japanese and Chinese poetry and Fascist ideology in Italy, the University of Iowa fostered young artists in a state known for its conservative, rural values.

Painting, sculpture, theatre, dance, and imaginative writing prospered in Iowa City during the roaring twenties. Then, just as a decade of severe economic depression hit the world, Iowa's creative writing programme began to gain in status and prestige. In 1931, Mary Hoover Roberts's collection of poetry, *Paisley Shawl,* was the first creative writing master's thesis approved by the university. Other theses soon followed by such writers as Wallace Stegner and Paul Engle. Engle's thesis, *Worn Earth,* the 1932 winner of the Yale Younger Poets Award, became the first poetry thesis at the University of Iowa to be published (Wilbers 1980: 39). Norman Foerster, director of the School of Letters, pushed forward with the creative writing programme throughout the 1930s. But when Engle joined the faculty in 1937, he jump-started the Iowa Writers Workshop and became its official director in 1943. He laid the foundation for an institution that would make its mark on the worldwide writing community.

Engle, a hard-driving, egocentric genius, possessed the early vision of both the Writers Workshop and the International Writing Program. He foresaw first-rate programmes where young writers could come to receive criticism of their work. A native Iowan who had studied in England on a Rhodes Scholarship and travelled widely throughout Europe, Engle was dissatisfied with merely a regional approach. He defined his ambition in a 1963 letter to his university president as a desire 'to run the future of American literature, and a great deal of European and Asian, through Iowa City' (Wilbers 1980: 85–6).

During his twenty-four years as director, Engle took a group of fewer than a dozen students and transformed it into a high-profile programme of 250 graduate students at its peak in 1965 (Wilbers 1980: 83). More importantly, he made decisions about creative writing that still define the academic field. For instance, he divided the Workshop into genres – poetry and fiction – to make classes easier to teach, took a personal interest in each student, and functioned as both mentor and godfather. In an essay entitled 'A Miranda's World' in Robert Dana's *A Community of Writers: Paul Engle and the Iowa Writers' Workshop* (1999), Donald Justice describes how Engle picked his wife and himself up from the Iowa City bus station on a cold January day, found them an apartment, and then gave the young poet one of his own wool suits to see him through the bitter winter.

Throughout the years, Engle brought to campus the hottest literary names of the time including Dylan Thomas, W. H. Auden, and Robert Frost. Engle then went on to found the International Writing Program where he poured this same kind of energy into spreading his literary enthusiasm around the globe. Engle's model of rigorous, genre-based workshops, close-knit communities formed around mentors, and highly respected visiting writers became the standard in the field.

The Iowa Writers Workshop MFA graduates fanned out across the US, and many entered the ranks of academe. English departments, experiencing dwindling numbers of majors, began to open up their doors to creative writers whose classes quickly filled. The black berets and cigarette holders of a previous era were traded in for the tweed jackets and pipes of faculty life. The turbulent late 1960s and early 1970s saw a growth spurt for creative writers in academe, as students not only demanded the end of the Vietnam War and greater civil rights, but more seemingly relevant course work.

Iowa Workshop graduates, in turn, set up their own writing programmes at other universities and produced their own graduate students, who once again set up more programmes. In the UK, creative writing in academe began to take hold as well. In 1969, the University of Lancaster was the first to offer an MA in creative writing. Even when the US academic job market inevitably tightened, academically trained writers found their way into teaching in community colleges in high schools, in state-run writers-in-the-schools programmes, in the prisons, and in youth shelters, retirement homes, elder hostels, and other short, focused noncredit workshops and conferences.

From the fall of 1996 to 2001, according to Andrea Quarracino's report in the *AWP Job List* (2005), the number of tenure-track academic job openings listed with the Association of Writers and Writing Programs (AWP) ranged from forty-six to seventy-two but later jumped to more than 100 twice, in 2002 and 2004. In 2013, AWP listed more than 800 creative writing programmes or concentrations. The literary community at large has grown to the point that it touches almost every city in the States. By 2005 in the UK, creative writing had become the fastest growing and most popular field in higher education, with nearly every college and university offering creative writing courses at the undergraduate and graduate levels (Beck 2005).

With this growth, 50 PhD programmes in creative writing emerged by 2013. New kinds of MFA programmes surfaced. In 1976, Goddard College in Plainfield, Vermont, was one of the first institutions to offer a high-profile but low-residency graduate MFA programme in creative writing. Students and faculty came together for two intense, on-campus weeks twice a year, then conducted their courses through one-on-one correspondence. Students and faculty could then retain their existing jobs while taking part in the programme. There was no need for relocation nor for financial aid in the form of teaching assistantships. Since the early 1970s, low-residency programmes in the US now number more than 50, according to AWP, and exist in the UK as well.

With the turn of the twenty-first century came specialisation within MFA creative writing programmes. In 2004, Seattle Pacific University launched an MFA programme highlighting writing about spirituality. The programme's website describes its mission:

> The low-residency MFA at SPU is a creative writing program for apprentice writers – both Christians and those of other traditions – who not only want to pursue excellence in the craft of writing but also place their work within the larger context of the Judeo–Christian tradition of faith.

Both Chatham University and Iowa State University began to offer MFA degrees that focus on particular topics. Chatham's MFA emphasises place-based writing and social justice and allows students to work across genres. Iowa State's creative writing programme has defined its mission this way:

> Under the broad rubric of 'environment', our MFA program in Creative Writing and the Environment would offer an original and intensive opportunity for gifted students of nonfiction, fiction, poetry, and drama to document, meditate on, celebrate, and mourn the reciprocal transformation of humanity and our world/s. (Iowa State University 2005: 2)

By 2013, the University of Alaska Anchorage now had a low residency program with an option of a special emphasis on writing about the relationships between people and place, landscape, nature, science and the arts, no matter where these relationships exist or how they are expressed. And the MFA Program in Utah had a modular approach with emphasis in Environmental Humanities, History of the American West, and Book Arts. Likewise, in the UK, students can now earn MAs, MPhils, and PhDs with an emphasis in creative writing in the traditional categories of poetry, fiction, and playwriting but can also link creative writing with science, critical theory, journalism, or the teaching of creative writing (Beck 2005).

As writing programmes mature and develop, the field is also re-thinking its pedagogy. Until around 1990, most creative writing faculty followed the Engle teaching model without much reflection. A workshop teacher led small groups – *The AWP Directors' Handbook* (2003: 5) recommends no more than fifteen, with twelve as ideal, but recognises that most workshop groups now are between eleven and twenty – through peer oral critiques of completed poems, stories, chapters of novels, or plays. In the Engle model, the criticism was meant to be tough and could save the writer years of individual trial and error. But the criticism could also become personality-driven or downright nasty. Little emphasis was placed on structure, work in process, or revision.

Currently, many workshop faculty across the US and UK have adapted Engle's model, are experimenting with creating new approaches to teaching creative writing, and are distinguishing methods used in graduate courses from those used in undergraduate courses. Some teach from assignments on technique and structure, whereas others initiate a process of constant revision. Some lecture to huge rooms of students on technique, then break into smaller workshops. Others emphasise working exclusively in even smaller groups of four or five students.

Texts such as *Power and Identity in the Creative Writing Classroom* articulate current practices and suggest new possibilities, in this case offering

> various ways to configure authority: as the expertise of the teacher or of the students, as agency or action for accomplishing things, as a set of mutually beneficial or agreed-upon guidelines for fostering success, as a set of evaluation criteria, as seemingly inherent forces in writing and teaching, and even as authorship itself. (Leahy 2005: i)

In 2004 in the UK, *New Writing: the International Journal for the Practice and Theory of Creative Writing* was launched under the editorship of Graeme Harper. This journal, published by Multilingual Matters, includes peer-reviewed pedagogy articles as well as shorter creative work. *Can It Really Be Taught?: Resisting Lore in Creative Writing Pedagogy* (Ritter and Vanderslice 2007) is a collection asserting that creative writing has too long been a separatist pedagogy based on undocumented and uncritical lore. The editors and authors examine this lore and argue for reframing the discipline and most importantly its pedagogy in relation to intellect rather than ego. Some of these same faculty members on both continents who have helped to restructure writing workshops have also made an effort to provide their own students with pedagogical training. More recent books about creative writing pedagogy include *Teaching Creative Writing* (Beck 2012) and *Does the Writing Workshop Still Work?* (Donnelly 2010). In addition, *The Program Era* (McGurl 2011) analyses the effects that the rise of creative writing in the academy has had on literary fiction published in the US. Many MFA programmes, such as those at Cardiff University, Antioch University of Los Angeles, and Indiana University, offer internships, courses, or postgraduate certificates in Teaching Creative Writing.

Writing workshops abroad, too, are now commonplace. A budding writer can go off for a summer to study creative writing in a number of international cities including Dublin, Paris, and Prague. The University of Iowa's Nonfiction Writing Program offers its writers study-abroad workshops in a different location every year; recent destinations have included the Philippines, Greece, and Cuba. In 2005, Iowa State University set up the first international writers-in-the-schools programme – a form of service learning – in Trinidad and Tobago, where Iowa State graduate students taught creative writing in K-12 schools in a Caribbean country with virtually no creative writing curriculum. Now that creative writing has established itself as an academic pursuit, its programmes are expanding, especially as academic options expand more generally.

Approaches to creativity and pedagogy

The Iowa Writers' Workshop declares on its website: 'Though we agree in part with the popular insistence that writing cannot be taught, we exist and proceed on the assumption that talent can be developed, and we see our possibilities and limitations as a school in that light'. The 'model for contemporary writing programs', by its own accounts, bases itself in part upon the most widely influential theory underpinning creativity and creative writing: the Romantic myth. The premises of this approach to creativity include that talent is inherent and essential, that creative writing is largely or even solely an individual pursuit, and that inspiration not education drives creativity. For the Iowa Writers' Workshop, that means, 'the fact that the Workshop can claim as alumni nationally and internationally prominent poets, novelists, and short story writers is, we believe, more the result of what they brought here than of what they gained from us'. The Romantic myth is a positive influence on creative writing in a variety of ways. This approach values the very act of creation that is difficult for writers themselves to articulate and values the relative isolation that, even in academe, seems necessary to write. In addition, it links writing with concepts of beauty and originality.

To state openly and confidently that creative writing cannot be taught, however, puts the field at risk as a serious *academic* pursuit. If creative writing cannot be taught, then it might also follow that student work cannot be evaluated and programmes cannot be assessed; creative writing does not, then, fit easily into academic contexts.

Brent Royster in 'Inspiration, creativity, and crisis: the Romantic myth of the writer meets the postmodern classroom' (2005) points to many aspects of the Romantic myth as problematic for the field. He demonstrates the dominance of Romantic ideology in popular culture as well as in the field's own venues such as the *AWP Writer's Chronicle* and *Poets & Writers*. Royster turns to the work of Csikszentmihalyi:

> Csikszentmihalyi's model, simply put, refutes the idea that solely the individual generates a creative work. On the contrary, though his dynamic model of creativity still illustrates the individual's role in the creative process, equal agency is distributed among the social and cultural systems influencing that individual. (2005: 32)

What feels like inspiration to the isolated writer can be articulated instead as a dynamic set of forces coming together:

> Rather than claiming that this inspiration came from somewhere beyond the writer, it seems more apt to suggest that the mind of the artist has reached an opportune moment in which rhythms, sounds, and connotations seem to arise unbidden from memory. (Royster 2005: 34)

This approach allows the writer to define him- or herself as an active participant in a larger, dynamic process. This view of creativity values both individual writer and culture or community and supports the concept of the multi-vocal workshop-based classroom.

The University of Cardiff offers a graduate degree in the 'Teaching and Practice of Creative Writing', according to its website, thereby claiming that creative writing can be taught and that the combination of creativity and pedagogy is an important emerging area: 'With increased interest in the relevance of creativity to current educational practices, this degree will place students advantageously for many types of teaching opportunities'. Programmes like this one and the graduate programme at Antioch University of Los Angeles reconfigure the field to include teaching. As a whole, the tension between the Romantic myth and various responses to it seems productive, allowing for a variety of approaches and debates that recognise the seriousness and rigor of the pursuit and the field's distinct pedagogical theories and practices.

Those who teach writing are very often situated in academe just down the hall from literary scholars, and most writing instructors would agree that good writers read a lot and that understanding written texts offers models, tools, and ideas for one's own writing. Elaine Scarry argues that beauty begets itself, that to read a beautiful sonnet urges one to reproduce that beauty, and that 'this willingness continually to revise one's own location in order to place oneself in the path of beauty is the basic impulse underlying education' (Scarry 1999: 7). Neurologist Alice Flaherty asserts, 'writer's block is not an inevitable response to masterpieces. They can inspire' (2004: 106). Indeed, creative writers can use literature and literary theory to help them understand and respond to the tradition (see Lauri Ramey's chapter, 'Creative Writing and Critical Theory', in this section). Madison Smartt Bell implies that grasping form through reading is foundational for writers: 'The reader who wants to write as well has got to go beyond the intuitive grasp of form to the deliberate construction of form' (1997: 22). In other words, teaching writing depends upon the study of existing texts in order that students comprehend how to construct texts of their own. Kim Addonizio and Dorianne Laux (1997: 105) offer a similar stance for poets:

> Poets need to tune their ears as finely as musicians; that's why reading poems aloud is a good idea . . . You need not be familiar with meter to gain an appreciation for the rhythms of writers' lines, and to begin to work with this principle yourself.

Moreover, Addonizio and Laux put the necessity of studying literature bluntly: 'To write without any awareness of a tradition you are trying to become part of would be self-defeating' (1997: 13). Reading literature and understanding it is part of being a writer.

Our other colleagues down the hall, at least in the US, are compositionists, who have been variously at odds with and in league with creative writers. Composition is often perceived as the department's curricular service to the university and creative writing is often perceived as the frivolous pursuit of eccentrics. Many creative writing teachers in the US today have drawn from graduate-school training in teaching composition and from composition theorists. Wendy Bishop is the lead example of a theorist who straddled the fence between composition and creative writing, who attempted to bring the theories underpinning the two disciplines together, and who brought not only composition approaches to creative writing but also vice versa. One of the important arguments that Bishop (2003: xi) and other compositionists have made to counter the assertion that writing is less rigorous than literary study is that writing courses have content and that writing is 'important *work*'. Bishop (2003: 234) argues that students 'should approach composition classes and creative writing classes in pretty similar ways. Overall, both types of classrooms need to encourage *and reward* risk taking and experimentation as you learn to conform to and break genre conventions'. Some argue the possibility that composition and creative writing are versions of the same field, while others argue that despite commonalities, discipline distinctions must be respected.

Cognitive science and creative writing share some history, in that both fields made great gains as academic pursuits only in the last half-century. Linguists like George Lakoff have been studying metaphor, cognition, and the arts for decades. Bell (1997), in the first section of *Narrative Design* entitled 'Unconscious mind', discusses the cognitive processes of creative writers, though he does not use terminology or specific theories of cognitive science. Likewise, Addonizio and Laux claim: 'We continually make comparisons and connections, often without realizing that we are doing so, so comfortable are we with seeing in this way' (1997: 94). Flaherty also discusses the cognitive process of creativity, in which we are able to make new, unexpected connections. These comparisons and connections that become images and metaphors in our poems are results of cognition and are of primary concern to Lakoff and others.

Existing theories of cognition underpin current pedagogical practices such as the workshop-based classroom and the battle against cliché as well as how the theories might improve our teaching. John T. Bruer notes:

> Instruction based on cognitive theory envisions learning as an active, strategic process . . . It recognizes that learning is guided by the learners' introspective awareness and control of their mental processes. It emphasizes that learning is facilitated by social, collaborative settings that value self-directed student dialogue. (1999: 681)

The workshop-based creative writing classroom – a nontraditional academic approach – presents writing as this sort of active, strategic process: all students must actively engage, student-writers become increasingly aware of how their own and others' decision-making affects written work, and the writing process is situated within an interactive, dynamic classroom where students share informed criticism. We are using a pedagogy that is supported by findings in cognitive science.

Studies show, too, that students' embedded knowledge structures and prevalent misconceptions are resistant to traditional instruction. As Bruer (1999: 682) states: 'The result is that students encode, or learn, schemata that are very different from those which teachers are attempting to impart'. To apply this problem to creative writing, we might consider, for instance, how schemata of narrative are embedded in our students' brains through interaction with television and video games. Or, we might consider students' relative unfamiliarity with poetry, or their deeply embedded schemata of poetry based on nursery rhymes, as an opportunity to build new schemata or build upon existing schemata of language's rhythm.

Cognitive science, too, offers ways to categorise learning and memory. Henry L. Roediger III and Lyn M. Goff offer an overview: '*Procedural memory* refers to the knowledge of how to do things such as walking, talking, riding a bicycle, tying shoelaces. Often the knowledge represented is difficult to verbalize, and the procedures are often acquired slowly and only after much practice' (1999: 250). Procedural memory is a way to understand learning in creative writing classrooms as slowly accumulated knowledge deeply internalised through practice that emerges as if known all along. Flaherty (2004: 242) offers a similar take: 'on its own the sensation of inspiration is not enough . . . Perhaps the feeling of inspiration is merely a pleasure by which your brain lures you into working harder'. If we think of inspiration as a cognitive event, how can creative writing courses best create the conditions for it and foster the work of writing?

With its workshop model, creative writing is a field with what Lee Shulman has termed, though he used professions like law and medicine as examples, 'signature pedagogies', which are distinct and commonly recognizable

> types of teaching that organize the fundamental ways in which future practitioners are edu-cated in their new professions. In these signature pedagogies, the novices are instructed in critical aspects of the three fundamental dimensions of professional work – to *think*, to *perform*, and to *act with integrity*. (2005: 52)

We must continue to define, support, and improve upon our signature pedagogy. Ultimately, of course, the burden and the opportunity for both teacher and student is to write.

Applying theory to practice in creative writing courses

Creative writing has defined itself in opposition to established practices in higher educa-tion, and this stance as much as any theory has contributed to classroom practices. This stance has also resulted in an approach to teaching markedly different from other disci-plines: no lectures, no exams, decentralised authority, and student ownership of the learn-ing process. Before composition theory touted the importance of audience and process, creative writing professors recognised that writers benefit from an immediate and worthy audience for their emerging work. The workshop, therefore, attempts to create a sort of literary café in which students earnestly analyse a classmate's poem or story, pointing out how it succeeds and what the writer might do to improve it and offering perspective that enables the writer to re-envision and revise, often for a portfolio of polished work.

Although different professors and tutor-writers implement the workshop – the signature pedagogy – differently, common practices exist, and the advent of online teaching has not altered that pedagogy significantly. Most often, before coming to class, students post each other's works to the course website or provide print copies of their works to classmates, who prepare for the upcoming class by reading and annotating the works with thoughtful, formative criticism. During class, the instructor leads discussion of the student works by asking questions, keeps the comments grounded in relevant and meaningful criteria, and maintains civility and respect among all students. Along with students, professors offer suggestions for improving not just the piece under discussion but also the approach to and understanding of craft and of the creative process. To minimise attempts to justify the work under discussion and to maximise introspection, the writer remains silent while the class discusses his or her draft. Professors also work individually with students during confer-ences, lecture on specific techniques, and assign practice writing exercises. By reserving official, final, or summative evaluation – the grade – of the creative work for the end of the academic term, the workshop approach privileges process over product and emphasises the complexity and time-consuming nature of the creative arts.

While student works comprise the major texts for the course, many professors assign reading from literature anthologies as well but approach and discuss these texts with a writerly slant. Pulitzer Prize-winning author Jane Smiley (1999: 250) maintains that, for writers, the study of literature provides distance from the ego and allows students to see the connections their work has to other literature. In *On Becoming a Novelist*, John Gardner notes that the writer 'reads other writers to see how they do it (how they avoid overt manipulation)' (1983: 45–6). He advises writers to read to see how effects are achieved, to question whether they would have approached the situation in the same way and to consider whether their way 'would have been better or worse, and why'. Similarly, R. V. Cassill, in *Writing Fiction*, explains that 'what the writer wants to note . . . is how the story, its language and all its parts have been joined together' (1975: 6). Great literature, therefore, models technique for writers.

As the popularity of creative writing classes has increased, more textbooks focusing on technique have emerged for use alongside student work and published literature. The *AWP Hallmarks of an Effective BFA Program or BA Major in Creative Writing* suggests that undergraduate creative writing courses 'require craft texts and literary works (anthologies, books by individual authors, literary periodicals) that offer appropriate models for student writing'. Most creative writing textbooks present chapters discussing specific elements of various genres and offer exercises to help students master these techniques. While textbooks acknowledge the difficulty of articulating foolproof guidelines, the authors assume would-be writers benefit from instruction on craft. In her introduction to *Write Away: One Novelist's Approach to Fiction and the Writing Life*, for example, Elizabeth George explains that for those who teach creative writing, 'craft is the point'; it is 'the soil in which a budding writer can plant the seed of her idea in order to nurture it into a story' (2005: x). Similarly, Addonizio and Laux state that 'Craft provides the tools: knowing how to make a successful metaphor, when to break a line, how to revise and rewriting – these are some of the techniques the aspiring poet must master' (1997: 11). Heather Sellers, in *The Practice of Creative Writing*, tells students that creative writing is 'about crafting language – words on a page – so that a reader (a stranger!) will have a specific kind of emotional experience. Design is the key word' (2013:4).

Unlike texts for other disciplines, creative writing texts seldom provide instructor's editions or supplements that ground the instructions and exercises in theories about learning to write, in part because even the teacher is yet another writer in the classroom. The hallmarks for successful undergraduate and graduate creative writing programmes in *The AWP Directors' Handbook* state that creative writing faculty consist of 'writers whose work has been published by nationally known, professional journals and presses respected by other writers, editors, and publishers' (2003: 15). These hallmarks stipulate, 'the criteria for promotion, assignment of classes, and tenure of creative writing faculty focus on publication of creative work, demonstrated ability as teachers of creative writing, and contributions to the university and greater literary community' (2003: 15). In other words, the leading organisation that promotes creative writing as a discipline values writers who teach more than teachers who write, as do other practice-based professions like medicine and graphic design.

More so than other disciplines, however, creative writing must contend with questions of validity and scholarship. While the blogosphere may allow such criticism to proliferate, the questions have lingered for decades. Flannery O'Connor's now famous remark that universities 'don't stifle enough' writers still holds sway, and pejorative labels such as *workshop story* or *McPoem*, a term coined by Donald Hall, reflect the disdain many feel for the writing that emerges from creative writing programmes. Even some who teach creative writing question its existence as an academic subject. For example, Lynn Freed in her memoir 'Doing time' (2005) confesses that she does not know 'how to pretend to unravel the mystery' (68) of what makes a good story and admits that she sometimes feels as if, by attempting to teach creative writing, she is participating in 'a sham' (72). Most professors of creative writing do not share Freed's opinion, but they share her despair at the prospect of articulating clearly and accurately what they do. As Richard Cohen states in *Writer's Mind: Crafting Fiction*, 'Technique is what can most efficiently be taught in classrooms, but technique is not the essence of writing' (1995: xvi). George Garrett makes a similar point in 'Going to see the elephant: our duty as storytellers' by claiming that the creative process is magic and mysterious: 'It breaks all the rules as fast as we can make them. Every generalization about it turns out to be at best incomplete or inadequate' (1999: 2).

Nonetheless, creative writing professors do and must make generalisations. 'If the teacher has no basic standards', Gardner writes, 'his class is likely to develop none, and their comments can only be matters of preference or opinion. Writers will have nothing to strive toward or resist, nothing solid to judge by' (1983: 84). Bishop and Ostrom's challenge to 'reexamine what takes place in creative-writing classrooms' (1994: xxii) has resulted not in a uniformity of standards and common learning objectives but in a meaningful dialogue by which professors can make clear what they expect students to learn. The AWP annual conference, for example, features dozens of panels on pedagogy and its website provides a wealth of pedagogical tools. Books such as *What If?* (1990), *The Practice of Poetry* (1992), *The Portable MFA in Creative Writing* (2006) and *Naming the World* (2008) compile exercises and advice from published authors with extensive classroom experiences. Julie Checkoway, former President of the AWP Board of Directors, writes that the successful writers and teachers who contributed to *Creating Fiction* 'have staked their reputations on the notions that when it comes to writing, teaching is at least as important as talent, nurture at least as important as nature' (1999: ix).

How best to teach and nurture writers changes as the population of students and the venues for creative writing classes change, and that comes across in responses to much of the criticism in the blogosphere and also comes across in recent pedagogy scholarship. Like professors in other disciplines, creative writing professors have responded to the influx of students whose different assumptions, expectations, and life experiences necessitate a change in pedagogy. Mark L. Taylor, in 'Generation NeXt: today's postmodern student – meeting, teaching, and serving' points to research suggesting: 'In our postmodern culture, the traditional models of premodern religion and modern science/reason must compete with postmodern consumerism/entertainment and hedonism/immediate needs gratification on a playing field that is level at best' (2005: 104). Current undergraduates, he contends, tend to be accepting of 'everything except people who believe in the hegemony of their chosen model'. Recognising that a student does not enter the classroom a *tabula rasa* and that the aesthetic values inherent in great works of literature may appear arbitrary, exclusive, or contrary to publishing trends or to students' embedded cognitive schemata, creative writing professors have developed strategies for identifying assumptions about literature and reconciling these with other notions of how a text communicates. In his essay, 'On not being nice: sentimentality and the creative writing class', for example, Arthur Saltzman (2003: 324) laments the sentimentality that students bring to the classroom – their tendency 'to be passionate according to formula' – and he strives to 'expose the evaluative criteria that they invariably bring to the discussion' of poetry. Discussing both his and his students' assumptions about poetry allows Saltzman to help students develop 'more specific and involved responses' with the hope that they 'become more demanding of the poems they encounter and produce' (2003: 325).

Being explicit about evaluative standards is in the interest of students, but articulating learning objectives also helps legitimise the difficult work students and teachers do in creative writing classrooms. Although institutional assessments may have limited value in determining whether students will be successful writers, six regional accrediting bodies in the US require institutions to develop, articulate, and assess standards and to improve student learning. The UK has the Quality Assurance Agency for Higher Education as its regulating body, which requires module-by-module assessment and external examiners to an even greater extent than is required in the US. More importantly, creative writing professors and tutor-writers have taken ownership of the ways in which creative writing is evaluated. In a creative writing class, marks or grades reflect comprehension and application of specific writing strategies as well as prolific writing. Many professors provide numerous and varied opportunities to demonstrate competency, including exercises, analyses of published work, and even quizzes or exams along with the portfolio of creative work.

As creative writing continues to define itself as a rigorous, academic discipline, professors will need to take into account the technological and demographic changes taking place. Online courses and programmes as well as online magazines, hypertexts, and blogs offer the prospect of reaching specific audiences and challenging assumptions about what constitutes publication. Cathy Day, for instance, is a creative writing professor and blogger who is redesigning her workshops for the twenty-first century and writing about it as she goes. How are professors addressing these new venues and texts? What teaching strategies have they developed to accommodate diverse groups of distance learners and to maintain the high standards for which college-level courses in creative writing are known? How successfully is the workshop environment being translated to the Internet? What are the standards by which different texts are judged?

At the same time, changes in the publishing industry limit some opportunities for novice writers while opening up other possibilities. Despite the number of writing courses and programmes, according to the National Endowment for the Arts' *Reading at Risk: A Survey of Literary Reading in America* (2004), the percentage of book readers at all ages has declined significantly over the past two decades. A follow-up study in 2007 revealed that 'teens and young adults read less often and for shorter amounts of time compared with other age groups and with Americans of previous years'. At the same time, more people are choosing to read e-books, to order books online, or download books illegally for free, the result being that many smaller presses and local bookstores have vanished. One of the few increases in literary activity has been in creative writing. These trends raise questions regarding who reads the works produced by writers from now more numerous creative writing programmes. Many authors turn to other avenues to find readers for their works, choosing, for example, to self-publish, publish online, or use software to produce downloadable novels and story and poetry collections. Whether publishing online or in print, writers more and more are responsible for promoting their works. Such changes offer the field opportunities to continue to refine and expand curricula, to explore the theoretical foundations on which the curricula are based, and to contribute to literary excellence within and outside of the academy.

Conclusion

Creative writing is an academic pursuit with a documented history that shapes its current theories and practices. The field has become increasingly varied in its curricula, moving away from foundations of literary scholarship to the signature pedagogy based on the workshop model and, more recently, to manifestations in low-residency, service-learning, and web-based iterations so that creative writers in academe – both professors and students – not only develop talent and craft but also bear witness to contemporary culture and develop transferable cognitive and communicative skills. Creative writing has borrowed and reshaped theoretical approaches from literary criticism, composition studies, linguistics, and even cognitive science. These foundations underpin a rigorous, rewarding academic experience in creative writing classrooms in the US, the UK, and increasingly around the globe. Though Dorothea Brande found the way creative writing was taught to be problematic seventy years ago, her claim in *Becoming a Writer* about our endeavour holds true today: 'there is no field where one who is in earnest about learning to do good work can make such enormous strides in so short a time' (1934: 27). Though challenges in the field still exist – perhaps *because* they exist – creative writing has come into its own within academe over the last four decades.

References

Addonizio, Kim and Dorianne Laux (1997), *The Poet's Companion: A Guide to the Pleasures of Writing Poetry*, New York: W. W. Norton.

The Association of Writers and Writing Programs homepage, www.awpwriter.org (accessed October 2005).

AWP Hallmarks of an Effective BFA Program or BA Major in Creative Writing, https://www.awpwriter.org/library/directors_handbook_hallmarks_of_an_effective_bfa_program_or_ba_major_in_creative_writing (accessed June 2013).

Beck, Heather (2005), email to Mary Swander.

Beck, Heather (ed.) (2012), *Teaching Creative Writing*, London: Palgrave Macmillan.

Behn, Robin and Chase Twichell (eds) (1992), *The Practice of Poetry: Writing Exercises from Poets Who Teach*, New York: HarperCollins.

Bell, Madison Smartt (1997), *Narrative Design: Working with Imagination, Craft, and Form*, New York: W. W. Norton.

Bernays, Anne and Pamela Painter (1990), *What If? Writing Exercises for Fiction Writers*, New York: HarperCollins.

Bishop, Wendy (ed.) (2003), *The Subject Is Writing: Essays by Teachers and Students*, Portsmouth, NH: Boynton/Cook.

Bishop, Wendy and Hans Ostrom (eds) (1994), *Colors of a Different Horse: Rethinking Creative Writing Theory and Pedagogy*, Urbana, IL: National Council of Teachers of English.

Brande, Dorothea ([1934] 1981), *Becoming a Writer*, New York: Tarcher/Penguin.

Bruer, John T. (1999), 'Education', in William Bechtel and George Graham (eds), *A Companion to Cognitive Science*, Malden, MA: Blackwell, pp. 681–90.

Cassill, R.V. (1975), *Writing Fiction*, New York: Prentice Hall Press.

Cohen, Richard (1995), *Writer's Mind: Crafting Fiction*, Lincolnwood, IL: NTC/Contemporary Publishing Group.

Dana, Robert (ed.) (1999), *A Community of Writers: Paul Engle and the Iowa Writers' Workshop*, Iowa City: University of Iowa Press.

Day, Cathy, www.literarycitizenship.com (accessed June 2013).

Donnelly, Dianne (2010), *Does the Writing Workshop Still Work?*, Clevedon, UK: Multilingual Matters.

Flaherty, Alice W. (2004), *The Midnight Disease*, New York: Houghton Mifflin.

Freed, Lynn (2005), 'Doing Time', *Harper's Magazine*, (July) 311: 65–72.

Gardner, John (1983), *On Becoming a Novelist*, New York: W. W. Norton.

Garrett, George (1999), 'Going to see the elephant: our duty as storytellers', in Julie Checkoway (ed.), *Creating Fiction: Instruction and Insights from the Teachers of the Associated Writing Programs*, Cincinnati: Story Press, pp. 2–12.

George, Elizabeth (2005), *Write Away: One Novelist's Approach to Fiction and the Writing Life*, New York: HarperCollins.

Gradschools.com, http://gradschools.com/listings/out/creative_write_out.html (accessed October 2005).

Iowa Writers' Workshop, www.uiowa.edu/~iww/about.htm (accessed June 2013).

Johnston, Anthony Bret (2008), *Naming the World: And Other Exercises for Creative Writers*, New York: Random House.

Leahy, Anna (ed.) (2005), *Power and Identity in the Creative Writing Classroom: The Authority Project*, Clevedon, UK: Multilingual Matters.

McGurl, Mark (2011), *The Program Era*, Cambridge, MA: Harvard University Press.

Meyers, D. G. (1996), *The Elephants Teach: Creative Writing Since 1880*, Englewood Cliffs, NJ: Prentice Hall.

Moxley, Joseph (1989), *Creative Writing in America: Theory and Pedagogy*, Urbana, IL: National Council of Teachers of English.

National Endowment for the Arts (2004), *Reading at Risk: A Survey of Literary Reading in America*, www.nea.gov/pub/ReadingAtRisk.pdf (accessed November 2005).

National Endowment for the Arts (2007), *National Endowment for the Arts Announces New Study*, http://www.nea.gov/news/news07/trnr.html (accessed May 2013).

New Writing: the International Journal for the Practice and Theory of Creative Writing, www.multilingual-matters.net/nw/default.htm (accessed November 2005).

The New York Writers Workshop (2006), *The Portable MFA in Creative Writing*, Cincinnati: Writer's Digest.

Proposal for MFA in Creative Writing and Environment (2005), Iowa State University English Department.

Quarracino, Andrea (2005), 'Annual Report on the Academic Job List', *AWP Job List: October 2005*.

Ritter, Kelly, and Stephanie Vanderslice (2007), *Can It Really Be Taught? Resisting Lore in Creative Writing Pedagogy*, Portsmouth, NH: Heinemann.

Roediger III, Henry L. and Lyn M. Goff (1999), 'Memory', in William Bechtel and George Graham (eds), *A Companion to Cognitive Science*, Malden, MA: Blackwell, pp. 250–64.

Royster, Brent (2005), 'Inspiration, creativity, and crisis: the Romantic myth of the writer meets the postmodern classroom', in Anna Leahy (ed.), *Power and Identity in the Creative Writing Classroom: The Authority Project*, Clevedon, UK: Multilingual Matters, pp. 26–38.

Saltzman, Arthur (2003), 'On not being nice: sentimentality and the creative writing class', *Midwest Quarterly*, 44:3, 322–35.

Scarry, Elaine (1999), *On Beauty and Being Just*, Princeton, NJ: Princeton University Press.

Seattle Pacific University website, www.spu.edu/prospects/grad/academics/mfa/index.asp (accessed June 2013).

Sellers, Heather (2013), *The Practice of Creative Writing: A Guide for Students*, New York: Bedford/St. Martin's.

Shulman, Lee (2005), 'Signature pedagogies', *Daedalus*, 134:3, 52–9.

Smiley, Jane (1999), 'What stories teach their writers: the purpose and practice of revision', in Julie Checkoway (ed.), *Creative Fiction: Instruction and Insights from the Teachers of the Associated Writing Programs*, Cincinnati: Story Press, pp. 244–55.

Taylor, Mark (2005), 'Generation NeXt: today's postmodern student – meeting, teaching, and serving' in The Higher Learning Commission (ed.), *A Collection of Papers on Self-Study and Institutional Improvement*, Chicago, IL: The Higher Learning Commission, pp. 99–107.

Wilbers, Stephen (1980), *The Iowa Writers' Workshop*, Iowa City, IA: University of Iowa Press.

2

The Evaluation of Creative Writing at MA Level (UK)

Jenny Newman

Can creative writing be assessed?

When the first creative writing MAs in the UK were founded in the late 1960s and early 70s, many traditional scholars and academics argued that no one could teach the mysterious and fascinating process of literary creativity, and that such courses had no place in a university. Their objections have been overturned, partly, it must be said, because of student demand for accredited creative writing courses from under-funded and money-hungry universities. A few literature dons, however, still follow the critic John Carey in maintaining that the evaluation of works of art is purely subjective and thus cannot be codified (Carey 2005: 52). Others say, with the novelist and former lecturer David Lodge, that no one can teach you 'how to produce a text other people will willingly give up their time – and perhaps their money – to read, although it has no utilitarian purpose or value' – and that the more advanced the course, the more heartbreak is likely to be associated with it (Lodge 1996: 176). Other lecturers and writers feel that good art overturns the rules, and that subjecting potential poets, playwrights and novelists to a series of tasks for assessment stifles genuine creativity.

Most tutor-writers would agree that they cannot impart originality or perseverance. But they do claim that they know how to foster talent in an academic environment where students can learn through workshops with fellow writers, and have access to libraries, conferences and electronic resources. Also, like university painters and musicians, tutor-writers know how to teach tradition and technique. Nor need they find it impossible to tell good writing from bad. Generations of critics and lecturers (including John Carey) have written books assessing writers past and sometimes even present. Although pundits fall out over individual cases, societies as a whole seem able to form a consensus even about what has only just been written. The Pulitzer, the Man Booker, the *Palme d'Or*, the Whitbread, the *Prix Goncourt*, the Orange and the International Man Booker: major prizes – and hundreds of minor ones – proliferate. Judging panels proclaim their manifestos, and their long lists and shortlists spark passionate and often knowledgeable debate on review pages, television and radio arts programmes, and among panels of experts and celebrities. New films, fiction, poetry and plays are judged good or bad by critics who offer their reasons at length. Fortified by generations of successful graduates, and by having road tested their grounds for awarding high and low marks, many tutors now assert that 'criteria for creative writing should be no more difficult to ascertain than for any other subject area, creative or not' (Atkinson 2000/2001: 26).

This chapter is intended to explore the evaluation of creative writing at postgraduate level, to help you choose the MA with the 'assessment pattern' best suited to your needs, and to enable you to avoid some of the pitfalls awaiting postgraduate writers.

Choosing a course

There is no standard curriculum for Creative Writing MAs, and they vary dramatically in their approach to writing, their teaching methods, their links with theatres, screenwriters, agents, publishers and production companies, and in their graduates' success rate. Some courses allow you to choose between poetry, fiction, screenwriting or scriptwriting, and to study full-time (typically a year) or part-time (typically two years). Though most Creative Writing degrees are not, strictly speaking, professional qualifications, many have 'modules' or 'pathways' which enable you to learn how to run a writers' workshop in a school, hospital, prison or hospice, or to edit a magazine, or to sample jobs in publishing, or film, or in the growing field of writing and mental health.

Not all university websites are user-friendly, but it is worth taking the time to search them for inspiration. Even if you are confined for personal reasons to a specific locality, you may have more choice than you think. As a subject, Creative Writing is booming, and more MAs are being offered every year, even by highly traditional universities. Do not be deterred if you do not have a first degree, or are older than the traditional student. Many institutions value life experience, and consider a promising portfolio and a strong commitment to writing, to be more important than formal qualifications. Students' ages range from twenty-one to sixty or even seventy, and some courses have a median age of thirty-eight or higher.

No website can tell you all you need to know, so you will need a brochure, or ideally a range (most websites allow you to request one online). Find out the names of the tutors, and read their plays, novels or poems; but remember that, though likelier to attract the attention of agents and publishers, a prestigious course may not best suit your needs. The ways in which an MA will develop and evaluate your writing are more important than its reputation in the national press, so ask yourself which one will best foster in you what Graeme Harper describes as 'creative practice and an understanding of creative practice' (Harper 2003: 1). If those courses near you seem unsuitable, or if you live in a remote spot, you could consider enrolling on an online or distance learning MA. Make a shortlist of those that interest you, and if you still cannot choose, email your queries to the admissions tutors, or ask for a telephone discussion, or a preliminary and informal interview.

What follows are some typical enquiries from potential MA students about the way their writing will be assessed:

- Do I have to submit an entrance portfolio? If so, how long should it be and what are the criteria? When is the deadline for submission and when will I be told the result?
- Will I be interviewed? Are you willing to interview over the telephone? What sort of students are you looking for?
- Do you accept students writing in their second language?
- Will I be able to switch from full-time to part-time if my financial circumstances change?
- Does the group size vary between lectures and workshops?
- As the course is by correspondence, does it include residentials or summer schools, locally run workshops, or online chatrooms in 'real' time?

- I think I might be dyslexic and I've been out of education for years. Do you offer study skills support?
- How many contact hours can I expect, and is there an attendance requirement?
- Will I be made to submit work in more than one genre (for example, scriptwriting, fiction, or poetry)?
- Does the MA have a critical or academic component, or will it focus exclusively on my writing?
- How much feedback will I be given and in what form? Will I get one-to-one tutorials from real writers? Can I choose my tutor?
- What are the course's links to publishers, agents and screenwriters?
- How successful are its graduates? Do you provide a list of former students whom I can contact to ask about the course?
- Who teaches the course, and how many visiting writers and publishers are invited?

The Assessment Pattern

An 'assessment pattern' is a list of the written, practical (if any), oral (if any) and online (if any) assignments you will be required to submit in order to graduate. Under regulations formulated by the Quality Assurance Agency for Higher Education in England and Wales (QAA), tutors can only assess what they have formally taught. The assessment pattern can therefore be seen as a more accurate guide to the course itself than what tutors may maintain is important. Although no student can fully understand its rationale before completing it, it is well worth knowing its requirements in advance, and in written form.

According to QAA guidelines, an assessment pattern should include a semester-by-semester schedule, a credit rating for each module (and a total of 180) which enables you to gauge the importance the course team attaches to each assignment, and information about word lengths. The submission dates will be carefully timed and posted well in advance.

Creative writing courses do not have as yet the explicit national standards or 'benchmarks' for assessment that have been compiled for many other longer established subjects. Most Creative Writing MAs teach more than creative writing (see the range of assessment tasks, below) and have several methods of assessment. The majority of courses have an academic or critical component. In some universities the latter is as high as 40 or 50 per cent, and courses are taught mainly by academics, not writers.

But assessment isn't only a test or a barrier. It is intended to motivate you to acquire and practise new techniques, to read widely, to analyse what you have written and read, and to reflect on your creative processes. Your assignments should also allow your tutor to gauge your progress, to diagnose errors and enable you to rectify them, and to offer you expert feedback and advice. A good assessment pattern can add variety to your experience of being a student and will also allow you to recognise your achievements, and monitor your development as a writer.

What follows are some popular examples of MA assessment tasks, plus a brief rationale of each.

Analytical essay

Good writers are avid viewers or readers, and all postgraduate courses encourage their students to become aware of the tradition in which they work, and of contemporary fiction, poetry or scripts. This process is often assessed through an analytical essay on significant work already published or produced, in which the student demonstrates his or her power to read or view for technique.

Critical commentary

This typically accompanies a piece of the student's creative writing. Its purpose differs slightly from course to course, but it is often used to place student work in a tradition, and in relation to recent or contemporary performances, films or publications. Rather than interpreting their writing, students can describe their intentions, their creative processes, the methods they used to resolve any challenges to technique, and the extent to which they felt they were successful. By identifying and analysing problems, a Critical Commentary can allow the tutor to reward ambitious creative writing which did not fully succeed. In some institutions the Critical Commentary is called a Supplementary Discourse, involving the separate discipline of poetics. Though most courses do not award the Commentary a specific proportion of the overall mark, it is often graded out of a notional 20 per cent, and the piece of creative work it accompanies out of a notional 80 per cent.

Oral presentation or pitch to the student group

This assesses the student's ability to talk about his or her work as if to agents, publishers, producers or readers, or to an interviewer on television or radio.

Website

Increasingly agents and publishers scout for talent on the web. At least one British MA programme teaches students to build their own writer's website, and to showcase their work, make links to other relevant sites, and present themselves as writers.

Précis or synopsis

Such material can help students to clarify their aims, understand their future market, and consider some of the writing or publishing industry's social, geographical or economic determinants.

Little magazine

Many courses ask students to learn editorial and group skills by collaborating over a platform for their work. This is often accompanied by research into other outlets, national, international or online.

Drafting and notebook-keeping

While these activities cannot – and perhaps should not – be formally assessed, some MAs require evidence of both.

Workshops

Sessions in groups of preferably no more than eight enable students to present their work to their tutors and peers (see 'Types and processes of assessment: Workshops', below).

Though verbal contributions should probably not be measured formally, the experience can feed into students' writing, as well as into their Commentaries or Supplementary Discourses.

Editing or proofreading exercise

This tests students' ability to identify and correct errors of punctuation, typography and spelling on a piece of published or unpublished work.

Analytical essay on a piece of original work by a fellow student

This assignment requires wide reading and research, and hones ideas about technique, and critical skills. It is particularly useful for those who will later earn their living as publishers or editors.

Creative writing

The portfolio that you build up during your course is likely to have the highest credit rating in the assessment pattern, and will be your 'calling card' when you contact agents or publishers. Find out the overall word length in advance. Some courses demand a whole novel, for example, or a collection of poetry, or two full-length scripts, and may allow you a year or more after the end of the taught component in which to complete your manuscript, supported by timed tutorials. Others ask for only twelve to fifteen thousand words or equivalent, and will expect you to submit them within the one- or two-year span of the course.

How your writing will be assessed

Criteria

Clear and thoughtful criteria 'owned' by all your tutors can be seen as a manifesto of the departmental spirit and of what it seeks to develop and impart. They may also endorse a university's 'mission', and play to the tutors' expertise and areas of research.

Though students often ignore them until an assignment is due, assessment criteria should be consulted in advance. They explain what tutors reward and penalise when they mark your work, and will be referred to in your written and oral feedback. The criteria will also inform workshop discussions, and both written and oral self and peer appraisal, and any Critical Commentaries you write to accompany your original work.

Criteria form the grounds for the discussions between your tutors about the marks they award you, and the annual exercises in which they grade anonymous scripts, then compare and discuss their verdicts. Criteria also form the basis of any appeal against a tutor's decision (see 'Appeals procedures', below). On some courses creative writing criteria vary from genre to genre, in others not. Either way, subsidiary sets of criteria are usually applied when the course includes diverse assessment tasks.

All criteria should be readily available in student handbooks and on the university website.

Grading

Most MAs are Pass/Fail degrees with the possibility of a Distinction. Your work, however, is usually awarded a percentage, and criteria are subdivided according to the standard BA degree classification system (1st, II.i, etc.).

What follows is a set of typical creative writing criteria, which has been adapted and amalgamated from those of five well-established MA creative writing programmes, most of which had poetry, prose and script components. Its categories are intended to give helpful and detailed feedback, but not to be prescriptive or exhaustive, or to reduce your tutors' thoughts to a simple grid. The divisions can better be seen as overlapping sets of guidelines rather than watertight compartments.

70 per cent + (Distinction)
Impressionistically, work in this range can be said to delight and excite through its ability to engage the reader or viewer or listener at a sophisticated level. More formally, it demonstrates an overall coherence of tone, control of narrative strategies, an inventive use of language and a distinctive 'voice'. It displays evidence of original observation, of a knowledge – if only implied – of varieties of structure, and of the tradition(s) in which the student is working, or choosing to subvert. Dialogue and idiom, if used, are effective, and spelling, grammar, punctuation, syntax and editing are impeccable. Presentation is to the standard normally required by agents and publishers when considering work for publication.

60–9 per cent (Pass)
Work in this category could be described as ambitious, with a clearly discernible narrative voice, though not as assured or coherent as that of work in the highest category. Nevertheless, the writing will show a strong understanding of its chosen form or genre, and of its artistic or literary context and tradition. The subject matter will be freshly approached, dialogue and idiom well handled, and the use of description and detail effective. The presentation will be almost of the standard required for submission to agents and publishers.

50–9 per cent (Pass)
Work awarded a mark in this band will generally have reached a satisfactory standard of invention and proficiency, with a clearly discernible narrative or theme, though there may inconsistencies of characterisation or plot. The conception may not be as fresh or striking as that of work in the higher categories, and tend towards the derivative or 'safe'. Though there will be evidence of redrafting, the use of technique might at points be limited or clumsy, with a sometimes indiscriminate choice of language or a reliance on cliché. N. B.: Even in these days of what some see as 'grade inflation', the work of half or more of a new MA group may fall into this band, and a mark at the upper end, in particular, should be seen not as grounds for discouragement, but as no mean achievement.

40–9 per cent (Pass)
This is the lowest bracket of work deemed worthy of a pass. Although it may show some understanding of the potential of its form, writing in this category is usually limited in conception and approach. It may demonstrate some fluency and technical competence, but lack coherence and clarity. It may also be structurally weak, with a patchy control of style and tone, stereotypical situations or characters, and hackneyed details. The layout may be confusing, and spelling, syntax and punctuation will probably be erratic.

Below 40 per cent (Fail)

Work in this category is deemed unworthy of a pass at postgraduate level, and will generally be poorly conceived and clumsily written. Though it may show some grasp of what is required, it may be rambling, difficult to follow or just plain boring. It may show little evidence of observation and descriptive skills, and lack a coherent tone, or knowledge of tradition, and be substantially under or over the required word length. The writer's purpose may remain unclear, and presentation will typically be careless, with repeated mistakes of spelling, syntax, layout and punctuation.

Types and processes of assessment

Formative and summative

Your coursework will be assessed in ways that are known as 'formative' and 'summative'. Formative assessment is not linked to a mark, and focuses on strengths and points for improvement. Summative assessment often involves an element of the formative (such as a feedback sheet or a tutorial), but crucially awards a mark to a piece of work that counts towards your final result.

What follows are the main forms of each activity.

Formative assessment by a tutor

No tutor, no matter how good a writer, can tell you what to write; but he or she will understand the creative process, be aware of your aims and ambitions, and help to guide and inspire. His or her formative role is to read and analyse your writing, to help you identify strengths and weaknesses, to answer your questions about technique, to recommend suitable reading and to prompt revision, in a workshop or one-to-one tutorial, or on a feedback sheet. In this kind of feedback a diligent and knowledgeable tutor can resemble the best professional editor imaginable.

Summative assessment by a tutor

When they award marks which contribute to your degree, tutors formally represent the institution, and are responsible for maintaining academic standards (see 'Marking procedures', below). This is the course's most official aspect and the most likely to be contested (see 'Appeals procedures', below).

Formative assessment by students

Learning how to evaluate and comment on your fellow students' writing most often occurs in workshops, and in the preliminary reading for workshops, and is a highly valued aspect of the course (see 'Workshops', below).

Summative assessment by students

Although peer assessment is usually formative it sometimes, as the course progresses, becomes summative: that is, a student may award a percentage to a peer's workshop submission which will contribute to the peer's final award, though usually to a very limited extent;

and, like all marks, that percentage will be subject to moderation. A detailed comment sheet written in accordance with the assessment criteria usually accompanies and justifies summative peer assessment.

Self-assessment

This formative skill is more demanding than peer assessment, and probably the most important aspect of the course, which will stand you in good stead throughout your writing life. Self-assessment involves learning how to gauge your intentions, to be a responsible parent to your work, and to deepen, revise and edit it. It can be most clearly demonstrated in the Critical Commentary which in many courses accompanies each piece of original work. Here the student reflects on his or her creative practice, the challenges overcome or the flaws which might remain. A student can also anticipate tutor feedback, or invite it on a particular point, so that work in progress resembles a dialogue or a practice space. Written self-assessment is often subject in its turn to formative or summative tutor assessment.

Workshops

Though the work is usually assessed formatively rather than summatively, most students see the creative writing workshop as the heart of the course, and its most beneficial and memorable component. Ground rules are best agreed by students and tutors in advance, and in accordance with their university's Equal Opportunities policy (see 'Equal opportunities', below), so that everyone feels they are being treated fairly and with respect.

Material for discussion should be photocopied and distributed at least a week in advance. To be just to your fellow students, you may need to familiarise yourself with the tradition in which they are writing, read their work several times, and allow yourself time to reflect. All work submitted is work in progress, and part of your fellow students' development as writers, so never be destructive, or fail to offer a creative solution. Feedback which describes and analyses developments of, for example, character, plot or tone, is more helpful than that which simply reaches a verdict, or describes a piece of work as 'boring' or 'not my thing'.

When it is your writing's turn to be considered, remember that readers' impressions are valuable, and may be in short supply when the course is over. Listen to the views of your tutors and fellow students rather than debating them, or defending your work. Although concurring opinions deserve serious consideration, you need to take time to consider them rather than agreeing straightaway. Though no one will oblige you to implement all – or any – suggestions, workshops can contribute substantially to the redrafting process, and to the Critical Commentary which accompanies a piece of creative writing (see 'The assessment pattern', above).

Because a range of spoken opinions on one's writing can be hard to assimilate, each contributor should compile a sheet of written feedback for the student whose work they assessed. The scripts themselves should be annotated and returned, with attention paid to matters such as style, punctuation and layout.

Marking procedures

University marking procedures are monitored by a national body linked to the Higher Education Funding Council (HEFCE) and known as the Quality Assurance Agency for

Higher Education (QAA). The QAA requires that procedures should be 'transparent' to you as a student and made explicit through your handbooks. Grading should follow the established criteria, and work should be marked anonymously where possible.

Major pieces of work should be second marked, and the run of all marks (of tutors, and of students, where submitted) should be moderated by the course or module leader. In British Universities, these processes are scrutinised by an External Examiner who is usually an experienced tutor from a parallel institution, and whose role is to ensure that Quality Assurance Procedures are followed, and that standards tally with those of similar courses. Marks are ratified by a University Examination Board of which the External Examiner, the programme leader or head of department, the course team and a senior administrator are members.

Benefits of assessment

While writing this chapter I distributed a questionnaire to a sample of twenty-five students from three courses. The range was almost evenly balanced in terms of gender, and its median age was twenty-nine. All had at least two part-time years' experience of postgraduate creative writing. The first question was: 'What benefits (if any) have you derived from the assessment of your writing?' (For the second question, see 'Troubleshooting', below). No student was totally negative, and over half listed four or more benefits. What follows is a sample of their replies:

- It gave me a goal and made me organise my time. I'd never have finished my work without the deadlines.
- [Assessment] made us really think about what the tutors were trying to put across.
- The written feedback from students and tutors definitely helped me improve my writing.
- The wide range of things we had to do made us experiment and extend ourselves. Without it, I would never have written a radio play.
- The course took off with the workshops – they were wonderful. My group continued to meet right through the summer, and we'll keep on getting together after the course is over.
- The workshops helped us monitor our progress, and let us know where we stood in relation to other young writers.
- My tutor was a brilliant writer, and my one-to-one tutorials were like a master class.

Troubleshooting
Many tutor-writers value their role in developing and cherishing new writing, including – or sometimes especially – experimental or even quirky writing of high literary merit that may not be market-driven, or readily find a publisher. But not all budding writers thrive on university courses, and not all students are as happy about assessment as those quoted above. Course duration is not organic but artificial, governed by university schedules rather than by writers' growth. Some students feel they are not allowed enough time to assimilate knowledge and develop their techniques. Others feel that their course has let them down when their marks fail to improve – or even grow worse. A few clash with their tutors or fellow students; or find the process of being assessed – or, as one student expressed it, of 'putting myself and my writing on the line' – more challenging than anticipated, and believe that it fosters unhealthy competition.

Some tutors, likewise, have reservations about contemporary aspects of assessment. Writing is not a career path, and even great talent can be erratic or sometimes wane, as can be seen from the output of lifelong writers such as Wordsworth, Tolstoy and Hemingway.

Yet universities are required to provide HEFCE, their funding body, with assessment data, and to undergo QAA inspections, which means that matters such as admissions, failure rates or student withdrawal from courses are subject to government strategies and sometimes even directives. Furthermore, as British university professor Frank Furedi points out, 'lecturers certainly do not have the right to lecture material for which the learning outcome cannot be demonstrated in advance' (Furedi 2004: 76). If, as he and others believe, assessment changes the nature of what is assessed, then student writing might at points become instrumental and even 'bite-sized' to fit cost-cutting timetables, and corporate agendas. As Graeme Harper puts it, 'Both order and disorder produce results for creative writers, yet the University has increasingly become a place of ordered existence' (Harper 2003: 8).

The following comments are culled from the questionnaires from which I quoted in 'Benefits of assessment', above, and were made in response to the question: 'What, if anything, have you found difficult or problematic about the assessment process?'

- I felt I was being judged, and not just like on a normal course. I'd handed over something of myself and it damaged my self-esteem.
- My workshop tutor was an academic not a poet, and she didn't know anything about the creative process or how to help me shape a poem.
- I was the only Black woman on the course and I was writing out of a different tradition to the rest. Sometimes they just didn't get it.
- Having my work scrutinised and graded made me very self-conscious. For the first time in my life I got writer's block. We should have been taught how to give and take criticism before the course started.
- I'd never felt competitive about my writing before but I became very aware of what the tutor's favourites were doing and started comparing myself with them.
- Some of the others didn't seem very committed and their work was quite weak. I was surprised that none of them failed. The tutors seemed to be protecting their [the students'] self-esteem instead of grading them as they deserved.
- There was a tension between the creative and the critical parts of the course, which didn't interest me. I felt I was being turned into an academic – and only because they didn't have enough writers on the staff.
- I didn't like my tutor's novels and felt that he didn't understand what I was trying to write.

Appeals procedures

If you have met all your deadlines and obligations, and have taken into account the assessment criteria, yet feel an assignment has been unfairly graded, you have the right to ask for it to be remarked. But before you begin, do some simple arithmetic: a few marks either way in one module will seldom make a significant difference to your overall result. Remember also that the world beyond the course of agents, producers, publishers, editors and (if you are both lucky and successful) critics and reviewers can be far harsher, more discouraging, more public and more arbitrary-seeming than being assessed in the microcosm of a university, where you will at least receive thoughtful feedback, and will have the support of your peers.

If, however, you remain dissatisfied, or continue to feel demoralised by your mark, ask first for an informal consultation with your tutor, and find out how his or her decision relates to the assessment criteria. If his or her reasons still remain unclear to you, and if your work has not been second-marked, you may be able to ask your tutor to pass it to a colleague, remembering that your work might be marked down as well as up. Even if your original mark is confirmed, you nevertheless may be able to ask for your work to be referred to the External Examiner, beyond whom there is no further court of appeal (and remember that he or she might also mark your work down). All final, heavily credit-weighted pieces of writing such as portfolios are invariably second- or even third-marked within the department, and a sample (including all Distinctions, Fails and Borderlines) is sent to the External Examiner, then ratified at a University Examination Board. After that you will have no grounds for appeal against its decision unless you can prove a serious injustice or procedural irregularity.

Equal opportunities

All universities have an Equal Opportunities policy which is promulgated in student handbooks and on the university website. Such policies are designed to enable all students and staff to achieve their full potential unhindered by prejudices relating to race, gender, age, disability, religion and sexual orientation.

For writers, however, such matters are not always clear-cut, as can be seen from the threats and debates that raged around Salman Rushdie's *Satanic Verses* (1988). Each student brings a different life experience to the course and, especially when submitting work in progress, may wish to test boundaries or even defy censorship. Such challenges need a sensitive and well-informed response from tutors and peers alike, and are best seen in the context of a national and international debate about contemporary writing. Parallel issues, such as the (sometimes necessary) use of character stereotypes, and the representation of those perceived as members of minorities, might be usefully discussed in early workshops, along with related matters such as the use of dialect and idiolect, non-standard speech patterns, and writing in a second language.

Study skills

If you have been out of education for some time, or have a disability (such as dyslexia) which might affect the way you are assessed, inform the admissions tutor before you start the course. If you wish, he or she will treat the information as confidential; or else notify appropriate members of staff, and arrange for you to receive the support you require (for example, study skills workshops, financial benefits such as the disabled student's allowance, access to photocopies and websites suitable for partially-sighted students, or extended deadline dates).

Plagiarism

As will be made clear in your student handbook, the term 'plagiarism' (sometimes known as 'academic impropriety') generally covers cheating, collusion or any other attempt to gain an unfair advantage in the way you are assessed. It includes not only verbatim copying (of the work of a peer or of a published author, online or in print, without acknowledgement), but also the close paraphrasing of another's work without acknowledgement, or passing off someone else's writing as your own, or appropriating another author's language or ideas.

Fortunately, most MA students are too busy finding and developing their individual 'voice' to copy the work of their fellow students, or of a published writer. Also, many courses require you to submit draft material with your creative writing, or to discuss your work in progress with their tutors, or in a workshop group – processes which make plagiarism almost impossible. But all good writers assimilate what they read or view, and the line between cribbing and what film buffs call an 'homage' (or deliberate and respectful quotation from a work which has influenced your own) is sometimes wavy.

You can see your course is a chance to learn about:

- The liberties the law allows you to take. For example, there is no copyright on titles or ideas. Furthermore, books are born out of other books, and many acclaimed novels, such as Jean Rhys's *Wide Sargasso Sea* (1966) and Valerie Martin's *Mary Reilly* (1990) 'write back' to earlier work, out of copyright. Kathy Acker's *Great Expectations* (1982) quotes tracts of Dickens' novel of the same name.
- Straightforward ways of avoiding illegality in critical books and articles through the use of quotation marks, footnotes, endnotes and bibliographies.
- Intellectual copyright, and the (sometimes protracted and expensive) ways in which you can assert ownership of work you have published in book or magazine form, and even online, or that you have had screened or performed.

Assessing the assessors

Universities are obliged by HEFCE to monitor both tutors and students, and university methods and practices of assessment must conform to a nationwide Code of Practice for the assurance of what is called academic quality and standards. This code has been devised by the QAA, and QAA-trained teams of academics visit universities on a rota to review, among other procedures, how tutors design their courses and have them 'validated' or approved by university committees, the documentation available to students, the quality of feedback to students on their work, the principles, timing and range of assessment tasks, marking procedures, and assessment panels and boards. The QAA also monitors student performance and charts their progress during their course, and ensures that their work is on a par with that submitted on similar programmes of study.

As a twenty-first century student you will have more say in how your courses are run than students have ever had before – if only because in part you are perceived (by university managers and accountants, not by tutors) as a client and consumer. At the end of every module you will be given (or sent online) an evaluation form. Be altruistic, and fill it in: it will help your tutors to identify points of good and bad practice, and to amend and streamline the MA. The results will be collated and included in an annual report which will be forwarded to a monitoring committee and made available to QAA assessors.

You will also have elected student representatives with whom you can raise matters of concern informally during the semester, or in special end-of-semester sessions where no tutor is present. Or perhaps you are a representative yourself, and required to pass on student opinion to the course team, and then to a committee that monitors MA programmes and whose minutes are available for inspection by assessors.

Assessment criteria are not a gold standard but are – and should be – influenced by changes in the culture at large. Although, as a postgraduate, you might not have been directly involved in establishing them, you could, in the light of your experience of the MA, help to modify or expand them. By doing so, you will help to update and improve the course for students of the future, by which time you will be testing what you learnt against the judgement not of the university but of the world at large. Good luck.

References

Atkinson, Ann, Liz Cashdan, Livi Michael and Ian Pople (2000/2001), 'Analysing the Aesthetic: a new approach to developing criteria for the assessment of creative writing in Higher Education', *Writing in Education* 21 (Winter): 26–8.

Carey, John (2005), *What Good Are the Arts?* London: Faber & Faber.
Furedi, Frank (2004), *Where Have All the Intellectuals Gone? Confronting 21ˢᵗ Century Philistinism*, London: Continuum.
Harper, Graeme (2003), 'Creative writing at university: key pointers', *New Writing: The International Journal for the Practice and Theory of Creative Writing* 13777: 1–8.
Lodge, David (1996), *The Practice of Writing*, London: Secker & Warburg.

3

The Creative Writing MFA

Stephanie Vanderslice

The Creative Writing Master's of Fine Arts or MFA is an American phenomenon that originated at the University of Iowa in the 1930s, in part as an answer to the problem of geographic isolation that confronted writers working in the US, especially those without access to large cities. Still one of the country's most august graduate writing programs, the Iowa MFA has graduated a long list of luminary writers, including Flannery O'Connor, Philip Roth, Jane Smiley, and Richard Bausch, to name a few. Not surprisingly, many of these graduates fanned out across the country and formed their own programs in the image of their Alma Mater. As a result, today there are 109 MFA programs in the United States (Association of Writers and Writing Programs), a number which does not include the growing number of PhD programs, MA programs with a creative writing emphasis, and undergraduate writing programs.

The MFA emerged from two distinct traditions, the studio arts tradition from which it borrowed its moniker, and the English literature tradition, that is, it is usually (but not always) the English department that houses the program. Consequently, most programs reflect one or another tradition in their philosophies or are often an amalgam of both. The MFA degree is distinguished by being longer than the MA, with expanded credit hour requirements, such as a thesis, or substantial body of creative work and special coursework. Like its counterparts in the applied arts, then, the MFA is technically a *terminal* degree, requiring no other degree to qualify its holder to teach at the university level. However, in the US the terminal nature of this degree has been challenged by the rising number of doctoral programs in creative writing in the past two decades.

Understanding and evaluating MFA programs in the US is a recursive process, one that involves surveying the field, understanding the role that the MFA serves in literary culture, examining specific programs that interest you in great detail, as an educated consumer, if you will, and returning again and again to these important issues as you consider your options. But the first thing you must be educated about is yourself, that is, who you are as a writer. What are your writing needs? What kind of creative writing MFA program can best meet these needs?

Fortunately, in terms of the information available to you, there is no better time to be educating yourself. In fact, a great deal has changed since I meekly declared my interest in pursuing an MFA degree in the office of my undergraduate writing professor almost two decades ago. At her suggestion, I checked out the books of professors at several programs, sent for a handful of brochures, worked hard on my portfolio, and hoped for the best. Largely thanks to the web, today's MFA aspirant has any number of information portals literally at her fingertips in divining the right program for her, portals we will discuss in detail as we examine the pursuit of the MFA in America. But first thing's first.

You, the writer

As I mentioned earlier, before you begin to consider an MFA in creative writing, you must first look deeply at who you are as a writer. Where do you see yourself going? How will an MFA help you move toward these goals? Are you currently frustrated at trying to fit writing in at the thin edges of your life and hoping that an MFA will finally give you a few years time to concentrate on your writing and a supportive culture to do it in? Do you currently have an unwieldy writing project you've been working on that you want to bring into a community of expert and dedicated writers, in the hopes of shaping it into something publishable? Do you feel – or have you been told by those who ought to know – that your writing potential is right on the cusp and a few years among like-minded souls, under the tutelage of experienced wordsmiths, may be what you need to hasten its development, not to mention perhaps giving you a few publishing and academic contacts? Do you hope to earn your living as a writer, journalist, or as a teacher of writing, or as a mix of the three, or do you consider yourself, like insurance executive Wallace Stevens, librarian Marianne Moore or physician William Carlos Williams, a writer who happens to pursue other professions to pay the bills? Do you see yourself spending one to three years focusing on writing and obtaining this degree in residency, or do you think a low residency MFA, which you work on throughout the year with a faculty tutor but which only requires intense ten-day to two-week campus residencies annually or semi-annually, might fit better with your current situation?

Understanding your answers to these questions will help you to determine, whether, how, and what type of MFA program may be useful for you. What's more, as if repeatedly holding garments up to your body in a dressing room, these are answers you will need to return to again and again in determining the right MFA fit for you.

Assessment

Before we go on to look in depth at how to analyse and evaluate the dizzying number of types of MFA programs that exist today, it will be helpful to get a general sense of how programs assess their own effectiveness as well as how student work, within these programs, is assessed.

Programs in general

Unlike in the UK, American MFA programs have no assessment organisations, like the Quality Assessment Association (QAA), to which they must answer. Although the Association of Writers and Writing Programs (AWP) is the primary literary arts advocacy organisation in higher education, it is neither a governing body nor an accrediting agency. As a result, MFA programs in the US have emerged quite independently, a state of affairs that has a long list of pros and cons which we don't have the time or space to devote to here. Nonetheless, the AWP does make advisory statements towards making MFA programs more universally useful to their participants, suggestions readily available in the AWP

Director's Guide, online at www.awpwriter.org One of these statements is the idea that MFA programs *should* participate in some form of self-assessment, although this assessment can be as varied as listing alumni publications, analysing retention rates or employing an exit survey and analysing – and ideally acting upon – the results.

A sample exit survey is also available in the Director's Guide at awpwriter.org and can not only shed light on the aims and effectiveness of an MFA program (Do they give such a poll? How do they use the results?) but also on the kinds of considerations one should take into account in exploring any program. Questions about quality of teaching and relevance of courses are all beneficial to ask of a program at the outset. We'll get to other pertinent questions later in this essay.

Student work in particular

In general, it is safe to say that in most US graduate writing programs, grades are not as important as the student work itself and how the professor's *response*, both formative and summative, can enhance improvement in the student's writing, the objective of any workshop. Moreover, entrance into most MFA programs is highly competitive; the student's motivation and dedication to success is usually a given in most courses. Consequently, then, neither the students nor the professors tend to pay much attention to grades; rather, the focus remains on the student's work, often intensely so. Assessment, then, may come more frequently in the form of extended oral or written response to the work at hand, usually in the workshop. With the exception of the final thesis, moreover, there are no second readers or external examiners involved. However, the workshop and the writing assessed within it often isn't the *only* work required of students in a graduate creative writing program. Indeed, assignments and coursework can vary as much as the programs themselves and are an important factor for prospective students to investigate. Some programs include traditional literature courses in the degree, taught by literature faculty and assessed by traditional means – analytical papers, essay exams and so forth (also read by one reader – the professor – unlike in the UK). Other programs offer reading courses in which students are taught to read literary models as writers, and are often led in this endeavour by creative writing faculty who may ask them to write critical analyses about how a particular author or literary work informs their own. Still others offer editing courses or internships at publishing houses or literary journals that also include reflective analyses of the student's experience. Finally, some programs require students to read self-directed reading lists of relevant authors and most require a thesis of some sort, a lengthy capstone creative work. Students work closely with faculty advisors on their theses in the production of a work of publishable quality. Usually, they also write a critical introduction to the work, bringing to bear what they have learned about literary history and culture to locate their work in a contemporary context. Such an introduction is also known more commonly in the rest of the English-speaking world as the exegesis. In exploring MFA programs, then, it is important that you try to find out about courses, typical assignments and how they are assessed, in determining those most suited to you.

Evaluation

Throughout this chapter it has been impossible *not* to touch on areas a student might consider in evaluating and selecting a prospective MFA program. In light of the current abundance of information available, moreover, such areas warrant further consideration. Once you've thought hard about where you are in your development as a writer and how and what kind of MFA might help you, the first place you should turn is your local resources. If you are a current or recent undergraduate, most likely the creative writing faculty at your institution will be able to shed considerable light on different programs, since many of them will have experienced them first-hand. Meeting with these faculty members is a good place to begin, although keep in mind that they will have individual biases based on their own experiences.

Another resource worth checking into at the outset is the *AWP Official Guide to Writing Programs*, a detailed guide to creative writing programs that has long been considered a touchstone in the field. Recently, however, two additional books have been published which stand to add considerably to the discipline: Amy Holman's *An Insider's Guide to Creative Writing Programs: Choosing the Right MFA or MA Program, Colony, Residency, Grant or Fellowship* and Tom Kealey's *The Creative Writing MFA Handbook: A Guide for Prospective Graduate Students*. Both are seasoned writers and MFA alums and have spent considerable energy educating writers on professional issues; both have a web presence and Tom Kealy even has a blog (see Online resources) that discusses MFA programs extensively and even offers an advice column for prospective students. Reading the archived questions and answers for this column is an education in itself. At any rate, both books provide detailed, long-overdue guides to graduate study in creative writing.

Talking with mentors and arming yourself with information from available guides should help you to begin to narrow your choices to the MFA programs that will best suit you. Once you're ready to focus your search, it's time to begin using the internet to its fullest advantage. Most if not all MFA programs have websites that provide a window into their institutions and you should mine these sites as much as possible. While the majority of programs offer basic information on faculty and coursework as well as program philosophy, some also offer course syllabi, information on student and alumni publications and even online student newsletters and discussion boards. All of these can be enlightening for prospective students. In fact, the more information a program provides on its website, the more that you can infer that it is an open, student-centered place.

In addition to formal websites, the web also has much to offer prospective creative writing graduate students in terms of unofficial information. In addition to Tom Kealey's blog, many current MFA students have blogs that can shed some – albeit highly subjective – light on the student experience at various programs. Moreover, simply searching the names of faculty on the program and learning about their work and their philosophies on writing and teaching, through lists of publications you can pursue, and interviews you can read, will add to the arsenal of information that can help you decide on the suitability of a program.

Much has been made of the global changes in publishing that have made it increasingly difficult for most writers to make a living solely via their writing. If you are looking at the MFA as a career step, then, it is important to consider the extent to which the program is realistic about what it can offer students. Is it a program that purports to offer only space and time to write as well as expert teaching, without raising student expectations about publishing or landing a plum job in academia without significant book publication? Or is it one designed to provide students with experiences which can render them better qualified to take on other jobs in teaching, publishing or arts administration in order to support their writing? In addition, you might consider the size of the program (an entering class of five versus twenty-five), and the character of the students (traditional-aged, residing near campus, commuting students who have other jobs or careers) when examining a particular program. For example, a program admitting a small number of students, though perhaps more competitive, *might* be more committed to mentoring those students and providing individual attention than one with a significantly larger student body. Moreover, a program that caters to commuting students who often work in other careers may be less focused on job opportunities for students and more intensely focused on the literary work alone.

In making such an important decision, it is also wise to look at available funding for graduate study. In the US, there are often many scholarship options available for qualified students. In addition to the small number of fellowships (no-strings attached scholarships) available which are often intensely competitive, many programs often offer teaching assistantships in which students either team-teach large courses with mentoring faculty or solely teach the first-year composition course common in American universities. Not only do these assistantships offer a stipend and tuition remission, they also provide students with an opportunity to pick up important teaching skills that can help them support their writing with part-time, adjunct positions.

Finally, in researching an MFA, it is also important to try to gauge the program's commitment to mentoring students and helping them to navigate the publishing world and to maintain a sustainable writing practice after the program is over. This can be accomplished through interviews with program faculty and administrators as well as students, whose contact information may be available via the website or contacting the program itself. Armed with this array of information, as well as with a clear understanding of how an MFA program can meet your needs as a writer, you will be able to make a highly-informed decision on the program that is right for you, a decision that is the first step in successful MFA – and, subsequently, writing – careers.

Online resources

www.awpwriter.org The website for the Association of Writers and Writing Programs, which offers abundance of information on writing and MFA programs, including discussion boards and information on the annual conference.

http://creative-writing-mfa-handbook.blogspot.com Tom Kealey's blogsite.

www.pw.org The website for Poet's and Writer's magazine, an excellent source of information on the writing scene in America, which includes MFA programs.

www.amyspublishingnotebook.blogspot.com, www.amyholman.com, Amy Holman's website and blog.

References

Fenza, D. W. (ed.) (2004), *AWP Official Guide to Writing Programs*, Paradise, CA: Dustbooks.

Holman, Amy (2006), *An Insider's Guide to Creative Writing Programs: Choosing the Right MFA or MA Program, Colony, Residency, Grant or Fellowship*, New Jersey: Prentice Hall.

Kealey, Tom (2006), *The Creative Writing MFA Handbook: A Guide for Prospective Graduate Students*, New York: Continuum.

4

Creative Writing and Critical Theory

Lauri Ramey

Background on the 'creative' versus 'critical' opposition

Slightly more than one hundred years ago, it was arguable that there was such a field as literary study. Language was a proper field of study, but some late nineteenth-century figures including James Russell Lowell, Thomas H. Hunt and Calvin Thomas began to argue that if philology were to be made practical, it could be applied usefully to literature. The most frequent rationales for the academic study of literature were that poems, novels, essays and plays often showed the greatest skill in the use of language; their mastery was a valuable intellectual and moral exercise in putting one's knowledge of languages to work; and properly chosen texts could exemplify the most admirable human traits and aspirations. Lowell provided this metaphor in 1889: instead of teaching 'purely the linguistic side of things', language study should lead to

> something better. And that something better is Literature. The blossoms of language have certainly as much value as its roots, for if the roots secrete food and thereby transmit life to the plant, yet the joyous consummation of that life is in the blossoms, which alone bear the seeds that distribute and renew it in other growths. Exercise is good for the muscles of the mind and to keep it well in hand for work, but the true end of Culture is to give it play, a thing quite as needful. (Lowell 1889: 1737)

The two aspects of literary study are harmoniously connected in Lowell's vision of roots representing the literary and linguistic past and blossoms as the creation of new writing. But his metaphor points ahead to precisely the pedagogical and intellectual schism that later arose in the post-philology development of literature and creative writing in the drive for connoisseurship combined with the pragmatics of inspiring new literature. The bifurcation of the field of literary studies was inherent from its inception. For example, when Stanford University was founded in the 1890s, two pre-eminent scholars were hired for its newly-formed department of English: Ewald Flugel, trained as a philologist in Leipzig in the scientific study of language; and Melville Best Anderson from Iowa, a poetry specialist who viewed literature as a source of moral uplift (Carnochan 2000: 1958–9).

Creative writing as an academic subject developed at approximately the same time as English, and out of the same desire, which was to rectify the 'impracticality' of philology. In the US, the first classes in creative writing were taught at Harvard College by Barrett Wendell in the 1880s, whose English 12 class was designed 'to turn out men with something like a professional command of the art in which to practice' (Adams 1993: 52, quoted by Lim 2003: 154). The class stressed 'practice, aesthetics, personal observation and creativity' as opposed to the 'theory, history, tradition and literary conservation' taken as the concerns of newly developing departments of English (Fenza 2000: 15). Creative writing had become institutionalised within the academy by the 1920s (Lim 2003: 155). By the 1940s, postgraduate degrees in creative writing were offered by a number of American universities, including Johns Hopkins University, University of Denver, University of Iowa and Stanford University. Several recent studies of the growth and development of creative writing and its pedagogy (see Lim, Myers, Dawson and Fenza 2000 and 2002) offer varying perspectives on whether the field was intended more as a subjective and personal corrective to the rigid linguistic and historical orientation of philology (Myers 1996: 3), or a means of 'giving play' to Culture by developing professional writers.

Some critics suggest a correlation between the development of creative writing and intellectual movements such as New Humanism, Progressive Education and New Criticism, and later the Sputnik-era concern with educational reform, including wide-spread views by the mid-to late-twentieth century that 'the teaching of English was "a disaster area"' (Lopate 1979: 15; see also Kohl 1976). Views that literary studies had experienced a loss of identity were exacerbated by the growing dominance of critical theory, seen by many as shifting the field's focus on literature as an inherently valuable object of attention to literature as a means of gaining insight into other academic fields such as psychology, sociology, history and cultural studies.[1] Others have suggested that part of creative writing's attraction and popularity was precisely its lack of reliance on theory and pragmatic focus on the production of new literature. Robie Macauley, a visiting lecturer at the University of Iowa in the 1940s, dismisses suggestions that theory exerted any kind of influence on the Iowa Writers' Workshop and Paul Engle, who became its director in 1941:

> The idea of Paul, like some grand Teutonic professor, initiating anybody into the grand theory is ludicrous. Paul was a practical critic pure and simple . . . Andrew Lytle, of course, knew all the N.C. [New Critical] writing, but it didn't affect him a great deal – and he certainly didn't propound it in teaching during his short stint in Iowa . . . Of course the New Criticism was talked about some (as the reigning critical theory) and most people had read Brooks and Warren but (as far as I can remember) none of us tried to apply it – the N.C. – to writing fiction in any specific way. (Correspondence to Sarah Fodor, 22 May 1991, used by the recipient's permission)

Other programs saw creative writing as a valuable adjunct to literary studies so long as the field incorporated historical knowledge and critical rigour into the practice of generating new writing. Jean McGarry's 'A brief history of the writing seminars at Johns Hopkins University' explains that in 1947, the poet Elliott Coleman 'was assigned the task of founding a department, within the humanities, to train young poets and fiction writers in a context of academic rigour appropriate to Hopkins. How the study and craft of writing could be blended into a traditional liberal-arts program was part of Coleman's experiment'. Coleman created a program which produced early graduates (including poet Karl Shapiro and novelist John Barth) who would 'do honor, nonetheless, to their strong studies in English and French literature, aesthetics, linguistics, history'. Stress on interdisciplinarity, practicality and scholarship has continued as the hallmark of Johns Hopkins's program. McGarry describes John Irwin, who became director in 1977, as 'the very fulfilment of the Coleman mandate, combining, in his work, meticulous scholarship, heady criticism and (on the side) the practice of poetry', as he hired other 'scholar-writers' to maintain 'the intellectual and aesthetic rigor of the program' which encourages experimentalism, innovation, varied styles and 'brainy ferment about traditions and genres' (McGarry 2005).

Critical theory and creative writing in higher education today

As D. G. Myers points out, the teaching of writing at mid-twentieth century – whether creative or academic – was still 'an experiment in education' (Myers 1996: 3), a concept which continues to figure importantly in the description of Johns Hopkins's Writing Seminars and some other creative writing programs, whilst the term 'experimentalism' rarely appears in descriptions of English programs. This pivotal word's absence and presence in these two contexts suggests that the qualities entailed in experimentation – such as exploration, unpredictability, uncertainty of outcome, and innovation – which still characterise self-descriptions of many creative writing programs may partly explain the split between these two approaches to literature if they are considered to be mutually exclusive. For example, on the website of the MFA program in creative writing at the University of Illinois at Champaign-Urbana, Alex Shakar offers his thoughts on teaching, specifically the benefits of the writers' workshop as the central creative writing pedagogical tool:

> What must be avoided is an atmosphere in which the out-of-the ordinary is castigated while the reflexive and habitual go unquestioned. I try to make the writing workshop a place where aspiring artists feel safe taking risks, both stylistic and emotional, with their works-in-progress. If this kind of freedom is encouraged, the workshop can really be a workshop in the best sense of the word: a smithy of techniques, a laboratory of experimentation, and a forum of ideas. (Shakar 2005)

In contrast, the MA program in English at the same university stresses research, theoretical fields in which to specialise, interdisciplinary study, teaching experience, financial support and affordability, as well as the professional benefit – whether in English or another field – of obtaining this degree. Foremost, the MA in English 'is designed to provide students with the training in research and teaching that they need to obtain academic jobs' (University of Illinois 2006). In addition to what is stated in Illinois's English program description, words are absent of the type used by Shakar which suggest poesis in the classical sense of doing or making, such as 'smithy' and 'laboratory'. Processual terms referring to uncertain outcomes such as 'risks', 'freedom' and 'experimentation' have been replaced by references to concrete fields of knowledge and employability. Rhetoric similar to Shakar's is characteristic of many postgraduate creative writing programs, although goals and methods discussed in these terms would be highly unconventional for English programs. Equally noteworthy is Shakar's omission of techniques other than the workshop or mention of critical skills, precise informational content and literary history.

This case in point highlights the differing opinions on the identities of literary studies and creative writing, as well as the relationship between these fields. Consider Green's description of creative writing as 'literary study's wayward cousin' (Green 2003: 47), Marcelle Freiman's use of postcolonial theory to frame creative writing as a marginalised subject in relation to the dominant discourse of English (Freiman 2001: 1), Fenza's contention that the role of creative writers is to rescue literature from critical theorists and English departments (Fenza 2002: 53) or Radavich's statements that creative writing is a source of trouble and contention within English departments (Radavich 1999: 106–12). As these examples suggest, most of what has been written on the subject of 'creative writing and critical theory' addresses the historical antipathy between these two approaches to literature, instead of discussing their shared roots (to re-invoke Lowell), the long tradition of combining critical thought with the production of new writing, or how critical theory could be incorporated practically as a valuable element in the teaching of creative writing.

Unlike English, creative writing has not been amenable to the development of its own body of theory (although many argue that the critical theory of English does not belong to English at all, but has come from other disciplines including psychology, philosophy and sociology). A comparison often is made to the field of studio art in contrast with art history. If the goal is to make new art rather than analyse art which already exists, theory has tended to be perceived as antithetical to creative writing's fundamental stress on freedom, receptivity to the new and unfamiliar, and experimentation. These assumptions – which have generated lively debate as to whether or not creative writing as an academic subject has or should have specific content – explains why theories from other areas of the humanities and social sciences have not routinely been grafted on to creative writing similarly to their adoption by English.

Critical theory is not widely applied in the teaching of creative writing, although a small number of programs exist where the separation between the two is viewed as artificial and unconstructive.[2] The new MA in Creative and Critical Writing at the University of Sussex announces itself as the first of its kind, and is

> designed to enable students to combine an interest in intellectually challenging critical and theoretical ideas with an interest in creative writing. The new MA is based on the supposition that 'theory' and 'practice' are not opposites, though the relations between them may entail productive tensions and paradoxes. It is impelled rather by the sense that the critical and the creative are necessarily intertwined. Many great writers in English, at least since Milton, have also written important criticism. Good writers are invariably also good readers. The MA in Creative and Critical Writing offers students courses that combine 'theory' and 'practice', focusing on critical writings, for example, specifically with a view to encouraging and clarifying a sense of how to write creatively and well, and how to think creatively and differently about the possibilities of writing. (University of Sussex 2006)

Although they remain the exception, some other programs throughout the world routinely incorporate critical theory into creative writing. The MFA program in Creative Writing at the University of Maryland states:

> The general objective of the MFA in Creative Writing is to provide a professional course of study for graduate students seeking to perfect their ability to compose poems, stories, and novels. While primarily affording students intensive studio or practical work in their chosen genre, the MFA in Creative Writing requires that students incorporate such work with a traditional study of literature. Therefore the objective of the MFA in Creative Writing is not only to provide an atmosphere in which students can perfect their skills as writers, but also to give students a theoretical and historical understanding of their craft. (University of Maryland 2006)

At the University of British Columbia Okanagan, there is a newly formed Faculty of Creative and Critical Studies (FCCS) where

> the Faculty of Creative and Critical Studies (FCCS) plays a central role in the cultural education of students at UBC Okanagan by mobilising immense creative expertise and critical acumen to help students to balance their study across subject boundaries. FCCS strives to produce students who are not only great performers or artists, but who also understand the academic and philosophical connection that the creative and performing arts and their related academic and theoretical disciplines have to the other endeavours of the University. (University of British Columbia Okanagan 2005)

At California State University, Los Angeles, MA students in the Creative Writing Option are required to enrol in classes in Historical Criticism and Contemporary Critical Approaches and take classes in a variety of periods and genres of English, American and world literature. Daniel Green expresses a perspective shared by other critically educated creative writers that creative writing may even be the answer to the problems in the field of English by serving as the primary lens through which literature may be viewed and considered, and suggests the development of hypothetical Departments of Creative Writing and Literary Criticism (Green 2003: 50). The University of Luton proposed the actualisation of such a course in 1998 by offering the majority of its literary theory in modules in creative writing and media rather than English, formally discontinuing its Department of Literary Studies whilst preserving its creative writing program.

Examples of using critical theory in creative writing classes

For many creative writers who are open to such possibilities, the philosophical, social, historical, cultural and psychological apparatus of critical theory has helped them to discover their central literary purposes and goals, whilst also enabling them to recognise antecedents, connections and methods that can powerfully generate new ideas and practices for the benefit of their writing. Critical theory enables writers to learn to write not by following prescribed external critical dictates, but by seeking principles to use selectively and thoughtfully as a guide to reveal the values that are important to them as individuals and members of a community, partly by forming a more precise awareness of audiences and reading practices. Postgraduates in creative writing often approach their work without a clear goal in mind but with the primary motive of desiring to write. Wishing to write and enjoying writing are fine reasons for becoming a creative writer – even necessary. But they may not be sufficient over time to facilitate the greatest literary development in their essential self-reflexivity which often fails to engage large and compelling ideas. One of the most powerful results of using critical theory in creative writing is that it deepens and enhances a sense of what one wishes to write and why.

In my own practice, some of the first questions that I ask creative writing students are 'What are a writer's responsibilities? Why do you write? Whom do you write for?' The most common responses are 'I've never thought about that', even amongst students who have studied creative writing extensively and may hold degrees in the subject. These are questions to contemplate over a lifetime, where answers may change, but it is difficult to imagine producing writing of substance and lasting value where the writer has not at least contemplated philosophical questions of purpose. A common reaction to the idea of introducing critical theory in creative writing is 'It will take away my creativity' or 'If I know too much, I won't be able to write "naturally"'. I have not encountered any other academic discipline where students view the acquisition of new knowledge as anything other than precisely the point, or as potentially detrimental. Far from disempowering writers through rules, the opposite often takes place. Ideally, critical theory is the adoption or recognition of a personal ethos – the discovery of what we most value as writers. Once such realisations are made, how can they fail to infuse the act of writing and the resulting work of literature with even greater senses of clarity, passion and purpose? Connecting critical thinking and creative writing provides mutually energising ways of approaching literary production and reception that writers prior to the twentieth century would not have seen as separate, as the Sussex program description suggests.

When teaching critical theory in creative writing classes, I often begin with the classical roots of critical thought. Starting with foundational texts helps dislodge students' prejudices about critical theory by embarking from an unfamiliar vantage point (few creative writing students either in the UK or US, in my experience, have a strong background in history and theory of criticism). This is helpful insofar as it breaks through some conventional, and often negative, notions about critical theory as didactic, political, polemical, rigid and impenetrably jargon-laden. Using extracts from Horace, Dante, Lucretius, Quintilian, Tertullian, Plotinus, Longinus, Plato and Aristotle makes it possible to show that many contemporary critical debates have ancient foundations and relevance across borders of time and culture.

As a case study, here is one unit from an MA class that I teach called Critical Theory for Creative Writers, to serve as a template which may suggest a variety of other combinations of creative and critical readings and corollary writing exercises. The template reflects the standard structure of my teaching, which includes a mini craft lecture, writing assignment, discussion and workshop. The reading list of this unit includes Longinus, Sappho, Aristotle, Joyce, Edward Young, Marx and Edward Bond, progressing chronologically from the first century AD to the late twentieth century. We start with this extract from Longinus's 'On Sublimity' (first century AD):

> Real sublimity contains much food for reflection, is difficult or rather impossible to resist, and makes a strong and ineffaceable impression on the memory. In a word, reckon those things which please everybody all the time as genuinely and finely sublime. When people of different trainings, ways of life, tastes, ages, and manners all agree about something, the judgement and assent of so many distinct voices lends strength and irrefutability to the conviction that their admiration is rightly directed. (Longinus 2001: 139–40)

As a starting point for discussion, I provide a list of what Longinus considered to be the five sources of sublimity:

> The power to conceive great thoughts.
> Strong and inspired emotion.
> Figures of thought and figures of speech.
> Noble diction which includes choice of words and the use of metaphorical language.
> Dignified and elevated word arrangement.

To link Longinus's critical thinking to a practical application in creative writing, the class next addresses Sappho's Fragment 31 and Longinus's discussion of the fragment in relation to his theory of the sublime, which is a piece of critical writing as subtle and sensitive as the poem itself:

> Do you not admire the way in which she brings everything together – mind and body, hearing and tongue, eyes and skin? She seems to have lost them all, and to be looking for them as though they were external to her. She is cold and hot, mad and sane, frightened and near death, all by turns. The result is that we see in her not a single emotion, but a complex of emotions. Lovers experience all this; Sappho's excellence, as I have said, lies in her adoption and combination of the most striking details. (Longinus 2001: 140–1)

After discussion, the students receive this exercise based on Longinus's explanation of the sublime, its five major sources, the Sapphic fragment and Longinus's commentary on the sublimity of Sappho's poem:

> Create a fragment using the techniques that Sappho uses – metaphor, emotions connected to physical responses; attention to detail; form and structure intended to reflect the physical and emotional state as it is being experienced; direct first person address of the person who is both subject and object of the poem; and measured pacing to focus with great intensity on the experience being described simultaneous with the persona's experience of it. Employ these specific features, and heighten them even further by using Longinus's five sources of the sublime as much as possible to create your own sublime fragment on a subject of your choosing.

The students share the poems they have produced, which consistently result in works of impressively multi-layered complexity that often surprise the writers themselves. Certainly these works would not have been possible without encountering the intersection of the creative and critical through the 'dialogue' between Longinus and Sappho.

Aristotle in *Poetics* (fourth century BC) identified one of the central dilemmas faced by creative writers: the wish both to be original and understood. Section 22 of *Poetics* is the next reading that I provide, where Aristotle argues that diction's perfection lies in using clear and ordinary words which make writing comprehensible, balanced with metaphors and strange words which make the writing distinguished (Aristotle 1998: 109–10). According to Aristotle, a writer must use both forms of diction to keep the ordinary words from becoming prosaic and the deviant words from becoming a riddle or a barbarism. I ask the class to put Aristotle's theory into practice by reading the first twenty-four lines of the Anna Livia Plurabelle section of James Joyce's *Finnegans Wake* (Joyce [1939] 1967: 196). Once again, the purpose is to illuminate critical theory's utility in a creative context, tie the literary past to more familiar modern texts, serve as a useful spur to creative inspiration, expand processes of cognition, connect cultures and texts in fresh ways to stimulate creative thinking, and show how critical ideas often lie hidden in creative endeavours. Here is the exercise based on Aristotle and Joyce:

> How does this extract relate to Aristotle's view of literary quality in terms of perfection in diction? How many different techniques can you identify in Joyce's passage relating to the ordinary and the strange? Produce your own creative work in any genre where you employ Joycean techniques and produce a work which follows Aristotle's dictum regarding balance in diction.

In introducing Aristotle and Joyce, I explain that we are so accustomed to holding originality in creative writing as a positive and reasonable goal that we may not realise that it

of authors and texts speaking to each other through allusion, one of the most ancient literary tropes. T. S. Eliot wrote in 'Tradition and the Individual Talent' (1919) (another excellent text for creative writing and critical theory) that a new literary work enhances the present but also the past because literary history is read differently in light of this new contribution (38).

Writers speak to their own times and places, and also to earlier and contemporary writers who, in turn, struggle to reflect their own identities and cultures. As writers aiming to use knowledge of literary history and critical thought to our advantage, we must recognise literature as a network of conversations. The operation of allusion invites us to decipher the relationship between new literary works and pre-existing pieces of writing to which they refer. We also need to decide what the earlier writer and literary work signify to the alluding writer. This is the lesson gained from the chain of communication that we have constructed linking Aristotle, Longinus, Sappho, Young, Joyce and Bond across periods and cultures, which serves as a model for you to enter the process.

It is impossible for good writers to be devoid of beliefs. Theory is the awareness and expression of beliefs in our writing. It does not imply that we always know precisely what we think, that our beliefs are static or that we are fully aware of all of our creative goals for a work in process, especially if we are attempting something new. But if we take ourselves seriously as writers, we are at least asking these questions and seeking answers as to what we value and why we write. Sometimes we will figure it out in advance and deliberately use those ideas in our writing. Sometimes we will not be fully conscious of our views and discover them through the process of writing itself, or even through the responses of readers. But we each have an ethos and so do our readers. If those can mesh and meld through conscious effort, we have formed a connection. Critical theory for creative writers reflects who we are as individuals in relation to the literary examples of the past. It is a way of entering into tradition in order to express our unique voices and visions in the present.

The extract from *Lear* read by the class in conjunction with this mini craft lecture (which in its full version includes instruction in Marxist theory to show Bond's use of social theory in creative form) is a parable. Its inclusion exposes students to the use of a genre within a genre as a double framing device. In this parable within the play delivered to the audience by King Lear (III, ii), a bird steals a man's voice – something of a trickster myth – resulting in a conflation where the bird possesses the man's voice whilst the man becomes caged and is able to feel the bird's pain in a poetic and evocative philosophical interlude within the play. Close focus on the passage offers a rich example of the postmodern imagination through non-genre bound uses of form, technique, allusion and ideology.

This linked pedagogical sequence closes by connecting the parable of the bird to Young and Marx, whilst inviting a summary engagement with all of the readings in a critical and creative culminating task:

> Can you identify your own theoretical perspective in terms of your most important values, beliefs or ideology? Forming into small groups, explain and discuss what you consider to be your ethos as a writer. Using Bond as a stimulus, write a parable which exemplifies those ideas or ideals. It may take the form of a soliloquy, dialogue, prose poem, poem or chorus, and may be written individually or collaboratively.

I have used this curriculum, or the same structure with varying texts, with undergraduates and postgraduates in the US and the UK. The students consistently handle the material adeptly, resulting in fine writing that reflects some remarkable ways in which the students have been stretched in craft and cognition through the cross-mappings of theoretical and creative domains.

Benefits of combining critical theory and creative writing

Literary studies – where critical theory has played a major role for at least two decades – and creative writing have a history of being in tension to varying degrees; but this situation reflects educational structures and not literary thinking itself, as we are reminded by Lowell's metaphor of roots and blossoms. Historically, critical and creative ideas and their expression have been fruitfully and necessarily interconnected. There is an illustrious lineage of writers whose creative and critical thought is mutually enriching, including William Blake, Alexander Pope, Samuel Taylor Coleridge, Henry James, Gertrude Stein, Ezra Pound, T. S. Eliot, Charles Olson, Langston Hughes, Charles Bernstein, Susan Howe, Adrienne Rich, Kamau Brathwaite, Italo Calvino, Umberto Eco and other equally distinguished examples whose critical and creative writing may be fruitfully paired in teaching creative writing. Many modern and contemporary writers interested in the relationship between creative and critical writing produce essays and use techniques such as self-reflexivity, pastiche, parody, irony and other frame-breaking operations to explore metaphorically the creative process itself. Other writers intentionally blur distinctions between genres, and between the creative and critical, so their work enacts both purposes simultaneously. Writers associated with Dada, Futurism, Negritude, L=A=N=G=U=A=G=E Poetry, Beat Movement, Black Arts Movement, Caribbean Arts Movement and Black Mountain School have continued the tradition of putting their critical knowledge to inventive uses, or using their creative practice as a means of articulating the underlying theoretical stances which generated it. In fact, it is difficult to imagine many of our finest writers achieving their level of literary greatness without the philosophical underpinnings that informed their work.

Critical theory for creative writers is intended to encourage students to think more deeply about the process, goals, style, content and reception of writing – issues that should be paramount to any creative writer. For our most important writers, a critical ethos is present to be articulated. That is what is meant by incorporating critical theory in creative writing, if we think of critical theory in the open, interrogative and generative senses of encouraging writers to think about their authorial identities, audiences, purposes for writing and ways of best achieving their literary aims with direction and self-awareness. Most practitioners in the field today would agree that the purpose of creative writing is to guide, nurture, educate and support developing writers for the purpose of producing fine new literature. The role of the critical theorist is to decipher the meaning of works of literature in social, philosophical, psychological, cognitive, historical and cultural contexts. Literature is the focal point of both disciplines. The analytical study of literature by means of critical theory provides historical background, philosophical rigour, a sociological framework and formalist knowledge that would benefit any creative writer, which brings us full circle to the original intent of both fields: to preserve the past 'to give it play' by creating new writing in the present.

Notes

1. Since the 1990s, issues of major scholarly journals including *PMLA* and *Profession* have been devoted to the topic of 'What is our subject and where are we going?' The English Subject Centre

sponsored a conference in 2003 called 'English: The Condition of the Subject' which aimed to 'reflect upon how English has been constituted in the classroom through the changes of the last ten years . . . and what the future of English might be' (*Council for College and University English News* 2003: 19). Craig Hamilton was blunt about the outcome: 'Most of us would fail an exam that tested our ability to define "English Studies" accurately. Those who went to this year's "Condition of the Subject" conference looking for such a definition no doubt returned home empty-handed' (Hamilton 2004: 12). In 'Imagining the coherence of the English Major', Jonathan Culler contrasts the current uncertainties of English with Northrop Frye's past sense of cohesion: 'I suspect that many of us do not know or no longer know this sense of the unity of the subject and have to posit it by an act of imagination' (Culler 2003: 86). For other perspectives on what the 'problem' is with English, see Dasenbrock, Lewalski, Krieger, Motion, Fenza and Levine, including critics writing on the post-theory era or the death of theory, such as Tikhanov.

2. I have restricted my examples to MA and MFA programs in creative writing, where the greatest diversity of opinion exists regarding the intersection of creative writing and critical theory. At the BA and PhD levels, creative writing and critical theory are more often joined in the same program (though typically in separate modules, not actually brought into direct relation in the same class), but for antithetical reasons. Creative writing for undergraduates generally is not regarded as career preparation, but as a means of encouraging self-discovery and self-expression in a humanities or liberal arts education. At the doctoral level, degrees in creative writing generally are viewed as career preparation because the majority of students earning PhDs in the humanities are interested in pursuing academic careers. It is a common perspective that creative writers hoping for careers in the academy will be more attractive job candidates if they also are prepared to teach in other areas, with composition and rhetoric, critical theory and English literature as the most likely cognate subjects.

References

Aristotle (1998), *Poetics*, in David H. Richter (ed.), *The Critical Tradition: Classical Texts and Contemporary Trends*, Second Edition, Boston: Bedford Books.

Bond, Edward [1971] (1993), *Lear*, in *Plays: Two*, London: Methuen.

Carnochan, W. B. (December 2000), 'The English curriculum: past and present', *PMLA*, 115:7, 1958–60.

Culler, Jonathan (2003), 'Imagining the coherence of the English Major', *Profession*, New York: Modern Language Association, 85–93.

Dasenbrock, Reed Way (2004), 'Toward a Common Market: arenas of cooperation in literary study', *Profession*, New York: Modern Language Association, 63–73.

Dawson, Paul (2003), 'Towards a new poetics in creative writing pedagogy', *TEXT*, 7:1 (April), www.gu.edu.au/text/school/art/text/april03/dawson.htm

Eliot, T. S. (1919) 'Tradition and the Individual Talent' in Frank Kermode (ed.), *Selected Prose of T. S. Eliot*, New York: Farrar, Straus and Giroux.

Fenza, David (2000), 'Creative writing and its discontents', *Writing in Education*, 22 (Spring), 8–18.

Fenza, David (2002), 'Annual report to the members of AWP', *The Writer's Chronicle*, 50–5.

Freiman, Marcelle (2001), 'Crossing the boundaries of the discipline: a post-colonial approach to the teaching of creative writing', *TEXT*, 5:2 (October), www.gu.au/school/art/text/oct01/freiman.htm

Green, Daniel (2003), 'Not merely academic; creative writing and literary study', *REAL: The Journal of Liberal Arts*, Nacogdoches, Texas, 28:2: 43–62.

Hamilton, Craig (2004), 'Anglo-America IV: Nottingham and Maryland', *Council for College and University English News*, 18 (Winter): 12–13.

Joyce, James (1967), *Finnegans Wake*, New York: Viking.

Kohl, Herbert (1979), 'Interview with Herbert Kohl', in Phillip Lopate (ed.), *Journal of a Living Experiment: A Documentary History of the First Ten Years of Teachers & Writers Collaborative*, New York: Teachers & Writers.

Krieger, Murray (2000), Letter, *PMLA*, 115:7 (December), 2008–9.

Levine, George (1993), 'The real trouble', *Profession*, New York: Modern Language Association of America, 43–5.

Lewalski, Barbara (1993), 'Critical issues in literary studies', *Profession*, New York: Modern Language Association of America, 41–2.

Lim, Shirley Geok-lin (2003), 'The strangeness of creative writing: an institutional query', *Pedagogy: Critical Approaches to Teaching Literature, Language, Composition and Culture*, 3:2, Duke University Press, 151–69.

Longinus (2001), 'On sublimity', in Vincent B. Leitch et al. (eds), *The Norton Anthology of Theory and Criticism*, New York and London: W. W. Norton & Co.

Lopate, Phillip (1979), 'Roots and origins', in Phillip Lopate (ed.), *Journal of a Living Experiment: A Documentary History of the First Ten Years of Teachers & Writers Collaborative*, New York: Teachers & Writers.

Lowell, James Russell [1889] (2000), 'Presidential address', *PMLA*, 115:7, 1734–8.

Marx, Karl [1859] (1978), 'Preface to A *Contribution to the Critique of Political Economy*', in Robert C. Tucker (ed.), *The Marx-Engels Reader*, 2nd ed., New York: W. W. Norton.

McGarry, Jean (2005), 'A brief history of the writing seminars at Johns Hopkins University', www.jhu/~writsem/history02.html (accessed July 2005).

Motion, Andrew (2001), 'Creative writing', *English Subject Centre Newsletter*, 1 (February), 17–18.

Myers, D. G. (1996), *The Elephants Teach*, Englewood Cliffs: Prentice Hall.

Radavich, David (1999), 'Creative writing in the academy', *Profession*, New York: Modern Language Association of America, 106–12.

Shakar, Alex (2005), www.english/uiuc.edu/mfa/content/faculty/ashakar.shtml

Tikhanov, Galin (2004), 'Why did modern literary theory originate in Central and Eastern Europe: why is it now dead?' *Common Knowledge* 10:1 (Winter), Duke University Press, 61–81.

University of British Columbia Okanagan (2005), http://web.ubc.ca/okanagan/creativeandcritical/welcome.html (accessed 2005)

University of Illinois at Urbana-Champaign (2006), English website www.english.uiuc.edu/-graduate-/english/general.html (accessed 14 July 2006).

University of Maryland (2006), English website www.english.umd.edu/programs/CreateWriting (accessed 14 July 2006).

University of Sussex (2006), English website www.sussex.ac.uk/Units/publications/pgrad2006/programmes/English+literature/12647 (accessed 2005).

Young, Edward [1759] (1967), *Conjectures on Original Composition, In a Letter to the Author of 'Sir Charles Grandison'*, in James Harry Smith and Edd Winfield Parks (eds), *The Great Critics: An Anthology of Literary Criticism*, New York: W. W. Norton.

5

Literary Genres

David Rain

There's an anecdote about a board meeting at Desilu Studios in Hollywood, circa 1964, where Lucille Ball presided over the TV production empire she had set up with one-time husband Desi Arnaz. According to Desilu vice-president Herbert F. Solow, Lucy seldom said much during meetings. But one day, as Solow was about to update the board on series in development, network deals and the like, Lucy said suddenly: 'Herb, what's happening with that South Seas series?' Solow was perplexed. There was no South Seas series. Lucy said, 'You know, Herb, that South Seas series you mentioned last time'. Solow, Lucy insisted, was producing a show about USO performers entertaining the troops in the South Seas during the war. Solow did not know what she was talking about. He said he had never mentioned a USO show. 'Oh yes you did,' cried Lucy. 'Oh, yes, you did, Herb. You called it *Star Trek*!' (Solow and Justman 1996: 21–2).

What had happened? When writers pitch ideas for film, television, even books, it is often thought a good idea to describe the proposed work in terms of another. A film, for example, might be *Moby-Dick* meets *The Terminator*, or *Macbeth* among the gangs of East LA. *Star Trek* creator Gene Roddenberry had pitched the series to Desilu as '*Wagon Train* to the stars' – after a Western series, top-rated in its day, in which a party of pioneers travel intrepidly, and interminably, across the not-quite-final frontier of the Old West (Solow and Justman 1996: 15). Lucy, evidently, was thinking about a wagon train *of* the stars. What could a show called *Star Trek* be about, after all, but stars on a trek? The USO business was her own invention. What Lucy had failed to grasp was the *genre* of the show. The anecdote not only answers the much-debated conundrum, 'What was Lucy's contribution to *Star Trek*?', it also illustrates that we understand stories and story-ideas on the basis of our previous assumptions. Give us just a little, and we take a lot. We never begin with a blank slate.

This is what genre is all about. In this chapter, we will look at what genre means, in practical terms; at how genres develop, using the novel as an example; at the notion of 'literary' versus 'genre' fiction; and at ways in which we, as writers, may work with genre – or, to put it another way, with our awareness of the past, of everything that has already been written, and not by us.

Genre, form and mode

To define genre is not as simple as it looks. At a basic level, it's easy. A French word denoting 'kind', related etymologically both to 'gender' and 'genus', 'genre' has been used in English since at least the early nineteenth century to refer to a form, a type, a variety of literature or art. But how specific a kind?

Old-style English exams often carried rubrics warning, 'Students must show competence in the three main genres' – in other words, answer on poetry, drama and fiction. By these lights, a literary genre is defined by whether it is written in verse, dramatic form, or narrative prose. This is a simplified, modern version of an older three-way definition, dating back to classical times. Aristotle and Horace weren't much concerned with prose versus poetry. Literature *was* poetry, but there were three types of it: lyric, where the poet speaks to us directly; drama, where the characters do the talking; and epic, where the poet appears as narrator, and the characters speak as well (Wellek and Warren 1976: 227–8).

It may seem contrary to common usage to talk about poetry or drama or fiction as a 'genre'. A better word perhaps is 'form', or 'medium', suggesting the essential containers in which writing comes, irrespective of subject matter or style. But things are not immediately clear if we assume that genre is only concerned with these finer distinctions.

Take tragedy. In classical terms, a tragedy is a work written in dramatic form and encompassing a specific action: the noble protagonist, the tragic flaw, the catastrophic fall. Tragedy emerges in ancient Greece, and Aristotle's *Poetics* (fourth century BC) is its how-to-write manual. Famously, Aristotle insists on the primacy of plot, on the point-by-point structuring of events and revelations to achieve the maximum emotional impact on the audience: the celebrated *catharsis*, or purging of pity and fear. It's not a question of shocks and surprises. Greek audiences didn't want to be told a story they'd never heard before. Everybody knew already what happened to Oedipus: Sophocles' skill lay in how he put the story across. But even if we don't know the story of a tragedy, we know what kind of story to expect – and what kind of ending. Drama has its origins in ritual. This is a key insight not only in the understanding of drama, but of the whole concept of genre. Genre is, in a real sense, the enactment of ritual.

Both tragedy and comedy are basic literary 'kinds' which can be associated with specific structural features and methods of presentation. They also represent deeper, more fundamental literary impulses. Northrop Frye's schema in the influential study *Anatomy of Criticism* (1957) sets forth four archetypal literary kinds – comedy, romance, tragedy, satire – which persist across human history and correspond to the four seasons: respectively, spring, summer, autumn, winter. Another classic critical study, William Empson's *Some Versions of Pastoral* (1935), takes what might have been thought a distinct, easy-to-recognise genre, and expands its meaning. Originally, pastoral was a form of poetry – the *Idylls* of Theocritus, the *Eclogues* of Virgil – in which the city-dwelling poet longs for an idealised notion of simple, rural life. To Empson, 'pastoral' is any work which, even implicitly, contrasts simple and complicated ways of life, favouring the former; his 'versions of pastoral' therefore include Shakespeare's Sonnet 94 ('They that have power to hurt, and will do none'), 'The Garden' by Andrew Marvell, John Gay's eighteenth-century satirical play *The Beggar's Opera*, and Lewis Carroll's *Alice's Adventures in Wonderland*. We could add more: A. E. Housman's poem-sequence *A Shropshire Lad*, *The Waltons* and *Little House on the Prairie*, *The Lord of the Rings*, 'Rocky Mountain High' by John Denver. If genre is to mean anything, it has to mean something more specific than this.

In Frye's archetypes and Empson's 'versions', we are dealing not with genres, as commonly understood, but 'modes'. Satire is a mode, and can appear in many forms: Pope's mock-epic poem *The Rape of the Lock* (1714), Voltaire's scathing parable *Candide* (1759), Orwell's *Animal Farm* (1945) and *Nineteen Eighty-Four* (1949), Kubrick's film *Dr*

Strangelove (1963). All are satires; all, in the classical definition, 'expose folly and vice'; but the means by which this is done, and the form, tone and style employed is different in each case. A mode, therefore, is a way of approaching material. Where it gets complicated is when a mode is also, in a more limited sense, a genre. Often what begins as a genre – tragedy, pastoral – expands over time into a mode. Conversely, a mode or other broad literary effect – fantasy, suspense – may come to characterise a genre.

What most people mean by genre – as applied to literature, film and the like – is a particular type of subject matter. A Western is a Western whether it is a novel by Zane Grey or a film starring John Wayne. *Rebecca* (1938), the novel by Daphne du Maurier, and *Rebecca* (1940), Alfred Hitchcock's film version of the book, are both romantic suspense stories. But it isn't always so easy. Is the sonnet a genre? It is certainly also a form in any sense of the word, defined by the number of lines and the rhyme scheme, as opposed to what it is about. The ode, on the other hand, is an ode because of its subject (serious) *and* its style (elevated) *and* its form (elaborately arranged stanzas).

Our distinctions can seldom be hard and fast. If 'genre' means a fundamental, essentially permanent type of writing – say, comedy – it has also come to suggest a rapid, more or less ephemeral succession of styles: bodice-rippers, sex-and-shopping novels, cyberpunk. Taxonomic critics such as Wellek and Warren in their *Theory of Literature* worry about this. Are we to have an endless line of genres, based solely upon subject matter? 'Our conception of genre should lean to the formalistic side', they sternly advise (Wellek and Warren 1976: 233). Biology might be helpful: if poetry is the genus, the sonnet is the species. Alastair Fowler in *Kinds of Literature* (1982) analyses genre theory in exhaustive detail, but in the end offers no simple system to make all clear. It cannot be: genre is not a precise business, and any attempt to divide genres definitively from sub-genres, or to keep them distinct from form and mode, is doomed to failure.

Theory gets us only so far. History is more instructive.

Genre in the novel: a case study

What is a novel? The word has come to suggest any fictional narrative, on any subject, so long as it is written in prose (usually) and is of some length – say, 40,000 words at a minimum.

The definition was once stricter. Prose fiction can be found far back in history, and all around the world. In a remarkable book, *The True Story of the Novel* (1997), Margaret Anne Doody argues for a 'history of the novel' spanning numerous cultures and thousands of years; but this, perhaps, is to stretch to breaking point the notion of 'the novel'. When we talk about the novel, we usually mean a form of fiction that developed in Europe. Familiar literary history goes like this: once, the dominant form of narrative fiction was 'romance' (a word originally meaning 'in the Roman language'). Written in prose from the fifteenth century onwards, romances in the original sense were elaborate tales of chivalric deeds, courtly love, and pastoral enchantments, flagrantly 'unrealistic', frequently invoking magic. In English, Sir Philip Sidney's *Arcadia* (1581–93) is the dominant example of the form; Shakespeare's *As You Like It* (c.1600) is an adaptation of a once-celebrated prose romance, Thomas Lodge's *Rosalynde* (1590).

Already, Boccaccio's *Decameron* (1349–51) in prose and Chaucer's *Canterbury Tales* (c.1387) in verse had suggested the possibilities of realism. The sixteenth century brought the Spanish 'picaresque' – episodic, low-life comic stories about a *pícaro*, a rogue or trickster – exemplified in the anonymous *Lazarillo de Tormes* (1554). The same realistic, comic impulse infuses Cervantes' *Don Quixote* (1604–14), which subjects the romance to the withering barbs of parody. Driven mad by the reading of romances, Quixote sets out on a life of adventure, not realising that, far from being a valiant knight on a noble steed, he is really just a silly old man on a broken-down nag. In exploring illusion, reality, and the gap between them, Cervantes discovers the quintessential theme of the classic novel, one we can trace through works as diverse as Austen's *Pride and Prejudice* (1813), Dickens' *Great Expectations* (1860–1), Dostoyevsky's *Crime and Punishment* (1866), and Fitzgerald's *The Great Gatsby* (1925).

In eighteenth-century England, realistic narratives come dramatically into vogue. At first, such books purported not to be fictional at all. Defoe's *Robinson Crusoe* (1719) was apparently the autobiography of a real shipwrecked sailor. Richardson's *Pamela* (1741) was presented as an authentic collection of letters from an unusually literate servant girl, telling how she married her master after first fending off his attempts on her 'virtue'. The pretence of authenticity didn't last long: the point was, the story *could* have been real, happening in the real world to believable characters. Books of this sort came to be called 'novels' because the stories they told were *new*. As Ian Watt remarks in *The Rise of the Novel*, 'Defoe and Richardson are the first great writers in our literature who did not take their plots from mythology, history, legend or previous literature. In this they differ from Chaucer, Spenser, Shakespeare and Milton' (Watt 1963: 14).

In contrast to Defoe's mock-autobiographies or Richardson's collections of letters, Fielding's bawdy comic adventure story *Tom Jones* (1749) is delivered to us in elaborately artful third-person narrative, complete with direct addresses to the reader. But all the time, Fielding makes his claim on truth. Watt usefully distinguishes 'realism of presentation', the novel's illusion of reality, and 'realism of assessment', its depiction of the realities of human nature (Watt 1963: 300–1). It is because of its truthfulness, Fielding declares, that the novel is superior to the romance: 'Truth distinguishes our writings from those idle romances which are filled with monsters, the productions, not of nature, but of distempered brains' (Fielding 1966: 151).

The distinction between novel and romance soon became commonplace. In her critical study *The Progress of Romance* (1785), Clara Reeve puts it like this:

> The Romance is an heroic fable, which treats of fabulous persons and things. – The Novel is a picture of real life and manners, and of the time in which it is written. The Romance in lofty and elevated language, describes what never happened nor is likely to happen. – The Novel gives a familiar relation of such things, as pass every day before our eyes, such as may happen to our friend, or to ourselves; and the perfection of it, is to represent every scene, in so easy and natural a manner, and to make them appear so probable, as to deceive us into a persuasion (at least while we are reading) that all is real, until we are affected by the joys or distresses, of the persons in the story, as if they were our own. (cited in Allott 1959: 47)

As it happened, Reeve was also the author of a book called *The Old English Baron* (1778), an early example of the 'gothic' vogue which established itself in the wake of Horace Walpole's *The Castle of Otranto* (1764). Walpole's absurd ghost story is a famously bad piece of writing, and its historical significance is far in excess of its merits. Almost as soon as the realistic novel had established itself, the romance, in effect, broke back through, with its 'fabulous persons and things'. But it was not a simple reversion: in the preface to the second edition, Walpole claimed that his book 'was an attempt to blend the two kinds of romance, the ancient and the modern' – the old romance, in other words, and the novel.

The limitations of the novel were clear: 'the great resources of fancy have been dammed up, by a strict adherence to common life'. Invoking Shakespeare as his model, Walpole claimed that he wrote about realistic characters, but placed them in 'realms of invention' (Walpole 1969: 7). The stage was set for the first great flowering of the 'gothic novel', which peaked in Ann Radcliffe's curiously hypnotic saga of a girl imprisoned in a mysterious castle, *The Mysteries of Udolpho* (1794). Not the least aspect of Radcliffe's importance is her unprecedented development of descriptive writing. Previous novelists had spent little time showing what the world of their characters looked like; Radcliffe, eager to arouse wonder and awe, immerses her reader in a rapturous dream-world of exotic, wild scenery.

The gothic marks the first great schism in the English novel. Walpole used the term 'romance' as a catch-all for 'prose fiction' ('the two kinds of romance, the ancient and the modern'), but later commentators increasingly used 'novel' as the default term, the novel being the form of which 'romance' was a genre. Often it was a dubious one. 'Romance' suggested something less serious than the novel proper, an unlikely adventure story, perhaps a book for children: Dumas' *The Three Musketeers* (1844–5), Ballantyne's *The Coral Island* (1857), Haggard's *King Solomon's Mines* (1886), Baroness Orczy's *The Scarlet Pimpernel* (1905). Only in the twentieth century did 'romance' come to mean simply a love story.

Today's major varieties of popular fiction can all be traced back to the gothic. In 1794, anarchist philosopher William Godwin publishes *Caleb Williams*, a tale of flight and pursuit about a man unjustly accused of a crime, struggling vainly to evade capture. The story is set in the England of Godwin's day. There are no castles, no clanking chains; there is evil, crime, darkness, but no ghosts, no demons. In *Caleb Williams*, the crime thriller is born.

When Edgar Allan Poe writes the short stories 'The Murders in the Rue Morgue' (1841) and 'The Purloined Letter' (1845), the gothic obsession with crime and darkness turns into one of its most productive pathways: the detective story. Poe, like Matthew Lewis in *The Monk* (1796), a festering tale of depravity that allegedly shocked even the famously dissolute Lord Byron, also pushes the gothic towards its most intense form – horror – in stories such as 'The Fall of the House of Usher' (1839). Later American literature offers further permutations of gothic, in the nineteenth-century novel of symbolism and psychological allegory – Hawthorne's *The Scarlet Letter* (1850), Melville's *Moby-Dick* (1851) – and the twentieth-century 'Southern gothic' of novels such as Faulkner's *The Sound and the Fury* (1929). Meanwhile, Jane Austen's celebrated satire of gothic, *Northanger Abbey* (1818), does for Radcliffe and her imitators much the same as Cervantes had done for the old romance.

Sir Walter Scott draws on the gothic in a different way. Radcliffe had presented a world of the mysterious past, steeped in an atmosphere of stagy medievalism. Scott shared Radcliffe's feeling for history, adopting her elaborate, evocative scene-setting, but drawing on an altogether more credible past. *Waverley* (1814) lays out the classic formula for the historical novel. In Edward Waverley, Scott presents a fictional hero caught up in real-life events – in this case, the Jacobite rising of 1745 – with historical figures in supporting roles. Shakespeare's history plays had concentrated on the main players: Julius Caesar, Henry V. In writing *Waverley*, rather than, say, *Bonnie Prince Charlie*, Scott achieves greater imaginative flexibility in terms of plot, and allows the reader a more compelling sense of identification through the device of the ordinary person caught up in extraordinary events.

Scott was by far the most influential British novelist of the nineteenth century. Both Hugo's *Les Misérables* (1862) and Tolstoy's *War and Peace* (1863–9), are working, if more brilliantly, in Scott's vein, as are twentieth-century popular novels such as Margaret Mitchell's *Gone With the Wind* (1936) or Herman Wouk's Second World War saga *The*

Winds of War (1971). Not until Robert Graves' *I, Claudius* (1934), purportedly the memoirs of the Roman emperor, did a rival conception of the historical novel come to the fore. It remains less widely imitated.

The most celebrated take on the gothic is Mary Shelley's. The story behind the writing of *Frankenstein* (1818) is legendary: the ghost-story competition one wet summer on Lake Geneva where the young Mary and Percy Bysshe Shelley were staying with Byron, inspiring a dream from which Mary woke in terror. Mary Shelley was William Godwin's daughter, and her novel partakes of the claustrophobic atmosphere of her father's *Caleb Williams*, complete with elaborate details of flight and pursuit. Where it differs is in its treatment of the monstrous. In *Caleb Williams*, the monster is a metaphor: the novel is a story of human beings, and the monsters they make of themselves through pride, envy, and lust for vengeance. In *Frankenstein*, metaphor is reality. But what is most important is the reason why: Frankenstein's creature is not the product of magic, but of science. As Brian W. Aldiss argues in *Billion Year Spree* (1973), *Frankenstein* – more than any rival precursor – marks the beginnings of science fiction.

How genre works

In the movement from romance to novel, to gothic novel and beyond, we see that genres develop not through one process but several. The predominance of one type of work (romance) calls forth another (realism) that seems quite unlike it, as if to illustrate the law that for every action there's an equal and opposite reaction. But it's not quite the tug-of-war it seems. Richardson's *Pamela* purports to be a realistic novel. The setting is not Arcadia, but contemporary England; the heroine is a defiantly 'low' character, a servant-girl, not a princess or noble lady. But the story – rags to riches, basically – is just fantasy in another key. This is inevitable: all storytelling depends for its effect upon the creation for the reader of a desirable fantasy, and this is as true of Irvine Welsh's squalid story of drug addiction, *Trainspotting* (1993), as it is of C. S. Lewis's children's fantasies, *The Chronicles of Narnia* (1950–6). The reader is invited to participate vicariously in a world that may or may not be attractive, but is – to the right reader – *exciting*, offering an imaginary but powerfully satisfying extension of experience.

New movements in literature and art frequently purport to be more realistic, closer to the truth of life, than what has come before. Wordsworth, announcing a poetic revolution in his preface to *Lyrical Ballads* (1798), rejects the paraphernalia of eighteenth-century verse, with its elevated style, its classical allusions and forms. By contrast, he claims, he will write about 'ordinary life' in 'the language really spoken by men' (Wordsworth 1969: 164). Wordsworth's influence on nineteenth-century poetry was immense, but by the early twentieth century the mournful evocations of landscape, rural life, and the passing of time which followed in his wake had become the merest convention, and the language of poetry again seemed remote from the language of life. In 1913, the American poet Ezra Pound announced a new revolution. 'Imagism' would be a hard, unsentimental poetry with no superfluous words, no abstractions, no meaningless ornamentation. Poetry would evoke, not explain. And of course there would be none of the clutter of rhyme, scansion, and other features of traditional form (Pound 1972: 130–4).

We could put it like this: yesterday's realism is today's romance. The novels of Jane Austen are realism's response to the romances of Ann Radcliffe. But Austen herself is now read largely as a species of romance, and modern novels which draw on Austen are romantic, as in the 'Regency romances' of Georgette Heyer, such as *The Grand Sophy* (1950), or the fantastical reconfiguration of Regency England in Susannah Clarke's fantasy *Jonathan Strange and Mr Norrell* (2004). Realism and romance are the fundamental poles of literature, and the history of literature is of an oscillation between them. Literature wants both to escape and to confront reality. Realism is waking and romance is dream, and we desire both equally.

But if genre develops through a process of rebellion, it also involves a tree-like branching. We see this in the case of the gothic, in which the implications of a style or subject are progressively explored, with different writers making different emphases. In the modern era, new genres are identified rapidly. This has not always been the case. When Aldiss calls Mary Shelley a science fiction writer, he is not using a term she would have recognised. H. G. Wells saw his novels such as *The Time Machine* (1895) or *The War of the Worlds* (1898) as 'scientific romances'. It was only with Hugo Gernsback's magazine *Amazing Stories*, launched in the US in 1926, that the world began to speak of 'science fiction' – and then only slowly: a 1928 Gernsback editorial boasts of 'The Rise of Scientifiction' (Frewin 1975: 56).

Literary versus genre

In any gathering of science fiction writers, one theme soon emerges: the unending clash between 'genre' and 'mainstream' or 'literary' fiction. Science fiction writers are used to being dismissed by the literary establishment, and resent it.

The use of 'genre' as a term of disparagement is a recent phenomenon historically, reflecting the rise of branded 'category fiction' in the twentieth century. The delineation of genre in this sense is far more of a problem in literature than it is in cinema, where the Westerns of John Ford are considered classics, and Hitchcock's status as 'master of suspense' does not prevent him also being regarded as perhaps the finest of cinema's *auteurs*. But there is a paradox here: in so far as Hitchcock's *Vertigo* (1958) is seen as a masterpiece, it is, of necessity, elevated above the merely generic. *Vertigo* is no ordinary crime thriller.

Used negatively, 'genre' suggests not the basic properties of a work in terms of content or form – a level on which, say, Dostoyevsky might be considered a crime writer – but an implication of formula, of joining the dots. Nor is the charge unjust: the strict guidelines issued by publishers of 'category romance', such as Harlequin or Mills and Boon, are notorious. Writers of ambition are repelled by such rules, which seem to militate against creativity itself, making blatant the writer's role not as self-directed creative person but mere servant of editors and marketing departments, dutifully fulfilling the apparent expectations of an audience pictured as inattentive, easily bored, and petulantly impatient with the unexpected or the difficult. 'Genre fiction' by definition is *like something else* – fiction that resembles other fiction. It is for this reason that 'serious' fiction is assumed to be nongeneric, the product of a unique imaginative act.

It need hardly be said that this is seldom the case. A cursory analysis of literary or 'mainstream' fiction reveals a series of genres or sub-genres which are not branded as such: the novel of middle-class marriage, the sensitive study of adolescence, the upmarket romance, the upmarket historical, the literary fantasy or magical realist novel, the feminist novel, the multicultural or 'minority' novel, the experimental novel, the cultish youth novel. Literary fiction includes a great deal of genre fiction, more or less successfully disguised: for example, Kazuo Ishiguro's *Never Let Me Go* (2005), in which cloned children are reared as organ donors in an alternative version of contemporary England, is a science fiction novel in all but name. A work like this is generally felt by critics to 'transcend' the genre it resembles.

One might say it transcends it in so far as it is published in a non-genre jacket. Yet this is not quite fair. Science fiction stories tend to fail artistically to the extent that the author is seriously interested in science or technology or predicting the future. Ishiguro cares about none of this, presenting his story as a metaphor of human destiny rather than as a commentary on biotechnology, to be praised or blamed for its success or failure as scientific extrapolation.

Genre transcendence is a real phenomenon. The 'revenge tragedy' was a recognised genre in Shakespeare's time. But when we have said that *Hamlet* (c.1601) is a revenge tragedy, we have not said much. A celebrated African–American novel, Toni Morrison's *Beloved* (1987), is a ghost story – a murdered child comes back from the dead. But to say this is to say nothing. In any literary work that aspires to art, basic features of content are never ends in themselves. They are a vehicle: in Morrison's case, for what she wants to say about motherhood, race, slavery, time and death.

The critic Harold Bloom has written compellingly of the 'strangeness' that marks out those writers we think of as great (Bloom 1995: 4). Writers are considered 'great' in the proportion to which we view them as original. The great writer is felt to be *sui generis* (one of a kind, unique – literally, outside of genre). We value Shakespeare to the extent that he is 'Shakespearean'; Dickens is 'Dickensian'. In the later eighteenth century, there was a vogue of 'Shandean' texts, inspired by Laurence Sterne's bizarrely digressive comic novel, or anti-novel, *The Life and Opinions of Tristram Shandy* (1759–67). The sub-genre has sunk almost entirely into oblivion, and it is not difficult to see why. Sterne's eccentricity is the whole point: he cannot be systematised. The same is true of twentieth-century experimental writers such as James Joyce or Virginia Woolf. There are incidental features one can take from Joyce's *Ulysses* (1922), but the performance as a whole is unrepeatable – indeed, there would be no point in doing it more than once.

We might feel that Joyce, like Sterne or Woolf, is an influence of far less immediate value to other writers than, say, Shakespeare or Austen or Hemingway, who, for all their individual brilliance, are *enabling* to other writers in a way that Joyce is not. The word 'experimental', as applied to art, is misleading, implying a scientific or technological notion of progress which can hardly describe the movement from Homer to Dante, from Shakespeare to Milton, from Dickens to Joyce to Stephen King. It is perhaps inevitable, however, that literary historians see a writer's supposed 'innovations' as the benchmark of literary value, akin to a scholar's contributions to scholarship – as if literature *were* a science and the duty of each writer were to carry out experiments that would bring it, in due course, to a final perfection. This is not how writing works. It is not a competition to get the right answer. Writing is a matrix of possibilities, a vast interconnected web, and *Ulysses* and *Pride and Prejudice*, *Superman* comics and the *Bhagavad-Gita* and the fairy tales collected by the Brothers Grimm, Edgar Rice Burroughs' *Tarzan of the Apes* (1914) and William Burroughs' *The Naked Lunch* (1959) are all part of that matrix. This awareness can help us as we consider how to work with genre.

Working with genre

Genre is the most important decision a writer makes. It's not always an easy one. Beginning writers are often uncertain even about whether to write poetry or drama, fiction or screenplays. Of course we need not choose one form, and one only; but the writer who excels in multiple forms is rare. One of the most successful writers of the twentieth century, W. Somerset Maugham, triumphed first as a playwright, then as a novelist, a short story writer, and an essayist. George Bernard Shaw, by contrast, wrote five unsuccessful novels before discovering his true calling as a dramatist. Most writers find themselves only through much trial and error. In the meantime, each work has to be written in one form or another, and the writer needs to understand the strengths and weaknesses of the given form.

What works in one form doesn't always work, or work well, in another. Moody, unresolved first-person introspection of the sort suitable in lyric poetry rapidly becomes tedious in prose fiction. Fiction is narrative: it has to *move*. Drama is characters interacting. Every creative writing teacher has read more than enough go-nowhere stories which are all description and memory, or screenplays drowned in narrative voice-over, with nothing happening on the screen. An opposite problem is the 'television novel' filled with thinly-described characters flitting back and forth in a succession of brief, insignificant scenes, or the 'blockbuster movie' novel stuffed with rapid-fire special effects which can hardly have the impact on the page that they will be presumed to have in the cinema.

But form is just the beginning of our problems with genre. Genre is about all that has gone before, the heritage of writing that lies behind us. And by now, this is a long heritage. Belatedness is our fate.

This is a burden, and it is pointless to deny it. In *The Anxiety of Influence* (1973), Harold Bloom sets out a theory of poetic influence not as a matter of casual borrowings but of deathly struggles, in which the 'belated' poet must battle against the 'precursor' – the 'father' whose work must be distorted, deliberately 'misread', by the poetic 'son', in order that he may claim his own imaginative space. As Terry Eagleton observes, 'What Bloom does, in effect, is to rewrite literary history in terms of the Oedipus complex' (Eagleton 1983: 183). Bloom's theory remains controversial, but the 'anxiety of influence' is a felt reality to any writer who has looked at a previous writer's work and felt, despairingly, that it has all been done – and so much better than one could do it oneself. The 'postmodernism' associated with American writers such as John Barth, Donald Barthelme or Thomas Pynchon, built on the parody and subversion of previous literary forms, is one way of approaching belatedness. The self-conscious dialogue with the classics in novels such as Jean Rhys's *Wide Sargasso Sea* (1966) – the story of the 'mad wife' from Charlotte Brontë's *Jane Eyre* (1847) – or Geoff Ryman's *Was* (1992), a latterday take on L. Frank Baum's *The Wizard of Oz* (1900), is another. John Barth expresses two views of contemporary literature in an illuminating pair of essays, 'The literature of exhaustion' (1967) and 'The literature of replenishment' (1980). The past, he suggests, is an opportunity as much as a burden.

We do not choose what we write as if from a smorgasbord of every available possibility. In the end, we write what we *can* write – to advance in writing is to become aware of limitations as much as of new horizons. As writers, it is the mission of each of us to find the material, the form and the style that best expresses our particular talents. Inevitably, this involves negotiation with literary history. Look at any work that is successful – in any sense – and what you find is the transfigured past. This is as true of T. S. Eliot's great poetic echo chamber of quotations and allusions, *The Waste Land* (1922), as it is of the Harry Potter books. J. K. Rowling's borrowings are obvious: *Harry Potter and the Philosopher's Stone* (1997) and its sequels combine the English boarding school story – a genre seemingly dead by the 1990s – with the 'magic portal' story of the *Narnia* kind, Enid Blyton's 'holiday adventures' such as the *Famous Five* series, and the weird grotesquerie of Roald Dahl. The US television series *Lost*, which premiered to much acclaim in 2005, is an inventive update of a very old standby, the 'Robinsonade', or story about being marooned on a desert island: *Lord of the Flies* meets *The Twilight Zone*, in this case.

Often there is a standard way in which a particular genre is treated. A productive approach is therefore to treat it differently. The reputation of Ray Bradbury rests largely on his use of a poetic, 'literary' style to render the sort of material which had hitherto formed the basis of pulp science fiction. In a classic Bradbury story such as his vision of nuclear holocaust, 'And There Will Come Soft Rains', from *The Martian Chronicles* (1950), Bradbury brings out the poetry and mystery and sadness and longing which had always implicitly inhered in the science fiction genre. Stephen King transforms pulp fiction in a different way. His basic plots are standard horror-fantasy material, not remotely original. What King does is to develop this material in a context of domestic fiction, the novel of character and relationships. A traditional horror writer would have written *The Shining* (1977) as a short story and sold it to the magazine *Weird Tales*. In what is probably the finest twentieth-century novel of the supernatural, *Interview With the Vampire* (1976), Anne Rice took an obvious, indeed hackneyed theme, and turned it on its head, presenting the one-time villain as hero, and showing us the world from his point of view. Two much-admired American novels of the late twentieth century, Larry McMurtry's *Lonesome Dove* (1985) and Cormac McCarthy's *All the Pretty Horses* (1992), are strikingly literary versions of another old pulp staple – the Western.

No literary property is inherently good or bad. Harriet Hawkins' critical study *Classics and Trash* (1990) is a good sourcebook for those wanting to see how elements of junk culture, so-called, circulate productively with high art – the hidden links between Shakespeare and Disney and George Eliot, Andrew Lloyd Webber and *Gone With the Wind*.

Screenwriting students are likely to be familiar with the 'hero's journey' laid out by Joseph Campbell in *The Hero With a Thousand Faces* (1949). Campbell, not a literary critic but a folklorist, claimed to have found a master-story which underlies the classic stories of mythology, a deep structure applicable to stories of all kinds. Filmmaker George Lucas famously used Campbell's model in writing the original *Star Wars* (1977), and the approach has since been popularised in screenwriting handbooks such as Christopher Vogler's *The Writer's Journey* (1992). The point of the 'hero's journey' is that it is an archetypal pattern, and appeals – and keeps on appealing – because it addresses basic human needs. Genres are repeating patterns of the same kind. To work with genre, the writer must understand not only how a given genre is structured, but what it *means* – what desires and fears we confront and perhaps allay in contemplating this quest, this crime, this tale of the Old West, this satisfying completion of fourteen iambic lines. To consider this is the beginning of at least one kind – one genre – of writer's wisdom.

References

Aldiss, Brian (1973), *Billion Year Spree: The True History of Science Fiction*, New York: Doubleday.

Allott, Miriam (1959), *Novelists on the Novel*, London: Routledge and Kegan Paul.

Aristotle (1970), *Poetics*, trans. Gerald F. Else, Ann Arbor: University of Michigan Press.

Barth, John (1984), 'The literature of exhaustion' and 'The literature of replenishment', in John Barth, *The Friday Book: Essays and Other Nonfiction*, Baltimore: Johns Hopkins University Press, pp. 62–76, 193–206.

Bloom, Harold (1973), *The Anxiety of Influence*, New York: Oxford University Press.

Bloom, Harold (1995), *The Western Canon: The Books and School of the Ages*, London: Macmillan.

Campbell, Joseph [1949] (1993), *The Hero With a Thousand Faces*, London: Fontana.

Doody, Margaret Anne (1997), *The True Story of the Novel*, London: HarperCollins.

Eagleton, Terry (1983), *Literary Theory: An Introduction*, Oxford: Blackwell.

Empson, William (1935), *Some Versions of Pastoral*, London: Chatto and Windus.

Fielding, Henry [1749] (1966), *The History of Tom Jones*, Harmondsworth: Penguin.

Fowler, Alastair (1982), *Kinds of Literature: An Introduction to the Theory of Genres and Modes*, Oxford: Clarendon Press.

Frewin, Anthony (1975), *One Hundred Years of Science Fiction Illustration*, New York: Pyramid Books.

Frye, Northrop (1957), *Anatomy of Criticism*, Princeton: Princeton University Press.

Hawkins, Harriet (1990), *Classics and Trash: Traditions and Taboos in High Literature and Popular Modern Genres*, Hemel Hempstead: Harvester Wheatsheaf.

Pound, Ezra (1972), 'A few don'ts by an imagiste', in Peter Jones (ed.), *Imagist Poetry*, Harmondsworth: Penguin, pp. 130–4.

Solow, Herbert F. and Robert H. Justman (1996), *Inside Star Trek: The Real Story*, New York: Pocket Books.

Vogler, Christopher [1992] (1998), *The Writer's Journey*, 2nd edn, London: Pan.

Walpole, Horace [1764] (1969), *The Castle of Otranto*, Oxford: Oxford University Press.

Watt, Ian (1963), *The Rise of the Novel*, Harmondsworth: Penguin.

Wellek, René, and Austin Warren (1976), *Theory of Literature*, Harmondsworth: Penguin.

Wordsworth, William, 'Preface to *Lyrical Ballads*', in William Wordsworth and Samuel Taylor Coleridge [1798] (1969), *Lyrical Ballads*, ed. W. J. B. Owen, 2nd edn, Oxford: Oxford University Press, pp. 153–79.

6

The Writer as Artist

Steven Earnshaw

For I know very well what the temptations of the Devil are, and that one of his greatest is to put it into a man's head that he can write and print a book, and gain both money and fame by it . . . (Cervantes 1986: 468)

It's 1940 and Gomez is visiting the Museum of Modern Art in New York. His life as a revolutionary in the Spanish Civil War has been overtaken by global events, and his wife and daughter remain in France, fleeing a Paris that is now ablaze. Gomez is given a job as an art critic and his first assignment is to write a piece on Mondrian, who is all the rage. But Gomez can see no point to Abstract Expressionism – it does not ask 'awkward questions', the kind of questions that a Europe coping with the rise of Fascism has to ask itself, the kind of questions Rouault, Picasso and Klee ask. His guide at MOMA is Ritchie, an American who counters that art is a chance to rise above these horrors – Ritchie goes to MOMA to *escape* the world (Sartre 2002: 26–32).

What, exactly, are the motivations for making art? The quotation from *Don Quixote* ironically suggests fame and fortune, but by its own artistic endeavour the novel hints that the real reason is elsewhere, whilst the scenario from Sartre's novel *Iron in the Soul* prods the reader in the direction of political seriousness over and above mere entertainment. There are assumptions in both which inform an understanding of the making of art. For one kind of artist, art has something to say about the world in order that it might be changed. Simultaneously, and sometimes in opposition, art is a means of transcending or removing oneself from reality, as if the world as we comprehend it is too much: Cervantes' novel plays on a confusion between the two as it lays before us his knight's attempt to transport chivalric texts into real life and thereby transform life itself. Whether as critique, mirror or escape, art exists within culture at the most profound levels. Which would seem to suggest that the artist, too, is a significant being. Yet it is more often the case than not that artists struggle to make a living out of their art. Is it only bad artists who suffer? A market interpretation would suggest so, but few, I suspect, would subscribe wholeheartedly to that. How do and should artists view themselves, and what language best describes what an artist does, the process of creativity the artist is engaged in, the role the artist finds him- or herself in? Or is it wrong to see the artist as engaged in a tussle with art and life; should we instead see the artist as a worker no different from any other who must find his or her way in the world, as a plumber, nurse or stockbroker has to do? Is being an 'artist' a vocation? Is being a 'stockbroker'? Is the artist simply another member of the audience?

You may have noticed that I have been talking of 'artists' rather than 'writers'. Are writers artists? Or has the notion of 'artist' been narrowed to the field of fine arts, leaving writers to assign to themselves the moniker of 'poet', 'novelist' or 'screenwriter'? For writers to call themselves 'artists' these days might seem pretentious, or foolhardy given the criticism modern art attracts (see below), or pointless since being a 'poet' or 'novelist' speaks to all these concerns in any case. However, part of the idea behind this chapter is that writers might think of their roles as working within the broader field of art, and that they are 'artists' whose concerns are broader than those of 'writing' only.

Such a distinction between 'writers' and 'artists' would certainly not have been a point of dispute in the first half of the twentieth century, as the title of Joyce's novel about the growth of a writer, *A Portrait of the Artist as a Young Man* (1916), indicates. The hero of the title, Stephen Dedalus, is steeped in aesthetics and couches his future life in terms of vocation and ambition from within the domain of art, not just writing. When Virginia Woolf advises readers how to approach the strange new works we now term 'modernist', she writes: 'You must be capable not only of great fineness of perception, but of great boldness of imagination if you are going to make use of all that the novelist – the great artist – gives you' (Woolf 1966: 3). Modernist writers assumed that they were part of a general artistic endeavour – to contribute to the possibilities of art in the making of art, to take it upon themselves to challenge themselves and the world. Joyce's novel ends on a note of high artistic seriousness: 'Welcome, O life! I go to encounter for the millionth time the reality of experience and to forge in the smithy of my soul the uncreated conscience of my race' (Joyce 1993: 218). However, a grand statement like this is likely to make today's writer unhappy, even though we know that it comes from the mouth of a self-consciously callow youth who might conceivably be forgiven for so blatantly reaching so high.

Why write? The Romantics

Even though Joyce's work is from the age of Modernism, Stephen is declaiming in the language of the Romantics. It is them we have to thank for the notion that the writer or artist is a different type of being from the rest of the world, someone who has a privileged vision and to whom the nature of the world is revealed: it is the artist who is inspired and has the ability to pass on such insights to mere mortals. There is no question here of *not* writing – the artist only has to be inspired, touched by the muse, to create. For Shelley, writing in 1821, the artist is an exceptional being, uniting the characters of legislator and prophet: 'For he not only beholds intensely the present as it is, and discovers those laws according to which present things ought to be ordered, but he beholds the future in the present, and his thoughts are the germs of the flower and the fruit of the latest time' (Shelley 1995: 958). But not only is the poet exceptional, the effects and scope of his work on society are virtually incalculable: 'Poetry is indeed something divine. It is at once the centre and the circumference of knowledge; it is that which comprehends all science, and that to which all science must be referred' (965). An artist making such claims now would be regarded as a deluded egomaniac, deluded about his or her own abilities and (possibly) about the power of art. Nevertheless, the language of the Romantics has continued to dominate ideas about the artist. In the twentieth century the sculptor Jacob Epstein said: 'A wife, a lover, can perhaps never see what the artist sees. They rarely ever do. Perhaps a really mediocre artist has more chance of success' (Epstein, quoted in Simpson 1988). Epstein's view is a direct descendant of the Romantics' view, and echoes the idea that because the (better) artist has a special insight, it may be that the general audience will have difficulty understanding the art on offer: art that is rejected or misunderstood may simply be an art that is beyond its audience. And so with the notion of inspiration inevitably comes a notion of hierarchy – the artist's heightened perceptivity places him or her not just outside the audience, but above it. No wonder then that many artists can be uncomfortable with the language of art when it is phrased in Romantic terms; they may want to use the term 'inspired' to indicate a very real, bodily feeling in the process of creation, yet will not want to lay claim to any special powers. Yet, rather oddly, the Romantic notion, at the same time as it appears to make the individual something of a unique case, denies the notion of the artist as the origin of his or her creation, since the artist is merely the medium through which the work of art comes. It places artists in a paradoxical position: wanting to lay claim to possession of the fruits of their labour, yet avowing that the driving force is not theirs at all. Whilst the Romantic notion of the artist continues to permeate contemporary culture, eighty or so years later a new grouping of artists advanced the idea that the artist was an irrelevance and that the work of art itself was what was most important. This too has had a forceful legacy in our understanding of the role of the artist.

Why write?: the modernist aesthetic

Modern artists do not necessarily want to be identified too closely with the 'content' of their work when it comes to interpretation and appreciation, certainly not so closely that the work is seen to wholly embody who they are; they would mostly want to reject the idea that artists and the work they produce are interchangeable. There is a horror that an audience (or interviewer) will crudely assume that the central character, theme or emotion is the pure expression of the life experience of the artist. This contemporary separation of the work of art from the artist derives mainly from the modernists.

The modernists saw a different world from their immediate forebears, one that placed greater emphasis on subjective experience, on the workings of the mind, and on the building blocks of art itself: language, narrative, form, colour, sound. To get at the newly perceived reality demanded attention to inner worlds and the artistic tools at hand to represent those worlds. One consequence was that art from the modernists moved away from an art that always had its audience in mind. Joseph Conrad wanted to make the reader 'see' (Conrad [1897] 1997: 128–31), but not in the same way as Dickens had wanted to open his readers' eyes to the appalling social conditions of the day which they lived next door to but could not 'see', or chose to ignore; Conrad's understanding of 'seeing' is that it is constructed through language, narrative, and cultural and social convention, not simply revealed or obscured by social upbringing or status. The emphasis is on the work of art itself. The modernist aesthetic is determined to make the work of art stand alone, to be autonomous. The young man in Joyce's novel argues that the artist should remain incognito: 'The artist, like the God of the creation, remains within or behind or beyond or above his handiwork, invisible, refined out of existence, indifferent, paring his fingernails' (Joyce 1993: 187). The work of art remains a law unto itself, each piece unique and with it its own set of rules, completely independent of the writer and its audience, self-directed, 'autotelic'. Another famous declaration from the modernist period is T. S. Eliot's essay 'Tradition and the individual talent' (1922), which also wishes to remove the writer from the equation by calling for an 'impersonality' of art, where the writer has to somehow be capable of excising what is personal from his or her artistic endeavour:

> There are many people who appreciate the expression of sincere emotion in verse, and there is a smaller number of people who can appreciate technical excellence. But very few know when there is expression of *significant* emotion, emotion which has its life in the poem and not in the history of the poet. The emotion of art is impersonal. And the poet cannot reach this impersonality without surrendering himself wholly to the work to be done. (Eliot 2005: 18)

This is both a theory of how art should be appreciated (non-biographically) and how it should be written (objectively). The artist is removed both from the process of creativity and from the creation. It is possible then to see that one of the modern difficulties for the artist is that there is a strong aesthetic derived from modernism, from modernist artists themselves, which demands a sidelining of the artist as important. We can have the art, but not the artist. This may explain the diffidence of many contemporary artists in talking about themselves and their works – although not all, of course.

Why write?: truth, politics, art

While modern artists might wish to distance themselves from the Romantic notion of the artist as hierophant, and also remain distanced from their work after the modernist fashion, it is also the case that it is rare for contemporary artists to assert that their work is primarily about raising social awareness in the manner that the novels of the nineteenth century did, in the way that the work of Dickens and Gaskell, for instance, did. Documentaries and investigative journalism would appear to be much better situated for this kind of work. It is not that modern artists refuse to comment on the modern world, it is that openly 'social' art – where the drive is primarily 'political' rather than 'artistic' – is categorised as 'propaganda' and therefore not good art.

It is not always the case. George Orwell gave four reasons for writing: 'Sheer Egoism', 'Aesthetic Enthusiasm', 'Historical Impulse' (the desire to see things as they are and record them) and 'Political Purpose' ('desire to push the world in a certain direction') (Orwell 1968: 3–4). Initially mainly motivated by the first three reasons, the Spanish Civil War 'and other events in 1936–7 turned the scale and thereafter I knew where I stood. Every line of serious work that I have written since 1936 has been written, directly or indirectly, *against* totalitarianism and *for* democratic socialism, as I understand it' (5). Dorothy Allison in a piece entitled 'Believing in literature' says that the reason for her writing is the desire to tell the truth in a publishing world which has difficulty appreciating her particular social, sexual and political context: poor, lesbian and Southern. She aims to tell the truth because mainstream publishing only reflects its own prejudices (Allison 1995: 178–93). On the other hand, we have a writer like John Banville who sees no overt moral or social intent in art. If there is anything moral to emerge it is just that 'the work of art represents the absolute best that a particular human being could do – perhaps even a little more than he could do' (Banville 2005: 51). E. A. Markham has this to say:

> Once, when asked why he wrote, John La Rose said: 'Because they lie about you. They pretend to speak for you and they lie about you.' I was encouraged by this, for I thought if anyone should

lie about me, I should be accorded that privilege. Though I would aim, naturally, to tell the truth. (Markham 2002: 94)

The problem is that 'truth' is not what it used to be (as Markham recognises), and again, from the modernists onwards, it has been difficult to lay claim to 'truth' in the way that the Victorians, for instance, did, or to share the kind of absolute political faith Orwell evinces at a time of political crisis. And the 'truth' about what? Subjective, experiential truth, vouchsafed for by artists themselves, is one thing; social or political truths are another.

It is a commonplace that bringing politics into art is the quickest way to bad writing. It will replace any artistry with vulgar preaching, replace entertainment with the didactic. Yet, if politics is taken in the broader sense of wanting to make some kind of intervention in the order of things, as Orwell takes it, in what sense could any serious work of art not be political? The Banville quotation might be the counter-argument, an argument that rests on aesthetics, a version of art-for-art's sake. But even here, surely, the intervention is in the possibilities of art, that the best art will expand art's horizons, and as such have significance in that way. But is that politics? Isn't that precisely the retreat from politics, the visit to MOMA to *escape* the world. Turning to John Burnside, here talking about his volume *The Asylum Dance* and its interest in 'dwelling', suggests that there is simply a reluctance for the writer to say what he is writing 'about', as if this is to betray oneself as unsophisticated, or not an 'artist', underlying which is no doubt a sense that what the writer does is work on his or her materials in order to create something that is not reducible to paraphrase:

> I have no desire – and do not presume – to write openly polemical poetry 'about' the environ-
> ment, first because I tend to dislike, as a matter of personal taste, poetry that is 'about' anything
> (no matter how worthwhile the subject matter); second, because the poetry I most value tells,
> as it were, in an oblique way, rather than directly.

Yet he concludes: 'Nevertheless, I do consider the poetry in this book meaningfully politi-cal (amongst other things), in that it tells – obliquely – some stories about dwelling, and about estrangement – which are, I believe, vital questions with regard to our participation in the life-world as a whole' (Burnside 2003: 24).

Burnside's predicament would seem typical of the contemporary artist: he wants to validate the importance of the artist whilst at the same time subscribing to the modernist aesthetic, Joyce's artist 'paring his fingernails' or T. S. Eliot's 'impersonality'. He wants to say something but not be caught doing it; he doesn't want to say anything but wants to say it well, since anybody can 'say' something, since anybody can have an opinion. It is the artist's 'purist' dream, perhaps, the novel that is all blank pages, the piece of music that is silence, the film that is one long unedited shot, the show that is a 'show about nothing'. Ian McEwan, in conversation with Zadie Smith, puts it like this: 'The dream surely, Zadie, that we all have, is to write this beautiful paragraph that actually is describing something but at the same time in another voice is writing a commentary on its own creation, without having to be a story about a writer' (Vida 2005: 225).

The desire to say things in such a way that they are not reducible to paraphrase, court-ing the charge of 'difficulty', 'inaccessibility' and 'elitism', is the modernist attitude of the artist, and, like the Romantic stance, can appear arrogant and anti-democratic. On the other hand, a modern artist who gives interviews, who is accessible to the public through readings, is faced, as we have seen, with the conflation of themselves with their works of art in a way which detracts from the art. Here is an example of a writer experiencing this very difficulty, of trying to be open to an audience yet struggling with its 'misapprehension', its desire to ascribe both a biographical connection and a social imperative:

> I did a reading a couple of months ago that was opened for questions from the audience at the end. One man asked if I'd had a particular set of tower blocks in mind when writing a poem that talks about tower blocks. I said yes, and explained which ones. He then asked me if I had been trying to 'draw our attention to something' by writing the poem, and burbled something about social problems. It wasn't so much steely incomprehension as cheerful misapprehension. I didn't really know how to respond, so I just laughed and said that if you're trying to draw attention to something then a poem probably isn't the best way to go about it. But it was disheartening to be confronted with the idea that people might read this particular poem and try and ascribe some kind of crude sociological agenda to it – 'Look at these poor people, look at how they live' – rather than the slightly subtler, less dogmatic treatment I had deluded myself into thinking I'd achieved. (Leviston 2006)

The public perception of modern art

Modern art itself is open to charges of elitism that brings it, and by natural association, artists, into disrepute. 'Is modern art off its head?' is a typical headline (Lawson 2006: 30), but this particular debate and perception about 'modern' art is at least a century old. Tolstoy in *What is Art?* (1898) fumed against the new art of his time – particularly the decadents and aesthetes – and the argument that it takes a cultured person to understand this kind of art, an art which is inaccessible to the majority of the population:

> Nothing is more common than to hear said of alleged works of art that they are very good but very difficult to understand. We are used to the assertion, and yet to say that a work of art is good but incomprehensible is the same as saying of some kind of food that it is very good but people cannot eat it. (Tolstoy 1995: 80)

More recently, John Carey's *What Good are the Arts?*, from which the Lawson commentary takes its cue, detects a similar disaffection amongst 'the masses' for

> various kinds of conceptual art, performance art, body art, installations, happenings, videos and computer programmes. They arouse fury in many because they seem . . . to be deliberate insults to people of conventional taste (as, indeed, they often are). By implication such artworks categorize those who fail to appreciate them as a lesser kind of human being, lacking the special faculties that art requires and fosters in its adherents. In retaliation, those who dislike the new art forms denounce them as not just inauthentic but dishonest, false claimants seeking to enter the sacred portals of true art. (Carey 2005: x)

Carey locates the decline in the appreciation of 'new' art in the 1960s, with the demise of painting, rather than with the emergent modernism so detested by Tolstoy. He identifies the role of the artist to be a fairly useless one, since art in itself is relatively useless. Many of the claims of importance that art often makes for itself are thoroughly demolished in his book: art does not represent a unique realm of culture; there is no work of art which can be said to have universal greatness; it does not make you a better person; there is no objective distinction between 'high' art and 'low' art – it is simply a matter of cultural construction; art's value in education is unprovable; experiencing art may lead to feelings of ecstasy, but then so might football violence. He comes to a conclusion at the end of the first section that rather than being an activity confined to social or class elites, art needs to be democratised:

> Perhaps if more money had been spent on, more imagination and effort devoted to, more government initiative directed towards art in schools and art in the community, Britain's prisons would not now be so overcrowded . . . It is time we gave active art a chance to make us better. (Carey 2005: 167)

It may seem that what we are talking about here has no relation to writing, it is about the use of art as a social panacea in opposition to the kind of modern art that is 'off its head'. However, it is related in two ways. First, writing falls within the realm of art, even if it is not (on the face of it) the kind of 'expensive' art Carey is discussing (paintings and sculptures, for instance). Secondly, the arguments in defence of modern art that he trashes are precisely the same arguments that are often used in defence of 'literary fiction', poetry and theatre. Interestingly, and bizarrely, in the second half of the book Carey advances writing and literature as the very cure-all for the ills of contemporary society he says is needed, whilst acknowledging he has no basis for his argument other than his own subjective taste and the benefits he has seen of introducing writing programmes into prisons, and the (unsupported) argument that providing an accessible, social art in schools will prevent the need for prisons in any case. The stakes for valuing art would appear to be extremely high, whilst at the same time there would appear to be no basis for identifying what counts as art, and if we were to know it when we saw it, it would have to be readily accessible to a general public in the manner that Tolstoy once argued. The modern-day writer wishing to take his or her art seriously does not have an easy time of it with a general audience or with certain critics. It should also be noted that Carey talks of 'the arts' and not of artists, again accentuating a modernist aesthetic that validates the work of art (after a fashion) but not its creator.

The Author in criticism and literary theory

Scott McCracken (in this book) remarks that when student writers are presented with literary theory and criticism they can often seem hostile to it:

> Ideas such as the 'death of the author', which can seem fresh and exciting in a third year undergraduate seminar on a traditional English degree, can appear absurd in a room full of struggling novelists; and their derision is hardly likely to be contradicted by a creative writing tutor who writes to live.

The response is not surprising, either from student writers or, indeed, from published authors. The history of twentieth-century literary criticism is one where the text itself has become all-important (mirroring the importance of the work of art at the expense of the artist), and the writer as an existing or once existing living person disappears from critical or theoretical attention. This is broadly the case throughout the twentieth century, although from about the 1960s onwards the reasons for dismissing the author change from those reasons advanced earlier in the century. More recently there has been work to reintegrate the author into literary theory and thus critical practice, complicated or smoothed by the increasing amount of interest in creative writing as an activity within the academy, from writers themselves and from academics. There is now a body of writers within the academy which is itself cognisant of what literary critics and theorists do and say about them, although this in itself does not necessarily negate what hostility there may be.

We have already seen that the separation of the work of art from the artist is initiated by writers and artists themselves at the beginning of the twentieth century. Once the work of art is finished and in the public domain the artist is no longer required either by the work of art, the artist or its audience. Following on from this, literary criticism from the 1920s onwards appeared to take the writers at their own words and argued that yes, indeed, writers were of no importance when it came to evaluating or interpreting literature. In practice 'Practical Criticism' in the UK and 'New Criticism' in the US became an ideal model for teaching and scholarship – the critic approaches the text as a verbal construct full of ambiguity, linguistic balance, and nuanced meaning organically organised, which then requires the wit of a trained academic to uncover and explicate. Students are given texts with no contextual information – everything they need is present in the 'well-wrought urn'. The killer blow to the writer came with Wimsatt and Beardsley's essay 'The Intentional Fallacy' (1946) in which they claimed that the reader can never know what the author's intentions were, and in fact, the authors themselves might have difficulty telling you. The intentional fallacy still holds strong today in theory and criticism, as Carey illustrates: 'Literary theorists effectively disposed of intentionalism as an evaluative procedure in the mid-twentieth century' (Carey 2005: 22).

What people are no doubt most familiar with, however, is the phrase 'the death of the author'. Rather than just an extension of what has already been said about the modernist aesthetic and the intentional fallacy, the arguments for killing off the author in literary theory and practice change in the second half of the twentieth century. 'The death of the author' derives from a Roland Barthes essay of that name (1968). Here is a passage from its opening.

> In his story *Sarrasine* Balzac, describing a castrato disguised as a woman, writes the following sentence: '*This was woman herself, with her sudden fears, her irrational whims, her instinctive worries, her impetuous boldness, her fussings, and her delicious sensibility.*' Who is speaking thus? Is it the hero of the story bent on remaining ignorant of the castrato hidden beneath the woman? Is it Balzac the individual, furnished by his personal experience with a philosophy of Woman? Is it Balzac the author professing 'literary' ideas on femininity? Is it universal wisdom? Romantic psychology? We shall never know, for the good reason that writing is the destruction of every voice, of every point of origin. Writing is that neutral, composite, oblique space where our subject slips away, the negative where all identity is lost, starting with the very identity of the body writing. (Barthes 1994: 114)

We cannot know 'who is speaking', or, put another way, we cannot identify 'an author', because writing itself, or text, or textuality, has a certain characteristic which removes 'voice' and 'origin'. This is a poststructural viewpoint, that everything exists as an inter-related text, unpickable, everything is text, including the world (pretty much). There is no such thing as individual identity, either for writers or for texts. In the poststructural view we, you and I, are 'subjects', constructed out of a myriad of historical and cultural forces. There is nothing unique about any of us, therefore there can be no unique individual called 'an author' to which or to whom we can refer if we want to understand what a text is saying. All of these notions – Romantic inspiration, the modernist aesthetic, the intentional fallacy, and the death of the author – remain potent forces in contemporary culture, and certainly do contribute to an overriding feeling that the artist has little to offer in terms of insight with respect to their own work. Comments they might make have no greater weight than comments by any other member of the public. To take the opposite point of view – that the artist naturally has the greatest insight into his or her work – has the tendency to move the discussion back onto the grounds of biographical understanding, towards which, as we have seen, artists themselves often have a great antipathy.

'The death of the author' view was in the ascendancy until the 1990s. In theory and criticism it probably still is the norm – somebody would have to do a lot of special pleading for proposing or assuming that his or her critical work could be based on something like authorial intention. However, there has been some renewed interest in the role of the author, although with certain caveats. The main proponent of returning attention back to the author is Seán Burke:

> When one also takes into account the sheer incomprehensibility of 'the death of the author' to even the finest minds outside the institution, it is clear that the concept functioned to keep the non-academic at bay: thereby, one more obstacle to the re-emergence of a culture of letters was put in place. (Burke 1998: ix)

Burke wants to return the author to theory using a language that does not have the difficulty of much of literary theory. However, the book is subtitled *Criticism and Subjectivity in Barthes, Foucault and Derrida* and so most of the book is engaged with close readings of these theorists. If ever you wanted to maintain the barrier between a culture of letters and a rarefied academic environment this is surely the way to do it. Undoubtedly there is something odd about telling a world of writers that 'the author is dead', but having to return the author to the living via Derrida is equally alienating, and it may be some time yet before the author is restored to both theory and a culture of letters.

The (self)-manipulating author: the writing 'I'

Nevertheless, Burke's path to the return of the author more generally might be quite helpful: 'This issue . . . is the need to arrive at a model of situated subjectivity. We are a long way off any such model, but the spectre of the inconceivable should not deter us from its adventure' (Burke 1998: ix). The problem then, as Burke sees it, is that the postmodern notion of subjectivity predominates and that any new theory would have to take this into account. (It could be argued that 'postmodern subjectivity' – the concept that we are not autonomous beings at all, but are merely the sum total of our historical and genetic circumstances – may appear just as counter-intuitive to 'the finest minds outside the institution' as does the argument about 'the death of the author', and therefore just as jargon ridden.)

There are a number of authors who have agreed with the postmodern view of subjectivity, or pretended to agree, so that just as there was a meshing of modernist aesthetics and the critical and theoretical work that followed, there has been a similar meshing in postmodern art and postmodern criticism and theory. Not only have they agreed with it, but used it to their advantage in creating art and a complex authorial persona that infects and informs the art itself. For example, here is Jorge Luis Borges toying with our view of 'him':

> The other one, the one called Borges, is the one things happen to. I walk through the streets of Buenos Aires and stop for a moment, perhaps mechanically now, to look at the arch of an

> entrance hall and the grillwork on the gate; I know of Borges from the mail and see his name on
> a list of professors or in a biographical dictionary. I like hourglasses, maps, eighteenth-century
> typography, the taste of coffee and the prose of Stevenson; he shares these preferences, but in
> a vain way that turns them into the attributes of an actor. (Borges 1964: 282)

Borges is making capital out of the distance between the author in the public domain and the living, psychological entity, the writer writing. The writer only recognises his existence as a definable author in an amused, affected manner. The public can only know the writer as a public construct, an 'author', which the writer himself may have had a hand in manipulating. The situation is further complicated because the status of the piece 'Borges and I' is unclear: is it an autobiographical note or a short story (in my copy it is actually in a section headed 'Parables', which creates further difficulties)? 'Borges and I' ends: 'I do not know which of us has written this page' (283). Roy Fisher's poem 'Of the Empirical Self and for Me' begins: 'In my poems there's seldom / any I or *you* –' followed by an indented 'you know me, Mary; / you wouldn't expect it of me –' only for the remainder of the poem to veer off into a landscape which appears impersonal and disconnected from the opening gambit, disappointing the reader who has been led to believe that there will either be some kind of 'I' revelation, or at least a further disquisition on this very subject matter. The poem itself is dedicated '*for M.E.*', which could either be Mary or a split self, m/e (Fisher 2005: 239). Without actually delving into Roy Fisher's life, or phoning him up, I have no way of knowing, and even then both interpretations might remain open.

This kind of writing foregrounds the issue of authorship and subjectivity: the gaps between writer (the living, psychological and physical human being), the author (public perception and construct attached to the name of the writer), the artist (the wider, public role). The very fact that we have the works of the writer/author/artist before us as an index of these three elements makes the network virtually intractable in terms of understanding it (and see Aaron Kunin's chapter in this book for more discussion on the 'I' in literature). Alice Munro's collection *The Moons of Jupiter* has a number of writers as narrators, and in the story 'The Moons of Jupiter' we are presented with this interesting scenario:

> I was tired from the drive – all the way up to Dalgleish, to get him, and back to Toronto since
> noon – and worried about getting the rented car back on time, and irritated by an article I had
> been reading in a magazine in the waiting room. It was about another writer, a woman younger,
> better-looking, probably more talented than I am. I had been in England for two months and
> so I had not seen this article before, but it crossed my mind while I was reading that my father
> would have. I could hear him saying, Well, I didn't see anything about you in *Maclean's*. And
> if he read something about me he would say, Well, I didn't think too much of that writeup.
> His tone would be humorous and indulgent but would produce in me a familiar dreariness of
> spirit. The message I got from him was simple: Fame must be striven for, then apologized for.
> Getting or not getting it, you will be to blame. (Munro 2004: 218–19)

Within the passage many of the concerns of a contemporary writer are apparent: other writers, the public perception, the writer's own status, the double-edged sword of fame, the varying degrees of 'recognition', of being validated as a 'writer'. But at the same time the reader cannot but help wonder about 'Alice Munro', the writer behind the author of a piece of writing concerned about being a writer/author. Is the writer in the story like Alice Munro in any way? But the writer in the story feels second-rate to another author. Does Alice Munro seriously suffer such an inferiority complex? Given her reputation that would seem unlikely? But then I check the date of publication – 1978 – when I suspect Alice Munro didn't then quite have the reputation as one of the world's greatest short story writers (but I may be wrong – how will I find out?). Or perhaps the joke is that it is the *other* writer – the more talented one – who is closer to the real Alice Munro? All futile speculation, of course, cleverly set off by the story's craft, but again, like the Borges and the Fisher, exploiting to the full the contemporary cultural position of the writer/author/ artist. There is nothing new about writers appearing as characters in writing – Cervantes 'the author' appears in *Don Quixote* – but the relation between the work of art and its creator would seem more complicated than ever within this 'crisis of subjectivity'. If there is nothing 'centred' or 'autonomous' about individuals, it makes it doubly difficult to discuss 'the author' or 'the writer' as something or someone singly identifiable within contemporary culture.

Timothy Clark's *The Theory of Inspiration* (1997) quotes from a number of writers showing how the very act of writing is itself a split in subjectivity, with at least two 'I's involved: 'Derrida quotes Merleau-Ponty: "My own words take me by surprise and teach me what I think"' (18), and Brewster Ghiselin on the process of writing: '"Now I began to see more clearly and fully what I was trying to say"', with Clark noting 'an unacknowledged disjunction here between the first and second "I," (Compare Virginia Woolf's diary entry: "I begin to see what I had in my mind")' (19). It is as if in the process of writing, it is what is written which doubles back on writers to confirm them and clarify what it is they are really thinking: there is a writing 'I' and a writer 'I' who, through the writing, comes to understand what the writing 'I' was doing all along. Clark takes this even further by showing how some times what we might call the writer-I only emerges at the time when writing occurs, and that calling up this writer-I can be a surprise to the everyday-I. That might account for the disjunction between the public's awareness and expectations of an author, and the ability of the author in the public arena to fulfil those expectations.

Although 'inspiration' is a somewhat discredited term in literary theory and criticism, it is clearly of interest to writers themselves, and in the way it is framed by Clark perhaps offers some kind of rapprochement between contemporary ideas of subjectivity and writing. Along the same lines, 'creativity' might be of interest as a subject for artists, and there is a lot of research ranging from the cultural to the neuroscientific (Sternberg 1999; Pfenninger and Shubik 2001; Pope 2005), but it remains outside the remit of much work in literary theory. Nevertheless, a book like Celia Hunt and Fiona Sampson's *Writing: Self and Reflexivity* (2006) is a sustained attempt to integrate awareness of these theoretical issues with advice about creative writing for the writer (and see Sampson's chapter in this volume), and Lauri Ramey (this volume) shows how literary theory can be positively used in the teaching of creative writing. Perhaps one should bear in mind the dangers of not being able to articulate the disjunctions apparent between the everyday 'I', the writing 'I' and the writer 'I'. In Muriel Spark's first novel *The Comforters* (1957), the central character 'hears' the tapping out of the novel she is writing, literally, leading her to wonder about her own sanity. It parodies Romantic theories of inspiration, conflated with the religious 'hearing' the voice of God, and yet at the same time provides an accommodation of the modernist distancing of the work from the artist producing it which itself seems open to question.

The role of the artist

The language of the artist is not often that of literary criticism or literary theory. Nor, as we have seen, is it often the language of its audience, an audience that wants to identify the writer with the works as closely as possible in terms of biography. When nineteenth-century writers addressed their 'dear reader' there was a context of intimacy, of an author speaking to his or her public, even if the possibility of there ever being such a direct, uncomplicated connection is now disputed. A 'dear reader' address now might have the appearance of unadorned communication, but it would be difficult to take at face value. The contemporary artist wants a knowing public, wants an audience that is aware of the sophistication of his or her art, a sophistication that is obviously felt to be lacking when the art is understood biographically. It is not easy to navigate through the demands of self, writing, being 'an author', the desire for a public that wants the art and not the artist (well, not all the artist), indeed the artist's desire for a public that wants 'art' rather than 'comfort', and the artist's desire for a critical acclaim that is not necessarily written in the language of criticism.

References

Allison, Dorothy (1995), 'Believing in literature', from 'Skin: talking about sex, class and literature', in Jack Heffron (ed.), *The Best of Writing on Writing*, vol. 2, Cincinnati: Story Press, pp. 178–93.

Banville, John (2005), in conversation with Ben Ehrenreich, in Vendela Vida (ed.), *Believer Book of Writers Talking to Writers*, San Francisco: Believer Books, pp. 43–58.

Barthes, Roland (1994), 'The death of the author', in Philip Rice and Patricia Waugh (eds), *Modern Literary Theory: A Reader*, 2nd edn, London: Edward Arnold, pp. 114–18.

Borges, Jorge Luis (1964), *Labyrinths*, Harmondsworth: Penguin.

Burke, Seán (1998), *The Death and Return of the Author: Criticism and Subjectivity in Barthes, Foucault and Derrida*, 2nd edn, Edinburgh: Edinburgh University Press.

Burnside, John (2003), in Clare Brown and Don Paterson (eds), *Don't Ask Me What I Mean*, London: Picador, pp. 23–4.

Carey, John (2005), *What Good are the Arts?* London: Faber.

Cervantes (1986), *Don Quixote*, Harmondsworth: Penguin.

Clark, Timothy (1997), *The Theory of Inspiration*, Manchester: Manchester University Press.

Conrad, Joseph [1897] (1997), 'Author's note' to *The Nigger of the 'Narcissus'*, London: Everyman.

Eliot, T. S. (1922), 'Tradition and the individual talent', www.bartleby.com/200/sw4.html (accessed 12 July 2006).

Epstein, Jacob, in *Simpson's Contemporary Quotations* (1988), www.bartleby.com/63/11/5711.html (accessed 12 July 2006).

Fisher, Roy (2005), *The Long and the Short of It. Poems 1955–2005*, Tarset: Bloodaxe.

Hunt, Celia and Fiona Sampson (2006), *Writing: Self and Reflexivity*, 3rd edn, Basingstoke: Palgrave Macmillan.

Joyce, James (1993), *A Portrait of the Artist as a Young Man*, R. B. Kershner (ed.), Boston: Bedford Books.

Lawson, Mark (2006), 'Is modern art off its head?', *The Guardian* 16 June, p. 30.

Leviston, Frances (2006), post to Hallam Poets Forum, www.poetburo.org, 10 June.

Markham, E. A. (2002), *A Rough Climate*, London: Anvil Press.

McCracken, Scott (2007), 'The role of the critical essay', this volume.

Munro, Alice (2004), *The Moons of Jupiter*, London: Vintage.

Orwell, George (1968), 'Why I write' in *The Collected Essays, Journalism and Letters of George Orwell. Volume 1. An Age Like This 1920–40*. London: Secker and Warburg, pp. 1–6.

Pfenninger, Karl H. and Valerie R. Shubik (eds) (2001), *The Origins of Creativity*. Oxford: Oxford University Press

Pope, Rob (2005), *Creativity. Theory, History, Practice*. London: Routledge.

Ramey, Lauri (2007), 'Creative writing and critical theory', this volume.

Sampson, Fiona (2007), 'Writing as "therapy"', this volume.

Sartre, Jean-Paul (2002), *Iron in the Soul*, London: Penguin.

Shelley, Percy Bysshe (1995), 'A defence of poetry' in Duncan Wu (ed.), *Romanticism: An Anthology*, Oxford: Blackwell, pp. 956–69.

Spark, Muriel (1963), *The Comforters*, London: Penguin.

Sternberg, Robert J. (ed.) (1999), *Handbook of Creativity*, Cambridge: Cambridge University Press.

Tolstoy, Leo [1898] (1995), *What is Art?*, London: Penguin.

Vida, Vendela (ed.) (2005), *Believer Book of Writers Talking to Writers*, San Francisco: Believer Books.

Wimsatt, W. K. R., Jr, and M. Beardsley (1954), *The Verbal Icon: Studies in the Meaning of Poetry*, Kentucky: University of Kentucky Press.

Woolf, Virginia (1966), 'How should one read a book?' in *Virginia Woolf. Collected Essays*, Vol. 2, London: The Hogarth Press.

7

The Future of Creative Writing

Paul Dawson

Originating in American universities in the early part of the twentieth century, Creative Writing has undergone an international expansion since the 1990s. Creative Writing programmes continue to grow in popularity despite perennial scepticism about their pedagogical value and their academic rigour, and despite their seemingly anomalous position within the modern research university. Perhaps an inevitable corollary of this expansion is the fact that Creative Writing has now become an object of scholarly enquiry, emerging in the new millennium as a distinct field of academic research.

It is no longer possible for Creative Writing to maintain its romantic ideal of a garret in the ivory tower, a community of writers made possible by the patronage of the university. And it is not sufficient to define Creative Writing pedagogy as the passing down of a guild craft from established practitioners to a new generation of writers. Writing programmes now exist in an intellectual environment of interdisciplinarity, critical self-reflection and oppositional politics on the one hand, and in an institutional environment of learning outcomes, transferable skills and competitive research funding on the other. What effects will this academic environment have on how the subject is taught, and on the creative work produced? This is the crucial question confronting teachers of writing in the New Humanities.

An object of study

For much of its history, formal reflection on Creative Writing has been largely restricted to writing handbooks which recast the evaluative and taxonomic language of formalist criticism in the 'practical' language of craft and technique, backed up by dilettantish musing on the creative process and the question of whether writing can be taught. Some critical commentary on the subject emerged in the 1980s, but this tended to be hostile rather than investigative, bemoaning the absorption of mainstream literary culture into the academy, and blaming writing programmes for the mediocre state of contemporary American literature.

While anxieties about the effects of Creative Writing on literary culture still exist, from the 1990s there has been a massive increase in scholarly material written about the pedagogical strategies and institutional location of writing programmes. Commentary on Creative Writing has become much more sophisticated and academic in focus, animated by self-reflexive theoretical and historical enquiry into the discipline and focusing on how to understand its place within the modern university. Handbooks continue to flourish, but the refereed journal article, the academic conference paper, even the scholarly book, now accompany creative work as regular publications produced by Creative Writing departments. The discipline of Creative Writing has become a growth area of academic research in America, and even more so in Australia and the UK where writing programmes proliferated in the last decade of the twentieth century.

TEXT, the electronic journal for the Australian Association of Writing Programs (AAWP), has published refereed articles about Creative Writing since its establishment in 1997. *New Writing: The International Journal for the Theory and Practice of Creative Writing* was launched in 2004 through the UK Centre for Creative Writing Research Through Practice. American scholarly journals such as *College English* and *Pedagogy* continue to publish articles on Creative Writing. There are several international conferences on Creative Writing held annually, including AAWP conferences in Australia, and Great Writing conferences in the UK. And the discipline now has its own institutional histories to accompany those of English and Composition which proliferated in the 1980s. D. G. Myers' *The Elephants Teach: Creative Writing Since 1880* appeared in 1996, providing a comprehensive historical account of the emergence of Creative Writing in American universities. My own book, *Creative Writing and the New Humanities*, was published in 2005 and provides an international account of the disciplinary history, theoretical underpinnings and pedagogical future of Creative Writing.

There are now sufficient key texts and identifiable debates, with specific national differences, to justify the existence of a field of 'Creative Writing Studies' within which academics can establish a research profile, and which can be packaged and taught to students. What happened in the 1990s to promote the emergence of this field? By this stage in history the intellectual paradigm shift of knowledge in the humanities produced by the rise of Theory had effected permanent disciplinary changes within English studies. In his 1993 book, *Cultural Capital*, John Guillory pointed out that the word 'theory', while most commonly associated with deconstruction, is a 'unifying name of manifestly heterogenous critical practices', but the *name* of theory is 'a sign both defining and defined by a syllabus of texts' (Guillory 1993: 177). This 'canon of theory', comprising 'master theorists' such as Derrida and Foucault, now supplements the traditional literary canon in graduate school curricula, as both an area of specialisation and a way to provide new methods for reading literary works. Guillory's argument is that Theory represents the technobureacratic knowledge of a new professional-managerial class, replacing literature as the cultural capital of the old bourgeoisie. Conflict over 'opening up' the literary canon, which Guillory argues wrongly conflates literary representation with political representation, is merely symptomatic of this crisis in the cultural capital of literature itself. Whether or not one agrees with this assessment, the very existence of Guillory's argument demonstrates the extent to which Theory had flourished in the academy. In other words, by the 1990s it could not be ignored.

The challenge of theory

By the time Guillory's book had been published it is noticeable that discussions about Creative Writing in America had shifted from concerns about the effects of writing programmes on literary culture to concerns about the division between Creative Writing and Theory within the academy, and this is precisely because of the influence of the Theory canon on graduate school education. In a 1986 review article Marjorie Perloff argued that conflict in American poetry between the conservative mainstream and a postmodern avant-garde is one that takes place 'largely within the academy', a battle 'between the Creative Writing Workshop and the Graduate Seminar in Theory' (Perloff 1986: 45). The fact that Perloff's characterisation of the 'A Team' workshop versus the 'B Team' seminar is one of the most-quoted lines in Creative Writing criticism demonstrates the extent to which a recognition of this institutional division set the tone for subsequent analyses of the relationship between the emerging discipline of Creative Writing and the increasingly dominant influence of critical Theory.

There was good reason for Perloff's characterisation of this divide. The classic critique of Creative Writing from the position of critical Theory is Donald Morton and Mas'ud Zavarzadeh's notorious 1989 article, 'The cultural politics of the fiction writing workshop'. In this tiresome rehashing of theoretical dogma, the authors criticise writing programmes for their outmoded neo-romantic belief in authorial 'voice' as the unmediated expression of selfhood, and the complicity of this belief with the ideology of the capitalist state. What is at stake in this caricature of the writing workshop is, as Guillory might say, the cultural capital of literature versus that of Theory. The article can be seen as a justification for setting the 'canon of Theory' on reading lists in the writing workshop as well as the graduate seminar, implying that writers are themselves unequipped to understand how literature really works, and that their craft requires explication by master theorists:

> The creative writing student who knows theory and who has read Marx, Lacan, Foucault, Lenin, Kristeva, Derrida, Gramsci, Heidegger, Cixous, Deleuze, Althusser, Luxemburg, Adorno will not approach the workshop with the same naïveté or accept its orthodoxies as will the student who has read the traditional syllabus of the literature department, which is entirely composed of poems, novels and stories. (Morton and Zavarzadeh 1988–9: 169–70)

By and large, the industry of critical Theory has not been concerned with Creative Writing, and it would be easy to dismiss Morton and Zavarzadeh's critique as an exercise in professional aggrandisement were it not for the fact that their basic criticisms of the workshop have been shared by many teachers of Creative Writing themselves. In the 1989 anthology, *Creative Writing in America: Theory and Pedagogy*, Eve Shelnutt articulated a frustration with the culture of anti-intellectualism within writing programmes, and this chapter has been regularly cited as a clarion call for a productive dialogue with Theory. The subsequent increase of interest in Creative Writing as an international field of academic research has largely come from within, and has resulted precisely from the discipline's formal engagement with Theory. This engagement has tended to see Creative Writing and Theory as incommensurable discourses, dramatising the professional divisions between these two areas as a series of intellectual binary oppositions (between practice and theory, creativity and criticism, writing and reading) which need to be negotiated. For instance, in the 1992 British anthology, *Teaching Creative Writing: Theory and Practice*, Robert Miles wrote: 'I believe that at bottom there is an irreducible tension between the manoeuvres of contemporary theory and the practice of teaching writing' (Miles 1992: 36).

In responding to this 'irreducible tension', some commentators have provided staunch resistance to the intellectual challenges and aggrandising critiques of literature offered by the 'fashions' of Theory, even positing Creative Writing as an antidote to the disciplinary malaise wrought by Theory, the last place for the art of literature to be appreciated as English departments are absorbed by Cultural Studies (see Fenza 2000; Green 2003).

Many teachers argue, however, that drawing upon the insights of Theory is necessary to 'demystify' the Creative Writing workshop, not simply as an exercise in criticism (such as Morton and Zavarzadeh's essay which approaches the workshop as a 'text' to be read against the grain) but as part of a genuine desire to reform the pedagogical practices of Creative Writing. Here the oppositional politics of Theory and the discourse of critical pedagogy are employed to challenge the commitment of writing programmes to a middle-class reading culture and a literary marketplace dominated by multinational publishers; and to uncover the 'false consciousness' of students, empowering them to develop a critically engaged and socially responsible awareness of their own work (see Amato and Fleisher 2001; Green 2001). Then there are those who argue that the writing workshop can establish a mutually profitable dialogue between literary practice and literary theory, introducing theoretical debates to workshop discussions which, in turn, offers a practical interrogation of Theory, thus establishing a formal pedagogical link between the two (see Cooley 2003; Newlyn and Lewis 2003).

These approaches rely on a rhetoric of opposition between Creative Writing and critical Theory, perpetuating this opposition as the very premise of their argument even as they seek to negotiate or collapse it. This rhetoric has been a necessary part of disciplinary self-exploration, but it will quickly become tiresome if taken as the basis for 'reforming' Creative Writing or 'integrating' the subject with literary studies. There are only so many times a teacher can use the workshop to stage debates about the 'death of the author', intertextuality, reader-response theory, identity politics, canonicity, etc. This is similar to the difficulties associated with Gerald Graff's suggestion, in *Beyond the Culture Wars* (1992), of 'teaching the conflicts' in relation to disciplinary debates within English studies: teachers find themselves compelled constantly to revisit the canon debate each time they teach the classics, maintaining a kind of polemical stasis.

As a response to the culture wars, Creative Writing studies has reconfigured literature from an artistic tradition which students enter by producing their own writing, to a contested epistemological category within the modern academy which can be investigated by the pedagogy of Creative Writing itself. However, Creative Writing is not a subject in 'crisis', the solution to which is to 'teach the conflicts' between literary practice and critical Theory; it is a subject which has gained disciplinary identity precisely because a new generation of teachers who perceive themselves as writers *and* critics have engaged with Theory to reassert the cultural capital of literature as intellectual work in the New Humanities. Creative Writing is thus an exemplary discipline of the post-Theory academy.

The post-theory academy

The concept of an age of post-Theory does not imply that the intellectual fashion of post-modernism has passed through humanities departments and that we can now return to the traditional goal of upholding Western humanist culture. Theory has irrevocably changed the way in which research and teaching is conducted in the field of literary studies. To say that contemporary critical thought is post-Theory is to recognise that the age of Grand Theory or High Theory in the 1970s and 1980s has effected disciplinary changes which are now being worked through.

One of the promises of Theory, particularly that offered by structuralism, was the possibility of a unifying methodological approach to the study of literature which could address foundational questions about what constitutes an object of study within the discipline, and which could provide a rigorous method for reading texts of all descriptions, manifested in exemplary fashion by the project of 're-reading' canonical works. In the 1990s, this grand enterprise of Theory fragmented and dispersed into diverse fields of enquiry: race studies, gender studies, postcolonial studies, media studies, etc. This is the result of both professional specialisation in an increasingly broad disciplinary field, and the pragmatic, localised and eclectic deployment of Theory within specific critical practices. Furthermore, a number of critics on the academic left have taken stock of the legacy of Theory, mindful that its radical promise can be dulled by institutional entrenchment. Post-Theory criticism in this sense is concerned with how politically-engaged criticism can operate in the modern university as well as agitate for social change. And it can be argued that the interdisciplinary enterprise of Cultural Studies has emerged as the post-Theory heir to English Studies. Indeed the slogan of the journal *Cultural Studies*, established in 1987, is 'Theorising politics, politicising theory'.

For me, the most significant and productive discussion of the post-Theory phenomenon is provided by Jeffrey Williams' 'The posttheory generation' ([1995] 2000). Williams' focus in this article is not on abstract debates but on the institutional conditions of criticism after the age of what he calls 'big theory'. For Williams the realities of 'a drastically reconfigured job market, pinched in the vice of a restructured and downsizing university' (25) are as important as the dispersion of Theory into various specialised studies, for this has influenced the orientation towards more modest and publicly accountable criticism which is being produced by 'the generation of intellectual workers who have entered the literary field and attained professional positions in the late 1980s and through the 1990s' (25). This posttheory generation, Williams asserts, has been educated in an academic climate governed by Theory and its 'hermeneutics of suspicion', but nonetheless possesses a sense of belatedness, of appearing after the revolutionary polemics of poststructuralism, Marxism and feminism became institutionally sanctioned as part of graduate school training and as a mark of professional attainment. 'In short, the posttheory generation was taught to *take theory* – not traditional scholarly methods, not normal practical criticism – *for granted*, and theory in turn provided a threshold stamp of professional value' (29).

Much of the research into Creative Writing as an academic discipline has been undertaken by members of this posttheory generation. According to Kelly Ritter: 'there is most certainly a generational divide between the pre-1980s hires in creative writing, most of whom hold the MA or MFA, and the current crop of new hires, many of whom will hold the MA or MFA and PhD' (2001: 216). In other words, Creative Writing students who have been exposed to the canon of Theory in the graduate school curriculum are now theorising their own discipline. According to Patrick Bizarro, there are several stages which Creative Writing has gone through in its emergence as an academic discipline in America: investigation into how the subject is taught; contextualisation of the subject in relation to other subjects in English studies, particularly composition; then, 'once it became economically feasible and desirable to do so, a new advanced degree in creative writing, the PhD, was established' (2004: 308). Bizarro points out that the research conducted by graduates of PhD Creative Writing programmes has been the next stage in defining for Creative Writing its 'epistemological difference from other subjects' (308).

As I pointed out earlier, a major reason for the emergence of an international body of research into the discipline of Creative Writing is the development of writing programmes in Australian and English universities. Creative Writing shares a remarkably similar institutional trajectory in these two countries. Courses in Creative Writing were first taught in vocational institutions in the tertiary sector: Colleges of Advanced Education in Australia; and polytechnics in England. When these institutions entered the university system in the early 1990s Creative Writing developed a large-scale presence, particularly at the postgraduate level.

What is significant about this history is that Creative Writing developed in both these countries *alongside* Theory and Cultural Studies as part of a challenge to traditional literary education. There is no long-standing tradition of Creative Writing in these countries which needed to be 'reformed', and no perceived contribution to an impoverishment or standardisation of literary culture. For instance, at the same time that Marjorie Perloff characterised an institutional divide between the A Team and the B Team in American graduate education, Ian Reid's 'The crisis in English Studies' (1982) and Colin McCabe's 'Broken English' (1986) argued that creative writing pedagogy could be enlisted in the *service* of Theory to interrogate the assumptions of traditional English studies.

By the time Creative Writing had attained a strong institutional presence and professional identity, the discourses of critical Theory had become embedded in university curricula and research output. And by making Creative Writing an object of critical scrutiny in order to establish its professional integrity as a new academic discipline, scholars in the field have been compelled to engage with prevailing modes of contemporary criticism. In other words, Creative Writing in Australia has developed its disciplinary identity *through* an engagement with Theory, rather than changing in *response* to it. In 2005, Jeri Kroll and Steve Evans commented that:

> anyone engaged in criticism nowadays, in fact anyone contemplating a higher degree in creative writing, has to be aware of theory, even if they are not converts to a particular tribe such as the poststructuralists or the new historicists. In Australia our discipline has been theorising its practice and its brand of research for more than ten years. (16)

A whole generation of graduates in Creative Writing who have gone on to teach in universities now takes Theory for granted, and this will continue. The post-Theory generation in Australia is also composed of established academics in literary and cultural studies who also publish creative work, and for whom the recent development of Creative Writing has offered the opportunity to combine their two interests. More and more teachers of Creative Writing across the world will thus be comfortable shifting between academic and literary modes of writing, and with combining the two, as well as investigating links with contemporary theory. For instance, in a 1999 essay about the hybrid mode of writing known in Australia as fictocriticism, Helen Flavell describes the eclectic interests of a typical student in the New Humanities:

> Anna is 24 and a postgraduate student. Her university doesn't have sandstone arches and ivy creeping; she's been brought up on a transdisciplinary diet of various subjects levelled under the umbrella of 'communications'. She's studied creative writing, journalism, won a prize for an essay in cultural studies, and thrives on reading contemporary theory. (105)

Creative Writing 'studies' will continue to grow, partly as a means for teachers to be considered 'research active' in a bureaucracy where research funding formluae do not acknowledge creative work, but mainly because it is inevitable that the proximity of writing programmes to other disciplines within the academy will facilitate a cross-pollination of ideas. Negotiating Theory for most teachers has involved finding ways to address productively critiques of authorship, representation and aesthetic autonomy; to challenge the hegemony of formalist and New Critical concepts of literature; to develop in students an awareness of the critical and social context of the work they are producing; and to encourage experimental writing rather than mainstream literary genres. If post-Theory criticism relies on what individual theorists or critical insights offer as the best help for the project at hand, then the same applies to post-Theory Creative Writing pedagogy. The usefulness of Theory to the teaching of Creative Writing (as opposed to the study of the discipline) relies largely upon the idiosyncrasies of teachers and their academic research interests. As Siobhan Holland says in her 2002 report to the English Subject Centre in the UK: 'Lecturers in Creative Writing differ in their views on the value of critical theory as a tool in the development of students' writing and such diversity in approaches to teaching Creative Writing is to be welcomed' (4).

Teaching the craft

In practice, the goal of the writing workshop and of postgraduate supervision will always be the same: to improve the student manuscript. What remains at stake is just what criteria are employed to guide and judge the success of this goal. I think a new aesthetic has emerged in Creative Writing in the New Humanities. There has been a shift from the 'sublime' (operationalised in the workshop by praising the well-wrought line, the striking metaphor, the finely constructed scene, the authentic 'voice') to the 'avant-garde', the goal of which, in Peter Burger's well-know formulation, is 'to reintegrate art into the praxis of life' (1984: 22). This avant-garde aesthetic encourages and rewards formal experimentation, subversion and renovation of genre, dialogic engagement with non-literary discourses, intellectual curiosity, political awareness and social responsibility.

In a 2001 article, 'Materializing the sublime reader', Chris Green argued that 'before asking how students can better write "good" poems, I propose we look beyond the gaze of the sublime reader and ask how students can write useful poems' (159). By useful he means 'a workshop where the class readership acts to represent the rhetorical circumstances of interpretive communities outside the university' (154). Green acknowledges that he is drawing upon the established discourses of Cultural Studies and reader-response theory to reorient the workshop towards a concept of community service. So the 'usefulness' of a manuscript comes down to the reading practices employed in the workshop. I have written elsewhere that in the workshop 'how a work is *composed* by the student is not as important as how it can be *read* in terms of the critical approach of Creative Writing' (Dawson 2005: 88). This means a student manuscript 'is evaluated according to its potential to sustain critical scrutiny, to be approved by specific practices of reading' (2005: 117). These reading practices have shifted in the post-Theory academy from a New Critical focus on unity and aesthetic autonomy, to a poststructuralist focus on open-ended play (see Freiman 2005) and a Cultural Studies emphasis on social context.

It would be instructive here to compare two handbooks on writing published in Australia by Allen & Unwin during the period which I have been discussing: Kate Grenville's *The Writing Book: A Workbook for Fiction Writers* (1990) and Hazel Smith's *The Writing Experiment: Strategies for Innovative Creative Writing* (2005). In a sense the difference between these two books is simply a product of the different aesthetic sensibilities of their writers: Grenville is a writer of realist fiction, while Smith is a writer of experimental poetry with a particular interest in multimedia and hypermedia technologies. Smith is also an academic with research interests in contemporary theory and poetics. In a broader historical sense, however, these two books demonstrate the difference between Creative Writing before and after its engagement with Theory.

There are many generic similarities between the two. According to Grenville, 'writing is one human activity that seems to respond better to well-developed intuition than well-developed logic. What this book tries to do is give those under-developed areas a chance to practise' (xi). Smith claims that her book is based on 'incremental strategies which recuperate, at a conscious level, the less accessible or unconscious aspects of the writing process' (vii). Both writers also rely on the standard handbook practice of exercises and examples. However, Grenville is concerned with helping writers gradually build up a coherent manuscript, while Smith is more concerned with suggesting open-ended 'strategies' for writing. And Grenville's examples are from the modern canon of Australian fiction, while Smith draws on not only a wider international and generic range of literature, but examples of student writing from her previous classes.

This approach indicates that there is a crucial difference in audience. Grenville's book has been on many recommended reading lists in writing classes since its publication, but it is designed for anyone who is interested in writing. Smith's book on the other hand is 'designed for university students enrolled in creative writing courses and for their teachers. Its aims are to suggest systematic strategies for creative writing, and to theorise the process of writing by relating it to the literary and cultural concepts which students encounter on other university courses' (vii). Smith realises that the presence of these concepts means a contemporary handbook needs to do more than simply duplicate the standard devices/taxonomies of fiction, which is what Grenville's book does with titles such as 'Point of View', 'Voice', 'Dialogue' and 'Description'. Smith's book, on the other hand, has chapter titles such as 'Genre as moveable feast', 'Writing as recycling'; and 'Postmodern f(r)ictions'. Grenville's book suggests drawing upon observations of life and is implicitly geared towards realist fiction. Smith claims that her book 'makes a connection between the analytical ideas of some major literary theorists and the process of writing, and puts theory into practice' (xii). In other words, it is an aesthetic engagement with Theory in order to generate innovative approaches to writing, not an attempt to educate students about the canon of Theory, or to establish an inter-disciplinary rapprochement.

The writing workshop is not simply a place for writers to pass on practical knowledge about their craft, but a site of contestation over various theories of literature, and a site for the exchange of pedagogical links with other disciplines. If the question which once dominated discussions of Creative Writing was, 'Can or should writing be taught?', it is now, '*What* should we be teaching students?' This question typically means 'Should we be teaching students Theory?', and 'What sort of Theory will be useful to them as writers?' An equally important question is 'What sort of writing should we be encouraging students to produce?' The aesthetic of post-Theory Creative Writing pedagogy is clearly geared towards experimental modes (anti-linear, discontinuous, multi-generic, self-reflexive, and so on) because these are more amenable to contemporary criticism. There is a danger here of promoting certain types of writing over others, rather than promoting a spirit of experimentation in all genres, 'conservative' or otherwise. It also begs the question of an ideal audience, and hence the way Creative Writing positions itself in relation to the literary marketplace.

The corporate university

The most pressing concern for the discipline of Creative Writing is not how to accommodate Theory in a traditionally anti-intellectual subject, but how Theory might help situate the discipline in what Richard Kerridge, in his editorial for the inaugural issue of *New Writing*, calls the 'audit culture' of the modern corporatised university, a culture which assumes that 'the main purpose of all subjects in higher education is the provision of transferable skills for employment' (2004: 3). This is an institutional environment in which 'generic definitions have confronted teachers in all subjects with the disconcerting new language of key skills, programme specifications, level descriptors and learning outcomes, terms that imperiously take from teachers the prerogative of identifying values' (3). Kerridge's argument is that Creative Writing 'lives in the borderland between the academic and the vocational' (4) and thus is well-poised to counter this audit culture.

There is in fact an uneasy synergy between the corporate language of this audit culture and the critical discourse of Cultural Studies which now dominates the New Humanities. They are both utilitarian, but one emphasises vocationalism and profit, while the other emphasises activism and critical consciousness. In his 2005 article, 'Cultural Studies in the corporate university', Jonathan Rutherford posits an historical link between the two, suggesting that the success of Cultural Studies 'as a multidisciplinary field of study that crosses the boundaries of economic, social and cultural life was both enabled by and also helped to legitimise the modularisation and marketisation of Higher Education' (309). And Simon During argues that Cultural Studies has replaced English in the corporate university because it has responded to both student demand for training in the culture industries, and the demands of a global economy for national competitiveness (During 1997). The debate between literary practice and critical Theory in Creative Writing Studies is, ultimately, not one over types of cultural capital represented by competing 'canons', but part of a wider debate about what transferable skills graduates need in the new economy. For instance, in the pages of *TEXT*, Jen Webb posed the question, 'What do writing students need?'

> My response to this question – a response predicated on my other-other identity as a cultural theorist – is that one of the skills writing students need is in understanding the politics of identity and representation; and that the active incorporation of cultural studies methodologies within the creative writing program is a good starting point for its provision. (2000: 1)

Webb justifies this in professional terms rather than in terms of overcoming intellectual naivety, 'on the grounds that it broadens students' skill bases' (2). While in America much is written about how outmoded assumptions of Creative Writing need to be reformed (or about how it can resist these reforms for the sake of literature), in Australia and the UK Creative Writing claims the post-Theoretical dynamism of the new, drawing on the rhetoric of praxis to distinguish it from traditional English studies and position it within the new economy of the Creative Industries. In describing a power shift within the university system which Creative Writing is poised to benefit from, Nigel Krauth writes:

> English and Humanities Departments, that once held sway in terms of offering studies for generic and analytical interpretative language skills, are now facing notions of 'productivity-value' not previously encountered. Reading and criticising texts, as opposed to producing them, doesn't cut so much ice with the clientele anymore. In the 1990s, the 'real world' focus of university training has added a practical 'can do' aspect to the receptive 'will do' orientation of English departments and traditional arts degrees. (2000: 5)

In other words, the response to a perceived decline in the cultural capital of literature has not been to set up a rearguard action or to embrace the canon of Theory; it has been to recognise 'creativity' as the cultural capital of the new Creative Class, which Richard

Florida defines as 'people in science and engineering, architecture and design, education, arts, music and entertainment, whose economic function is to create new ideas, new technology and/or new creative content' (Florida 2003: 8).

The term 'creative writing' has traditionally operated as a synonym for literature, and one which emphasises literature as a process rather than a product, but the fact that the word creative now refers in common parlance to any form of human endeavour, and the fact that the word writing is itself genreless, means that Creative Writing is almost by definition limitless in its disciplinary application. This is why the subject is taught in a range of disciplines in Australian universities, alongside literary and cultural criticism, the visual and performing arts, journalism, advertising and public relations, and new media technologies.

The PhD in Creative Writing

The growth of the PhD as a degree option in the subject is the most salient feature of Creative Writing in the post-Theory academy. It is important because the sort of doctoral education provided to a new generation of teachers will not only define Creative Writing as a research-based discipline, but also determine the future direction of the way the subject is taught at all levels.

As writing programmes proliferated in American universities after the Second World War, the Master of Fine Arts (MFA) became the most common degree in Creative Writing, and is still recommended by the AWP as the 'terminal' degree in the discipline, and as the equivalent of the PhD in literature. The MFA is conceived as a practical studio training for aspiring artists rather than a research oriented education for future intellectuals and teachers, and this system has taken the brunt of criticism about the role of Creative Writing in the academy and its impact on literary culture. The small but growing number of PhDs in Creative Writing are now being offered as a solution to some of the intractable problems associated with the discipline, particularly in relation to its intellectual narrowness.

In 2001 Kelly Ritter pointed out the declining value of the MFA, suggesting the degree is no longer considered a sufficient qualification for a university teaching position unless the candidate has several books published. Hence the PhD has become an important additional degree for MFA graduates who hope to teach in the academy. However, for this doctoral degree to justify its existence, Ritter argues, it needs to be marked as professionally distinct from the MFA. Her suggestion is that the PhD in Creative Writing be reconfigured towards teacher training, specifically 'the ability to teach undergraduates in the field' (208). Patrick Bizarro makes a similar point in his 2004 article, arguing that if Creative Writing is to operate as a discipline in its own right it must offer a distinct doctoral degree. For Bizarro this would involve the systematic teaching of skills employed by writers which are equivalent or analogous to those of scholarly research, and it would involve the teaching of skills required by writing teachers.

Both Ritter and Bizarro emphasise the need to provide PhD candidates with discipline specific skills rather than those offered by standard doctoral courses in literary research and composition teaching. In neglecting to discuss the creative dissertation itself, they demonstrate a belief that what defines Creative Writing as an *academic* discipline (rather than the master-apprentice system offered by the MFA) is its ability to be taught in a scholarly self-reflexive fashion, as opposed to its ability to produce new writing. In other words the creative dissertation is still conceived as a literary work to be circulated outside the academy instead of a contribution to disciplinary knowledge.

The PhD is a more widespread option in Australian universities, which Nigel Krauth claims are 'international pioneers in developing the creative writing doctorate' (2001). The reason for the growth of this option throughout the 1990s is again largely economic: in the modern research university the PhD is now an essential academic qualification for aspiring teachers; and universities are keen to enrol large numbers of students because they attract research funding from the federal government. Many established teachers of Creative Writing who were initially hired on the strength of their creative publications have undertaken doctoral study for professional reasons: in order to achieve promotion, or to meet standard requirements that supervisors of doctoral candidates should themselves possess a PhD. And a growing trend has been for PhD programmes to accept for candidature well-established writers with national and international literary reputations, many without strong academic backgrounds or any aspirations to work in the academy. For these writers the three-year federal scholarship for doctoral study offers a substantial alternative to grants from government arts bodies such as the Literature Board for the Australia Council.

The debates over the PhD in Australia and the UK have differed from those in America because the degree structure itself is different. Whereas in America doctoral students must complete substantial coursework and language requirements as well as sitting for comprehensive examinations before submitting their dissertation, in these countries there is no formal coursework and the degree is assessable by thesis only. The thesis consists of a creative dissertation and a substantial critical essay, often referred to as the 'exegesis', of up to 50 per cent of the word limit. This model comes from research degrees in the visual and performing arts, where a formal reflection on the creative process provides an interpretive guide to examiners for ephemeral performances or non-verbal artefacts.

Whereas in America debate exists over how coursework requirements can encourage reflection on Creative Writing as a teachable subject, in Australia debate exists over how the exegesis can encourage reflection on the creative dissertation as an intellectually rigorous enterprise. In the exegesis students will typically theorise their own creative process, reflect on the theoretical underpinnings of the creative work and its dialogic engagement with non-literary discourses, or contextualise the creative work in relation to specific genres, critical movements, etc. Hence requirements for some sort of relationship between the exegesis and the creative dissertation provide a formal opportunity for students to explore intellectual links between literature and critical Theory as modes of writing (as opposed to links between the teaching of writing and the study of Theory). The dilemma over how the relationship between the two components of this hybrid thesis is to be assessed has generated many articles by both students and academics in the pages of *TEXT*, providing a fundamental focal point for disciplinary investigation.

The debates I have outlined demonstrate a marked shift away from a conception of Creative Writing as formal training for new writers, and towards a conception of it as practice-oriented research. They are debates not just about doctoral education, but about how Creative Writing defines itself as an academic discipline in the New Humanities. The future of the discipline hence resides in how it theorises and manages the traditional nexus between research and teaching in the modern university.

References

Amato, Joe and Kassia Fleisher (2001), 'Reforming creative writing pedagogy: history as knowledge, knowledge as activism', *Electronic Book Review*, 12, www.altx.com/ebr/riposte/rip2/rip2ped/amato. htm (accessed 9 February 2004).

Bizzaro, Patrick (2004), 'Research and reflection in English Studies: the special case of creative writing', *College English*, 66:3, 294–309.

Burger, Peter (1984), *Theory of the Avant-garde*, trans. Michael Shaw, Minneapolis: Minnesota University Press.

Cooley, Nicole (2003), 'Literary legacies and critical transformations: teaching creative writing in the public urban university', *Pedagogy: Critical Approaches to Teaching Literature, Language, Composition, and Culture*, 3:1, 99–103.

Dawson, Paul (2005), *Creative Writing and the New Humanities*, London/New York: Routledge.

During, Simon (1997), 'Teaching culture', *Australian Humanities Review*, 7. www.lib.latrobe.edu.au/AHR/archive/Issue-August-1997/during.html (accessed 9 February 2004).

Fenza, David (2000), 'Creative writing and its discontents', *The Writer's Chronicle*, 32:5, http://awp-writer.org/magazine/writers/fenza1.htm (accessed 12 February 2003).

Flavell, Helen (1999), 'The investigation: Australian and Canadian fictocriticism', *Antithesis*, 10, 104–16.

Florida, Richard (2003), *The Rise of the Creative Class*, Melbourne: Pluto Press.

Freiman, Marcelle (2005), 'Writing/reading: renegotiating criticism', *TEXT*, 9:1, www.gu.edu.au/school/art/text/april05/freiman.htm (accessed 13 August 2005).

Graff, Gerald (1992), *Beyond the Culture Wars: How Teaching the Conflicts Can Revitalize American Education*, New York: Norton.

Green, Chris (2001), 'Materializing the sublime reader: cultural studies, reader response, and community service in the creative writing workshop', *College English*, 64:2, 153–74.

Green, Daniel (2003), 'Not merely academic: creative writing and literary study', *RE:AL: The Journal of Liberal Arts*, 28:2, http://libweb.sfasu.edu/real/vol28-2/notmerelyacad.htm (accessed 8 July 2005).

Grenville, Kate (1990), *The Writing Book: A Workbook for Fiction Writers*, Sydney: Allen & Unwin.

Guillory, John (1993), *Cultural Capital: The Problem of Literary Canon Formation*, Chicago: Chicago University Press.

Holland, Siobhan (2002), *Creative Writing: A Good Practice Guide – A Report to the Learning and Teaching Support Network (LTSN)*, English Subject Centre, London: English Subject Centre.

Kerridge, Richard (2004), 'Creative writing and academic accountability', *New Writing: International Journal for the Practice and Theory of Creative Writing*, 1, 3–5.

Krauth, Nigel (2000), 'Where is writing now?: Australian university creative writing programs at the end of the Millennium', *TEXT*, 4:1, www.gu.edu.au/school/art/text/april00/krauth.htm (10 February 2004).

Krauth, Nigel (2001), 'The creative writing doctorate in Australia: an initial survey', *TEXT*, 5:1, www.griffith.edu.au/school/art/text/april01/krauth.htm (accessed 10 February 2005).

Kroll, Jeri, and Steve Evans (2005), 'How to write a "How to Write" book: the writer as entrepreneur', *TEXT*, 9:1, www.gu.edu.au/school/art/text/april05/krollevans.htm (accessed 13 August 2005).

MacCabe, Colin (1986), 'Broken English', *Critical Quarterly*, 28, 1, 2, 3–14.

Miles, Robert (1992), 'Creative writing, contemporary theory and the English curriculum', in Moira Monteith and Robert Miles (eds), *Teaching Creative Writing: Theory and Practice*, Buckingham: Open University Press, pp. 34–44.

Morton, Donald and Mas'ud Zavarzadeh (1988–9), 'The cultural politics of the fiction workshop', *Cultural Critique*, 11, 155–73.

Myers, D. G. (1996), *The Elephants Teach: Creative Writing since 1880*, Prentice Hall Studies in Writing and Culture, New Jersey: Prentice Hall.

Newlyn, Lucy and Jenny Lewis (eds) (2003), *Synergies: Creative Writing in Academic Practice*, St Edmund Hall: Chough Publications.

Perloff, Marjorie (1986), '"Homeward Ho!": Silicon Valley Pushkin', *American Poetry Review*, 15, 37–46.

Reid, Ian (1982), 'The crisis in English Studies', *English in Australia*, 60, 8–18.

Ritter, Kelly (2001), 'Professional writers/writing professionals: revamping teacher training in creative writing PhD Programs', *College English*, 64:2, 205–27.

Rutherford, Jonathan (2005), 'Cultural studies in the corporate university', *Cultural Studies*, 19:3, 297–317.

Shelnutt, Eve (1989), 'Notes from a cell: creative writing programs in isolation', in Joseph M. Moxley (ed.), *Creative Writing in America: Theory and Pedagogy*, Urbana: National Council of Teachers of English, pp. 3–24.

Smith, Hazel (2005), *The Writing Experiment: Strategies for Innovative Creative Writing*, Sydney: Allen & Unwin.

Webb, Jen (2000), 'Individual enunciations and social frames', *TEXT*, 4:2 www.gu.edu.au/school/art/text/oct00/webb.htm (accessed 9 February 2004).

Williams, Jeffrey [1995] (2000), 'The posttheory generation', in Peter C. Herman (ed.), *Day Late, Dollar Short: The Next Generation and the New Academy*, Albany: State University of New York Press, pp. 25–43.

Section Two

The Craft of Writing

PROSE

8

Reading, Writing and Teaching the Short Story

E. A. Markham

1. Preparing for the short story

Reference

Of the couple of dozen names of writers you might be expected to encounter during the exploration of the short story, special attention should be given to the following: Anton Chekhov (1860–1904, Russia); James Joyce (1882–1941, Ireland); Guy de Maupassant (1850–93, France); Katherine Mansfield (1888–1923, New Zealand); Jorge Luis Borges (1899–1986, Argentina); Ernest Hemingway (1889–1961, USA); Jean Rhys (1894–1979, West Indies); J. D. Salinger (b. 1919, USA); Alice Munro (b. 1931, Canada); Donald Barthelme (1931–89); Raymond Carver (1938–88); Angela Carter (1940–92, Britain); T. Coreghassen Boyle (b. 1948, USA); Haruki Murakami (b. 1949, Japan); Mia Couto (b. 1955, Mozambique).

We can narrow this down to an arbitrary dozen or so stories to start with:

1. 'Lady with a Lapdog' (Chekhov)
2. 'The Dead' (Joyce)
3. 'Bliss' (Mansfield)
4. 'Hills Like White Elephants' (Hemingway)
5. 'Funes the Memorious' (Borges)
6. 'Mannequin' (Rhys)
7. 'A Perfect Day for Bananafish' (Salinger)
8. The 'Juliet' stories (Munro)
9. 'The Flight of Pigeons From the Palace' (Barthelme)
10. 'The Company of Wolves' (Carter)
11. 'Neighbours' (Carver)
12. 'The Elephant Vanishes' (Murakami)

How to read the short story – an overview

Most critics agree that the history of the short story can be made sense of by seeing its trajectory from the nineteenth century (Gogol, Turgenev, Chekhov . . .) to the contemporary (Barthelme, Boyle . . .) as a move from naturalism (or, perhaps it's better to call it social realism) to formal experimentation and forms of surrealism. Though the most challenging figures defy this easy categorisation, the familiar names from the past – for example Chekhov, Joyce, Mansfield – seem to have a great deal in common with, say, Raymond Carver and his 'dirty realist' colleagues such as Richard Ford, Tobias Wolff, Andre Dubus – who seem to practise a pared down form of naturalism.

Nevertheless, everyone can agree that Borges (with a trail of magical realists in South and Central America behind him), challenged Aristotle's beginning, middle and end 'well-made' story concept, set in a world conforming to traditional logic. That is to say, a world view which assumes that if you accurately depict what's on the surface, you might usefully suggest or reveal what's under that surface.

Some people would claim the experience of the Second World War as ushering in a change of sensibility (see the rise of the Theatre of the Absurd in France). Others, like C. L. R. James, the West Indian Marxist historian and critic, would date the concept at the First World War, with the millions killed in the trenches having a coarsening effect on those who survived at home – 'barbarism' he called it. The theory is that at some point in the twentieth century something (Freud? World Wars? Concentration camps? Repressive regimes?) caused us to break faith with Aristotelian verities of the golden mean and an assumption of rationality and the claims of naturalism. The result? Psychological instability (Pirandello – his stories, his plays) and Symbolism in Italy – particularly in the fables of Italo Calvino (1923–85); magical realism in central and South America, the 'pop sociology' of Barthelme and the 'epic realism' of T. C. Boyle, and others.

2. Revision

We assume that by now you have written something. So, to start with, have you:

- properly identified the setting for your story
- established a character: who is s/he and what is s/he doing here
- actually told a story?

Now: if you were to change the setting, what else would need to change?

- Is the character or the setting more important to the telling of this story?
- Are there people, not shown, affected by the actions of characters in the story?
- How will you communicate this?

This brings us to the question of how the story relates to the world of the story. The world of the story is usually larger than the story which is set in that world. The trick of the story that has resonance is to suggest that larger world without having to flesh it out.

So, to start with Revision, means that the emphasis is going to be on the *writing* of the short story, and to do that successfully (consistently, as opposed to a lucky one-off), you need to read and you need to revise.

Revision is important as it concentrates the mind on the practice rather than the theory of story writing. The notion of revising is useful to the writer as it implies that whatever is written can usually be improved upon; and it helps that mental transition from being a consumer of texts (the casual, even the critical reader) to being a practitioner. Being a practitioner not only helps you to focus on the art (craft) of making, but it informs your reading of published work, and invites you to ask new questions of it.

Plucking a story almost at random from those above, let's consider for a moment Hemingway's 'Hills Like White Elephants'. Nothing is spelt out in this excellent 'minimalist' story. It is cryptic, elliptical and, indeed, 'Hemingwayesque' to a degree. Briefly, a young man and woman are at a small railway station in Spain (they are not Spanish) waiting for a train. We pick up from their conversation at the bar/café that she is distressed and he is, in a sense, reassuring her. She is distressed because he wants her to do something that she doesn't particularly want to do (we think it's to have an abortion); she is asking (obliquely – or openly, according to your interpretation) for reassurance but he is emotionally incapable of providing it; and in the end she becomes hysterical and asks him to shut up.

Now, he is not only emotionally immature (or cruel) he is off-hand and impolite (to the waitress) and we begin to wonder why someone who comes across as unattractive to the reader still manages to hold on to the affections of the young woman. We want to have a view of them beyond and outside this sketch. Has the man's behaviour always been like this? If so, we must form a view of the young woman's judgement, and perhaps modify our impression that she is purely a victim. (Reread Chekhov's 'Lady with a Lapdog' with this in mind. Why does Anna, in that story, so seemingly privileged and not under threat choose unsuitable men as her husband and lover?) We might begin to ask ourselves why the lady in the Hemingway story willingly goes along with what seems like emotional abuse. But does she willingly go along with it? We don't know for sure, because there is no 'back' story; there is no hint that the man has been different at different times in the past or in different circumstances. Is it merely the pressure of the situation that makes him odd? We can go on speculating but, after a while, this is what we are doing: we are no longer reading the text. It is at this point that we might ask of this (excellent) piece of writing, if some slivers of 'back' story might not have clarified (rather than explained) it, might not have made it an even better story. This is an example, then, of how we might approach revision without prejudice to the excellence of the draft in front of us.

3. The opening paragraph

It doesn't do any harm to ask where stories come from and whether they need to grow out of your personal experience because we all, presumably, know things about ourselves that others don't, and we find some of these things interesting, or hilarious or painful enough to want to share them with others. (We do this all the time, in conversation, and are puzzled if our listeners don't react with interest or concern.) So one thing that drives the story might be the conviction that your experience is unique. Or it may be the opposite impulse, that what has happened to you is something shared by others. Either way, a narrative will, hopefully, bring the experience to the engaged attention of others. (Of course, if the writing is successful, you are likely to discover new things about yourself that you didn't quite 'know' – or want to acknowledge – at the start).

As you write you'll be pleased (or alarmed) to discover that there are no rules about where to start. Anything – a memory, a smell, a sound and, of course, an incident – might trigger a story. (A writer once said to me, 'I write because I want to answer back. They tell lies about me, about us; and I want to put the record straight'. Nothing much wrong with that, and the energy in wanting to put the record straight could usually be relied on to keep a narrative buoyant. But a writer of fiction – as opposed to one of journalism, say, or documentary – must be careful to 'answer back' in ways that are not predictable.)

So to the mechanics of starting. Some writers – and the American Bernard Malamud comes to mind – present us with a mass of clues in the opening paragraph, each of which suggests a separate storyline. The effect of this being that we, the readers, are forewarned of the possible developments of the story almost before we get going, and this primes us as we read along. We won't, of course, make the same connections as the writer does, but the consciousness of hints being realised or not as we read, adds to the richness of experience for the reader (and to the text).

Talking of the opening paragraph, how about being playful and start your story where someone else's story ends? Not in the conventional way of adding to the previous writer's narrative but by working backwards. Take a short story collection down from your shelf, turn to the end of a story and read the final paragraph. Then reconstruct the story (a story) from that final paragraph. The aim isn't to second-guess the author, but to show how a narrative can be teased out by working back from a given ending. How will you know if you have succeeded? Having constructed your story by working backwards from another's ending, then – and only then – read the original story. Is it richer than your own reconstruction? If it is, revise. Or start again with another story. And again.

Finally, in talking about starting your story, I am attracted to something that the American dramatist, David Mamet once said in connection with putting a script together. 'Get in late, get out early'. The first part, 'Get in late', seems very useful advice for the short story. Assume that things have happened before your story opens. Then you have the option, during the writing of the story, to refer back to some of those things.

Before we illustrate let me stress that of course we can start, like many traditional novels start, with the birth of the hero and continue with a strict chronology of events (I'm thinking of, say, *Robinson Crusoe* here: 'I was born in the year 1632, in the city of York . . .'); but often we need a novel's length to do justice to that approach. So, granted that we don't have 70,000- plus words at our disposal in a short story, it is good to start farther on in the story and leave room for the 'back story' that can be dipped into at will.

Consider this opening:

> Mary lived in Manchester. She was a student. . .

This might be acceptable, because then we could be made interested in Mary, in her being a student; and in Manchester. But wouldn't it give us a greater sense of lift-off if we assumed more of the story before we started? For example:

> Mary was late for College again today. It took two buses from Openshaw . . .

Here, we add another storyline (the lateness) but more importantly we give the opening greater force, greater sense of buoyancy, by making Mary habitually late for College. (Is the – presumably – difficult journey from Openshaw a reason or excuse for lateness: how organised is Mary in other areas of her life?)

How does Mary deal with being late? Do we need to know what she is studying? Is she living away from home? Is she an influence on or more influenced by her friends? (How much of her world are we minded to bring in?)

Doesn't the specificity of Openshaw suggest the writer's greater intimacy (knowing something more about it) with the tale about to be told?

So, here are more 'getting in late' lines, at random, that might open up space (rather than shutting it down) for the story:

> On her first day/last day at university . . .
> She didn't want to go back to Huddersfield.
> She was looking forward to going back to Huddersfield.
> Her sister visited that weekend. (A sister, another story line; a lot of 'back
>   story' to be dipped into . . .)
> She dreaded what would happen this weekend.
> She was packing to go home.
> The first time it happened she didn't know what to do.
> Michael saw her first.

In the first sentence she can contrast her first day at university with the time before university. Better still, if it were the last day she'd have not just her time before university to draw on and the prospect of what happens after university to speculate about, but she would have the university experience to explore (to look back on with relief or regret) to work into the narrative. Similarly, there is Huddersfield and there is time away from Huddersfield. You can compare/contrast, etc.

Look at the last example, 'Michael saw her first'. What are the possibilities for the narrative? Already there are three possible storylines. Michael's, the woman's, and the person who didn't see her first. If this was a question of a woman and two men, we might be talking of a tale of rivalry. Even if – though this is less likely – there are only two people involved, Michael and the woman, and that Michael saw her before she saw him, there are two storylines; and the decision to point out who sees whom first almost suggests parallel narratives (or levels of perception).

Another question here is 'Who is to tell the story?' It is sometimes useful to write the narrative from one person's point of view and, in revision, give the story (or bits of the story) to someone else, and in further revision, see which angle of telling is the more effective. You might push this technique to the limit and attempt multiple narration!

Exercise

Look at an opening paragraph of a typical Bernard Malamud story (where many story lines are introduced), and try that approach for yourself: that is, hinting at many storylines that might be woven into the story – or at least be seen, in retrospect, to frame or establish the larger world of the story.

By the time you have worked through these various challenges you will have a substantial amount of the story written down – enough to read over, reassess and revise.

4. Revision: 2 – paying attention to detail

Sometimes your prose isn't convincing because the scenes you try to invoke come over as being generalised, not specific. It is best to assume at this stage that a person is not like another person. See your character as an individual. Only when you've successfully done that do the similarities with others reveal themselves. So, in revision, write some descriptions – as if you're doing a documentary – of some of the following. These needn't lead to stories, they are your equivalent to the pianist's five finger exercises.

> Waking up (time, where, with/without whom?)
> Using the bathroom (Sharing? Are things in the right place? What's your
>   gaze like first thing in the morning?)
> Breakfast (How is it organised?)
> Starting the day (getting ready for school, college, office, shop, factory,
>   etc.)
> Lunch with a friend. (Describe the friend. Then imagine the friend
>   describing you.)

Now, can you imagine someone who doesn't have access to most of the above? Is there a narrative to be teased out there? We're moving from observation to the use of the imagination.

5. Shape: structure and form

Structure

If structure is something to do with the chronology of events, then the idea of a journey or of a quest would seem a natural shape for a story. The story of a life is one we can all attempt. But this might consume too many words (a novel). So, how about: going to the supermarket/ hairdresser's/ train station and coming back (either immediately or after a gap in time). Think of one unusual thing that happens on the journey. How did you (the character) deal/fail to deal with it?

Many stories are about a quest, sometimes external, sometimes internal. That gives a shape or direction to the narrative: Will the character accomplish the quest? Who will frustrate or facilitate the exercise? And why?

When you re-read published stories are you impressed by those where the quest is *more* or *less* overt?

Building the story around an incident

An incident, for example, such as an encounter with a pickpocket or a burglar (in the house)? A potential rapist? But it needn't be grim: how about: an encounter with a future husband/wife/partner?

If art is a marriage of content and form, the art is the more sophisticated when content and form would seem to fit in a way that excites interest in its aliveness – the opposite of being mechanically correct. Some traditional forms, following the Aristotelian principle of *beginning, middle* and *end* work well (hunt out new examples). Some modern writers shuffle this order – end, beginning, middle; middle, end, beginning – or dispense with some elements of it. (Think of Borges, Calvino, Barthelme, Boyle, etc. Or even, nearer home, J. G. Ballard in *The Atrocity Exhibition*.) They delight in creating new and unfamiliar structures. These shapes/structures range from the muted, for example the diary form (Jean Rhys, 'Fishy Waters'), the exchange of letters (Alecia McKenzie, 'Full Stop') to the more overtly daring: the Review, the Report, the Lecture, the rewrite of a non-existent classic characteristic of Borges ('Pierre Menard, Author of the Quixote'), Barthelme ('The Flight of Pigeons from the Palace'), and others.

Fiction versus essay

It's often a good idea to try to enlarge the space where fiction happens. We've hinted that 'getting into the scene late' might be one way of doing it. Another way would be to introduce the second character (we should have been practising this by now) bringing with her or him a new storyline (or set of storylines) to wrench the narrative away from the 'essay' structure, and make it easier to give your narrative 'social depth'. The dynamic between characters usually (though not inevitably) helps to enlarge the space for your fiction. For not only does each character have her own story, back story, life experience to date, and fantasies of the future, but some aspects of this are likely to conflict with the other character(s). The fictional world thus becomes more socially complex. If the world created isn't large enough to live in, that in itself is a theme of the story – whether stated or not.

Study the plays of Samuel Beckett to see how a space seemingly large enough to live in can be conjured from the most cramped – physical and emotional – circumstances.

6. Revision 3

There have to be some rules by which you revise, by which you decide that some stories are better than others, and it's useful to share those rules with others with a professional interest in fiction. Would you agree, broadly, with the consensus, that, say, Chekhov might not be a great stylist and there are loose ends in some of his stories, and sometimes there might be less narrative tension than a contemporary writer might employ *but* that his tone is humane, his approach is non-judgemental (which is, in a way, a form of respect for his characters); that in his tendency to understatement he doesn't bully the reader; that his characterisation is acute – and that these last are some of the qualities that make him special and attractive to the reader?

Assessment is often contentious. I would suggest three very simple rules as a guide to this. The 'rules' were formulated by the Council for the Encouragement of Music and the Arts (CEMA) established in London after the Second World War to encourage appreciation of the arts in Britain. The guidelines for assessing literature were:

- linguistic vitality
- formal innovation
- emotional truth.

Do these need explaining?

'Linguistic vitality' means freshness of language and the absence of cliché. You will not be willingly read if your language seems borrowed or second-hand, if the imagery is stale ('Football is a game of two halves') or if it is weighed down by unnecessary adjectives and adverbs. Remember, in imaginative writing, effectiveness is not communicated only by the grammar of what is said. To say 'She goes quickly' to the door, or 'She goes slowly' to the door does, of course, communicate something of the sense of anticipation or reluctance with which the person in question goes to the door. But it might be useful to ask yourself whether 'quickly or 'slowly' communicates enough of the 'colour' or 'buried drama' contained in those particular actions.

Similarly, to write 'This is a sad moment' or 'This is a happy moment' very soon has diminishing results. How does this particular person demonstrate or communicate sadness or happiness at this moment? That's what you want to show. It is your ability to convey that, not the idea of it, that helps to create convincing fiction.

With 'formal innovation' (innovation of form), we mean that it is important to have a knowledge of (or a feel for) the *genre* in which you're working. Your reader is likely to have certain expectations (from prior reading, from films, from television) of how other writers have treated it. And you can't afford to be less sophisticated than your reader.

'Emotional truth' is difficult to describe. But if you are urging writers to avoid cliché in language, in form – and also in thought – it is important not to cheat where the feelings or emotions are concerned. Do not confuse sensibility with sentimentality. One way of distinguishing between empathy (something to strive for if the situation warrants) and sentimentality (to be avoided at all costs) is to subject the relationship of author and character to the 'empathy with' or 'sympathy for' test. Avoid 'sympathy for' (it's 'undemocratic', it makes the emotional relationship between writer and character unequal). Encourage 'empathy with'.

In attempting to avoid sentimentality do not go too far the other way and brutalise feeling. Remember that the object of the exercise of writing is not to show off, not to demonstrate how clever or knowing you are, but to present something effectively and convincingly true to your reader. Don't make your characters do things merely because those things are unusual or bizarre. Think of your characters as having their human rights, so that anything they do must be in response to their situation, and stem from their personality.

7. Character

We have more or less said something about character. There are lots of books on this by David Lodge and others. It might be useful, too, to read how people from the theatre – for instance, Stanislavsky, the first director of Chekhov's plays – write about this. You might have a look at Julian Barnes' essay, 'Justin: a small major character', collected in *Something to Declare* (Barnes 2002). Remember the same care must be taken over the minor character as over the major one. A waiter in a restaurant who comes to your fictional table might have only a few lines, but get the vocabulary, the idiom, the tone of address right so that we know not just where he's from but from his tone what sort of time he's having in the kitchen.

Always give the impression that the character is living a life which the story just happens to shed light on (to break into), and that that life will continue to be lived (unless the person dies in the story) after the story's end. So it's useful for the writer to know – though not necessarily for the reader to be told – what the character was doing five minutes before that character was introduced into the story.

But what is character?

A woman in an early John Updike novel has a stroke. Her speech patterns change. What else has changed: is she the same 'character' as before? If you were to change the character's name a couple of times during the course of the story for no dramatic reason, just to show that what unites the figure is more than a name, would the confusion caused be tolerated as more than a gimmick? What about fraught relations between the character and the author?

There is a character in a Pirandello story who is in revolt against the author. In 'A Character in Distress' we have the author (Pirandello) one night reading a manuscript of someone else's rather dull novel. The only lively character in the book is a Doctor Fileno. Next morning, which is Pirandello's time of day to meet *his* characters (that is, to write, to think about writing, to engage with writing), at the place and time where his characters jostle for his attention, Doctor Fileno turns up, and battles his way to the fore of Pirandello's characters, protesting to the new author first of all about his name, which he does not like. Furthermore, in the original novel Fileno has himself authored a work entitled *The Philosophy of Distance*. Fileno is proud of that but insists the way he is used in the plot of the novel demeans an author (himself) so elevated. He complains that instead of Fileno, another character, a solicitor, should have been made to take on a foolish woman as her second husband, and so on.

Is this a joke too far? Or is this a useful way in which an author might (in revision) think about character before releasing the work to the public. (It might be instructive that this story is called, 'A Character in *Distress*', not 'A Character in *Revolt*'.)

8. Dialogue

The old image of the iceberg is a good one when considering dialogue. Let the visible dialogue communicate a sense that two-thirds of the action is hidden underneath. To spell it out, to over-write is to lose credibility, is to risk self-parody.

It is useful to remember, also, that the application of dialogue must not give the appearance of conveying information, it must be to characterise. Of course it must convey information, but it must not give the appearance of doing so. (For examples of excellent dialogue, look again at those early dramas of Harold Pinter, those collected in *A Slight Ache and Other Plays*.) The Methuen series of monologues, dialogues and scenes from popular dramas are worth looking at here. They would be useful, also, for your study of character.

9. Literary conceits and extended metaphors

Writing involves discipline and hard work, but that doesn't preclude having fun. There is a sort of intellectual conceit, hinted at already – often a play with form – which, when it works, gives both author and reader tremendous fun. And you don't have to push it through to 70,000 words! To the experiments with form already mentioned, have a look at Donald Barthelme's one sentence story, 'Sentence'. Or read again 'The Flight of Pigeons from the Palace', the story where the print has to jostle for position with graphics for space on the page. Or look at J. G. Ballard's story, 'Index', which is nearly all index. (If it were all index it would not be particularly interesting as a story, but as a clever puzzle.) That it is not all index (see the first page) makes it an effective, experimental story.

10. Advanced exercises

Read a classic

Read a 'classic' story and see if there is a minor character in it who deserves her or his story to be more fully told (for example, Lily the caretaker's daughter in James Joyce's 'The Dead' from *Dubliners*). Seek out other examples and write the 'unwritten' stories.

Why limit it to the short story? How about doing something similar for Lucy in Virginia Woolf's *Mrs Dalloway*?

Non-human consciousness

Try composing a narrative where the mode of consciousness might not be human. For example, how do you capture the aliveness of a tree in leaf in its own terms; the *riverness* of river, the *stoneness* of stone?

This is perhaps the most difficult of all exercises. We might want to seek the assistance of the poets as we wrestle with this one.

Research

Of course everyone who writes does 'research'. If you are writing a story set in the 1960s, and the main character (or any character) is partial to popular music, you would inevitably check to see what was on the hit parade at the time the story was set. But most research is more than 'checking'. It is to familiarise yourself with subject and setting (often remote from your own) so that you can then present both without making either exotic.

You might look to the contemporary historian, the best of whom, in their narratives, manage to convince us that the lives and thought processes of people who lived in the past are very much like our own.

Short shorts

The production of the mini-short story is now suddenly made popular by Dave Eggers. But, as a feature of the genre, it has always been with us (not counting the fables of Aesop, etc.) from Kafka through Saki, Kelman to Frederic Raphael (*Sleeps Six and Other Stories*), etc. An issue of the *Translantic Review* was devoted to short shorts.

The test of the successful short short is no different from that of any other story: is it more than a sketch or a fragment? The special effect that the best short shorts have is the quality of parable.

An exercise for male writers

Try writing a mini-biography of a woman – or a series of women. Now revise. Delete those bits of the writing that are about yourself. Revise again. Delete those other (less obvious) bits of the writing that are about yourself. Start again.

11. Revision 4

Revision for an 'advanced' exercise is no different from revision at an earlier stage of the writing process; that's the important thing: the story, the scene, the character must convey the same degree of credibility as if you were writing about someone you know sitting down to breakfast and being casual about the brand names of the things on offer.

So, with an exercise that is particularly challenging, don't forget that your story is like a picture in a frame, and that there is something happening (or at least, existing) outside that frame: it helps to animate, or to read better what's inside the frame. So, in revision, ask yourself the usual range of questions. If your character is in a room, mentally sketch the rest of the house, furnish it (though don't necessarily tell us that you've done that) so you know where the bathroom is, and if there is a fixed-line telephone; if there are other people in close proximity: this visual map, among other things, will help to particularise that person's way of inhabiting her space.

Then there is the revision that comes about when you shift position from writer to reader, when you become your own critic: is the sensibility of the tree the same as that of the river? And is that what the author intended?

Or again, having seen that film, read that book - since having produced the last draft of your own - or having had a strange parting with a friend, do you now feel that the texture of your piece no longer feels quite right. Revision ideally continues until the work is abandoned (ideally, because it has been published) and you're now working on the next piece.

12. Pace and tone

One of the organisations that gives prizes for stories, and hence must assess them, distributes a list to its judges of categories to be ticked off in pursuit of the winner. The categories include: Characterisation, Dialogue, Narrative, Voice, etc. But also Pace and Tone.

Pace

Lack of pace is perhaps easier to detect and put right than tone. For when the interest begins to flag, when you find yourself, as a reader, struggling to continue – even though the story is well-written, is free of cliché, is well-characterized and there is precision in the writing – chances are that the problem is lack of pace. If it seems flat or static or bogged down, you're likely to tick the box: 'loss of pace'. Better still, think of having a conversation with your friends, recounting a story of something that happened to you. You are not managing to hold the attention of your audience: your story is losing pace. You try embarrassingly to recapture their attention – you cut things out, you bring the end forward . . . Employ this method when you write.

Tone

With the problem of tone, what it means is that the author is getting in the way of her character. The child narrating has been given the experience – the sensibility and vocabulary of the adult author. That violates the tone. Remember that the author is at the service of her characters, not the other way around.

On another level, think again of the work of Katherine Mansfield. The great short story, 'Prelude', has a nervy, restless, anxious, impressionistic feel that makes the reader unsurprised to learn, in retrospect, that the story was written in a mood of anxiety and grief following Mansfield's brother's death on the Western Front in 1915. The impression we get from reading the stories, though, is one of vitality, youthfulness, the joy of discovery. Even in 'Bliss', where we learn at the end that the husband is having an affair, this febrile quality is maintained. And remember for much of this time Mansfield knew she was dying of TB. The shadow is present behind the glow, but doesn't overwhelm it. Mansfield has complete control of tone. She doesn't confuse seriousness with solemnity.

Questions

1. Talking about pace, does Chekhov's 'A Dreary Story' avoid being boring?
2. Talking of tone does Katherine Mansfield's 'The Garden Party' avoid sentimentality?

13. Sharing the 'back' story

The collection

We move on now from the individual story to the collection – the book of stories. Naturally, for a first book, it makes sense to put together a selection of 'best pieces'. But publishers will tell you – rightly – that it is difficult to market a book of stories. Unless they are genre stories. Our favourite detectives – from Sherlock Holmes through Pierrot to Inspector Rankin – hold their respective collections together.

Alternatively, we can build up a world from the individual story, by setting other stories in the same place, and be loyal to the 'facts' established at the beginning. The most spectacular instance of this is that of R. K. Narayan's imaginary 'Malgudi', now a 'village' on the map of India. Others have used the combination of the same setting and characters popping in and out of that setting, to create a larger world of the story. Sandra Cisneros' *The House on Mango Street* is an example of this.

The device of creating the storyworld goes back to Chaucer's *The Canterbury Tales*. The simplicity and effectiveness of getting each pilgrim to tell a story on their way to Canterbury is exemplary. Behind Chaucer, of course, was the inexhaustible Bocaccio of *The Decameron*.

My own experiment here, presenting a literary canvas larger than your conventional story can manage, but without the tight formal disciplines of the novel, is represented in *Meet Me in Mozambique* (2005), where one character, Pewter Stapleton, appears (or is referred to) in all fifteen of the stories, and where the same scene is sometimes animated by different characters in different stories. The trick is to try to be loyal from one story to the next to the details established (as in Narayan's 'Malgudi', the characters might display new facets of their personality in the new story, but they shouldn't change character). The process is perhaps taken a bit further in *At Home with Miss Vanesa*, the 2006 companion volume to *Meet Me in Mozambique*. Of course we've had hints of this from many writers. F. Scott Fitzgerald's Pat Hobby, Hemingway's 'surrogate', Nick Adams, etc.

Cross-story revision

When you look back over the collection you'll need to adjust names, professions, places where people went on holiday, who they were with at the time, and so on to make the collection consistent. For example, in one story your character is called Marcus but in another Michael. Which name will you settle for? Would you have to alter his nickname in another story? Why is there no reference to a character's children in one story when in another she seems attached to them? Is this character's hobby (prominent in a later story) recently-enough acquired not to have been mentioned in the earlier one? And so on.

14. Additional reading

This is not less important than the list at the start of this study. Suggestions here would include Colette (1873–1954, France); Joyce Carol Oates, among the American 'dirty realists'. Also from the US: Eudora Welty, Flannery O'Connor and Jamaica Kincaid (Antigua/US). All the writers mentioned in this chapter are worth dipping into.

In addition, a good English dictionary (as much for browsing as for checking spellings); 'Why I Write' (essays by various authors: George Orwell [1968], David Lodge [1988]); *Good Fiction Guide*, Jane Rogers ed. (2001); *Thinking About Texts*, Chris Hopkins (2001); *Reading Groups*, Jenny Hartley (2001); Assorted Literary magazines such as: *Ambit*, *Granta*, *London Magazine*, *Paris Review*, *Wasafiri*.

References

Ballard, J. G. (2001), *The Atrocity Exhibition*, London: Flamingo.

Barnes, Julian (2002), 'Justin: a small major character', *Something to Declare*, London: Picador.

Barthelme, Donald (1987), 'The Flight of Pigeons From the Palace' in *Forty Stories by Donald Barthelme*, New York: Putnams.

Borges, Jorge Luis (1974), 'Funes the Memorious' and 'Pierre Menard, Author of the Quixote' in *Labyrinths*, Harmondsworth: Penguin.

Carter, Angela (1986), 'The Company of Wolves' in *The Bloody Chamber*, Harmondsworth: Penguin.

Carver, Raymond (1995), 'Neighbours' in *Where I'm Calling From*, London: Harvill.

Chekhov, Anton (1970), 'A Dreary Story' in *Stories 1889–91*, London: Oxford University Press.

Chekhov, Anton (1975), 'Lady with a lap dog' in *Stories 1898–1904*, London: Oxford University Press.

Cisneros, Sandra (1992), *The House on Mango Street*, London: Bloomsbury.

Hartley, Jenny (2001), *Reading Groups*, Oxford: Oxford University Press.

Hemingway, Ernest (1968), 'Hills Like White Elephants' in *The First Forty-Nine Stories*, London: Jonathan Cape.

Hopkins, Chris (2001), *Thinking About Texts*, Basingstoke: Palgrave.

Joyce, James (1972), 'The Dead' in *Dubliners*, Harmondsworth: Penguin.

Lodge, David (1988), *Write On: Occasional Essays 1965–85*, London: Penguin.

Mansfield, Katherine (2002), 'Bliss', 'Prelude' and 'The Garden Party' in *Katherine Mansfield. Selected Stories*, Oxford: Oxford University Press.

Markham, E. A. (2005), *Meet Me in Mozambique*, Birmingham: Tindal Street Press.

Markham, E. A. (2006), *At Home with Miss Vanesa*, Birmingham: Tindal Street Press.

McKenzie, Alecia (1992), 'Full Stop' in *Satellite City and Other Stories*, London: Longman.

Munro, Alice (2006), The 'Juliet' Stories in *Runaway*, London: Vintage.

Murakami, Haruki (1994), 'The Elephant Vanishes' in *The Elephant Vanishes*, London: Vintage.

Narayan, R. K. (1995), *Malgudi Days*, London: Penguin.

Orwell, George (1968), 'Why I write' in *The Collected Essays, Journalism and Letters of George Orwell. Volume 1. An Age Like This 1920–40*, pp. 1–6, London: Secker and Warburg.

Pinter, Harold (1961), *A Slight Ache and Other Plays*, London: Methuen.

Raphael, Frederic (1979), *Sleeps Six and Other Stories*, London: Cape.

Rhys, Jean (1976), 'Fishy Waters' in *Sleep it off, Lady*, London: André Deutsch.

Rhys, Jean (1976), 'Mannequin' in *Tigers are Better-Looking*, London: André Deutsch.
Rogers, Jane (ed.) (2001), *Good Fiction Guide*, Oxford: Oxford University Press.
Salinger, J. D. (1948), 'A Perfect Day for Bananafish', *The New Yorker*, 31 January 1948, pp. 22–5.
Woolf, Virginia (1976), *Mrs Dalloway*, London: Grafton Books.

9

Writing the Memoir

Judith Barrington

What is memoir?

This chapter is about literary memoir. If that sounds a little pretentious, I use the word 'literary' because, although all memoirs recount life experiences, the kind of book I'm describing here aspires to affect its readers through the quality of its writing rather than through the scandalous or gossipy nature of its subject. In order to write this kind of memoir, you don't have to be famous but, rather, to want to turn your life experiences into well-honed sentences and paragraphs.

The literary memoir has recently surged in popularity, but it has been around for a long time. In 1920, Virginia Woolf was part of 'The Memoir Club', a group convened by Molly McCarthy with many of the writers and artists we know of as 'The Bloomsbury Group'. Before that, the groundwork for the memoir was laid by many of the great essayists.

In trying to define the modern memoir, it is important to understand that it is a different genre from autobiography. A quick key to understanding the difference between the two lies in the choice of a preposition: autobiography is a story *of* a life; memoir is a story *from* a life. The latter makes no pretense of capturing the whole span from birth to the time of writing; in fact, one of the important skills of memoir writing is the selection of the theme that will bind the work together and set boundaries around it. Thus you will discover, if you read Vivian Gornick's *Fierce Attachments* (1987), that her chosen theme is her relationship with her mother, described in the context of their walks together in New York City. The author resists the temptation to digress into stories that have no immediate bearing on the subject, and indeed Gornick's book tells nothing about many other aspects of her life. By setting boundaries such as these, whether the memoir is book-length or just a few pages, the writer keeps the focus on one aspect of a life and offers the reader an in-depth exploration.

Of course memoirs can be about any kind of life experience. Some are lighthearted and in places laugh-out-loud funny like Gerald Durrell's *My Family and Other Animals* (1956). Others, like *Survival in Auschwitz* by Primo Levi (1996), blend a personal story into an important historical record. J. R. Ackerley's *My Dog Tulip* (1956) is a small gem rooted in domestic life while Ernest Shackleton's *South: A Memoir of the Endurance Voyage* (1998) embraces huge frozen tracts of an unfamiliar world.

It may seem obvious that memoir is also different from fiction; after all, one is 'true' and the other imaginary. But the line between these two genres is not always clear. Not everything in a memoir is factually accurate: who can remember the exact dialogue that took place at breakfast forty years ago? And if you can make up dialogue, change the name of a character to protect his privacy, or reorder events to make the story work better, then how is it different from fiction?

One way that memoir is different is that it prompts readers to approach it differently. When you name your work 'memoir' or 'fiction', you are entering into a kind of contract with your reader. You are saying 'this really happened', or 'this is imaginary'. And if you are going to honour that contract, your raw material as a memoirist can only be what you have actually experienced. It is up to you to decide how imaginatively you transform the facts – exactly how far you allow yourself to go to fill in memory gaps and make a good story out of it. But whatever you decide, your reader expects you to remain limited by your experience, unless you turn to fiction, in which you can, of course, embrace people, places, and events you have never personally known. While imagination plays a role in both fiction and memoir, the application of it in memoir is circumscribed by the facts of your life experience, while in fiction it is circumscribed by what the reader will believe.

Writers of memoir vary in how much they feel free to reorganise their experience. One thing to bear in mind, though, is that you will gain little of value if you end up abusing the reader's trust. Making up a 'better ending' to your story, while presenting it as true, or, worse still, inventing a whole piece of your life because it makes a good memoir, will often backfire.

Even if no one ever finds out that you tampered with the facts, your memoir will suffer if you are dishonest. It is very difficult to be both candid and deceptive at the same time, and a memoir does need to be candid. Tampering with the truth will lead you to writing a bit too carefully – which in turn will rob your style of the ease that goes with honesty. Dishonest writing is very often mediocre writing; it has a faint odour of prevarication about it.

None of this should prevent you from speculating. Your readers will appreciate an honest desire to make sense of the facts, however few you may have. Musing on what might have been the tale behind that old photograph of your grandmother, or telling the reader how you've always imagined your parents' early lives, is not the same as presenting your speculations as fact. Mary Gordon, for example, in *The Shadow Man* (1996), speculates about her father who died when she was seven, using imaginary conversations and, at one point, actually writing in his voice. But none of this is presented as anything other than her search for the real man behind the idealised figure she had preserved over the years.

Retrospection or musing

What I call 'musing' is an important ingredient of literary memoir. You try to tell a good story, as you would if writing a novel or short story, using the fictional techniques of scene and summary to move through time. But unlike the fiction writer, you can also reflect out loud on your own story, bringing retrospection to bear on the events.

In this respect memoir is similar to personal essay. As Montaigne said, 'in an essay, the track of a person's thoughts struggling to achieve some understanding of a problem is the plot, is the adventure'. When you write memoir, like the essayist, you invite the reader into your thinking process, going beyond the telling of a good story to reveal how, looking back on it, you now understand that story, perhaps asking questions like, 'How did it affect my later life?' or 'What was the full significance of these events?'

This brings up one of memoir's unique challenges. When you write in this genre, you have to wear at least three different hats: that of the narrator who tells the story, that of the interpreter who tries to make sense of the story, and that of the protagonist or hero of the story.

Often the musing is buried inside the narration, and the reader merely gets the sense that the memoirist has done a lot of thinking about his or her experience. But sometimes it stands out separately, as an interruption of the narrative thread. This example may help make clear what I mean by musing. My book, *Lifesaving: A Memoir* (2000) begins like this:

> I must have been twelve when my father, my mother, and I participated in the Shoreham to Littlehampton yacht race. Actually, I did that race more than once, but I'm talking about the only time my mother came along – the time that turned into full-blown family story.
>
> The way I see it, the story is about my mother's lifelong terror of the sea and my father's pigheadedness. Or perhaps it is about the absurd pretenses of the British middle-class, particularly the male of that species, whose dignity must be preserved at all costs . . . (Barrington 2000: 13)

This speculation about the underlying meaning of the story continues for another four sentences. Then the third paragraph picks up the narrative again with the words, 'It should have been an easy day's sail: straight down the river from the yacht club'.

If you interject this kind of speculation into the narrative, it is important how you transition in and out of it. In the above example, I introduced the musing with the phrase, 'The way I see it'. It is clear at that point that I, who have begun as the storyteller, am about to become the interpreter, using retrospective wisdom, to shed some light on the meaning of the story. When transitioning back into the narrative, the reference to sailing is enough to cue the reader back to the yacht race that was introduced in the first paragraph.

The nuts and bolts of memoir

In many ways, memoir calls upon your narrative skills much as fiction does. You need to understand how to handle the passage of time, using summary techniques to cover a long period in a few pages or sentences, and breaking this up with scenes that slow down the action and move in close to your characters.

One way of understanding scene and summary is to think of them in cinematic terms: the summary is the long shot – the one that pulls back to a great distance, embracing first the whole house, then the street, then the neighbourhood, and then, becoming an aerial shot, it takes in the whole city. This view can include a lot of details, but they are all seen from the same distance, none apparently more important than another.

A scene, on the other hand, is the close-up, the camera zooming in through the kitchen window, picking out the two figures talking at the table and going up close to the face of first one speaker then the other. Many details of the kitchen are lost with this shot: maybe a blurry blue pitcher on a sideboard can be discerned; perhaps there is a vague impression of yellow walls and an open door. But in this scene it is the speakers' mannerisms and what they say that matter.

A summary uses verbs that don't refer to what happens on any particular day. If it were written in French or Spanish, it would use the imperfect tense to indicate the ongoing nature of what is being described. But we don't have that tense in English. Thus, Esmeralda Santiago, in her memoir, *When I Was Puerto Rican* (1993), begins a section with the words,

'I started school in the middle of hurricane season'. Never focusing on a particular day or week, she captures a whole chunk of time with her verbs: 'I loved the neat rows of desks lined up', 'I walked home from school full of importance', 'I learned that there were children whose fathers were drunks' (Santiago 1993: 30).

This is very different from a scene. Here is the opening of a scene taken from the same memoir:

> Sunday morning before breakfast Abuela handed me my piqué dress, washed and ironed.
> 'We're going to Mass,' she said, pulling out a small white *mantilla*, which I was to wear during the service.
> 'Can we have breakfast first, Abuela. I'm hungry'.
> 'No. We have to fast before church. Don't ask why. It's too complicated to explain'.
>
> (Santiago 1993: 96)

As you can see, this pinpoints the exact time ('Sunday morning before breakfast'). When you read a past tense verb such as 'handed' or 'said', you know it happened on a particular occasion, just that one time. It's not ongoing like the summary.

Many scenes, like this one, contain dialogue. To do this well, you must not only listen carefully to how people actually speak, but you must also select judiciously from all the things they might say. It's no good protesting, 'but that is exactly what she said', even if it is. A transcript of real life does not make for an engaging story. Your job is to shape, to select, and to add focus.

Some of the most common mistakes in writing dialogue involve the attributions (the 'he saids' and 'she saids'). These are needed much less than you might think, since the usual practice is to use a new line for each new speaker. If the conversation only involves two speakers, you'll hardly need any attributions. It is also unwise to shore up the dialogue with descriptive verbs such as 'he snapped' or 'she mused', or to qualify the verbs with phrases like 'in an endearing tone', or 'with a sarcastic edge to her voice'. If you pick the right words within the dialogue itself, you won't need this kind of clarification.

These techniques are common to most narrative prose. What is more specifically related to memoir is the question of retrospection. You can use scene and summary to narrate your way through the many different time periods. But in memoir there is another time that is always present, either explicitly or implicitly, and that time is *now*. The reader must have a sense that the narrator is rooted in a particular moment from which he or she may look back, may speak in present tense, or may even look forward to the future. It doesn't matter what the exact date, or even the decade, of the 'now' is: all that matters is that the reader senses that it exists and that it anchors a logical time span. It is from this 'now' that the memoirist muses on the story being told.

Because there is always an implied now, difficulties sometimes arise if you choose to narrate the events themselves in present tense, which has become a somewhat popular narrative style in recent times. Here is an example of past-tense narration, which, in turn, moves further back in time using the past perfect tense: 'When I turned fourteen, I decided to sell my pony. Several years earlier, I had sworn I would keep him for his whole life'. Here is that narrative in the present tense: 'When I turn fourteen, I decide to sell my pony'. All right so far, but what comes next? 'Several years earlier, I had sworn . . .'? Or is it, 'Several years earlier, I have sworn . . .'? Or perhaps, 'Several years earlier, I swore . . .'? None of these sounds perfect to my ear, but we do somehow manage to land on a tense that conveys the meaning adequately.

The real problem arises if we want to add a piece of musing: perhaps a sentence like, 'I feel ashamed of being so fickle in the face of teenage temptations'. If this sentence is inserted into the past tense narration, it is perfectly clear that it is a piece of retrospection on the part of the adult speaking now. On the other hand, if it is inserted into the present tense narration, it becomes ambiguous: 'When I turn fourteen, I decide to sell my pony. Several years earlier, I had sworn I would keep him for his whole life. I feel ashamed of being so fickle in the face of teenage temptations'. The third sentence here might be a continuation of the narrative, describing how the narrator felt *at the time*, or, equally, it might be retrospection from much later – from *now*. You will have to juggle your words to make clear which it is.

Writing about living people

There are sticky ethical questions that may come up when you set out to write a personal story. It might involve less-than-flattering portrayals of family members, friends, associates, or simply those who crossed your path and left you with an unfavourable impression of them. Sometimes, when you set out to write a memoir, your anxiety about these issues becomes a concern about legal matters: you worry that someone will sue you. But in almost every case, this is a misplaced anxiety. People are not at all inclined to sue, since it is expensive and will bring more attention to whatever they don't want made public. In any case, although the law varies in different countries, generally anyone upset by your work would have to prove both that it is untrue and that it causes them actual harm, rather than simply hurt feelings. Your anxiety is much more likely to stem from your own fears of dealing with the person concerned, or your own difficulties in reliving the story.

This is not to say you should disregard the consequences to others. You must weigh up your need to write a story that is true to how you experienced it, with the harm that might be done to others. You might be writing about a failed relationship; perhaps your memoir involves your closeted gay brother, your teenage daughter's first period, or a close friend's mental breakdown. There are often solutions to these problems that go beyond the simple choice of telling or not telling. You can be selective about what to include. You can show the person concerned what you've written and find out how he or she feels about it. You can change names, disguise places, and so on. But if you decide to make some of these adjustments, you should leave them until you have finished writing the memoir. It's only when your work is published that these things matter. Aim for absolute honesty while you are generating it.

Believe it or not, we often overestimate the power of our words. In interviewing memoirists, I discovered that several writers who had feared the reaction of family members or friends, actually had good experiences as a result of their writing. People were sometimes able to talk about something that had previously kept them apart.

On the other hand, we must not underestimate the consequences our words could have in some situations. I have a friend, for example, who wrote about her time as a teacher in China. Describing her relationships with friends she made there was not likely to be solved by changing names. At the time, associating with someone from the West was frowned upon in China and making those friendships public could have resulted in people losing jobs, or losing their right to leave the country. Similarly, publishing true stories about illegal immigrants or doctors who assist in a suicide, can bring trouble to those we depict. As writers, it is our business both to think about and to understand fully what can happen to people when we reveal what we know about them.

If you want to write about someone who severely hurt you, it is particularly difficult to tread a path to good writing, which is always the ultimate goal. You may find yourself not caring, or even delighting in, the consequences to family members, medical professionals, teachers, or others who abused their power over you in the past. But be aware of revenge as a motive for the writing. Your readers will be uncomfortable if they sense that you are retaliating. It may be anger that gets you started, but your writing will not flourish until you give your full allegiance to the story itself, letting go of any desire on your part to gain sympathy from readers or to punish the wrongdoer.

Two memoirs that in my view tread this difficult path successfully are: Lorna Sage's *Bad Blood* (2000) and Alexandra Fuller's *Don't Let's Go to the Dogs Tonight: An African Childhood* (2001).

Pitfalls

There are many hazards in writing a memoir. Tone, for example, is important. Since you are writing about yourself, it is important not to strike your reader as self-aggrandising. You can be funny or serious, but whatever your choice, you should aim for being self-revealing without seeming self-obsessed. Work hard on not beginning paragraphs with 'I'; vary your sentence structure to bury the first person inside it; and check for all those unnecessary phrases like 'I thought', 'I looked', or 'I heard'. Just give the thought, the sight or the sound without inserting yourself between it and the reader.

Another possible pitfall is that your memoir will become too internal. By this I mean that it will become a story entirely about your psyche or your emotional development. Readers don't want to feel as if they're eavesdropping on a therapy session, but, perversely, they do want to understand how you were affected by your story and what you learned. These things can become apparent through the storytelling, without inserting lengthy passages about your personal growth, your dreams, or your journal writings. Follow the old, but good, advice: show it, don't tell it.

An engaging memoir is set in a real world. It conveys a sense of period by including details from the culture, from public events, or from the history within which your personal story took place. Don't get so absorbed in your own life that you forget to include the music that played on the radio or the war that broke out while you were coming of age.

One last challenge is the difficulty of working with a writing group or with an editor on your manuscript. By the time you show the work to someone else, you should be ready to look at it and to discuss it as a piece of writing. This is why, when I teach memoir, I suggest that anyone giving feedback be scrupulous about his or her language. They should not refer to the narrator as 'you', but as 'the narrator', even though they know perfectly well that the narrator is, in fact, you. Surprisingly, this will help you to separate criticism of the writing from what you might perceive as criticism of your life. Imagine an editor saying, 'Well, on page 76, when you lose your temper with your frail old mother', as opposed to, 'Well, on page 76, when the narrator loses her temper with her frail old mother'.

I set out a more detailed blueprint for such critique sessions in my book, *Writing the Memoir: From Truth to Art* (Barrington 1997: 167).

Exercises

Here are a few exercises to get you started.

1. Think of an incident in your life that one or more people see very differently than you. Tell the story beginning with the words, 'This is how I see what happened'. Do not reveal how anyone else sees it.

2. Pick a season from your childhood and write an account of it all in summary. From that summary, write two full scenes with dialogue.

3. If you wrote the story in exercise 2 in a past tense, re-write it narrating in the present. If you wrote it in present, switch to the past. Note what works better and what is difficult in each rendition.

4. Choose a house you once lived in and remember well. Draw a plan of one floor, showing rooms, doors, windows, pieces of furniture, etc. Ask someone else to randomly mark an 'X' in one room (or if necessary, close your eyes and do it yourself). Write a detailed description of that room, paying attention to all five senses. Then write something that happened, or didn't happen, in that room.

References

Ackerley, J. R. (1956), *My Dog Tulip*, London: Secker and Warburg.

Barrington, Judith (1997), *Writing the Memoir: From Truth to Art*, Portland: The Eighth Mountain Press.

Barrington, Judith (2000), *Lifesaving: A Memoir*, Portland: The Eighth Mountain Press.

Durrell, Gerald (1956), *My Family and Other Animals*, London: Hart-Davis.

Fuller, Alexandra (2001), *Don't Let's Go to the Dogs Tonight*, New York: Random House.

Gordon, Mary (1996), *The Shadow Man*, New York: Random House.

Gornick, Vivian (1987), *Fierce Attachments*, New York: Farrar Straus Giroux.

Levi, Primo (1996), *Survival in Auschwitz*, New York: Simon & Schuster.

Sage, Lorna (2000), *Bad Blood*, London: Fourth Estate.

Santiago, Esmeralda (1993), *When I Was Puerto Rican*, New York: Addison-Wesley.

Shackleton, Ernest (1998), *South: A Memoir of the Endurance Voyage*, New York: Carroll & Graf.

10

Introduction to the Novel

Jane Rogers

'How do you begin to write a novel?' There are two answers to this question, and the first is, 'I don't know'. I've written seven and I still don't really know. Ask a number of novelists where their novels begin and you will get some of the following replies: they begin with an idea, a feeling, an image, a mood, a face, a place, a plot, a dream, an autobiographical experience, an item in the news, a story from history, family, friends, Shakespeare, the bible, myth or fairytale; or more probably, a mixture of several of these. What this adds up to is that anything can be the starting point for a novel. My favourite answer of this type comes from Virginia Woolf:

> *To the Lighthouse* is going to be fairly short; to have father's character done complete in it; and mother's; and St. Ives; and childhood; and all the usual things I try to put in – life, death, etc. But the centre is father's character, sitting in a boat, reciting. We perished, each alone, while he crushes a dying mackerel. (Woolf 1953: 76)

It is daunting, the notion of finding this beginning, because by its very vagueness it might not be a beginning of a novel. It might be a great baggy mess of life love the universe and everything, the literary equivalent of a drunk at a party. Or it might simply be the beginning of a short story.

The second answer to 'How do you begin to write a novel?' is much simpler, 'Start writing words on a page'. I am always reassured by this. No matter how complex or ethereal the inspiration for a novel is, what it boils down to, is writing words on a page. Which pulls the whole thing back into the realm of the practical and possible. Woolf goes on to say, 'I must write a few little stories first and let the Lighthouse simmer, adding to it between tea and dinner till it is complete for writing out'. So it seems that the way to begin writing a novel is to ring-fence a time to do it in – I prefer morning to 'between tea and dinner' myself, but that may be because I don't have a cook – and to begin putting words on paper. What you begin by writing may not figure at all in the finished novel; and indeed, it is easier to begin writing if you have told yourself that what you're writing is provisional and can easily be thrown away. But what you are doing is writing yourself into it, you are finding out what it is, you are edging your way into defining the book's territory. And best of all, by writing something down, you are providing yourself with something concrete to work on, even if it is only to cross out.

There is another breed of writers, who work out whole novels – plotting, chronology, even precise sentences – in their heads before putting pen to paper; my guess is they may not need to read about beginning to write a novel, so I won't address myself to them. For the rest of us, the early stages of a novel are a period of exploration. Whatever the story, there will be lots of different possible ways of telling it. Sometimes, instinctively, one hits on the right way from the start; sometimes it takes a lot of playing around and trial and error to discover the right way. What follows in this chapter are a number of thoughts and suggestions for what to do in the early stages, to encourage wider exploration of the material, and to help with structuring it. Given that, as a writer, you are choosing every twist and turn of the plot, every detail of characterisation, every sentence structure, every single word you write, it is important to make the best choices possible – and to be able to do this, it's important to have some sense of the range of options open to you. The exercises are about playing with the way you write, and trying out different techniques. Obviously, there is interplay and overlap between the elements of the novel which I have here crudely singled out.

Subject matter and theme

No one can tell you what to write about: it must be your own obsession. And if you don't have an idea for a novel, please don't write one, it will be better for everyone if you don't. It is also worth bearing in mind that there are some subjects which people may not much want to read about; these change according to fashion but may currently include wretched childhoods of abused children, and the amusing plight of thirty-something single women. What is important to remember is that a good novel usually contains more than one theme. Anita Desai's *Clear Light of Day* (1980) is about a rift between a brother and sister, but it is also centrally about the passage of time, about childhood and age, love (both familial and romantic), and about the wounds inflicted upon individual lives by the partition of India and Pakistan. Its themes are both personal and public; it is this range and complexity which make it so satisfying. If you have written a few thousand words of your novel and can only find one theme in it, it may be happier as a short story.

Narrative voice

Narrative voice is the most important single choice I make about the novel I am working on. Finding the right voice makes the writing of the book possible; the narrative voice or voices tell the story, their vocabulary and style and tense determine the texture and mood of the novel. There are a number of options, and I find it useful to play with them and try them all, before settling upon one.

First person ('I')

This is preferred by many first-time novelists because of its immediacy. It draws the reader straight into the narrator's head, it is easy to write in the sense that it is a limited, circumscribed point of view; it is fun to write, *because* it is circumscribed. A first person narrator cannot know everything, and therefore will sometimes misinterpret information or other characters; so they can be exposed to the reader as unreliable, providing a detective role for the reader. The first person voice is dramatic – indeed, it is a monologue. And the character of the narrator is revealed in the most direct way possible, by the language he uses. Consider how much we learn about Mark Haddon's narrator from this sentence, with its pedantic, logical thinking, its simple vocabulary and inadequate punctuation, and the odd formality of the narrator not using contractions:

> I decided that the dog was probably killed with the fork because I could not see any other wounds in the dog and I do not think you would stick a garden fork into a dog after it had died for some other reason, like cancer for example, or a road accident. (Haddon 2003: 1)

There are conventions of first person storytelling which you can adopt and which readers accept without question; the diary, letters, a confession, a 'I have decided to write my story in an attempt to understand what happened' or simply, an internal monologue.

The chief disadvantages of first person are that a single voice can become rather relentless, particularly if it has a limited vocabulary, and that it is sometimes difficult to find ways of conveying essential information to the reader, if that information is unknown to the narrator. Both difficulties can be overcome using such means as more than one narrator, or including information via a medium like newspaper articles. Look at Peter Carey's *True History of the Kelly Gang* (2001) to see how he frames a first person narrative with an informational third person account of the shoot-out which finished off the gang, and of Ned's death – information the reader needs to know, but which the narrator, Ned, cannot furnish for obvious reasons.

Exercise
Your character, writing as 'I', takes a walk down the street. What does she see? Is it external? Internal? Is she looking at other people, cars, flowers, litter, sunshine, dogshit, or is she oblivious to it all, and if so, what is she seeing in her mind's eye? Think about the language you are using, which is defining your character.

Second person ('you')

This is rarely chosen, and can feel rather contrived. But in the hands of some writers it is even more compelling than the first person, leading the reader to identify strongly with the protagonist. B. S. Johnson's *Albert Angelo* (1964) has a section in the second person from the point of view of a supply teacher who has found some boys messing about in a painting class:

> You walk slowly up and demand the painting. In the foreground are hardly identifiable animals with television aerials on their heads, yoked to a sleigh. Underneath each is a series of brown splodges, and, leaving no room for dubiety as to what was represented, an arrow and the word *shit*. You conceal your amusement with difficulty, confiscate the drawing for your collection, and stand the boys out in the front facing the board. (Johnson 1964: 27)

Second person is often used for short passages within a first or third person narrative, when a character is (schizophrenically) talking to herself as 'you'. Some writers, like James Kelman, have their protagonist move fluidly between all three voices within one novel, and this is an interesting exercise to try.

Exercise
Transpose a paragraph you have previously written in the first person, into the second person. You may find it necessary to change more of the language than simply the I/you

and the verbs. (Note how Johnson generates humour, above, by the contrast between the formality of the language, and the intimacy of the narrator's inwardly childish response.) Compare your two versions, considering how different an impact the second person makes.

Third person ('he' or 'she')

This breaks down into two further choices. The first of these is the God-like third person voice of many nineteenth-century novels, the authorial voice who has created the world of the novel and who knows the thoughts and feelings of every character in it. In contemporary writing it is uncommon, but Annie Proulx's *The Shipping News* (1993) is a fine example. It opens 'Here is an account of a few years in the life of Quoyle, born in Brooklyn and raised in a shuffle of dreary upstate towns. Hive spangled, gut roaring with gas and cramp, he survived childhood . . .' and moves effortlessly through the thoughts and feelings of all its characters, revealing and commenting upon them. Note how elegantly this third person voice allows her to leap over swathes of time.

Exercise
Try the all-knowing third person. Describe the scene in a courtroom where a woman is awaiting sentence for infanticide. Her husband and parents are present, as the jury files in.

The second choice, for third person, is use of restricted point of view. A novel may be restricted to the point of view of one character, as in J. M. Coetzee's *Disgrace* (1999). This has many of the advantages of first person, in terms of intensity and leading the reader fully into the protagonist's head, but it makes the summarising of information easier, as can be seen in these thoughts of David, the central character in *Disgrace*:

> He has not taken to Bev Shaw, a dumpy, bustling little woman with black freckles, close-cropped, wiry hair, and no neck. He does not like women who make no effort to be attractive. It is a resistance he has had to Lucy's friends before. (Coetzee 2000: 72)

Imagine how informational this would feel, transposed to the first person. Coetzee creates an added sense of alienation by presenting his protagonist's story in the third person, as if David himself is at a slight remove from his own experiences; the first person would make him more intimate with the reader, which would work against the grain of this chilly, deeply disturbing novel. The lack of any other point of view reinforces the sense of David's isolation, his inability to understand those around him.

A third-person novel can also range through the restricted points of view of a number of characters, moving from one to another within the course of a page, or separating them out into distinct chapters. John Updike's *Rabbit Run* (1960) is centrally the point of view of Rabbit Angstrom, but also contains sections from the point of view of his wife and his mistress and a handful of minor characters, which reveal to us, almost shockingly, that Rabbit is not actually the centre of the universe. This is used to brilliant effect after Rabbit's wife (whom he has walked out on) accidentally drowns their baby, and the point of view shifts to Lucy, a woman who dislikes Rabbit and is simply concerned about how his behaviour impinges on the life of her Rector husband (Updike 1964: 215).

Exercise

Select a day of crisis in your protagonist's life, and write in the third person about an action he performs from the point of view of someone with different values or concerns. It could be a pet, a door-to-door salesman, a plumber, an airline hostess, a child. Use the new point of view to attempt to find meaning in the protagonist's action, and to reveal how it affects the character whose point of view you are using.

The storyteller

This is really a subsection of 'first person', but the effect is so entirely different that it deserves considering on its own. The storyteller is a device occasionally employed by novelists ranging from Dostoevsky to Conrad to F. Scott Fitzgerald. Storytellers are not players; they simply observe and record, and occasionally, pass judgement. They put a frame around the story. In Dostoevsky's work, look at the difference between the in-your-face unreliable first-person narrator of *Notes from Underground* (1864), and the shadowy storyteller who is not even a character in the novel, in *The Brothers Karamazov* (1880). The storyteller is not the authorial voice, but is privileged to an overview and a wide-ranging knowledge of events, which characters in the thick of the action cannot have. Philip Roth in *American Pastoral* (1997) gives this device an extra tweak by having his storyteller, Zuckerman, admit that he is making up those parts of the story of which he could not realistically have knowledge:

> I dreamed a realistic chronicle. I began gazing into his (Swede Levov's) life – not his life as a god or a demigod in whose triumphs one could exult as a boy but his life as another assailable man – and inexplicably, which is to say lo and behold, I found him in Deal, New Jersey, at the seaside cottage, the summer his daughter was eleven . . . (Roth 1998: 89)

From here the story homes in on Swede and his daughter, leaving Zuckerman's life behind. A storyteller uses her own language to present the story, and thus interesting contrasts can be generated, for example between emotional subject matter and a distanced, measured narrative voice; irony and humour can arise from the gap between the protagonist's feelings and the storyteller's attitude.

Exercise

Use the voice of a cynical and weary journalist to narrate the story of a joyful incident in your protagonist's life, for example winning a prize. The journalist is a neighbour of your protagonist, but is not a close friend.

Characterisation

Fictional characters are often partly based on real people known to the writer, or on aspects of several different people, run together into one fictional character. But creating a character in fiction is rather like acting. The writer needs to enter, imaginatively, into that character's head; see as he sees, think as he thinks, feel as he feels. Creating a convincing character is often about pushing one aspect of your own personality to an extreme. Most writers are not murderers, but, to write about a murderer, you need to be able to imagine inhabiting a murderer's skull, understanding and believing in the motives that prompt him, embracing the contradictions and confusions he feels. You need to know your characters well enough to sympathise with them. A writer who sets out to present the murderer as bad will write a two-dimensional character.

It is worth drawing up a list of the ways in which writers can reveal character, and then testing your own writing against the list – to see how many of the available techniques you have used, and to consider whether trying some that you have not used, might be a way into more interesting or complex characterisation. Some 'ways of revealing character' are listed below.

Physical description

For example 'the babysitter came to loll in front of the television set – Mrs Moosup with arms too fat for sleeves' (Proulx [1993] 1994: 14). Note here that one telling detail can be more effective than a page of photographically accurate description. Be wary of over-description, and cut down on your use of adjectives.

Action

This example is from *True History of the Kelly Gang,* and follows a scene in which Ned has just shot two men: 'we knocked up an old man in a nightgown Coulson were his name. I counted out the price for what we took telling him my name so he could tell Ned Kelly were no thief' (Carey 2001: 246). Quite apart from the curious revelation that he is anxious not to be thought a thief, after admitting to being a murderer, note how Kelly's language reveals his lack of formal education.

Speech

This outburst is from David Lurie in *Disgrace*: 'I have not sought counselling nor do I intend to seek it. I am a grown man. I am not receptive to being counselled. I am beyond the reach of counselling' (Coetzee [1999] 2000: 49).

Possessions or setting

This example is a description of the London room furnished by Nazneen's husband Chanu, in *Brick Lane*:

> The carpet was yellow with a green leaf design. One hundred per cent nylon and, Chanu said, very hard-wearing. The sofa and chairs were the colour of dried cow dung, which was a practical colour. They had little sheaths of plastic on the headrests to protect them from Chanu's hair oil. (Ali 2003: 15)

Note the economy here; the room is described from Nazneen's point of view and we can see that it is hideous, but she does not pass this judgement herself. Her description tells us as much about her as it does about Chanu.

Thoughts

In Valerie Martin's *Property*, the protagonist watches her husband's sadistic sexual exploits with young black boys, and reports, 'Often, as I look through the glass, I hear in my head an incredulous refrain: *This is my husband, this is my husband*' (Martin [2003] 2004: 5). The character's extreme self-control and her powerlessness to change her situation are succinctly revealed by this thought.

Speech or thoughts of other characters

Other characters may give their view of this particular character, as in *Clear Light of Day*: 'Bim watched her sister in surprise and amusement. Was Tara, grown woman, mother of grown daughters, still child enough to play with a snail?' (Desai [1988] 2001: 2).

Language and style

In the first person, the language *is* the character; but also consider the choice of language you are using about the character in the third person, whether it is colloquial or formal, direct or circumlocutory, etc.

Exercise
Try any of these ways of revealing character which you have not already used, for example, through describing possessions. Describe your character's bedroom. How have they personalised the room?

Setting

Setting in a novel is not background; it is a key, vital element. In the best novels it permeates and determines the characters' behaviour; it thwarts or facilitates their actions. It may echo their moods or present an ironic contrast. Consider the role of contemporary South Africa in *Disgrace*, Delhi and Partition in *Clear Light of Day*, nineteenth-century Louisiana in *Property*, and London in *Brick Lane*. Setting may be simply geographical; but more often it is also politics, class, public events, all of which impinge upon the lives of your characters. Setting needs thorough research and convincing writing, even if it is a fantasy setting. (See Peter Carey's *The Unusual Life of Tristran Smith* [1994] for a meticulously imagined alternative world, complete with footnotes detailing its history.)

When researching historical setting, first-hand accounts are always the most useful. Look at diaries, letters, and travellers' accounts. When researching *Promised Lands* (1995), I was able to build up for myself a very real sense of Australia in 1788 through reading four journals by different members of the First Fleet. Diaries give the kind of specific detail (what they ate for breakfast, how clothes were washed, the weather on a certain day) which history books omit.

Exercise
Write a scene where the external world impinges on your character's life and changes it. For example, a storm, a riot, threat of a terrorist bomb, a fire. Or it could be something as simple as being stung by a bee.

Plotting and structure

Plot and structure often change as a novel grows. But it is still necessary to know what they are from the beginning: if writing the novel is a journey of exploration, then the plot and structure you have in your head at the beginning is the map. The map may turn out in the end to be wrong in some respects, or even entirely useless. It will need redrawing numerous times along the way; but still, it's no good setting off without one. And in fact the maps of plots are all very well known. People will argue about exactly how many plots there are in the world, but it is generally agreed to be a limited number (somewhere between seven and eleven). The bones of one of these key plots can be found in all novels, and most of the best novels contain at least four.

This is my list of the basic plots; your own list might vary.

1. Rags to riches – the Cinderella plot. For this plot reversed, see *Disgrace*.
2. Love – succeeding after being thwarted. See *The Shipping News*. Or, for an interesting inversion, *Brick Lane*.
3. Transformation – which may be literal, children growing into adults (*Clear Light of Day*) or psychological (*Disgrace*, *Brick Lane*).
4. Disaster – how does the protagonist cope under ever-increasing pressure? As in Yann Martel's *The Life of Pi* (2001). This is a plot more commonly used in films than novels.
5. Good v. evil – for example *True History of the Kelly Gang* (with the twist that the outlaw Ned is good, and the police and society are evil).
6. The Outsider – someone strange comes to town. This is the central plot of much Science Fiction and many Westerns, but also literary fiction like *The Curious Incident of the Dog in Night-time*, *Property* and *Brick Lane*.
7. Quest or mission – the protagonist has to find or accomplish something. See *American Pastoral*, *The Curious Incident of the Dog in Night-time*.

Most good novels contain elements of most of these plots. Crossing from one plot to another creates suspense; look at the structure of the great Victorian novels written for magazine serialisation, switching from one storyline to another, chapter by chapter. Or look indeed at soap opera, as we cut from one family's story to the plot of another set of characters.

Exercise
This is a crude exercise, but can be helpful in exposing weaknesses in an idea. Check how many of these archetypal plots feature in your novel. A plot represents questions for the reader to ask, and assumptions the reader will make; questions you can avoid answering, by twists and turns, thereby creating suspense, and assumptions you can foil by taking off in another direction. Since the blueprint of these plots is already in all readers' heads, you can play against it, you can do the unexpected.

Structure is the shape of the book; baldly, it is the sections it is divided into (for example, four parts, thirty chapters). It is the order in which the plot is told, which may be chronologically, or backwards in flashbacks, or from the point of view of a minor player, or through conflicting points of view, or counterpointed with another story (or stories) altogether. It is composed of sequences of writing in which contrasts of pace and tension, comedy and tragedy, action and reflection, lead the reader through a range of emotions, always asking questions.

It is something the writer needs to be aware of from the start, but it is infinitely open to change. It is perfectly possible to write a book and completely change its structure when it is finished. For example a novel may consist of two characters' contrasting views of a love affair; first one, then the other. It could be restructured by chopping them up, re-ordering, and intercutting the two voices, with an eye to varying pace and increasing suspense. For the novelist at the beginning of a novel, an idea of structure is vital because it breaks the novel into manageable chunks. It is difficult to sit down and write a novel. It is less difficult to sit down and write a ten-page chapter. Invent a structure to begin with, even if you need to change it as you go along.

And once you have a draft, test it against received notions of what structure should be; not necessarily in order to change it to fall in line with these, but to see if they will help to reveal weaknesses. The five-point structure pattern for novel which is most frequently cited goes: (1) inciting incident, (2) major climax around page 80, (3) midpoint crisis where underlying motives are revealed, (4) climax, (5) resolution. I am not recommending anyone to set off writing a novel to this formula. But applying it to a first draft can help to diagnose problems. If I had known of it when I was writing my first novel, I may have been able to work out why the ending feels so abrupt: there is a climax but no resolution.

Exercise
Analyse the structure of your three favourite novels. Consider use (or non-use) of parts, chapters, divisions. Write a brief summary of what happens in each chapter or section, note crises, time gaps, changes of voice, etc. Now do the same for your own novel-in-progress. Although this will throw up problems, it usually makes the writing seem more manageable, and there may be aspects of the structure of the novels you have analysed which you decide to borrow. Bear in mind that there are no rules about writing. You don't have to begin at the beginning. If there is a difficult section, leave it till later. Very often, the way to tackle it will emerge mysteriously, from somewhere in the back of your mind, while you work on other things. And allow yourself to work on from bad writing to good, don't waste days repeatedly crossing out that awful first sentence.

The most important preparation for writing a novel is to read. Look at how other writers have constructed novels, created characters, generated suspense, evoked powerful settings. Look at the voices they have invented, the language they use, the structures into which they have composed their work. The more you can read and gain understanding of how other novels are put together, the more tools you have at your disposal in the creation of your own novel. Once you have read, you can begin to write.

References

Ali, Monica (2003), *Brick Lane*, London: Doubleday.

Carey, Peter (1994), *The Unusual Life of Tristan Smith*, London: Faber.

Carey, Peter (2001), *True History of the Kelly Gang*, London: Faber.

Coetzee, J. M. [1999] (2000), *Disgrace*, London: Vintage.

Desai, Anita [1998] (2001), *Clear Light of Day*, London: Vintage.

Dostoevsky, Fyodor [1864] (1972), *Notes from Underground*, London: Penguin.

Dostoevsky, Fyodor [1880] (1992), *The Brothers Karamazov*, London: Vintage.

Haddon, Mark (2003), *The Curious Incident of the Dog in the Night-time*, Oxford: David Fickling Books.

Johnson, B. S. (1964), *Albert Angelo*, New York: New Directions Books.

Martin, Valerie [2003] (2004), *Property*, London: Abacus.

Proulx, E. Annie [1994] (1993), *The Shipping News*, London: Fourth Estate.

Rogers, Jane (1995), *Promised Lands*, London: Faber.

Roth, Philip (1998), *American Pastoral*, London: Vintage.

Updike, John (1964), *Rabbit, Run*, London: Penguin.

Woolf, Virginia (1953), *A Writer's Diary*, London: The Hogarth Press.

11

Crime Fiction

John Dale

Over the past twenty years as a writer and teacher of creative writing I have read more than a hundred writing guidebooks and found that less than a third of these were of any value. Usually if a developing writer receives one solid piece of advice from a writing book then he or she is doing well. The worst how-to-write books eschew the practical in favour of the abstract, their authors speak in generalities and say things such as, 'We read fiction to know what it is like to be human'. Well no, what attracts me above all else to fiction and non-fiction is story. A sense that the writer is taking me on a journey where I am not ahead of her, where the dialogue is not flat and predictable, where the prose is accomplished. As much as I admire *Ulysses* I now reach for *The Odyssey*. Great narratives survive for a reason and not solely because of Jung's archetypes. All fiction needs movement, a sense that we are getting somewhere. Without forward movement a story feels slow. Without digression a story can be unsatisfying. Narrative drive is related to plot, to things happening. Digression is related to character, a revealing incident from a character's past. In crime fiction with few exceptions plot is more important than in literary fiction. Crime fiction tells a story, and that is its great and lasting appeal.

What follows in this chapter contains practical information for crime writers and teachers of crime fiction writing with the emphasis on narrative. If you can take away two useful pieces of advice from this chapter then I will have done my job.

Crime fiction, and the thriller in particular, has its structural roots in the novella form: a short, sharp, tightly-written narrative consisting of a series of increasingly intense climaxes where something happens to the protagonist(s) who comes under increasing pressure. John Buchan's *The Thirty-Nine Steps* is in many ways the perfect example of the thriller form except that it lacks the female element and so remains a boy's own adventure; nonetheless it is an excellent example of a continuous stream of action moving through a series of rising climaxes and focused throughout on a single character. The thriller, and crime fiction generally, suits the novella, which covers a shorter time span than the novel; and this adds a sense of urgency to the story.

Thrillers, whodunits, mysteries, police procedurals – all of these sub-genres come under the umbrella term of crime novel and many of them share similar features, but the crime novel has moved a long way from the traditional detective story. The constant dilemma for the crime writer is how to make the genre new, to take the old conventions and formulae and inject them with energy and innovation. Just as Hammett and Chandler took murder out of the English drawing rooms and dropped it back into the streets, so it is the emerging writer's job to make crime writing relevant to today.

Where to start?

There is nothing more difficult to write than the beginning. It is the beginning passages of a story which tell us how to read it and also whether we want to read it. From the beginning we learn about content, tone, and subject matter. A good beginning must do many things and do them all at once. It should raise questions, set up character and situation and hook the reader in by suspense, atmosphere, and a promise of things to come. Sam Reaves' *A Long Cold Fall* is a memorable example of a crime fiction beginning: 'By the time he reached 26th Street, Cooper was hoping he hadn't made a mistake. Things were too quiet in the back seat' (Reaves 1991: 7). There are no preliminaries, no introductions. Reaves begins as near as possible to the action with his taxi-driver protagonist encountering a dangerous fare at night. What is set up from the outset is tension. Writers are often advised to start a crime story with a bang, but not too big a bang, because where do you go from there? Many crime novels employ a dual narrative, switching between the personal emotional story and the external action. This allows the writer somewhere to go when the narrative flags. The more different narratives there are and different points of view the easier it is to switch, but the disadvantages are a loss of identification and sometimes confusion for the reader.

The best crime narratives contain both internal and external conflict. Generally, for the writer, internal conflict is more important than external conflict. Raymond Chandler believed that readers only thought they cared about nothing but action, but really what they cared about, and what he cared about, was the creation of emotion through dialogue and description. The emotional narrative is what counts. One of the most effective exercises to get any crime writer started is to describe in ten sentences a character in action who has just committed (or witnessed) a crime. Do not state what this crime is, but let the sentences raise questions in the reader's mind. Describe the character in action. She can be running away, driving from the scene, but whatever role she plays in the narrative, use her thoughts, actions and dialogue with others to intrigue and capture the reader's attention and above all, to raise questions.

Character and dialogue

When you think of crime fiction the first thing you think of is the protagonist: Marlowe, Robicheaux, Scarpetta, etc. It is not crucial to have an original protagonist, but it helps. Look for what hasn't been done yet. As popular as crime novels with private investigators are, it is difficult to disagree with James Ellroy's remark that the last time a PI investigated a real murder was never.

A far more believable protagonist than the PI is the ordinary man or woman – the taxi-driver, the house-breaker, the journalist, someone with a real job – who gets caught up in a crime or with the consequences of a crime. Whatever protagonist you choose it is advisable when introducing your main character to let the facts emerge gradually. Only let out as much as the readers need to know. As in real life we get to know a character by sight, smell and sound and a few snatches of dialogue, or more often by what is not said. There is nothing more boring in life or in fiction than a character who blurts out her personal history at the first meeting. Do not under any circumstances use mirrors or shop windows to describe physically your main character. Much of the information about a protagonist does not surface in the narrative, but making a comprehensive profile allows a writer to know their main character intimately and how they will react. Ian Rankin never physically describes Inspector John Rebus in *Set in Darkness*, but from reading just one Rebus novel I learned the following details about the detective inspector: he drinks malt whisky and ale in Edinburgh's ungentrified hotels; he drives a Saab; he is an expert on 1960s rock music; he is a loner, bad-tempered and divorced, yet older women appear to find him attractive. Such information will come out indirectly through dialogue and action, but the writer needs to know it first. It also helps to have some unspoken complication from your protagonist's past as well as something from the present. Usually this is an emotional obstacle. Too often in crime fiction it is alcoholism or a murdered spouse, but an emotional wound is part of the territory. Whatever complications exist in your character's past, don't reveal them too early.

Once you have your character, then you need to find that character's voice. How do you reveal character through dialogue? What is dialogue's main function? Dialogue moves a story forward, it communicates information to the reader, it reveals character and establishes relationships between characters. Dialogue should do many things all at once. It should never be predictable; it should rarely answer a question directly; it should be cryptic and build tension; it should keep the narrative on track; it should never tell the reader what they already know. Good dialogue is the hardest thing to write. Writers who have a brilliant ear for dialogue include George Higgins, Elmore Leonard and Cormac McCarthy. Elmore Leonard once said he learned everything about writing dialogue from reading Higgins' *The Friends of Eddie Coyle*. And Higgins learned to write his dialogue from listening to Federal wire taps. Read *The Friends of Eddie Coyle* and then write four pages of razor-sharp dialogue between your main character and someone of the opposite sex. Put it away for twenty-four hours and then go through it thinking what you cut out, then revise until half the length. Spend as much time on your dialogue as you do on your prose. Leave out redundancies. Avoid tags wherever possible. Never use an adverb to modify the verb 'said'. Nothing indicates the amateur or hack more than the habit of attaching an explanatory adverb to every line of dialogue, he said tediously. Use adverbs and exclamation points sparingly! Above all, good dialogue should be character-driven far more than plot-driven.

Setting, atmosphere and the city

G. K. Chesterton maintained that the reason for the detective story's significance was its poetic treatment of the city. The detective story was the earliest form of popular literature to express a sense of the poetry of modern city life, the urban environment. The importance of the city as the milieu has been apparent since Edgar Allan Poe's M. Dupin sallied forth into the streets. Setting not only determines atmosphere, mood, characters, plotline, the nature of the prose, setting *is* character. Think of Philip Marlowe, Sherlock Holmes, V. I. Warshawski, Dave Robicheaux, Cliff Hardy and the cities of LA, London, Chicago, New Orleans and Sydney spring to mind. Apart from the protagonist and antagonist, setting is your most important character.

In his ten deadly sins of crime writing Elmore Leonard urges the writer never to open a book with the weather. What Leonard means by this, presumably, is not to go into great detail about the weather at the outset; however weaving the weather into the fabric of your narrative adds texture. Weather is connected to the senses. In a city like Sydney the weather affects everything: what your character is wearing, eating, doing and drinking, the type of pubs, the cafés, the water restrictions. For most readers what remains long after the plot has faded of a thriller like Peter Høeg's *Miss Smilla's Feeling for Snow* is the feel of wintry Copenhagen or icy Greenland. When describing weather or other aspects of setting and atmosphere be specific and concrete. Ideally the writer requires that readers fill in the gaps and pick up on the hints. Reading good fiction is not passive like watching bad TV, it requires engagement, concentration to enter the fictional world. Setting and atmosphere help to create and reinforce this relationship between writer and reader.

Think of a city (or suburb) that your protagonist knows intimately. Don't write this city down. Jot down twenty words, phrases, sentences that describe this place. Think of unusual details. Use the senses: sounds, smells, touch, sight, taste. Now show your writing partner. Don't tell them the name of the city (suburb) but see if they can figure out where it is. Decide which phrases, details have evoked your setting most effectively and throw the rest away.

Structure, plot and patterns of the generic formula

It is said there are two kinds of writers, those who start from plot, an idea, and those who start from a character in a situation: a lonely woman needs a lover, a crim gets out of jail. Many new writers have a problem with plot and structure and confuse the two. However, structure is more than plot. Structure refers to the overall design of your piece of fiction. If you write a story using alternating points of view, with a male and female detective, or four contrasting characters, then this is part of the structure. Plot is also related to time. How long do you need to spend on a particular incident? Scene and summary set up a rhythm in your writing. Use scenes (dialogue, physical reaction, senses) for emotional highpoints. Use summary for the rest.

Another way to think about plot is to decide what your character wants. In Christopher Cook's *Robbers*, Ray Bob wants a pack of cigarettes, goes into a convenience store and shoots the clerk, which starts the narrative rolling. Elmore Leonard uses 'wants' in most of his books – someone wants to get into movies or record producing. The most common 'want' in crime fiction is money; others are revenge or sex. Once you have the 'want', then think of obstacles that stand in the way of your character achieving it. Crime fiction and most screenplays work with a want and obstacles. The detective wants to find a missing woman. Maybe she is not a woman, maybe she is not really missing. Reversals or turning points work well in crime fiction especially where the readers' expectations are turned around. This is not to advocate using tricks. Stay true to the fictional terms of the piece. Don't use surprise endings that come from nowhere. As a novel or story draws to a close, each word gains weight. Think carefully about the words you use to end a piece. Although ambiguity is closer to real life, closure in crime fiction is often believed to be more satisfying. But not closure that is rushed and contrived. Many detective novels end badly because the writer strives to tie everything up neatly. In many ways this is a weakness of the genre. Even Truman Capote's classic non-fiction novel *In Cold Blood* is marred by its mawkish end, a corny scene at the cemetery, which clashes with the gritty realism of the rest of the book. It is difficult to think of many crime endings that have resonance: one memorable exception is Chandler's *Farewell, My Lovely* where Marlowe rides the lift down and walks out onto the steps of City Hall: 'It was a cold day and very clear. You could see a long way – but not as far as Velma had gone' (Chandler 1949: 253).

Voice and point of view

In contemporary fiction one may do anything one pleases with point of view as long as it works, but the writer should do it for a reason other than it seemed a good idea at the time to use twelve different characters. Elmore Leonard used an alligator's point of view in *Maximum Bob* and Tolstoy used the point of view of a dog in *Anna Karenina*. First person, second and third person all have their advantages and disadvantages and there is not the space to go into them here other than to say that detective fiction has traditionally been written in first person; that second person is rare in crime fiction and works best when drawing the reader into the subworld of the mental institution, jail or detention centre; that third person objective, where the narrator refrains from entering any character's mind, can be a strangely unsettling choice in crime fiction. There are no rules other than consistency. Point of view is merely a tool that a writer chooses in order to tell the story in the most effective manner.

When we talk about voice there are two meanings: the author's voice and the character's voice. A writer like James Ellroy has an unique voice in crime writing, frenetic, flamboyant, explosive; his authorial voice is everywhere in his tightly-plotted novels, *American Tabloid* and *LA Confidential*. There are other crime writers, however, who can adapt their voice and command a variety of borrowed voices. Perhaps the most versatile technique for representing narrative voices is free indirect discourse (FID), a technique effectively employed by Elmore Leonard. FID is sometimes referred to as 'coloured narration' or 'double-voiced discourse' because it incorporates the voice of a character within the narration thereby colouring the prose rather than explicitly marking it out as separate speech or thoughts with attribution. FID has the capacity to reproduce the gangster's speech, thoughts and perceptions within the narrator's reporting language, thus contributing 'to the semantic density within the text' (Rimmon-Kenan 1983: 114). Leonard utilizes FID in all his later books narrating the story in third person limited, usually through the eyes of four, sometimes five contrasting characters each with their own distinctive and idiosyncratic voice: 'Here was this dink talking right up to him. It took Elvin a moment to adjust, resetting his hat again where it would stick to his forehead' (Leonard 1992: 102).

What gets eliminated with FID are the 'he thoughts', the 'she wondereds', the unnecessary authorial interpositions. FID is particularly useful for a crime writer like Leonard who is more concerned with developing character than plot. Slipping in and out of FID is more difficult than it seems and many new writers struggle to make the transition smoothly. Very often these transitions to FID occur immediately after a sentence containing a verb of perception: 'Elvin came out of the dark into the spotlight looking at the Volkswagen parked there by the open garage. She was here, no doubt about it, and that was too bad. Ms Touchy, she was a salty little thing for being as cute as she was. Spoke right up to you' (Leonard 1992: 121).

Suspense and tension

Suspense is tied up with anxiety, and therefore is generally superior to surprise. The bomb that we know is about to go off in a crowded cinema is more effective in creating tension in an audience than the bomb that goes off without warning. Suspense and surprise, however, can work together in a complementary way. The role of suspense is crucial in any crime novel and in most fiction that strives for a wide readership. All narratives need to create some uncertainty. Questions are thrown up, secrets hinted at, information suppressed. As a reader you anticipate what these characters will do next, the choices they will have to make. These may involve life or death decisions or suspense may depend whether or not to open a door. With suspense you can never be too certain of the outcome. The writer presents the situation and then teases the reader with various possibilities and by delaying gratification rather than moving directly towards the solution. Delay makes the process more thrilling, even within minor scenes. There is a scene in one of Chandler's novels when a crucial letter arrives. Marlowe leaves the letter on the desk toying with it while the reader is anxious to know the contents. A page or so later Marlowe opens the letter providing the vital information. Suspense is the way you make your audience worry and the more involved your readers become with your characters the more tension they will feel. The highest kind of suspense, according to John Gardner, 'involves the Sartrean anguish of choice; that is, our suspenseful concern is not just with what will happen but with the moral implications of action' (Gardner 1991: 162).

Certainly suspense works best with highly-developed characters. With comic-book characters who tend to be either black or white there is little real suspense for we can easily predict what action they will choose. When characters are presented in shades of grey and are, therefore, more human, suspense is heightened as readers are uncertain about the outcome and worry over which choice the characters will make and ultimately what the results will be. Foreshadowing is an important part of creating suspense. Ideally in crime fiction every episode prefigures something to come. Every action has a consequence. Suspense is created by foreshadowing, by withholding the revelation. A good task is to devise two scenes, a foreshadowing scene and a realisation scene to create suspense. Think of something original or subtle. Don't use a bomb or a gun. Then think of delays in between.

When characters are going to decide something, there should always be friction, some uncertainty as to which way they'll go. Will she go in the bedroom, will she stay out? This stay-go dilemma is used to create tension in all drama so that even the smallest scenes have inherent conflict and these in turn build to make up larger scenes. Tension on every page is perhaps the best piece of advice a teacher can give the writer of crime fiction, but it is easier said than done. This does not mean melodramatic conflict with characters screaming and throwing furniture at every opportunity; on the contrary, it means that lurking behind even casual conversations should be a sense of menace, that minor scenes should contain some kind of conflict either spoken or unspoken. The crime writer builds tension and does not release it until the end. If a scene does not have conflict then cut it out.

Style

Raymond Chandler maintained that the time comes when the writer has to choose between action and character, between menace and wit. There are a handful of crime writers who can do humour well: Carl Hiassen, Elmore Leonard, Shane Maloney to mention a few, yet even the wit of the best crime writers such as Chandler fades with the years. Generally, if you can write funny then write it; if you can't – and most of us can't – then choose menace and suspense. Promise your readers something and hold off supplying it until the end. Use internal monologue to heighten doubts, increase tension and make sure that your readers turn those pages.

The best style for a crime writer is the one that appears to be no style at all. Elmore Leonard tries to leave out the parts that readers skip. James Lee Burke evokes the landscape and weather of the bayou country yet he does it with a lyrical effortlessness. The crime writer must strive to find their natural voice, by avoiding overwritten prose and long slabs of beautiful but dull description. Try not to be too obviously literary. Or self-conscious. It is fair to say that most good writers care deeply about language, but that most readers don't. People don't go out and buy Dan Brown's *Angels and Demons* for the language, they go out and buy it for the story. That is not to say crime writers can't write a great story and do it with style. Thomas Mann said that a writer is somebody for whom writing is more difficult than it is for other people. And it's true. Good writing is hard work and looks easy. It has energy yet never appears rushed.

Avoid italics like the plague, especially long passages which readers are inclined to skip, and try to avoid the major fault of style connected with crime writing, namely sentimentality. Present your characters calmly and coolly and let the reader supply the emotion.

Research and authenticity

Unlike other genres, crime fiction is based firmly in real life. It's no longer the case that a crime writer can make it up as she goes along. Research is an integral part of being a crime writer and unless you are successful enough to employ your own researcher then this involves going out into the world yourself and finding facts about the criminal justice system, about DNA evidence interpretation, or the best ways to pick a lock (never with a credit card). Research should not be viewed as a chore; it is the closest point that the crime writer comes to being a real detective. The most effective task I use with postgraduate writing students is to compile a list of places in the city for them to visit individually or in pairs — the City Detectives, Supreme Court, Long Bay Jail, the Wall in Darlinghurst (a pick-up place for gay prostitutes), the triage ward of a major public hospital, the city morgue – and for students to report back with details from their authentic research of how these places operate. The only proviso is that their research must be gathered first-hand and the information not widely known. This task always provides fascinating results. In a sense we are all detectives trying to make sense of our world and the crime writer's job is to explore their city, to uncover the hidden connections that exist between criminals, police and powerful members of society. The detective is linked to the *flâneur*, the idler who travels through the city observing people and places and sometimes uncovering crimes by reading the signs.

In the end, a crime writer needs to do a lot of things well: character, plot, dialogue, tension and suspense. Technique and theory, however, can only take you so far. Above all, a writer needs persistence. The ability to keep going through the bad times, when no one believes in your work, when everything you touch is leaden and lifeless. But the committed writer keeps going through the tunnel, for the day will come when your dialogue is sharp, when your prose is taut and your plot unfolds faster than your fingers can type. Only then will you know why it is you must write.

References

Buchan, John (2004), *The Thirty-Nine Steps*, London: Penguin.
Capote, Truman (1967), *In Cold Blood*, London: Penguin.
Chandler, Raymond (1949), *Farewell, My Lovely*, London: Penguin.

Cook, Christopher (2002), *Robbers*, New York: Berkley Publishing Group.

Gardner, John (1991), *The Art of Fiction*, New York: Vintage Books.

Higgins, George V. (1972), *The Friends of Eddie Coyle*, New York: Knopf.

Høeg, Peter (1994), *Miss Smillas' Feeling for Snow*, London: Flamingo.

Hiney, Tom, and Frank MacShane (eds) (2001), *The Raymond Chandler Papers: Selected Letters and Non-Fiction 1909–59*, London: Penguin.

Leonard, Elmore (1992), *Maximum Bob*, London: Penguin.

Reaves, Sam (1991), *A Long Cold Fall*, London: Serpent's Tail.

Rankin, Ian (2000), *Set in Darkness* (Inspector Rebus), London: Orion.

Rimmon-Kenan, Shlomith (1983), *Narrative Fiction: Contemporary Poetics*, London: Methuen.

12

Writing Science Fiction and Fantasy

Crawford Kilian

Science fiction and fantasy seem unlikely partners. SF, after all, is about what could happen, given what we currently know about the universe. Fantasy is about what could never happen, because science has shown it to be impossible.

But science itself uses fantasy to make its points, and fantasy tries to work out its own implications in a consistent manner. Science imagines elevators that fall forever, and spaceships that display clocks running slower and slower as the ships near the speed of light. Fantasy imagines the logical consequences of a spell, and the ecological niche of dragons. These are all 'thought experiments', ways of using fantasy to look at the world and ourselves outside the limits of ordinary experience.

Whether you write SF or fantasy, you are conducting such a thought experiment: could a human love a robot, and could the robot requite that love? If magic worked, what would it cost? In both genres, you are really exploring the human mind under conditions that reveal something new – or something old, familiar and ingrained that we have taken for granted until you make us look at it again. Just as some rocks and flowers reveal unexpected colours under ultraviolet light, human nature looks different in the light of a distant star, or of a sorcerer's glowing staff.

In this chapter I want to throw some light on the similarities of the two genres as well as their differences. This will involve their history, their conventions, and their future. But mine is just one writer's view; I hope that your own vision of your genre will be far more imaginative and original than mine.

Origins of Science Fiction and Fantasy

Fantasy arises from myth, folk tale, and fairy story. It began as an effort to personify the mysterious forces that rule our world: lightning, rain, sunlight, ice, and earthquake. Sometimes those forces were seen as gods, or as 'little people', or as supernatural beings inhabiting trees or rivers. Obviously this view of the world is psychologically satisfying: the gods make us in their image, and we return the compliment.

SF's ancestry is almost as old, but distinctively more upper-class. It stems from 'Menippean satire', also called 'anatomy', which was written by scholars who enjoyed poking fun at one another. Fantasy personalises natural forces and human traits; anatomy personalises abstractions. The Canadian literary scholar Northrop Frye calls anatomy a vision of the world in the light of a single idea. Both genres, as we'll see, share a fascination with language.

Both genres also eventually crossbred with heroic romance, itself a descendant of myths about gods and their half-human, half-divine offspring. Folk tale offered simple advice (don't talk to wolves you meet on your way to grandma's), and anatomy parodied scholarship (here are the customs of the Utopians). But heroic romance actually turned both genres into narratives, stories that illustrated, glorified, or criticised a society's values.

This evolution occurred relatively recently. Swift's *Gulliver's Travels* is largely anatomy, but Gulliver is a typical quest hero out of romance. In fact, he is an ironic antihero, a variation on Don Quixote.

Before we consider the modern genres, and where we might take them, we should look at some of their ancestral elements. They may still appear in your work, consciously or not, and you should be aware of them. Anatomy, for one, has several elements that have persisted since More's *Utopia* in the sixteenth century:

An isolated society
A society which is distant from us in time or space. It may be an island (Utopia, Lilliput, Airstrip One), or in the future (*The Time Machine*), or in a self-contained spaceship like the Enterprise in *Star Trek*.

A morally significant language
Orwell's Newspeak is a superb example, but so are Tolkien's languages and the Utopians' Greco-Latin patois . . . which implies that even a pagan society could do much better than Christians have done.

An inquisitive outsider
The outsider stands in for us; he or she has to learn what the society's people all know from childhood. So Gulliver learns about Lilliput and Brobdingnag, and Genly Ai, in Ursula K. Le Guin's *The Left Hand of Darkness*, learns about the strange world called Winter.

The importance of documents
Orwell gives us *The Theory and Practice of Oligarchical Collectivism*, which describes the world of Oceania. *The Lord of the Rings* claims to be based on various written sources, and Vonnegut's *Cat's Cradle* keeps returning to the *Book of Bokonon*, a religious text.

A 'rational' or ideological attitude toward sex
In Zamyatin's novel *We* (which influenced both Huxley and Orwell), any citizen can claim the sexual services of any other citizen. In *Utopia*, those engaged to be married can see each other naked before the ceremony, so they know what they're getting. In *The Left Hand of Darkness*, people change gender every month, more or less at random.

Fantasy has borrowed many of these elements, and its own elements show its descent from myth – which is about gods, beings who are superior to humans in every way. Frye argues that myth evolves into romance, whose characters are superhuman but not divine. So while anatomy shows people in conflict with their own minds (they know less than they think they do), fantasy shows people in conflict with enormously powerful beings.

The hero's quest

In western literature, myth is about tyrant fathers overthrown by rebel sons, and about the uneasy relations between gods and humans. Events are fated, but not always as we might suppose. Humans (including those with divine ancestors) can sometimes use magic as a kind of godlike power.

So fantasy tends to deal with people, usually young, in conflict with enormously powerful beings who play a kind of parental or elder role: giants, dragons, sorcerers, witches, and even Tolkien's Ents. From heroic romance, fantasy borrows the great themes of the quest and the social redeemer. Just as Zeus and Jesus escape the murderous intent of ruling father-figures, the quest hero survives childhood and survives to overthrow the old order.

The quest hero is the central figure of both science fiction and fantasy, so it is worth revisiting that hero's life stages:

- an unusual birth, with a prophecy of a great future
- menace from the father-figure, who tries to subvert the prophecy by killing the child
- pastoral childhood, with the hero growing up in seclusion among simple rustics, close to nature
- early signs of the hero's special qualities
- departure from the 'paradise' of childhood on a quest; the hero leaves reluctantly, and often only after three challenges
- the quest itself, often with companions; the events of the quest are a sequential test of the hero's skills and character
- the confrontation, when the hero faces a major struggle with the evil adversary, armed with whatever skills and values he has demonstrated on the quest
- the hero's death, real or symbolic; in the latter case, a journey underground is a metaphor for death
- the return to life, and the hero's triumph and recognition as a social saviour; like his death, his resurrection may be merely symbolic, with a new society forming around the memory and achievements of the lost hero.

I have not bothered to give examples, because you can supply them from your own reading. With countless variations, this is the basic plot of science fiction and fantasy. Implicit in the plot is the basic theme of both genres: power. What is it, who holds it, who should hold it, and with what results?

Science fiction and fantasy enable us to imagine power as a fulfilment of our deepest desires and dreams, or as the nightmarish destruction of those desires. Like gamblers who hope to win the one big pot, to buy the winning lottery ticket, we keep returning to science fiction and fantasy to help us visualise the quest for power and its achievement.

The writer's challenge

As a new writer of science fiction or fantasy, you are like a quest hero rusticating in Arcadia: you read of great deeds being done long ago, in galaxies far away, and you dream of doing some yourself. In some ways you have opportunities undreamed-of a generation ago. Readerships are large, and publishers must crank out more titles every month.

But these advantages have their drawbacks. Most readers, unfortunately, tend to like the same kind of story, over and over again. Write such a story and editors will reject you as too derivative. Try for originality, and they'll reject you as too far out for their readers. You are working as a craftsperson, even as an artist, but what you create is essentially a raw resource for an industry that tries to satisfy a market.

I recommend that you go for originality. Science fiction and fantasy are now compartmentalised into subgenres: alternate history, military SF, epic fantasy, urban fantasy, and so on. Every one of those subgenres resulted from some author breaking into new territory. Robert Heinlein's *Starship Troopers* launched military SF. Tolkien created epic fantasy with *The Lord of the Rings*. In the past half-century, no imitator has surpassed the originals. In effect, as such authors open our eyes to a new genre, they close the door to followers.

Those followers form two tribes: the worshipful plagiarists, who change only names and details, and the parodists who put an ironic spin on their versions of old stories. Irony is often useful in science fiction and fantasy, but only when it is useful to you and your story – not when it simply reports your own dislike for some bogus classic.

The blended future of Science Fiction and Fantasy

I believe the two genres share a future that could take them in alternate directions. One is what I call 'bottom-line' fiction, where the focus (whether in SF or fantasy) is on the economy and technology of your imagined world. Walter Jon Williams has pointed the way to this in his fantasy novel *Metropolitan*, where a planet-covering city is run by 'plasm', a kind of supernatural source of energy. We still need science-fiction novels about the future economies that can make starships financially attractive projects, likely to return a profit to their investors. I would also love to read a novel about a US president in 2061 who has to talk the taxpayers into terraforming Mars for the sake of thirty-first-century America.

The other direction is what I call 'mythotropic': we assume that science (or magic) has made economics irrelevant, and the people in our worlds are free to act out their own psychological desires in any way they choose. I tried to do this in my novel *Gryphon*, where interstellar contact with advanced civilisations has meant the reduction of humanity to a few million extremely powerful individuals; everyone else was killed in wars using alien technology. The survivors are not always very nice people, but they are free to do anything they like.

So you might consider stories involving political intrigue over funding a new stardrive, or the stormy romance of two godlike individuals who quarrel by flinging asteroids at one another.

However original you are, of course, you are still working within the conventions; originality means finding something new in what seems to be an exhausted genre. Can you tell a new story about time travel? A new kind of military SF story? Do it!

Ernest Hemingway said that all American literature comes from one novel, *Huckleberry Finn* – because that novel established American vernacular speech as a literary language as expressive and powerful as any. In the same sense, all modern fantasy comes from *The Lord of the Rings*, which synthesised a range of literary styles and conventions into a form never seen before.

If fantasy is your genre, then you should regard *The Lord of the Rings* as mainstream writers regard James Joyce's *Ulysses*: a must read that it is pointless to imitate. Introduce elves or dwarves or magic objects into your story, and you waste all your efforts and imagination. (The same is of course true of the Harry Potter books, which must have made many readers try their hands at writing Potteresque fantasy.)

If you must take something from Tolkien or Rowling, let it be inspiration – that you too can write a magnificent book, original and ambitious, in this genre. It may have a quest; it may rely, like anatomy, on strange languages and obscure documents. But it will still have something new and exciting to say.

Research and soul search

Where do you get your ideas? In a word, everywhere – *except* science fiction and fantasy. Of course you'll read in your preferred genre, but authors in either genre should be polymaths, reading both broadly and narrowly in history, anthropology, the sciences, politics, the arts, and everything else. You should be reading journals of archaeology and psychology, not to mention popular magazines like *Discover, New Scientist,* and *Scientific American* (this applies to fantasy writers also). You'll discover that scientists are often very imaginative, but they don't, and won't, take the three extra steps you can take with their findings and speculations.

Think also about the stereotypical thinking behind many stories, like the barbarian nomads besieging the civilised world. It's fun for the Conan fans, but go back to the history those stereotypes are based on. Genghis Khan, for example, was a politically advanced leader who created the concept of diplomatic immunity, built a meritocratic social system to replace the old Mongol aristocracy, recruited scholars to staff his empire, promoted free trade, and decreed absolute freedom of worship within his realm. So perhaps the barbarians in your fantasy world could be the progressives, battling to transform a decayed civilisation.

You should consider the history and cultures of non-European societies: Arab, African, Asian, Polynesian, Native American. What are their political systems like? How does magic work in the Bolivian Andes, or among Montreal's Haitians? Would a Jordanian community on the moon be different from one in suburban Amman? What would a Vietnamese space station sound like and smell like?

That's the research part of your writing. The soul search is just as important. You should brainstorm with friends (especially those who share your taste in fiction), kicking around ideas that you love or hate in other writers' work. (Doing this over coffee with a friend one morning, I came up with an idea that turned into a radio drama produced by the Canadian Broadcasting Corporation – a very good return on the price of a pot of coffee.) The key to such brainstorming is to avoid being negative. Instead of saying, 'No,' participants should say: 'Yeah, or . . .' and 'Yes, and how about . . .' That's how the creativity keeps flowing.

You can even brainstorm by yourself. Start with the kind of letter that you'd send to an editor, pitching your story – but you're writing this letter to yourself. It will force you to create details about the story and its characters, and about how it differs from earlier treatments of the same idea. Before you know it, you'll have at least a rough outline of your story, and quite a few details about your characters. I have written such letters to myself for almost all my novels, and I still marvel at how well they help to clarify my thoughts about a story.

But don't stop there! Start keeping a journal or diary about your story. It's not just a place to record how many words you've done today, but also a place to do some hard thinking about the story's strengths and weaknesses. Chances are you've gone many pages into a story and then run out of steam. Something's wrong with the story, but you can't be more specific than to say, 'This is awful'. The story goes in a drawer, or stays unprinted on your hard drive, and you repeat the same sorry process with the next story.

But if you let your 'inner editor' criticise the story in progress, you'll be amazed at the results. As soon as you start writing, 'This is awful because . . .' the reasons for the story problems become clear. As you're stating those problems in clear, complete sentences, the solutions come to you, sometimes faster than you can type them down. You see where the plot needs patching, or the heroine's character needs sharpening, or the dialogue could convey more than mere exposition.

This kind of 'metawriting' can also help you put ideas together. A starfaring society must have more gadgets than just big rockets or warp drives. What other advances has it made, and what consequences have resulted? Suppose, for example, that we can simply teleport from Earth to other planets. No one bothers to use spacecraft any more, so interstellar space has been abandoned. Just as people still sail solo around the world when they could book airline flights, your characters might deliberately choose spaceflight as a form of recreation. One such hobbyist-astronaut might then discover something unexpected out there between the stars.

Your sorcerers' empire has a long history, even if your novel deals with only the three weeks before its cataclysmic collapse. What's happened in the past century or two that could influence your characters and their destinies? (You don't have to go to the lengths that Tolkien did, but even a few paragraphs about your world's history may give you still more ideas.)

What if and what's more

In other words, your story is not just 'what if?' It's 'what if, and what's more!' You are trying to evoke a world that is plausibly, vividly different from ours in at least a couple of important ways. Your interstellar empire is not just the nineteenth-century British empire with starships, but an empire of its own kind, with its own problems and successes, with people who may or may not like the empire they live in.

Even some of the Golden Age greats could miss the 'what's more' details. In 'Delilah and the Spacerigger', Robert A. Heinlein examines the problems of a construction foreman on a space station when a female worker shows up. Heinlein pokes some rather advanced women's-lib fun at the outraged foreman. But it would have been a better story – a better science-fiction story – if he'd taken female astronauts for granted, and the conflict had arisen from something less obvious: What if a woman helped build the first space station . . . and what's more, she was black, or lesbian, or a better engineer than the foreman?

Anyone can predict the automobile, old SF writers used to say. The trick is predicting traffic jams and making out in the back seat. That's the 'what's more'.

This puts you in an interesting predicament. Stick to 'what if', and your story is dull and predictable. Explore 'what if and what's more', and you find yourself satirising your genre's basic theme power and its proper use.

For example, you may portray humans who are starfaring immortals, or ancient wizards, but they will still suffer from at least some of our own follies and vices. They may deal with a better class of problem than we do, but we can identify with the challenges they face. Otherwise, how would we understand them?

When you consider 'what if and what's more', don't forget your critical element: the implications of some aspect of science, or the function of magic. Both grant us a power over the material world, but it's a power that reflects our own psychology.

So whether we're dealing with a world where magic works, or an earthlike world orbiting a gas giant, it's a world that reflects our fears and desires, and even personifies them.

Satire and irony are often present (hobbits, for example, are ironic treatments of standard quest heroes). But the science or magic really serves by helping to dramatise our personal struggles with love, sex, death, and social relationships.

Satire and superpowers

So on one hand you are portraying people with 'superpowers', people who fulfil our own desires to know more and do more. At the same time, you're showing those people forced to fall back on the same resources we have: courage, patience, intelligence, loyalty, and so on.

Satire implies irony, and in irony the reader knows more about your characters than the characters themselves do. In fact, the great target of Menippean satire is the educated ignoramus, the wizard without wisdom. A crude version of this character is the mad scientist of the comic books. A more sophisticated version is Saruman, the wizard who rationalises his alliance with Sauron. Dr Strangelove is another example, inspired by the much less funny scientists who designed the first nuclear weapons and then developed plans for fighting suicidal wars with them.

The unwise wizard doesn't have to be evil, and doesn't even have to be a wizard. The villains in your SF or fantasy should never think of themselves as bad; they think of themselves as sadly misunderstood and hard done by. But they are also people who don't care if they hurt others by exercising power. Saruman and Dr Strangelove alike think they're being 'realistic' in pursuing their catastrophic policies. If people get hurt, well, it's in the service of some higher good.

By contrast, your hero understands very well that misusing power can be disastrous. That's why Gandalf and other characters in *The Lord of the Rings* are terrified of the One Ring, and Frodo's near-failure to destroy it shows how right they are to be terrified.

Bear in mind that the best satire is the least obvious. When we satirise, we invite our readers to look down on our characters from some moral height; we and our readers should be detached enough to see the absurdity of the characters' actions and values, but close enough to recognise how much like ourselves they are. Imagine a photo of yourself that makes you look the way you want the world to see you . . . but also makes you look a little silly. That's the effect the satirist wants to create in the reader.

Five modes of literature

Satire in science fiction and fantasy is a bit more complex, however. Northrop Frye argues that literature has five modes that reflect the power of the characters.

Myth
Myth is stories about gods who are superior to us in power and in kind. The Roman, Greek and Norse myths are all examples.

Romance
Romance describes superhumans who are superior to us in power, but are still recognisably human. Hercules and Achilles and Superman are such superhumans.

'High mimetic'
This portrays aristocrats who are superior to us in social status but otherwise ordinary humans. ('Mimetic' means 'imitating reality'; the 'high' refers to class.) *Hamlet* and *Julius*

Caesar are high mimetic. 'Low mimetic' is about people whose power and knowledge are equal to our own. This includes most mainstream fiction, whose middle-class characters are a lot like us.

Irony

According to Frye, irony portrays characters who are inferior to us in knowledge or power. We know more than they do, or we have more freedom of action than they do. Winston Smith in *Nineteen Eighty-Four* is a classic ironic character; we know him better than he knows himself, and we have more freedom. At least we hope we do! Satire makes us think again about ourselves and what we take for granted.

You could read each mode of fiction as a satire on the one above it. A superhuman looks ironic compared to a real god; consider the fate of superhuman Icarus, who aspired to heaven and fell to his death. An aristocrat, for all his privileges, is a pretty sad excuse for a superhuman, and a middle-class hero imitating an aristocrat (like Leopold Bloom imitating Ulysses) is equally ironic. An ironic character like Winston Smith looks simply pathetic in his search for the kind of life we take for granted.

So your hero may be a starfaring astronaut who reminds us of Ulysses, but the astronaut is likely to seem comparatively trivial compared to the larger-than-life Ulysses.

I have discussed literary history and theory at considerable length because whatever you write will reflect everything you have read so far. If you had no idea what a quest hero is supposed to be, your stories would still have quest heroes – because all the stories you've read have had them, and your stories would subconsciously imitate what you've read.

But if you consciously exploit literary theory, and you consciously know how the Greeks and Romans told stories, your stories will be far more effective.

Twelve techniques for SF and Fantasy writers

1. Don't be in a hurry

Too many writers cram all the exposition into the first chapter. That's like putting all your furniture just inside the front door. Even a short story has a lot of room, and a novel has even more. Give us background information when your readers need it – and in many cases they won't need it at all.

So if your story is set in Titanopolis, on Saturn's largest moon, don't feel you have to give us a potted history of the settling of Titan. Just establish the setting, maybe with a custom like no drinking until Saturn rises above the horizon.

Much of the earlier material in your story will therefore be a bit confusing to your readers. That's all right – they know you'll get around to explaining things in good time. In the meantime, they'll keep turning pages because they want to learn more about this weird world you're giving them.

2. Make the setting a character

In a novel set in Cornwall, the author is saying that only in Cornwall could such a story happen. Cornish culture will affect the events and the outcome, and in the process we'll learn about Cornwall as well as about how Cornish girls catch their boys. Similarly, something about Titanopolis and its residents will influence the outcome of your story.

This is important, but exposition will only hurt matters. The culture of Titanopolis should emerge naturally as we watch its inhabitants go about their business. But your characters, especially if they're visitors, may 'naturally' consult some tourist guide or history of Titanopolis.

3. Make the science or magic critical to the story

Spaceships and magic spells are important for more than simply taking us to the setting of the story. The science or spells should advance the story at every point, creating both obstacles and solutions.

In my fantasy novels *Greenmagic* and *Redmagic*, I assumed that using magic would exhaust the magician, so after a big spell he would be useless for days or weeks. I also assumed that magic had to be spoken. So my hero had an advantage (he didn't get tired after casting spells), but when he lost his voice by another sorcerer's spell, he was crippled; he would have to deal with life using brains and muscle, like everyone else.

4. Make your characters insecure

When people do amazing things for stupid reasons, it's melodrama. When they do amazing things for absolutely real reasons, it's drama. So it's not enough to have a brave hero or a hostile heroine. The hero should be scarred by some earlier failure to be brave, and the heroine should be nursing a broken heart. The talented young sorcerer wants to master magic to avenge his family, or to make life secure for his people.

In other words, motivation is critical. Something awful has happened in every character's life, in effect an expulsion from paradise. Now your characters are struggling in a harsh world, trying to regain paradise or to replace it with the Heavenly City. They will stop at nothing to achieve that goal.

Here's a way to get into a character's soul: write a first-person account by that character, describing the worst thing that ever happened to them. It may not get into the story, but it will give you some surprising insights into the character. When I did this with the hero of the novel I'm now working on, I was astonished by his emotional flatness as he described the destruction of his company, his career, and his marriage. I realised he's a very angry, very repressed man, so his anger may explode at some point in the story.

5. Make your characters concrete

This doesn't mean description of hair colour or height or clothing. Instead, write a résumé for each of your major characters. But don't include just education and job history. What about sexual orientation, personal relationships, family, social status, income, taste in furniture, anxieties, philosophy of life, attitude toward death? Again, you may not use all the data you come up with, but it's often helpful – and it can give you ideas for how your character might develop.

6. Experiment with 'periscope writing'

I do this when I'm starting a novel and want to learn more about its world. So I write a scene or two, just to find out what my viewpoint character sees as he or she moves around. It can be amazing to see how much detail pops out at you: not just Saturn rising above the horizon, but the smell of recycled air in the Titanopolis Bar & Grill. In effect, you're letting your 'inner writer' take over for a while, creating images and problems that may be useful in the story itself.

7. Build your 'back' story

The story should begin at the moment when it becomes inevitable – when something happens to your protagonist that forces him or her out into a hostile world. But you should know what's been going on in your characters' lives for years or even decades before the start of the story. *The Lord of the Rings* takes place over a span of a few months, but the 'back' story covers thousands of years . . . and it affects the story again and again.

8. Foreshadow your ending

The opening scenes of your story should describe some kind of appropriate stress – for example, your hero is tested under fire and fails the test. This humiliation will motivate him to redeem himself, and the climax will echo the opening scene in some way. The opening scenes will also tell us what is at stake in this story: the hero's self-esteem? The fate of the sorcerers' empire? The survival of humanity against the alien onslaught? Whatever it is, we should care about the outcome.

9. Keep style consistent with the point of view

A blunt-spoken veteran warrior will notice almost everything around her, but she'll think about it in short sentences with a simple vocabulary. A minstrel will pick up emotional moods that the warrior misses, and he'll express his thoughts with more words (including quotes from appropriate songs and ballads). So when the minstrel is the POV character, you'll write in a richer, more luxuriant style than when you're showing us the world through the warrior's eyes.

If your point of view shifts regularly, your style should also shift. The veteran will view a sunrise in far different terms from the minstrel – and a vampire's view of sunrise will be still more different.

As the author you will sometimes have to tell us things that your characters can't. Keep such interruptions as few and brief as possible, and avoid 'fine writing' – it will only distract readers from the story to you and your supposed talent.

10. Remember the moral importance of language

Tyrannical bureaucracies will use euphemisms: 'Human resource reallocation' could be a term for 'exile to the Titan Penal Colony'. In *A Clockwork Orange*, written during the Cold War, the British thug Alex uses Russian slang – hinting at some unfortunate future Soviet influence over Britain.

People from different cultures in a fantasy novel may use brief expressions in their own languages, which should sound like the cultures: Elvish is lovely and musical, while the Orcs' language is harsh and rasping. You will find it very helpful to develop vocabularies in various languages; these will give you the basis for names of characters and places.

Be careful, though, about using a real-world language in a fantasy-world setting. Your readers will find it jarring if familiar words and names pop up in a world where they shouldn't. (I did this in my novels *Greenmagic* and *Redmagic*, but my premise was that ancient tribes on Earth had been mysteriously transported to a world where magic works . . . so one tribe spoke Proto-Indo-European and another spoke ancient Irish.)

11. Use symbols appropriately

Seasons, times of day, youth, age, weapons and tools, gardens and wildernesses – these all have symbolic resonance going back thousands of years. If you use them in some reversed form (a sword that kills but never liberates, for example), you are using them ironically. That's fine, but know what you're doing.

When your sorceress-heroine is a little girl, she might consider her mother's herb garden a wonderful place; when she must flee for her life and the garden is destroyed, you've got a traditional expulsion from Eden. A memory of a poisonous plant in that garden might later help the sorceress to triumph over her enemies. But if Eden nurtured poisonous plants, just how innocent and happy was it?

12. Keep your characters in constant trouble

Stress reveals character, but different challenges will reveal different aspects of that character. Each aspect is going to be needed to help get your characters from problem to problem, and finally to the climactic struggle. Until then, they live in either the frying pan or the fire.

Even if you give your hero a chance to kick back and have a beer while en route to Titan, that peaceful moment should be a time for him to fret about how ill-prepared he is, how ferocious his enemies are, and how easily everything could go wrong. That in turn will show us that your hero is a worrier – and we'll keep reading to see if that helps him anticipate trouble, or sink into indecision.

Is it worth doing?

Science fiction and fantasy are genres with mixed reputations. Millions of readers love them, and millions of other readers think they're terrible. Even the publishers regard science fiction and fantasy in one of two ways: commercial, or unpublishable.

I have argued here that you should try for the most original, unusual kind of fiction you can write, and not to worry about publishing. That's because the first person to benefit from your writing is you . . . and if you write imitative, derivative stuff, you will not advance as a writer or as a person.

Any kind of writing tends to rewire your brain, to make you more observant, more articulate about your own experience. This is especially true of science fiction and fantasy, which challenge us to look at our experience in a very different light. So both you and your writing will be better if you push for the strangest, most personal kind of writing you can produce – publishable or not.

Think of Tolkien, spending the war in Oxford and slowly following the Fellowship of the Ring across a world that existed only in his imagination. Would his book ever be published? It didn't matter – what mattered was the creation of a world like no other.

I tell my own students that I enjoy walking my dogs three or four times a day. It's good exercise, and it gives me time to think about my own imaginative worlds, while the dogs explore the woods. We both come back in better shape. Sometimes, I actually find a coin in the street, and that's nice too. But if I come home without finding a coin, that doesn't make me a failure as a dog-walker.

By the same token, you are not a failure as a writer if you don't publish. You are a success as a writer if you write what seems true to you, and what teaches you to go on to write still better work.

Is writing science fiction and fantasy worth it? Yes!

References

Burgess, Anthony (2000), *A Clockwork Orange*, London: Penguin.

Dr. Strangelove (1963), dir. Stanley Kubrick.

Frye, Northrop, *Anatomy of Criticism* (1957), Princeton: Princeton University Press.

Heinlein, Robert A. (2000), 'Delilah and the Space Rigger' in *The Green Hills of Earth*, New York: Baen Books.

Heinlein, Robert A. (2005), *Starship Troopers*, London: Hodder & Stoughton.

Kilian, Crawford (1992), *Greenmagic*, New York: Del Rey.

Kilian, Crawford (1995), *Redmagic*, New York: Del Rey.

Kilian, Crawford (2000), *Gryphon*, New York: toExcel.

Le Guin, Ursula K. (1987), *The Left Hand of Darkness*, New York: Ace.

More, Thomas (2003), *Utopia*, London: Penguin.

Orwell, George (1981), *Nineteen Eighty-Four*, Harmondsworth: Penguin.

Swift, Jonathan (1979), *Gulliver's Tales*, Harmondsworth: Penguin.

Tolkien, J. R. R. (1972), *The Lord of the Rings*, London: Allen and Unwin Ltd.

Vonnegut, Kurt (1971), *Cat's Cradle*, London: Victor Gollancz Ltd.

Wells, H. G. (2005), *The Time Machine*, London: Penguin.

Williams, Walter Jon (1996), *Metropolitan*, New York: Eos.

Zamyatin, Yevgeny (1999), *We*, New York: Eos.

13

How Language Lives Us: Reading and Writing Historical Fiction

Brian Kiteley

Gained in the translation

Oscar Wilde said, 'The one duty we owe to history is to rewrite it'. Writers of contemporary historical fiction seem to say the one duty we owe to history is to reread it. The main character Omar Khayyam Shakil, in Salman Rushdie's *Shame*, says his namesake, Omar Khayyam, the twelfth-century poet and astronomer,

> was never very popular in his native Persia; and he exists in the West in a translation that is really a complete reworking of his verses, in many cases very different from the spirit (to say nothing of the content) of the original. I, too, am a translated man. I have been borne across. It is generally believed that something is always lost in the translation; I cling to the notion – and use, in evidence, the success of Fitzgerald's Khayyam – that something can also be gained. (Rushdie 1984: 24)

Poetry is very difficult to translate – more like an idiolect or a personal language than the King's English or a master code, although fiction is comparatively easy to translate. Historical fiction, a once undistinguished genre, fails the translatability test, as most poetry does. It is hard enough to write about the present. Even the recent past needs to be resuscitated. When writing about a more distant past, one is essentially translating from another language, losing great chunks of idiosyncratic detail, and worried that contemporary meanings will not correspond. But something can also be gained: prose styles erupting out of close readings of and interactions with secondary and primary texts and a healthy rethinking of the relationship between the past and the present. When a writer rewrites history, by taking over other texts and elaborating on them, the result is history reread and revised. Much contemporary historical fiction takes a simple idea – of reading the past – and elaborates on the process in surprising and imaginative ways.

A kind of historical omniscience has developed in the past forty years that reads and rereads the past. The research is often exposed quite casually to its readers, fixing on the page a self-conscious method of understanding the past by inserting imaginative dreamscapes between the words and sentences of primary and secondary sources. Rushdie's tongue-in-cheek theory that something can also be gained in translation is a useful metaphor for this new fictional historiographic thinking.

Gandhi was asked what he thought of Western civilisation, and he is supposed to have said, 'I think it would be a good idea'. So, too, historical fiction. Arguments against historical fiction have often been that it is impossible and simply a disguised comment on the present, rather than a recreation of the past. I think all fiction is historical fiction.

Public vs. private

Ian Watt in *The Rise of the Novel* traced the sources of the genre to the idea that truth can be discovered by the individual through his senses, which was at the heart of the Enlightenment. He felt the novel was concerned with the individual, not the group or the community. Early novels introduced first and last names: 'Proper names have exactly the same function in social life: they are the verbal expression of the particular identity of each individual person' (Watt 2001: 18). E. M. Forster saw the portrayal of 'life by time' as the distinctive role which the novel has added to literature's more ancient preoccupation with portraying 'life by values'. Time was abstract before the novel. After the novel, Watt said, 'We have the sense of personal identity subsisting through duration and yet being changed by the flow of experience' (Watt 2001: 24).

There were historical novels before Walter Scott, but in the nineteenth century, historical material became a fairly standard subject matter for the form. The individual in *War and Peace* or *The Tale of Two Cities* is not much different than the individual in *Moll Flanders* or *Don Quixote*. Roland Barthes, in *Writing Degree Zero*, saw a parallel between the writing of the great spherical novels of the nineteenth century and the great histories of the same period, when some form of historiography in the modern sense was born (Barthes 1967: 29).

During the period of high modernism, history and the epic treatment of the individual fell out of fashion. The early twentieth century saw an inward spiral toward ahistorical – or certainly unhistorical – subjects, although the tentacles of references crossed centuries of other literary works.

Samuel Beckett took a long walk from Paris to south central France, during the Second World War, after he found the Gestapo in his apartment (he said to them, turning on his heels, 'Sorry, wrong flat'). He and his girlfriend, both working for the underground and in grave danger, walked for many days, starved, frightened, but by all accounts philosophical about their chances for survival – they retold the story of this journey many times to friends. None of the actual history of this momentous walk made it – in biographical or even biological details – into the artistic form Beckett chose for it: *Waiting for Godot*. But *Godot* is nevertheless a record of that long walk, ripped from time and history (Knowlson 1996: 343).

Lennard Davis, in a review of Martha Nussbaum's *Poetic Justice: the Literary Imagination and Public Life*, talks of how the 'two cosmopolitan entities, the "public" and the "novel", made their joint appearance in Anglo-Europe during the eighteenth century, and throughout the nineteenth century, these two *flâneurs* strolled arm in arm down the pollarded boulevards of the social imagination' (Davis 1996: 40). Contemporary forms of historical fiction have followed the path of other forms of modern and postmodern fiction, which is inward, toward more private methods of expression (or opposing private life and public life). Listen to the opening of Christa Wolf's lovely novel, *No Place on Earth*, which is an exploration of a possible (but not probable) relationship between Kleist and a much less well-known female poet who died at sixteen, Karoline von Günderrode:

The wicked spoor left in time's wake as it flees us.

You precursors, feet bleeding. Gazes without eyes, words that stem from no mouth. Shapes without bodies. Descended heavenward, separated in remote graves, resurrected again from the dead, still forgiving those who trespass against us, the sorrowful patience of angels or of Job.

And we, still greedy for the ashen taste of words. (Wolf 1982: 3)

The intimacy of these lines and of this book is startling. Wolf did some research into the two subjects, and she appears in the telling of the story from time to time, but she also gives herself license to invade the minds and souls of these two writers, inventing (or 'resurrecting') where there is no other evidence to counter the inventions – and the big invention is in placing von Günderrode and Kleist in a romantic relationship.

History and collage

In the last third of the twentieth century, large numbers of fiction writers began exploring history again, with new methods and styles – Rushdie, Doctorow, Wolf, DeLillo, Byatt, Coover, Yourcenar, Galeano. The novelist Paul Horgan, who won both the Bancroft and Pulitzer Prizes for his 1954 book *Great River: the Rio Grande in North American History*, says in the preface:

> To do my subject anything like justice, I have hoped to produce a sense of historical experience rather than a bare record. This required me whenever possible to see events, societies, and movements through human character in action. While respecting the responsibilities of scholarship, I took every opportunity, when the factual record supported me, to stage a scene. (Horgan 1984: vii)

Staging a scene and showing human character in action – usually methods of the novel – have fallen out of fashion in academic history writing (Horgan was not an academic until late in his writing career; he was primarily a novelist). When Roy Mottahedeh mingled a history of the Iranian revolution with a fictionalised portrait of a mullah who left Iran shortly after the revolution (fictionalised to protect his identity), in his 1985 book *The Mantle of the Prophet*, the community of historians generally condemned the experiment.

Linda Hutcheon, in *A Poetics of Postmodernism*, comments on the recent desire to intermingle history and fiction:

> In the [nineteenth] century . . . historical writing and historical novel writing influenced each other mutually: Macauley's debt to Scott was an overt one, as was Dickens's to Carlyle, in *A Tale of Two Cities*. Today, the new skepticism or suspicion about the writing of history found in the work of Hayden White and Dominick LaCapra is mirrored in the internalized challenges to historiography in novels like *Shame*, *A Public Burning*, and *A Maggot*: they share the same questioning stance towards their common use of conventions of narrative, of reference, of the inscribing of subjectivity, of their identity as textuality, and even their implication in ideology. (Hutcheon 1988: 105, 106)

Through a keyhole

Henry James dismissed the historical novel, saying it was 'condemned . . . to a fatal cheapness'. But James also famously used the example of Anne Thackeray, in his essay 'The Art of Fiction', to explain how a good writer finds the right details of a subject he or she is not intimately familiar with: 'once, in Paris, [Thackeray] ascended a staircase, passed an open door where, in the household of a [Protestant minister], some of the young Protestants were seated at table round a finished meal. The glimpse made a picture; it lasted only a moment, but that moment was experience' (James 1984: 52). James makes the point that genius finds a way to understand human nature, no matter how far afield from the home world of the genius, no matter how little information is available, which would seem to go against his distrust of historical fiction.

Further back, Flaubert devoted a good deal of his writing career to historical subjects, and he chose to treat even his contemporary subjects the way an irritably objective historian might. About his novel *Salammbô*, he said, 'Few will be able to guess how sad one had to be in order to resuscitate Carthage'. But Flaubert revelled in his depressions. He preferred his study, his books, and his upside down life (sleeping away the daylight and writing and reading all night) – he preferred to read about life.

Life's residues

I started a book of historical fictions, *The River Gods*, in 1995 (and haven't finished the book yet). I was sidetracked for a year trying to write another more intimate history, about my brother Geoffrey, who died of AIDS in 1993. I found that book difficult to write – it was sad; I had little real evidence about my brother's life; and, aside from an almost inexpressible understanding of him, I discovered I did not know him – or large parts of his life – all that well. My brother Geoffrey offered me very few written clues about his life.

When I wrote my first novel *Still Life with Insects*, I started with a bare-bones outline, in the laconic field notebooks my grandfather kept of his beetle-collecting. I used a handful of these locality notes as a springboard for the novel. I turned from my brother as subject to my home town because there was so little evidence to work with (the subject just kept slipping away). *Still Life* was a historical novel that advanced up to the present time in which I was writing it. The last scene took place a few years after I started the book, when I was aware I was writing a life and observing it – my grandfather visited me on Cape Cod for a long weekend in 1985. He understood the parallax and did not seem to mind the literary intrusion into his life. Most of the rest of the novel was true historical recreation, using his notes, but mostly taking oral family stories and fleshing them out. Like Flaubert, I prefer to read life and life's residues: '*To read what was never written*. Such reading is the most ancient: reading before all languages, from the entrails, the stars, or dances', Walter Benjamin says, in 'On the Mimetic Faculty' (Benjamin 1986: 336). I have always been partial to this other reading of the word *read*.

In *The River Gods*, I've based an encounter between Wallace Stevens and William Carlos Williams in Northampton in 1944 on a sentence from the Paul Mariani biography of Williams: only Williams was in Northampton, overnight, for a visit to his publishers in Cummington. I read other biographies and letters. I devoured the poetry, finding myself siding with one, then the other poet, for long periods. Wallace Stevens and William Carlos Williams stand for something quite personal. For *Still Life with Insects*, I read biographies of both men as tangential research for my character, my grandfather, who was a chemist at a grain milling company all his working life but in his spare time – passionately so – a beetle collector. These two poets, who had full-time jobs (a small-town doctor and an insurance executive) but did their poetry passionately in their free hours, were two important analogues for my grandfather's story. I stepped into William Carlos Williams' voice as easily as I stepped into my grandfather's voice – they had, I noted, in the earlier research, the same kinds of sense of humour, the same wry sweet outlook, the same darkness at the edge of their sunny dispositions.

Writers educate themselves to a large degree and the rest is often imagination, extrapolation, or hypothesis. Aristotle made the distinction between history and poetry: an account of what happened versus an account of what might have happened. I once caught my brother red-handed in an untruth (and I asked how he could have sounded so sure of himself when it turned out he was wrong) – it was a rare thing for me to be able to prove he was wrong about anything, because he seemed to know everything about everything. My brother said, 'Brian, you must first of all act like you're telling the truth. Usually, truth follows confidence in the truth'. Nietzsche said more or less the same thing: 'what can be thought must certainly be a fiction'.

The novel and research

Historical fiction often inserts fictional moments into what is relatively accepted as factual events (which can be verified by first-hand accounts, but who's to say how accurate first-hand accounts are?). Fiction slows history down and therefore it *has* to fictionalise events, because no matter how thorough a historian is, there are still yawning gaps between moments, multiple and contradictory explanations for causes and effects.

William Vollmann says in the 'Sources and a Few Notes' at the end of his historical novel *The Rifles* that what he's written is 'often untrue based on the literal facts as we know them, but whose untruths further a deeper sense of truth. Here one walks the proverbial tightrope, on one side of which lies slavish literalism; on the other, self-indulgence' (Vollmann 1994: 377). Vollmann's method is scrupulously honest, despite this coy disclaimer, which introduces a long list of his sources. *The Rifles* reconstructs the last, fatal expedition John Franklin made in the mid-1800s to find the Northwest Passage from the Atlantic to the Pacific, and Vollmann interlaces the historical fiction with descriptions of his research – the reading, the trips to some of the places Franklin visited. He claims that the narrator (whose name starts out as William or Bill [as in Vollmann], but settles into Captain Subzero) is a reincarnation of John Franklin. This sleight of hand allows Vollmann to erase the boundaries between this past and the present of the novel. It also makes his essentially research-oriented novel into a romantic quest for a past life, rather than merely a dry intellectual pursuit.

Just the facts

A few years ago there was an argument about fiction in biographies. A biographer of Ronald Reagan grew depressed by his subject and was unable to proceed with the process for almost a year. Edmund Morris overcame this block against telling the life of a man he could not relate to by inventing a fictional version of himself who knew Reagan in his youth when Reagan might have been a more likeable fellow. The reaction to this fictionalising, particularly in the political press, was amazing: he was just plain wrong to do this, and because he chose to fictionalise a small part of his biography, everything else in the book was tainted. There has also been a general distrust of contemporary memoirs, on somewhat the same grounds. I'm amused at the very notion that anything a biographer or a memoirist writes is not, essentially, fiction. In the end, the writer who claims historical subjects may have lived their lives the way the writer says they lived – this writer is doing the same thing a novelist who appears to make it all up is doing.

In *The River Gods* I was very interested in how history works – or how individual characters (both my own fictional creations and historical figures) came alive against the grain of the events we often think of as historical events – and they came alive by means of what they said or wrote – or what I wrote for them. In my fiction generally, language is the key – language lives us. One translates the past, one fills in the many details that must be filled in between the great gaps, one finds appropriate language to bridge these gaps. When I have read the book to audiences, I'm often asked what is true and what fiction, and one person suggested I colour-code the fictional sections so readers would be able to distinguish between the two dangerously different types of narrative.

I decided early on in writing *The River Gods* to use some of the historical documents I found either as direct inspiration or as a shadow thrown against the prose I was trying to compose. My colleague Jan Gorak suggested I'd stumbled onto a crisis between history as research or lumber and history as meaning or novel. He thought writers of historical fiction were now between times rather than above time. I believe in using the words of the past and inserting fictions – or like-minded prose – between them to create another version of both past and present, not necessarily interpretation of past, but illumination of the passage of time with language as its fuel.

Palimpsest exercises

Exercise

I use an exercise in my History and Fiction class. I suggest students take ten sentences from the first paragraph of E. L. Doctorow's novel *Ragtime* and add a sentence between each sentence – an explanation, a connective tissue, a reason for going from one sentence to the next (which is not always clear in *Ragtime*). As they're doing this, I write on the blackboard: Associative prose. Associative means the process of forming mental connections between sensations, ideas, or memories. Psychoanalysts ask patients to free-associate from a word ('bird' causing a patient to think of his mother's hawk-like nose and the habit she had of watching him sleep every night from his bedroom doorway, her hawk nose the only identifying characteristic in the dark). The opposite of this is cause and effect, which is how traditional narrative operates. What I'm getting at in this exercise is an understanding of how Doctorow's sentences work – he lists things, presenting a collage of objects and ideas from the past, in an attempt to catalogue the dizzying multiplicity of past details. Here are the first ten sentences (more or less) of *Ragtime*:

> Teddy Roosevelt was President. The population customarily gathered in great numbers either out of doors for parades, public concerts, fish fries, political picnics, social outings, or indoors in meeting halls, vaudeville theaters, operas, ballrooms. There seemed to be no entertainment that did not involve great swarms of people . . . Women were stouter then. They visited the fleet carrying white parasols. Everyone wore white in summer. Tennis racquets were hefty and

the racquet faces were elliptical. There was a lot of sexual fainting. There were no Negroes. There were no immigrants. (Doctorow 1996: 3, 4)

Notice, for instance, between the sentences about sexual fainting and Negroes the possible connection: women fainting at the mere sight of a Negro male.

Exercise

The following is a short piece from my historical novel *The River Gods*, an Oulipo-like exercise that takes two pieces of someone else's writing and creates a bridge of prose between them:

> 1943
>
> I don't know much about gods, but I think the river is a brown god – sullen, untamed, untrust-worthy, and, in the end, just a riddle for builders of bridges. My job was to hammer the hot rivets into the support beams of the new bridge, following the orders of men who were also following orders. We took our lunches on the I-beams, even when there was no platform under us. The Connecticut River in May is a syrup, sluggish and hypnotic. My mate Sabin, the one man who died while we made the bridge, often fell asleep at lunch, dangling fifty feet above water (not a fatal plunge), jerking awake with bad dreams about his sister and her boyfriend. He died on solid earth, when someone dropped a pail of box end wrenches on his head. I did not know I could get used to such dying. When we trained for our bombing runs in New Jersey and then in Hampshire, we lost four planes and all but three men of the crews. It was a relief to be in combat, in some ways. You knew you were going to die. Training missions wasted our anxiety muscles. There was a moment, before the shrapnel ripped me apart, when I thought I was on the nearly completed Coolidge Bridge. Gusts of sweet river air, unfastened from the dream of life. I awoke to black flak and Messerschmitt 109s. They washed me out of the turret with a hose.

Oulipo is a group of writers and mathematicians in France who have since 1960 been dreaming up writing exercises (with sometimes severe restraints that distract writers while their creative unconscious does the interesting work). At the beginning of this piece of mine are some revised lines from T. S. Eliot's *Dry Salvages*, and at the end, lines from Randall Jarrell's 'Death of the Ball Turret Gunner'.

Here are the instructions for the Bridge exercise from above, which I wrote for my book, *The 3 A.M. Epiphany*:

> Choose two good, useful, and thrilling paragraphs from other writers of fiction, letters, or non-fiction. Then make a prose bridge between the paragraphs, although you don't need to make the matter between the two paragraphs equal to the two bookend paragraphs. There are all sorts of ways of approaching this problem – you could choose two paragraphs that could not possibly fit together and somehow make them fit. Or you could choose two different voices that might, with a little sharpening, become one voice. (Kiteley 2005: 181)

The difficult pleasure of writing this exercise was not only that I had to connect these dissimilar thoughts (from Eliot and Jarrell), but also that I had to make this fit into the scheme of the novel, which was, simply, about Northampton, Massachusetts. I had been reading on Calvin Coolidge, mayor of Northampton early in the twentieth century, but

I had also been thinking of the depression era bridge that connects Northampton and Amherst. Having this other set of coordinates (Jarrell and Eliot) to worry about helped me discover this ghostly bridge builder and ball-turret gunner, who returned after his death to the site of his greatest pride.

I used this exercise often when I was writing *The River Gods*, sometimes taking two pieces of first-hand historical material that shouldn't fit together, sometimes going far afield from the subject of my study (because I got bored). It is telling that this exercise was so fruitful: history is made up of these layers upon layers of fact and opinion and stray thoughts, so that one cannot always decide if one is reading one layer or another – some details shine through more brightly than other details. A palimpsest is a piece of paper written on several times, with the earlier erased text barely visible. When we read anything, we see erasures from other reading and writings. History is the reading we make of this subjective, visually complex activity.

References

Barthes, Roland (1967), *Writing Degree Zero*, New York: Hill and Wang.

Benjamin, Walter (1986), *Reflections*, New York: Shocken.

Davis, Lennard (1996), Review of *Poetic Justice: The Literary Imagination and Public Life*, by Martha Nussbaum, *The Nation*, 18/22 July 1996.

Doctorow, E. L. (1996), *Ragtime*, New York: Plume.

Horgan, Paul (1984), *Great River: The Rio Grande in North American History*, Middletown, CT: Wesleyan.

Hutcheon, Linda (1988), *A Poetics of Postmodernism: History, Theory, Fiction*, New York: Routledge.

James, Henry (1984), *Henry James: Literary Criticism*, New York: The Library of America.

Kiteley, Brian (1989), *Still Life with Insects*, Boston: Ticknor & Fields.

Kiteley, Brian (2005), *The 3 A.M. Epiphany*, Cincinnati: Writer's Digest Books.

Knowlson, James (1996), *Damned to Fame: The Life of Samuel Beckett*, New York: Grove Press.

Rushdie, Salman (1984), *Shame*, New York: Aventura.

Vollmann, William (1994), *The Rifles*, New York: Penguin.

Watt, Ian (2001), *The Rise of the Novel: Studies in Defoe, Richardson and Fielding*, Berkeley: University of California Press.

Wolf, Christa (1982), *No Place on Earth*, New York: Farrar Straus Giroux.

14

Writing Humorous Fiction

Susan Hubbard[1]

Let other pens dwell on guilt and misery.
Jane Austen, *Mansfield Park* (Austen [1814] 1983: 375)

The best humorous writing, like the best magic act, appears to be almost effortless. The audience becomes so engrossed in the story unfolding that no one notices the sleights of hand until the unexpected happens, provoking the magic of laughter. Paradoxically, it's the effort, or craft, behind the writing that produces the illusion and the laughter.

Humour results from incongruous juxtapositions (Paulos 1977: 113). We read or listen to humour in expectation that we will be entertained in surprising ways. The simplest form of humour – the joke – aims to elicit laughter through an unexpected punch line; literary short stories and novels use humour to provoke insight, as well. Most jokes are expository, but they have a structure similar to that of a story (and to that of a magic trick). We meet the principal characters and conflict is introduced; tension is generated and builds; then comes crisis/revelation/punch line/surprise. Each of these elements is developed briefly, if at all. A joke or a comic sketch doesn't aspire to the complexity of a humorous story or novel. As American fiction writer John Dufresne notes, 'Jokes and anecdotes don't make good stories, though good stories can be inspired by them. Anecdotes do not explore or reveal character. Stories do' (Dufresne 2003: 162).

Vladimir Nabokov's interpretation of the purposes of writing is worth repeating here: the writer may be considered a storyteller, teacher, and/or enchanter (Nabokov 1980: 5). By orchestrating the classic aspects of fictional craft (characterisation, setting, plot, theme, and style), the writer of humorous fiction can simultaneously entertain, enlighten, and enchant.

So we begin our explorations in conjuring laughter. After a brief review of some theories of humour, we'll consider aspects of its fictional craft, focusing in particular on those related to creating character, setting, and plot. Each section on craft includes examples and exercises designed to help writers incorporate humour into their work. Books and stories are cited as examples in hope that you may be enticed to read the unfamiliar ones. In the end, there's no better way to learn to write humour than to read it.

Some general principles and theories

In medieval times, a humour was thought to be a fluid – blood, phlegm, choler, or bile – coursing through the human body, capable of influencing one's disposition. A person behaving oddly was suspected to have an imbalance or dominance of a particular fluid and was called a 'humourist' – a term later extended to those who wrote about odd behaviour.

Writing about oddities, or incongruities, seems a natural tendency. Unless you have a very fancy prose style, writing about the commonplace tends to be dull.

But why do we want to be funny? From a vast number of serious books addressing that question, I culled a list of reasons:

1. To keep the devils at bay
2. To commune with the gods
3. To celebrate the joy of existence
4. To lighten the burden of reality
5. To change the world.

Humour may seem benign or malicious. Theorists tend to find its origins in the darker sides of human nature. In the Bible, in Homer, and in many medieval tales, laughter often is associated with scorn and mockery. Aristotle found comedy far inferior to tragedy, and he considered laughter base and ignoble (O'Neill 1990: 34–5).

In *Sudden Glory*, Barry Sanders traces the history of laughter and deems it essentially ambiguous: 'Throughout time, laughter never shakes its dual character; it is always associated with both the devilish and the angelic, with both the positive and the negative' (Sanders 1996: 69).

Sanders, along with Kant and Kierkegaard, finds laughter a basic, universal response to an incongruous situation that surprises us, jars us out of the rut of civilised behaviour. Plato and Aristotle thought laughter stemmed from feelings of superiority over others. In *The Republic*, Plato expressed concern about the power of laughter to disrupt order even as he noted its usefulness as a means of moral reform.

Herbert Spencer and Sigmund Freud considered laughter a release of pent-up energy. In his early twentieth-century writings on creative writing, as well as those on humour, Freud stressed repressed instincts and emotions as the wellspring of the creative process. Sanders notes the power of the derisive laugh as a means of social subversion:

> I call Freud the father of stand-up comedy because, through jokes, he articulated an acceptable way for the discontent, or marginal malcontent, to break the law, to upset the status quo, with impunity . . . Every comic is a social scofflaw who could be charged with breaking and entering – with breaking society's rules and restrictions, and with entering people's psyches. (Sanders 1996: 252–3)

In *Writing Humor: Creativity and the Comic Mind*, Mary Ann Rishel defines humour as 'playful incongruity', and says humour depends on departures from the logical and normal. But she notes that humour can go too far – beyond absurdity, nonsense, and silliness – to confusion and meaninglessness (Rishel 2002: 34–6).

Satire has classically been associated with using humour for a moral purpose. A great deal of literary fiction that attempts humour is satiric.

'Black humour', a term widely used to describe the work of writers as varied as Kurt Vonnegut and John Hawkes, goes beyond classical satire's penchant for moralising. It focuses on a kind of cosmic irony by creating surreal worlds inhabited by one-dimensional characters. In 1939 André Breton used the term *humour noir* to describe the subversive power of writers (such as Poe, Nietzsche, Kafka, and Lewis Carroll) who take on subjects considered taboo in polite society (O'Neill 1990: 28).

No matter how subversive or moralistic your writing aims to be, it will usually be more effective if it incorporates humour. Humourless writing, like a humourless person, is difficult to tolerate for long.

Some elements of craft

Character

Historically, humorous characters have often enjoyed a shady reputation. Even when they embody moral principles, they've been dismissed as mere plot vehicles. The difference between a comic sketch and a humorous story often lies in the degree of complexity of the characters.

E. M. Forster wrote in *Aspects of the Novel*: 'Flat characters were called "humorous" in the seventeenth century, and are sometimes called types, and sometimes caricatures. In their purest form, they are constructed around a single idea or quality: when there is more than one factor in them, we get the beginning of the curve towards the round' (Forster [1927] 1995: 41).

Built around a single idea or quality (which often is exaggerated), flat characters don't change and never surprise us in realistic ways, as round (complex) characters do. Flat characters are a staple of satire and of black humour. As Forster notes, flat characters have one great advantage: they tend to be memorable by virtue of their very flatness. Daniel Defoe's *Moll Flanders* (1722), for instance, features an unforgettable protagonist who manages her life like a balance sheet, calculating the cost of every trick she plays and ultimately trumping the conventional morality she pretends to espouse. And Charles Dickens' schoolmaster Thomas Gradgrind, in the novel *Hard Times* (1854), will forever remind us of the folly of equating fact with wisdom.

More modern fiction uses humorous characters in more complicated ways, making us sometimes question Forster's notion of flatness and roundness. American novelist Joseph Heller's protagonist Yossarian, in *Catch-22* (1951), is flat in the sense that he doesn't change in the course of the novel – his circumstances are altered, but he remains essentially the same sceptical anti-hero, bent on surviving an absurd war and an absurd world. Yet Yossarian is capable of surprising us, often humorously. When he has an uncharacteristically sincere, romantic encounter with an Italian woman named Luciana, he professes love and proposes marriage (a surprise); Luciana offers him a slip of paper with her name and address on it, then retracts it, saying Yossarian will 'tear it up into little pieces the minute I'm gone and go walking away like a big shot because a tall, young, beautiful girl like me, Luciana, let you sleep with her and did not ask you for money'.

Yossarian protests; she relents and gives him the paper. Yossarian seems to have matured, from a callous young man who patronises prostitutes to someone embarking on a relationship that truly matters to him.

> Then she smiled at him serenely, squeezed his hand and, with a whispered regretful 'Addio,' pressed herself against him for a moment and then straightened and walked away with unconscious dignity and grace.

The minute she was gone, Yossarian tore the slip of paper up and walked away in the other direction, feeling very much like a big shot because a beautiful young girl like Luciana had slept with him and did not ask for money. (Heller 1971: 167)

The double surprise, like so many in *Catch-22*, seems to put the reader and Yossarian right back where they started. Yet both are a little wiser as a result of this scene.

In *Money: A Suicide Note* (1986), British novelist Martin Amis uses his characters and his style as Heller does: to continually set up and dispel readers' logical and sentimental expectations. Amis's protagonist, John Self, often engages in dialogue with the reader. 'Memory is a funny thing, isn't it. You don't agree? I don't agree either. Memory has never amused me much, and I find its tricks more and more wearisome as I grow older' (Amis 1986: 30). Self is a consummate unreliable narrator; even he can't trust himself.

One of the essential traits of humorous literary fiction is a compelling protagonist. Both Yossarian and Self are highly effective protagonists, given their novels' grand designs. Yossarian, an Air Force bombardier, and Self, a commercial director and aspiring movie producer, defy the stereotypes associated with their respective professions. Yossarian is no typical war hero; he is selfishly and solely determined to prolong his own existence (arguably an act of heroism in itself), yet he commands the respect of his fellow soldiers. Self is not the slick, confident con-artist he imagines himself; rather, he's a dupe of others, constantly being conned, and he's at least partially aware of the con as it happens. Both of these characters have oddly endearing flaws: Yossarian's propensity to sit naked in trees, for instance, and Self's unceasing appetite for exaggerated quantities of junk food and alcohol, both of which habits he continually pledges to kick. By existing somewhere between flatness and roundness, these characters are sufficiently complex to haunt us long after we've finished their books.

Exercise: moving beyond the flat humorous character

Begin constructing a protagonist by listing characteristics associated with his or her professional stereotype. Say your character is a funeral director. You might list such adjectives as these: sombre, tall, gaunt, dark, bespectacled, plain-dressed and plain-spoken, brooding about eternity, given to playing classical music and driving black automobiles.

Now consider a character in a very different sort of profession: a disk jockey who spins records at a club. A list of this character's stereotypical aspects might include these: muscular, self-assured, shaven head, earrings, piercings, trendy clothing, fond of fast cars and fast relationships, living for the moment.

Blending the stereotypes is the first step in creating a more compelling protagonist: a muscular funeral director fond of piercings and fast cars, say, or a sombre disk jockey who broods about eternity. The second step is to introduce traits that blur the stereotypes further; let the funeral director be a gourmet vegetarian chef, say, and make the disc jockey addicted to watching TV shows about fishing or golf. Creating tension among your protagonist's passions is a useful way to build a humorous character.

Exercise: what's in a name?

The easiest way to make a humorous character fatally flat is give that character a too-cute name. The card game 'Happy Families' is rife with such names: Mr Snip the Barber, Mrs Bun the Baker's Wife. Names that seem incongruous with the character's profession tend to be funnier: in real life I've encountered a realtor named Pirate and a doctor named Risk, not to mention a fund-raiser named Death.

Other names may strike you as funny for no reason in particular. It's not a bad idea to begin keeping a list of names with humorous potential. Daily newspapers and telephone directories are good sources. In a quick scan of my local directory, the following names caught my eye: Wayne Spelk, Damon Stankie, Betty Almond, Melanie Gooch, and J. P. Pronto. (I cheated and put different first names with last names, and so should you, to avoid unduly embarrassing anyone.)

Setting

Sometimes setting is so important to a story that it acts as a character does: as an agent of action that advances the plot. In humorous fiction, setting is also used as a means of displacement. A character at odds with a particular world tends to be either tragic or comic. When Adolf Hitler is a character in a novel set in Liverpool (Beryl Bainbridge's *Young Adolf*, 1978) he manages to be both.

Cold Comfort Farm (1932) is a good example of using setting both as character and as plot catalyst. The Sussex countryside entraps and manipulates the Starkadder family; when the sukebind weed is in bloom, some characters are helplessly driven to fornicate. Author Stella Gibbons used a florid prose style to great advantage, and even went to the trouble of putting stars next to her most overwrought passages to help readers and reviewers tell 'whether a sentence is Literature or whether it is just sheer flapdoodle' (Gibbons 1978: 8–9). The following excerpt rated two stars:

> **Dawn crept over the Downs like a sinister white animal, followed by the snarling cries of a wind eating its way between the black boughs of the thorns. The wind was the furious voice of this sluggish animal light that was baring the dormers and mullions and scullions of Cold Comfort Farm. (32)

The farm and its environs provide a challenge for protagonist Flora Poste, a model of commonsensical English gentlewomanliness, who goes to battle with gothic nature itself in her efforts to reform the Starkadders.

In *Scoop* (1938), Evelyn Waugh contrives to put his protagonist, John Boot, in a setting entirely at odds with his sensibility. Boot, self-professed Countryman and nature columnist, given to writing sentences such as 'Feather-footed through the plashy fen passes the questing vole' (Waugh 1999: 25), is mistakenly sent to Ishmaelia in Northern Africa to serve as war correspondent for the *Daily Beast*. Utterly the wrong man for the job, Boot's bumblings bring him improbable success – of a sort – and allow Waugh to satirise war coverage in general and the English press in particular.

Other writers of humorous fiction opt to use setting as definition and reinforcement for their characters. In the 1980s and 1990s, Lewis Nordan and James Wilcox each published several novels set in the American South in which setting is depicted sensually and sincerely (albeit humorously) as a formative force in characters' lives. During the same period, John Irving and Richard Russo were writing fiction set in the American Northeast. My first satiric novel, *Lisa Maria's Guide for the Perplexed*, was set in a fictionalised version of my hometown. These works all use a sense of place in humorous ways to evoke characters' moral, social, ethnic, and political identities and conflicts.

Whether you choose to use setting as contrast or complement to character, remember that specific sensory details are critically important in creating a vivid fictional world.

Exercise: our house, in the middle of our street

Choose the place you lived longest while you were coming of age. Draw a map of the house and make a list of rooms. List the objects, colours, sounds, textures, and smells that you associate with each room. Finally, write a scene set in one of the rooms, featuring a character or two very unlike the actual people who lived there. Putting unfamiliar characters in familiar places is an effective way to generate humorous tension.

Exercise: products of one's environment

Create a setting whose nature embodies some of the important traits of your protagonist. Make a list of your character's principal descriptors, and then try to list an element of setting that conveys each one. Showing your character through setting reduces the need for exposition, and it's far more interesting to the reader to be shown, not told, the nature of your protagonist.

Plot

Humorous plots often involve exaggeration, mistaken identity, reversal of fortune, and the meeting of opposites. Odd characters in strange situations and settings tend to generate plots – sequences of actions – all by themselves.

Avoid planning your story's plot too far in advance of writing. One student of mine liked to outline his short fiction, much as he did his essays; the results were wooden. It's fine to have a destination in mind for your characters, but don't be surprised if they change their minds along the way and never reach it.

To consider the range of possibilities with plot, let's look at three classic stories involving dogs: Mark Twain's 'The Grateful Poodle' (1878), Dorothy Parker's 'Mr. Durant' (1944), and Anton Chekhov's 'Kashtanka' (1887).

Twain's story is the simplest of the three: a kind of parable about a physician who one day treats a stray poodle's broken leg. Next day the poodle returns with another stray dog with a broken leg; the physician mends it. In ensuing days the physician treats an exponentially growing number of dogs with broken legs. Finally, when the mass of needy dogs far exceeds his (and his newly-hired assistants') abilities, he decides to shoot them. But as he goes forth with his gun, he happens to step on the tail of the original poodle, who bites him. A month later, the physician, on his deathbed as a result of the bite, proclaims to his friends: 'Beware of books. They tell but half of the story. Whenever a poor wretch asks you for help, and you feel a doubt as to what result may flow from your benevolence, give yourself the benefit of the doubt and kill the applicant' (Twain 2002: 714). Then the physician dies. (Are you laughing yet?) Like many moral tales, this one is largely expository, with its satiric moral neatly spelled out at its end. Development of character and setting are sketchy at best.

Dorothy Parker's 'Mr. Durant' also has a moral, but it's slightly more embedded in the story's plot. The title character is a chronic womaniser, a married family man who recently impregnated one of his secretaries. After paying for her abortion, he goes home, ogling fresh possibilities on his way, to find that his children have taken in a stray dog. They beg him to be allowed to keep it, and in a benign mood engendered by his skilful dispatch of his secretary, he promises to let it stay. But soon afterward he is disgusted to discover that the dog is female. He tells his wife, 'You have a female around, and you know what happens. All the males in the neighborhood will be running after her' (Parker 1973: 46). Durant reassures his wife that his children won't think he's broken his word; he'll simply get rid of the dog while they're sleeping.

The parallels between Durant's treatment of his secretary and his dog give this satirical story a rather rigid structure, relieved only by Parker's authoritatively detailed depiction of her protagonist's thoughts and actions.

The Chekhov story has the same ingredients of the first two: characters, a moral message, and a dog. But here we find more complex development of our protagonist, a mongrel who resembles a fox. Kashtanka, lost by her abusive owner, is found by an animal trainer and transported to a world of relative luxury. She consorts with a trained gander and a clever pig, as well as a snob of a cat, and has a nice dinner every evening. But when Kashtanka herself is taught to do tricks, performs in public, and is reclaimed by her original owner (a drunken carpenter), she readily leaves her exciting new life to resume the derisive neglect of her original owner. And her time away seems to her only a dream.

Without humour, all of these stories would be unbearably bleak. With humour, their serious themes gain significant dramatic power.

Defining the theme of a work of fiction is a task some authors avoid completely. But, if pressed, many writers of contemporary humorous fiction would admit that their themes involve some sort of alienation. A writer pal of mine says all of his stories have the same theme: 'Us versus death'.

Whatever notion of theme you may have, let it inform your writing style. Martin Amis's and Joseph Heller's depictions of absurd, even surreal, worlds are reinforced by their use of consecutive contradictory sentences and scenes. Lewis Nordan's celebration of the pervasive power of the Mississippi Delta on its inhabitants is lyrically conveyed through his lush, idiosyncratic prose style.

Exercise: seeing the forest as well as the trees
You've finished writing a first draft of a story or novel and are ready to revise. Writing a synopsis of the work will help you see its plot in clear relief. List the key fictional events on index cards, one per card. Tape the cards to a flat surface, arranging their respective heights to reflect rising or diminishing dramatic tension. Do you see anything resembling a dramatic arc? If not, move the cards around. If no arc emerges, consider rewriting or reordering scenes. Consider opposites: what might happen, for instance, if your character stayed home instead of running away? What if, instead of heartbreak, the protagonist found requited love – but with the wrong person?

A final exercise
A challenge for aspiring writers of humour is to keep a diary, over a period of three or four days, listing every incident that makes them laugh. (Good luck.) Such a list may provide inspiration for one's fiction – or, at the very least, some insights into one's own warped psyche. Be forewarned that the act of keeping the list may inhibit laughter.

For most of us, laughter is a necessary part of our daily conversations with the world – a physiological response to situations that may be social, political, or downright silly. If you ever meet someone who never laughs, keep a close eye on that person; at the very least, he or she might be worth writing about.

Note

1. The author gratefully acknowledges the research assistance of Elizabeth Hastings, graduate student in Creative Writing at the University of Central Florida.

References

Amis, Martin (1986), *Money: A Suicide Note*, New York: Penguin.

Austen, Jane [1814] (1983), *Mansfield Park*, New York: Bantam Books.

Bainbridge, Beryl (1978), *Young Adolf*, London: Duckworth.

Berger, Arthur Asa (1977), *The Art of Comedy Writing*, New Brunswick: Transaction Publishers.

Chekov, Anton (1986), 'Kashtanka', in *The Tales of Chekhov, Vol. 12: The Cook's Wife and Other Stories*, New York: Ecco.

Critchley, Simon (2002), *On Humour*, London: Routledge.

Defoe, Daniel [1722] (2004), *Moll Flanders*, New York: W.W. Norton & Co.

Dickens, Charles [1854] (1981), *Hard Times*, New York: Bantam Classics.

Dufresne, John (2003), *The Lie That Tells a Truth*, New York: W. W. Norton & Co.

Forster, E. M. [1927] (1995), 'Flat and round characters', in Michael J. Hoffman and Patrick D. Murphy (eds), *Fundamentals of the Theory of Fiction*, Durham: Duke University Press.

Freud, Sigmund (1963), *Jokes and Their Relation to the Unconscious*, trans. James Strachey, New York: W.W. Norton.

Galef, David (1993), *The Supporting Cast: A Study of Flat and Minor Characters*, University Park: The Pennsylvania State University Press.

Gibbons, Stella [1932] (1978), *Cold Comfort Farm*, New York: Penguin.

Heller, Joseph [1951] (1971), *Catch-22*, New York: Dell Publishing Co. Inc.

McManus, Patrick F. (2000), *The Deer on a Bicycle: Excursions into the Writing of Humor*, Spokane: Eastern Washington University Press.

Nabokov, Vladimir (1980), 'Good readers and good writers', in *Lectures on Literature*, New York: Harcourt Brace.

Nash, Walter (1985), *The Language of Humour*, London: Longman.

O'Neill, Patrick (1990), *The Comedy of Entropy*, Toronto: University of Toronto Press.

Parker, Dorothy (1973), 'Mr Durant', in *The Portable Dorothy Parker*, New York: The Viking Press.

Paulos, John (1977), 'The logic of humour and the humour of logic', in Antony J. Chapman and Hugh C. Foot (eds), *It's a Funny Thing, Humour*, Oxford: Pergamon Press.

Rishel, Mary Ann (2002), *Writing Humor: Creativity and the Comic Mind*, Detroit: Wayne State University Press.

Sanders, Barry (1996), *Sudeen Glory: Laughter as Subversive History*, Boston: Beacon Press.

Twain, Mark (2002), 'The grateful poodle and sequel', in Joe Queenan (ed.), *The Malcontents: the Best Bitter, Cynical and Satirical Writing in the World*, Philadelphia: Running Press.

Waugh, Evelyn [1938] (1999), *Scoop*, New York: Back Bay Books.

15

Writing for Children

Alan Brown

I believe that writing for children is the most important writing of all. It helps establish reading (or non-reading) patterns that last for life. It helps children grow intellectually and emotionally by giving them vicarious experience. But children's literature is never pretentious. It is always entertainment, always fun.

In this short chapter, I intend to focus on what I see as particular about writing prose fiction for children (hereafter called WFC). I will leave aside writing for teenagers which is the subject of another chapter, along with non-fiction, drama and poetry in their specialist aspects.

Much of what has been written elsewhere about the craft of writing applies to WFC. The market is equally demanding as regards quality, although what this means may vary. When children are bored they stop reading. Successful WFC will be, by and large, fast paced with at least some humour.

A few words of caution about such statements.

Rules are notoriously made to be broken. In the 1990s, writers were being advised by their agents that the supernatural would not sell (to publishers). So no witches or wizards, please. Joanne Rowling seems not to have had the benefit of this well-meaning advice. Along comes Harry Potter and the rest is history.

This example brings us to another important aspect of WFC. Success can be huge. Writers such as Rowling and Philip Pullman earn more than most if not all other living writers. Part of their success is that their work is also read by adults (so-called 'crossover' books). However, Theodore Geisel's sales as Dr Seuss make him one of the most successful writers of all time and his work is probably read only by or to children. Children read more than adults, and the generations are quickly replaced.

WFC is as diverse as all adult writing put together, and then some. It has the genres of adventure, romance, comedy, horror, animal, sci-fi/fantasy, biography and history and no doubt more I haven't thought of. Booksellers look for marketing categories, and main-stream 'literature' is much less important than for adults.

There are also the different formats of board books (and others such as so-called 'mechanicals'), picture books, illustrated stories, comics, longer stories, and short novels. Each of these can be defined by interest age, but reading age may be different, which will influence length, vocabulary and grammatical structure.

Material for reluctant readers must have an interest level several years older than its reading level. This is a relatively specialist schools market where National Curriculum and

National Reading Strategy are important considerations. Work is invariably commissioned from known authors.

The short story does not have the same meaning in WFC as it has in adult writing. A short story becomes a book for the younger reader. Short stories may be linked by their characters to form longer books. Anthologies are found mainly in the schools market, or as tasters of longer work published for marketing reasons or for charity. Adult-style short stories tend to be aimed at an older readership by established novelists (Almond 2000).

WFC is special in other respects. Many books are bought not by child readers but by parents, teachers and librarians. Publishers have to guess what these other adults will choose. Most of the decision-making adults in this industry are women, though the consequences of this are a matter of debate.

Initial publication may be something of a lottery. There is an inevitable degree of censorship. Children are given what is thought to be appropriate to their age and development. Some 'unsuitable' books do get published, but who knows how many fall by the wayside.

This goes hand in hand with the popularity of 'issue' books. The limits of acceptability are constantly being revised, sometimes becoming more liberal, at other times more restrictive. Broken homes seem now to be the norm in modern writing for young children. As soon as topics such as asylum seekers and terrorism enter the news they become the themes of older children's books. The work of Robert Swindells shows how these large-scale matters can become fine storytelling on the individual level.

A frequent theme in children's books is, of course, growing up. Keen child readers are eager to read up the age-range. They often like a central character who is older than they are. The later Harry Potter books about the pubescent problems of a teenage wizard are devoured by the pre-teen audience as soon as they have finished his younger adventures.

The fantastic is a common element in children's books. There are a number of possible reasons for this. It is often said that the child's imagination has not yet been blunted by the transition to adulthood and that they are more willing to suspend disbelief. Fantasy worlds or magic realism are ways of delivering the fast paced action that children demand in a real world where they are increasingly protected and restricted.

All this may seem a long preamble to practical writing advice, but studying the field and understanding what WFC is and is not can help you. WFC is not simply writing about children. For example, a book such as Arundhati Roy's *The God of Small Things* (Roy 1997) is about children but it is an adult book in its sophisticated style, sexual content and tragic ending. Some teenagers and young adults might love it, but younger children would probably find it boring.

Stories for younger children are almost always fully resolved by a happy ending. This is one of the things that make them fun to write.

Finding the young voice – a writing exercise

The right voice will vary according to target age and format, but is likely to be younger than the one you use with other adults. This applies to the narrative voice as well as to dialogue. You really do have to know how children speak and be able to adopt a young voice for your written words.

Does this mean that you must have children of your own? Well, it helps, just as it helps to work with children. Or have done these things and have a good memory.

Knowing the latest slang is not required. The latest today may be ridiculed as old-fashioned by the time your work is published.

It is more a matter of point of view, in the broadest sense. The best children's books might just conceivably have been written by a child. Their authors know what is important to children and how children would see these things. Their writing style does not use long words where short ones will do. Their sentence structure and grammar is not needlessly complex.

Writers for children have adult skills but have not lost touch with the child they once were, the child within.

I suspect that each of us has a particular voice with which they are most comfortable. I think mine is about nine years of age. I can remember what it felt like to be nine better in many ways than at any other time of my childhood. Specific memories of that time seem to glow, though not all were happy. Those memories and feelings have become important parts of what I see as my personal 'mythology' – the 'dreamtime' of my life. This is the source or inspiration for many of my stories.

Try this as a writing exercise. Think of an episode from your childhood that you remember at least in outline. Write as much as you can about it, in the third person. Elaborate patchy areas creatively. Introduce fictional characters if necessary to generate some kind of storyline. Give people words to speak. Try for the language and style of a child one or two years younger than your remembered self.

The reason I suggest that you use the third person is to encourage you to go beyond what you can strictly remember, into remembered remembering and imagination. I suggest that you try in the first instance for a younger voice than your subject to counter any adult tendency to overestimate children's reading ability.

Does it work for you? I hope so.

The early years – baby books to picture books

The earliest years are a very specialist area. Board books, waterproof bath books, word games of many kinds are as much works of design as authorship. Artist and author is often the same person, perhaps having child development experience or training. The 'books' use all of the senses – smell, touch and sound as well as visual stimuli.

In picture books the design element continues to be strong. There are mechanicals such as 'pop-up' books, books with sliders to push or pull, boxes and letters to open (see Alan Ahlberg's *Jolly Postman* books). There may be windows or holes in the pages that allow one page to be temporarily superimposed on another, as in Eric Carle's classic *The Very Hungry Caterpillar* (Carle 2002). It is generally recognised that it is the look and feel of even the most straightforward picture book that primarily determines its success. No coincidence then that some of the most successful authors illustrate their own books (for example, Albrough, Sendak), sometimes as a series featuring the same character(s) such as Butterworth's Percy the Park Keeper.

Nevertheless, picture books are the first format where a writer can independently create a stand-alone storyline and sell it to a publisher who then commissions someone else as illustrator. *Guess How Much I Love You* (McBratney 1997) was written by Sam McBratney and illustrated by Anita Jeram and is perhaps the single most successful picture book of all time, selling many millions of copies.

A picture book is radically different to an illustrated story, in that the illustrations carry their share of the storyline. The text should give the artist opportunities and not duplicate what is obvious from their pictures. An intending author has to study the way the format works.

The story is usually spread over twelve double pages, and sometimes uses the single page at front and back. There may be one illustration on a page, or a number of linked pictures, but the writer can consider each page or double page as like a miniature scene in a film. Each time the child opens the book at a new place, what they read and see has a unity of meaning, whilst also leading on to the next scene. The ultimate scene is of course the dramatic highpoint, with some revelation, surprise or joke.

I do not mean to suggest that the picture book story hops about in time and place. On the contrary, it is commonly set in a single time and place with a small cast of characters. The storyline is usually quite simple with a few twists and turns along the way. It helps if there is some interest for the adult who may have to read the book over and over to their child.

Picture books are aimed at children from two or three years of age up to six or seven, who differ greatly in terms of emotional and intellectual development, linguistic and reading skills. Their books are correspondingly diverse in theme and style. They have in common that the present tense is often used, with lots of speech and humour.

If you love writing picture books, sooner or later you will want to write a text in verse. Agents and publishers seem reluctant to accept them on the grounds that rhymes do not translate into the foreign language co-editions needed to make publication worthwhile. Clearly, some of the most loved picture books ever published are in verse, so perhaps rhyme is just a convenient criticism of an inadequate text.

A picture book writing exercise

Write a very short and simple story about animals. Animal texts are very common for the very young. Story animals can be smarter and more adventurous than children themselves. So what if they are people in animal skins? Children love them.

If you get stuck for ideas, just recount a day in the life of your chosen animal, your own pet perhaps. Aim at 500 to 1,000 words.

Now try to cut your story into twelve more or less equal parts. You may find it helpful to draw twelve boxes and write your text into them.

Does it work? If you are used to writing only older stories, or adult short stories, the chances are that it doesn't. There will be too much 'rationale' and not enough action. Some boxes will be bursting with text, others almost empty.

So change your story until it does work. Consider the point of each scene. What is it really about? If there is nothing of interest there, cut it out. Develop what is lively and moves the story along.

You can repeat yourself. Picture books often use fairytale threes. For example, a character looking for something may have to look in the cupboard and behind the sofa before finding it under the bed. They would find something interesting each time.

Don't worry if the last page punch-line seems predictable to you. Very young children love repetition and anticipation. If they take to your book they will read it dog-eared.

I would not submit a text with my own pagination. Editors like to make their own decisions about such things. They may want very little text on some pages. The last might have just one word.

If your text is seriously considered for publication the commissioning editor will make up a package that includes samples from an illustrator, input from a design editor and commitment to co-editions from publishers abroad. Then it is examined by the accountants and marketing people. Along this long, hard road you are likely to be asked to make many changes to your text. You will be one of a project team.

Picture books may be short but each is polished to as near-perfection as the team can achieve. The time between submitting a text and seeing it in a bookshop is unlikely to be much less than two years.

First story books

Children who take to reading soon want something meatier than a picture book but with some of the same visual appeal. First story books are a hybrid form, perched between the text heavy novel and the illustration heavy picture book. As well as text, they have pictures on most pages, sometimes in colour but often black and white.

These pictures may add to the story but they are not expected to carry meaning essential to the storyline that the text does not. You will not usually be asked to change your words to fit the illustrations.

The text will contain the rationale and scene linking that is minimal in picture books. In fact, a 'scene' is now a chapter in the style of a novel. Each chapter has its own structure and moves the story along, though it may be very short.

The sophistication and word length of early story books varies according to target age, with series for each age group. Each publisher divides up the field in a slightly different way, and a useful source of information about how they do so is contained in the annual *Writers' & Artists' Yearbook* (A&C Black annual). Make a trip to your bookshop to read some samples for yourself.

New and aspiring writers often debate the value of agents. A neglected factor (because you don't see it if you don't have one) is that your agent will pass on requests by publishers for contributions to new series such as these. Their letter will set out the aims, style and topics wanted. This is the point at which you are most likely to get a story accepted.

You might get this information by writing regularly to every children's publisher, but it is unlikely that you or they would have the patience to do so.

A first story book writing exercise

School is one of the first big adventures for children, and is very useful for writers because parents are mostly absent. It can be a pretty scary place. Teachers have a parental role but with a tough core of authority most parents lack. Other children may be friends, but their friendship may be fickle. They may be rivals or bullies.

School stories rest upon the fact that schools are where important social interactions take place. This is their hidden agenda, if you like.

Think back to the earliest school days you can remember. Don't worry if there have been changes since then. Concentrate on the emotions that you felt at the time, or imagine you felt. Children today will be not be so very different.

Populate your classroom with characters – best friends, enemies, teacher, and class pets. Invent what you can't remember. Imagine the everyday routine of registers, lessons, dinner time and breaks.

Now think of an event that breaks this cosy routine and you have the basis of your story. A visitor, human or otherwise, a new student, a change of teacher, an accident. How do you and the class react?

Write your story in a lively style, and be humorous if you can. For five-to seven-year-olds aim for five chapters of about 300 words each. For seven to nines extend the total length to about 3,000 words.

Longer story books

Even a casual glance at the books on offer will tell you that the boundaries between categories in terms of age and length are quite flexible. The categories themselves are much firmer, because they correspond to the sales strategies of the bookshops. All books might be presented in alphabetical order of author's name, but they are not. For better or worse, they are categorised by age and other more transient marketing devices.

Many children from the age of eight or nine are ready to tackle stories of 8,000 words or more, and writers and publishers are keen to provide them. They may be series, or stand-alones linked by a series format.

A popular author may write all the titles in a series, or there may be many authors. The supposed author may not exist or have written only the first titles. Thereafter, some series are written by jobbing authors working from a brief supplied by the publisher. This kind of work should not be demeaned. It is a good way of learning the craft and acquiring useful contacts.

Many classic books have been written for this age group, for example Roald Dahl's *Charlie and the Chocolate Factory* (2004) and Dick King Smith's *The Sheep-pig* (1999).

These story books are fun to write; long enough to allow substantial plot and character development, but short enough so that the writing never becomes heavy labour. These 'mini novels' usually have illustrations, but only one or two per chapter, of which there may be ten or twelve.

A longer story book writing exercise

Children are often obsessive about their hobbies. They are avid collectors. A child may, for example, be fascinated by dinosaurs. They will then collect anything about dinosaurs – models, fossils, books of fiction, books of facts – anything that remotely bears upon those fabulous beasts.

Did you have such a hobby? Do you still? Think of something that children in the pre-teen years might find fascinating. The endless possibilities include princesses, monster trucks, spaceships and ponies. Choose one that you like too, and let your enthusiasm shine through your writing.

Now all you need is a storyline that gives a child protagonist what the child reader dreams about in relation to that hobby. Not too quickly or easily, but with some ups and downs, twists and turns. Remember that the essence of dramatic storytelling is unfulfilled desire and conflict between characters.

So your heroine living in an apparently ordinary family might discover that she is really a princess. Your hero might find a spaceship at the bottom of the garden.

A villain is invaluable for generating conflict, and from this age onward villains can be really villainous. A usurper imprisons our princess to keep her from claiming the throne. A rogue scientist steals our hero's spaceship.

The issue of gender is also becoming important. We can more easily be politically correct with younger children. Girls of five or six may like the engine stories of the Rev.

Audrey as much as do boys, but most people would admit that by age ten differences between the sexes are emerging.

So, some books will probably appeal to one sex more than the other. Much of the work of Jacqueline Wilson is unashamedly aimed at girls and she is Britain's most borrowed author in public libraries. Publishers make great efforts to keep boy readers, knowing that they are more likely than girls to lose the reading habit as they grow older. There is a whole genre of football stories, for example, from the likes of Michael Hardcastle.

In your story, you will generally appeal more to boys with a male chief protagonist, and vice versa. If you can have a gang of mixed gender, so much the better. Enid Blyton's famous and secret gangs were always so.

You have your characters, a setting and the rudiments of a plot. Is it time to start writing the story? Perhaps so, if you can write 8,000 words without any formal outline. I find a written outline essential for longer story books and novels. Do whatever works for you.

Short novels

Fluent readers of age ten and average readers of just a few years older (the early teens) want a substantial book in 'grown-up' novel format. These are dealt with in the chapter 'Writing for Teenagers'.

In conclusion

WFC invites children to identify with characters in situations both strange and familiar, allowing them to imagine how they themselves might act in such situations. Remember to make your young heroes and heroines as proactive as possible in order to keep your novel firmly for children and not just about them. Let those heroes and heroines achieve their own resolutions to problems. By empowering your characters, you empower your readers – of which may there be many.

References

Alborough, Jez (2006), *Hit the Ball, Duck*, London: HarperCollins.

Ahlberg, Allan and Ahlberg, Janet (ill.) (2006), *The Jolly Postman or Other People's Letters: 20th Anniversary Edition*, London: Little, Brown and Company.

Almond, David (2000), *Counting Stars*, London: Hodder Children's Books.

Carle, Eric (2002), *The Very Hungry Caterpillar*, London: Puffin.

Dahl, Roald (2004), *Charlie and the Chocolate Factory*, London: Viking.

McBratney, Sam and Jeram, Anita (ill.) (1997), *Guess How Much I Love You*, London: Walker Books.

Roy, Arundhati (1997), *The God of Small Things*, London: Flamingo.

Smith, Dick King (1999), *The Sheep-pig*, London: Puffin.

Writers' & Artists' Yearbook (annual), London: A & C Black.

16

Writing for Teenagers

Linda Newbery

Teenage fiction, young adult fiction, 'crossover' books – these terms seem to be used inter-changeably, and therefore confusingly. In bookshops and libraries, the shelves labelled 'teenage fiction' often display books aimed at readers who are two or three years short of their teenage years; the term 'crossover' is used sometimes to indicate suitability for older teenagers and adults, but elsewhere to mean a book written primarily for children, and with child characters but also adult appeal, such as Philip Pullman's *Northern Lights* (1995) or Lewis Carroll's *Alice's Adventures in Wonderland* (1865). Young adult fiction is more clearly defined in the US and Australia than in the UK, and is given a standing and a critical attentiveness which most UK authors only dream of; on the other hand, a large proportion of the world market has little concept of teenage or young adult fiction, making sales of translation rights difficult.

For the purpose of this chapter, I'm concerning myself with fiction likely to be enjoyed by capable readers of thirteen or fourteen and up, and possibly by adults. From about 2002 onwards, highly successful 'crossover' titles such as Lian Hearn's *Across the Nightingale Floor* (2002) and Jennifer Donnelly's *A Gathering Light* (2003) have won prizes and hit bestseller lists. It would be easy to think that the phenomenon of the upper-end of fiction for the young – titles which could be, and have been, published with equal success on adult lists – has only now been invented by publishers and authors. That isn't the case, though: fiction of adolescence has been around for a very long time. J. D. Salinger's *The Catcher in the Rye* (1951), Jane Austen's *Northanger Abbey* (1818), Dodie Smith's *I Capture the Castle* (1949), Sylvia Plath's *The Bell Jar* (1963), *To Kill a Mockingbird* by Harper Lee (1960), Mervyn Peake's *Gormenghast* trilogy (1946–59) and *All Quiet on the Western Front* by Erich Maria Remarque (1929) – to pick just a few of the best-known – could all fit into this category, or rather span these categories. All these were first published on adult lists, and several have reached teenage readers via an exam syllabus rather than because publishers saw 'crossover' potential. Fiction of adolescence isn't new, but newly-branded.

The concept of teenage fiction didn't arrive in the UK until the 1970s – which is odd, as teenage fashions, music, and magazines were very much in evidence, so why was fiction so slow to catch up? It's possibly because fiction has to be filtered through large numbers of adults before reaching its audience, and it seems to be felt that young people must be protected in their fiction reading from the realities of modern living which are so appar-ent in the magazines, films and TV available to them. Writers such as K. M Peyton, Jane

Gardam, Jill Paton Walsh, Aidan Chambers and Jean Ure in the UK, and S. E. Hinton, Robert Cormier and Katherine Paterson in the US, were among the first to write challenging fiction for readers at the upper end of the youth market, with US writer Judy Blume topping bestseller lists – and causing shelving anxieties for librarians – with *Forever*, in which she was determined to show that sex need not be guilt-ridden, nor first love for ever.

Issues-driven?

Since then, this upper end of the children's market has had its ups and downs before reaching the 'crossover' boom in around 2005. In the UK, by the late 1980s, every publisher was keen to leap on the teenage bandwagon, and several imprints appeared such as *Teen Tracks* from HarperCollins, *Plus* from Puffin, *Topliners* and *Limelight* from Macmillan, all of these given a distinctive branding to separate them from the core nine to twelve fiction the publishers were known for. Teenage fiction tended at that time to be dominated by issues-driven fiction, and some might argue that it still is. Anorexia; squabbling or separating parents; sibling death; racism; drug-taking; unemployment; bullying and other forms of peer pressure – topics such as these made easy marketing hooks, and assured teenage readers, often perceived by publishers as reluctant, that they would find stories relevant to their own lives. Although some of this, as publishers rushed to fill the teenage gap, could be formulaic, there were also enduring and satisfying novels from the authors mentioned above, and others.

Publishers and authors soon found, however, that it was (and still is) hard to achieve the same levels of sales with a teenage title that might be achieved by a younger book. Books for the core nine to twelve age-group and younger are bought for children by parents and relatives; teenagers are more likely to choose and buy books for themselves, but have many other demands on their money. Even for a well-established author, it's hard to make a living by writing teenage fiction alone. Many well-known writers for this older age group earn their bread-and-butter by writing for younger children as well.

Reaching readers

It can be particularly hard, I think, for fiction of adolescence to reach readers. As I've mentioned, 'teenage' shelves in bookshops and libraries are often dominated by books aimed at ten or eleven and up. (Although publishers use the term 'pre-teen' or 'aspirational' for this just-below-teenage fiction, most shop or library shelving doesn't distinguish.) The unfortunate result is that readers of fifteen or sixteen are often deterred from browsing by the belief that they've outgrown teenage fiction. And, as in every area of publishing, shops give more shelf and table-space to the highly-promoted books with immediate mass appeal and a big marketing budget, with the result that books produced without fanfare can be overlooked. It can be depressing, on scanning the shelves, to see ephemeral but glossily-produced books and series given prominence. Faced with this apparently large but in fact limited choice, it's not surprising that some teenage readers feel patronised by the fiction targeted at them, and consider that it has little to offer them by the age of thirteen or fourteen.

Undoubtedly, the children's book world benefits from an enthusiastic army of support, composed of teachers, librarians, volunteers helpers, reading-group organisers, journalists, knowledgeable booksellers and suppliers, who are devoted to bringing books and readers together. Many children and teenagers have daily access to a good school library, with a keen and well-informed librarian, reading clubs, fresh and appealing stock. But, regrettably, too many are not reached by this network. Their experience of books will then be limited to the drab and outdated stock in a library they're unlikely to visit voluntarily, or to the local bookshop – if they choose to go there. The sad fact is that the greater proportion of books published each year remains invisible to most readers.

Why write for teenagers?

Why write for this age-group, then? You're unlikely to get rich, unless you're phenomenally successful with high 'crossover' sales or a film deal. Your audience is possibly the hardest to reach, the hardest to please, and the least likely to spend their money on books. Yet writing for and about adolescence can be immensely satisfying, offering – among other things – the immeasurable reward of reaching young people at this crucial stage of their lives.

Many writers for the young say that they remember some particular stage of child-hood with particular clarity. Many reviewers have commented on Roald Dahl's ability to speak so directly to child readers. Chris Powling, himself a children's author, wrote of Dahl: 'When asked how he can communicate so successfully with eight-year-olds he once replied, "I am eight years old". And so he is – or five or ten or fifteen years old, as necessary' (Powling 1983: 69).

Maybe you have a particular closeness to teenagers, through work or family; maybe you *are* a teenager! Or maybe you rely on your own memories. Whatever your circumstances, if you feel that you can re-experience the peculiar intensity of teenage years, with all their anxieties, exhilaration, disillusionment, wild hopes, passions, frustrations, yearnings, inse-curities, soaring ambitions and acute sense of injustice, then maybe you can write a teenage novel, whether you choose to set it now, in the past or in the future.

One of the attractions for me is that if I write about a character aged fifteen, sixteen or so, I'm focusing on a stage of life at which many things will imminently change. A sixteen-year-old, within the next ten years, will inevitably be faced with many decisions, will encounter new people and places, will develop and change values, and will make discoveries about his or her own strengths, weaknesses and qualities. People of this age can have a fair amount of independence, too – travelling unaccompanied, going around on bikes, walking home at night, etc. (One of the problems faced by authors of stories for younger children is the need to separate them from controlling parents or teachers. Unlike the Famous Five or the Swallows and Amazons, twenty-first-century children don't, unless in exceptional circumstances, set off for islands, forests or ruined castles without adults in attendance.) Since I always assume that I'm writing for *readers*, I can write a substantial and complex novel which absorbs and challenges me in the writing; I can experiment with structure; I can set up puzzles and questions for the reader; I can use contradictions, irony, juxtaposition. In other words, I can do whatever suits the story I'm telling.

Writers are frequently asked who they write for, but not all of them know the answer. I tend to have far more idea of an intended readership if I'm writing, say, a story for six-year-olds. With my older fiction, I don't particularly consider that I write 'for' teenagers, or indeed 'for' anyone other than myself. The needs of the story determine the style, structure, tone and pace, not the response of an imaginary reader. More important than aiming at any supposed readership is to be as honest as I can in portraying my characters and their concerns. What *is* crucial, in any kind of writing for the young, is that the actions or choices of the young protagonists must be significant. The main characters must affect the development of the story, whether through actions, allegiances or decisions, right or wrong; they can't simply have things happening *to* them.

Not a genre

As with many areas of writing, it's possible to try too hard to give publishers or readers what you think they want. This presupposes that editors and readers *know* what they want, before they get it. Teenage fiction is not a genre, though it's often spoken of as if it is. Mention the term, and a number of likely subjects and characters spring to mind: first love and sex, rivalries, teenage pregnancy, drugs, independence, conflicts at school, exam pressures, clashes of values, etc. But successful fiction cannot be produced by ticking off items on a check-list. The best novels of adolescence don't, to my mind, have a self-conscious focus on obvious teenage interests, or a crowd-pleasing intent. They are simply novels in which the main character or characters happen to be at some stage of adolescence. Good fiction – for whatever age group – should offer, not narrowness, but widening and expansion. Paradoxically, it can be the assumption of some editors that teenagers have to be prised away from computers or TV to read at all, and must be offered undemanding plot-driven fare in which everything's spelled out for them, that risks driving away more discerning readers.

'Teenagers', obviously, range from thirteen to nineteen, which is a vast stretch in anyone's life, and reading tastes vary as widely as for any other age group. I find it as patronising to assume that teenagers are solely interested in fashion, sex, fame and rock groups as it would be to assume that thirty-year-old women only want chick-lit, or that young men will always choose sex, cars and football; but a glance at bookshop shelves – particularly at series fiction – shows how prevalent this assumption is. That's only the surface, however. You might have to look a little harder to find them, but some of the most striking and compelling novels for this age group fit no formula, and might have been considered unmarketable or at least unlikely to sell well. For example, Ann Turnbull's *No Shame, No Fear* (2003), set in England in the seventeenth century, is about religious persecution and the relationship between a Quaker girl, Susanna, and William, the son of a wealthy wool merchant. Not a subject that the marketing department would gleefully seize upon: but the quality of the writing ensured that the book was shortlisted for two major prizes, the Guardian and the Whitbread awards, and thus found readers who would not otherwise have come across it. Aidan Chambers' *Postcards from No Man's Land* (1999) combines two stories, that of a Dutch family protecting an injured soldier after the Battle of Arnhem in the 1940s, with the present-day experiences of Jacob who is visiting Amsterdam, and an elderly woman who has chosen euthanasia as the preferred end to her life. This outstanding novel won the Carnegie Medal, bringing its author to a wider audience than his previous novels had reached. Neither of these authors began by taking a survey of teenagers and their interests, nor by scanning teenage magazines to see what's topical, but with the story they had to tell.

Taking issue with issues

Earlier, I mentioned the prevalence of 'issues-driven' fiction. As the author Melvin Burgess points out:

> There are some stout defenders of these kind of books, and rightly so – many of the very best novels are set in areas of social tension. But the discomfort people feel about 'issue' books is

also justified. In some ways, the problem is bad writing – books that twist life to suit an educational purpose. But a more insidious effect has been what I'd like to call educationalism – the
idea that a book is somehow better because it is useful in socialising young people. (Burgess
2005: 14–15)

My own novels certainly include elements that could be termed 'issues' – confusion over
sexuality, prejudice, religious doubts in *The Shell House*; racism, alienation and belonging,
in *Sisterland* – but then, that is what life is made of. I resist saying that my novels 'deal with'
any particular subject, which suggests that a topic is being given a decisive sorting-out and
laying to rest. The risk of issues-led fiction is that the author can seem to be writing *on
behalf of* a particular group of people, such as asylum-seekers, or sufferers from anorexia.
This can produce a sense of duty to the reader, which is not quite the business of fiction. For
instance, it would be hard to imagine a teenage novel focusing on anorexia which ended
with the central character obstinately persisting in the face of all offers of help, advice or
treatment. Such books almost invariably contain a 'self-help' element. David Fickling, of
David Fickling Books, made a similar point in an address to the Scattered Authors' Society
(Oxford, 2004): 'The danger of issues is that you appear to know what is good. And then
you are not writing a story but a lecture'.

Young readers are very alert to any attempt to teach them through fiction, and quite
rightly so. In this, they are no different from adults. Most of us willingly absorb information
about, say, the American civil war or managing crop-rotation on a smallholding through
reading *Cold Mountain* (Frazier 1997); this is one of the pleasures of reading fiction, and a
particular pleasure of literature in translation or of reading about an unfamiliar culture or
period. But being bludgeoned with an overt message or moral is not the same at all, and
young readers resent being patronised just as much as adults do.

I'll quote myself here, referring to my young adult novel *The Shell House* (2002):

> Fiction does not concern itself with offering helpful advice, but with inhabiting the conscious-
> ness of one or more characters. In *The Shell House* I did not aim to represent all teenage boys
> in doubt about their sexuality, as Greg is, nor all teenage Christians experiencing a crisis of
> faith, as Faith does. I tried to *be* Greg; experiencing, from inside his mind and body, confusion,
> doubt and denial. My treatment of Faith was different, as she is not a viewpoint character, so I
> tried to see her as Greg does: to find such respect for her conviction, even though he does not
> share it, that he wants to help her regain her wavering belief. The question 'Does God exist?'
> certainly looms large in the novel, but, of course, I made no attempt to answer it . . . Questions
> are as important as answers – perhaps *more* important. (Newbery 2004: 13)

Adolescence is a stage of life at which values, priorities, politics, moralities are likely to be
questioned more than at any other time. Stimulating fiction for this age group not only permits
but provokes questioning, allows for more than one interpretation, and encourages re-reading.

Who's talking?

First-person or third-person narrative? Since the creation of Holden Caulfield, with his
direct and unmistakable voice (Salinger 1951, *The Catcher in the Rye*), first-person narrative has been widely used to engage teenage readers. The single first-person viewpoint
can be colloquial, confiding, recognisable, and can give the impression that the narrator
is speaking directly to the reader as an equal. There are inherent risks, though. One is

that first-person narrative must usually use the slang of the period, and thus, if set in the present, risks dating rapidly; a second is that vocabulary and expression must be limited to that of the narrator. Such literary ventriloquism can be more authentic than interesting. Where used skilfully, though, it can work magnificently, as in David Klass's *You Don't Know Me*, in which John is a most engaging narrator – witty, self-mocking, with an eye for detail and absurdity even through the painful experiences he relates. Alternating voices are effectively used by Robert Swindells in *Daz 4 Zoe* (1990) in which episodes by articulate, middle-class Zoe are offset by the illiterate but expressive account of Daz, denied an education in this near-future Britain in which affluence and poverty are exaggerated and forcibly segregated. First-person narrative can work well in historical fiction, too, carrying the reader through an initial sense of strangeness. Ann Turnbull effectively uses the alternating-narrator structure in *No Shame, No Fear,* and Celia Rees' *Witch Child*, Mary Newbury, speaks to us directly from the seventeenth century.

Third-person narrative may at first seem to be more removed from the reader, but it doesn't have to be the voice of an author obviously present in the text; it can be endlessly flexible, allowing for single- or multiple-viewpoints without restricting vocabulary. An example of third-person narrative deftly handled to include multiple viewpoints is *Deep Secret*, Berlie Doherty's moving novel about a Derbyshire community threatened by the flooding of their village for a new reservoir.

A trawl through recent publications would suggest that all taboos have now been broken, and that there's no subject that can't be used in young adult fiction: *Boy Kills Man* by Matt Whyman and *Looking for JJ* by Anne Cassidy (2004) are both about children who kill; Melvin Burgess's *Junk* (1996) and *Doing It* (2002) concerned themselves with heroin and sex respectively, the latter including an exploitative relationship between a teacher and a student; Julie Burchill's *Sugar Rush* (2004) must be one of the first novels on a teenage list which ends with lesbians in a happy and trusting relationship. But the shock or novelty factor will only take you so far. An intriguing plot or a catchy marketing hook might get your typescript as far as an editor's desk, but then it's over to the writing. And if you want to get enduring satisfaction from the writing itself, rather than (or as well as) from advances and royalties, then the most important person to please is yourself. If you want to write for teenagers, I suggest that it's better to start from the position of wanting to write fiction, and to write it as well as you possibly can, than by wanting to write specifically for a teenage audience.

Not only for teenagers

Aidan Chambers, who 'accidentally' became an editor as well as author in the 70s when he created the Macmillan *Topliners* series, had this to say:

> I do *not* believe teenage literature is *only* for children or teenagers; I do *not* believe that young people should *only* read what is published for them, and nothing else. Far from it. The sooner children and teenagers reach into the mainstream of our literature the better. But I do believe that most people will reach into it more vigorously, more willingly, and with a deeper understanding of the pleasures it offers if they have encountered on the way a literature which is for them ... and which is written with as much dedication and skill as is the best of the mainstream work. (Chambers 1985: 86–7)

This is just as true twenty years later. Without diverse, stimulating, challenging fiction to take readers through their teens, the risk is that they lose the reading habit; they may forget the pleasure they had from reading as children; they may even consider it childish. At the time Aidan Chambers published *Booktalk*, readers may have been discouraged by a dearth of books; now, they're more likely to be overwhelmed by the baffling quantity. But, however fashions change, and whatever we choose to call it, fiction of adolescence will always be crucially important. Publishers will always be looking for writers who can tune into the adolescent years, and can take readers with them.

References

Austen, Jane (1818), *Northanger Abbey*, London: John Murray.

Blume, Judy (1975), *Forever*, New York: Bradbury Press.

Burchill, Julie (2004), *Sugar Rush*, London: Macmillan.

Burgess, Melvin (1996), *Junk*, London: Andersen Press.

Burgess, Melvin (2002), *Doing It*, London: Andersen Press.

Burgess, Melvin (2005), 'What is teenage fiction?', *Books for Keeps*, no. 152, 14–15.

Carroll, Lewis (1865), *Alice's Adventures in Wonderland*, London: Macmillian.

Cassidy, Anne (2004), *Looking for JJ*, London: Scholastic.

Chambers, Aidan (1999), *Postcards from No Man's Land*, London: The Bodley Head.

Chambers, Aidan (1985), *Booktalk*, Stroud: Thimble Press.

Doherty, Berlie (2003), *Deep Secret*, London: Penguin.

Donnelly, Jennifer (2003), *A Northern Light*, New York: Harcourt Brace. Published in the UK, (2003), as *A Gathering Light*, London: Bloomsbury.

Frazier, Charles (1997), *Cold Mountain*, New York: Atlantic, Monthly Press.

Hearn, Lian (2002), *Across the Nightingale Floor*, London: Macmillan.

Klass, David (2001), *You Don't Know Me*, London: Viking.

Lee, Harper (1960), *To Kill a Mockingbird*, Philadelphia: J. B. Lippincott.

Newbery, Linda (2002), *The Shell House*, Oxford: David Fickling Books.

Newbery, Linda (2003), *Sisterland*, Oxford: David Fickling Books.

Newbery, Linda (2004), 'How the authors of children's books perceive their audience', *Books and Boundaries: Writers and their Audiences*, Pat Pinsent (ed.), National Centre for Research in Children's Literature papers 10, London: Pied Piper Publishing.

Peake, Mervyn, *The Gormenghast Trilogy*: (1946) *Titus Groan*, (1950) *Gormenghast*, (1959) *Titus Alone*, London: Eyre and Spottiswoode.

Plath, Sylvia (1963), *The Bell Jar*, London: William Heinemann.

Powling, Chris (1983), *Roald Dahl*, London: Hamish Hamilton.

Pullman, Philip (1995), *Northern Lights*, London: Scholastic.

Rees, Celia (2000), *Witch Child*, London: Bloomsbury.

Remarque, Erich Maria (1929), *All Quiet on the Western Front*, trans. A. W. Wheen, London: G. P. Putnam's Sons.

Salinger, J. D. (1951), *The Catcher in the Rye*, Boston: Little, Brown.

Smith, Dodie (1949), *I Capture the Castle*, London: William Heinemann.

Swindells, Robert (1990), *Daz 4 Zoe*, London: Hamish Hamilton.

Turnbull, Ann (2003), *No Shame, No Fear*, London: Walker Books.

Whyman, Matt (2004), *Boy Kills Man*, London: Hodder.

17

The 'Everything You Ever Wanted to Know About Creative Nonfiction, But Were Too Naïve or Uninformed to Ask' Workshop Simulation

Lee Gutkind

Scene 1: sucking them in

I usually begin this workshop by telling students I am not going to define creative nonfiction for them. No one asks a poet to define poetry or a novelist to provide a meaning of fiction, because art defines itself. Rules and regulations are for journalists and government officials – not writers.

Creative nonfiction demands what the name implies: that a writer find an interesting and compelling way – a creative approach – to communicating information and teaching readers something they don't necessarily want or need to know.

It is easy to write for an audience geared to a particular subject; for example, animal lovers or people who live in the country will be interested in an essay about a farm veterinarian. But how to attract readers with little interest in animals, medicine, or rural life? That's the challenge. You do so by telling a story – a true story about real people – that captures their attention and engages their imagination. Along the way, readers learn a great deal about whatever it is the writer is trying to teach them – in this particular case, the problems and challenges of a working farm veterinarian. But you have enticed them with story, not with an informational pay-off. That is what I say in my real workshops. I can hear it now, as I write.

'That's creative nonfiction in a nutshell', I say. The story is the 'creative' part and the information (also called 'the teaching element') is the 'nonfiction' part. I do not mean 'story' here in the generic sense the way in which reporters often rely on the term, as in 'I have to write my story' or 'Did you see the story in today's paper?' I mean 'story' with a beginning, middle and ending. I mean story with drama, suspense, and conflict – a story that compels a reader to say, 'I couldn't put it down'.

At this point, I inform my students that the workshop is over. I have told them everything they ever needed or wanted to know – and I begin to pack up my papers.

Scene 2: the yellow test

My students may think I am a bit of a fool at this point, but since they are not asking for their money back – yet – here's what I say next: 'OK, you get the story idea here. The building blocks of creative nonfiction are scenes, or little stories, that are pieced together in such a way that they tell a larger story'. I make a big point of this 'building block' concept, and repeat it over and over again so they will not forget.

As my students discover, the concept of writing in scenes is easier to digest – intellectually – than to practise. Journalists, especially, have trouble 'seeing' a story or a series of stories because their work is often so formulaic. So, we move on to the 'yellow test'.

'Get yourself a highlighter', I say, 'and go to the books or magazines you like to read. Look for the writers you appreciate and respect'. I name a few very prominent creative nonfiction writers, like Gay Talese, Tom Wolfe, and Annie Dillard. 'Read them carefully and with your marker, yellow-in the scenes or little stories. Guess what? Anywhere from 50–70 per cent of the text will glare back at you in yellow'.

Scene 3: what's a scene?

Creative nonfiction allows – in fact, encourages – the writer to use basic literary techniques once previously and primarily employed by the fiction writer rather than the journalist. By 'literary techniques' I mean the obvious stuff, like description. What do the characters and places about which you are writing look like? Make material come alive visually by evoking specificity of detail to provide three-dimensional texture.

'There's specific details and what we call "intimate details"', I say. By 'intimate' I don't mean sex and drugs and rock-and-roll, but stuff that your readers won't necessarily or easily imagine. There's the old story about Gay Talese's classic profile of Frank Sinatra, published in the mid-1960s in *Esquire* Magazine. Talese was prohibited from interviewing Sinatra when he arrived in California because 'Old Blue Eyes' had a cold and wasn't in the mood to chat with anyone. Talese followed Sinatra around and interviewed his entire entourage – from bodyguards to PR flaks. He eventually happened upon a little old blue-haired lady who carried around a hatbox and shadowed Sinatra virtually anywhere he went. This woman, he discovered, was Sinatra's wig lady. She tended to his toupees. This was an intimate detail – something a reader would not easily imagine. Not only was the existence of a full-time wig lady a telling detail about Sinatra, but it also enhanced Talese's credibility by reflecting a level of awareness and intimacy about his subject that was deeper and more thorough than other writers' Sinatra efforts. Description with specificity and intimacy of detail is an anchoring element of a good scene.

So is dialogue. In creative nonfiction, characters are sometimes interviewed and quoted – this is often a necessity – but people more often than not talk with one another. Dialogue increases the pace of the essay and helps make the characters more human and accessible. Sometimes interviews can be made to simulate a conversation between writer and subject. Rather than a Q and A experience with a table and a tape recorder dividing the two 'adversaries'.

And while use of the first person 'I' is not a requirement of creative nonfiction, it is not (as it is in traditional journalism) anathema. In creative nonfiction the narrative determines the writer's point of view and presence. The idea always is to make the narrative seem natural; there's no reason to strain to keep yourself out of the story if you are part of it – or in the story if you are not.

Scene 4: don't hold back

You are free to say what you think about the people you meet. Creative nonfiction encourages, though it certainly does not require, subjectivity. The writer's particular orientation, should he or she choose to share it, adds an eye-opening three-dimensional element to what might normally be a more conventional, hesitant observation.

Under certain circumstances, writers can also see their world through the eyes of the people about whom they are writing. This technique, used frequently by fiction writers, is called inner-point-of-view. Inner-point-of-view helps establish a direct link between reader and the story, without a writer in the middle as an interpreter or filter.

'So you've got dialogue, description and detail, inner-point-of-view, personal voice – what else?' I ask.

Invariably, in these workshops students eventually say, 'Action'.

'This is a good word,' I answer. But action is not enough – you don't want action without some sort of resolution. Something has to happen. Something big and memorable. The action can also be small, as long as there is a happening – a beginning and end.

At this point, I raise the Magic Marker I have been using to write down the anchoring elements of a scene on a whiteboard and wave it in the air, saying, 'The professor lifts the Magic Marker in the air. That's the beginning of a scene. If he drops it, well then, something happens. And even if he doesn't drop it – but only threatens to drop it – that's also a happening'. An action is initiated. Tension is established – and suspense is created, if only for a few seconds. ('Will the professor throw the Magic Marker? At whom? Will he put it down and walk away?') The reader will usually stick around to see the end if he or she is intrigued in the beginning.

Scene 5: the nonfiction part

And speaking of the beginning, I next take my students back to the way my presentation started, by reminding them about what creative nonfiction is all about – style and substance.

'The story is the style part', I say, 'and it acts as a receptacle for the information or reportage you are doing. So what you try to do is embed or include information about your subject inside the scenes you write, and then you also embed information between the scenes you write. So it is kind of like a TV show. First there's a story, and the audience is hooked by what's happened. Then, when you know you have them in the palm of your hands, you give them a commercial. You tell them what you want them to know about your subject. Then, when you think they might be getting bored, you continue the story until they're hooked again. Any time you get the chance, you also put information into the story itself. It is kind of like a dance: Story, information inside the story, information between the stories, then more story'.

Scene 6: frame and focus

I now ask students to notice the different ways in which the scenes are rendered. A scene can be recreated with dialogue, description, and other literary techniques, or it could be straight monologue with the subject simply telling a story. Another scene could be a combination of quotation and paraphrasing by the writer. Remember that scenes can also be stories told to you, so when you interview your subjects, keep in mind that you are not doing a Q-and-A. Ask questions which will lead into stories – get them to set the scene, supply characterisation and description. Talk to them and squeeze out the details. Let them do the writing for you. Good writing begins with good material. Digging out the details is the writer's responsibility and the ultimate challenge.

Each scene should have a beginning and an end. Something happens. Some scenes contain information, some scenes don't. But in between those scenes that don't should be blocks of information.

'OK?' I ask. 'Does everybody understand? The building blocks are scenes. The scenes aren't scenes unless they have a beginning and an end. Something has to happen. Information – the reporting – is embedded in the scenes and between the scenes. That's the rhythm and that's the dance, whether it is an essay or book chapter or even the entire book. OK?' I repeat.

'Yes', they say.

'Are you ready to go home?' I ask, even louder.

'Yes', they yell.

'No', I tell them. 'You haven't learned the "F" words. Creative nonfiction won't work until you can use the "F" words'.

Now they are really interested. The 'F' word' gets their attention. But I am about to disappoint them. 'How is this essay framed?' I ask.

'Framed?' they say.

'Good creative nonfiction is put together in a series of scenes or stories – moving pictures', I explain. 'But you can't just throw eight stories together and assume they will fit. There must be an order – a "structure" to it. And in the story-oriented genre of creative nonfiction, even the structure or the frame must be shaped like a story'.

'Frames are almost always timelines', I say. A day in the life, a year in the life – even a minute in the life of a person, place or thing.

Tracy Kidder, a Pulitzer Prize winner, is famous for his 'year in the life of' books, which include stories about nursing homes and elementary schools. One of his early books, *House*, begins with the moment a husband and wife decide to build a new house for their growing family. We meet the architect, the contractor, carpenters, electricians – everyone having anything to do with the conception and construction of the house. In the interim, we learn vividly about the complications, challenges and frustrations of home building from these many different perspectives. The book ends when the family moves into their new house. Thus the frame begins with a dream and ends with the fulfilment of that dream. That's the frame. Every essay has a frame.

'Sounds kind of boring', a student says. 'Every essay put together in a chronology'.

'It *would* be boring if every essay ever written had a "this happened first, this happened last" chronology', I agree, 'but that's not the case. A writer can manipulate time – can start in the middle or even at the very end – and backtrack before working back to the beginning. How many people saw the movie *Forrest Gump*?' Everybody in the room raises a hand. I always use *Forrest Gump* as an example because it has been so eminently popular. 'Where does it start?'

'On a bus stop bench'.

'Yes, Forrest is sitting on a bus stop bench, and he turns to a stranger sitting beside him and starts to tell his life story. We are immediately carried back to his birth and his mom's story. In a little while, we are back at the bus stop bench. Forrest turns in the other direction and he is talking to another stranger – and continuing his story. This happens at least a half-dozen times. It takes half the movie before we work our way back to the present and learn why Forrest is waiting for a bus'.

Writers often move back and forth in time. You can even start at the end and then go back all the way to the beginning to explain how and why your story ended in that particular way. James Baldwin's classic, *Notes of a Native Son*, starts with his father's funeral procession and ends when the procession arrives at the cemetery – twenty minutes later. But it takes Baldwin 15,000 words of background and flashback to get there.

Baldwin's essay was long, but he had a lot to say about racism, poverty, fatherhood and being black in America. And indeed, having a message – saying something to a reader – is very much part of the reason creative nonfiction is going through such an explosion of popularity. This leads to the second creative nonfiction 'F' word: 'focus'. In order for creative nonfiction to be creative nonfiction, it must be framed *and* focused. We get focus when phrases and ideas recur throughout the scenes.

Focus is the second way in which the scenes must be organised. The first 'F' – frame – means organising by time and shape, and the second 'F' – focus – means organising by meaning and content. In order for the scenes to fit together, they must reflect the same or similar focuses.

'And when you put it all together', I tell my students, 'You get creative nonfiction: story and information, style and substance, frame and focus. That's all there is to it'.

It's like this essay, this workshop simulation. I have provided a lot of information about the genre and the classic structure of the creative nonfiction essay. But I have also shaped the presentation in order to make the information more compelling and accessible to the widest possible reading audience. If this works – I mean, if you find this engaging and are still reading – then I have done my job; I have written a compelling and informative chapter for a textbook, and I have had fun in the process. And that's what this genre is all about – engaging the reader, as well as the writer in the writing and reading experience.

References

Baldwin, James (1984), *Notes of a Native Son*, Boston, MA: Beacon Press.

Dillard, Annie (1998), *Pilgrim at Tinker Creek*, London: Harper Perennial.

Kidder, Tracy (1999), *House*, New York: Mariner Books.

Talese, Gay (1995), *Fame and Obscurity*, New York: Ivy Books.

Talese, Gay (2003), *The Gay Talese Reader: Portraits and Encounters*. Introduction by Barbara Lounsberry. New York: Walker Publishing.

Wolfe, Tom (2005), *The Right Stuff*, London: Vintage.

Zemeckis, Robert (1994), *Forrest Gump*.

POETRY

18

Introduction to Poetry

Sean O'Brien

In order to gain the greatest benefit from writing and studying poetry on a postgraduate creative writing course, there are number of matters to be borne in mind and acted on. Some of them are perfectly obvious; some may be completely new to you; and some of them have a significance which may not be immediately apparent. They are discussed under various headings below, but what they have in common is the aim of helping you to see your poems not simply in isolation but in relation to the art of poetry as a whole, its practices, history and traditions. The practising poet needs to occupy several roles, among them those of reader, critic, advocate and, perhaps, performer. We read and write poetry for pleasure – a pleasure intensified by knowledge and understanding. The poet studying on a writing course should feel free – no, should feel obliged – to be imaginatively and intellectually gluttonous. You may never have a better opportunity. Enjoy it!

Suggested reading

Eliot, T. S. (1951), 'Tradition and the Individual Talent', Selected Essays, London: Faber.

Herbert W. N. and Matthew Hollis (eds) (2000), *Strong Words: Modern Poets on Modern Poetry*, Newcastle upon Tyne: Bloodaxe Books.

Preminger Alex and T. V. F Brogan (eds) (1993), *The Princeton Encyclopaedia of Poetry and Poetics*, Princeton: Princeton University Press.

Wandor, Michelene (2003), 'A creative writing manifesto', in Siobhan Holland (ed.), *Creative Writing: A Good Practice Guide*, London: English Subject Centre.

1. Vocation

Only a lunatic or a charlatan would consider poetry as a possible career. It can, however, be a vocation, in the sense of 'a calling', rather than in the present-day sense of an occupation requiring practical training (although writing poetry is, of course, a wholly practical activity). In 1903 the German poet Rainer Maria Rilke (1876–1925) wrote the first of a series of *Letters to a Young Poet*, addressed to a military cadet, Franz Xaver Kappus, in which he tried to answer the young man's questions about poetry and being a poet. Rilke's first letter includes this very famous passage:

> You must seek for whatever it is that obliges you to write … You must confess to yourself whether you would truly die if writing were forbidden to you. This above all: ask yourself in the night, in your most silent hour – *Must* I write? If there is an affirmative reply, if you can simply and starkly answer '*I must*' to that grave question, then you will need to construct your life according to that necessity. (Rilke 2000: 174)

Rilke's words are both stirring and intimidating. Who would not aspire, at least with part of themselves, to satisfy that stern central enquiry? One is also tempted to irreverence: for most of his working life Rilke lived like an aristocrat, that is, without having to make a living, which took care of the construction of life. He lived separately from his wife and took a fairly distant interest in his daughter. Many of us have obligations other than poetry, and we would not willingly neglect them. Yet if writing poetry is to matter to us, if it is to stand at the centre of our imaginative lives, we must make a contract with ourselves to keep its importance in view. We must, in fact, have enough selfishness to go on tending and deepening our interest. Poetry is uncompromising. Rather than take second place, it may simply go away. Many of those undertaking writing courses are returning as mature students, often with family responsibilities. To enrol on an MA is an assertion of freedom which may well require a degree of courage. Yet experience shows, even at this stage, how often and how easily students' interests are pushed aside in favour of other claims. One consequence is frustrated literary development, a fragmentary poetic education in which bad habits go unchallenged and important areas of the poetic repertoire remain unexplored. It is sometimes said that poetry suits a crowded life better than fiction, but the grain of truth such statements might contain is often tainted with an inhibiting modesty about the value of the undertaking, and by formal timidity. The poet must find a *modus vivendi*, a time and a place to work with neither infringement nor the sense that poetry is being privileged beyond its 'real' importance. This remains as true for the poet now as it was for the novelist Virginia Woolf when she wrote 'A Room of One's Own' in 1929.

Suggested reading

Rilke, Rainer Maria (2000), *Sonnets to Orpheus and Letters to a Young Poet*, trans. Stephen Cohn, Manchester: Carcanet.
Woolf, Virginia (1998), *A Room of One's Own*, Morag Shiach (ed.), Oxford: Oxford University Press.

2. The status of poetry

In our time poetry has little cultural prestige. As Dana Gioia puts it, the residual respect for poets is like that accorded 'to priests in a town of agnostics' (Gioia 1992: 1). The reasons for this are complex, but among the most important is poetry's accessibility – not to readers but to writers. It is often said that poetry has more writers than readers. It costs nothing to write a poem, but to make a film or stage an opera is an expensive business, beyond the reach of the amateur. The economic accessibility of poetry to participants is, in a sense, one of its problems. Anyone can have a go. The question is: have a go at what? What do the millions of amateur poets consider themselves to be doing? Somewhere among the motives, though perhaps not named as such, is the idea of self-expression. That self-expression is an undeniable good is a tenet of modern orthodoxy, and this is not the place to dispute it. Applied to poetry, however, self-expression becomes problematic when it is assumed to be identical with artistic success.

The confusion of art with the self is in part an unintended consequence of the late eighteenth- early nineteenth-century Romantic period, when the self of the artist, and his/her interior life, became eminent and urgent matters for poets such as Wordsworth, Coleridge, Keats and Shelley. To the uninstructed, to write of what is 'personal' has gone on being the 'real' task of poetry. The border between poetry *as an art* and related but different activities such as diary-keeping and personal testimony, has ever since been breached in the popular mind; there, authenticity, truth to feeling and the fact that these-events-actually-happened-and-not-only-that-but-they-happened-to-me becomes the final court of artistic appeal, beyond the reach of serious critical authority because true (though rarely beautiful).

By this article of faith, poetry is thus bound up with its creator in an especially privileged way. At its crudest, according to this confusion, to slight the poem is to demean its maker, an attitude which invokes discourses of rights, empowerment and identity, whose concerns are not ultimately with art as art but with the esteem due to the self or the group. Much has been written in recent years from the perspectives of ethnic minorities, feminism and sexual preference. Such political preoccupations are of course an inalienable part of poetry. The problem arises (as with any other interest group, white bourgeois males included) when the fact of making oneself heard is viewed as identical with the creation of art – that is, when craft is subordinate to sincerity. To need to state this so baldly indicates the tenacity of the error.

To have something to say is fundamental to poetry, but subject matter is not the same as art.

Suggested reading

Gioia, Dana (1992), *Can Poetry Matter?* St. Paul: Graywolf Press.
O'Brien, Sean (1998), *The Deregulated Muse: Essays on Contemporary British and Irish Poetry*, Newcastle upon Tyne: Bloodaxe Books.
Paterson, Don (2004), 'The dark art of poetry', London: Poetry Book Society, www.poetrybooks. co.uk

3. The poem

It is in the nature of poetry that the attempt to define a poem remains unfinished. The place to begin is by reading Aristotle's *Poetics* (c. 350 BC), after which there is a vast body of description and analysis from which a number of phrases have entered common usage, including 'emotion recollected in tranquillity', 'memorable speech', 'the best words in the best order', 'no ideas but in things,' 'negative capability', 'objective correlative', 'what oft was thought but ne'er so well expressed' and 'imaginary gardens with real toads in them'. As time passes and as needs and interests shift, new possibilities are added to the store of working definitions. The poems written by the New York poet Frank O'Hara (1926–66) would not have been thinkable for John Milton or William Wordsworth; equally, however, all three poets were writing with an intense consciousness of the *medium* in which they were working – as distinct, that is, from the instrumental, prosaic view of language appropriate to a letter from one lawyer to another, or for supplying instructions for the assembly of a flat-pack bookcase (though these language-uses can also be subverted into poetry). In his poem 'Poetry', O'Hara addresses the art itself, attempting to convey both its immediacy and its emerging historical context:

All this I desire. To
deepen you by my quickness
and delight as if you
were logical and proven,
but still be quiet as if
I were used to you; as if
you would never leave me
and were the inexorable
product of my own time.
(O'Hara 1991: 18)

We can note the conflict from which this poem derives its energy. The poem is an imaginative construction, a set of propositions qualified by the repeated phrase 'as if': the poem is not literally the case, but clearly the poet appears to need to believe that it is and that the poem can bridge the gap between the possible and the actual. And while we note the built-in reservations, we note too that the poem makes present to us possibilities (for example, that 'you would never leave me') even as it seems to deny them. This relationship to fact – which is, to put it mildly, ambiguous – is part of the power of poetry. It appeals to an authority beyond mere literal truthfulness, making present what is not literally there. In the *Poetics* Aristotle drew a distinction between the poet and the historian: 'the one says what has happened, the other the kind of thing that would happen' and goes on: 'For this reason poetry is more philosophical and more serious than history. Poetry tends to express universals, and history particulars' (Aristotle 1996: 16). Poets might want to insist that the way to the universal is through the particular, but otherwise would be pleased to accept this ranking. Sir Philip Sidney in his *Defence of Poetry* (1595) wittily rephrased the poet's privileged condition. The poet he says, cannot lie, since 'he nothing affirmeth, and therefore never lieth . . . Though he recount things not true, yet because he telleth them not for true, he lieth not' (Sidney 1966: 25). Sidney has Plato in mind here: in the *Republic* (written c. 375 BC) the Athenian philosopher (427–347 BC) has Socrates argue that poets must be excluded from the ideal society because they deal in illusions, in imitations (Plato 2003: 335–53). Sidney also suggests that Plato, manifestly far from immune to the pull of art and fiction, was himself a poet (Sidney 1966: 19).

To consider poetry as a power of such an order, capable of unsettling philosophers (and, perhaps more to the point, political rulers) is a useful and heartening corrective to the impression we might gain from the mass of relatively unambitious, frequently and flatly anecdotal poetry to be found in magazines. The misapplied democratising impulse of the times often seems to have shrunk the conception of the poetic to a condition of modesty so extreme as to produce work which is more or less invisible and inaudible. It should be noted that when we speak of modesty we are not speaking of subject matter or length – an epic is not in this respect superior to a brief lyric – but of imaginative compass, the three-dimensional sense of all that is possible for a particular poem to offer through the poet's alertness to image, music, tone and so on. In this sense, a brief, quietly spoken poem such as Edward Thomas's 'Tall Nettles' (Thomas 2004: 111) is an ambitious piece of work, alert to every implication of its material, alert to the power of quietness itself in making the world present to us. A similarly brief poem, William Blake's 'The Sick Rose' (Blake 1997: 216–17), vastly different in tone and address, manages to blend two scales of perception – the cosmically vast, the intimately particular – in a single utterance. Different again is

Sylvia Plath's 'Ariel', a wonderfully compact dramatic lyric rendering a complex sensuous and emotional experience (Plath 1981: 194).

The Greek root of the word poem – *poiesia* – means *making*, an act dependent on artistry, skill, practice and – let it be said – a capacity not merely for taking endless pains but for enduring perpetual dissatisfaction. Our works, for example the poems we write, serve as our judges and give us the measure of ourselves. The court of poetry can be severe in its sentencing. But any poet worth the name is a recidivist.

Suggested reading

Aristotle (1996), *Poetics*, trans. Malcolm Heath, London: Penguin.

Plato, (2003), *Republic*, trans. Desmond Lee, London: Penguin.

Sidney, Philip (1966), *Defence of Poetry*, Jan van Dorsten ed., Oxford: Oxford University Press.

4. Form

Form, which is discussed in detail in W. N. Herbert's essay in the next chapter, is a term so important in poetry as to seem almost synonymous with it. Like poetry itself, form resists ready definition, but it is useful to think of it as a series of fruitful constraints whose function is both to exclude accidents and to provoke them. Rhyme, rhythm and metre, refrains, the stanza, enjambment, local and extended musical effects, all these will come under the heading of form, but form is also difficult to separate from matters such as sentence structure and rhetorical devices involving balance, contrast, amplification and repetition.

Poetic form can be illuminated by a comparison with prose. The fiction of Henry James (1843–1916), for example, is elaborately formal at both local and structural levels: for James, this organising power, applied to the psychology of his characters – which it's hard to resist calling poetic – is what elevates the novel to the status of art. Poetry carries the organising process a stage further, its thematic motifs not merely shaped by, but *coming to being in* the music of verse. Moreover poetry invites or teases the reader to notice (or at times insists upon) formality in action. Though form often works subtly, it can, equally, be a means of display, and of artistic assertion. Form is a source of authority: the octet, the turn, the sestet and the resolution of a sonnet all enforce the poem's persuasive power. Form is a means of memorability, as playground rhymes and football chants indicate. In pre-literate societies, poems for recital were learned with the aid of mnemonic devices whose traces persist in early written poems such as Homer's *Iliad* and *Odyssey* (c.750 BC). Perhaps the first poetic form is the list.

Given that poetry and form are inextricable, the subject creates a surprising degree of unease. Form involves a specific craft skill – the ability to organise words and sounds into patterns of varying complexity – a skill which exists independently of attitude or opinion and cannot simply be supplanted by them. Anthony Hecht puts the matter plainly:

> not a few poets, under the pretext of freeing themselves from the bondage of prosodic and formal considerations, have found ... a convenient way to avoid the very obvious risks entailed by submission to form and meter: unskilled attempts are instantly to be detected, and on these grounds alone it is literally *safer* to play the poetic role of independent radical. (One such radical has recently affirmed that anyone who observes formal constraints is unambiguously a fascist.) (Hecht 2004: 2)

The widespread present-day confusion and ignorance about form provide another example of unintended consequence – in this case, derived from early twentieth-century modernism. When Ezra Pound, T. S. Eliot and others began to employ free verse or *vers libre* they were attempting to overcome a crisis in English poetry, believing that Romanticism had run into the sand, and that its formal methods had lost their imaginative urgency and become merely habitual and decorative. Pound succinctly approved of Eliot's view of free verse, commenting: 'Eliot has said the thing very well when he said, "No *vers* is *libre* for the man who wants to do a good job"' (Pound 1954:12), that is, that free verse is not an *abandonment* of form but, rather, a *version* of form, an addition to the existing repertoire of formal possibilities. Traditional, newly devised, free – whatever form a poem takes, it must be more than an accident, must be able to give an account of itself, even when, as is to be hoped, its effects exceed the poet's deliberate intent.

Lip-service is often paid to form nowadays. The Japanese *haiku* is widely used 'as a form' in a merely arithmetical sense. More elaborately, creative writing students are often encouraged to write villanelles, though there is perhaps no other form as likely to expose the merely mechanical nature of the exercise, not to mention the banality of the content. Form as exercise is only valuable as part of the continuity of writing, not as the arcane requirement of an imaginary examination board which, once satisfied, can be forgotten. If you want to write villanelles you should study versions of the form such as Auden's 'Miranda's Song' from *The Sea and the Mirror* (Auden 1991: 421) and variations such as William Empson's 'Missing Dates', 'Success' and 'The Teasers' (Empson 2000: 79, 80, 86) before, or perhaps instead of, embarking on your own attempts. Similar reservations apply to the sestina. It is altogether more urgent to be able to master writing in iambic metre, to control a passage of blank verse, to be at ease with ballad form, with couplets, quatrains and sestets, to develop an accurate ear not just for stress and syllable count but for effective combinations of sound, and to understand how free verse alludes, directly or by contrast, to the forms from which it departs. At the same time, as a poet you need to develop an understanding of the powers and consequences of sentence structure, which is certainly as important (even when fragmentary) in poetry as in prose but which, like verse form, is often ignored or uneasily evaded.

Suggested reading

Donaghy, Michael (1999), *Wallflowers: a Lecture with Missing Notes and Additional Heckling*, London: The Poetry Society.

Carper, Thomas and Derek Attridge (2003), *Meter and Meaning*, London: Routledge.

Hecht, Anthony (2004), 'On Rhyme', and 'The Music of Form' in *Melodies Unheard: Essays on the Mysteries of Poetry*, Baltimore: Johns Hopkins University Press.

Hollander, John (1981), *Rhyme's Reason: A Guide to English Verse*, New Haven: Yale University Press.

Pound, Ezra (1954), 'A Retrospect' in *Selected Literary Essays*, T. S. Eliot (ed.), London: Faber.

Wainwright, Jeffrey (2004), *Poetry: The Basics*, London: Routledge.

5. Analysing

Diverse experiences and attitudes mean that some of you will be comfortably accustomed to the academic context; others will be returning after long absence; yet others may be coming to the setting for the first time. For a significant proportion of each of these rough groupings, along with the students' identification of themselves as writers there comes, in many cases, suspicion and fear of 'academic' approaches, of analysis and reasoned criticism, of a tendency to 'kill' material by 'dissecting' it. If you intend to write poetry seriously you will need to recognise these fears as hindrances to the development of your work, and that they can be outgrown and shed. If it is true that, as Wallace Stevens puts it in 'Man Carrying Thing', 'The poem must resist the intelligence / Almost successfully' (Stevens 1984: 350), the effort and the pleasure of understanding, with all the nuances which the word 'understanding' carries, form a major part of reading poetry. Our love of poems – a love, if we're lucky, which is formed in childhood – may begin in a mixture of fascination, uncertainty and recognition, and a desire to follow this creature further into the wood, to learn its names and its habits. Reading as adults can intensify such pleasures by opening the question of *how* the poem exerts its effect on us. Its meaning is inseparable from its method. Sound effects, rhythm, timing, imagery, sentence structure, figures of speech, allusiveness, and all that comes under the heading of poetic gesture, are all working parts of the poem, and what they work on is the reader. T. S. Eliot was right to attribute to poetry the power to communicate before it is understood (Eliot 1951: 238); the task of the poet-as-reader, though, is to value and enrich that communication by enquiring into its methods – without expecting ever to exhaust the enquiry.

It is not true to say that only poets can write about poetry, but the critical writing and informal observations of poets on their art are often among the most interesting and illuminating, perhaps because they arise from the poets' efforts to clarify or justify their own practice, or to solve problems with which the poetry has presented them. Such writing is historically situated but remains at the core of discussion about poetry. We could go back to Sidney's *Defence of Poetry* and work – very selectively – forward through Johnson's *Lives of the Poets*, Wordsworth's *Preface to Lyrical Ballads*, Keats's letters, Coleridge's *Biographia Literaria*, the essays of Eliot, Pound, William Empson and W. H. Auden, Elizabeth Bishop's letters, Randall Jarrell's reviews, the essays of Seamus Heaney and Tom Paulin and many others.

Suggested reading

Scully, James (ed.) (1966), *Modern Poets on Modern Poetry*, London: Collins.
Hamburger, Michael (1970), *The Truth of Poetry*, London: Penguin.

6. Reading

In her crisp and practical 'Creative Writing Manifesto', Michelene Wandor is surely correct to state that one of the primary purposes of undergraduate creative writing courses – and this applies equally to postgraduate courses – is 'to create more hungry readers' (Wandor 2003: 13). For many of you, reading will prove to be the most important and permanently influential part of the course. It is essential for you to read as widely as possible, not simply among contemporary or modern poets but in the whole tradition of poetry in English and in the poetic traditions of other languages too. Clearly, this is not a finite project, but that fact should reduce it neither to a hobby nor an option. Experience indicates that even strongly committed postgraduate students may in fact have read very little and that what they have read is often narrowly confined to the contemporary. There may also be resistance to items of required reading, on the grounds of difficulty, unfamiliarity or alleged 'irrelevance'. These terms have become part of the informal orthodoxy (formerly known as cant) of the age. Before sitting down to write this paragraph, I heard a BBC Radio 4 continuity announcer explaining that the next programme would be about *Macbeth*. My interest turned to gloom when she went on to say that the task of the director was 'to make the play relevant and accessible to a modern audience'. How strange that the play had survived 400 years without such assistance. The challenge (and the pleasure, the more intense for being at times hard-won) is to equip ourselves to read poetry, not to adjust poetry to our limitations. As Robert Frost put it, 'A poem is best written in the light of all the other poems ever written. We read A the better to read B (we have to start somewhere; we may get very little out of A). We read B the better to read C, C the better to read D, D the better to go back and get something out of A. Progress is not the aim, but circulation' (Frost 1966: 97).

Suggested reading

Keegan, Paul (ed.) (2005), *The Penguin Book of English Verse*, London: Penguin.
Ferguson, Margaret Mary Jo Salter and John Stallworthy (eds) (1996), *The Norton Anthology of Poetry*, New York: F. W. Norton.
Padel, Ruth (2002), *52 Ways of Looking at a Poem*, London: Chatto and Windus.
Ricks, Christopher (ed.) (1999), *The Oxford Book of English Verse*, Oxford: Oxford University Press.

7. Company

Douglas Dunn's poem 'The Friendship of Young Poets' opens: 'There must have been more than just one of us, / But we never met' and adds 'My youth was as private / As the bank at midnight' (Dunn 1986: 38). It is natural to seek the company of the like-minded. Those coming to postgraduate writing courses have often been members of workshops before and now seek a more formal setting in which to develop their work. The university may – in fact, should – also supply new and fruitful informal groupings. As well as sharing a literary passion, most poets need mutual support, acknowledgment and the recognition of their peers. It is worth being careful and demanding about the company you keep. Just as the border between poetry and testimony has been smudged, so in workshops the distinction between criticism and therapy is sometimes lost. There is a fear of giving and receiving offence, and often this is accompanied by a vague, impressionistic way of discussing poems, heavy on affirmation, light on explanatory detail and the examination of technique. Michelene Wandor offers a succinct account of an approach which begins in the classroom but should extend into informal workshops:

> Work to develop a critical vocabulary which outlaws all subjectivist responses: 'I like', 'I dislike', 'I prefer': all distract from the analytical process. Value judgements, if used at all, should be left to the END of the analytical process. I have found that if illuminating and exciting textual analysis takes place, value judgements effectively become unnecessary. This doesn't mean that anything goes; rather, it constantly recreates a notion of the use of 'criticism', as a meaningful analytical process, which leads to understanding why certain approaches to writing work better than others, and thus encourages good practice. Notions such as 'positive' or 'negative' criticism, which accrue as correlatives to premature value judgement, thus also become irrelevant. (Wandor 2003: 14)

If only it were so simple in practice! But Wandor's severe clarity is bracing. She has no time for notions of writing as therapy or comfort, or for cosy mutual support. What she demands, without making it explicit, is that the poet be able to consider the poem as a work separate from the self, with its own life to live. This is, of course, extremely difficult, and the difficulty is by no means confined to novices.

8. Audience

In fact, the people that students of writing are most keen to meet are not others like themselves, but publishers, agents, producers and anyone else with access to the business. The economics of poetry, as I suggested earlier, are relatively constrained, but the anxiety to publish is at least as powerful among poets as among novelists – perhaps because for most poets publication is likely to have to be its own reward. Writers want readers and audiences, understandably. The problem arises when public readings and publications are assumed to be proof of quality in themselves. In this respect there are districts of poetry which at times resemble the sub-cultural worlds of some kinds of genre fiction or music, existing beyond the reach of general interest or serious critical scrutiny – and intended, indeed, to occupy such a place of safety. It's a free country; people may treat their work as they choose, but the real challenge of finding and addressing an audience is more exacting. Moreover, an indifferent MA in Writing is not infrequently used as a credential for teaching writing, which helps to perpetuate a cycle of mediocrity. Go where the difficulty is – the best magazine, the strenuous workshop, the impossible publisher.

9. Activities

In his essay 'The Poet and the City' W. H. Auden imagined a poetic academy where the students would engage in activities such as learning poetry by heart, the study of ancient and modern languages, translation, parody, cooking, care of a domestic animal and the cultivation of a garden (Auden 1963: 77). The emphasis would be on *doing* what may not come easily, since originality can, in a sense, take care of itself. As indicated earlier, basic forms need to be acquired. For blank verse read Shakespeare, Milton, Wordsworth; for ballads see the Border Ballads and modern exemplars such as Auden and Louis Simpson; for sonnets you might begin with Don Paterson's anthology *101 Sonnets* (1999). More tailored workshop activities need to produce a friction between habit and challenge – to make you look again at fundamentals such as careful observation and the influence of sentence construction; to enhance your sense of the *dramatic*, three-dimensional possibilities of poetry; to offer specific technical challenges.

1. Just the facts, Ma'am

Read Edwin Morgan's 'Glasgow March 1971' from the sequence 'Instamatic Poems' (Morgan 1996: 217). Attempt a similar brief factual presentation of a single event without commentary. Then read 'Ellingham Suffolk January 1972' (223) from the same sequence and consider how depiction crosses over into suggestion and interpretation. Follow this by reading August Kleinzahler's 'Snow in North Jersey', Carol Ann Duffy's 'Prayer', Douglas Dunn's 'The River Through the City' and Elizabeth Bishop's 'The Bight'. One of the most powerful symbolic properties is *the fact*.

2. The rules

Use postcard reproductions of paintings, photographs, movie posters, wartime propaganda posters, advertisement, etc. Assume that each card contains the equivalent of a movie trailer for an entire world, consistent in every way with what is shown on the card. Devise a set of rules – one sentence for each – governing this world. These can be commands, prohibitions and statements of fact. Now write a poem in the first person from the point of view of an inhabitant of this world (that is, write a dramatic monologue). Only one topic is forbidden: you must not specifically refer to the rules. You may prefer to exchange cards and rules with another member of the group. Read Robert Browning, 'My Last Duchess', Philip Larkin, 'Livings' and Charlotte Perkins Gilman's story 'The Yellow Wallpaper'.

3. The Poem Noir

Parody and popular cultural references are significant elements in contemporary poetry. See Alice Notley's 'A California Girlhood' and, for our present purpose, Charles Simic's 'Private Eye'. The aim of this activity is to explore and take possession of a prominent example – the intimately related hardboiled crime novel and Hollywood film noir.

The Poem Noir Manifesto

'To make a movie only takes a girl and a gun'. – Jean-Luc Godard

1. It is alleged that the demands of contemporary life prevent people having time to read – in particular the classics of nineteenth- and early twentieth-century fiction. Students of literature, for example, are often heard to say this.

2. It is alleged that the visible image film, video, digital art – has displaced the written word in the affections of the world: the triumph of passivity.

3. It is alleged that *film noir* of the 1940s and 1950s is the most *poetic* of film genres because of the unity of form and content on which it depends, and because, too, of the secret artistry of writers, directors and cameramen working in the world of the B movie.

4. It is alleged that of the surviving written genres the crime novel is among the most enduring. Praise of such novels is often framed in approving comparisons with *film noir*.

5. It is alleged by the poet X that the best day's work he ever did was writing the back cover blurb for a paperback reissue of a hardboiled crime novel. There is, he argued, a poetics of the blurb – economy, vocabulary, tone, a particular realm of detail and suggestion – which might assure such work the status of a secret art, a poem read by the many.

6. It is alleged that we must adapt or die.

7. Therefore let us write the secret poem that all the world will read.

8. Let it take the form of a blurb – which is to say a combination of synopsis and evocation.

9. Let it exploit the language and style of *film noir* and the hardboiled crime novel to reclaim the world for poetry.

10. Let this *poem noir* be laid out like a poem (no one will notice).

11. When people read nothing, they will still read blurbs.

Examples of Existing Blurbs

Dashiell Hammett – The Maltese Falcon (1930)

Sam Spade is hired by the fragrant Miss Wonderley to track down her sister, who has eloped with a louse called Floyd Thursby. But Miss Wonderley is in fact the beautiful and treacherous Brigid O'Shaughnessy, and when Spade's partner Miles Archer is shot while on Thursby's trail, Spade finds himself both hunter and hunted: can he track down the jewel-encrusted bird, a treasure worth killing for, before the Fat Man finds him?

James M. Cain – Double Indemnity (1936)
Walter Huff is an insurance investigator like any other until the day he meets the beautiful and dangerous Phyllis Nirdlinger . . .

Manda Scott – No Good Deed (2002)
Orla McLeod knows too much for her own good. She knows about pain, she knows about guilt and she knows about survival . . . There's no way Orla McLeod's going to let anyone else take care of Jamie Buchanan. Not when Jamie's the sole witness to Tord Svensen committing an act of savagery of the kind that's rapidly turning him into one of the most feared criminals in Europe . . .

Kenneth Fearing – The Big Clock (1946)
George Stroud is a charming, yet amoral executive working for a magazine empire run by Earl Janoth. Stroud embarks on a dangerous affair with Janoth's mistress and when Janoth kills the woman, Stroud is the only witness who can pin him to the crime. The catch is that Janoth does not know that the man he saw in a shadowy street was Stroud – and he gives Stroud the job of tracking down the witness.

James Hadley Chase – You've Got It Coming (1955)
'The world is made up of smart guys who get rich and suckers who stay poor', Harry Griffin tells his girl friend, Glorie. 'I've been a sucker too long, now I'm going to be smart'.

4. Revisions

One of the hardest things to do is to manage the revision of your poems in a sufficiently detached way. There may be parts that, while immensely appealing, should be sacrificed for the greater good. Read A. E. Housman's 'Tell Me Not Here, It Needs Not Saying' and Louis MacNeice's 'Meeting Point'. Argue the case for removing one stanza from each.

5. Restorations

Tone and register are vital features of poetry. To recognise what is apt, to marry art and feeling in the gradient of a poem, to have the sense of imaginative hinterland – a poem will falter if these obligations are not met. Translation, and related activities such as restoration, can help develop our understanding and control of these factors.

Restore the missing parts of this text. It is thought to consist of six three-line stanzas, of which there survive: the first; a fragment of the first line of the second; the second and third lines of the fourth; and the first and second lines of the fifth.

> When I see the silver
>   Coiling waterways
>   Like necklaces detached
>
> From throats
>   Please God no
>   Calm or oblivion
>
> Will occupy my heart,
>   Or close it. Listen . . .

The original can be found in Christopher Middleton (trans.) (2000), *Faint Harps and Silver Voices: Selected Translations*.

6. English is a foreign language

Style is double-edged, offering both authority and entrapment. We sometimes need to go out and come in again. Imagine that English is a foreign language to you, which you must translate into your own tongue. We begin with two medieval examples. N. B. avoid reading any glossary which accompanies the poems.

Example 1
Erthe tok of erthe
   Erthe with wogh;
Erthe other erthe
   To the erthe drogh;
Erthe leyde erthe
   In erthene through;
Tho hevede erthe of erthe
   Erthe ynogh.
          Anonymous, 1300–50

Example 2
Gloria mundi est:
Alse a se flouwende
Als a skiye pasende
Als the sadwe in the undermel
And als the dore turnet on a quell.
          Anonymous, 1300–50

Example 3
Supply a second, decisive stanza for this example:
I am the ancient Apple-Queen,
As once I was so am I now.
For evermore a hope unseen,
Betwixt the blossom and the bough.
        (? 1891)

Example 4
Attempt a translation of William Empson's 'Let it Go'.

(The first two poems can be found in *The Penguin Book of English Verse*, edited by Paul Keegan. Avoid reading the glosses until you have completed the activity. The last two poems can be found in *The Oxford Book of English Verse*, edited by Christopher Ricks, 1999).

7. Line-breaks

1. List as many factors influencing line-breaks as you can think of. Then apply your list to the passage from T. S Eliot's 'Burnt Norton' IV, lines 1–10, beginning 'Time and the bell have buried the day'.

2. Ask a colleague to supply two anonymous pieces – one a free verse poem printed as prose, the other a prose poem. Decide which is the conventionally lineated poem and supply the line-endings.

8. *The prose poem*

1. Read and discuss the following: Rimbaud, from *Les Illuminations*, xli 'Jeunesse', in French and in parallel translation by Oliver Bernard; Zbigniew Herbert, 'To Take Objects Out', translated by John and Bogdana Carpenter; Francis Ponge, 'La Valise', in French and as translated by John Montague.
2. Write a suite of three prose poems – one about a city, one about a room, one about an object.

9. *Sentences*

1. The group divides in half.
2. The members of one half each write four lines in iambic pentameter taking the form of a command. At the same time, the members of the other half each write four lines in iambic pentameter in the form of a question.
3. When the pieces are written, the members of each half-group exchange work with the other half-group.
4. On a separate piece of paper, those who wrote the commands each reply to the questions with four lines each of iambic pentameter in the form of a single sentence.
5. On a separate piece of paper, those who wrote the questions each reply to the commands with four lines of iambic pentameter in the form of a single sentence riposte.

10. *Ways in*

A miscellany of possibilities which may stimulate your work.

1. A recipe
2. Instructions for how to get there
3. The Best Man's speech
4. The verdict of the court
5. Exchanges in the Personal Column
6. Last Will and Testament
7. A Christmas Round Robin
8. A review of a book of poems
9. How to use this equipment
10. Instructions for an original activity at a poetry workshop
11. A manifesto
12. Dear John
13. A curse
14. A prayer
15. This news just in . . .
16. A history of Spengler, Traum and Bubo Ltd

17. Blankness!
18. Sex Tips for Dead People
19. What I Always Say
20. I wouldn't mind, except
21. Acceptance speech
22. Hagiography
23. Welcome to Xenograd: a guide for visitors
24. Oh, look, darling: lots of giant crabs
25. An epitaph

Suggested reading

Keegan, Paul (2005), *The Penguin Book of English Verse*, London: Penguin.
Ricks, Christopher (1999), *The Oxford Book of English Verse*, Oxford: Oxford University Press.
Sweeney, Matthew and John Hartley Williams (1996), *Writing Poetry and Getting Published*, London: Hodder.
Twichell, Chase and Robin Behn (2002), *The Practice of Poetry: Writing Exercises by Poets Who Teach*, New York: HarperCollins.

10. Conclusion

1. A poem is not an explanation but an event.
2. Consider language not as a vehicle for transporting meaning but as the place in which meaning is constituted.
3. The literal truthfulness of a poem is not an aesthetic defence of it.
4. Form is not a container. It is a creator.
5. 'Relevance' is a term of use to administrators, not to poets. The 'real world' is frequently mentioned, but its proponents never go there.
6. 'Gesang ist Dasein' – 'Singing is Being' – (Rilke 2000: 18–19)
7. 'I have come up with a proposal as to why poetry seems difficult for readers of literature in general. In prose you can say that your main purpose is *telling*. In poetry it is *making*. A poem is analogous to a painting, a piece of sculpture or a musical composition. Its material is language, and often that language will be almost mosaically fitted together, with words as the pieces of the mosaic. A novel, an essay and a TV sit-com also use words but without the oppressive need to honour them outside their utility in conveying meaning and feeling. These are turbulent waters: poetry is charged with meaning and feeling also, but first it has to satisfy the turbulence of its hope . . . as we write the poem we pitch it both forward into existence and backwards to its need to exist.' (Peter Porter, 'The poet's quarrel with poetry' [Porter 1998: 171–2])

In 'Musée Des Beaux Arts' Auden writes that the ship in Breughel's painting 'The Fall of Icarus' 'Had somewhere to get to and sailed calmly on' (Auden 1991: 179). Where is there to get to in poetry? Though we may take degrees in writing it, poetry does not consist of a series of qualifications. Nothing of poetry is ever finished: the challenge of writing poetry, of studying it, and of serving it as a reader, extends perpetually, and should be accepted in the light of that fact. In the same way, the pleasures intensify and the discoveries extend without limit.

References

Aristotle (1996), *Poetics*, trans. Malcolm Heath, London: Penguin.

Auden, W. H. (1963), *The Dyer's Hand and Other Essays*, London: Faber.

Auden, W. H. (1991), *Collected Poems*, Edward Mendelson (ed.), London: Faber.

Bishop, Elizabeth (1983), *Complete Poems 1927–79*, London: Chatto and Windus.

Blake, William (1997), *Complete Poems*, Alicia Ostriker (ed.), London: Penguin.

Browning, Robert (2005), *The Major Works*, Adam Roberts and Daniel Karlin (eds), Oxford: Oxford University Press.

Carper, Thomas, and Derek Attridge (2003), *Meter and Meaning*, London: Routledge.

Coleridge, Samuel Taylor (2000), *The Major Works*, H. J. Jackson (ed.), Oxford: Oxford University Press.

Donaghy, Michael (1999), *Wallflowers: a Lecture with Missing Notes and Additional Heckling*, London: The Poetry Society.

Duffy, Carol Ann (1994), *Selected Poems*, London: Penguin.

Dunn, Douglas (1986), *Selected Poems 1964–83*, London: Faber.

Eliot, T. S. (1951), *Selected Essays*, London: Faber.

Eliot, T. S. (1963), *Collected Poems*, London: Faber.

Empson, William (2000), *The Complete Poems*, John Haffenden, ed., London: Allen Lane.

Ferguson, Margaret, Mary Jo Salter and John Stallworthy (eds) (1996), *The Norton Anthology of Poetry*, New York: F. W. Norton.

Frost, Robert (1966), 'The Prerequisites' in *Selected Prose of Robert Frost*, Hyde Cox and Edward Connery Lathem (eds), Austin: Holt, Rinehart, Winston.

Gilman, Charlotte Perkins (2003), 'The Yellow Wallpaper' in Joyce Carol Oates (ed.), *The Oxford Book of American Short Stories*, Oxford: Oxford University Press.

Gioia, Dana (1992), *Can Poetry Matter?* St Paul: Graywolf Press.

Hamburger, Michael (1970), *The Truth of Poetry*, London: Penguin.

Heaney, Seamus (2003), *Finders Keepers: Selected Prose 1971–2001*, London: Faber.

Hecht, Anthony (2004), *Melodies Unheard: Essays on the Mysteries of Poetry*, Baltimore: Johns Hopkins University Press.

Herbert, W. N. and Matthew Hollis (eds) (2000), *Strong Words: Modern Poets on Modern Poetry*, Newcastle upon Tyne: Bloodaxe Books.

Herbert, Zbigniew (1977), trans. John Carpenter and Bogdana Carpenter, *Selected Poems*, Oxford: Oxford University Press.

Hollander, John (1981), *Rhyme's Reason: A Guide to English Verse*, New Haven: Yale University Press.

Housman, A.E. (1997), *Collected Poems*, Archie Burnett (ed.), Oxford: Oxford University Press.

Johnson, Samuel (2000), *The Major Works*, Donald Greene (ed.), Oxford: Oxford University Press.

Keats, John (2002), *The Selected Letters of John Keats*, Robert Gittings (ed.), Oxford: Oxford University Press.

Keegan, Paul (ed.) (2005), *The Penguin Book of English Verse*, London: Penguin.

Kleinzahler, August (1995), *Red Sauce, Whisky and Snow*, London: Faber.

Larkin, Philip (1988), *Collected Poems*, Anthony Thwaite (ed.), London: Faber.

MacNeice, Louis (2003), *Collected Poems*, Peter MacDonald (ed.), London: Faber.

Middleton, Christopher (trans.) (2000), *Faint Harps and Silver Voices: Selected Translations*, Manchester: Carcanet Press.

Milton, John (2003), *The Major Works*, Stephen Orgel and Jonathan Goldeberg (eds), Oxford: Oxford University Press.

Morgan, Edwin (1996), *Collected Poems*, Manchester: Carcanet Press.

Notley, Alice (1994), 'A California Girlhood', in *Postmodern American Poetry*, Paul Hoover (ed.), New York: F. W. Norton.

O'Brien, Sean (1998), *The Deregulated Muse: Essays on Contemporary British and Irish Poetry*, Newcastle upon Tyne: Bloodaxe Books.

O'Hara, Frank (1991), *Selected Poems*, Donald M. Allen (ed.), Manchester: Carcanet Press.

Padel, Ruth (2002), *52 Ways of Looking at a Poem*, London: Chatto and Windus.

Paterson, Don (1999), *101 Sonnets from Shakespeare to Heaney*, London: Faber.

Paterson, Don (2004), 'The dark art of poetry', London: Poetry Book Society, www.poetrybooks.co.uk

Paulin, Tom (1997), *Writing to the Moment: Selected Critical Essays 1980–95*, London: Faber.

Plath, Sylvia (1981), *Collected Poems*, London: Faber.

Plato (2003), *Republic*, trans. Desmond Lee, London: Penguin.

Ponge, Francis (1998), *Selected Poems*, Margaret Guiton (ed.), Margaret Guiton, John Montague, and C. K. Williams (trans.), London: Faber.

Porter, Peter (2001), *Saving from the Wreck*, Nottingham: Nottingham Trent University.

Pound, Ezra (1954), *Selected Literary Essays*, T. S. Eliott, ed., London: Faber.

Preminger, Alex, and T. V. F. Brogan (1993), *The Princeton Encyclopaedia of Poetry and Poetics*, New Jersey: Princeton University Press.

Ricks, Christopher (ed.) (1999), *The Oxford Book of English Verse*, Oxford: Oxford University Press.

Rilke, Rainer Maria (2000), *Sonnets to Orpheus and Letters to a Young Poet*, trans. Stephen Cohn, Manchester: Carcanet.

Rimbaud, Arthur (1962), *Collected Poems*, Oliver Bernard, trans., London: Penguin.

Scully, James (ed.) (1966), *Modern Poets on Modern Poetry*, London: Collins.

Shelley, Percy Bysshe (2003), *The Major Works*, Zachary Leader and Michael O'Neill (eds), Oxford: Oxford University Press.

Sidney, Philip (1966), *Defence of Poetry*, Jan Van Dorsten (ed.), Oxford: Oxford University Press.

Simic, Charles (1999), *Jackstraws*, London: Faber.

Simpson, Louis (2003), *The Owner of the House: New Collected Poems 1940–2001*, Rochester: Boa Editions.

Stevens, Wallace (1984), *Collected Poems*, London: Faber.

Sweeney, Matthew and John Hartley Williams (1996), *Writing Poetry and Getting Published*, London: Hodder.

Thomas, Edward (2004), *Collected Poems*, London: Faber.

Twichell, Chase, and Robin Behn (2002), *Poetry in Practice: Exercises by Poets Who Teach*, New York: HarperCollins.

Wandor, Michelene (2003), 'A creative writing manifesto', in Siobhan Holland (ed.), *Creative Writing: A Good Practice Guide*, London: English Subject Centre.

Wainwright, Jeffrey (2004), *Poetry: The Basics*, London: Routledge.

Woolf, Virginia [1929] (1998), *A Room of One's Own*, Morag Shiach (ed.), Oxford: Oxford University Press.

Wordsworth, William (2000), *The Major Works*, Stephen Gill (ed.), Oxford: Oxford University Press.

19

What is Form?

W. N. Herbert

Iambic pentameter. There now, I've said it. Please form an orderly queue to flee from this chapter. What other two words in the poetry world excite such intimidation, boredom, cantankerousness and, yes, passion? (Though 'reluctantly rejecting' or 'talentless guff' may come close.) 'Iambic pentameter' gives off the musty scent of the academy, with perhaps a topnote of formaldehyde – it's Greek, for God's sake, though apparently not in the way 'ouzo meze parakalo' is Greek. And it functions as shorthand for a host of terrors: metre, stress, stanza, and above all, form. Form consists of all the structural conventions within which most poetry in English has been written inside and outside the last hundred years. It is to the aspiring practitioner of literature as theory is to its critic. It is also the undisputed hero of this essay, even if it is an abstraction.

Whether you are a new writer approaching this issue for the first time, a resolute anti-formalist, or someone in their seventh year of fruitless struggle with the trochee, you are haunted by form. If you haven't got to grips with it, says that over-familiar inner voice, then you're not serious about this whole poetry business. If your inner voice happens to be Baudelaire, he's even blunter: 'I pity the poets who are guided solely by instinct; they seem to me incomplete' (Auden 1987: 53).

If you go to writers' groups, you'll find that form bores proliferate with their coronets of sonnets or praise of the amphibrachic foot. You'll also find their opposites are just as bonkers about their anti-academic performance schtick, their aleatoric principles for generating text, or their Old Believers-type devotion to the ampersand. The temptation to shrug it off, to keep shrugging it off, seems entirely natural; to concentrate instead on the intricate, careful work of giving each poem its own combination of music and structure, according to one's own principles of rhythm and discipline. To keep verse, as the vernacular has it, free.

This essay tries to present both what form is, and the arguments for its use, in as clear a way as possible, in order to encourage you to engage with it if you haven't, and to reconsider it if you have. Because they are just that, arguments for form, it cannot claim to be impartial, and I suspect it won't entirely avoid the perils of the form bore. But I will attempt to confront the phantom, and to articulate the principles which might be behind that inner voice.

My own practice as a writer is to use form and various types of free verse (and indeed anything else that seems to work), depending on the demands of the given poem. My conviction, after the usual years of obscure struggle, is that the two types of writing are not in implacable opposition, but rather shade into each other in ways that demand closer study. My final assessment is, first, that all poetry is more or less consciously in a form; and, secondly, that consciously formal writing is, in certain cases, simply able to do more than what we think of as free verse. It does more in terms of the numbers of levels it functions on – particularly in terms of the types of allusion it can make – and it frequently does this more succinctly. Of course the same can also be argued about free verse in particular instances, but I will try to prove that this generally occurs because of principles we only discover through the study of form; that we can only say something meaningful about how such poems work using the language of form.

Writing poetry is very much about engaging the senses, especially the ear, and perhaps the most basic thing we can say about form is that it too is firmly based in auditory perception. Just as you hear musical patterns in words as the vowels and consonants combine in assonances and consonances, so too you can hear the stresses in ordinary conversation form rhythmic patterns. Just as you can arrange the sounds into interesting shapes, so too you can arrange the beats. Indeed, just as in music, the melodiousness or otherwise of poetry is largely dependent on our manipulation of its rhythms.

And just as in music, you can have an instinct for these things, in which case metre can seem too obvious to worry about, or even just a tool of the trade, a mode of notation. Or you must work to hear rhythms, and work harder still to note them down. Neither position is 'correct', neither is permanent (poets can both lose and refine their sense of rhythm), and neither is proper justification for any argument for or against form.

So the first thing every writer has to learn to do is listen, both to themselves and to other writers. 'Listening' means reading yourself and other poets with pen in hand, trying to hear if there are specific recurrent rhythmic patterns in their verse (and whether there should be in yours), and, if so, finding a simple way of marking these down.

Books about metre will supply you not only with bewildering explanations of the straightforward phenomenon of stress, but will also provide rather too many ways of indicating it. Philip Hobsbaum, for example, rather relishes telling us there are four different levels of stress according to the Trager-Smith notation (Hobsbaum 1996: 7) – about as helpful to the rookie ear as being told there are four tones in spoken Chinese. The succession of marks suggested by Thomas Carper and Derek Attridge are so complex you may feel they are sending you subliminal messages in some kind of manga cartoon shorthand (Carper and Attridge 2003: 19–41). So let's not add to the confusion: whatever you go for, keep it simple.

What I go for is ˘ above an unstressed syllable, and ´ above a stressed syllable, and | to divide one group of these off from the next. (If it helps, you could vocalise ˘ as a light 'duh' noise, and ´ as a heavier 'dum'. | doesn't need a sound.) The word 'syllable', for instance, would be sýllăblĕ (dum duh duh). This is what most poets do who aren't nutters (and a few who are). Every word can be analysed for stressed or unstressed syllables ('stréssed' is always stressed, whereas the 'ĕr' in 'either' isn't). The stress patterns of most words are fixed by usage; others can be stressed or unstressed according to context: the 'or' in 'stressed or unstressed' isn't stressed; but it's possible to say 'OR, we could just let him go', and place a lot of emphasis on that first syllable. It's a matter of listening carefully.

What people are doing when they use words like 'iamb' and 'trochee' is straightforward: they're noticing the recurrent shapes that stresses fall into, and they're giving them names. Helpfully in Greek. 'Noticing', not 'imposing': all English is stress-based, and an iamb is a unit for indicating this. We call these units 'feet', which at least indicates their purpose is to get us somewhere.

This act of noticing is what Wordsworth was on about when he said: 'The only strict antithesis to Prose is Metre; nor is this, in truth, a *strict* antithesis; because lines and passages of metre so naturally occur in writing prose, that it would be scarcely possible to avoid them, even were it desirable' (Wordsworth 1994: 439–40). Notice how Wordsworth is quite strict about being strict, because what he's talking about isn't, strictly speaking, a stricture. It's a description.

Iambs describe what we do when we say 'coŭrgéttes': we go duh dum. Trochees depict us saying 'frŷĭng' (dum duh). There are lots of other combinations (anapaests go ˘˘´ (duh duh dum), or 'ĭn á pán'; dactyls go ´˘˘ (dum duh duh), or 'gárlĭckў'), but the crucial thing to spot is that they do this whether we notice them or not. If we rejigged those examples, and ran them together with a divider between each foot, they'd go

> gárlĭckў | coŭrgéttes, | frŷĭng | ĭn â pán.

I know, it's not a great line, but it shows how natural patterns of stress can be gently adjusted into form. Having read it, being an obsessive, I'm strongly inclined to rearrange it as two lines with two stresses in each.

> gárlĭckў coŭrgéttes,
> frŷĭng ĭn ă pán.

Now I've taken those dividers out you can see and hear the two phrases are rhythmically parallel. The line break helps to make that clear. So iambs, trochees, anapaests and dactyls are descriptors. Their only job is to help us hear rhythms clearly, and their interaction with the poetic line is the thing that sets rhythms – even workaday normal rhythms like these – into patterns. And rhythmic patterns are the rudiments of form. (By the way, that 'in' in the second line is one of those instances where usage could make the stress slightly stronger: 'frŷĭng ín ă pán'. What do you think?)

The simplest way to attune the ear to metric feet is to find and create examples of them. Next time you find yourself admiring what someone has said, whether in conversation or in a newspaper, or a book, a film, or a TV programme, write it down. Analyse it for stress; see if you can find out if your admiration had to do with its rhythm. See if you can write something else in the same rhythm, and whether you like that imitative statement too. And next time you write up a shopping list, try arranging the items into groups according to their metric structure: it may not help you navigate the supermarket, but it might help prove how built into our daily lives these little rhythmic units actually are.

So far so simplistic, but the repercussions of this kind of observation are important: form is not something imposed on language, it is derived from something naturally arising within it. So by the simple act of listening attentively, we can perceive rudiments of form in any piece of writing. Equally, by overlooking the essentially stress-based patterns of English, we can fail to see how closely form is linked to speech, and thereby the central error of the formal verse/free verse schism comes into being.

When people think of metre, line and stanza as carapaces, shapes into which language must be forced, where it sits the way an invertebrate's flesh is contained in a shell, they lose connection with the rhythmic roots of speech. When they write free verse and think of themselves as cracking the old moulds in which words used to be straitjacketed, they overlook the pattern-building facility which drives all verse from nursery rhymes to renga, from the ballad to the calligramme. In other words they assume that a metrical writer has divided structure from content, whereas their proper practice is to unite these in a unique event.

A writer who managed to express some of the functions of form succinctly was, perhaps unexpectedly, Robert Louis Stevenson. Writing in a period when conventional assumptions about verse were being challenged by French prose poems like those of Baudelaire, and America's more rhetoric-driven structures, typified by Whitman, and being familiar with the experiments in free verse of his close friend W. E. Henley, Stevenson showed himself sympathetic to both innovation and tradition:

> Verse may be rhythmical; it may be merely alliterative; it may, like the French, depend wholly on the (quasi) regular recurrence of the rhyme; or, like the Hebrew, it may consist in the strangely fanciful device of repeating the same idea. It does not matter on what principle the law is based, so it be a law. It may be pure convention; it may have no inherent beauty; all that we have a right to ask of any prosody is, that it shall lay down a pattern for the writer, and that what it lays down shall be neither too easy nor too hard. (Stevenson 1905)

This is admirably even-handed, and still applicable today if slightly incomplete, as is what he goes on to say about line:

> Hence . . . there follows the peculiar greatness of the true versifier . . . These not only knit and knot the logical texture of the style with all the dexterity and strength of prose; they not only fill up the pattern of the verse with infinite variety and sober wit; but they give us, besides, a rare and special pleasure, by the art, comparable to that of counterpoint, with which they follow at the same time, and now contrast, and now combine, the double pattern of the texture and the verse. Here the sounding line concludes; a little further on, the well-knit sentence; and yet a little further, and both will reach their solution on the same ringing syllable. The best that can be offered by the best writer of prose is to show us the development of the idea and the stylistic pattern proceed hand in hand, sometimes by an obvious and triumphant effort, sometimes with a great air of ease and nature. The writer of verse, by virtue of conquering another difficulty, delights us with a new series of triumphs. He follows three purposes where his rival followed only two; and the change is of precisely the same nature as that from melody to harmony.

What Stevenson is suggesting here is that the poetic line is fundamental to our sense of verse as something structurally distinct from prose. This helps us to build up a theory of the line, one that can function independently of our sense of it as a metric unit. I've just been arguing that a sense of the metric foot is crucial to our understanding of rhythm. In the same way, a sense of line contributes to our sense of form. But for the moment, let's put aside the issue of lines formed from metric feet.

This is because the way the poetic line interacts with the flow of the sentence (which can be regarded as continuing to observe prose norms of syntax and grammar in the vast majority of cases) is actually the same for free verse and formal verse. There are essentially two options: to interrupt the flow of the sentence, or to coincide with it.

Let's have an example of the first. Here is Jo Shapcott's Mad Cow at the exact moment when she falls over:

> . . . and then there's the general embarrassing
> collapse, but when that happens it's glorious
> because it's always when you're traveling

most furiously in your mind. My brain's like
the hive: constant little murmurs from its cells
saying this is the way, this is the way to go.
                    (Shapcott 1992: 41)

Here we can see that a line break which does not coincide with a pause in the structure of the sentence, whether that is a temporary pause for breath, a comma or a full stop, breaks into that flow and imposes the different unit of the line upon it. Whether that unit is syllabic, metrical or more instinctual, it has an effect on our reception of the sentence: the momentary pause while the eye travels to the beginning of the next line causes us, however subliminally, however involuntarily, to consider the fragment contained by the line ('the general embarrassing'), and to question the sentence so far. This can send us on to that following line with our curiosity piqued, in which case it speeds things up; and it can lodge the alternative sense of that fragment in our unconscious.

Now an example from Julia Darling, called 'The Recovery Bed':

I am riding a raft that was made by kind women

who have left me here, who gave me a key,
for I was forgetting to look out of the window, but now,

I shall float home, firm as this mattress.
You will find me quite sure, convalesced.
                    (Darling 2004: 46)

Here those line breaks which coincide with a pause, a piece of punctuation, be it a comma or a full stop, slow things down and affirm the sentence. Each time, the line silently underscores the pause and redoubles its impact. In doing this it is implying there is consonance between the progression of each sentence and that of the poem, between the form of all the sentences and the form of the whole poem. As this unspoken agreement builds, its conclusion can sound like the resolution of a harmonic progression.

Poetry which is aware of the play between the sentence and the line is filled with a sense of pace and elasticity. Poetry which is not feels either loose or hobbled: loose because there's no tension in the way syntax overflows the line; hobbled because the line-breaks meekly and continuously agree with the syntax.

You can experiment with this with your own drafts: take a poem and rearrange its lines so they always coincide with syntax; then rearrange it again, so they never do. In each case note the points at which the line break feels most effective. Then rearrange the poem a third time to accommodate the best of both options, as it were. Finally, compare this draft to your original layout: is it exactly the same? Are any of the changes improvements?

So far so free. To bring metre back into the equation, we can now say it tests our sense of line by imposing a structure which interacts not only with the sentence but with our instinctive sense about when to break the line. When a formal restraint stretches or compresses that instinct, it challenges it: it shows us when we care passionately about a line unit, and when we are indifferent. Clearly it is not going to be enough to be indifferent. When a formal restraint matches our own instinct seemingly exactly, it affirms sentence, line and structure: there is a triple underscoring of what the poem is saying.

Frequently, when we are writing formally, the demands of fitting phrase to metre and sentence to line cause us to say something we wouldn't come up with normally. Opponents of form regard this as unnatural; proponents find it as natural as any other act of communi-cation. Composing within form is a dialogue with form, even a debate. In passionate dia-logues, in arguments, we may say things we didn't expect to – something gets blurted out. Frequently we say that we didn't mean it; secretly, we sometimes discover that we do. What is drawn from us in the dialogue with form lies close to the point of writing poetry at all.

Poetry is a means whereby we can discover what we didn't know we knew. Form is a means of generating these unknown messages. What we have to say to satisfy the form can be judged quite starkly: it is either false or a new truth. And the line is the unit within and across which these outbursts, these new truths, are tested and found sound or wanting. The line is a unit of attention for the reader, and a unit of intent for the poet. It is the place where both meaning and formal scope are discovered. It is the unit within which these two essential elements of a poem are found to be either ignorant of each other, or in opposition; in harmony with each other, or even identical, one indisputable impulse.

Let's take a retrograde step, and look at how a genuine old master handles iambic pentameter. You may protest that I should at least be citing a contemporary example, but be assured, there will prove to be method in my antediluvianism. So here is Wordsworth, describing birds in Spring with no less energy than Jo Shapcott, and with as much attention to line-endings as Julia Darling, but with the clear formal design of iambic pentameter:

> They tempt the sun to sport among their plumes;
> Tempt the smooth water, or the gleaming ice,
> To show them a fair image, – 'tis themselves,
> Their own fair forms, upon the glimmering plain,
> Painted more soft and fair as they descend,
> Almost to touch, – then up again aloft,
> Up with a sally and a flash of speed,
> As if they scorned both resting-place and rest!
> (Wordsworth 1994: 247)

Wordsworth distends his sentence for as long as possible, allowing his phrases to pause at the line-endings, and using a strong break within the line – what's known as caesura – to catch the rapid shifts of the flock. He sets the stability of pentameter against the instability of his subject, in other words, reassuring the ear with long lines and definite end-of-line pauses, and destabilising that reassurance with more abrupt internal phrases. He gains the same effect within his lines as Shapcott does at the ends of hers, implying chaos can be contained within an underlying and finally affirmative order. So when he concludes line, verse paragraph and sentence with that triumphant exclamation mark, there is a real sense of fulfilment as well as release. His use of pentameter serves several purposes at once. Used well, form is always multi-tasking.

The purpose of form is sometimes described as pleasurable or mnemonic. Though it is both of these things, this is too narrow a definition. As Wordsworth shows us, it actually gives us another way of speaking within the poem. Stevenson talks about the interplay of the line with the sentence. To this we should add the way that form interacts with subject, approaching and shying away from mimesis. And this isn't all.

Yes, form dictates the length of that line Stevenson speaks of, setting its regularity against the irregularity of the sentences. It plays with the patterns of the speaking voice, reforming what we normally say without losing the thread of how we normally say it. But it also engages in a dialogue with past examples of itself. It is not too large a leap to say that Wordsworth's glad birds, celebrating the end of winter with aerial acrobatics, echo and contrast with Dante's famous image of the souls of adulterers in the Inferno, constantly blown around on a scouring wind.

In this sense not only is the Paradise of the English Lakes being set against the Peninsula's conception of Inferno, the iambic pentameter itself is being compared with Dante's terza rima as its British rival and equivalent. And this crucial ability of form to speak to form, present to speak with past, is a dialogue free verse would appear to deny itself.

Everyone is aware of a slight sense of intimidation when they write a line in iambic pentameter because they are conscious of Wordsworth, Milton and Shakespeare standing over their efforts. This sensation is even more pronounced when we use the pentameter as a building block in something larger – say the sonnet – because everyone knows something of the illustrious history of that form (Auden, Keats, Shelley, WordsworthMiltonShakespeare). One response to the terror of how to create something new in an old form is parody (or pissing in the ear of Ozymandias). Abandoning such forms altogether is another response, and both have their roots in timidity as well as a desire to free yourself from the burdens of a heritage.

But form in the best sense rehabilitates parody, because it establishes it as a dynamic dialogue with the past. This is a matter of structural allusion, for instance choosing a stanza form with a specific history, and it can occur alongside verbal allusion. (Verbal allusion has a similar relationship with pastiche, and, as Eliot taught us, a similar capacity for serious purpose.) Form is about treating structure as recyclable, and finding new uses for it each time, uses that have specific resonances with past instances. Instead of ridiculing or denying the past, form acknowledges and engages in dialogue with it.

Most of us hope our work will resonate with future readers, whether five, fifty or 500 years ahead – a space we obviously can know nothing about. Form teaches us that we can relate to and resonate with the past, whether with those works that have proven their longevity, or with those we choose to resurrect, becoming their most receptive future readers. The sense of continuity this generates might even create a little momentum to carry us a short distance into that unpredictable future. Here is Douglas Dunn considering the suicide in the early nineteenth century of the Paisley poet, Robert Tannahill:

> Gone, gone down, with a song, gone down,
> My Tannahill. The tavern town
> Said one book was your last and frowned.
>   The River Cart
> Ran deep and waste where you would drown,
>   Your counterpart.
>
> (Dunn 1981: 73)

Here Dunn uses a form Tannahill worked in, the Burns stanza or Standard Habbie. As its name suggests, use of this form harks back to Robert Burns, another poet from the labouring classes, and is thus, in itself, a reference to Dunn's theme of the unacknowledged autodidact bard. Into that form he pops a verbal allusion to another Scottish writer, William Soutar, 'Gang doun wi a sang, gang doun', changing his vigorous resistance to death into a lament (Soutar in Dunn 1981: 73). So this poem is engaging with its predecessors and addressing its successors, and, crucially, it uses its form as eloquently as its content.

You can experiment with this use of previous form by picking the structure of a formal poem you are fond of and writing something of your own to fit exactly into that metric shape. Don't try and match your subject to that of the original, but don't fight it if some form of echoing or contrast creeps in. Now select a number from three to six, and another number from five to eight. You can combine these two numbers to form a stanza structure, in which the first will be the number of feet you'll be using, and the second the number of lines per stanza. Rewrite your draft so that it conforms to this new shape. Does your poem 'belong' in the original, borrowed form, or is it just as happy (or indeed just as unhappy) in the new, invented stanza? Is there something you can do to the new stanza to make it feel more at home? Shorten a line length, say, or introduce a rhyme scheme? Or is there another subject matter which would now seem more appropriate for the original?

So in a formal poem, not just imagery and music, or sentence and metre, but also verbal and structural allusion are all in dialogue with each other as well as with the subject of the poem: this is language in a heightened state of perception. And it's the dynamics of these interchanges which make it difficult for the formal poet to divide structure from content: structure is in the best instances creating or influencing content. The argument that metre forces language into a pre-arranged shape, bruising or mutilating the voice, is too aggressive an interpretation: form is certainly an act of will, but its purpose is to transcend the will. We surrender to form in order to find out what it enables us to say, and in those best instances we find it generates further meaning, even further levels of meaning.

None of this invalidates free verse in the slightest: almost any verbal structure can become a form in the terms discussed here (though from that point we might go on to raise questions of its flexibility and resonance). It is certainly the case that many experimental forms from the last two centuries were intended to replace form, to become new forms, and by now there are very few of them with which it is not possible to have that structural dialogue which I have been relating to, and would suggest is a transcendent use of, parody.

The thing to note is that the freedom or freshness associated with breaking away from established form is momentary: it belongs to the writer in the act of composition, the reader in the first apprehension of the new text. Strictly speaking, it belongs to the writer intoxicated by the moment of creation, the reader distracted from their memory of other work. Crucially, it doesn't belong to the text. Because the moment at which the piece settles into its final draft coincides with the moment at which it acquires the status of a new form, the moment at which it starts to become independent of its author. Compositional space is anterior to this, but, since it is where the pleasure of writing takes place, for the new or unpublished writer, or the inexperienced reader, it is easy to equate this space with that inhabited by finished works. In fact these are connected yet separate zones, adjoining chambers: the completed poem is still charged by the energy of creation, but it is more responsive to its ancestors, more open to its successors, than it is beholden to its creator.

> Toll a muffled peal from the bells;
> Hang flags halfway on the standards, on spires, and on steeple;
>   hang flags half mast on the ships that come from afar;
> Hang crape in the churches – on the galleries, on the pews, on the pulpits –
> The good old town is gone, irrevocably gone, dead, vanished!
>
> (Geddes 1991: 99)

Few people reading these lines by the minor Scottish poet James Young Geddes, for example, could read them as doing anything other than alluding to the work of Whitman, and in doing so they are clearly treating Whitman's verse as a definable form. In the hands of Allen Ginsberg, that allusion goes beyond imitation into a discovery of new uses for the long, breath-based rhetorical line that equal the reinvents of the sonnet or the ballad we see in generation after generation of British poets.

> I saw you Walt Whitman, childless, lonely old grubber,
> poking among the meats in the refrigerator and eyeing the
> grocery boys.
>   I heard you asking questions of each: Who killed the
> pork chops? What price banana? Are you my angel?
>
>   (Ginsberg)

(Why not try the exercise suggested above for formal verse for a free verse poem you admire? Analyse its structure as closely as you can, then write a new poem to fit it. Then revise the poem so that it finds its own best form: will this be another free verse shape, or does it require some kind of formal framework?)

Similar tactics to Ginsberg's can be seen in Tom Leonard's relocation of William Carlos Williams to Glasgow; Barry MacSweeney finding a home, half-Geordie, half-Cambridge, for, among others, Michael McClure; or many British and American poets' rephrasing of the distinctive tropes of Frank O' Hara or John Ashbery, from Ted Berrigan to Mark Ford. Formalists who are reluctant to concede this are as hidebound as experimentalists unable to contemplate writing a single line in pentameter.

These are all cases of writers who are aware of the formal tradition they are working in, even if in some cases they have had to invent that tradition. But what many apprentice writers produce under the heading of free verse is more based in bookless assumption than any sense of continuity. And there is a structural weakness inherent in the pursuit of the apparently liberated voice.

Where there is no perception of form in terms of metrics, and so no sense of an underlying support to decisions about line, the writer frequently must rely instead on the restraints of rhetoric. The integrity of the poetic voice becomes the strongest principle holding a poem together. This places pressure on the poet to produce significant utterance. That pressure of course already and always exists, but now the intensity of that utterance is directly related to the structural competence of the poem: it must be sound, in both senses of that word. There is therefore an inherent temptation to pump up the rhetoric and with it the status of the poet producing it, to become overblown. Ironically, form, by providing a simple means of validating poetic structure, acts as a restraint against this type of potential strain: it is a protection against preciosity.

Of course there are other strategies the poet can employ before turning to formal metrics. The American poet Jane Hirshfield, for instance, places emphasis on the integrity of the syntax in her poetry. The weight of utterance in her work is comfortably held by the interaction of line break and grammar, by the clarity of punctuation:

> Brevity and longevity mean nothing to a button carved of horn.
> Nor do old dreams of passion disturb it,
>   though once it wandered the ten thousand grasses
>   with the musk-fragrance caught in its nostrils;
>   though once it followed – it did, I tell you – that wind for miles.
>
>   (Hirshfield 2005: 29)

But, muscular as this writing is, people who express some commitment to form would argue that metre provides the essential vertebrae, the skeletal structure onto which those muscles should fit, on which the flesh of subject hangs, into which the organs of its imagery may all be placed exactly. This is as fundamental to them as the music of a poem, or the way metaphors and similes can combine or contradict each other, and complement or contradict the sense of the text. In fact, Glyn Maxwell would use the same physical imagery to argue that a sense of metre is above all a bodily function: 'Poetry is an utterance of the body . . . It is the language in thrall to the corporeal, to the pump and procession of the blood, the briefly rising spirit of the lung, the nerves' fretwork, strictures of the bone' (Maxwell 2000: 257–8).

If this seems an extreme position, ask yourself this: what are we acknowledging in a free verse poem through the interplay of sentence and line, if not the ghost of metric structure? What are we engaged in, other than the unwitting imitation of form through the use of unmeasured linebreaks and unscanned stresses? Here is the real phantom of form, and these are its lineaments: pentameter, tetrameter, trimeter, dimeter, and (very rarely) monometer; iamb, trochee, dactyl, anapaest, and (occasionally) pyrrhic. Let these words haunt us in the same way as the shapes they refer to haunt our verse. If we are fully aware of them we can make structures as elaborate and strange as Gray's Pindaric odes (which contain deft combinations of many of the above). Without awareness of them, we can only make structures which look as elaborate and strange as those odes. In this particular sense, free verse can only be an imitation of formal verse.

Of course we don't have to go this far. Of course well-made intelligent poems exist which are not in thrall to metre, which do not use stanza in the dialogic form I'm suggesting above. Of course poems which do utilise such techniques can be accused of a certain obscurity if their references are not commonly understood (and so few are these days, even among poets). But there is a difference between deciding not to write in metre in a given instance, and always writing in despite of it. The first decision accords your poem its own formal space alongside other forms, it acknowledges those forms but appeals to its right to operate differently. Implicitly, it acknowledges that the author may not have read everyone, but is at least aware that they might exist. The second not only denies those other forms relevance, it denies those other writers influence, and it denies itself formal analysis of its own success or failure.

The unique poem has unique problems. While a formal piece can allude structurally to the context it comes from, the poem that refuses even to acknowledge that it has a context has to teach the reader its strategies and goals at the same time as revealing its subject. Just as much of the obscurity complained of in modern poetry stems from this as from references to examples of previous writing – which can at least be researched. But if the author of the unique poem fails to acknowledge the pressure on that poem to explicate itself as well as to pronounce, the reader is left without any field of reference for the techniques or devices it deploys.

This is particularly true of typographic innovation: should its gaps represent a notation for performance or a graphic representation or an indication of some inner space? Without reference to previous practitioners, be they Guillaume Apollinaire, e. e. cummings or Charles Olson, how shall the reader know which way to proceed? All truly innovative experimentation needs to be formally aware, otherwise it is either incoherent, or an unwitting repetition.

So how do we become aware, specifically, of metric form; of how line and stanza interact to create a device, or indeed to devise a creature, which addresses contemporary and future readers and even poetic ancestors with one and the same voice? Well, we read, in exactly the same way as I suggested earlier that we listen, that is, we read as much for form as for content (sometimes, as in the case of Gray's odes, we read despite content). We read with pen in hand making marks all over those neat printed pages (that's what all that white space is for: for you to think in).

But reading for a writer is never far away from writing, in the same way thinking is always close to practice. Try every structural device you become aware of on for size. Accept that 90 per cent will be arid exercises (that way you might loosen up enough for more than ten per cent to succeed). Examine everything you're writing in any case and check whether any of it has a hidden structure – if two or three lines fall into anapaest, consider the rest; if two stanzas rhyme ask yourself if you've seen this pattern before. Don't just wonder if something would be better recast in tetrameter, try it out.

But above all, be patient. Success is so rarely automatic in poetry I should hardly need to say this, but metrical ability, stanzaic competence, even the decision whether or not to write in free verse, are all dependent on developed skills, not your current opinions. In the same way as a musician or dancer must repeat an action enough times for the neural pathways to be established, for the body to learn what is required of it, so too rhythmic awareness needs time to accommodate itself to verbal dexterity. What is happening is a double effect: you are becoming more and more aware of how your voice fits, say, the pentameter; and the pentameter is becoming more and more aware of you. Your voice must develop as a result of interacting with metre, in the same way as it obviously changes in response to all life experiences. What must begin as deliberate is sinking back into the instincts where it belongs.

An understanding of form is fundamental to our understanding of poetry because it brings to our awareness the particular poise of consciousness from which poetry springs. We must be as aware as possible without self-consciousness – the self is of interest only as another subject matter. We must be technically adept without the need to display mere technique – form is not a decoration, it is a function. We must be responsive to instinct and inspiration without becoming slaves to one or idolators of the other. Above all we must be as aware as possible of what our language is doing, how it combines as sound and stress as well as how it builds up sense – form is the means by which we bring one into harmony with the other, and our skill in doing so, not just our eloquence or our message or our social role, is what makes us makers. Or, to use the Greek, poets.

References

Auden, W. H. (1987), 'Making, knowing, judging' in *The Dyer's Hand*, London: Faber.

Carper, Thomas and Derek Attridge (2003), *Meter and Meaning*, London: Routledge.

Darling, Julia (2004), 'The Recovery Bed' in *Apologies for Absence*, Todmorden: Arc Publications.

Dunn, Douglas (1981), 'Tannahill' in *St Kilda's Parliament*, London.

Geddes, James Young (1991), 'The Glory Has Departed' in *Dundee: A Dundee Anthology*, Dundee: Gairfish.

Ginsberg, Allen, 'A Supermarket in California' in *Howl*, www.writing.upenn.edu/~afilreis/88/supermarket.html

Hirshfield, Jane (2005), 'Button' in *Each Happiness Ringed with Lions*, Tarset: Bloodaxe.

Hobsbaum, Philip (1996), *Metre, Rhythm and Verse Form*, London: Routledge.

Maxwell, Glyn (2000), 'Strictures' in W. N. Herbert and Matthew Hollis (eds), *Strong Words: Modern Poets on Modern Poetry*, Tarset: Bloodaxe.

Shapcott, Jo (1992), 'The Mad Cow Talks Back' in *Phrase Book*, Oxford: Oxford University Press.

Soutar, William (1992), 'Song', in Douglas Dunn (ed.), *The Faber Book of Twentieth-Century Scottish Poetry*, London: Faber.

Stevenson, Robert Louis (1905), 'Essays in the art of writing', http://robert-louis-stevenson.classic-literature.co.uk/essays-in-the-art-of-writing/ All references to Stevenson are to this source.

Wordsworth, William (1994), *Selected Poems*, John O. Hayden (ed.), Harmondsworth: Penguin.

20

New Poetries

Aaron Kunin

Two reasons for studying new poetry are suggested by Arthur Rimbaud in *A Season in Hell* where he writes that 'one must be absolutely modern' (Rimbaud 1945: 87). The mood of this sentence is ambiguous. 'Must' could be a wish, implying that modernisation is a duty (poets should work hard to become as modern as possible); or, alternately, 'must' could be grimly deterministic, implying a historical necessity (poets are modern because they live in the modern period).

Consider the wish-reading. You must always be completely modern because novelty and originality are the primary criteria of value, as in the motto adopted by Ezra Pound in *The Cantos*, 'Make it new' (Pound 1940: 11). To make something, such as a poem, that has no precedent in the history of forms is a heroic act. This reading is based on a romantic notion of poetic composition (you invent an image out of your unique self and project it beyond yourself, like a lamp, which consumes its own fuel in order to illuminate the world) as opposed to a classical one (you follow an assigned pattern, like a mirror, which receives an image from outside, from nature).

The limitations of the romantic aesthetic for any account of new poetries are:

- Novelty and originality are never the only values.
- A lot of the best new poetry is explicitly anti-romantic, introduces no new ideas, uses exclusively pre-fabricated material, and attempts to dismantle the individual human speaking subject. (See the section on 'Non-intentional writing' below.)
- Poetry is almost never original. New poetry typically authorises itself in reference to its own encoded history. Even Pound uses models from Confucian China, Jeffersonian America, and fascist Italy to authorize his practice of making new.

These limitations are visible in some of the unwieldy names by which the subject of this chapter is known in criticism: 'innovative poetry' (which implies that poetry has an expiration date), 'non-traditional poetry' (which implies that poetry could exist apart from any tradition of reading and writing), 'experimental poetry' (which implies a lack of finish or polish – 'Whoops! Well, there's my experiment, back to the drawing board, etc.' – or, more sympathetically, a Baconian attitude, as though one might make a discovery or proof in the process of writing), 'avant-garde poetry' (which implies a progressive and militaristic history of literature), and 'post-avant poetry' (which defaults on the possibility of any future avant-garde activity).

Here is one further illustration of these limitations. John Cage, whose characteristic works are based on chance operations, always maintained that he was not interested in novelty. Cage tells a story in which a friend observes that the 'most shocking thing' he could do when invited to lecture would be to give a normal lecture – no one would expect that. Cage's response to this proposal is that he doesn't write and deliver lectures in order to shock people, but rather 'out of a need for poetry' (Cage 1961: x). Cage, one of the most radical artists in history, is careful to distinguish shock from poetic value. His point is well taken. Some gaps in the history of form-making are felicitous; not all untried forms would represent an improvement on the available ones.

Now consider the determinist reading of 'must'. You are already modern, whether you want to be or not, whether you know it or not. This is a very good reason for studying new poetry, no matter what kind of poetry is important to you. A question for all poets in the first years of the twenty-first century is: what do we want the poetry of the next century to be? If a well-tempered poetry is what you want, you will have to look at many examples of different kinds of poetry in order to determine the rules according to which they operate or should operate. Also, remember that many ways of writing poetry, which no one has seen yet, are possible. Even if you want to resist or reject old or new models for writing and understanding poetry, you still may need to study them, simply because they are part of your culture, and because sheer ignorance may not be the most effective mode of critique. In short: new poetry is whatever we poets do. That is both a threat and a promise.

What have poets been doing for the past century? Here are some generalisations. The most advanced art of the modern period:

- Is interested in the elemental and primordial (medium and object specificity)
- Includes process in product (a procedural aesthetic)
- Is structured as theme-and-variations (a recursive rather than progressive paradigm)
- Privileges the non-recurrent element (non-commensurability).

We will fill in some of the details as we proceed.

Intentional writing

In his lectures on Shakespeare, Samuel Coleridge distinguishes between what he calls 'mechanical form', in which a limit on what a poem can and can't say is imposed from outside, and 'organical form', which he prefers, where a poem discovers its own limits (Coleridge 2004: 325, 515). Confusingly, his examples of organic form are trees and people rather than poems. Sol LeWitt makes a more precise statement of this distinction in his 'Paragraphs on conceptual art'. According to LeWitt, there are two strategies for making art. In the normal, intuitive, organic way, you're constantly discovering new problems and improvising responses to them. What colour should this be? What materials should I use? What scale am I working on? You have to make a whole new set of decisions at every stage of the project. In the other, conceptual way, you make all the decisions before you start working 'and the execution becomes a perfunctory affair. The idea becomes a machine that makes the art' (LeWitt 1996: 822). In the conceptual way, all the creative energy goes into the idea. It isn't necessary to do the labour of turning the idea into an object, and you certainly don't have to perform this labour yourself; you can hire someone to 'fabricate' the object. The distinction, whether organical/mechanical or intuitive/conceptual, is not between imposing form and not imposing form, because LeWitt believes that you can't have art without some degree of control. The question is: 'At what point in the process are you going to introduce the controls?' Either you plan ahead, or else you have to improvise.

The international literary society called the *Ouvroir pour la littérature potentielle* (Workshop for Potential Literature, or Oulipo) represents an extreme commitment to planning. This group, formed in the 1960s by the writer Raymond Queneau and the mathematician François LeLionnais, was originally supposed to explore links between poetry and mathematics, with special attention to the design of a poetry-writing machine. An important early work in this mode is Queneau's book *Cent mille milliards de poèmes*, a collection of ten sonnets in which each line, helpfully printed on a separate strip of paper, can be combined with others to produce the astronomical number of formally exact, thematically coherent poems given in the title. This is a work of 'potential literature' in that no single person, including its author, can read all the possible poems in a lifetime. The Oulipo has become increasingly identified with 'restrictive forms' – historical ones such as the sonnet, sestina, and lipogram (writing without a chosen letter of the alphabet, a formal procedure made famous by Georges Perec's novel *La disparition*, which does not include the letter 'e'), as well as recent inventions such as the septina, devised by Jacques Roubaud. Some members of the group believe that these restrictive forms are of conceptual and aesthetic interest in their own right (such as Perec, who always made his process of composition explicit in the work or in prefaces addressed to his readers), while others believe that the restrictive forms are of merely practical interest (such as Queneau, who tried to avoid making his arcane compositional systems available to readers and critics).

The use of restrictive forms is obviously intended as an expression of control. Particularly for Queneau, control is an ethic: nothing should happen in a text that has not been planned by the writer. Artists should be fully aware of the rules governing their decisions, because otherwise they are 'slaves to rules of which they know nothing' (Queneau 1986: 64). However, one advantage for writers who work with restrictive forms is the loss of control in later stages of composition. John Ashbery has said that writing a sestina is like riding a bicycle downhill, when the pedals start pushing your legs instead of the other way around (Packard 1974: 124); the six repeating end-words of the sestina effectively become 'a machine for making art', as LeWitt might say. Placing a limit on one area of decision-making encourages surprising inventions in other areas. You think what you would not otherwise have thought, and write what you would not otherwise have written.

Non-intentional writing

For some writers, the goal, which may be an impossible one, is not to express an intention, or not to have an intention at all. This is an ancient idea: for example, the classical poet is often imagined as a conduit through which a divine voice speaks. In the twentieth century, William Yeats used his wife's automatic writing, ostensibly dictated by spirit voices, as a source of 'metaphors for his poetry'. The use of automatic writing and dream imagery in surrealist poetry was supposed to connect poets not to a spirit-world but to a deeper reality than that of conscious awareness. Similarly, William Burroughs used chance operations (cut-ups, fold-ins, etc.) to make his novels subject to a 'third mind' not his own. Jack Spicer called his mature poetry 'dictated' in that it consisted of messages from an outside source that he sometimes described as 'Martians' or 'ghosts' but that he was apparently not curious to identify. Hannah Weiner called her mature poetry 'clairvoyant' in that it was based on words that she either 'saw' (on objects, on the bodies of people, and sometimes suspended in air) or 'heard' (here she made a difficult distinction between words that had a determinate physical source, words that had no apparent source, and words that were spoken 'silently') and then transcribed and interpreted.

A more sustained, rigorous effort to divest poetry of intention occurs in the work of John Cage and Jackson Mac Low. Cage's use of chance operations in order to generate writing is not as well known as his chance-based musical compositions, but is part of the same project. His typical procedure as a writer was to 'write through' another text, such as Ezra Pound's *Cantos* or James Joyce's *Finnegans Wake*, using a mesostic. Cage would start with a keyword, usually the name of his subject (for example, 'Ezra Pound') then write a poem using words from *The Cantos* containing letters from the keyword. The resulting poem *Writing through the Cantos* is planned by Cage but does not express his intentions, opinions, or (this claim is dubious) his taste; its diction and syntax are determined solely by the source text and the keyword.

The ultimate aesthetic ideal for such poetry would be to perform an action, such as writing, without leaving a trace. Failing that, the ideal would be to make the smallest possible intervention, as in the work of the minimalist sculptor Carl Andre, who made a series of sculptures using blocks of wood as materials in which each block received exactly one cut from a radial arm saw. For writers, the advantage of using chance operations is that you don't have to be special – you can write poetry without being a genius and without having a privileged relationship with an outside source (gods, muses, spirits, Martians, etc.). You can write poetry in mundane circumstances, even when you don't feel like a genius. Moreover, the labour is not taxing. Cage liked to quote the following Zen poem: 'without lifting a finger I pound the rice' (Cage 1995: 174).

Another recent iteration of this project is Kenneth Goldsmith's 'uncreative writing'. Goldsmith's main activity as a writer is transcription – of a phonetic event (his book *No. 111* collects instances of the schwa), of every word spoken by Goldsmith in a week (*Soliloquy*), of a taped verbal commentary on every physical movement performed by Goldsmith in a 24-hour period (*Fidget*), or of a copy of *The New York Times* (*Day*). Goldsmith's work is important, interesting, and readable, but neither his practice nor his theory is as rigorous as Cage's. *Fidget*, his best book, is incomplete, because Goldsmith got so drunk in the sixteenth hour of the project that he was later unable to transcribe his slurred verbal commentary on his intoxicated bodily existence; instead of giving a record of the last few hours, the final chapter presents the first chapter in reverse. According to Goldsmith, this failure proves that the project itself is impossible; actually, it proves that Goldsmith was unable to do it. Another artist might not encounter the same problems, and might realise the project more fully, if not perfectly.

The most serious problem for this kind of writing is that it is often a blatant exercise in taste-making. Cage always makes interventions in canonical modernist masterpieces by writers he personally admires; when he writes 'through' Joyce and Pound, he is also identifying with them, channelling them, going inside their heads, or trying to. The 'writing through' projects thus become inadvertent portraits of great modern artists, as well as self-portraits insofar as they are expressions of personal appreciation. Cage's use of Joyce to authorize his practice as a writer is particularly egregious and almost delusional. The aesthetic ideal implied by a novel such as *Finnegans Wake* would seem to be the exact opposite of the chance aesthetic: a book in which every available space has been marked, and in which the smallest mark reflects a coherent intention. Goldsmith's *Fidget* has a similar problem, in that it takes place on June 16 – in other words, 'Bloomsday', the day Joyce describes in *Ulysses*. This coincidence effectively recasts Goldsmith's external monologue as an experiment in stream-of-consciousness writing; it also signals an impasse for conceptual writers who keep returning, as if by compulsion, to Joyce as a model. These problems, however, present opportunities for future writers.

Jackson Mac Low, originally Cage's student, is more various in his use of chance- and intention-based writing procedures; his poetry is alternately spontaneous, planned, machine-assisted, personal, notational, performative, mesostic, and diastic. Some of Mac Low's writings are based on word lists generated randomly by computer programmes; his intervention as a poet is then to recognise the poem delivered by the machine. Mac Low is also somewhat more realistic than Cage in his claims for non-intention. In interviews and statements, Mac Low always insisted that poets can't get away from intention regardless of the formal procedures they're following, because 'the ego is implicit in everything you do' (Bezner 1993: 110). Mac Low thus supports Sol LeWitt's point that art can't exist without the exertion of some control.

Which brings us back to the beginning. As a poet, you have three kinds of decisions to make: selection (why this word rather than some other word?), order (why this word before the next word?), and division (what is the compositional unit – the word, the line, the fragment, the sentence? What marks the boundary between units?). We will consider each of these sites for decision-making in turn.

Vocabulary

Here is a simple way of thinking about poetry: a poem is a list of words. Slightly more complicated: a poem is an attempt to define one word (that is, the poem is still a list, but some of the words on the list are more important than others). Even more complicated: a poem creates a community in which its language is the only one. Only these words can be spoken in the space of this poem. Or finally: the words themselves are the community. Modern poets tend to insist on one of these formulations. In *A Textbook of Poetry*, Jack Spicer says that a poem first establishes a vocabulary, takes a cut out of the English language, then says: 'Imagine this as lyric poetry' (Spicer 1975: 177). Similarly, William Carlos Williams: 'A poem is a small (or large) machine made of words' (Williams 1988: 54). And Stéphane Mallarmé: 'Poems are made of words, not ideas' (Mallarmé 1956: 145).

Poets who insist on words as materials are making a claim about medium specificity. The project is to say what can only be said in the form of a poem and can't be said in the form of a painting, novel, film, dance, etc. Is there such a thing as medium specificity? Not insofar as poetry is conceived as a technology of representation. If a poem can describe a film or a painting (the technical name for this kind of mixed-media image-making is 'ekphrasis'), it can include anything that the film or painting might do. Any medium of representation is always capable of including and outflanking all the others. If, however, you are committed to object specificity as well as medium specificity, representation is not an issue, because you assume that the replacement of any object (such as a film or painting) with a convenient image (in the form of a poem, say) is going to fail, or, in any case, is morally wrong.

Many poetic revolutions have been founded on vocabulary. In their *Lyrical Ballads*, Wordsworth and Coleridge make a theoretical claim for ordinary language (not 'plain language' but 'scenes from common life . . . in a selection of language really used by men') as a useful, interesting material for poetry (Wordsworth 1984: 596–7). Whether any of the poems collected in *Lyrical Ballads* actually uses such a language is debatable. In the modern period, Ezra Pound makes a different claim for ordinary language as opposed to literary language (for example, words that appear only in poems, such as 'eglantine') in the name of clarity. The principle is '*nothing* that you couldn't, in some circumstance, in the stress of some emotion, *actually say*' (Kenner 1971: 81). For Pound, ordinary language is not valuable because it is the language of a particular class (Wordsworth's 'common life') but because it effectively communicates ideas and experiences. In the 1950s and 1960s, Barbara Guest put 'eglantine' and other super-literary words back into circulation. Such flagrant archaisms are a signal of the expansive vocabulary available to New York School poets: Guest reserves the right to use any word she wants. This expansiveness is thematised and exemplified in the flat, prosaic diction and syntax of John Ashbery's *Three Poems*. The book begins by distinguishing between two compositional practices: 'I thought that if I could put it all down, that would be one way. And next the thought came to me that to leave all out would be another, and truer, way'. Ashbery then gives some examples of leaving out: 'clean-washed sea/ the flowers were' (Ashbery 1972: 3–4). 'Leaving out', then, is the exclusive, artificial language that marks a boundary around poetry. With eyes fully open to the implications of his decision, Ashbery dedicates himself to what he has identified as the less true way – the use of a language that does not draw attention to itself as poetic.

Other poets work valiantly to expand their vocabulary beyond the personal – see, for example, Tom Raworth's poem 'Sixty Words I've Never Used Before' (Raworth 1999: 10–12). Perhaps the greatest vocabulary in all new poetries is that of Clark Coolidge. For Coolidge, the very fact that a poem has a vocabulary is a deplorable expression of human finitude. It is unfortunately impossible to have all experiences, to be all persons in history, to know every language; it is impossible even to use all the words in one's native language. Most people, poets included, use a few words, a tiny piece of English, over and over, in every conversation and in every poem. Poets normally respond to this fact by ignoring it or by inventing a poetic persona which becomes an emblem for a different language. Coolidge responds, first, by ransacking dictionaries to find new, unfamiliar materials for poems. Coolidge also carries out these investigations on a micro-level in books such as *Ing*, where division occurs below the level of the individual word, allowing part-words such as 'ing' and 'ness' to become bearers of meaning.

Excursus on plagiarism

One essential formal feature in new poetries is collage, which means that the compositional unit is not the individual word (or something smaller, such as a part-word), but a larger prefabricated language piece often called a fragment. The term 'fragment' could imply that the unit is grammatically incomplete or miniature in scale, but this is not necessarily the case; the fragment can be a phrase, a line, a sentence, a paragraph, etc. In poetics, its actual valences are:

- the fragment has another context outside of the poem;
- the edges of the fragment are not coextensive with those of the poem.

We will consider the problem of the fragment's edginess later (under 'Syntax' and 'Measure'). Here we are concerned with the problem of the fragment's original context, a problem sometimes identified as appropriation, and sometimes, more bluntly, as plagiarism.

To whom do words belong? Montaigne: 'I myself am the substance of my book'. Rimbaud: '"I" is an other'. Both of these quotations occur, unattributed, in Walter Abish's book *99: The New Meaning*, a collection of sentences and paragraphs copied from other books and arranged, or as Abish says 'orchestrated', to give them a new meaning (Abish 1990: 9, 16). (The title piece takes passages from the ninety-nineth page of ninety-nine different books.) If the three kinds of decisions writers have to make are selection, division, and order, Abish has tried to limit his decision-making, as much as possible, to order. Although he gives no author citations for any of the passages, he is careful to give an exact word count for each one.

The Montaigne and Rimbaud quotations may be understood as the conceptual limits of his project. Both are statements about how the person relates to writing. Montaigne, whose essays grow out of short tags copied from ancient poetry, identifies with the materials of writing. This writing, this ancient poetry, is Montaigne. Rimbaud, on the other hand, is alienated from the materials of writing as he receives them. The language is contaminated by other voices on the most elemental level. Even the personal pronoun 'I' is useless; Rimbaud will have to invent a new term to designate himself. The only completely satisfying solution would be to invent a new language every time he sits down to write.

The quotation marks inside the Rimbaud quotation tell a different story. They are intended as a distancing device. They mean: that isn't my word. That isn't my voice. That isn't me. Are the quotation marks enough of a shield to protect Rimbaud from what this sentence is actually saying? Is the disagreement between subject and verb, a grammatical error, enough of a shield? The words of the sentence may be too close to be entirely detached from one another and from the writer. The meaning of the sentence finally cuts across boundaries imposed by punctuation and grammar.

In the Montaigne sentence, on the other hand, the subject is not as stable as it wants to be. It is curiously doubled: 'I myself'. The 'myself' is redundant. It's there only for emphasis. But its presence suggests a problem: Montaigne isn't exactly the substance of his book. The book doesn't even look like him. The distance from 'I' to 'my book' is a full sentence. That distance could be bridged to an extent; the relation could be expressed as 'I = book' or Ibook or boIok. But there will always be some distance between Montaigne and what he writes, just as there's a necessary distance between 'I' and 'myself'. They are different words.

The positions that Montaigne and Rimbaud want to occupy are impossible. They are theatrical performances of absolute proximity and absolute distance. Abish manages to include both of them in one piece 'What Else', an arrangement of sentences and paragraphs that he describes in a prefatory note as his 'pseudo-European autobiography', in that the sentences are all written in the first-person singular. In 'What Else' the word 'I' is a lie. It conceals many voices, many unnamed authors. We know this much from the preface. But we can't help putting it together anyway – constructing a character, a personality, a life story, out of the fragments. And we also know that the 'I' isn't entirely a lie. There is an organising intelligence behind this anthology. 'What Else' is a personal record of a lifetime of reading. A person selected these passages and put them in order. Isn't that always what we do when we write? We select words – which, usually, we didn't invent – and arrange them. Abish is just using larger language pieces – complete sentences and paragraphs.

Can 'I' ever be a lie? 'I', the personal pronoun, the word we use to designate ourselves, the word that we identify with at the most profound level, doesn't belong to anyone. Everyone says 'I'. We are all part of it. Abish is manufacturing an autobiography that anyone could have, making himself anonymous, flattening his own 'I' against an unnamed, faceless European past. Acts of literary collage, such as Abish's, are incorrectly described as theft, appropriation, plagiarism. Collage is really about letting go, becoming another person, in the same way that we become other people when we read books.

Syntax

Collage procedures usually do not involve a laborious or painstaking selection process. Finding fragments to use as materials is not much more difficult than recognising a poem delivered by one of Jackson Mac Low's word generating programmes. Instead, collage puts pressure on the other sites of decision: order (what principle determines the arrangement of the fragments?) and division (what principle determines the boundaries of the fragment?). To understand the issues involved in ordering a composition, it may help to adopt or at least consider some more precise definitions of our terms.

Collage is sometimes used as a synonym for montage, but sometimes is opposed to montage. Strictly speaking, collage may designate only the introduction of fragments from other media. Thus, a poem becomes a collage when it incorporates drawings, photographs, newspaper clippings, labels ripped from cans, jars, and bottles, etc. The precise name for a poem that incorporates only pieces of other texts is montage.

However, the terms collage and montage are also sometimes used to make another useful distinction: collage designates a spatial arrangement of fragments for visual effect; montage designates the arrangement of fragments in chronological sequence (that is, the order of the pieces is the order in which they should be read). Finally, montage is sometimes thought to have a special political significance because of its association with photography. In Soviet constructivist film theory (most notably that of Sergei Eisenstein), montage gives viewers power to interpret images actively. Presented with two images that have been edited together, the viewer creates a new, third image to connect them. In a similar spirit, the German photomontage artist John Heartfield claimed, falsely, that the etymology for montage is from 'Montour' (or 'factory worker'), implying that the act of assembling photographic images is equivalent to production on an assembly line.

These precise definitions may not be satisfactory in that they are not congruent among themselves and not universally agreed-upon. However, the distinctions they make are extremely useful. Consider the first one, which is based on medium specificity. The introduction of a fragment from a different medium (collage in the strict sense) announces the embeddedness of the fragment in another context, but the introduction of a fragment from the same medium (montage in the strict sense) does not. A flower pasted into a poem clearly originated elsewhere, but a description of a flower, regardless of whether it's quoted from another text, looks about the same as the other words in the poem. The distinction is crucial. In the work of some writers, the syntax emphasises the prior embeddedness of the fragments in another context. For example, Marianne Moore usually puts quotation marks around fragments to show that someone else is speaking, and gives bibliographical information to show where the fragments came from, giving an overall impression of polyvocality. This sharp use of collage also emphasises the difficulty of writing itself, the labour of the artist who puts the pieces together. Other writers who use fragments arrange them so that they present a relatively seamless surface, with narrative, thematic, and stylistic coherence. For example, T. S. Eliot's 'The Journey of the Magi' incorporates phrases and images from a variety of poems, sermons, and memoirs, but the poem is presented as a univocal performance. (The 'different voices' of *The Waste Land* are presented more crisply.)

This distinction becomes even more interesting when it is politicised, as it spectacularly is in Language writing, a poetic and intellectual movement from the 1970s and 1980s.

The Language writers are radical formalists in their deployment of a broad range of formal devices, their sense that whatever a poem does is its form; in their tendency to make formal devices visible in their writing (the meta-device called 'estrangement' in Russian formalism and 'alienation' in Brecht's 'epic theatre'); and in their insistence that poetic form has political effects. (The earlier Objectivist poets – Zukofsky, Oppen, Niedecker, and others – whom the Language writers frequently claim as models are equally committed to a radical politics and to formal experimentation in poetry, but not to their co-articulation; instead, they insist on the separation of political and poetic activities. Thus, George Oppen did his most effective work as a labour organiser during the decades when he was not writing poetry.) The political effects are explained in Charles Bernstein's lucid essay in verse 'Artifice of Absorption'. Synthesising the poetic theory of Veronica Forrest-Thomson and the art history of Michael Fried, Bernstein distinguishes between poems that conceal artifice, pretending to ignore their readers in order to absorb them more effectively into an imaginary world; and poems that foreground artifice, challenging their readers with difficult interpretive problems. The first kind of writing is escapist fantasy; the second kind encourages readers to become active participants in the construction of meaning, and also, perhaps, to become more alert in their engagement with other cultural and social objects.

I have written elsewhere that this is a rather weak and unappealing way of giving power to readers, and that readers always have the option of aggressive reading tactics, regardless of whether they are reading Language poetry or confessional poetry or the newspaper, because texts do not set limits on our ability to interpret them. (For an illustration, see the exercise 'Page from a Tale' below.) However, I agree that formal decisions have political consequences. In fact, poetic form is only interesting insofar as it produces a social relation or an image of one. Form can produce a social relation rhetorically (for example, a poet uses a formal device to have an effect on the minds and bodies of readers) or it can define a community of people who have read the same poems or write in similar forms, such as the Language writers. Form can also be understood as political allegory; however, any form is capable of several allegorical interpretations. For Pope, the closed couplet indicates an enlightened community in which people live in harmony and their knowledge can be externalised, grasped, and transferred to others. For Milton, the closed couplet indicates an imposed order that should be resisted. For Bernstein, the artificiality of the closed couplet represents a deliberate refusal of an unseen order imposed on ordinary language; the couplet helps to make that order visible, and thus is a useful tool for resisting it.

The Language writers attribute special political significance to parataxis, a syntax in which compositional units (typically not verse lines but sentences, or, in Ron Silliman's terminology, 'new sentences') are sequenced without implying chronology (one thing happens before another), etiology (one thing happens because of another thing or so that another thing can happen), or hierarchy (one thing is more important or more valuable than some other thing); without conventional transitions or other connective material; or (a device learned from Ashbery) with misleading connective material – for example, a non sequitur beginning 'Therefore . . .' or 'And yet . . .' Here is an example from Carla Harryman's 1987 collection *Vice*. As often happens in Language writing, this example both performs and theorises parataxis:

> Twenty-five years later the words that had passed between them were unalterably compromised by everything they had come to know in the meantime.
>
> I believe in an order that does not exist, will never exist, and that one must seek in order to preclude its existence. The impulse of the painting I have turned you around in is dissatisfied

with a place to go – so as not to have been here, we have come up with a monochrome by which your remarks are masked.

Here, syntax is initially a spatial relation, one that occurs on the page between two sentences or paragraphs; then, a psychological one that occurs in the distance 'between' people; then, a historical one that occurs across time ('twenty-five years later'); finally, an artistic one, in which the first-person singular commits to a self-defeating search for order so that it 'will never exist'. This kind of writing is sometimes called 'disjunctive', but the only disjoining going on here is my own act of quoting this passage apart from the context of Harryman's book. Her work might be described more accurately as conjunctive, in that she proceeds by conjoining language pieces paratactically. It is also conjunctive in its wish to provoke a new social organisation.

Excursus on repetition

In his late autobiographical statement on poetics *A Vision*, Yeats describes the experience of reading Pound's first drafts of *The Cantos*. Yeats immediately recognises the structure as one of theme-and-variations. Instead of progressing toward a goal, the development of the poem is recursive. The compositional elements of this 'poem including history' are historical fragments arranged ahistorically, producing a flat chronology in which a painter from renaissance Italy can appear to engage a colonial American architect in conversation. Yeats is comfortable with this structure, which he knows from his own work. However, he notes that 'some of the elements' in Pound's long poem 'do not recur', and this failure puzzles and irritates him (Yeats 1966: 4).

What is the significance of the non-recurrent element? Instead of translating people from contingent into absolute reality (as Yeats does in 'Easter, 1916', where the names of the Irish nationalists can be 'written in a verse' only after their bearers have been killed and thereby made efficacious in history), Pound locates value in the contingent: events, people, and things that occur only once in history. For the same reason, Gertrude Stein's highly repetitive writing rejects the possibility of repetition. Each person, thing, and event is different, unique, unrepeatable. You can't repeat a word any more than you can repeat a person. The same word is no longer the same when it occupies a different space.

Few writers have attempted the difficult task of repeating no compositional element, so that there is no consistent narrative, argument, or style, and each step forward is a step into new territory. Lyn Hejinian's early book *Writing Is an Aid to Memory* makes some gestures in this direction. (The title is partly a joke on the difficulty of memorising a poem in which almost nothing is repeated.) Christian Bök makes non-recurrence one of the formal constraints on his progressive lipogram *Eunoia*, each chapter of which uses words with only one vowel; for each vowel, Bök tries to exhaust the available vocabulary and to avoid repeating individual words. Lisa Jarnot embraces repetition as a structuring device, building poems around anaphoric repetitions and distortions of a keyword or phrase. One of Jarnot's characteristic productions is her 'Sea Lyrics', a series of statements centred upon the first-person singular speaking subject that Language writing would like to dismantle. Also worthy of note in this regard is Tan Lin's 'ambient stylistics' project, a perverse response to Bernstein's aesthetic theory that tries to take the literary technology of absorption as far as it can go, in order to produce a writing that would be 'relaxing', environmental, like wallpaper (Lin 2002: 109). Lin pursues this project by taking the materials of popular culture personally – for example, rewriting restaurant reviews, wedding notices, and obituaries as though they were about him as an individual subject instead of addressed to him as a member of the collective readership of *The New York Times*.

Measure

One of the oldest and most beautiful ideas about poetic form is that it is a system of measurement. Specifically, the line measures. What does it measure? The traditional answer is time. In classical prosody, you're measuring time in units called long and short syllables that have precise lengths. Because it measures time, this kind of poetic line also implicitly measures human life. It may also be thought to regulate, therefore to institute or control time, to stop time, or to shield objects from the effects of time. As in Shakespeare's Sonnet 15: 'And all in war with time for love of you,/ As he takes from you, I engraft you new', whatever the speaker might mean by 'engraft'. Lyn Hejinian's *My Life* is an unusual example of a prose poem in which the compositional unit, the sentence, measures time – not the time it takes to say the sentence, which is not precisely regulated, but a year. The number of sentences per paragraph is the number of years Hejinian has lived at the moment of composition as well as the number of paragraphs in the book. (Hejinian first wrote *My Life* at age thirty-seven; then revised it according to its own internal logic at age forty-six, adding sentences to each paragraph to close the gap; then invented a new time regulation system for the most recent sequel *My Life in the Nineties*.) Miles Champion's poetry does not measure time notationally, but time becomes an issue because of his reading speed, which is just at the limit of intelligibility. Champion writes slowly but reads very fast; each line is thus subjected to intense dilation in time at the moment of composition, then contraction in time at the moment of performance. The result is a postmodern version of sublime: an aesthetic experience that almost outstrips one's capacity to enjoy it because it happens too quickly.

'Time' is still a very good answer to the question of what poems measure. The typical, modern, vernacular answer is voice. In traditional English prosody, you're measuring voice in units called long and short syllables that bear a precise stress. It might not sound as though very much is at stake in the modern conception. Time sounds like a profound concept; accent doesn't, maybe because everyone has a distinct accent. No one speaks exactly the same English, no one puts stress in the same places or pronounces a stressed syllable in the same way, or not all the time. But that's what makes the reduction of voice – of a particular, accented voice – to a uniform, abstract pattern so ambitious. The project of measuring accent is really a wish for a universal language, and, beyond that, a common world. There's a poem by the nineteenth-century German poet Christian Morganstern in which only the title, which translates as 'Fishes' Nightsong', is in German; the rest of the poem is written in accent marks. When you diagram voice as a pulse, human language looks the same as fish language.

After the twentieth century, there are many possible answers to this question. For example; for the Black Mountain poets (Charles Olson, Robert Creeley, Denise Levertov, and others), the line measures breath, which could mean that the end of the line marks the assumed limit of the speaker's lung capacity, or that the line break is notational, marking a place where a reader would be expected to pause. The line in Zukofsky's poetry often has a consistent word count, so something is measured, but the measure is not universalised; the word count has a private numerological significance for Zukofsky and does not regulate time or voice. The implication of Zukofsky's frequent practice of homophonic translation – re-articulating foreign poems to make them sound English – is the same: the rules governing the behaviour of the voice are private. Zukofsky himself is the measure.

Other poets reject the impulse to measure, which is considered inaccurate at best (because time and voice are not fully accessible to one person), violent at worst (because measurement is thought to introduce divisions in nature that were not previously there). The various marks of division in Leslie Scalapino's writing – which include, but are not limited to, dashes, brackets, and quotation marks – and their tendency to occur at unpredictable intervals and to interrupt line units and grammatical units, may indicate the co-presence of several measuring systems, or an effort to reject measurement altogether. For example:

> so the man – as gentle – for
> causing the fine – in that situation of
> being on the subway – when the cop
> had begun to
> bully him – at its inception
>
> > and – a senseless
> > relation of the
> > public figure – to his
> > dying from age – having that
> > in the present – as him to us
>
> as is my
> relation to the mugger – a
> boy – coming up behind
> us – grabbing the other woman's
> purse – in his running into the park

By contrast, the marks of division in Alice Notley's poetry represent a traditional voice regulation project. The quotation marks in *The Descent of Alette* represent the presence of different voices and the fact that Notley is alienated by any language that she did not invent herself; the spaces and ellipses in *Close to Me and Closer . . . the Language of Heaven*, indicate the voice of a particular speaker, Notley's father: 'you will be given a strange gift/ a number no one has seen before/ the number [unrepresentable]// the magic number . . . ness'.

Final excursus on the page

The father in *Close to Me* who presents 'a number no one has seen before' is proposing a new prosody in which divisions occur below the level of the individual word – so that 'ness', for example, becomes a complete unit – but using the language of traditional prosody. As in Alexander Pope's *Essay on Criticism*: 'But most by Numbers judge a Poet's Song,/ And smooth or rough, with them, is right or wrong' (337–8). 'Numbers' here means the tendency of prosody to reduce a specific grouping of words to a universal, abstract pattern. The sound of the words becomes a diagram. The term 'numbers' has the same meaning in baseball, where every player and every action can be replaced by a number or a long list of numbers. It's one of the three or four things that baseball players are allowed to say in interviews: 'I'm not thinking about my numbers, I'm just glad that my team got the win'. For Pope, the function of the numbers is rhetorical: 'The Sound must seem an echo to the Sense' (365). Here, the relation between form and content is redundant. Formal devices are always bearers of meaning, and their meaning is always the same as the semantic content of the line. Thus, a line that describes 'a smooth stream' is enacted 'in smoother

Numbers' (367). The numbers function to reinforce, below the level of literacy, a meaning already in the words.

The radical formalism of some new poetry links poetic form to social organisation by analogy, exactly as in Pope. However, other new poetries are committed to formal properties that exceed the production of meaning, so that the relationship between form and content is one of tension rather than redundancy; the sound effects may have a meaning different from or opposite to the semantic content, or they may be conceived as purely formal and meaningless. Susan Howe's poem 'A Bibliography of the King's Book, or Eikon Basilike' provides examples of all of these tendencies. The graphic eccentricities in Howe's writing are sometimes used as political emblems (for example, a line that can only be read intelligibly when the page is oriented differently, which may signify resistance to convention), sometimes as notation for vocal performance (so that different typographic conventions represent distinct voices or characters), sometimes as purely visual objects (for example, lines crossing each one another or printed directly on top of one another so that they become illegible). Here, the page becomes a field or canvas. It may include notations for sound effects, but its most interesting formal properties are based in sight rather than sound. Unfortunately, prosody has no vocabulary for naming or measuring visual effects.

I want to conclude by recalling two other uses of the page in new poetries that may be productive sites for future work. Ronald Johnson's *RADI OS* is a poem based on the first four books of Milton's *Paradise Lost*. Most of the words have been removed, and are represented by Johnson as white space; the remaining words take their positions from an 1894 edition of Milton. Johnson uses Milton, and a nineteenth-century editor, to make all of the decisions in the area of order (the sequence of the words is that of *Paradise Lost*), and most of the decisions in the area of selection (the words are chosen by Milton) and division (the page layout is determined by the nineteenth-century editor). He only allows himself to make negative decisions about selection and division; as he puts it, 'I composed the holes'. A related project from roughly the same period is Tom Phillips's *A Humument*, described by the author as a 'treated Victorian novel'. Phillips performs extraordinary interventions on H. R. Mallock's novel *A Human Document*, drawing and painting over the pages to make most of the original text illegible, drawing 'channels' or 'rivers' of space between words and phrases to create a new syntax among the remaining islands of legible text, combining pieces of text from several pages into one page, and introducing new divisions above and below the level of the individual word to form new contractions and compound words (for example, the hero of the first edition of *A Humument* is a figure named 'Toge', a word that appears nowhere in Mallock's novel). The only rule for these interventions is that the collage has to be internal. Johnson's and Phillips's books are inspiring not just because of what they achieve but also because of their limitations. Although Phillips is primarily a visual artist, *A Humument* is more interesting as a verbal composition than as a visual one. The visual interventions are mainly illustrational – for example, a text piece naming or describing 'steps' is laid out by Phillips as a set of steps. Future writers may be interested in exploring the possibility of stronger tensions between text and image.

Exercises

'*Page from a Tale*'
A group of people divide a text between them so that everyone has a page. (If there are ten people, the text should be ten pages long.) Each person reads the assigned page carefully and becomes an expert on it. The text thus is divided over the consciousness of

the entire group. The group then meets to reconstruct the complete text based on their shared knowledge.

The point of this experiment in reading is that any idea you have about a text is a reading of that text. On any page, there are energies of many kinds, possibilities for many different continuations, which tend to disappear when you put the page together with others. Reading is normally conceived as a process of imposing control on the disparate energies of the page, making the words line up so that they all appear to be saying the same thing. This exercise is a way of articulating the possible continuations before they disappear.

This exercise can also be used as a germ for a series of writing exercises based on the assigned page. For example: write a poem using only words from your page; or write a poem without using any of the words from your page; isolate the textures on your page and write a poem with them; circle all words containing the letter 's', draw lines between them, and write a poem about the resulting constellation; write a poem by crossing out words on the page.

Another reading experiment

Put this book under your pillow and sleep on it. Or, if you can't sleep with the book under your pillow, read the book continuously until it puts you to sleep. Then write a poem based on your dream.

This exercise is based on Carl Jung's analysis of Joyce's *Ulysses*, which is actually an analysis of the dream Jung had after falling asleep over the novel.

'Inverted sonnet'

Write a fourteen-line poem in which the first word in every line is a rhyme-word from a sonnet.

'Reducing the sauce'

Write a poem. Write another poem by removing most of the words from the first poem. Write a third poem by removing most of the words from the second poem. Write a fourth poem by paraphrasing the third poem (not using any of the words from the first poem).

Other ways of reducing the sauce. Remove all the people from a poem. Remove every trace of human civilisation from a poem. Write a resumé of the people who appear in a poem and comment on their actions (morally, intellectually, aesthetically, personally). Write a review of a poem that you would like to write. Write a rejection letter for a poem you would like to write. Determine the keywords in a poem; write a glossary for them. Imagine that a censor will go over everything you write and remove certain references (to sex, politics, religion, and technology); rewrite your poem so that it can be submitted to the censor.

'The lost suitcase'

Reconstruct the life of a person based on the contents of a suitcase.

'Physical symptoms'

Write 'automatically' – in other words, making a direct connection between your unconscious and your hand, if such a thing were possible. After five minutes, switch hands and continue writing. (If you're right-handed, switch to your left hand; if you're left-handed, switch to your right; if you favour neither hand, put the writing instrument in your mouth, hold it between your toes, or close your eyes).

The point of this exercise is that when you write, you have a body. This is also the case when you read – the best way to remember the second point is by placing the book at a distance slightly greater than your comfortable reading distance. Writing and reading are normally conceived as the elimination of physical awareness and confrontation.

Exercises in confrontation

Write a poem that will make readers laugh. Write a poem that will make readers cry. Write a poem that will disgust readers, nauseate them or make them throw up. Write a poem that will arouse readers. Write a poem that will put readers to sleep. Write a poem that will cause readers to commit violent acts (such as: fall out of their chairs, throw your poem out the window, tear the poem into bits, etc.). Write a poem that will make readers hungry. Write a poem that will make readers sweat.

Write a description of an action that can be read in the time it would take to complete the action. Write an abbreviated description of an extended action. Reverse the chronology of the action. Reduce the action to its smallest components. Write about everything that happens prior to or following the action. Write a scene in which all actions are facilitated by servants.

'Blow Up'

Write three pictorial descriptions of an action or event: one from inside the event, where you experience everything as it happens without being able to predict where it's coming from or explain why it's happening; one from directly outside the event, where you see and understand everything that happens but are either powerless to stop it or enjoying it too much to want to stop it; one in which the event is in the background and you are unaware of what's happening or its significance for you.

'Blow Out'

1. As above, write three descriptions of an action or event relying exclusively on the sounds attendant to the scene or produced by it.
2. Write a poem in which words are used for sound value rather than semantic value.

'Memory palace'

Use lines from a poem to memorise a set of facts or instructions. Then use those lines to write a new poem about their new subject.

Monetary value

1. Put a monetary value on different parts of speech. Or put a monetary value on particular words. (You can imagine either that this is how much you will have to pay in order to use the word, or that a reader will pay more for certain words than others.) Now write a poem.
2. Put a monetary value on each line in a poem (as on a restaurant menu).
3. Write a poem using only numerals.

'Restraining order'

1. Write a poem in which there are five people; no more than one person can be named in a line; no two people can come within 100 feet of one another. Or write a poem in which five people are introduced in the first line. Or write a poem whose referents are limited to a ten-foot square space.

2. Write a poem in which there is only one object: a chair. Now write a poem about a universe in which there are two objects: chair and pencil. Now write a poem with chair, pencil, and umbrella. Finally, add a newspaper. (The newspaper allows you to do pretty much anything, because it is not just an object but also a technology of representation. Any object that can be represented in the newspaper can also be represented in the poem.) Questions to ask about objects. What does it look like? What physical properties does it have? How does it take up space? How does it appeal to senses other than vision? How does it relate to the human body – can you pick it up, is it constructed to accommodate your body in any way, does it resemble a human body? How does it relate to other objects? What activities can be performed with this object (including, but not limited to, the activities for which it was designed)?
3. Rewrite a poem so that people and things can be seen only from behind.
4. Take three sentences and distribute them over three pages, adding words, pictures, doodles, glosses, etc. There should be at least two significant graphic interventions on every page.
5. Write a poem about an abstract concept in which you substitute the homophonous name of a concrete substantive for the name of the concept (for example, 'bowtie' for 'beauty').
6. Write a poem that exactly copies the cadences of another poem.
7. Write a poem that can only communicate by quoting another poem (or song, novel, movie, etc.).
8. Write a poem that re-enacts another poem (knowingly, ritualistically, or against its will).
9. Derive a vocabulary from a poem; use the vocabulary to write a new poem.
10. Translate a poem into another vocabulary, keeping as close as possible to the paraphraseable content of the original.
11. Invent a new language and write a poem in it.

References

Abish, Walter (1990), *99: The New Meaning*, Providence: Burning Deck.

Andre, Carl (2005), *Cuts: Texts 1959–2004*, Cambridge: MIT Press.

Ashbery, John (1972), *Three Poems*, New York: Viking.

Bernstein, Charles (1990), *A Poetics*, Cambridge: Harvard University Press.

Bezner, Kevin (1993), 'Jackson Mac Low, Interviewed by Kevin Bezner', *New American Writing*, 11: 109–24.

Bök, Christian (2001), *Eunoia*, Toronto: Coach House.

Brecht, Bertolt (2003), *Brecht on Theatre*, trans. John Willett, London: Methuen.

Cage, John (1961), *Silence*, Middletown: Wesleyan University Press.

Cage, John (1979), *Empty Words*, Middletown: Wesleyan University Press.

Cage, John (1995), with Joan Retallack, *Musicage*, Middletown: Wesleyan University Press.

Champion, Miles (2000), *Three Bell Zero*, New York: Roof Books.

Coleridge, Samuel Taylor (2004), *Poetry and Prose*, Nicholas Halmi, Paul Magnuson, and Raimonda Modiano (eds), New York: W. W. Norton.

Coolidge, Clark (1968), *Ing*, New York: Angel Hair Books.

Coolidge, Clark (1970), *Space*, New York: Harper and Row.

Creeley, Robert (2006), *Collected Poems*, Berkeley: University of California Press.

Eisenstein, Sergei (1970), *The Film Sense*, trans. Jay Leyda, New York: Harcourt.

Eliot, T. S. (1971), *Complete Poems and Plays*, New York: Harcourt.

Gizzi, Peter (2003), *Some Values of Landscape and Weather*, Middletown: Wesleyan University Press.

Goldsmith, Kenneth (1997), *No 111 2.7.93–10.20.96*, Great Barrington: The Figures.

Goldsmith, Kenneth (2001), *Fidget*, Toronto: Coach House.

Goldsmith, Kenneth (2001), *Soliloquy*, New York: Granary Books.

Goldsmith, Kenneth (2003), *Day*, Great Barrington: The Figures.

Guest, Barbara (1973), *Moscow Mansions*, New York: Viking.

Harryman, Carla (1987), *Vice*, Elmwood: Potes and Poets.

Hejinian, Lyn (1987), *My Life*, Los Angeles: Sun and Moon Press.

Hejinian, Lyn (1996), *Writing Is an Aid to Memory*, Los Angeles: Sun and Moon Press.

Hejinian, Lyn (2003), *My Life in the Nineties*, New York: Shark Books.

Howe, Susan (1993), *The Nonconformist's Memorial*, New York: New Directions.

Jarnot, Lisa (2003), *Ring of Fire*, London: Salt Publishing.

Johnson, Ronald (2005), *RADI OS*, Chicago: Flood Editions.

Kenner, Hugh (1971), *The Pound Era*, Berkeley: University of California Press.

Levertov, Denise (2002), *Selected Poems*, Paul Lacey (ed.), New York: New Directions.

LeWitt, Sol (1996), 'Paragraphs on conceptual art', in Peter Howard Selz (ed.), *Theories and Documents of Contemporary Art*, Berkeley: University of California Press, pp. 822–6.

Lin, Tan (2002), 'Mary Mary Ellen Ellen', *Conjunctions* 38: 99–122.

Mac Low, Jackson (1986), *Representative Works 1938–1985*, Washington, DC: Sun and Moon Press.

Mallarmé, Stéphane (1956), *Selected Prose*, trans. Bradford Cook, Baltimore: Johns Hopkins University Press.

Moore, Marianne (1994), *Complete Poems*, New York: Penguin Books.

Morgenstern, Christian (1993), *Songs from the Gallows*, trans. Walter Arndt, New Haven: Yale University Press.

Niededeer, Lorine (2002), *Collected Poems*, ed. Jenny Penberthy, Berkeley: University of California Press.

Notley, Alice (1995), *Close to Me and Closer . . . the Language of Heaven and Désamère*, Oakland: O Books.

Notley, Alice (1992), *The Descent of Alette*, New York: Penguin.

Olson, Charles (1997), *Collected Prose*, Donald Allen and Benjamin Friedlander (eds), Berkeley: University of California Press.

Oppen, George (2002), *New Collected Poems*, Michael Davidson (ed.), New York: New Directions.

Packard, William (ed.) (1974), *The Craft of Poetry: Interviews from the New York Quarterly*, New York: Doubleday.

Phillips, Tom (2005), *A Humument: A Treated Victorian Novel, Fourth Edition*, London: Thames and Hudson.

Pope, Alexander (1963), *Poems*, John Butt (ed.), New Haven: Yale University Press.

Pound, Ezra (1940), *Cantos LII–LXXI*, New York: New Directions.

Queneau, Raymond (1961), *Cent mille milliards de poèmes*, Paris: Gallimard.

Queneau, Raymond (1986), 'Potential literature', in *Oulipo: A Primer of Potential Literature*, Warren F. Motte (ed. and trans.), pp. 51–64, Lincoln: University of Nebraska Press.

Raworth, Tom (1999), *Meadow*, Sausalito: Post-Apollo Press.

Rimbaud, Arthur (1945), *A Season in Hell*, trans. Louise Varèse, New York: New Directions.

Scalapino, Leslie (1988), *Way*, San Francisco: North Point Press.

Shakespeare, William (1977), *The Sonnets*, Stephen Booth (ed.), New Haven: Yale University Press.

Silliman, Ron (1987), *The New Sentence*, New York: Roof Books.

Spicer, Jack (1975), *Collected Books*, Santa Rosa: Black Sparrow Press.

Spicer, Jack (1998), *The House That Jack Built: The Collected Lectures*, Peter Gizzi (ed.), Middletown: Wesleyan University Press.

Stein, Gertrude (1998), 'Composition as explanation', *Writings 1903–32*, New York: Library of America, pp. 520–9.

Weiner, Hannah (1978), *Clairvoyant Journal*, New York: Angel Hair Books.

Weiner, Hannah (1984), *Spoke*, Washington, DC: Sun and Moon Press.

Williams, William Carlos (1988), *The Wedge*, in *Collected Poems*, Vol. 2, Christopher MacGowan, New York: New Directions.

Wordsworth, William (1984), *Major Poetry and Prose*, Stephen Gill (ed.), Oxford: Oxford University Press.

Yeats, William Butler (1966), *A Vision*, New York: Collier.

Zukofsky, Louis (1993), *'A'*, Baltimore: Johns Hopkins University Press.

Zukofsky, Louis (1997), *Complete Short Poetry*, Baltimore: Johns Hopkins University Press.

21

The Poet in the Theatre: Verse Drama

Sean O'Brien

I say that prose drama is merely a slight by-product of verse drama.
  (T. S. Eliot, 'A Dialogue on Dramatic Poetry' [Eliot 1951: 46])

Poetry is all I write, whether for books, or readings, or the National Theatre, or for the opera house and concert hall, or even for TV. All these activities are part of the long quest for a 'public' poem, though in using that word public I would never want to exclude inwardness.
  (Tony Harrison, 1987 [Astley 1991: 9])

Climate

In 2005 the BBC broadcast on its most popular television channel, BBC 1, a series of 'modernised' Shakespeare plays, that is, plays appearing under Shakespeare's name but not containing his language. This is not the first such effort, on either side of the Atlantic. In 2001 there was a television version of *Othello*, set in the present-day London Metropolitan Police, written by Andrew Davies, a leading literary adaptor for television. Anthony Hecht recalls a 1975 parallel text of *King Lear* 'with the folio text on the left hand side, and facing it, a version intended to appeal to modern readers' – in other words, a translation from English into English. Hecht comments with restraint:

> there must be others who feel no loss in the dignity of utterance of the original. Yet I can't help feeling that such dignity is conferred by . . . a species of music, which, while not simply a question of meter, cannot wholly be separated from it. (Hecht 2004: 278–9)

The contemporary verse dramatist faces two problems. The first is a widespread view of language as instrumental and readily transferable. It's *only words*. The second is a similarly widespread failure to understand the work of metre. Remove Shakespeare's language and the music where it lives, and you will have a completely different work, which should not in fact have his name attached.

The existence of such a work – Fakespeare – will help the gradual extinction of the ability to read the original. This process may have begun with a baffled, irritated sense of Shakespeare's difficulty among relatively educated but impatient people, but extinction is now the intention (albeit usually unwitting) of the vulgarisers, for whom the existence of the literature of the past has come to seem an intolerable reproof, to be resisted to the death with the weapons of 'relevance' and 'accessibility'.

The verse dramatist needs to bear this unfavourable climate in mind. She will be swimming against the tide – a good thing in many ways, but exhausting and often solitary. It would be unfair to generalise, for the theatre is a very broad church, but one could be forgiven for thinking that nowadays there seem to be fewer actors with the training and experience to handle Shakespearean language; and that likewise fewer directors and literary managers seem trained or inclined to read verse drama with appropriate understanding and to discriminate between good and bad examples of the form. Verse drama receives lip service but adequate textual attention is by no means guaranteed. Partly as a result, it is often assumed that verse drama is characteristically *undramatic.*

Audiences, too, are encouraged, in effect, to *fear* poetry, on the grounds that its difficulty will make them unhappy and expose their ignorance, as though people only watch plays to confirm what they already know, rather than to extend their experience or perhaps even confound their understanding. *King Lear* comes immediately to mind as a play which does both of these things. The fact that the assumption (verse drama is undramatic) and the fear (it will present an intolerable challenge) are both groundless is not the point: a cultural myth is in operation, and its assurances are more compelling than mere facts.

It is also widely assumed that verse drama is 'uneconomic', a description no more true of verse drama than of any other kind of new writing. Most serious drama of any kind in the British theatre, for example, has long depended on government subsidy in order to be written and initially staged. The desirable transfer to the West End is a matter of economic calculation, carried out once the play has a life, the makings of an audience and the potential to attract a larger one.

In the light of these conditions, the poet-dramatist in particular may conclude that the theatre is not 'literature' in the same sense as poetry and fiction. Theatre is a collective activity. Its preoccupations lie elsewhere than with literary quality and the kinds of detailed discrimination employed in framing the literary judgements with which poets are likely to be intimately familiar. A play can be 'too literary' for the theatre. It is hardly surprising that very few poets make a career in the theatre; less so that the theatre produces verse dramatists who have no reputation as poets offstage. If these conditions do not sufficiently discourage you, if you simply want to write the best verse play you can, then you should set to work.

The poet in the theatre

The theatre is a collaborative art form. You will hear this statement often, though perhaps more frequently from directors, producers, actors and designers than the poet herself, who may feel rather isolated from her surroundings, a bit like the pig described by Randall Jarrell, which wandered into a bacon-judging competition and was asked on what authority it was there (Jarrell 1997: 63). The poet's play is the result of an individual vision, a way of reading the world. It has its own integrity as a complex imaginative arrangement. She has come to the theatre in order to see that vision embodied on the stage. She may be in for a nasty shock.

Whatever their real level of enthusiasm, the other people involved in the production – director, actors, designer, composer and even the publicity and marketing staff – will need to think of the play as being as much theirs as the author's. Their labour and talent is being invested in the play; they themselves are in many cases artists; ergo they will need to leave their mark on it in some way. New plays usually undergo an extended period of drafting, interspersed with first readings, discussion, redrafting, perhaps a rehearsed reading and then the rehearsal of a final draft, which may still be subject to change, before the play reaches the stage, at which point changes may still be being made. The theatre is necessarily an extremely practical place, concerned with *what works* – though this, of course, is a matter for debate. Writers profess to enjoy the theatrical process, and to a certain extent this is true (it gets them out of the house), but it can also present a serious challenge to the writer's determination and self-assurance. The verse dramatist needs to have an extremely clear sense of what she has in mind before she goes into the arena of collective endeavour where prose is viewed as the normative and natural linguistic form. She will need to act as an advocate, an explicator and a propagandist for the kind of work she wishes to present, and to be prepared to engage in a much more basic level of explanation than she might have expected. She needs to bring a good deal more than the play itself into the theatre.

In order (to paraphrase Wordsworth) to create the taste by which they may be understood, dramatists have often created or led their own companies, Yeats and Brecht prominent among them. There is much to be said for doing the same, at any rate in the early stages of writing verse drama, though the labour is necessarily immense, and not every poet-dramatist possesses, or desires, the totalising vision necessary to see such a project through. After all, isn't that what the theatre is for?

Traditions

The contemporary verse dramatist may at times feel like an orphan. Where does she come from? The Greeks? Shakespeare? Tony Harrison? Although a good deal of modern verse drama has been written and staged, it has come to seem more like a series of interruptions to the dominance of prose than a continuous tradition of its own. Verse drama is like one of the ancient rivers that runs beneath a city, usually unseen and unheard but occasionally breaking out before being sealed away again.

Since 1900 there has been a good deal more verse drama than contemporary readers and audiences may be aware of. Ruby Cohn's essay on dramatic poetry in the *New Princeton Encyclopaedia of Poetry and Poetics* provides an extensive survey (Preminger 1993: 304–11). Verse drama has played a significant role in the German-speaking theatre into the present day, while in the UK, the US and elsewhere in the Anglophone world it has attracted some of the major poets of the time, among them W. B. Yeats, T. S. Eliot, Robert Lowell, Tony Harrison and Seamus Heaney – with Eliot and Harrison making an important part of their careers in the theatre. Among the other significant contemporary poets who have written verse plays are Simon Armitage, Douglas Dunn, Ted Hughes, Kenneth Koch, Derek Mahon, Glyn Maxwell, Paul Muldoon, Tom Paulin and Richard Wilbur. As in other literary forms, verse drama has produced famous names which have now lapsed from currency – Archibald MacLeish, Christopher Fry and Ronald Duncan among them. Leading American dramatists such as Arthur Miller (in the first draft of *The Crucible*) and David Mamet have at times used verse. So too have English playwrights including John Arden, Caryl Churchill and David Edgar. It is necessary, however, to draw a distinction between poets who work in the theatre, and playwrights who sometimes employ verse but have no status as poets. There is at times a desire to *include* poetry without having mastered the art, and the theatre's problems with that art take us back to where we came in.

Playwrights and language

The poet and critic Neil Powell has argued:

> the . . . development of cinema, television and video seemed to reinforce a general assumption that dramatic language should make some attempt at verisimilitude; the mainstream English playwrights of the post-war years – Osborne, Pinter, Wesker – are, despite their differences, essentially engaged in presenting a language which purports to be that of 'real life', in which characters are unlikely to speak poetry. (Roberts 2001: 561)

The reader may pause over Pinter's name here, since his interest *in language* is everywhere apparent, although his claims as a poet are limited to a handful of early pieces; but otherwise Powell accurately describes the naturalisation of prose as the pre-eminent theatrical form. He indicates that there is an underlying assumption that there is a 'natural' fit between prose and speech, although of course speech is not in fact a *written* form, as also between 'realism' (and naturalism) and prose – the total effect of which is to produce 'reality'. But drama (*pace* Brecht) deals in illusion, in the impersonation of reality, and its effects are stylised by convention: see most television soap opera for the ritualised degeneracy of dramatic 'realism'. The theatre of prose is engaged, however minimally, in a form of rhetoric – the employment of artistic persuasion. The verse dramatist would contend that the confinement of prose sets limits to the imaginative scope of that persuasion, limits by which verse drama is not bound.

For example, David Edgar's *Destiny* (1976) is an absorbing play, set in the English West Midlands, about the rise of the neo-Fascist National Front in the 1970s. *Destiny* treats serious subject matter with a great deal of skill. What it misses, however, is the further dimension imparted by a more-than-instrumental view of language, capable of carrying us beyond documentary earnestness towards the Shakespearean scope its theme deserves. Edgar himself has succinctly observed that 'the social-realist form has significant limitations when it comes to representing the contemporary world to itself' (Edgar 1987: ix). From a slightly earlier date, Trevor Griffiths' *The Party* (1974) is a play almost without action – set among a group of writers and intellectuals watching on television the 1968 street battles in Paris between students, workers and the forces of De Gaulle's tottering government. It is a play about the impotence and bad faith of the Left in Britain, notable for one great speech, originally delivered in the 1973 National Theatre production by Laurence Olivier, the Shakespearean actor *par excellence*, playing the part of the elderly Marxist, John Tagg. This is a *tour de force* of passion and political analysis, and it stands on the border of poetry – from where it probably helped to sink the play by outshining a context in which, inert though it was, critics and audiences felt more or less at home. Griffiths's work, always problematic in theme and method, has been superseded by the current leading contemporary political playwright in Britain, David Hare, a bourgeois 'playwright of ideas', whose writing harks back to the 'well-made play' dominant in English theatre before the arrival of John Osborne in 1956. It is an honourable tradition (it encompasses Terence Rattigan, for example), but its core language is that of the English middle class, and like that of the more intellectually spectacular Tom Stoppard, it cannot help seeming disempowered. The brooding repetitions and silences of Pinter, and the abraded last-ditch language of Beckett, are much more alert to the medium itself.

The classical model

The work of the three great Greek tragedians, Aeschylus, Sophocles and Euripides, continues to exert a powerful hold on the imagination of directors and poets alike. So does the comedy of Aristophanes. New versions of the Aescyhlus's *Oresteia*, the Theban plays of Sophocles (in particular *Antigone*) and Euripides' *The Bacchae* continue to be made; the same is true of Aristophanes's comedies, such as *The Birds* and *Lysistrata*. The tragedians' concern with order, violence, justice, freedom and fate remain the bedrock concerns of western literary culture; Aristophanes's (equally enigmatic) plays read the world in comic parallel. 'Relevance' is, of course, a term to be used with extreme scepticism, given that it so often serves a historical *dis*connection rather than a sense of human and historical continuity, but the reader should consult Terry Eagleton's *Holy Terror* (Eagleton 2005: 1–41) for a reading of *The Bacchae* in the shadow of the War on Terror which does justice to the psychological dimension of political intransigence.

The most sustained and successful commitment to re-presenting the Greek classic drama has been that of Tony Harrison (b.1937). Harrison has famously commented: 'Poetry is all I write' (Astley 1991: 9). He has also argued for the unique power of poetic language to comprehend (in the sense of containing, absorbing and responding to) the recurrent atrocities of the modern age, and has found in the Greek drama an enduring capacity to face, and give form, to the worst that life can do to the human race. Harrison, unsurprisingly, has little time for the conventions of realism. His plays are all manifestly *performances*, with the artifice of the verse (see his version of Molière's *The Misanthrope*) brandished as a means of engaging and delighting the audience. His original plays move readily towards music-hall (*Square Rounds*) and towards deliberate *naïveté* and doggerel in the story of the Airedale weaver-poet John Nicholson (*Poetry or Bust*). In a sense Harrison has been a one-man disproof of the inevitable dominance of prosaic realism. Seamus Heaney's translations of Sophocles, *The Cure at Troy* (from *Philoctetes*) and *The Burial at Thebes* (from Antigone) are dignified, impersonally faithful renderings of the plays. Versions of *Antigone*, including those by Tom Paulin and Blake Morrison are always timely, but dramatisations of the resistance of the individual (Antigone) to the arbitrary and peremptory power of the state (embodied by Creon) seem particularly urgent at present.

The Shakespearean model

Contemporary theatre is usually governed by the need for plays with small casts, so that to invoke the Shakespearean sense of scale and population-in-depth may seem utopian, but the world-creating opportunities of the Shakespearean-Jacobean model speak to the desire for 'history plays', capable of treating politics and society as a whole, plays capable too of rising to the intensity of tragedy. David Edgar describes a selection of his plays in the following terms:

> Most of the plays in this volume can be described as social-realist pieces . . . they present what
> aspires to be a recognisable picture of human behaviour as it is commonly observed, but, unlike
> naturalistic drama, they set such a picture within an overall social-historical framework. The
> characters and situations are thus not selected solely because that's how things are but because

they represent a significant element in an analysis of a concrete social situation. The most popular definition of this endeavour is by Lukács, who said that social realism presents 'typical' characters in a 'total' context. (Edgar 1987: viii)

The reference to Lukács helps to point out the indebtedness of social-realist drama to the nineteenth-century novel. The intention Edgar describes is a universalising one, but the separation between the actual and the typical reveals the problem of squaring that circle. In verse drama, the representative status of the persons of the play is taken for granted as a phenomenon present in the first place in a way that social realism (as Edgar describes it) can never be. What Edgar is gesturing at is a Shakespearean imaginative confidence and competence.

The contemporary interest in the verse dramas of the great German romantic Friedrich Schiller (*Don Carlos, Mary Stuart, Wallenstein*) indicates the persistence of a hunger for scale, political scope and linguistic richness. As Ruby Cohn has observed, 'It is . . . the English language, forever haunted by Shakespeare's ghost, that has hosted most twentieth-century efforts at dramatic poetry. Each generation seems to sound its own clarion call for a revival of poetic drama' (Preminger 1993: 308). That call was sounded in Britain in the years after 1945 by Christopher Fry in particular. Fry's gorgeously mounted rococo verse plays enjoyed a tremendous popularity for a time. The verse plays of Louis MacNeice (most notably *The Dark Tower*) were successfully broadcast on the old BBC radio Third Programme. Other names have almost vanished from memory, such as that of Ronald Duncan, a verse dramatist of repute in the 1950s. It is arguable that just as the 'well-made play' represented by Terence Rattigan was doomed by the unlikely but then massive success of John Osborne's *Look Back in Anger*, staged at the Royal Court Theatre in 1956, so the likes of Duncan must have seen the writing on the wall at the same time, though Duncan himself was involved in the setting up of the Royal Court. Duncan's *Don Juan* and *The Death of Satan* were programmed to follow a short run of *Look Back in Anger*, in the expectation that they would succeed at the box office where Osborne's play would probably fail. History has made its judgement in the matter, in favour of Osborne rather than what Mark Lawson has described as 'Duncan's unspeakable historical pieces [which] were pulled off after catastrophic reviews' (Lawson 2006: 16). What may be an unintended consequence was the seemingly widespread belief thereafter that dramatic *energy* was the preserve of prose, and that if the common man and the working classes were to be heard, it would happen in prose.

The assumption that verse drama is *undramatic* may arise in part from a contemporary unease with the ritual and statuesque mode of the Greek tragic drama to which poets are so often drawn. It is also felt that poetic language is often merely decorative, inclined to exert a brake on the action of the drama. A bad verse play will probably fail on both counts, quite aside from problems of characterisation and emotional engagement. *A verse drama is not a staged poem but a play in verse.* It has the same obligation as any other play to compel the audience's commitment and absorption, while *at the same time* offering poetry's greater suggestiveness, precision and musical power. The audience should rapidly come to accept poetic language as the drama's natural medium, and to enjoy its greater imaginative scope. Chorus in *Henry V* describes the epic possibilities of verse drama:

> O, for a Muse of fire, that would ascend
> The brightest heaven of invention!
> A kingdom for a stage, princes to act,

> And monarchs to behold the swelling scene!
> (*Henry V* I, i, 1–4)

The Muse (warlike, in this case) is invoked at the very beginning of the action, as a guiding power, with the audience enlisted as imaginative collaborators ('Suppose, within the girdle of these walls / Are now confined two mighty monarchies'), making present what Chorus professes only to long for. The ancient trope of poetic unworthiness is here laid bare in the service of imaginative triumphalism.

Which form the verse dramatist will adopt varies from writer to writer and play to play, but there is an argument for selecting blank verse or rhyming couplets. These methods clearly manifest themselves to the audience from the outset, offering an artistic contract signalled by a layer of formality which magnifies and intensifies the action in view, giving language a human eminence which even the most artfully scored of Harold Pinter's works cannot quite match. It is a mode of privilege, a gift to all its speakers, able to unlock tongues that would elsewhere be unready for their burdens. With this in mind, despite the problems discussed in this essay, the poet-dramatist may legitimately conclude that the very absence of a stable and generally recognised theatrical tradition for verse drama offers a unique opportunity to create the stage-world anew, as poetry.

References

Astley, Neil (ed.) (1991), *Tony Harrison*, Newcastle upon Tyne: Bloodaxe.

Eagleton, Terry (2005), *Holy Terror*, Oxford: Oxford University Press.

Edgar, David (1987), *Plays One*, London: Methuen.

Eliot, T. S. (1951), *Selected Essays*, London: Faber.

Griffiths, Trevor (1974), *The Party*, London: Faber.

Harrison, Tony (1992), *Square Rounds*, London: Faber.

Harrison, Tony (1993), *Poetry or Bust*, Halifax: Salts Estates.

Heaney, Seamus (1991), *The Cure at Troy: a Version of Sophocles' Philoctetes*, London: Faber.

Heaney, Seamus (2004), *The Burial at Thebes*, London: Faber.

Hecht, Anthony (2004), *Melodies Unheard: Essays on the Mysteries of Poetry*, Baltimore: Johns Hopkins University Press.

Jarrell, Randall (1997), *Poetry and the Age*, London: Faber.

Lawson, Mark (2006), 'Fifty years of anger', London, *The Guardian* G2, 31 March, pp. 14–17.

Preminger, Alex, and T. V. F. Brogan (1993), *The New Princeton Encyclopaedia of Poetry and Poetics*, Princeton: Princeton University Press.

Roberts, Neil (ed.) (2001), *A Companion to Twentieth-Century Poetry*, Oxford: Blackwell.

Shakespeare, William (1995), *The Arden Shakespeare: King Henry V*, T. W. Craik (ed.), London: Thomson Learning.

Shakespeare, William, adapted by Andrew Davies, *Othello*, broadcast on ITV 1, 23 December 2001, Granada International.

22

The Sequence and the Long Poem

George Szirtes

Can poems be long at all? Good question.

'Epic, lyrical or dramatic?' asked the Victorian poet, Robert Browning, when told that his excellency the Japanese ambassador, wrote poetry. 'His excellency's verse', replied the interpreter, 'is chiefly enigmatic'.

A lot of confusion can arise if we apply too rigid a framework to anything, but Browning's courteous question wasn't nonsense. The three likely categories for the ambassador's poetic activities were appropriate to most European poetry, epic being concerned with narrative, lyrical with states, incidents and moments, and dramatic with verse as spoken, sung or chanted in plays as part of a dialogue.

If it no longer occurs to us to think in these categories it may be because verse drama has become very rare on stage and fewer people – though there are exceptions – write epics. 'Why are there no verse dramas?' you may ask, or 'Why so few epics?'

The reasons are long and complex. Enough perhaps to say that linguistic naturalism or 'realism' on stage has come so far to dominate theatre that it might be difficult for audiences to hear or appreciate speech that is anything but immediate, colloquial, smacking of the language they themselves speak. They allow for productions of historical verse plays, and make headspace for operas and musicals where the conventions are familiar, but the notion of spoken verse seems artificial to them. There is a good argument to be made for certain plays by, say, Samuel Beckett or Harold Pinter, to be regarded as poem-plays if not exactly verse plays, simply because the language is so carefully weighed, so precise that it carries the power of poetry. But that is not quite the same as Shakespeare or Webster or Molière or T. S. Eliot, who wrote verse that functioned as drama rather than drama that felt like poetry.

Epic verse is not quite so rare as dramatic verse now but some of the functions of the epic have become problematic. The grand narratives of the epic required a hero and some kind of adventure – a war or a voyage or a process – that summed up part of the history of a people. It offered a mythic history as the common ground of a nation or tribe's idea of itself. 'This is how we got to be who we are', said the epic, but in modern nations where societies contain many elements the epic has restricted meaning, and in any case, people have grown suspicious of grand narratives of 'us' and 'them' – or so they say.

You will notice I say 'them' rather than 'us' in talking about audiences and readers, but we can safely assume that 'them' is as likely to mean 'us' as anybody else.

Are 'we' then left with the lyrical poem, that short piece of verse that rarely exceeds a page in length when written down? Is that what we think poetry is now? Some think so. A long poem, where such exists – if such exists – is only a series of short poems stuck together to make a series or sequence, they say and they might be right, pointing to T. S. Eliot's *The Waste Land* as an example: yes, a single complicated theme but not really a narrative, more a series of mysteriously related brief scenes and fragments, hardly telling a single story, or not as we would expect a story to be told.

One of the essential differences between prose narrative and poetry is that prose narra-tive is expected to maintain tighter story lines. What this means is that the language itself needs to be pushing on from one consequence to another. This has a moral dimension for when one action is a consequence of another we tend to wonder what the choice of original actions was, and whether the choice made was the right one. We identify with the choice-maker. The crudest interpretation of this dynamic is the one made by Miss Prism in Oscar Wilde's *The Importance of Being Earnest*, where she says: 'The good ended happily, and the bad unhappily. That is what Fiction means'. She is wrong of course in that this principle would make for very predictable novels, but not altogether wrong in the essential moral notion of consequence. And such consequence is exciting. There are so many 'wrong' choices one might make! You will have heard children telling stories in which the phrase 'and then' keeps recurring. 'And then' is narrative prose at its simplest. It is the exciting next thing, the cliff-hanger, the breathless operation of railway points to prevent the train crashing so that it may arrive safely at its destination, which in the case of tragic works can be a very sad and deserted station and not much more.

I began by referring to traditional distinctions between three kinds of poem, and sug-gested briefly why two of those kinds – the epic and the dramatic – were less frequently written now than they used to be. Long poems are, nevertheless, written, although it all depends what you mean by long. Some people might say anything over forty lines is long, but I think we ought to look for something longer than that, something at least the equiva-lent of the prose chapter in length, that is to say a good clutch of pages. It's not asking for much, is it? But how does it work when, or so it seems, the modern poem is restricted to the short lyrical form that fits on the page of a magazine, in a corner between a piece of, often, critical prose text about something else. If we look at it like this the poem is merely a commodity that has to struggle for its place among other available commodities. And – so the argument would go on – that real space 'out there' must surely carry an echo in the apparently virtual space 'in here', in the head. Our notion of possibilities must be influenced by that which actually seems to be possible, it insists.

Furthermore (we are still listening to the same voice) there is something about the way we live our lives that seems to prefer short attention spans to long ones, or, if we must have something long, to demand lots of distractions, loads of action: nothing we have to think about too much. Consumers prefer things that go down easily. And poems are relatively hard work, aren't they? They take all your attention. The language in them isn't neces-sarily the kind that slips down the throat. They are somehow denser, more packed than something of that length in prose would seem to be. Who would actually want to read a long poem that doesn't, by its very nature, come straight to a point that isn't in any case too far away. People might have done so once in a different society with different values, the voice may argue, but we have so many other things to absorb our attention, so many more commodities to choose from that our minds glide rather than meditate, are maybe even passive rather than active. Frankly, the argument might conclude, I can't really see why you bother with the poem at all: either (if the argument is put forward by a lover of commodities) because it is so unlike any other commodity, so stubbornly un-commodity-like, that you wouldn't want to bother with it – get a tattoo instead or a T-shirt with a message – or (if you are a critic of commodities) because having had to make its way in a world of commodities in which value is reduced to easy consumability and low price the poem cannot be worth much at all. In order to be consumed, it must become merely a prettified kind of commodity that fools you into thinking that you are having some kind of 'spiritual' experience. Get off the public page, the argument might insist. Nothing happens there. Go subvert instead. Well, yes – the same argument might go on – except subversion too can be bought in neatly packaged tubes.

There is, no doubt, something in both arguments though, and that something will be as true or false as you think and feel it is. What is true and what is misunderstood will depend on you. I, for my part, bear in mind what the poet Martin Bell, who had taught English schools for several years and later, at art college, taught me too, once said: 'Poetry should not be taught in schools. It should be a secret and subversive pleasure'.

Secret and *subversive* and a *pleasure*. Poetry can be all those things and more, once you enter it. It is never simply a neatly packaged tube. While the arguments above all apply, to some degree at least, to the public page, they don't necessarily describe the world in the dreaming head where space is less tidily compressed for consumption. It is true that we are not living in a world of unlimited possibilities. A poem has to appear somewhere and space is limited. If you want to appear in magazines you were probably best not to send them something that occupies a whole page, let alone several pages. And most people start publishing by appearing in magazines. So we come to think the poem is something short that fills a space in a context dedicated to something else, the glimpse of a small bird through the windowpane of a study, but the bird can fly a long way and we can follow it. Nor do we have to stay in the study.

But once out there, how can we get our minds around that longer journey, the long poem. Is it just a rhythmical, possibly rhyming version of the prose story set out in lines? Is it in fact a version – a subversive, submerged, altered version – of the epic? Is it just a collection of short lyric poems that happen to be strung together on some arbitrary string? A series of towns on the map that you can drive through if you really want to but with no particular connection between them?

Let me pursue the town analogy for a while, though later I want to switch to something less fixed and more fluid.

It is worthwhile thinking for a moment about the short lyrical poem – a single one of those 'raw towns' that W. H. Auden in his 'In Memory of W. B. Yeats' said 'we believe and die in'. It is, of course, the business of the whole poetry section of this book to deal with that question but perhaps I could offer a brief necessary handle on it, just so that what follows makes better sense. There are so many definitions out there that any new one is likely to be a vainglorious act of *chutzpah*, but let me have a go.

A lyrical poem, from the point of view of this chapter, is a poem of between roughly, say, six and forty lines, employing some variation on a regular rhythmical unit plus any possible number of known poetic and rhetorical devices to articulate and explore an experience that is registered on the consciousness as something important and vivid but to which you cannot do justice by simply describing it or talking about it. The point of the experience – of all experience when you come to think of it – is that it registers at several levels through memory, association, hope, fear, indifference, fascination, and has then to work its way into language, clearly, memorably, in a way that sings in the nerves like music but has the power of statement. Poetry, at its best, is about what it is like to be alive, now, in the passing minute. It has that kind of intensity, that kind of emotional drive. It is less interested in what happens next than in what exactly it is that is happening now. But that which is happening is not static. It cannot be simply 'described': it shifts and drifts all over the place. A poem has to move through some transformation in which the transformations that go on in any experience are enacted. Something, in all poems, is different by the end. Something moves and happens next, but the interest is not so much in destinations as in the sense of movement, in some crucial shift in the apparently frozen moment.

To sum up, a lyric poem is usually the enactment of a single experience that is associated with others, and a way of exploring how these others hang with the original one, so that by the end of the exploration we have arrived at a new point of understanding, an understanding that cannot be articulated any other way, that cannot be paraphrased, because the experience it makes is made in those specific words and in those specific order. To read a poem is not like measuring a field: it is rolling around in the grass. It is a way of understanding the field directly. A lyrical poem is that sort of experience.

There you are. It is pretty long as explanations go, but it's the excitement of it – the level of potential excitement – that matters, that mixture of music and statement. There's nothing fancy about it in itself. It's not mystical or intellectual stuff: it is just what *is* and how what we say embodies and transforms what *is*. That is our basic block, the bead we may be trying to arrange on a string, the town along the route we might drive through.

There are two main ways such a body of words may be joined together, one closer to straight prose narrative than the other, so let me start with the one in which the raw towns are clearly distinct and might even appear to be strewn a little off track: the poem sequence.

The sequence

A poem sequence, you might argue, is not exactly a single narrative poem, nor exactly a group of poems that happens to be about a particular subject. The ties between the poems that comprise it are looser than they would be in a story, but not quite so loose as in a batch of poems about the same thing, in which the order is of no particular importance, or is not, at least, conceived to be of importance. (A narrative impression may be created by a later ordering of poems and that impression may not be beside the point, but the issue here is the conception.)

A sequence, then, as the word implies, is a particular order without the 'and then'-ness too heavily inscribed in it. It is not a series of cliff-hangers in which we necessarily follow the fortunes of a single group of characters. What holds it together and gives it a sense of progression is more a sense of consistent, developing exploration. A sequence is a consecutive set of poems that embark on a journey to find something that is only guessed at in the beginning. It resembles the individual lyric poem in that it is an enquiry into the meaning of an experience or group of experiences, an enquiry that may well entail catching a flight to a distant city, or moving underwater to follow the faint scent of something that seems important enough to follow, but here one enquiry leads to another naturally connected one. It is a journey. The journey, as in fiction, as in any text or speech, is through language in the first place, but through the particular kind of language that has been developed for just this purpose, with just this instinct in mind, the language of poetics.

By poetics here I mean essentially any device that has a historical association with poetry, historical because we don't make language from scratch. Language carries its history with it and no more intensively perhaps than in poetry. As one of the greatest

American poets of the twentieth century, Elizabeth Bishop, put it in her poem, 'At the Fishhouses':

> It is like what we imagine knowledge to be:
> dark, salt, clear, moving, utterly free,
> drawn from the cold hard mouth
> of the world, derived from the rocky breasts
> forever, flowing and drawn, and since
> our knowledge is historical, flowing, and flown.
> (Bishop 1983: 66)

The knowledge in the poem is of the sea, but if even the sea is historical how much more must language be so. Language, for a poet, is something you put your hand in and feel.

Very well then, let us switch analogies from towns to seas and currents. Let us say a poem sequence is a journey through a medium that is, in Bishops' words to do with history, a history that is 'flowing and flown', and that its movement is less like that of a train, more like that of sea or water. That is to say it consists of currents and that the journey therefore is one of currents.

Poem sequences have been with us a long time. There are poem sequences in Latin, in all languages in fact, because the sequence is probably the most natural of longer poetic constructions. But let's take a modern – indeed early Modernist – poem as a possible example, Wallace Stevens's 'Thirteen Ways of Looking at a Blackbird' that begins:

> I
> Among twenty snowy mountains,
> The only moving thing
> Was the eye of the blackbird.
>
> II
> I was of three minds,
> Like a tree
> In which there are three blackbirds.
>
> III
> The blackbird whirled in the autumn winds.
> It was a small part of the pantomime.
>
> IV
> A man and a woman
> Are one.
> A man and a woman and a blackbird
> Are one.
> (Stevens 1997: 74–5)

These are all, clearly, about a blackbird, or about the sensation of seeing and hearing a blackbird. What does it mean to hear a blackbird? Could Stevens have organised his poem differently, starting with, say the fourth part? Or the third? Is this an arbitrary order of notations by some over-refined figure with too much time on his hands? But it might be just as well to set the scene first and those snowy mountains do serve to do that. Then we shift to the observer and the three trees. There is a quiet joke about being 'in two minds'. Then the blackbird takes off and the whole world seems like a pantomime. A woman appears, and the sense of love. The man and woman are watching the blackbird together: the blackbird brings them together; it is an aspect of the togetherness. It is a natural thing to be together. There is some kind of harmony between living creatures. But then the blackbird stops singing. That's rather nice too, that moment it stops but when you can still hear it in your head.

Granted, this is a kind of philosophical poem. It is the mind that is moving, not so much the actors, but there does seem to be a floating, singing kind of order in the movement. The poem is celebrating something (the blackbird), in fact two things (the language and the blackbird), in fact three things (nature, the language and the black-bird), etc. And so it resounds, though the blackbird, like Stevens, is 'historical, flowing and flown'.

But the sequence need not float quite so delicately and abstrusely through language, nor need it float in free verse. There are more formally structured approaches available, such as the Crown of Sonnets (also known as the Hungarian Sonnet) that consists of fifteen sonnets, the first fourteen ordinary sonnets related by theme but more closely joined by the last line of the first forming the first of the second, the last of the second the first of the third and so on down to the end of the fourteenth, the really demonic thing about the fifteenth being that it is made up of the fourteen first lines of the previous sonnets. It is an obsessive, intricate shape. A number of contemporary poets have used it including John Fuller, Peter Scupham, Nigel Forde, and I myself wrote a group of three such poems in what might seem a fit of madness for a 1998 book. Peter Scupham's poem, 'The Hinterland', written in the early 1970s, was about the First World War, and looked to place that war in the cycle of human history, a cycle in which the observer too was involved. The way the sonnets link together can be shown by joining the end of one sonnet (the third for instance) to the beginning of the next, like this:

> 3.
> . . .
> They were buried shallow and the putrid meat
> Soured through the grass, wept the green over
> 'So the cattle were observed to eat
> Those places very close for some years after.'
> > We fat the dead for our epiphanies,
> > But there's a no-man's-land where skull talk goes.

> 4.
> But there's a no-man's land where skull talk goes:
> She sits alone by the declining sea;
> Winds turn continually upon their course
> And all their circuits are a vanity . . .
> . . .

> the sonnet ending:

> . . .

> A hinterland to breed new summers in.
>
>   (Scupham 2002: 104)

And these are joined in lines four, five and six of the fifteenth and last sonnet like this:

> But there's a no-man's-land where skull talk goes,
> A hinterland to breed new summers in.
> The unfleshed dead refusing to lie down –
> . . .
>
>   (Scupham, 2002: 110)

It is an intricately linked series of events in the sea of language: it is the current that matters. There's room in the passage above for a quotation from another book ('So the cattle were observed to eat'), for the introduction of a woman sitting by the sea, for a little turn of the wind, for figures of speech that refer to emblems and moralities, but then that's the whole idea of the poem – or rather its mode of feeling – it feels the event of the war as it works its way into myth and memory. It isn't quite a narrative of course. It is not consequences that are linked along its journey, but a series of registerings. The mind registers this or that impression or experience and strives to give it, to give the combination of them, a shape in language.

Wallace Stevens and Peter Scupham are both contemplative, erudite poets. That is not to say they are merely cerebral because everything they think they also feel, and those feelings are very precisely and passionately registered. Stevens is interested in philosophy and aesthetics, Scupham in history and memory. Stevens is music, Scupham ghosts. But neither is exactly demotic, that is to say their voices are not of what tend to value as being of 'the street'. Their noise isn't street noise. I quote them to demonstrate the main aspects of the mechanism of the sequence, the almost intangible way in which passages that follow one another are linked by motif, association, theme and formal devices.

The sequence will support any kind of mindset though. You don't have to be an intellectual, a scholar or an aesthete to explore it. Poetry belongs to everyone. That is not to say it has to look too determined to endear itself to everyone. It is best as itself, not pretending. If it sings itself truly people will come to it.

The American poet Adrienne Rich's 'Twenty-One Love Poems' is exactly what the title says it is, twenty-one linked poems of roughly sonnet size about love, though the love is set as part of an exploration of feminism and is directed towards another woman. This is how it begins:

> I
> Wherever in this city, screens flicker
> with pornography, with science-fiction vampires,
> victimized hirelings bending to the lash,
> we also have to walk . . .
> . . .
> No one has imagined us. We want to live like trees,
> sycamores blazing through the sulfuric air,
> dappled with scars, still exuberantly budding,
> our animal passion rooted in the city.

II
I wake up in your bed. I know I have been dreaming.
Much earlier, the alarm broke us from each other,
you've been at your desk for hours.
   . . .
. . . and I laugh and fall dreaming again
of the desire to show you to everyone I love,
to move openly together
in the pull of gravity, which is not simple,
which carried the feathered grass a long way down the upbreathing air.
                                                        (Rich 1993: 77–8)

Beginning with impressions of the street, it describes the world in which the lovers live, a world of 'rancid dreams, that blurt of metal, those disgraces', then, in the second poem, zooms up close the way a film might, to give an intimate picture of the lovers before moving on, in the third poem, into memory of the past. It is something like a cross between a letter and a film in this respect, and the film is in fact a useful analogy for the sequence. (Analogies are always useful – all poetry is analogy – as long as we don't take the analogy literally, for the one thing poetry is not is 'literal'.) By film I don't mean a straightforward Hollywood kind of film but something more adventurous: the kinds of things you can do with film, narrative techniques explored in pop-videos of the less glossy or clichéd sort for example. Sharp cuts, changes in colour and angle, panning across to follow a moving figure, zooming in, dissolving, all these are reasonably useful ways of referring to the notion of the poem-sequence.

Then there is the theme of course. The journey – we mustn't forget the journey – is about following the glimpse of something that seems to matter for some reason. That thing we follow is a notion of the theme, but however formal the *poem* is, the *poetry* moves by its own underwater radar, sensing the currents.

The long poem

The long poem of the epic kind often involves gods and supernatural beings as well as people, usually engaged in some great emblematic war or voyage that entails conflict, such as the Iliad, the Odyssey, the Aeneid, the Nibelungelied, Beowulf, the Mahabharata, the Ramayana, or the Epic of Gilgamesh. There are many epics of various types, and most cultures possess one that draws on history and mythology offering the culture a definition of itself.

But long poems of other kinds exist. Some wars-and-voyages narratives are about creation or ancestry, others about the rationale for some particular world or social order. The affairs of the gods, in the thirteenth century Roman Catholic Dante's hands became a tour of the regions of Hell, Purgatory and Heaven. A little later in the fourteenth century Geoffrey Chaucer told stories of the Canterbury pilgrims in his *Canterbury Tales*, a series of colourful anecdotal narratives spoken by specific characters. John Gower also worked with tales in his *Confessio Amantis*. William Langland's *Piers Plowman* is a dream vision. Then comes the great age of poetic drama, of Marlowe and Shakespeare and Webster. In the seventeenth century Puritan John Milton's *Paradise Lost* considers God and the fall of humankind in great musical unrhymed narrative verse.

An alternative model arises in the eighteenth and nineteenth centuries once the activities of gods are seen in a more rational, less mystical framework. Humour and irony re-cast the epic. There are long satires by, for example, John Dryden in the late seventeenth century, his chief follower being Alexander Pope who writes a mock-heroic epic, *The Rape of the Lock*, as well as other long poems that are essentially about ideas. He deals with these through biting wit, an extraordinarily attuned ear and brilliant rhyme. His discursive poems give rise to a lot of imitations, with long poems about various subjects, from smoking and cooking through to cider and art. They generally use much the same techniques – Pope's – some well enough and entertainingly but none to such effect. Pope himself draws on discursive poems of the ancient Greek and Latin period: poems about ideas, about science, or art, or society, or work.

There is perhaps a limit to the excitement aroused by civilised rationality in the form of witty, polite conversation. In the Romantic period, it is the state of the individual and its relationship to nature, rather than God, that becomes the main theme. The great work in this field is William Wordsworth's autobiographical and philosophical poem *The Prelude* about the growth of the individual mind. Byron's *Don Juan* is a marvellous combination of adventure, romance, comedy and social satire and bears comparison with the poem known and quoted by all Russians: *Eugene Onegin* by Alexander Pushkin. Light and colloquial in tone but dramatic, romantic and philosophical in subject, and available in four highly readable translations, it has been an interesting influence on English language writing in the last twenty years or so.

But once the novel is established as the chief story-telling form – and that process begins in the eighteenth century and is more or less complete by the middle of the nineteenth – the work of social narrative and high adventure is generally taken over by prose. The rhetorical manners of the long poem begin to seem unnatural. The poem has to concentrate on what is its own specific, different province. The long poems of the mid-nineteenth century draw on medieval legends almost as an act of nostalgia, trying to re-establish some kind of natural order or code of behaviour, but though offering wonderful often sonorous passages they don't necessarily convince on the narrative side.

What does the long poem in our own time do? What kinds are there? And what can we ourselves do?

Here are a few examples of what has been thought possible.

The form of the epic voyage is revived by the Nobel Prize winning Caribbean poet, Derek Walcott in his book-length *Omeros* that plays directly on the *Odyssey*. Like the Odyssey it is a sea voyage with adventures and a return home. It springs in some ways from one of the best of Walcott's earlier poems, 'The Schooner Flight' that mixed standard English, with patois and bits of French to marvellous effect and gave some useful advice to those attempting long poems:

> You ever look up from some lonely beach
>   and see a far schooner? Well, when I write
> this poem, each phrase go be soaked in salt:
> I go draw and know every line as tight
> as ropes in this rigging; in simple speech
> my common language go be the wind . . .
>   (Walcott, 'The Schooner Flight', 1, 1986: 347)

That sense of the line as tight as ropes in rigging, in simple speech is necessary to most long poems that take the epic route. Walcott rhymes unobtrusively (beach / speech, write / tight, etc.) and his use of the loose enjambment gives the poetry the prose drive of the sentence without ever losing the wavelike rhythmic pulse of poetry. At sixteen pages 'The Schooner Flight' could be considered a long poem, but *Omeros*, written in a more standard English, comes in 325 pages, showing how flexible the definition is.

Les Murray's *The Boys Who Stole the Funeral* is a novel in sonnets, much like Vikram Seth's *The Golden Gate*. Murray's poem-novel is also about a return, to the Outback in this case. Seth's is a witty, social novel whose tone picks up from Byron and Pushkin: light, conversational, ingenious. Murray has also written a novel-length travelogue-epic, *Fredy Neptune*, about a man who loses his ability to feel, then travels around the world.

Like all poems that are also partly novels the work is subject to a two-fold criticism, firstly from those who read it as a poem, and then those who prefer to read it as a novel. The problem perhaps is that a long poem, even one of novel length, is not – indeed cannot be – a novel as such, because the novel itself is historically defined: it is not the whole enterprise of narrative, only one form of it.

Fiona Sampson and Deryn Rees-Jones have recently written long poems of short novella length. Rees-Jones's book, *Quiver* is a sort of detective story about a poet following up the discovery of her husband's old lover. It moves through a sequence of short poems that serve for chapters, some as short as nine lines:

> She takes my arm, says 'Ssssshhh',
> pushes a note in my gaping pocket.
> Her dark eyes are cool as a church,
> fixing on mine, both query and quest.
>
> Who's written this strange yet familiar script?
> Who's following who?
> Then she's off, and I'm left with her whisper,
> a mark on my arm where her grip was too tight,
> handwritten lines on an unlined page.
> ('Then', Rees-Jones 2004: 42)

The language is slightly more charged than it would be in prose here (those eyes, 'cool as a church', the wordplay on query / quest and on lines / unlined) but the story is clear, although it is told in mostly notational form by the central character who, being a poet, naturally thinks and writes like a poet, albeit a poet under the pressure of action. The book begins with a nod to Dante and with characters like Nate Devine (hinting at a divine birth) the story is clearly more than about a routine murder.

Sampson's *The Distance Between Us* is a more overtly philosophical search for the self in terms of narrative and sequence, in fact it is almost more sequence than long poem in that the narrative arc is secondary to the enquiry, which is conducted through meetings and reflections, as if there were an action but the poems had decided to work in the margins in order better to seek the meaning. Her reading of European poetry, of European states of mind, is an important part of the development:

> Scars on a map.
>
> The distance between us
> might be no more than fifty yards

under the proscenium arch
of a stairwell.

Might be no more than half an hour:
time stepped out of its daily clothes
every second febrile
as the hair's on a girl's skin . . .
              ('Brief Encounter', Sampson 2005: 31)

This complex, allusive poetry is far from the novel in terms of voice, but is driven by the necessity of a search. You could argue that the crime-novel, a genre developed chiefly in the twentieth century, has bred its own poetics, that the reader – or the watcher of the film derived from the book – is participating in a kind of poetry of moods and hidden meanings. So Raymond Chandler, for example, whose poetry-quoting detective Philip Marlowe has become the fount of all private-eye clichés since, lends himself to poetry, as do the films of Alfred Hitchcock and other directors of mysteries. *Time's Fool* by Glyn Maxwell is another mystery verse novel of wandering and seeking.

And it may be true that the syntax of film has entered the bloodstream of poetry, particularly of long poems, and that we may be able at some stage to talk of long poems in terms of establishing shot, tracking, zoom, fade-out and so forth, because all these are narrative devices, and because out common culture is as likely to be informed by films as by books.

There are light long poems by John Fuller on art forgers, by Ranjit Bolt (in rhyming couplets) on a girl's quest for romance. Pushkin stanzas, sonnets, rhyming couplets, *terza rima* and ballad are after all stories seeking song form. The storyline in these lighter textured poems may sometimes be fragmentary, but is rarely too far from the colloquial, so should make a natural enough read for the general reader.

It is clear that poets sometimes want to push at the edges of their craft and see whether the long arc of narrative can be accomplished by means other than prose with its relentless forward drive. Poetry itself seems to clamour for it. It will not always be crammed into the spaces between other things or be satisfied with a single breath or a single if complex perception. Rhythm, after all, is the most natural of instincts, and song follows close behind.

This is by no means an attempt to define a canon of long poems or poem sequences. If it were it would certainly include Basil Bunting's 'Briggflats', David Jones's 'In Parenthesis', Ted Hughes's 'Crow', Louis MacNeice's 'Autumn Journal', John Berryman's 'Dream Songs', Marilyn Hacker's novel in sonnets, 'Love, Death and the Changing of the Seasons', Anthony Hecht's 'The Venetian Vespers', Andrew Motion's 'Independence', Craig Raine's 'History, The Home Movie', Bernardine Evaristo's 'The Emperor's Babe', a number of poems by W. H. Auden, Peter Reading and many many other works, to mention only those written in the twentieth century. I have tried instead to establish one or two historical markers then pick up on contemporary work, particularly by younger writers. It is by no means a way of saying that the books I have discussed in brief are worth reading and the rest are less so.

References

Auden, W. H. (2004), *Collected Auden*, London: Faber.
Bishop, Elizabeth (1983), *Complete Poems*, London: Chatto & Windus, Hogarth Press.

Bolt, Ranjit (2001), *Losing It*, London: John Murray.

Byron, Lord (1982), *Don Juan*, London: Penguin.

Chaucer, Geoffrey (2005), *The Canterbury Tales*, London: Penguin Classics.

Dryden, John (2003), *The Major Works*, Oxford: Oxford University Press.

Eliot, T. S. (2004), *Complete Poems and Plays*, London: Faber.

Forde, Nigel (2003), *A Map of the Territory*, Manchester: Carcanet Oxford Poets.

Fuller, John (1996), *Collected Poems*, London: Chatto & Windus.

George, Andrew (trans.) (2003), *The Epic of Gilgamesh*, London: Penguin.

Gower, John (2005), *Confessio Amantis*, London: Penguin.

Hacker, Marilyn (1995), *Love, Death and the Changing of the Seasons*, New York: Norton.

Hatto, A. T. (trans.) (1973), *The Nibelungenlied*, London: Penguin.

Heaney, Seamus (trans.) (2000), *Beowulf*, London: Faber.

Homer (1992), *The Odyssey*, trans. George Chapman, Knoxville: Wordsworth Classics.

Homer (1998), *The Iliad*, trans. Robert Fitzgerald, Oxford: Oxford University Press.

Langland, William (1999), *Piers Plowman 'B' Text*, Knoxville: Wordsworth Classics.

MacNeice, Louis (1989), *Collected Poems*, London: Faber.

Maxwell, Glyn (2001), *Time's Fool*, London: Picador.

Milton, John (2003), *Paradise Lost*, London: Penguin.

Murray, Les (1989), *The Boys Who Stole the Funeral*, Manchester: Carcanet.

Murray, Les (1998), *Fredy Neptune*, Manchester: Carcanet.

Narayan, R. K. (trans.) (2004), *The Mahabharata*, London: Penguin.

Pope, Alexander (2006), *The Major Works*, Oxford: Oxford University Press.

Reading, Peter (1997), *Collected Poems: Poems, 1970–84, Volume 1*, Newcastle, Bloodaxe.

Rees-Jones, Deryn (2004), *Quiver*, Bridgend: Seren Books.

Rich, Adrienne (1993), *Adrienne Rich's Poetry and Prose*, Barbara Charlesworth Gelpi and Albert Gelpi (eds), New York: Norton.

Sampson, Fiona (2005), *The Distance Between Us*, Bridgend: Seren.

Sattar, Arshia (trans.) (2001), *The Ramayana*, India: Penguin.

Scupham, Peter (2002), *Collected Poems*, Manchester, Oxford Poets: Carcanet.

Seth, Vikram (1999), *The Golden Gate*, London: Faber and Faber.

Stevens, Wallace (1997), *Collected Poetry and Prose*, New York: The Library of America.

Walcott, Derek (1986), *Collected Poems*, New York: Farrar, Straus & Giroux.

Wilde, Oscar (2003), *The Complete Works of Oscar Wilde*, London: Collins.

Wordsworth, William (1995), *The Prelude*, London: Penguin.

SCRIPTWRITING

23

Introduction to Scriptwriting

Mike Harris

The argument

Beckett, Tarantino, Churchill, Shakespeare, Ponte, Buñuel, Wagner and the writers of The Archers all have something essential in common: if they want an audience to understand what they say, they have to keep us in our seats till they've finished saying it. The poet doesn't have to do that, and although the novelist needs the reader to keep turning pages, her task doesn't have to be completed in one sitting. Only the scriptwriter has to deal with the problem of passing time in this immediate and visceral way.

Scriptwriters create the interest and attention of an audience mainly through narrative. Even scriptwriters who subvert narrative can't do so without using its conventions. This is not surprising given that we're soaked in stories from the earliest age. What is surprising is that when we come to write we often focus on anything but narrative: the ideas or the language or the characters or our experience, as if narrative were a lower form of aesthetic life which can either be dispensed with or left to itself to evolve slime-like while we concentrate on these spiritually higher matters; and it's the main reason why scripts don't work. So this chapter is about dramatic narrative and its practical uses.

The basics

An exercise that establishes the basics is to give a group five minutes to write a simple story or anecdote (no dialogue or descriptions and no longer than a paragraph). Collect them in, un-named, re-distribute them and invite people to read out the one they got. Each will inevitably involve one or more of the essential building blocks (a specific world, a protagonist, an incident that starts the story off, a chain of events, plot twists, a theme, etc.) which can be identified and form the basis of further discussion.

In a drama things have to happen. Yes, really. Small children who write stories that are simple chains of events ('I got up, had my breakfast, walked to the bus stop, got scooped up by a passing pterodactyl and dropped my homework') have grasped the essentials. In *King Lear* our protagonist gives up his kingdom, divides it up on the basis of which daughter says she loves him best, disinherits the one who won't lie, marries her off to a Frenchman and then banishes the best friend who points out to him the folly of all this, and that's only scene one. What the plot of Lear has, which the child's story above doesn't, is plausibility.

Chains of plausibly-connected events keep people in their seats not only because they create anticipation and suspense but also because in them character is explored and thoughts provoked. Novelists editorialise and write down the thoughts of their characters at will. A scriptwriter can of course use soliloquy and narration and in radio drama all forms of direct address can be especially effective (see the chapter on 'Radio Drama') – but performances composed entirely of these put a heavy strain on audience attention: which is probably why Ancient Greek and Medieval priests added incident and dialogue to their ceremonies and thus gave rise to drama in the first place (See Thomson, *Aeschylus and Athens* [1980] and Chambers [1963], *The Medieval Stage* for detailed discussions of this).

In the main, therefore, Drama explores character and ideas through the medium of events, generally in the following way: when characters confront obstacles they have to act (or not act) in one way or another. The choice they make reveals them. We think *Macbeth* is a loyal subordinate but when ambition overcomes the obstacle of his conscience, he kills the King and we realise he's not so loyal after all. Robert McKee calls this a 'story event' (McKee 1999: 33–5). And that's a useful term because it makes a distinction between events in life, which are more often than not meaningless, and events in a play, which can't be.

The more 'story events' in a script, the more obstacles we see a character dealing with and the more various, the more we are likely to understand (or be puzzled by) him, and the more liable we are to ask questions: why do Vladimir and Estragon persist in waiting for Godot? Why do they not leave, or commit suicide? Why don't we?

The mechanics of this can be explored by inventing aloud a simple collective story in which the group can employ only physical obstacles. Here's one: a powerful woman dresses in a rush because she's late for the most important business meeting in her life but still pauses to hug her beloved poodle. She goes to the front door – and? Physical obstacle only, please. It won't open. OK so she looks for the key – and? She can't find it/it breaks/whatever. Fine, so she tries the back door all the windows and? The windows won't break, the phone won't work, people don't see her when she waves. Time-shift: a week later. She's eaten all the food in the fridge. What's she going to do? Eat the dog! shouts a cynic. Not yet, you reply, because she loves it, doesn't she? Time-shift three more days. Is she hungry enough to eat the dog now? Yes! Cry all but the most hardened pet-lovers. But she's got to catch it first and kill it, hasn't she? Stop the story and discuss how we've turned this sophisticated woman into a primitive hunter and tested the limits of her values; mostly by keeping the doors shut.

The list of story events in a play are its most basic structure and if we haven't got enough we haven't got a play. The approximate number of significant story events a script needs depends on taste, length, genre and medium. Full-length films tend to have more than full-length stage or radio plays. Action thrillers more than European art films. Writing by numbers is idiotic but given that most of us generally under-estimate just how many narrative ideas we need to tell our stories effectively, it's worth quoting (sceptically) a guesstimate. McKee reckons you need forty to sixty full-blown story events in a feature film and forty or so in a full-length stage play. Most first drafts I come across, including my own, certainly have far fewer, which is one reason why they aren't working.

Count the number of times in a great play or film when characters confront obstacles. Then count the number of times your own protagonist confronts obstacles. It will almost certainly be far fewer.

Obstacles in story events aren't just physical. They can also be the conflicting desires of other people: for example the younger son who resents his returning father in Andrei

Zvyagintsev's *The Return*; or social: for example the racism of the 60s deep South, against which Sidney Poitier's sophisticated New York cop has to struggle in order to conduct a murder investigation in *In The Heat Of The Night*; or psychological. In *Hiroshima mon amour*, we gradually realise that The Woman's rejection of The Man is a deep-seated response to the death of a lover when she was eighteen. The arena of such a script is primarily interior; its gladiators the competing impulses within a character: not Arnie with an Uzie, but that memory you don't want to walk over. Radio Drama is particularly suited to dramatising psychological conflicts.

Most story events in drama occur because Character A wants something different than Character B. This can be reduced to an equation, if you are so inclined. A wants x, B wants y and therefore z (where z is what happens as a result). If there is ever a moment in a script when A wants x and B wants x too, and they both get it, it's either the end, a third antagonistic force is about to ruin the idyll (for example, Martians, a psychopath, a Bad Thought, etc.) or your story just died. It may also suggest that you have characters who are too similar. A cast of characters should be as diverse as possible in order to maximise the range of possible conflict. The equation above is a crude but useful way of testing whether story events in an outline or in a scene are working, and what's wrong with them if they're obviously not. What does your A want? Is it different than what your B wants? If it isn't, why not? If it is, what happens as a result, if anything? If you don't know the answer to all these questions, why have you started writing?

Scenes and sequences

Whenever the narrative shifts in time or space, the scene changes, with the exception of single-room dramas. In these the location is fixed so the scene changes whenever the script shifts in time and, if you like, whenever a character enters or leaves thus affecting the balance of power, for example see *12 Angry Men*.

The essential core of any scene on stage, and a long scene (or a sequence of quick-cutting very short scenes) on radio or screen, is at least one story event. Most will have more. For example the two-page first 'scene' of Harold Pinter's *The Dumb Waiter* (between lights up and Gus retiring to the toilet) contains a couple of dozen small story events. There are long scenes that don't have any and most need to be dumped or re-written. Some might be giving or establishing essential information but they're a lower order of life and are altogether better if they contain a story event as well. There are lots of short scenes in film which simply give information. For example establishing shots which give us an external view of the location in which the next scene will take place, and travelling shots like the many we get of John Mills and co. trudging through blizzards in *Scott of the Antarctic*. Scenes in film can convey a simple single piece of information very quickly. More complicated meanings are often made by editing together lots of these simple shorter bits. This can also happen in radio drama, but it's less common. The basic narrative unit in film is frequently the scene sequence, for example the Polish wedding in the first act of *The Deer Hunter*, and then it's this that always needs at least one story event.

To all intents and purposes a scene or scene sequence *is* the story event that controls it. When we list story events, in the order in which we think they might occur, we have our most basic plan.

Prose descriptions of what's going to happen in a script are a good way of forcing oneself to think and plan. This is not a late intrusion of Hollywood into serious writing: 'The poet should first plan the general outline and then expand by working out appropriate episodes'

(Aristotle's *Poetics*, fourth century BC). Our reasons for not planning enough have nothing to do with seriousness and everything to do with the fact that thinking is much harder than writing screeds of bad dialogue; which is why we generally start writing dialogue before we know properly what we're writing it for and then run out of ideas. It's possible of course to finish a draft and then try to decide what it's all about. The problem is you might just decide it's not about anything and have to dump months of work, which is demoralising, wasteful and not viable on a serious writing course or with a commission because both have deadlines attached. An outline, or something like it, is therefore essential. You can discuss an outline with others and discover quickly that there's only three story events in it and then profitably wonder what's going to be going on for the other hour and three quarters? An outline can be re-drafted in far less time than a whole script and then repeatedly pulled apart and put back together until it's got enough plausible story events in it, so that if you start writing and get stuck on one scene you can drop it, write an easier one, and come back to the hard one later when, if you're lucky, you'll have figured out the first problem whilst you weren't looking.

Beginnings . . .

Of course, planning and organising aren't just a matter of listing in roughly the right order all the story events one can think of, although that's a good start. It's well known, for example, that every script has to have a beginning, a middle and an end. So why not start at the beginning?

Problem is, stories don't start at the beginning. They start when we know everything we need to know in order to understand the story when it *does* start. Take the panto script of Cinderella. Before we can make any sense of the main storyline involving a fairy godmother, a ball and a glass slipper test, we have to know that Cinders is badly treated by her step-mum and sisters, that she is deserving and beautiful, lives in an undemocratic state run by a bachelor prince who is looking for a bride, and also it's the kind of world in which magic can happen. That's the set-up, without it the story can't work and it's generally sensible to do it as quickly and as economically as possible. In *Die Hard* we need to know that Bruce Willis is an ordinary-Joe New York cop visiting his estranged and more successful wife in California, and that he still loves her. We get Cop when a fellow plane passenger sees his gun and asks about it. We get the back story on his marriage when a nosy chauffeur badgers it out of him. We understand some of the complexity of his feelings when he keys his wife into a computerised reception and discovers, resentfully, that she's reverted to her maiden name.

When the set-up's completed the story needs something to make it start. This is a very particular story event or a series of proximate and linked events – call it the Inciting Incident or Plot Point 1 or what you like (McKee prefers 'inciting incident', Syd Field 'Plot Point 1' – it doesn't matter) – but it's the big bang that disturbs the status quo of the fictional world, creates volatility and makes narrative life possible. 'The inciting incident' in the panto Cinderella is of course the fortuitous arrival of a Fairy Godmother after Wicked Step-mother has banned Cinders from the ball.

Robert McKee insists that 'the inciting incident' has to happen 'in the story' (McKee 1999: 189–94) and Syd Field that it happen no later than page thirty (Field 2003: 119) but the fact is that in drama outside mainstream Hollywood it occurs almost everywhere. In Chekhov's *Uncle Vanya* it's the arrival of the professor and his young wife months before the play begins; in the *Oresteia* of Aeschylus it happens in the mythic past when Tantalus feeds the Gods on his own son's flesh and so brings down a curse upon The House of Atreus. And in Christopher Nolan's back-to-front memory-thriller, *Memento*, it happens, quite remarkably, at the very end of the film. But it's normally a lot closer to the beginning of a script and tends to need to be if you want to avoid your audience turning off before you've even started. In *Die Hard* it's the classic twenty minutes in, when Alan Rickman's gang capture the building and Bruce Willis's wife but not Bruce himself. Elizabethan theatre-goers were as familiar with the conventions of stage kingship as we are with cop-show procedurals so the inciting incident of *King Lear* can occur early (before the end of Scene One). However, in *Brazil*, Terry Gilliam's quirky, complicated dystopia about a state dominated by a cruel but comically inefficient bureaucracy (and ventilation ducts), it takes nearly fifty minutes to arrive. In a long set-up it helps if there's a sub-plot in it to tide us over till the real story begins. In *Brazil* it's the wrongful arrest of the innocent Buttle instead of the renegade ventilation engineer Tuttle. It's even better if the sub-plot is a thematic variation on the main one, which Tuttle and Buttle is, so it not only grips us but also helps us understand the rules of the world we're in.

No matter where it occurs, however, the inciting incident obliges the protagonist to act, or leads us to expect that he will, eventually. In *Die Hard*, Bruce Willis has to because he's trapped and Alan Rickman's just kidnapped his wife. Hamlet thinks he has to because the ghost of his murdered father has just grassed up his step-dad.

Middles

. . . and then what? There's a whole series of obstacles in the way, of course. What keeps things going is the protagonist's persistence in seeking to overcome them and the insights we gain as that happens. Protagonists persist long after most of us would have given up and gone to the pub. That's how they get to be protagonists. Even Hamlet – the greatest prevaricator in world drama – doesn't actually give up, and *Macbeth* fights on even when he realises his death is inevitable because Macduff was Not of Woman Born.

There are of course dramas that don't have a single main protagonist. A good example is Paul Thomas Anderson's magnificent *Magnolia* in which the stories of half a dozen equally important characters are inter-cut throughout. Several things are instructive here: each character's story is plotted as carefully as if he or she were the sole protagonist; we then discover, to our great narrative satisfaction, that the stories gradually link up, and that they all are subtle variations on a common theme. Being unable to decide who is one's main protagonist, is not the same thing at all.

But most scripts do have a single main protagonist and they *are* very pro-active. Syd Field suggests that you can't have one who isn't. If this were true, drama would lose some of it greatest protagonists. For example, The Alienated Hero and an awful lot of Child Heroes. Alienated protagonists find it hard to act – because they are alienated. Hamlet decides he'd better kill his step-dad at the end of Act One and then spends the best part of the remaining four acts not doing it. Child protagonists in an adult world tend to be limited in what they can do. What happens therefore is that other characters act instead. In *Hamlet* virtually every other character in the play does what Hamlet says he ought to do: Ophelia commits suicide, Laertes acts to revenge the death of his father and so on. In Billie August's *Pelle the Conqueror* the child hero is primarily an observer of older lives but each is in some sense a trial run for what he might be when he grows up. As the alienated or child protagonist watches, or dithers, the narrative energy goes to the sub-plots of secondary characters, until he finally acts. Hamlet slaughters almost the entire cast, and Pelle, now pubescent, leaves to make his own life.

King Lear shows how obstacles in The Middle get progressively tougher. When Goneril tries to strip him of some of his rude retinue of knights, Lear goes to Regan in the hope of better treatment but she takes *all* his knights away and Lear, unable to reconcile himself to this or to do anything about it, goes mad.

The course of the plot through the middle doesn't have to be progressively Worse, it can get Worse then Better, or Better then Worse. But it does need to progress and the cost of action nearly always escalates.

Matters are generally forced by one or two major story events that cause things to change (reversals) or which bring the audience or the protagonist to a very different understanding of what has been happening (recognitions). (1) Macbeth kills Duncan and there's no going back, but Duncan's heirs escape. (2) He's consolidating his power at a banquet for the nobles when Banquo's ghost appears and throws him into embarrassing mental torment. (3) He goes back to the witches for re-assurance, they confirm that Banquo's descendants will inherit the throne but tell him his position is secure unless Burnham Wood comes to Dunsinane and he can't be killed by any man of woman born so he's happy, until . . .

When the consequences of one of these main story events, or 'plot turns', or 'twists', have run out and the next has not yet kicked in, the audience will start to fidget and it's time to reach for sub-plot again. In *Memento* when the love-interest, Natalie, proves to our protagonist that the man we saw him shoot at the start was the one who killed his wife, the main story seems to be over. At this point, Nolan gives us in flashback the vital sub-plot/ back story of how our hero discredited another amnesiac whilst conducting an insurance investigation and the tragic consequences that ensued. This holds us in place until we shortly realise that Natalie is not to be trusted and the main plot is on the road again.

Pick a genre and then list what always happens in it. Then pick another, and so on. If we know what generally happens in stories and therefore what the audience will be expecting, there's a chance of coming up with something different. Make everyone decide what genre they are writing in. Some will claim they aren't but they are and pretending not to be is the surest way to write the clichés of the genre in which we are, in fact, writing. *Hamlet* is a great play, in part, because Shakespeare uses the conventions of the Elizabethan revenge tragedy to do something different. *Thelma and Louise* works because it re-imagines the Buddy-Buddy adventure genre for two modern women. When we've worked out what genre or genres we're writing in it's possible to root out the clichés and make something different happen.

Ends

. . . and what happens in the end? The protagonist generally comes up against the greatest obstacle of all, which is usually in some form or other himself, and then he overcomes it, or not. In *Krapp's Last Tape*, Beckett's protagonist literally confronts his younger self in the form of a tape-recording, whilst the final obstacle The Woman in *Hiroshima mon amour* has to face is not whether she loves her new married lover enough to be with him, it's whether she can abandon her love affair with Death and, in the end, we're not sure whether, in choosing the lover, she's done that, or its opposite. This is the Ambiguous Ending. There are also, of course, the Happy and Sad ones. *Uncle Vanya* ends with Vanya and his niece going back to their farm accounts as they return to their life of provincial obscurity (Unhappy). In *Groundhog Day*, Bill Murray gets the girl and time stops repeating itself (Happy). Hollywood films now end with such idiotically predictable happiness that all reasonable people leave the cinema wishing the entire cast had died in a bath of acid instead. But a Happy ending is perfectly viable if you've earned it after inflicting lots of misery, and it's still plausible despite that.

Both McKee and Field require the penultimate sequence or section of a script to be in the opposite mood to the end. So a happy ending should always be preceded by an unhappy sequence and visa versa. This is one of the many reasons why it's possible to watch almost any current Hollywood movie and predict exactly what will happen. But that up-down-up-down rhythm is common in good scripts too. Just when you think it couldn't get any worse for Lear, Cordelia turns up with an army and you just know it's going to be all right, and then she's defeated and it gets much worse. There's a good reason for the prevalence of this pattern. A string of dialogue, scenes, sequences, turns or big story events written in the same emotional register runs the risk of inappropriate audience reaction. One unhappy bit = sad audience; two unhappy bits in a row = not quite so sad audience; three unhappy bits in a row = audience stifling inadvertent guffaws. Scripts that repeat Sad-Sad-Sad or Happy-Happy-Happy and get away with it have to play half-tones in scenes or descend into bathos and worse. In Sarah Kane's *Blasted*, eyes are sucked out, babies eaten and people try to strangle themselves to death in such quick succession that the tittering audience member begins to feel like he's just stumbled into Benny Hill's Theatre of Cruelty. Whereas, although scene after scene in *Magnolia* is unutterably sad, the bleakness is subtly interwoven with strands of dark comedy.

Literary critics merely describe plays. We have to make them better. To do that requires practical evaluative criteria. Academic debates about the impossibility of evaluation since it is always conditional on class, gender or history, or about the irrelevance of The Writer either because we're all dead or because our intentions are always fallacious, are deeply damaging to any writer who takes them seriously. We do exist and we do have to try and make our work better. The evaluative terms described above and below work for me and have proved useful in developing scripts with students, but they may not work for you. Suck them and see. For example: has a draft outline got an inciting incident, and does it start the story off convincingly? Has it got a couple of major 'turns' in the middle; if it's only got one, or none, that's why it feels flabby. Who's the protagonist? If the writer doesn't know (a surprisingly common phenomenon) that's why the whole thing feels unfocused. Look at the cast of characters. What motivates each one, and is it incompatible with what motivates the others? If not, why not? How many of these characters have stories of their own, apart from the protagonist? None? Then the script is going to feel very thin and you've got no sub-plot to play with. Kill characters who do nothing or merge them with another cipher to create a more interesting composite. Are characters being pushed far enough? People in plays are much less dull than people in life and do much more extreme things, even when they're supposed to be ordinary. For example Chekhov's 'ordinary' characters are much given to suicide, and waving guns around. Most important of all, what ideas or values are being explored in the drama? If none are, why are you writing it? Life is very hard to change. Drama on the other hand is an entirely virtual reality that the writer can fiddle with at will until it seems to work.

Dialogue

Most people think Drama is dialogue but they're wrong. Drama is about doing things. The word itself is ancient Greek meaning deed or action and in his *Poetics*, Aristotle lists in order of importance the constituent elements of Tragedy (the dominant dramatic form of his time): (1). Plot, (2) Character, (3) Ideas, (4) Dialogue. If you're disinclined to credit dead foreigners (even when their compatriots invented what you're trying to do) you might prefer to consult the Oxford English Dictionary which defines drama as, 'a series of actions or course of events leading to a final catastrophe or consummation'. It doesn't mention dialogue.

The most common fault in scripts is Too Many Words, which is understandable because the most obvious way of externalising thoughts and feelings is by having one character tell another character what he's really thinking and feeling. The problem is, if a character tells us everything about herself, what's left for the audience to find out and why should we carry on watching? Experience teaches that people aren't like that, anyway. What we say is rarely what we think and what we think is not what really motivates us and what really motivates us is, more often than not, a complete mystery: what is Hamlet's problem at bottom? Or Lear's? We're just not sure, so we keep thinking about them long after the play has ended and centuries after they were first written. Of course, fiction isn't reality and need not be held hostage by it, but when an aesthetic strategy is neither true to life nor dramatically effective, why use it?

The principle way we explore character in drama, as in life, is by comparing what people say, with what they do ('I love you more than word can wield the matter;/Dearer than eye-sight, space and liberty' – Goneril to Lear, [I.i]). Which is why it makes sense, when planning a scene, to start not with a list of things we think should be *said* but with the main story event in it. Dialogue will then happen if A and B happen to use words to get what they want. They may also use violence of course, or silence or gestures, or the merest glance. Moments of silence in drama are more expressive than the noisiest dialogue. Cassandra stands silently to enormous theatrical effect for most of the Second Act of Aeschylus's *Agamemnon*. Whole sequences on film can (and should) contain no dialogue at all. One of my favourites is the long speechless sequence in the middle of the Coen brothers' *Blood Simple*, which culminates in a good man burying his lover's husband alive because he can't bring himself to kill him. Perhaps most remarkable of all is the almost total silence of Anthony Minghella's protagonist in the radio script of *Cigarettes and Chocolate*.

Getting rid of unnecessary words: take a few bad or early draft scenes and set everyone to cut as many words as possible but still tell all the story. Very soon you can't see the black for the red. Then get them to re-write a sequence of their own scenes with very little dialogue – no more than ten or twenty words.

Dialogue in a scene based on conflicted desire is more dynamic and engaging because it involves a struggle for power the outcome of which is uncertain.

In a good scene or scene sequence power is held in contest and then shifts at least once from one character to another. In the *Oresteia*, Clytaemnestra urges Agamemnon to cross the blood-red carpet that will lead him to his death. He refuses, she persuades, he crosses and is lost. In the case of psychological drama, power passes between one aspect of a person's psyche to another. In Tyrone Guthrie's groundbreaking 1930 radio play *Matrimonial News* the thoughts of shop-girl Florence are personified and conflict with each other as she sits waiting for her blind date to arrive.

Conflicted dialogue can sound more like real speech with all its interruptions, half-finished phrases, non-sequiturs and so forth, as in Caryl Churchill's *Top Girls*. This is not because writers set out to copy 'real life' speech, because they don't, being primarily interested in the exploration of character and ideas within a particular aesthetic structure. And most 'real speech' is too unutterably dull to be worth copying, anyway. A tiny portion of it, however, embodies interesting struggles for power or status and we remember this as 'real speech' because it sounds like good dramatic dialogue.

b or at home. Each should l then read it out aloud. be power-play. It was this n't contain conflict. emanating from William : the scene as close to the before it can resolve. The ny first drafts ('Hello come :parture ensures that audi- d out what happens next. : start of *Lear*, Shakespeare an feel drearily functional

than Cornwall?

agreements can of course ood reason, characters tell se scenes in which a suc- ve accept the revelations e of Lorca's *Blood Wedding* nimself now married. The protesting too much, and the importance of making guests are arriving, adding on should be written into

:ets, in an outlining pro- main story event in every apart from talk. After that For example any dialogue carried, and anything else

e plenty of occasions in ...ess the audience but such passages generally dramatise either psychological conflict ('To be or not to be'), or are in conflict with what happens before or after it, for example Edmund's 'I'm the Bad Guy' soliloquy in Act One Scene Two of *King Lear* undermines Gloucester's defence of him in Scene One. And in every case soliloquies must move the drama on or we need to ask, why are they there? When Mozart was trying to re-invent the moribund form of Opera Seria with *Idomeneo*, he bombarded his old-fashioned librettist with demands that the lyrics embody the action and not simply repeat lyrically what the audience knows already (Anderson 1997: 662).

A Chorus can perform many different functions. In Greek Tragedy it sometimes becomes a character in conflict with or a confidante of the protagonist, for example the

Corinthian Women in Euripides *Medea*; at others it performs a holding operation at a moment of great suspense, making the audience wait whilst it reflects on what has gone before. Lorca re-invents this technique very effectively in Act Three of *Blood Wedding*. Greek Choruses often related violent offstage action or essential back story and, Greek Tragedy being closer to opera than modern drama, the lack of dramatic action on stage at these points was compensated for by music, movement and heightened verse. Which is precisely what happens in Steven Berkoff's *Greek* in which characters speak Mockney-Shakespeare and the sheer virtuosity of the language and the physical theatre (actors turning each other into motorbikes, etc.) almost blinds you to the fact that what you are watching is little more than a series of misanthropic music hall sketches. Narrators work like choruses. That is, best if they are part of the play's conflicts and best of all when unreliable. Direct address written simply to cover an inability to tell the story through dramatic action, is best avoided.

Strange worlds, minimalism and anti-narratives

It's widely believed that lots of dramas work without using narrative, or with so little of it that it doesn't signify. Richard Gilman, for example, thinks that Chekhov's *Three Sisters* abandoned, 'the usual linear development of a play . . . from a starting point, to exposition and development . . . to a denouement', and instead, 'worked toward the filling in of a dramatic field' (Chekhov 2002: ix). If this were true we would justifiably baulk at going to Chekhov to learn how to write minimalist dramas of ordinary life, for how does one teach, or learn, how to 'fill in a dramatic field'?

Fortunately, it's not true.

At the most basic narrative level, lots of things happen in *Three Sisters*: a weak, selfish woman marries their beloved older brother who becomes a wastrel and a gambler. His wife gradually takes over the family house, forces the sisters out and has an affair with his boss. Irene gives up her dreams of Moscow to marry the manager of a brick works, who is then killed in a duel by a thwarted admirer. Masha has an affair with an army officer who is unhappily married to a lunatic and then, when he leaves, finds out that her boring husband knew all along. Oh yes, and there's a major conflagration at the start of Act Three. These events all occur in regular time-sequence (not back to front, at random or in flashback) and the multi-narratives are organised into inciting incidents, progressive developments, sub-plots and a dramatic climax.

But Chekhov is very different from the writers of melodrama against whom he was in revolt because he does successfully create a sense of quiet unchanging lives riven by regret and despair. He doesn't do this by abandoning narrative but by using two of the oldest known narrative techniques to help give the impression that this is what he is doing. He sets his most melodramatic events (the duel, the fire and most of the adultery) offstage and tells the rest, 'on the cut', that is, in time-shifts between acts, leaving him free to devote onstage action and dialogue to what may appear to be 'ordinary life', but which, amongst other things is getting the audience up to speed on what's happened since the last act. We realise this soon into Act two, and are thereafter partly hooked by the need to find out not so much what's going to happen next, but what's happened since.

But if we want to boldly go beyond the merely humdrum to the Utterly Purposeless and Absurd, the best pilot is that master storyteller and all-round entertainer, Samuel Beckett. But not if we think that his plays, 'lack plot more completely than any other works', because they adopt 'a method that is essentially polyphonic . . . [confronting] . . . their audience with an organised structure of statements and images that interpenetrate each other and that must be apprehended in their totality' (Esslin 1976: 44). Try teaching that. 'Everyone interpenetrate your meanings in their totality *now* please!'

Luckily Beckett no more does this than Chekhov fills in fields. Take *Waiting for Godot*. He gives us four very distinct characters (Vladimir, Estragon, Lucky and Pozzo) who vie for status throughout a play which is, in essence, a simple one-room, invasion of space drama. There's an inciting incident: when Vladimir informs Estragon and us that they are waiting for Godot, which induces the wholly conventional audience anticipation that Beckett plays cat and mouse with for the next two acts. On several occasions in Act One he deliberately, Hitchcock-like, makes us think that Godot has arrived:

VLADIMIR	Listen!
	(*They listen, grotesquely rigid*)
ESTRAGON	I hear nothing
VLADIMIR	Hssst!

But of course he hasn't. Eventually, instead of him, Pozzo and Lucky arrive to inject danger into the play just when it's in danger of flagging. In between these conventional narrative tropes Becket occupies his waiting audience with stand-up patter and music hall slapstick routines. In the second half the pattern is often said to be identical but isn't. There's considerable development – the power relations between Pozzo and Lucky have been transformed, Vladimir and Estragon are more despairing and it is also, sensibly, much shorter than the first, because by then we know that Godot probably isn't coming and Beckett is too wily a storyteller to push us over the brink. He gives us the illusion of a purposeless, story-less world by invoking narrative expectations that he never, completely, fulfils but which allow him to portray ennui without making his audience feel it (too much).

When one turns to Absurdists like Ionesco and Ominous-ists like Pinter, the case hardly needs making. Ionesco's shtick is injecting highly conventional narrative with something ridiculous to see what effect this has on the audience. Thus the plot of *Rhinoceros* is *Invasion of the Body Snatchers* with rhinoceroses, and *The Lesson* is *10 Rillington Place* with added gibberish. Pinter's preferred mode is to put lots of pauses into highly conflicted, idiomatic dialogue whilst refusing ultimate explanation of his characters' generally violent or oppressive behaviour. *The Room*, for example is, like *Godot*, a conventional invasion of space drama, except we never learn exactly why Riley has come back for Rose or why Bert brutally kills him in the end.

And all these writers also maintain attention and interest second by second with dialogue that contains almost as much blocking and gainsaying per-scene as a soap.

Scripts that inhabit strange worlds are sometimes conflated with these 'anti-narratives' but they are generally even more conventionally structured. So only two additional points need to be made. First, the main plot in a weird world script ought to arise at least partly from the strange conditions of that world, otherwise what's the point? So, in *Delicatessen*, which takes place in a post-holocaust Gallic No-Time in which food is scarce and cannibalism rife, the unemployed clown-protagonist is (of course) in danger of being turned into steak fillets by his butcher-landlord. Secondly, the stranger the world the more helpful to the audience will be at least one conventional narrative strand. It's not an accident that *Delicatessen*, *Brazil*, and *Groundhog Day* (in which the protagonist experiences the same day over and over again) are all partly powered by a love-story.

References

Aeschylus (1977), *The Oresteia: Agamemnon, The Libation Bearers, The Eumenides*, London: Penguin.

Anderson, Emily (ed.) (1997), *The Letters of Mozart and his Family*, London: Macmillan.

Anderson, Paul Thomas (1999), *Magnolia*, screenplay: Paul Thomas Anderson.

Aristotle (2000), *Poetics*, London: Penguin.

August, Bille (1987), *Pelle the Conqueror*, screenplay: Bille August.

Beckett, Samuel (1979), *Krapp's Last Tape, Waiting for Godot*, London: Faber.

Berkoff, Steven (1989), *Greek, Decadence and Other Plays*, London: Faber.

Caro, Mark and Jeunet, Jean-Pierre (1991), *Delicatessen*, screenplay: Gilles Adrien.

Chambers, E. K. (1963), *The Medieval Stage*, vol. 11, book 3, Oxford: Oxford University Press.

Chekhov, Anton (2002), *Three Sisters, Uncle Vanya*, London: Penguin.

Churchill, Caryl (1993), *Top Girls, Plays 2*, London: Methuen.

Cimino, Michael (1978), *The Deer Hunter*, screenplay: Michael Cimino, Deric Washburn.

Coen, Joel (1984), *Blood Simple*, screenplay: Joel Coen, Ethan Coen.

Esslin, Martin (1976), *The Theatre of the Absurd*, London: Penguin.

Field, Syd (2003), *The Definitive Guide to Screenwriting*, London: Ebury.

Frend, Charles (1948), *Scott of the Antarctic*, screenplay: Walter Meade, Ivor Montague.

Gilliam, Terry (1985), *Brazil*, screenplay: Terry Gilliam, Tom Stoppard.

Goldman, William (1984), *Adventures in the Screen Trade*, London: Macdonald.

Guthrie, Tyrone (1931), *The Squirrel's Cage and Two Other Microphone Plays*, London: Cobden Sanderson.

Ionesco, Eugène (1962), *Rhinoceros, The Chairs, The Lesson*, London: Penguin.

Jewison, Norman (1967), *In the Heat of the Night*, screenplay: Stirling Silliphant.

Kane, Sarah (2001), *Blasted (Complete Plays)*, London: Methuen.

Lorca, Federico Garcia (1999), *Blood Wedding, Four Major Plays*, Oxford: Oxford University Press.

Lumet, Sidney (1957), *12 Angry Men*, screenplay: Reginald Rose.

McKee, Robert (1999), *Story: Substance, Structure, Style, and the Principles of Screen Writing*, London: Methuen.

McTiernan, John (1988), *Die Hard*, screenplay: Jeb Stuart.

Minghella, Anthony (1989), *Cigarettes and Chocolate, Best Radio Plays of 1988*, London: Methuen/ BBC Publications.

Nolan, Chris (2000), *Memento*, screenplay: Chris Nolan.

Pinter, Harold (1978), *The Dumb Waiter, The Room*, London: Methuen.

Ramis, Harold (1993), *Groundhog Day*, screenplay: Danny Rubin.

Resnais, Alain (1959), *Hiroshima mon amour*, screenplay: Marguerite Duras.

Scott, Ridley (1999), *Thelma and Louise*, screenplay: Callie Khouri.

Shakespeare, William, *King Lear, Hamlet, Macbeth* (Arden Editions), London: Methuen.

Thomson, George (1980), *Aeschylus and Athens*, London: Lawrence and Wishart.

Zvyagintsev, Andrei (2003), *The Return*, screenplay: Vladimir Moiseyenko, Alexander Novototsky.

24

Writing for the Stage
A blueprint, a suggestive text, a thrown gauntlet for aspiring, stalled, and practising playwrights

Brighde Mullins

Terms and conditions

The word playwright is in the same etymological family as that of a shipwright, a cart-wright, a wheelwright. The words shipwright, cartwright, wheelwright are descriptive: they summon up a craftsperson making a useful object – a ship, a cart, a wheel. A playwright is the maker of a script for the stage, a useful text. The second half of the word play-wright, then, emphasises the craft aspect of writing for the stage. Not that there isn't a good deal of artfulness, and a wealth of aesthetic complexity involved in playwrighting. But these elements are yoked to the psyche of the maker, so much so that they are idiosyncratic and unteachable. Exercises that can increase craft and make a playwright aware of existing models and practical techniques are highly teachable, and they are what will be focused on in this chapter.

Writing for the stage implies that you are writing words that will be spoken by actors and heard by an audience. If you are writing for actors, then actors are your vehicles, your instruments. This is the most important distinction between writing for the stage and writing for another genre. Poems and prose occur in a private space between the reader and the writer. The play, however, like a composer's score or an architect's blueprint, exists as a written text as a stop along the way. The play fully exists only in production, and therefore the single most vital element that a playwright has to shaping her craft is access to a theatre.

The most important information that a playwright can have is an arsenal of experiences in the theatre. By experiences I don't mean that you have to have worked on plays – although that is of course extremely useful. Indeed, one playwright I know (Paul Selig) has said that his best insights and ideas have come to him when he worked on running crew backstage and sat waiting for a cue light. There are some things that only proximity to stagecraft can transmit. If you cannot work in or on a production, the next best thing is to read and then to see plays in performance. If you live near a large city, such as London or New York or Paris, you are in luck on this count.

You should seek out as much theatre as possible, whatever productions you can find. I was raised in Las Vegas, Nevada, which may seem cosmopolitan, but at the time that I grew up (in the late seventies) was really a small town in the Mojave Desert, and the first theatrical productions that I saw were musicals on the Strip. But it was enough to whet my appetite, and as a teenager I started going to the Shakespeare Festival in nearby Cedar City, Utah. If you live in the provinces, or in the desert, then it is necessary to make pilgrimages every now and then to see plays in production. You may live in a city that has an 'underground' theatre scene: Austin, Texas; Los Angeles; Providence; Rochester; many places around the US have theatre scenes that happen in small spaces that are just off the radar of the official theatre culture. You should seek out these venues.

If you do have theatres in your area that are doing plays from the canon, that is also useful: ideally, you should read the script and then go to see the actual production. That is the most practical way to begin to understand the relationship between the page and the stage. A production is a somatic event, an experience that engages all of the senses. There is no substitute for witnessing live theatre. It is the necessary background. The full-immersion of a production is what any play is written towards. And so, seeing a play in production after reading it can help you to fill in the gaps. You can start to see and then to articulate the contributions that designers, actors and directors make in embodying the play. You start to be able to imagine your own writing as being breathed into a space where it can be met and taken up by a collaborator.

Many playwrights also have acting experience. Shakespeare, Molière, Sam Shepard, Athol Fugard and Christopher Durang, Erin Cressida Wilson, Harold Pinter and Tom Stoppard, to name a few. But acting is by no means a prerequisite. Some of our finest living playwrights are essentially very shy people, who would never dream of setting foot onstage. I am thinking of Caryl Churchill and Richard Greenberg. But facets of temperament aside, it is important that you are able to locate the sources of your connection to the theatre, and to read and see as many plays as you can before you start writing for the stage.

The primary thing, then, is to acquaint yourself with practical models, plays that you can read and then go to see in production. In this way, you can see the way that theatre works on the level of the pores: as a physical embodiment, a collaboration with actors and designers, and of course that other unstable but necessary element, an audience.

This chapter will include some writing exercises that I've developed in my ten years of teaching playwrighting at both the graduate and the undergraduate level. Many of these exercises were developed with playwright and film-maker Madeleine Olnek, who is one of the co-writers of the much-used acting textbook *A Practical Handbook for the Actor*, and trained by David Mamet at The Atlantic Theatre Company in NY. My background is also as a poet: and so this methodology brings together a very pragmatic approach toward practice (Mamet's work is heavily method-based) as well as my own more experimental, poetic foundation. It will also discuss ways to focus your writing through the lens of your own obsessions and themes. Writing for the stage starts with writing for the page. Your personal connection to your material, as in all genres, is paramount. Your private obsessions, ideas, ideals, recurring dreams, fondest hopes, greatest fears will be tapped if you are writing, as they say, from the heart and from the gut. All of this sounds abstract, but there is a real skill in being able to translate these areas into a story onstage.

A necessary step

A primary text, a tried and true, both railed against and derided, but always seminal, always indispensable text is Aristotle's *Poetics*. It is both a how-to book and a cook-book. It is also a very practical book to have in that it articulates the tools that a playwright needs to create a playable text. The *Poetics* introduces a vocabulary that is the foundation for thinking and conversing about plays. Whether a playwright misinterprets, over-interprets or attacks the

Poetics, Aristotle is always on some level being referenced. Beyond the fact that he is in our collective bone-marrow then, there is also the practicality of knowing his terms.

What are the ingredients of a play? Aristotle was interested in parsing how a play affects an audience. He was trained as a scientist, so his method was empirical. He was interested in the way that a story, shaped into a plot, was presented to the group-mind of the audience using all of the tools at the playwright's disposal. Aristotle names and describes six ingredients that he noticed as occurring in the plays. These ingredients may be emphasised or de-emphasised, but they are still the template of the dynamic of any play. The choices that the playwright makes in the script as far as emphasising or describing these ingredients are what will guide the production, both in terms of design interpretation, actors' and directors' understanding.

The first three, the most important elements, are the non-perishable elements. These are in the DNA of the script, they are written into the play by the writer. The second three are the elements that are more perishable, and, in Aristotle's understanding, are related to the interpretation or to a particular production. But there is a way to use these elements as well in our writing of plays, and I will emphasise my interpretation of these elements.

Aristotle's elements in a nutshell

1. Plot
Every play must have a beginning, a middle and an ending. This sounds disingenuous, but it isn't. A plot is not a story. Story is not as sculpted as plot. Plot contains elements of causality and consequence; this brings up necessity and inevitability.

2. Character
These are the agents that will enact your story. Aristotle divides characters into tragic and comic, flat and round.

3. Thought
Something is proved or disproved through the writing of the play, through the exploration of the material. We often write to effect a change upon ourselves or upon others.

4. Diction
Diction refers to the spoken rhythms of the language, according to Aristotle. Also, for a writer's purposes, the storehouse of words themselves that a character has at their disposal to describe, to change, to think about their predicament. Since language is a distinguishing feature of the contemporary theatre (film and television can do images so much better) it is worthwhile for a playwright to pay attention to this chapter of the *Poetics*.

5. Music
Again, Aristotle is thinking of production-specific effects, but again, this is not just a phenomenological situation. A play may be structured on musical lines: it can yearn toward a fugue-like structure.

6. Spectacle
Props and scenic design are probably the most perishable elements of all, according to Aristotle. But, again, for our purposes, which are generative, props and scenery can be suggestive. If you consider, for instance, Beckett's situational elements that entail writing

from a place onstage, such as the urns in *Play* or the mound of dirt in *Happy Days*, you see that these elements of place can help to dictate the action of the play.

Aristotle presents a wealth of useful ways of thinking about what it is to write a play. For instance, he emphasises action over narration; and the pleasure of imitation or mimicry. These are still baseline elements of a play, even in the most experimental work. Even the work of Sarah Kane, Mac Wellman and Chuck Mee capitulate to these ways of realising the form.

You can certainly proceed with the exercises in the rest of the chapter without reading the *Poetics*, but I suggest that you go get a copy of it if you don't already own one. I recommend Francis Fergusson's translation. And then, as an antidote and a corollary, read Bertolt Brecht's 'Short Organum for the Theatre'.

Approaches and temperament

There are various ways that playwrights approach writing a play: some work from subject (indeed, Aristotle says that 'the only thing is to have a subject'). The subject of the play is the material from which the play is formed. In psychological terms, the subject is 'one whose actions are studied', which blends into about how we think about the character as carrying the subject into the body of the play. In musical terms, the subject is the principal theme or phrase of a melodic composition.

In philosophical terms, the subject is perceived reality; and since the laws of human perception are our most valuable tools as playwrights, the modes of perceived reality are valuable to contemplate. These are useful distinctions, although at this point they may be a bit abstract-sounding. Some of your preparation for writing your play, for dwelling in the material and the ideas that you are exploring in the play itself, will be to steep yourself in what the play is 'about'.

Some of the play's about-ness has to do with why you are writing the play: perhaps you want to expose the conditions of the working class; perhaps you want to exorcise a personal demon; perhaps you simply want to tell a good story. No matter. The vital thing is that you have the originating impulse.

The writing exercises that follow are improvisatory, in the way that actors sometimes create movement and gesture in rehearsal or as warm ups.

Preliminary exercises

Exercise 1.

Brainstorming
An early exercise that I use with students who have a desire but no clear story yet is a series of generative exercises. The first of these is a writing warm up. Brainstorm a few ideas after writing down these words 'I want to write a play in which . . .' Anything can follow this jumping off point. The writer may want to see a certain image onstage, explore a complicated psychological situation, make people laugh, make people cry. This is a place to begin. It can help you to identify and start to narrow down what you want to work on.

After you write down the words 'I want to write a play in which . . .' start writing and keep writing for at least fifteen minutes. Some writers set an egg timer. Others listen to music. The point is to write in an uncensored fashion for fifteen minutes to write as much as you can generate. As Virginia Woolf writes: 'what is essential is to write *fast* and not break the mood' (Woolf 1981: 282). Then re-read what you've written and isolate and choose three ideas that have bubbled up.

Exercise 2.

Origins

Write about your first theatre experience, as either a participant or as an audience member. Again, write for fifteen minutes and generate as much material as you can. This exercise will put you back in touch with your earliest experiences in the theatre: these early emotions are ones that you should still be trying to graft onto your work, to recreate for yourself and for others. They are what initially got you hooked on theatre.

After re-reading and looking over what you've written, you may be able to locate a subject that interests you. If so, if you are going to work from a subject, you are in good company. Many playwrights work from a desire to understand, to investigate, to search out a terrain. This is the playwright as researcher, as hunter and gatherer. This has to do with channelling your obsessions and realms of interest into your work. This is the underneath of the play. A playwright such as Tom Stoppard writes from this methodology, these are plays of 'ideas'. Not that every play doesn't contain ideas, but Stoppard plays do so rather boldly. I am thinking of *Arcadia*, of *The Invention of Love*, of *Jumpers*. Caryl Churchill also has written from this category, plays such as *Mad Forest* and *Top Girls* take an area or topic (Romania, Victorian sexuality) and examine them from a theatrical stance.

Exercise 3.

Childhood map

Samuel Beckett once said, about Dublin: 'I have changed refuge so many times in the course of my route that I now cannot tell the difference between dens and ruins. I know only the city of my childhood' (Beckett 1997: 61–2). This map exercise is one that I learned from one of my first teachers, the novelist John Irsfeld.

1. Draw a map of a place that you lived in your childhood. Include everything that you can remember about this place on this map. It can be a neighbourhood map, of the locale that you frequented as a child. If you moved around a lot, as I did, choose one particularly resonant place that you lived.
2. Circle places where events happened: describe these events in one or two sentences.
3. Pick one event from your childhood map and write it down; describe it in detail. Use all of your senses in describing this event.

Now that you have a handle on the event, take the event and make it either a setting or part of a scene between two characters, A and B.

This scene may be the seed of a longer play, or a character study. The Irish poet Seamus Heaney has said 'I began as a poet when my roots were crossed with my reading' (Covington 1996) and this exercise takes the playwright's earliest memories and dislocations and brings them to the forefront of the writing.

Reading list

Plays to look at in relation to this writing exercise:

Barry, Lynda (1998), *The Good Times are Killing Me*, New York: Samuel French.

Bowles, Jane (1954), *At the Summer House*, New York: Random House.

Friel, Brian (1998), *Dancing at Lughnasa*, New York: Dramatists Play Service.

Kron, Lisa (2005), *Well*, New York: Theatre Communications Group.

McCullers, Carson (1993), *The Heart is a Lonely Hunter*, New York: Modern Library.

Rapp, Adam (2002), *Nocturne*, London: Faber and Faber.

Vogel, Paula (1999), *How I Learned to Drive*, New York: Dramatists Play Service.

Williams, Tennessee (1998), *The Glass Menagerie*, New York: Dramatists Play Service.

Exercise 4.

Images

1. Collect twenty images. These may come from anywhere: they may be from the newspaper, from magazines, from postcards. Cut them out into manageable sizes and shapes.
2. Look at your twenty pictures; look with an open mind for at least five minutes.
3. Look for some potential relationship among ten of these images.
4. Arrange those ten in some order. Take about five minutes to do this.
5. Write for fifteen minutes about what potential linkage there could be among them.
6. Write three to five lines of text to accompany the images.
7. Now take your pile of discarded images.
   Do the same thing with this pile of images.
   Look at your ten pictures; look with an open mind for at least five minutes.
   Look for some potential relationship between these images.
   Arrange them in some order. Take about five minutes to do this.
   Write for fifteen minutes about what potential linkage there could be among them.
   Write three to five lines of text to accompany the images.
8. Choose one of these scenarios to expand into a scene.

Reading list

Aristotle (1961), 'Spectacle' in *Poetics*, trans., S.H. Butcher, New York: Hilland Wang.

Artaud, Antonin (1966), *The Theatre and Its Double*, New York: Grove Press.

Brook, Peter (1995), *The Empty Space: A Book About the Theatre: Deadly, Holy, Rough, Immediate*, London: Touchstone Press.

Iizuka, Naomi (2003), *36 Views*, New York: Overlook Theatre Press.

Pirandello, Luigi (1987), *The Man with the Flower in his Mouth*, in *Collected Plays*, New York: Riverrun Press.

Vogel, Paula (1992), *The Baltimore Waltz*, New York: Dramatists Play Service.

Exercise 5.

Writing from character

1. Write down on a piece of paper a character that you are drawn to: in literature, mythology, film or public life. In one or two sentences describe why you are drawn to this particular character.
2. Now write down a character from your life, someone who intrigues you on the level of behaviour or appearance. This can be a stranger, someone you see in line at the kiosk, a favourite aunt, whomever. Someone who strikes you, although you aren't sure why.
3. Write two five-page scenes that includes these characters, both the characters from category one and from category two.

Reading list
Aristotle, 'Character and Character Types' in *Poetics*, trans. S. H. Butcher, New York: Hill and Wang.
Brecht, Bertolt (1991), *Galileo*, trans, Eric Bentley, New York: Grove Press.
Churchill, Caryl (1991), *Top Girls*, London: Methuen.
Greenberg, Richard (2003), *The Dazzle* and *Everett Beekin*, New York: Faber and Faber.
Guare, John (2003), *A Few Stout Individuals*, New York: Grove/Atlantic Press.
Kushner, Tony (1993), *Angels in America*, Theatre Communications Group.
Olnek, Madeleine, *Wild Nights With Emily*, unpublished.
Parks, Suzan Lori (2002), *Topdog/Underdog*, New York: Theatre Communications Group.
Stoppard, Tom (1994), *Jumpers*, New York: Grove Press.

Exercise 6.

Writing from place
Quidditas as Aquinas called it, is the ability, the desire to write from a landscape. Onstage this will manifest itself as a setting, and this is a vital place to begin. The setting often dictates what can happen, what kind of language can be used. The limitations are also the potential freedoms. 'To know who you are, you have to have a place to come from' Carson McCullers says (quoted in Heaney 1981: 135), and so a place also conjures up a way of speaking, a way of saying.

Write a treatment or précis, a prose description of an event that *must* take place in one setting. It can be a bar, a bus station, a coffee shop. But the characters must remain in that place. As research you may want to do a transcription exercise, in which you go to the place that you are using as a setting and you record the activities and language that you overhear as closely as possible.

Reading list
Albee, Edward (1998), *The Zoo Story and The Death of Bessie Smith*, New York: Dramatists Play
    Service.
Aristotle (1961), 'The Unities' in *Poetics*, trans. S. H. Butcher, New York: Hill and Wang.
Baraka, Amiri (1971), *Dutchman and the Slave*, New York: Harper Perennial.
Fugard, Athol (1996), *Valley Song*, New York: Theatre Communications Group.
Gorky, Maxim (2000), *The Lower Depths*, New York: Dover Thrift.
Stein, Gertrude (1995), 'Plays' in *Last Operas and Plays*, Johns Hopkins University Press.
Valdez, Luis (1992), *Zoot Suit and Other Plays*, Arte Publico Press.

Exercise 7.

Writing a playable scene
This exercise was learned from Madeleine Olnek, and owes its genesis to her own particular brilliance as well as her acting work with David Mamet. It encompasses all of the other exercises, and it also gets to the animating principle of all actable (in psychological terms) dramatic writing: it gets sub-text, action and conflict into a scene.

1. Take a piece of paper and tear it into three sections. Write one place on each slip of paper. Examples of *places* are: a high-rise apartment, a coffee shop, a swimming pool, etc.
2. Take a piece of paper and tear it into three sections. Write one relationship on each slip of paper. Examples of *relationships* are: mother–daughter, cop–perpetrator,

lover–ex-lover, etc. (By relationship what is meant essentially is: what two people mean to each other.)

3. Take a piece of paper and tear it into three sections. Write an object on each slip of paper. Examples of objects are: a bottle of expensive shampoo, a tube of lipstick, a dead seagull, etc.

4. Take a piece of paper and tear it into three sections. Write an action on each slip of paper. Examples of actions are usually written with an infinitive verb and describe an effect that one person wants to create in another. Examples of actions are: to put someone in their place; to open someone's eyes to the truth; to beg someone for forgiveness, etc.

Now take all of your slips of paper, fold them in half and sort them into piles for each of the categories:

Relationships, Objects, Places, Actions. You will be choosing slips of paper blindly, or randomly, from the piles, so it's important to fold them up.

Writing Round 1
Take one slip from the relationship pile and one slip from the place pile. Write a scene with these characters in this place.

Round 2
Take one slip from the relationship pile and one slip from the action pile. Write a scene with these characters playing this action. NB only one character plays the action.

Round 3
Take one slip from the relationship pile, one from the place pile and one from the action pile. Write a scene incorporating all of these elements.

Round 4
Take one slip from all of the piles: the relationship pile, from the place pile, from the action pile, the object pile. Write a scene incorporating all of these elements.

This exercise can be repeated indefinitely. It can also be done extremely successfully with students, or in a group of writers. Madeleine Olnek and I used to write scenes using this method, and then reading the scenes that we had just written aloud to each other. What is most vital about this exercise, what is solid gold about it, is that it shows you how a scene operates; how place can dictate an action; and how the animating factor of action is at the heart of writing playable txt.

Reading list
Beckett, Samuel (1954), *Waiting for Godot: A Tragicomedy in Two Acts*, New York: Grove Press.
Beckett, Samuel (1979), 'Play' in *Collected Shorter Plays*, New York: Grove Press.
Bond, Edward (2000), *Saved*, London: Methuen Modern Plays.
Chekhov, Anton (1989), *Uncle Vanya*, New York: Grove Press.
Churchill, Caryl (1994), *The Skriker*, New York: Theatre Communications Group.
Churchill, Caryl (1997), *Blue Heart*, New York: Theatre Communications Group.
Greenberg, Richard (2004), *Take Me Out*, New York: Dramatists Play Service.
Lorca, Federico Garcia (1997), *Blood Wedding*, London: Faber and Faber.
Miller, Arthur (2003), *The Crucible*, New York: Penguin.

Nagy, Phyllis (1995), *Butterfly Kiss*, London: Consortium Books.

Pinter, Harold (1979), *Betrayal*, New York: Grove Press.

Wallace, Naomi (2000), *The Trestle at Pope Lick Creek*, New York: Broadway Play Publishing Services.

Wellman, Mac (1994), 'The Hyacinth Macaw' in *Two Plays: A Murder of Crows and the Hyacinth Macaw*, Los Angeles: Sun and Moon Press.

Wertenbaker, Timberlake (1998), *Our Country's Good*, London: Dramatists Pub. Co.

Structure

As you continue to write plays, you will become more and more interested in the overall heft and structure of the play. As Samuel Beckett says:

> I am interested in the shape of ideas even if I do not believe them. There is a wonderful sentence in Augustine. I wish I could remember the Latin – it is even finer in Latin than in English. 'Do not despair: one of the thieves was saved. Do not presume: one of the thieves was damned'. That sentence has a wonderful shape. It is the shape that matters. (Schneider 1967: 34)

Keeping going

The limitations of the stage are also the places where the stage is unique and transcendent: exploring these boundaries is what writing plays is about. You can't explore them alone, though. There are no Emily Dickinsons in the realm of the theatre. You must work with actors, directors, designers and an audience. That is the necessary next step. You can look at *The Dramatist's Sourcebook*, or various other handbooks about how to get your play produced: the most important thing, though, is to find a theatre or a group of actors that you are *simpatico* with, and to find an artistic home. These homes can be found anywhere, not just in metropolitan centres: indeed, grass roots theatre activity is the future of innovative writing in the US, where I am based. There are vital theatre scenes happening in San Diego, California; Providence, Rhode Island; Austin, Texas, to name a few burgeoning theatre cities where cutting-edge work thrives. The advent of online publishing forums such as playscripts.com makes the baptism-by-fire of Broadway and the West End and the canonising powers of the Critics less of a part of what it is to be a produced playwright. There is more and more room for the idiosyncratic and the revolutionary voice. Indeed, the theatre is becoming more and more the antidote to what Brecht termed the 'bourgeois narcotics factory' of mass cultural entertainment. This chapter is meant as an introduction to writing and a smorgasbord of exercises that have proved useful over my years of teaching and writing. The making of plays is a broad church, and there are practitioners whose work is informative and inspiring, but who are less text-based, and so less useful for our purposes in generating texts for the stage. But part of writing is becoming acquainted with your own temperament as a writer. And so the work of the Wooster Group or of Cricot 2 may be what inspires you: the thing is to seek out your 'tribe' and as Emerson says, to be open to collaboration, since 'thought makes everything fit for use' (Emerson 1844).

References

Aristotle (1961), *Poetics*, trans. S. H. Butcher, New York: Hill and Wang.

Beckett, Samuel (1961), *Happy Days*, New York: Grove Press.

Beckett, Samuel (1984), 'Play' in *The Collected Shorter Plays*, New York: Grove Press.

Beckett, Samuel (1997), 'The Calmative' in *Samuel Beckett: The Complete Short Prose, 1929–1989*, Grove Press.

Brecht, Bertolt (1964), 'Short Organum for the Theatre' in *Brecht on Theatre: The Development of an Aesthetic*, trans. John Willett, New York: Hill and Wang.

Bruder, Melissa, and Lee M. Cohn, Madeleine Olnel et al. (1986), *A Practical Handbook for the Actor*, New York: Vintage Press.

Chuchill, Caryl (1990), *Mad Forest*, New York: Theatre Communications Group.

Chuchill, Caryl (2001), *Top Girls*, London: Methuen.

Covington, Richard (1996), 'A scruffy, fighting place', *Salon*, www.salon.com/weekly/heaney2.html, 29 April 1996.

Emerson, Ralph Waldo (1844), 'The Poet' in *Essays*, 2nd series, John Chapman. Source: Literature Online.

Heaney, Seamus (1981), 'The Sense of Place', in *Preoccupations: Selected Prose, 1968–1978*, New York: Farrar, Straus & Giroux.

Schneider, Alan (1967), 'Waiting for Beckett' in *Beckett at 60: A Festschrift*, London: Calder and Boyars.

Stoppard, Tom (1994), *Jumpers*, New York: Grove Press.

Stoppard, Tom (1994), *Arcadia*, London: Faber and Faber.

Stoppard, Tom (1997), *The Invention of Love*, London: Faber and Faber.

The Dramatists Sourcebook (2006), 24th edn, New York: Theatre Communications Group.

Woolf, Virginia, and Anne Oliver Bell (1981), *Diary of Virginia Woolf, vol. 3: 1925–1930*, 'Sunday, 12 January 1930', Harvest/HBJ Book.

25

Writing for Radio

Mike Harris

Radio drama is a hybrid. Like theatre, words are crucial. Like film, scenes can cut rapidly from any place or time to another. Like prose fiction, we consume the product alone, hearing, 'with our minds', completing the physical images of people and places in our imagination from the merest suggestions.

Radio plays that sound like theatre generally confine themselves to a few locations and try to tell the story entirely in dialogue. But sets, costumes and facial expressions are of course not visible on radio and non-verbal sub-text correspondingly hard to do. As a result the dialogue has more information to deal with. If it doesn't carry this extra burden lightly, the mike will pick it up and draw attention to every plodding line. So, it's best to detect the problems in the script before that happens. Here's a case in point from *At the Gellert* by Gillian Reeve:

> *(We are listening to rock music on a Walkman)*
> OLD WOMAN Karen, can I trouble you to lay the table?
> KAREN *(Walkman stops)* Sorry, course. [. . .] *(Pots being cleared under)* So when did you come here to England?
> OLD WOMAN After the revolution I found I had no reason to stay, my parents were dead, Andrash was taken away, our houses had been confiscated, my job was to inculcate my pupils with the communist view of history.
> KAREN I'd love to be in a revolution, it must be so exciting.
> OLD WOMAN It is an excitement I was happy to leave behind. Although you could say that Hungary has been in revolution ever since. It is in a big one now with capitalism taking over from communism. What shall I find when I go back next month? So much will have changed.
> KAREN You're going back next month?
> OLD WOMAN Oh yes. I told your mother when I came to look after your grandmother.
> KAREN Eastern Europe sounds so grim and depressing.
> OLD WOMAN Actually Hungary is in central Europe.

The lack of sub-text and dramatically significant in-scene activity, the weight of un-dramatised back story on the dialogue, and the failure to exploit potential sources of conflict ('Karen, can I trouble you to lay the table?' 'Sorry, course') turn the scene into a ponderous lesson in Hungarian history and geography ('Actually Hungary is in central Europe'). There are theatrical radio plays in which the quality of the writing triumphs over the essential perversity of choosing conventions that emphasise the limitations of a form more than its possibilities. Compare the opening scene of Jill Hyem's almost perfectly constructed psycho-chiller *Remember Me*:

> (*A music box plays an unsettling tune*)
> NANCY (*Approaching*) Mrs Weedon, Mrs Weedon (*door*)
> THELMA (*With us*) yes?
> NANCY There's someone on the phone, long distance, wants to know if you've got a double room for the coming week.
> THELMA Well you know we haven't – we're booked solid over the Easter holidays.
> NANCY Thought I'd better check, only they said they were acquainted with you.
> THELMA Oh. What was the name?
> NANCY I think he said Sutton.
> (*Music box lid slams shut. Music stops*)
> Would that be right?
> THELMA Yes, Nancy, yes, that's right, good girl. Leave it to me. I'll deal with it.

In which far less is said, to far greater, and appropriately ominous, effect.

On the whole, though, radio dramas that exploit its similarities to screen drama are a more interesting technical proposition. Here's a whole scene from Ken Blakeson's army wives drama *Excess Baggage*:

> (*Interior quarters*)
> DENNY Three Bedrooms, Sarge?
> SERGEANT Yes, three bedrooms . . .
> DENNY But I put in for two . . .
> SERGEANT Well you got three, didn't you! Three beds, one bath, one reception, one dining, one hall and one shithouse . . . you!

The mike then cuts like a camera from parade ground, to bedroom, to pub, and back, rapidly interweaving the stories of several army families. This 'cinematic' approach need not be confined to gritty realism. In *The Falklands Play* Ian Curteis inter-cuts seamlessly between Whitehall, Washington, Buenes Aires, mid-Atlantic plane flights and half a dozen other locations, to tell the political story of that war as a gripping drama-doc.

The novel and short story are both print-based, non-performance forms but radio drama's most distinctive output has more in common with them than either stage or screen. This is because voices on radio transfer directly from the studio mike to the listener's mind without the distraction of little people emoting in boxes, or actors gurning and gesticulating for the benefit of the back circle. As a result radio drama is at least as intimate as prose fiction and so direct address of all kinds can be especially effective.

Michael Butt uses the most apparently simple form of it in *A Fire in the West*. A mother, father, sister and former boyfriend talk directly to mike as each tries to understand why Cirea burnt herself to death. The style is so intimate and the dialogue so 'real' that we wonder if we're not listening to a documentary. Then, as the testimonies inter-cut and conflict, we slowly realise that this is an artfully constructed drama about the impossibility of ultimately understanding anyone. The technique is similar to a novelist using several narrative voices, but the impact is specifically radio. It brings the emotions and evasions of the characters right inside our heads.

It's not surprising therefore, that radio dramatists often allow their protagonists to address the listener directly with their thoughts. One of the earliest and best examples of this is Tyrone Guthrie's *Matrimonial News*. Florence, a thirty-something shop-girl who fears that she's 'on the shelf' is waiting for a desperate blind date in a café. And that's it. The rest is psychological. Guthrie does radio stream-of-consciousness:

> FLORENCE [. . .] Ten years younger that would make me twenty two –
> ten years younger that would make me tootaloo–
> twenty two to two tattoos at Tooting.
> I don't feel a bit different–
> Not a bit–

Characters appear and disappear in her thoughts in short, sometimes only one-line, montage scenes that summarise neatly great swathes of monotonous time:

> MAN (*Very quiet and very near*) Then you don't have any say in the management of the business?
> FLORENCE I hate the business.
> (*Shop bell*)
> CUSTOMER *Good* morning.
> FLORENCE *Good* morning.
> (*Shop bell*)
> I hate the business.

Giles Cooper's comic *tour de force Under the Loofah Tree* uses a similar approach, dramatising the rich fantasy life of Ted as he takes a long luxurious soak in the bath, harassed by his spouse, child and an encyclopaedia salesman. Gerry Jones puts it to more disturbing service in the Kafkaesque *Time After Time*, in which a character eventually decides that he's 'all alone talking to myself in the madhouse'.

Most radio dramas inter-cut between direct address and dialogue, so a lot of the art is deciding when, how and why to do that. But it should never be forgotten that radio drama is *drama*. So, whether you're telling the story using dialogue or direct address you're always doing it through action and conflict (see 'Introduction to Scriptwriting' for a more detailed discussion of the practicalities of this). In *Matrimonial News*, Florence's restless personified thoughts contradict each other constantly:

> ALICE Why you look a picture in that blue!
> FLORENCE Oh dear, I wonder if I ought to . . . I don't know *what* mother'd say.
> MOTHER What's that flo?
> FLORENCE Nothing mother.
> MOTHER Oh yes it is – you needn't try to have me on.
> FLORENCE Go away.
> MOTHER You needn't try to keep *me* out of your thoughts, you *can't* you know.
> FLORENCE *Can*.

When the direct address is continuous, be it in the form of un-personified thoughts or any other kind of 'monologue', it needs to conflict within itself – expressing doubts, contradictions and so forth etc – and/or to be in conflict with the dialogue on either side. Here's Stoppard doing both simultaneously, in *'M' is for Moon Among Other Things*.

> (*Alfred is reading the paper*)
> CONSTANCE (*Thinks*) [. . .] Thirty days hath April, June, is it? Wait a minute, the Friday before
>   last was the twenty-seventh . . .
> ALFRED (*Thinks*) 'I found her to be a smooth-as-silk beauty with the classic lines of thrust of
>   . . .'
> CONSTANCE Alfred, is it the fifth or the sixth?
> ALFRED Mmmm? (*Thinks*) 'surging to sixty mph in nine seconds . . .'
> CONSTANCE Fifth?
> ALFRED Fifth what?
> CONSTANCE What's today?
> ALFRED Sunday . . . (*Thinks*) '. . . the handbrake a touch stiff . . .'

Direct address *never* works when it's used simply because the writer can't work out how to convey information dramatically. Here's a bad lapse by Louis MacNeice in *Persons from Porlock* (our protagonist is pot-holing):

> HANK (*Calling*) Peter, you OK?
> PETER (*Calling*) I'm OK. How are you?
> HANK (*Calling*) Fine. (*to self*) I'm not though. Talk about back to the womb! Difference is the
>   womb was soft.

Nowhere else in the script are we given access to thoughts so their sudden arrival here simply draws attention to the fact that they're being used to clumsily dump information on us.

The one exception to this rule is when the words of direct address are so vividly written that the listener does not care whether they're conflicted or not. Norman Corwin was the grand master of American radio drama in its heyday, and his beautiful *Daybreak* is narrated by a pilot following dawn around the world. Here's how it starts:

> PILOT A day grows older only when you stand and watch it coming at you. Otherwise it is
>   continuous. If you could keep a half degree ahead of sun-up on the world's horizons, you'd
>   see new light always breaking on some slope of ocean or some patch of land. A morning
>   can be paced by trailing light. This we shall do . . .

So if you think you're that good, you can always try it. But it's over-used by bad dramatists who'd prefer to be writing prose fiction or poetry, and it shows.

Direct address works best of all within a framing device that complements the sound-only nature of the medium. Anthony Minghella employs an answer machine at the start of *Cigarettes and Chocolate*. Its messages deftly establish six different characters and kick off the story by making us wonder why Gail is not answering. A good part of the rest of the play consists of these people one by one visiting Gail to find out why she has, literally, stopped talking. Gail does not reply to them, so they deliver self-revelatory monologues straight to the mike, putting the listener in the position of the silent protagonist. In *If*

You're Glad I'll Be Frank Tom Stoppard imagines that the telephone speaking clock is not a recording but a constantly live telephone 'broadcast' given by Gladys, whose estranged husband Frank hears it and tries to rescue her. Tape recorders, call-centres, short-wave radio, letters, mobile phones, diaries, taxi-cab calls, intercoms, all-night radio call-ins, and many other such devices, all isolate or evoke the human voice, and provide appropriate contexts for inventive radio drama.

There's another possibility in radio drama worth mentioning, which is to experiment and self-consciously play with the form itself. Here's Beckett in *All That Fall*:

> MRS ROONEY All is still. No living soul in sight. There is no one to ask. The world is feeding. The wind – *(brief wind)*– scarcely stirs the leaves and the birds – *(brief chirp)*– are tired singing. The cows – *(brief moo)* – and sheep – *(brief baa)* – ruminate in silence. The dogs – *(brief bark)* – are hushed and the hens – *(brief cackle)* – sprawl torpid in the dust. We are alone. There is no one to ask.

Beckett is a dark comedian who never loses sight of character, conflict and popular art forms. The above clearly owes much to Spike Milligan's use of radio in *The Goon Show*. Experimentation in German radio drama (Horspiel) is rather different. Peter Handke's *Radio Play (No. 1)* abandons characterisation, consistent narrative and disassociates sound from words to produce an effect analogous to a Magritte painting:

> (*A screech owl cries. A car tries vainly to start*)
> [. . .]
> INTERROGATOR A Why do you speak of the cat's naked ear?
> INTERROGATED Do you sell peach preserves?
> INTERROGATOR A Why do you clap your hands in an empty room?
> INTERROGATED What do you mean by that?
> (*The tiger hisses. A brook splashes. Water gurgles. Whistle*)

His later work 'dispenses with language altogether to become a play of pure sound' (Handke 1991: 194) prompting the observation that a radio play that dispenses with narrative, character and language in favour of 'pure sound' isn't a play at all but either aural performance art or a form of modern programme music, for which one is more liable to receive an arts council subsidy than a Radio 4 commission.

It is of course one thing to describe what can and can't be done in general with radio drama. It's quite another to do it in detail. Here are some tips.

- Close your eyes and listen for a minute. Try and remember what you heard. If you're running a group ask everyone in turn. Differentiate between sound, words and music (if there were all three). That's radio drama. If you don't hear it, it's not there.
- Audiences can't see actors and locations in radio drama, so it's absolutely essential to answer three questions within a few lines of the start of nearly every scene: Where are we? Who's there? What's going on? This is how it's done:
- Characters need to name each other and keep doing so, without the audience noticing. Characters in a scene who don't speak and aren't referred to for any length of time simply 'disappear'.
- Music can give a general cultural signal at the start of a whole play or a new scene. Vaughan Williams' 'Lark Ascending' might suggest a yearning English summer. 'White

Riot' by The Clash is probably anticipating violent urban realism. Music can also help create atmosphere; adding pace and tension within a scene (as in *bring up driving rhythm*) or a mood (*run sad theme under*). It can also be used ironically. Go from, 'White Riot' to a cricket match on a village green and the listener will expect ructions in paradise.

- Sound effects pin things down more. If it's church bells after 'Lark Ascending', not only is it England in summer but we're in a village. Follow 'White Riot' by lots of spitting, and it's almost certainly a punk gig in 1977. Some music and sound effects can be instantly evocative but most aren't. For example, cicadas always mean 'hot and abroad' but rain on radio is just as likely to sound like someone rustling through long grass. Does a burst of Tchaikovsky mean we're in Russia, or just in a bit of an emotional state? And no combination of music and sound effects is going to tell you, 'Ibiza, Sunday Afternoon, 2005, Chantelle Smith applying sun-block to burnt skin'.

For a precise picture in the listener's imagination, you need words. You almost always need words, actually. For example, the very first scene of *Excess Baggage*:

> (*We are outside*)
> CORPORAL *(Shouts)* Squad will fix bayonets. *(Pauses)* Fix bayonets! *(Sound effects: ten men fix bayonets)* Squad . . . Squad shun!

An exterior acoustic would have given us 'outside' but it's the dialogue that tells us a squad is being drilled. The sound of fixing bayonets merely confirms it. Not all dramatic situations allow basic visual information to come out so unobtrusively. The classic bad radio line, 'put down the gun that you are pointing at me', illustrates the problem. Here's Norman Corwin solving it in *Radio Primer*:

> (*Desk drawer opening; something heavy being removed*)
> JB What are you doing?
> RM What does it look like?
> JB Like suicide. But don't be hasty *(shot)*.

The word 'gun' is never said. We hear a drawer being opened and the clunk of something heavy. JB's question, and the actor's delivery would suggest that something's wrong. The line, 'like suicide, but don't be hasty' does most of the rest and the shot clinches it. But most important of all, the information was transmitted within dramatic conflict, which is what the audience are paying attention to, not the slick technique. Here's Harold Pinter smuggling visual data inside a conflict of sensibilities in *A Slight Ache*:

> FLORA Have you noticed the honeysuckle this morning?
> EDWARD The what?
> FLORA The honeysuckle.
> EDWARD Honeysuckle? Where?
> FLORA By the back gate, Edward.
> EDWARD Is that honeysuckle? I thought it was . . . convolvulus or something.

But it's not just a question of Who, Where, and What at the start of each scene. We need to know where the characters are in physical relation to each other throughout the play. This is called 'perspectives' and it might seem complicated, but it's just about the microphone.

The mike in radio drama is like the camera in film. It does long shots, medium shots, close-ups, and tracking. Several actors two-three feet away from the mike are having a conversation or an argument. Two actors closer to it are talking privately. Two actors very close up are probably in bed, and an actor right on the mike is generally voicing thoughts. An actor coming into a location is *approaching* a mike. An actor leaving a location is *going* from the mike. When we *go with* an actor, the mike stays close to him whilst he simulates movement by walking on the spot and the other actors literally move away from it.

And that's it. There's no absolutely fixed way of writing this but the following vocabulary is OK: *approaching, going, we go with, off a bit, right off, close, very close*. Or you can simply write it out as we would hear it: *in her head,* or *thinking,* or, *leaving the room* or, *entering the room,* etc. Norman Corwin again, doing movement and perspective with great precision in *Appointment*:

> (*Cell door clangs shut; two pairs of footsteps on stone floor*)
> VINCENT (*Yelling further and further off mike as Peter and the guard walk down the corridor*) They can't do this to you! Peter! (*Rattling of steel door*) God in heaven, let me out of here! . . . Peter.
> TURNKEY What's the matter with that guy? (*Steps come to a stop*). In there. (*Wooden door. When it shuts, Vincent's uproar cuts off*)

The footsteps are appropriate here because they would be audible in a jail acoustic and in any case serve a dramatic purpose in the scene. Inexperienced radio writers over-use footsteps to suggest movement (footsteps on carpets?) but this is generally done more effectively by characters *approaching* or *going* and by them *speaking* as they do so.

Val Gielgud, Head of BBC Radio Drama from 1929 to 1963, suggests, rightly, that sound effects should normally be used sparingly and only for a dramatic purpose because their 'significance . . . decreases in proportion to the amount of their use' (Gielgud 1957: 89). Battle and action scenes can be confusing because, 'one sound effect unaided by sight is liable to be horribly like another' (Gielgud 1948: 51). The Rule is always, put it in dialogue as well.

And, in general, keep things simple, to begin with at least. Small casts (two or three) are easier to deal with than big ones (seven is liable to be your budget maximum anyway). Each character should be 'aurally distinguishable on immediate hearing' (Gielgud 1948: 22). Differing genders, ages, and accents are obviously good for this and should be specified.

The only other technical vocabulary worth using in radio scripts occurs at the end of scenes. They can *cut, fade out, fade in, fade to black,* and *cross-fade,* just like a film and with the same dramatic effects. It's more acceptable in radio than theatre to give directions to actors in the script ('angrily', 'long suffering', etc.) because rehearsal time is shorter and it can be helpful if there is ambiguity in the line and a particular interpretation is essential to the plot. Otherwise don't. Actors know what they're doing.

Let each member of a group choose one from several short and deliberately difficult radio scenarios and then try and write it in one half-page scene. Here's a couple from my list, but they're easy to make up:

1. Rachel, a pushy young journalist from a working class background, is being rowed down the river Nile at night by an Egyptian peasant who happens to be mute. Also in the boat is Ali, assistant chief of the Cairo police, who is risking his life to show her the secret installation. He also fancies her.

2. A child ages from three to the verge of death in old age. The subject has several different careers and lives in more than one country. You only have five lines of dialogue for the subject but can have in addition one line each for up to five other characters. Read the results and discuss what was easy, what was hard, and why.

Selling the play

Once the play is written, it has to be sold. In the UK, Canada, and Australia the national public service broadcasters are the main (effectively the only) significant national market. In the UK BBC Radio 4 and Radio 3 produce between them about 500 plays a year, and most of them are original, which is possibly more than anyone else in the world, in any medium. Therefore you've got a much better chance of selling a new play here to radio than to stage or screen. There's no point in writing a script longer than sixty minutes (about fifty to fifty-five pages, depending) because, outside Radio 3 (which tends to use well-established writers) there's no spot for it. Because there are more afternoon plays than any other, you've got a statistically better chance of selling one, so start at forty-five minutes (forty-ish pages).

You can send your script to any in-house producer at a BBC production centre (London, Bristol, Manchester, Cardiff, Edinburgh, Belfast). There's usually one with a special brief to develop new writers, or you can send it to specific new-writing initiatives that pop up every so often. Since ten per cent of radio drama is now 'outsourced' you can send it to independent producers as well. They can be hungrier for new material than the officials but they also have a statistically smaller chance of selling it. Go to The Radio 4 Drama website for addresses, contacts and detailed information about formatting and programme content. Make sure the script is formatted correctly and don't put clip art on the front page unless you want them to think you're barking. Then don't hold your breath. There's lots of you and not many of them. If the producer hasn't replied in, say, three months, a polite reminder is in order. In six, send another reminder, and after that try another producer (my record is two years waiting for an outline to be read, and I was an established radio writer by then). It's worth persisting. They pay, and the audience for an afternoon play in the UK can be as many as a million people (Radio 4 2005: 20).

In Canada information on writing for the CBC's Sunday showcase and Monday Night Playhouse (and contacts for specific producers) can be obtained from www.cbc.ca/show-case/writersguide.html. In Australia the only national producer of radio plays is ABC Radio National, www.abc.net.au/rn/

Acknowledgements

Radio drama is alive and kicking but almost no recordings are commercially available. The failure of the BBC to exploit either its current output or its vast back catalogue of great radio plays is, in the age of the audio book, truly remarkable, and a significant cultural loss to the nation. So if you're thinking of writing a radio play you need to listen to lots of them live, or catch up on the previous weeks output on the BBC website. Podcasts and online broadcasting now give anyone with a computer and the internet access to radio plays from all over the world.

Most of the published scripts listed here are out of print but can be obtained relatively easily from online second-hand sites such as abebooks.co.uk. The very best source of information on British radio drama and writers is not the BBC but the non-profit making, wholly unofficial 'Diversity' website http://web.ukonline.co.uk/suttonelms/ which I cannot recommend highly enough and to whose webmaster, Nigel Deacon, I am very much in debt for information, the loan of his personal recordings, and unstinting help and assistance.

References

Beckett, Samuel, *All That Fall* (TX Third Programme, 13 January 1957), *All That Fall*, London: Faber (1978).

Blakeson, Ken, *Excess Baggage* (TX Radio 4, 22 February 1998), *Best Radio Plays of 1988* (1999), London: Methuen/BBC Publications.

Butt, Michael, *A Fire in The West* (TX Radio 4, 6 September 2003).

Cooper, Giles, *Under the Loofah Tree* (TX BBC 3 August 1958), *Giles Cooper: Six Plays for Radio* (1966), London: BBC Publications.

Corwin, Norman, *Daybreak* (TX Columbian Broadcasting Service, 22 June 1941); *Radio Primer* (TX CBS, 4 May 1941); *Appointment* (TX CBS, 1 June 1941) in *Thirteen by Corwin* (1945), New York: Henry Holt.

Curteis, Ian, *The Falkland's Play* (TX BBC Radio 4, 6 April 1902).

Gielgud, Val (1948), *The Right Way to Radio Playwriting*, London: Elliot.

Gielgud, Val (1957), *British Radio Drama 1922–56*, London: George Harrap.

Guthrie, Tyrone, *Matrimonial News* (TX BBC, 1930 approx.) in *Squirrel's Cage and Two Other Microphone Plays* (1932), London: Cobden-Sanderson.

Handke, Peter, *Radio Play (No. 1)* (TX 1968) in *German Radio Plays* (1991), ed. Frost and Herzfeld-Sander, New York: Continuum.

Hyem, Jill, *Remember Me* (TX BBC Radio 4, 20 May 1978).

Jones, Gerry, *Time After Time* (TX BBC Radio 4, 30.05.79, 18.06.80, 25.04.84, 09.03.06).

MacNeice, Louis, *Persons from Porlock* (TX Third Programme, 30 August 1963), in *Persons from Porlock and Other Plays for Radio* (1969), London: British Broadcasting Corporation.

Minghella, Anthony, *Cigarettes and Chocolate* (TX Radio 4, 6 November 1988) in *Best Radio Plays of 1988* (1999), London: Methuen/BBC Publications.

Pinter, Harold, *A Slight Ache*, (TX BBC, 29 July 1959) in *Plays 1* (1997), London: Faber.

Radio 4 Commissioning Guidelines 2005 (sent to producers).

Reeve, Gillian, *At the Gellert* (TX Radio 4, unknown).

Stoppard, Tom, *If You're Glad I'll Be Frank* (TX BBC, 1966), *M is for Moon* (TX BBC, 1964), in *Stoppard the Plays for Radio 1964–1983* (1990), London: Faber.

26

Writing for Television

Stephen V. Duncan

In the highly competitive industry of television programming, weekly series come and go. Most experts agree, whether drama or comedy, the primary reason a series fails is the lack of excellent writing. For this reason, high-quality TV writers are in constant demand.

The Writers Guild of America[1] suggests series executives assign several freelance scripts each season, however, the Members Basic Agreement doesn't require this.[2] Essentially, freelancers compete for assignments against writing staffs. Therefore, in order to join the ranks of those sought-after writers, you must demonstrate the knowledge and talent to write for television. To this end, this chapter presents concepts to help you *begin* the journey toward becoming a successful television writer.

The television writing sample

Your primary task is to *mimic* the series by entangling its existing cast of characters in conflicts within the bounds of an *original* story that befits the series creator's week-to-week blueprint. Whether writing for a drama or comedy series, you must never breach this imperative.

The vehicle to prove your abilities is the *speculation script* (spec). The spec is a writing sample used to attract professional agents and managers[3] who assist writers in gaining employment. Your representative sends the spec to a series producer with the primary objective of setting up a 'pitch' meeting where you must present several original story ideas in order to land an assignment. Ironically, the specific show for which you've written a spec is generally the last one – if ever – your representative will approach. This is true because it's nearly impossible to impress the Executive Producers[4] who spend five days a week and entire seasons working on a series. Ideally, the writer-producers of series with a similar franchise should read your spec teleplay, for example, a cop show spec goes to other cop series. Of course, there are exceptions to this general practice. Regardless, those who read and judge the quality of a spec will do so against the series weekly formula.

Television series 'Hallmarks'

Become familiar with a series' 'Hallmarks' – the style and use of storytelling devices – integral from week-to-week. For example, the popular CBS TV forensic investigation series 'CSI: Crime Scene Investigation' (premiered in 2000) and its two spin-offs – 'CSI: Miami' and 'CSI: New York' – replaces expository dialogue with a distinctive visual device that illustrates for the audience what may or may not have happened at a crime scene through both the investigator's and suspect's points-of-view. In the HBO comedy 'Sex in the City' (1998–2004), voiceover from the main character drives each episode.

Whether writing drama or comedy, you must be aware of each character's moral values, speech pattern, and vocabulary. Be sensitive to the series Television Rating Code.[5] It's important to stay abreast of the nature of the relationships in the series since they are dynamic. The most prudent approach is if you materially alter the series established concept and/or character relationships in your spec, return it to status quo by 'The End'.

The 'nuts and bolts' of writing the spec

Once you decide which series to write, the next step is to develop the episode. This section addresses the critical elements to master both in drama and in comedy.

The one-hour drama

The storyline premise for the one-hour drama
Create an appropriate story premise (the underlying idea for a story). For established series, the obvious story premises have been generally considered, used, or discarded by producers, so strive to create unique storylines. Admittedly, this is difficult and pre-supposes that you must watch every single episode of a series. There are two solutions: utilise free internet websites such as www.tv.com[6] to research story summaries of produced episodes and purchase and view each season's DVD package.

Many drama series employ an 'ensemble cast' and you may need to invent more than one storyline premise per episode, called 'multiple storylines'. A concept called 'The Area' or 'Arena' which establishes each storyline's *central theme*, is of primary importance to this task. The one-hour drama is an ideal form to explore subjects such as date rape or international art thief or serial killing or euthanasia or police corruption. Interweave the beliefs and values of the characters that regularly appear in the series – called the 'series regulars' – into the Area and invent the following elements:

> The Problem-predicament: What is the primary source of conflict?
> The Protagonist: Who is the storyline about?
> The Protagonist's goal: What does the protagonist want to accomplish?
> The Antagonist: Who opposes the protagonist's efforts?

Writers can 'service' series regulars who do not have prominent roles in a major storyline by creating 'Runners'; these are not storylines, per se, but the exploration of conflict in relationships and can also be used to spawn future storylines. Generally, a Runner will have only a few scenes over the course of an episode. Carefully study the series and analyse numerous episodes to see how the series utilises Runners, and then mimic it.

The basic story for the one-hour drama
Following existing character problems in established plots can quickly render a spec teleplay obsolete since producers can change them at anytime. The '"Bottle" Story Concept' is a technique used by producers to curtail an episode's budget or to attract a wider audience

during ratings periods called Sweeps.[7] The series writers essentially 'bottle up' the characters in a small number of sets in one primary location. Use this concept to help you escape the grip of the dynamic nature of continuing plotlines. For example, after a big storm hits and knocks out the power and phone lines, trap the entire cast of a series in the basement of a building where personal dramas unfold at a heightened level of conflict. However, be careful. If you write the most obvious ideas for a Bottle Story, the likelihood of the series producers using that same idea is extremely possible. A Bottle Story should be, ideally, a 'one time' occurrence in the context of the series. The keys to writing an extraordinary spec Bottle Story are creativity, originality while faithfully duplicating the series Hallmarks.

Story structure for the one-hour drama
For advertising-based television networks, you must take into account commercial breaks. Over the 2004–5 Television Season, a typical one-hour episode ran forty-four minutes with each of the four acts unfolding in eleven minutes. However, in a spec teleplay, each act is written within thirteen to fifteen pages and its overall length falls between fifty-five to sixty pages. With the premiere of 'Alias' in 2001, the ABC Television network introduced the five-act structure in primetime, a structure which had previously only been utilised in first-run syndication. The net effect is shorter commercial breaks with the same amount of programming. As of the 2005–6 television season, the four act structure continues in general use.

For series on non-advertising based networks, such as HBO and Showtime, the pacing generally remains the same in terms of four acts since many of these series will eventually get syndicated on advertising based networks.

The 'Act Break' is an important element of storytelling in television since it provides the audience with a reason to continue viewing – with or without commercial breaks – by providing the audience with a dramatic highpoint. Think of the last scene in each act as a 'mini-climax' that motivates each protagonist to do more about the problem in the next act.

Each storyline uses an alphabet designation, that is, A-Story, B-Story, C-Story, etc. The fundamental story structure of a one-hour drama consists of Story 'Beats' (important developments in the plot). Here is the general format of a *Beat Sheet*, with Beats per Act for One-Hour Drama:

> *Beat Sheet*
> Write one to three sentences for each beat:
> *Act One*
> A1-Teaser
> B1
> C1
> R1-1
> A2
> *Act Two*
> B2
> C2
> A3
> B3
> A4

Act Three
A5
R1-2
B4
A6
R2-1
Act Four
C3-Climax
R2-2
B5-Climax
A7
A8-Climax

While the example illustrates *five* Beats per act, the number and order of your Beats will probably vary. However, this is more or less a typical quantity given the time constraints of television programming. From these Beats, you develop specific scenes whose number and lengths vary for each act depending on the storytelling style of the series.

The dramatic goals of each act
In Act One, the Teaser or Prologue is a part of the first act. Some dramatic series do not use Teasers but most do. The number of scenes in a Teaser varies. Series that use 'continuing storylines' often begin with a short segment containing 'Previously on . . .' voice-over which features short clips from previous episodes intended to bring the audience up-to-date; this is not a part of the Teaser and should not appear in your spec. The main purpose of the Teaser (or Prologue) is to 'hook' the audience into a storyline's problem-predicament. The Teaser is exceptionally dramatic and/or ends with a 'cliff-hanger' to motivate the audience to ask the question 'What's going to happen next?'

The Teaser usually presents only one major story Beat; in the case of a series that utilises multiple storylines, the first Beat in the 'A-Story' is presented. Some series that utilise the 'continuing stories' approach use longer Teasers to set up several storylines. Occasionally, series that utilise multiple storylines will open with a different Beat than the A-Story in order to stay fresh. Series producers sometimes break their own rules because they – not necessarily the audience – are bored with the series' weekly formula (or its Sweeps). This shouldn't distract you from the fact that it's more important to mimic the weekly formula and write a 'typical episode'.

Introduce the problem-predicament to the protagonist. Generally, each storyline's first Beat, at a minimum, appears in the first act. Runners do not strictly follow this rule, though each Runner should have conflict. End the act with a strong mini-climax, preferably in a cliffhanger.

In Act Two, the protagonist complicates the problem-predicament by getting involved and, in fact, causes it to 'get worse'. This Act Break is the most important one of all since it marks the half-hour point when programmes are starting on other networks. Use the cliffhanger device to motivate viewers to come back after the commercial break. Generally, this second mini-climax puts the protagonist in some kind of jeopardy or in a heightened emotional state because of having gotten involved with the problem.

In Act Three, the problem-predicament intensifies for the protagonist because he or she tries to solve it prematurely and fails in some way. This conflict escalation, called the 'reversal', is a *major setback* to the protagonist's efforts toward solving the problem in the storyline. The act break, again, is important because this third mini-climax shows the protagonist defeated and at the lowest point in the story. Again, the cliffhanger technique is the most effective technique for sending the audience into the commercial break wanting to know the outcome of the storyline.

Act Four. The protagonist(s) resolves the problem-predicament in a *final confrontation with the antagonist*, called the *climax*. The protagonist's discovery of a 'key thing' to solving the problem or removing the predicament from the story sparks him or her to try to solve the problem regardless of possible negative consequences. The more risky the effort – what's at stake if he or she fails – the more entertaining it will be for the audience. Each storyline should have its own climax in this final act. Be sensitive to the way a particular series typically ends its episodes. In fact, some series do not end every storyline with a happy conclusion.

Finally, it bears repeating, you should be as creative and original as you can while mimicking the series for which you're writing. Once you have a rough draft continue to watch new episodes of the series, as this will help unveil any weaknesses in your spec. After watching each new episode, pen notes directly onto the pages of your script, then execute a revision. Follow this process until you have a strong sample script that represents your talent and ability to write for the one-hour drama art form.

The half-hour situation comedy

There are some essential differences between the one-hour drama and the situation comedy (sitcom):

- programme length is one half hour
- story structure utilises two acts
- teleplay page format is more specialised for production
- the focus is on humour.

In nearly every sitcom series, the same basic two underlining themes are repeatedly used:

> 'We're all in this together.'
> 'It's OK to be yourself.'

When developing stories for a sitcom, it's wise to keep it simple. Most situation comedies are about some form of family whether it's domestic or, for example, the camaraderie of a group of girlfriends. This suggests that the series regular characters are metaphors for typical family roles such as father, wife, son, daughter – even the crazy uncle who lives in the basement. To create a story, exploit a predicament by putting the series regulars in situations that generate conflict in the 'family'. The more ridiculous the conflict is for the story or for the characters, the more potential there is for humour. In the sitcom, the 'Area' would most likely embrace such moral themes as 'faithfulness' or 'honesty' or the ever-popular theme of 'sex'. Sitcoms tend to stay away from serious themes such as murder and rape.

Writing 'funny'

When writing a sitcom 'spec', being funny is important and the humour should match the hallmarks of the series you are writing. If a series depends heavily on physical humour, then you must create physical humour. If a series depends on intellectual humour generated from the characters, then that's what you must mimic. The most essential skill a writer needs to learn is the art of writing comedic dialogue. The structure of funny dialogue uses the 'theory of "threes"'. To illustrate, I've taken creative licence with a classic Mae West joke:

> The straight-line: You told me to come up and see you sometime . . .
> The punch line: Well, big boy, is that a gun in your pocket or are you just glad to see me.
> The follow-up or Topper: You'd better come in before that thing goes off.

Physical comedy fits into the same construction. A look or reaction can be a straight-line, punch line, or topper. Alternatively, you can use a combination of dialogue and physical expression. Timing (where you place the humour) and rhythm (the length of the lines of dialogue) are also important.

To write humour, you must first recognise why people laugh. The true essence of comedy ironically embraces conflict (pain) with which the audience can relate (truth). This merger is important since the audience laughs because they are familiar with a situation. Therefore, the art is to *take out of context what the audience expects* to create an *unanticipated* result.

To put this technique into practice, utilise the concept of 'The Area'. Start with something on which to mine humour. Most times, it's a 'situation' (thus the nickname situation comedy). Let's say characters have to attend a funeral, therefore the 'Area' is 'a funeral'. A funeral is not funny in and of itself but there are ways to extract humour from the characters who attend a funeral. First, make a list of the normal or expected facets of a situation or activity, in this case, a funeral. Then use those as the basis of the humour. For example, mourners cry at funerals – have a character's quiet sob grow into a gut-gripping laugh. Mourners view the reposing corpse – create humour from the way different personalities perceive the actual dead body in the casket, for example, a character might say: 'He looks better dead then when he was alive'. Put the wrong banner on a funeral wreath: 'Congratulations' instead of 'Rest in Peace'.

The other component of this equation is to incorporate a character's personality, which is essentially comprised of attitudes and values. On the long-running American sitcom *Frasier* (1993–2004), much of the humorous dialogue emanates from the erudite, snobby view of life of two brothers who practise psychology in different ways. Let's say Frasier's line of dialogue is 'you're not going to make one cent on that scheme'. To make this line more humorous – and in keeping with the character's personality – he might say, 'You're not going to earn one Euro, Shekel or Botswana Pula on this ruse'. Deconstructing the line of dialogue, you see I used *three* different kinds of money – two of which *sound* funny. Some words do sound funnier. For example, it's funnier for a waiter with a tray of finger snacks to break the tension of a serious moment at a cocktail party by innocently asking *ramacki* rather than *hors d'oeuvre*. In my example, to indicate a well-travelled character, I used money from around the world. Replacing the word 'make' with 'earn' and 'scheme' with 'ruse' better captures the sense of Frasier's intellectual personality.

Story and structure for the sitcom
Start with an appropriate premise for the series you are writing. The half-hour comedy utilises simple story ideas. As I've already emphasised, focus on the *drama* of the story premise and use Area in order to create a foundation from which to evoke humour.

In terms of pacing, the sitcom teleplay uses two pages for each minute of screen time. Half-hour teleplays typically run between forty-five to fifty-five pages in length and much of the script is double-spaced to allow for production notes. That computes to an act running about twenty-five pages and twelve minutes. The page format is difficult to replicate in standard word processing computer software programs such as Microsoft Word®, so it's strongly recommended you use commercially-available screenwriting software.

The dramatic goals for each act

Some sitcoms do not use the Teaser; those that do, use it to grab and draw-in viewers. Unlike the drama, the Teaser can have absolutely nothing to do with the 'A-' or 'B-Story'. Sometimes, the Teaser sets a 'Runner' into motion. How to use the Teaser depends on the series. The length of a Teaser is, generally, less than two minutes; this computes to about four script pages or less. Above all, the Teaser should be funny.

In Act One, each protagonist becomes aware of the problem-predicament and intensifies it by getting involved. Accomplish this by placing the series regulars into a succession of situations that relate to the storyline's problem. The act break is often dramatic with a humorous spin, of course. On average, the length is twenty-five pages or twelve minutes.

In Act Two, each protagonist tries to solve the problem-predicament only to make it worse. Again, use situations that relate to the protagonist's attempts to solve the problem to draw out the humour. In many sitcoms, you can characterise these attempts as 'schemes'. These efforts should backfire and create a 'reversal' in the story. In sitcom writing, this is commonly called the 'the act two bump'. This bump (in the road) is usually an unexpected result or turn for each protagonist as well as for the audience. This event is what leads each protagonist to the climax or resolution of the problem-predicament. On average, the length is twenty-five pages or twelve minutes.

Note the sitcom structure collapses Acts One and Two dramatic goals of the one-hour drama structure into the first act. Then, in Act Two, collapse Acts Three and Four's dramatic goals.

A short scene called the Tag or Epilogue 'buttons up' the story's loose ends. In comedy, all the characters generally come back to where they started in the story. More often than not, the Tag punctuates the 'We're in this together' and/or 'Be yourself' themes and are topped with a laugh or a poignant moment. Since the 1980s, few sitcoms utilise the Tag as a dramatic element in an episode. So study the series for which you are writing your spec sitcom.

Other popular forms of television writing

The MOW: Movie of the Week

Television producers or studios generally acquire an idea and/or the rights to a story from individuals or publishers who own them. Rarely do producers purchase a spec movie teleplay. Therefore, if you own the story rights, it's wiser to write a 'treatment'; this is a synopsis of the story that is eight to ten double-spaced pages organised in a seven-act structure. Set up the story and its premise in the first page or two, and then write one page per act to create this 'sales tool'.

A completed teleplay would have the first act at twenty-five pages with Acts Two through Seven at fourteen pages each. These are, of course, averages. As series TV, indicate act breaks in the script's page format. However, non-advertising based television networks do not use the seven-act structure and are written like feature films.

Since audiences primarily watch TV for the characters, producers and networks prefer movies with strong social themes and universal appeal. MOW stories tend to be exceptionally emotional. Like series television, stories about families appeal to buyers and tales about the average woman succeeding against overwhelming obstacles are most popular. There's a short list of actors whose popularity draws big ratings.[8] You have a better chance of selling a TV movie if one of these actors is perfect casting for the lead role.

The daytime drama series

Commonly called the soap opera, this genre is, by in large, written by staff writers and supervised by a headwriter. Some staff writers specialise in writing certain character's storylines and dialogue. Others write 'Breakdowns' – a detailed scene outline for an episode. Breakdown writers are sometimes freelancers who are part of a pool that producers turn to because of the sheer volume of writing necessary for a series that airs five days a week. Some of these writers work via email and fax. If you're interested in writing for Daytime Television, you'll need an agent with good contacts in this genre.

The reality series

Game shows fall into this category and essentially use what is called 'researchers' to come up with questions and answers. Allegedly, the hosts 'ad-lib' their lines for the programme and provide them for the teleprompter. However, on some reality series, writers are being employed and receiving screen credits. The game show has transmuted outside of the studio set with such hits as 'Fear Factor' and 'Amazing Race'. Reality Drama Series such as MTV's 'Real World' and the CBS network's 'Survivor' technically do not use writers. However, these reality series do use the series episodic technique of multiple storylines and unfolding storylines using the two-or four-act structure based on a formula of activities the 'real' people are required to perform. Producers achieve this in the editing room applying the same principles used in writing a scripted episode. The skills you learn for writing scripted episodic teleplays are very useful in the reality genre. It won't be long before collective bargaining agreements are forcing this genre to employ writers beyond consultants or researchers.

The improvised series

The success of Larry David's HBO 'Curb Your Enthusiasm' (creator of the hit series *Seinfeld*) has set the creative pace for this new form of reality television since it hit premium pay cable in 2000. In this category of series, the writer comes up with a story and scene outline (and receives a screen credit as per the MBA) and the actors ad-lib the scenes during actual production, aided by the director and producers. This is a growing genre on television.

In closing . . .

Television is among the largest employers of writers in the entertainment industry worldwide. Becoming a professional takes training, commitment, stamina and, yes, some luck. As someone once said, 'writers who write the most are the luckiest'. This chapter has only addressed the fundamentals required to start a career as a TV writer. But to be truly successful, you must love television and watch a lot of it.

Notes

1. The Writers Guild of America (West and East) is the union for screenwriters and affiliates with other writing guilds around the globe. Go to www.wga.org for more information.
2. The Members Basic Agreement sets forth working rules to which all members and signatories must adhere.
3. In the US, writers need someone who can legally negotiate contracts in order to sell material to producers or have it read by executives.
4. Executive Producers are generally also writers who have worked their way up the ranks and earned the title 'Showrunner'. For more non-artistic information on being a professional television writer, go to the Writers Guild of America website and download their free publication entitled 'Writing for Episodic TV: From Freelance to Showrunner'.
5. TV ratings are divided into six basic categories: TVY and TVY7, which are just for children's programming and TVG, TVPG, TV14, and TVMA for all other programs. The ratings do not apply to sports coverage and news.
6. TV.com (formally known as tvtome.com) has over 2,500 complete guides covering nearly all the current shows and past series. The site also features over 250,000 people associated with TV, including the actors, writers, directors, and producers.
7. Rating Sweeps take place in November, February and May of a television programming year and serve to set the advertising rates for American networks.
8. 'TV-Q' is a service that measures the popularity of certain actors with the audience and often influence casting decisions of producers and network executives.

27

Writing for Television – UK Differences

John Milne

I'm sure you could not be better prepared for writing for American television than by reading and understanding Stephen V. Duncan's chapter. But at the risk of stating the obvious, American television is not British television. Put brutally, American television was developed to fill the spaces between adverts. Though the situation has since become more complex, the basic rationale persists. American television exists to make money for the people who make it, and the source of the money is usually advertising. The primary purpose, therefore, of American television is to stop people switching either over to another channel or switching off altogether. There has never been any other motive to American television production. Public Broadcasting in America is a rump. Oddly, subscription cable or subscription satellite TV in America raises its head from this singularly commercial approach from time to time. Once the bills are paid you can be a little more adventurous, and it might be that those capable of meeting the monthly subscription for, say HBO, need the 'Sopranos' or 'Curb Your Enthusiasm' or 'Six Feet Under' to keep their appetites whetted.

British independent television suffers from (or enjoys, depending on your point of view) a similar singularity of purpose. Once British independent broadcasters were from time to time reminded of standards required by broadcast regulators. Since the so-called 'light-touch' regime of recent years, designed to allow free-to-air ITV to stay competitive, producers have found themselves under more pressure than ever to deliver audiences from an increasingly fractured market. Shows which had audiences of twelve million less than ten years ago now have audiences of three million. This has some extraordinary results. If you stumble upon 'ITV play', for example, you will be watching gambling, not drama.

This pressure means drama broadcast on British Independent TV has to meet certain expectations, and this is achieved by a lighter version of the highly manipulative way of writing drama described by Stephen Duncan, as used in America. If you wrote for 'The Bill' (as I have done a great deal) at one time you might have expected to draw up a document containing formal storylines, teasers, ends of parts, reveals for the ends of eps (as they are called) and all the rest of it. This has relaxed a little at this at the time of writing (2006) because British audiences for main-stream free-to-air TV are middle-aged and didn't like it. The British middle-aged, lower middle-class *Daily Mail* type of taste is for something a little more organic, and research carried out in the 'focus groups' beloved of modern advertising men and women proved it.

I should point out that none of this highly structured, centralised approach to scriptwriting was ever there because the producers or script departments are by nature oppressive (some are, but not many). It existed simply because they have accountants breathing down their necks. Once the accountancy model spreads right through an industry (any industry) it means that everyone signs off on what everyone else does and only that which is capable of being 'signed off on' is achievable. This kind of self-fulfilling prophecy writing would have been unthinkable in the 1980s.

The BBC used to be different. Since the BBC is financed by what is in effect a public tax (the licence fee) its formal chartered purpose is to raise its head above that which is merely commercial. It should inform, educate and entertain. In the past, Reithian standards, referring to the first Director General of the BBC, prevailed. However, in an extraordinary inversion which George Orwell (himself a BBC employee under Reith) would have recognised, the theory got around in the 1990s that the BBC would have to deliver mass audiences to justify the tax (sorry, licence fee) and should therefore match ITV step for step. It did not lead but was led. At one time, whether a certain BBC executive's mother would watch a drama was reputed to be the benchmark. Things have improved since and the BBC's expansion into digital and cable have left the organisation with a wide variety of channels to feed, while poor old BBC 1 carries the burden of delivering what mass audience there is. Sometimes it's very successful but in general is rather conservative. The BBC also receives enormous income from its 'Worldwide' arm, and one wonders to what extent commercial pressures come from that corner. BBC drama is not generally sold to other organisations like itself but to commercial entities, and this may be the underlying reason why the BBC drama 'hour' has shortened and you have (in the UK) to watch endless puffs of other BBC programmes at the beginning or end of BBC dramas. The puffs are in the air-space which will be used by advertisers when the BBC subsidiary rights are sold on by BBC Worldwide.

What does all this mean for the would-be TV scriptwriter? Interestingly, the conservatism of both main channels and their rush for ratings do not necessarily find themselves reflected in the views of individuals in script departments of production companies. Originality and the ability to deliver powerful emotions and stories are still very high on the list of desirable qualities for a British TV scriptwriter. For this reason there isn't a lot of point in writing try-out examples of TV shows in an attempt to get hired on the show (as is the case in the US) – I can only think of one scriptwriter who broke in this way. However, theatrical work does seem to have some considerable 'cachet' for the guardians of the gate, the script editors and readers on whom producers and for that matter writers rely. They might be in a drudge job but their minds are not those of drudges, and if they are young they may very likely have come straight to the job after studying Renaissance drama for four years at university. So if I were to offer a single piece of advice for people wanting to be a *British* TV scriptwriter, it would be '*write a little play and get it put on somewhere*'. Anywhere. Above a pub, preferably in Islington or Edinburgh. Get it staged during the interval of another play, if you must, or in the foyer of a bigger theatre. You get the picture – just get something performed.

The other route which is available to writers for the British market is BBC radio, which is poorly paid and sometimes has wildly variable standards of both writing and performance, but will (like the play above the pub) give you the writer a professionally performed and original piece of work with which you or your agent can start bothering script editors. Good hunting.

28

Writing for Film

Bonnie O'Neill

Introduction

In my mind, there's no writing form that requires a higher degree of discipline than writing a feature-length screenplay. The purpose of this chapter is to take the mystery out of the filmwriting process by giving writers a method to create within this art form. Once you have mastered the process of screenwriting, it is my experience that writing in all facets of your life will improve dramatically.

First, let's clear up the often-confusing filmwriting/screenwriting/scriptwriting terminology. I consider filmwriting/screenwriting as writing for the 'big screen'. Today, however, that doesn't necessarily mean your screenplay will be shot on film. We have moved into the age of Digital Video and there may be no turning back. George Lucas has been at the forefront of this movement and soon theatres worldwide will be equipped to project Digital Video. It's less expensive and easier to manipulate than film, although it still has a 'flatter' look. So, chances are that in the future, your screenplays may be shot on video.

However, whether shooting on film or video, your feature-length projects should always utilise the traditional stacked Hollywood (theatrical) format. There are specific formatting rules that I will discuss later in the chapter. You should not overly concern yourself with formatting until you know the basics of developing your story. I will take you through each step. Do not write a single scene until you've completed these steps.

You will have an edge over other screenwriters if you develop film-viewing skills. Learn to look at films with a screenwriter's eye. Time the acts. It's important to be aware of film terms and formats; analyse film and television clips, shorts, tapes, and full-length films with emphasis on understanding the writer's perspective. You should also devour as many screenplays as possible. A good site for screenplay research is www.script-o-rama.com. Here, you can read hundreds of screenplays. Make note of this art form. There's nothing like it! And remember always to try to read the latest draft.

The skills utilised in feature filmwriting are applicable to other scriptwriting formats including half-hour and one-hour TV programmes, educational and training videos, documentaries, and video games. Sometimes the split page format is used for the above-mentioned projects. In this format, a page is 'split' into two vertical columns. The left column represents the video and the right column is where the sound and dialogue is written. The audio and video should be matched up, side by side in each column. These are usually referred to as scripts. If freelancing, always ask your producers for a sample script or screenplay so you know their preference from the start.

For the purposes of this chapter, we shall focus on the feature screenplay that is usually 120 pages long. The rule of thumb is one page per minute. Comedies are generally shorter, perhaps ninety pages. Regardless of the length, a screenplay should follow the 1:2:1 beginning, middle, end ratio. That is, the second act (middle) should be twice as long as the first and third act.

There are essential steps that should be followed when you write a screenplay. Don't skip the steps as you will likely end up with what I call 'the mess in the middle'. After all, I think we can all write a great beginning scene and a great ending, but it's usually that second act that kills the beast.

In a sense, writing a screenplay and marketing is a circular adventure. You must know the essence of your story, the tone and code of your story and who, ultimately, your audience is. If you follow the natural process for writing a screenplay and don't skip any steps, you will come full circle by the end so you can market your labour of love. If you skip steps, you won't have anything worth marketing.

Here are the steps I suggest you follow to avoid the typical screenwriter's struggles and come up with a product you are proud of:

> Know your premise.
> Research your genre and audience.
> Write a good, tight logline. Know your ending.
> Flesh out your characters.
> Write a synopsis.
> Know each step of your hero's journey.
> Create a working diagram of your Three-Act Structure.
> Write a treatment.
> Learn the proper screenplay format.
> Write your screenplay, scene by scene. Take your diagram with you everywhere.
> Rewrite, rewrite, rewrite.

Premise

Your premise is the arc of your theme. Theme = Subject. Let's take the theme of love. You might try to prove the following premise: Trust leads to love. How about ego as a theme? One premise could be: Bragging leads to humiliation. When thinking of the premise for your screenplay, consider what the moral lesson or discussion might be. Without a concrete premise, you will have no foundation for a film.

Genre and audience

What specific category of film would your story fit into? Search for a screenplay on the web that is the same genre you want to write. You might consider a romantic comedy, suspense thriller or action adventure. Or, you might be writing a sub-genre film such as a biopic, zombie or neo-noir film. For some enlightening information on film genres, go to Tim Dirks' website www.filmsite.org/genres.html

Define your audience and write accordingly. If you're writing a PG comedy, don't waste your time with strong language or nudity. Think of the kids, think of the parents who are buying their tickets. You can allude to adult humour, but don't get carried away. On the other hand, if you're writing an R zombie film, then extreme gore is expected.

Logline

After reading the screenplay, write your logline. A logline is the one to three sentence description of your screenplay. It's the condensed version of the plot. Plot = Situation. Think of how movies are described in a TV Guide or on a Cable scroll.

The logline for my screenplay *Screw the Golden Years* is: two eccentric, long divorced parents rebel when stuck into the same nursing home by their greedy children.

Next, think deeply about the screenplay you will be working on and then write its logline. In your mind, begin with the phrase – this is the story of . . . Keep it brief, snappy and to the point. Then trim it down with the goal of one line.

The logline doesn't have to give the ending away. However, you must know the ending of your screenplay before you write your first scene. Each scene should lead the audience up to the ending. If a scene doesn't establish something that leads to the end, then it doesn't need to be written. Ideally, your screenplay should be so tight that it would collapse with a single scene removed.

Characters

Creating interesting and compelling characters is at the heart of a good screenplay. To do this, you need to develop tridimensional characters. The character sketch needs to give the whole picture of your character from the inside out. Not only do you need to know how your character looks, but you also need to know how your character thinks, feels and why. A well-developed character sketch should be done before you start to write a single scene. This sketch has the potential to help you understand the extraordinary nuances of a character that can later be used to create believable and unique scenes. As you progress in your screenplay, your writing will be clear and come to you more easily if you do the preliminary character work. The character sketch should be broken into the following three categories:

1. Physiology
2. Sociology
3. Psychology

Following is an excerpt from a playwriting book that is considered an essential tool in the screenwriter's toolbox. Lajos Egri's *The Art of Dramatic Writing* (1972) is a must-have for the committed screenwriter.

Tridimensional Character Guideline

Physiology
1. Sex
2. Age
3. Height and weight

4. Colour of hair, eyes, skin
5. Posture
6. Appearance: good-looking, over- or underweight, clean, neat, pleasant, untidy; Shape of head, face, limbs
7. Defects: deformities, abnormalities, birthmarks; Diseases
8. Heredity

Sociology
1. Class: lower, middle, upper
2. Occupation: type of work, hours of work, income, condition of work, union or non-union, attitude toward organisation, suitability for work
3. Education: amount, kind of schools, marks, favourite subjects, poorest subjects, aptitudes
4. Homelife: parents' living, earning power, orphan, parents separated or divorced, parents' habits, parents' mental development, parents' vices, neglect. Character's marital status
5. Religion
6. Race, nationality
7. Place in community: leader among friends, clubs, sports
8. Political affiliations
9. Amusements, hobbies: books, newspapers, magazines

Psychology
1. Sex life, moral standards
2. Personal premise, ambition
3. Frustrations, chief disappointments
4. Temperament: choleric, easygoing, pessimistic, optimistic
5. Attitude toward life: resigned, militant, defeatist
6. Complexes: obsessions, inhibitions, superstitions, phobias
7. Extrovert, introvert, ambivert
8. Abilities: languages, talents
9. Qualities: imagination, judgment, taste, poise
10. IQ
     (Egri 1972: 36, 37)

Synopsis

A good synopsis is a one-page description of your story. It reads like a very short story, preferably with no dialogue. You should use the 1:2:1 ratio in your synopsis. Your first paragraph should represent the beginning, the second two paragraphs your middle and the last paragraph should explain the end of your film. Fully capitalise your main characters' names the first time they appear on the page.

The Hero's Journey

No one knew the role of good and evil better than the master of mythology, Joseph Campbell. His work was both a spiritual and scholarly adventure. What is commonly referred to as 'The Hero's Journey' was the culmination of years of studying ancient archetypes in order to bring that familiar story into our present consciousness.

So, what is The Hero's Journey? In essence it's the universal myth. It's the journey of a hero into conflict and back again. In his book, *The Writer's Journey*, Christopher Vogler recaps the twelve steps of the Hero's Journey:

1. Heroes are introduced in the ordinary world, where
2. They receive the call to adventure.
3. They are reluctant at first or refuse the call, but
4. Are encouraged by a mentor to
5. Cross the threshold and enter the Special World where
6. They encounter tests, allies and enemies.
7. They approach the inmost cave, crossing a second threshold
8. Where they endure the ordeal.
9. They take possession of their reward and
10. Are pursued on the road back to the Ordinary World.
11. They cross the third threshold, experience a resurrection, and are transformed by the experience.
12. They return with the elixir, a boon or treasure to benefit the Ordinary World.

Once the rhythm of the journey is in the writer's mind, its truth will become obvious in the heart. Like Aristotle's Three-Act Structure, the stages of the journey are flexible. A multitude of paradigms have thrived over time and will morph into the future.

Diagram

Before you create your diagram, you must understand the Three-Act Structure. Some writers get a bit rebellious at this step, believing that such structure will somehow inhibit their creativity. I have found the opposite to be true. Once my screenplay is fully structured and diagrammed, I can focus all my talent on creating masterful scenes – finding the perfect, concise phrases and dialogue that will make my screenplay a page-turner. Remember, you must know the rules before you can break the rules.

Act One is where you establish your screenplay. Here you introduce your premise, characters and conflict. It is the beginning of your story. It's where the tone, texture, and the place becomes clear. Act One establishes a problem for the main character and his or her dramatic need.

Act Two is where you build your screenplay. This is where you have a series of conflicts that will eventually lead to the resolution. It is the middle of your story. This act presents obstacles to the main character's dramatic need. It creates the rising conflict and action of the screenplay. Act Two raises the stakes for the character. It develops tension and/or suspense.

Act Three is where you resolve your screenplay. This is where your series of conflicts become a crisis and must get resolved. It is the end of your story. It presents obstacles to the main character's dramatic need. It creates the rising conflict and action of the screenplay. It presents a moment of change and discovery for the character. It allows the character to achieve or not achieve his or her dramatic need.

The first act is usually thirty pages long. The second act is usually sixty pages long. The third act is usually thirty pages long. Remember that this varies with genre. For example, comedies often run shorter, sometimes just ninety pages. Always remember that your screenplay should follow the 1:2:1 ratio. So, if you're writing a ninety-minute comedy, your first act would be twenty-two-and-a-half pages, your second forty-five pages and your third twenty-two-and-a-half pages.

There are just a few other page markers you must be aware of. Within the first act is the 'set-up' – this is on pages ten to twelve of your screenplay. Within Act Two is the mid-point of your screenplay. This lands on page sixty. Within Act Three is the 'climax' – this is on pages 110–12 of your screenplay.

Right before the end of Act One, there is a 'turning point' that spins the story around and catapults the audience into Act Two. Right before the end of Act Two, there is another 'turning point' that spins the story around and catapults the audience into Act Three. The short wind-up of the story that occurs after the climax, is often referred to as the denouement.

Now, you're ready to create your Three-Act Diagram. This is a portable screenwriter's tool that reflects the Three-Act Structure. Take a long, rectangular piece of paper (side by side copy paper is fine – you can tape the centre). Then, fold it so it reflects a 1:2:1 ratio horizontally. At the top, mark your important page numbers: 1 12 30 60 90 110 120.

You can use this to 'diagram' your screenplay. First, enter the twelve steps of your hero's journey. Steps one to five will be in Act One, six to nine will be in Act Two and steps ten to twelve will be in Act Three. This diagram is really the foundation for me. It's easily portable! I tend to write my first few drafts of my diagram in pencil and shift around constantly until I know that my set-ups and pay-offs are well planted. You can also trim post-its and manipulate them on the page. I prefer this method instead of lugging my laptop around. My diagram goes with me everywhere and rests on my nightstand for those sleepless brainstorm sessions.

Treatment

The treatment is the first written form of a film outlining the scenes, the major characters, action and locations. It's like the writer's storyboard. It looks very much like a short story. It's written in paragraph form, uses quotation marks for dialogue, and doesn't include camera angles. It's dramatic and full of action phrases.

Your treatment should be written in proportion to the Three-Act Structure. In other words, if your treatment is twelve pages long, the first three pages should represent Act One, the next six pages should represent Act Two and the last three pages should represent Act Three.

You may find when you are writing that great chunks of dialogue rush into your head. Add these as notes on the back of corresponding index cards. In general, the treatment is sparse on dialogue. There are two kinds of action that move a treatment forward – something happens to the character or dialogue. Just remember to only use dialogue that will move your treatment forward.

Your treatment should be dramatic yet easy to read. Write in the present tense with highly visual prose and include important scenes and turning points. This is just another part of the expansion process – premise, logline, synopsis, diagram, treatment and then . . . finally you can start writing your screenplay.

Format

The simplest way to format your screenplay is to use scriptwriting software. I use Final Draft which is considered by many to be the industry standard.

The following is a general formatting guideline most of which can be found in *The Complete Guide to Standard Script Formats* by Hillis Cole and Judith Haag. Margins are moving a tad to the right, so that's reflected in these tab settings which are always counted from the left-hand margin:

> Scene description 20–70
> Dialogue 30–65
> Parenthetical description 35–50
> Character name 40
> Page numbers 75
>> Do not use right-hand justification for any margins.
>> All sluglines start at the left margin.
>> Most angles are on the left margin.
>> All narrative description is single spaced, lowercase and starts at the left margin.
>> Double space between the sluglines and the description; between the description and
> the character's name.
>> Dialogue begins directly under the character's name.
>> Go to www.script-o-rama.com for examples.
>> Use sparse camera directions.

Scene by scene

Now that you're finally ready to write your first scene, take a good look at your diagram, treatment and index cards. Check out the following summary of script breakdowns. At this stage of the game, you might feel perfectly comfortable with all of your pre-work and ready to go on. Or, you might feel like something specific is missing or hasn't 'hit the mark'. Reflecting on these questions should help:

Set-Up (1–12)
Have you established who your main characters are? Is the place, time and mood clear? What is the story about? Who does the story belong to? Is the hero's goal clear? What are the hero's obstacles? Do we want to cheer for the hero? Does something significant happen to shift the story by the end of the set-up?

Turning Point (30)
Is there an event that forces a reaction, sets the hero firmly on a path to the goal?

Point of No Return (60)
Does something happen so that the hero, against all odds, must continue forward?

Lost Hope (90)
Does something huge happen to nearly discourage the hero from the goal? Does this event change everything, spin the story around?

The Heroic Effort (90–108)
Does your hero's actions intensify to get the goal? Does your hero get focused on the one specific action that will lead him or her to the resolution?

Climax (110–112)

Does your hero know what the final obstacle is? Is everything in jeopardy/crisis? Does the hero clearly fail or achieve the goal? Is the hero's obvious motivation resolved?

Unlike writing a novel, filmwriting is specific in that one must never write what is thought. Rather, you should quickly get into the habit of writing what is seen and heard. That's it. What is seen and heard. Period.

Every screenplay starts with the capitalised words FADE IN: which are flush on the left margin. It ends with FADE OUT. In between is where the fun begins!

Next comes your slugline which is all written in capital letters and tells whether the scene is interior (INT.) or exterior (EXT.), where it takes place and whether it is day or night.

Under the slugline comes your description. Pretend you are the camera. Describe what you see without using camera angles. Unless you are directing a film, you should only use specific camera directions when it's necessary to understand what needs to be established in a scene.

Dialogue is centred under the action line. You may use brief additional directions for the actor in parentheticals under the character's capitalised names. Use parentheticals only when necessary and use no more than sixteen letters and spaces.

If you've done all the steps leading up to actually writing that first scene, then don't stop to re-write. The set-up is the only section I recommend re-writing before the entire first draft is complete. Then you can (and will) re-write your heart out.

Re-write

Becoming a re-write pro is the screenwriter's spare key. At the most basic level, a 're-write' is writing a story for a second (third, fourth, fifth, sixth and so on . . .) time to add or delete information to make it more interesting to the reader. Screenwriters have the extra task of making sure it is presented in tiptop form. This is often a dreaded task – particularly when you think you have perfected your screenplay and a producer requests a major change. They'll call the next draft a second draft when it's probably your hundredth!

The sooner you learn how to approach a re-write, the more open you'll be to the process. Chances are, the more thought you put into diagramming your screenplay, the less severe the re-write will need to be.

Begin your re-write with a quick read through. Don't stop to take notes. Just get the overall feeling for your work. Do this all in one sitting whether it's for this lesson (just the set-up) or an entire screenplay. Don't break up this important read through. Don't take notes yet. Just formulate your fresh impression. Then, ask yourself a few questions:

> Does it work?
> Does it have a beginning, middle and end?
> Is it interesting?
> Is there a clear climax?
> Did the story lead up to the climax?

Now, do a detailed analysis. Focus on characters, settings, action and dialogue.

Characters

Do your characters have goals? Too many, too few? Do your characters evolve throughout the story?

Settings
Have you chosen interesting settings? Are they described in an interesting way without appearing to be written by a frustrated set designer? Are the settings too claustrophobic and stage-like?

Action
Have you over-described the action? Are you 'directing' in your screenplay, overusing camera angles and terms? Does the action advance the story or did you just write it because it was fun to write?

Scenes
Did you get into your scenes at the last possible moment? Did you get out of your scenes at the first possible moment? Do the scenes build on each other? Do you have any unnecessary scenes that can be cut?

Dialogue
Did you truly write dialogue or are your characters simply delivering the message? Good dialogue will always sound natural, but clever. It is lean, but not too 'on-the-nose'. I suggest that you start your re-write by reading all scenes out loud, paying particular attention to the length of the dialogue and how easily the words flow. If you have a 'chunk' of dialogue that is five lines, see if you can cut it to three, three to one and so on. Always try to write lines that are memorable. Don't overwrite. Make sure the dialogue fits the character. Don't be a lazy writer. Really try to put yourself in your characters' shoes and write like they would naturally talk. That means pauses and beats. Some ahhhs . . . Make sure your dialogue fits the situation. Avoid clichés. Remember, good dialogue is re-written dialogue.

When you re-write, I suggest that you drop (move) scenes and major dialogue pages to the end of your document. Nothing is more crazy-making than wanting that perfect scene or phrase back! If you drop it to the end of your screenplay, you can refer to it easily and (chances are) you'll realise it wasn't as perfect as you remembered, otherwise you wouldn't have dropped it.

Review the lessons from this chapter. Have you taken cues from all of them?

Conclusion

To be honest, it takes a couple of screenplays and screening hundreds of films really to get the experience needed to begin to write marketable screenplays. Don't attempt to market anything until you know in your heart it's ready to be shown. I'm a big believer in writers' groups. Find a group of trusted writers in your area who have also studied screenwriting. Share you work and learn to take criticism with an open mind.

Please check my website at www.cinetale.com for more information on The Art of Screenwriting.

References

Cole, Hillis and Judith Haag (1989), *The Complete Guide to Standard Script Formats*, CMC Publishing.
Dirks, Tim: www.filmsite.org/genres.html
Egri, Lajos (1972), *The Art of Dramatic Writing*, New York: Simon and Schuster.

O'Neill, Bonnie: www.cinetale.com

Script-o-rama: www.script-o-rama.com

Vogler, Christopher (1998), *The Writer's Journey*, 2nd edn, Studio City, CA: Michael Wiese Productions.

OTHER WRITING

29

Song Lyrics and Poetry[1]

Pat Pattison

'Her lyrics are pure poetry'. Really? Why does a statement like this create such diverse reactions: knee-jerk agreement or knee-jerk disavowal? Either 'Of course', or 'You've got to be kidding'?

I have been teaching both lyric writing and writing poetry at Berklee College of Music for nearly forty years, and have gained a bit of perspective in the process. I would like to make a few observations.

Since the invention of the printing press, poetry, once spoken and performed, has been delivered mainly to the eye. Lyrics are delivered mainly to the ear. Many consequences follow from this simple fact.

I

The first consequence: the poet can depend on the reader's being able to stop, go back, or even to look up words while reading the poem. A lyricist can't.

Since a poet can depend on the reader's being able to re-read, the poet can use quite complex language: less familiar words, ambiguity, multiple meanings, intricate metaphor. The density of poetic language is a poet's way of 'harmonising' ideas. Like putting chords under your words, it adds a new level of emotion. Poetry eats the whole animal and says the most it can with the fewest words. Phrasing, form and poetic meter add to this 'musical' underpinning. A good example of this is 'After Long Silence' by William Butler Yeats:

> Speech after long silence; it is right,
> All other lovers being estranged or dead,
> Unfriendly lamplight hid under its shade,
> The curtains drawn upon unfriendly night,
> That we descant and yet again descant
> Upon the supreme theme of Art and Song:
> Bodily decrepitude is wisdom; young
> We loved each other and were ignorant. (Yeats 1996)[2]

The poem has lots of nifty words. Just look at 'descant'. Why not say 'talk about'? There are several definitions in the dictionary that provide depth and colour to the idea 'talk about'.

Etymologically, the word means a voice (cantus) above, or removed, from others. It also means a lengthy discourse on a subject; or a counterpoint melody sung or played above the theme. One dictionary defined it as 'To discuss at length; To sing or play a descant'.

'That we descant and yet again descant . . .' These multiple meanings give texture to the idea, creating tone and depth, just as chords and melody would in a song. The language resonates on several levels, creating something akin to harmonic overtones.

Also, the rhyme scheme adds another undertone: two 'In Memoriam' stanzas, rhyming abba cddc, using consonance rhyme for the inner lines, dead/shade, song/young. The 'In Memoriam' stanza is taken from Alfred Lord Tennyson's poem of the same name, a eulogy. The form is a fitting choice for this descant on ageing. The way this rhyme scheme moves creates a feeling of longing all by itself (motion creates e-motion), and adds that emotion to the rest of the poem.

II

The language of a lyric can be simpler and more straightforward. There will be plenty of extra colour given by the notes that join the words, their relationships to other notes, and the rhythm they embody. If you think of melodies as 'nouns', then chords, the textures that colour them, are the 'adjectives'. Rhythm is the 'verb'. It activates the melody and harmony – it supplies the action. So the words themselves get a lot of help. For example, 'My Girl' by Smokey Robinson:

> I got sunshine on a cloudy day
> When it's cold outside, I've got the month of May
> I guess you'd say, 'What could make me feel this way?'

You can't help yourself. You hear the whole thing in your head. It all happens at once: you hear not only the instruments and melody, but an expressive human voice.

There's a lot going on, and it's one time through. In most cases, no stopping, no looking. No checking the dictionary. Even if we could, we usually wouldn't want to stop ourselves. The pleasure is in the continuous movement forward.

So, the more complicated a lyric's language, the more it limits its audience to those who understand complicated language easily. Not a majority. Take a look, for example, at the Genesis album, *Selling England by the Pound*. It is rife with allusions and quotes from Eliot's *The Wasteland*. Or, look at Steely Dan's song, 'Home at Last', an oblique re-telling of Odysseus and the Sirens. The lyrics beg for explication – if you are interested enough to explicate. Limiting the audience to those who care. Many people simply move on, not having been allowed entry on the first listen. For those who stay awhile, it may be for other reasons. If the guitarist or the singer is good, perhaps oblique lyrics will be ignored or put on the back burner while the singer wails and the guitarist flashes lick after lick.

It's a matter of choice: how deep do you want the lyrics to go? Most often, it's a trade-off: if the lyric is dense the music is simple, and conversely. Songwriter 'poets' like Bob Dylan and Leonard Cohen generally use pretty straightforward melody and harmony. Usually, something's gotta give: if everything is dense, nothing much is clear and there's limited communication – or at least, communication to a narrower audience.

Of course, the matter of density also affects poets. From pop poets like Rod McKuen to the density of T. S. Eliot or Ezra Pound, choice of language limits and determines audience. Between poets and lyricists it is more a difference of degree than kind. Some lyrics may use more complicated language than some poems. Some poems may use simpler language than some lyrics. But still, poems must stand on their own ground. Lyrics have extra modifiers to colour their words.

III

Another distinction between songs and poems is that, since the end of a line in poetry is a visual cue, a poet can end a line, yet let the grammatical meaning continue on to the next line, creating tension, but not confusion. An example of this is from 'Birches' by Robert Frost:

> You may see their trunks arching in the woods
> Years afterwards, trailing their leaves on the ground
> Like girls on hands and knees that throw their hair
> Before them over their heads to dry in the sun.

The tension between line three's ending and the idea continuing into the next line feels like the girls are actually tossing their hair.

In a song, the end of the lyric line usually has a sonic cue – the end of a melodic phrase. Because the song is aimed at the ear, if a lyricist tries to carry a thought into the next melodic phrase, it usually creates confusion, since there is a disconnect between the melodic roadmap and grammatical structure. I've arranged these lines from 'Eddie My Love' by Aaron Collins to match its musical phrasing:

> Eddie please write (pause)
> me one li-ine
> Tell me your love is
> Still only mi-ine . . .

Or take a look at this example from 'I Still Believe' by Doug Johnson, again arranged according to its melodic phrases:

> Sometimes it's easy & sometimes it's not
> Sometimes I can't think of one thing we've got (pause)
> In common to keep us from falling apart . . .

The result is almost comical. The melodic phrases give the ear its roadmap. The lyric phrases lose their way.

Because we can *see* lines on a page, poetry is able to counterpoint line against phrase. Because we only *hear* songs, the marriage of musical phrase with lyric phrase is essential.

With the recent movement toward performance poetry in spoken word and slams, poetry is once again being directed to the ear rather than the eye, where the grammatical phrase, once again, rules the roost. Like prose, it is grammatically driven, and where the natural phrase ends, it ends. When you don't see lines, then counterpointing line against phrase is no longer a compositional option, and we are dealing with 'a poetry of phrases'.

The fundamental unit of composition for 'prose' is the 'grammatical phrase', building into sentences, paragraphs, sections and so on. In slams and spoken word, the 'phrases' build the flow, and are often done with rhythm and syncopation, utilising the opportunities that a performance by a human voice can give: tone of voice, stopping and starting, extend-ing syllables, modulating pitches – in short, many of the things that the music of the song provides the lyric. Both are ear-directed.

By contrast, 'poetry' uses *two* fundamental units of composition: the grammatical phrase (tied to meaning) *and* the line (independent of meaning). It is made for the eye, as well as the ear. It is a poetry of both lines and phrases.

IV

These two fundamental units of composition for a poem – the grammatical phrase and the line – are both dependent on the page. Because a song lyric is directed to the ear, *rhyme* is important since it provides a roadmap for the ear, by showing relationships between lines, creating forward motion, creating either stability or instability in sections, and telling the ear where sections end.

Though rhyme is common in poetry it is less important, since the reader can see where a line or a section ends. Even when poems rhyme, they don't necessarily announce a phrase's end or a section's end, as in Percy Bysshe Shelley's 'Ode to the West Wind':

> O wild West Wind, thou breath of Autumn's being,
> Thou, from whose unseen presence the leaves dead
> Are driven, like ghosts from an enchanter fleeing,
>
> Yellow, and black, and pale, and hectic red,
> Pestilence-stricken multitudes: O thou,
> Who chariotest to their dark wintry bed
>
> The winged seeds, where they lie cold and low,
> Each like a corpse within its grave, until
> Thine azure sister of the Spring shall blow
>
> Her clarion o'er the dreaming earth, and fill
> (Driving sweet buds like flocks to feed in air)
> With living hues and odours plain and hill.

V

Clearly, the compositional strategies of the poet differ dramatically from the lyricist's. The vast majority of poems, whether fixed form, blank verse or free verse, are linear journeys, moving from idea to idea, line to line, until the end. Except in rare cases, such as the 'rondel', poetry's compositional strategy does not use *repetition of lines or sections*. Older ballade poetry sometimes uses repetition, but note that it was performed, and directed to the ear rather than the eye.

Lyrics, conversely, depend heavily on repeated content, usually refrains or choruses. The development of the lyric's ideas must take account of the repeated sections, and in the ideal case, transform or deepen the meaning of that same content each time we hear it. Watch the words 'What'll I do', from Irving Berlin's song, gain weight in each section because of the focus each section provides. First, the thought of distance from you; second, the danger you might be finding someone new; and finally, the heartbreaking news that our love is over:

What'll I do
When you are far away
And I am blue,
What'll I do?

What'll I do?
When I am wond'ring who
Is kissing you,
What'll I do?

What'll I do with just a photograph
To tell my troubles to,

When I'm alone
With only dreams of you
That won't come true
What'll I do?

VI

Another practical concern that is often overlooked is the fact that a lyricist has extremely limited space to work with. Normal commercial songs, lasting from 2½ to 3½ minutes, limit space dramatically. A commercial song cannot be too long and it cannot be too short. Not counting the repeated choruses or refrains, the average commercial song contains twelve to twenty lines. There are, of course, some exceptions, but not many. 'McArthur Park' (Jimmy Webb), 'Vincent' (Don McLean), 'Scenes from an Italian Restaurant' (Billy Joel), 'Paradise by the Dashboard Lights' (Jim Steinman). Very few long songs have commercial radio success – they take up too much time that could be spent making revenue by playing commercials. This space limitation no doubt affects, to some degree, choice of topic. Of course, that's equally true for fixed poetic forms – sonnet, terza rima, haiku and so on – but for the most part, the poem can be as long or short as it needs to be.

VII

Lyrics are far more dependent on regular rhythm than poems, since a lyric's rhythm is *set* to musical rhythm. A regular lyric rhythm prepares the words to snuggle into the alternating strong/weak/strong/weak patterns of 4/4 time, or the strong/weak/weak pattern of all the triple times, 3/4, 6/8, and 12/8. Musical rhythm, because it can extend a syllable's length or syncopate its regular lyric rhythm, can transform what, if spoken, would be mind-numbingly regular, into an interesting journey.

Great poetry contains its own theme and variation, setting a rhythm and syncopating against it. Look at the first two lines of John Keats's 'Ode on a Grecian Urn':

Thou still unravished bride of quietness   - / - / - / - / - -
Thou foster child of silence and slow time - / - / - / - - / /

The first four feet of line one are strictly iambic (‑ /, or weak‑strong). The last foot is pyrrhic (‑ ‑, or weak‑weak), creating a dimunendo that supports 'quietness'. The first three feet of line two are strictly iambic. The fourth foot is pyrrhic, supporting 'silence', while the final spondee (/ /, or strong‑strong) slows the line down, reinforcing the slowness of time. Neat.

And look at the rhythmic strategy of 'After Long Silence' by William Butler Yeats, where rhythm is again at work creating additional texture and making its own commentary. The poem is written in an iambic pentameter pulse, using substitutions expressively. In the first three lines, the rhythm seems to be shaking itself awake – clearing its throat after long silence: 'Spéech áfter lóng sílence; it is right'. This nine‑syllable line has a defective first foot, missing the unstressed syllable of the iamb, followed by a trochee (/ ‑, or strong‑weak), a spondee, and a pyrrhic before the final iamb. None of it moves forward. It creaks from age and disuse. None of the feet feel like substitutions, since a pulse has yet to be established:

> Áll óther lóvers béing estránged or déad.

After an opening spondee, the rhythm begins to move iambically, though 'being' threatens to feel like two syllables, disturbing the iambic motion:

> Unfriéndly lámplight híd únder its sháde.

The iambic pattern has been established by the time we reach 'under', a marvellous trochaic substitution that creates the feeling of being hidden beneath the shade. It interrupts the iambic motion at a particularly sensitive position – the fourth foot. It's hard to hear the last foot as an iamb, so the pattern is broken and must be re‑established by the next line.

> The cúrtains dráwn upon unfriéndly níght.

'Upon' is probably best scanned as a pyrrhic substitution. This is close, but we have yet to feel a perfectly iambic line. And so now we are prepared to arrive at the rhythmic tour de force of the poem:

> That wé descánt and yét agáin descánt.

This rhythmic release into the smooth iambic actually feels like we can't stop ourselves from talking. The rhythm itself, from the first line to this line, would have had the same effect without using words at all, just tapping it with a stick on a table. We would feel the fifth line release and push smoothly forward. The rhythm carries its own message. It assists the words.

Yeats meant to do all this. It is part of being a poet – to understand how to use the whole of language – its sounds, its rhythms, its stacked meanings. It is not simply a matter of jotting your feelings and insights down in chopped‑up sentences. Poetry is com‑position, from 'posito/positare – to place or arrange; to position', and 'com' – a prefix meaning 'together, in relation to'. Art is composed. It places things together for a reason. It creates, in Aristotle's words, a 'unity'. Everything working together.

Because a poem stands on its own ground, making its own rhythm and music, setting great poetry to music is about as futile and pointless as writing a lyric to a Beethoven piano concerto.

When combining works of art, say music and poetry, one or the other must always be in a position of servitude. Consider setting: 'Thou foster child of silence and slow time' (scanned ˘ / ˘ / ˘ / ˘ ˘ / /) to music. The line's rhythm makes its own 'music'. It makes a statement with the pyrrhic substitution in the fourth foot, creating a diminuendo that creates 'silence', while the spondee in the fifth foot slows down, supporting the idea 'slow time' nicely.

Music has two choices here, to create a different rhythm of its own, and therefore ruin the rhythmic statement of the line, or bow to the line's rhythm and orchestrate it. Note that in orchestration, the music is in service to the poem. It does not create something musically independent. The poem is driving the bus. Of course, setting light verse to music is easier to accomplish, since it thrives on regular rhythms, rhymes and common metre or matched tetrameter couplets – qualities typical of lyrics. (But in light verse, we are generally not talking about great poetry.)

This is not to say that you shouldn't try to orchestrate a poem. But to actually try to create a beautiful stand-on-its-own melody and harmony and stay precisely true to the music of the poem itself is a task. Musical motion makes its own demands, often tempting the composer to step away from the poem's music in favour of his own composition – to create a Piece. The raft of unfortunate settings of Frost poems should be enough to warn off any would-be composer. There is a reason they fail so universally, and it's not that the composers are bad composers. Their music is, by itself, rather lovely and creative. But alas, while the music is out on the town having a real good time, it mostly leaves the poetry dishevelled and wandering along the night-time roadside, hoping to hitch a ride home.

VIII

When talking about the similarities and differences with songs and poems, we might also consider history. The year 1066 was a pretty big one for poetry. The Norman (French) invasion of England (Celtic/Anglo-Saxon) produced a collision, not only of cultures, but also of languages.

Until that point, poetry in England was 'accentual' – that is, drawn from a Germanic base, featuring a wide dynamic range between stressed and unstressed syllables – so much so that stressed syllables were all that mattered in their poems. Celtic poetry usually consisted of lines of three or four strong stresses, usually accompanied by caesura at the half-line. Unstressed syllables weren't counted at all. Some of this strategy is preserved in nursery rhymes:

Hickory Dickory Dock	(three stresses)
The mouse ran up the clock	(three stresses)
The clock struck one, the mouse fell down	(four stresses)
Hickory Dickory Dock	(three stresses)

Across the Channel, William the Conqueror mobilised his army to invade England. He spoke French. But French is not an 'inflected' language: there is, relatively, less difference there between stressed and unstressed syllables. Thus Norman, or French Poetry, was a 'syllabic' poetry, counting syllables, not stressed syllables. The usual line of French poetry consisted of twelve syllables, often called a hexameter line.

As these two languages inevitably blended, the result was modern English. Poetry beginning with Chaucer began to merge French and English poetic devices, resulting in 'accentual-syllabic' verse, which counts both the number of syllables and the number of stressed syllables. William the Conqueror had no idea that he was creating the language of Shakespeare and Yeats, but he was.

Because English does not use its ending for grammatical purposes (as Latin does, or Spanish), English is restricted to position: because adjectives and nouns do not identify their alliance via the way they end, they must be physically adjacent. Typically, English sentences are ordered – they start with the subject – the noun or noun phrase. Nouns are identified as nouns by using an unstressed article, 'the', 'a', 'an', a grammatical function. So, the typical English sentence starts unstressed, and moves to the stressed noun, creating instant iambic motion from weak to strong. Thus, English is iambic. Latin, because it used endings to identify its nouns, adjectives and verbs, generally started strong (or 'long') and moved to weak (or 'short').

English poetry uses the dynamic contrast between stressed and unstressed syllables to create rhythms, to set a 'groove'. Most poetry, in any language, strives to create the longest line possible – a line that feels like one thing – that does not feel like it breaks or subdivides into smaller units. If you think of strong syllables as having 'weight', the strong syllables in Germanic poetry are quite heavy, only allowing three or four of them to sit on the branch before it breaks, making us feel like another line has appeared. The medial caesura in Germanic poetry attests to the density of the stressed syllables; they need to 'prop up' in the middle of the branch.

French poetry's 'stressed' syllables, its meaning functions, are much lighter (they do not weigh as much in this 'branch' metaphor), and you can line twelve of them on the branch (six units of two) without some of them falling off into the next line. In English poetry, which is not as inflected as German, and is more inflected than French, the branch can hold five feet (five iambs) without breaking – without subdividing into smaller units, as we can see with these lines by Frost:

> When Í see bírches bénd to léft and ríght
> Acróss the línes of stráighter dárker trees

Whereas with seven stresses in a line:

> When I see birches stánd alóne and bend to left and right
> Across the lines of óak and élm and straighter darker trees . . .

the branches get too heavy, and break into:

> When I see birches stand alone
> and bend to left and right
> Across the lines of oak and elm
> and straighter darker trees

Even hexameter lines (six feet) tend to subdivide from:

> When I see birches stand and bend to left and right
> Across the lines of elm and straighter darker trees

into:

> When I see birches stand
> and bend to left and right
> Across the lines of elm
> and straighter darker trees . . .

So, the longest non-subdividing line in English poetry is the pentameter line – a line of five feet. And the basic rhythmic figure of English is the iamb, moving from weak to strong. Thus, the staple line of the majority of poetry written in English is iambic-pentameter such as we see here:

> When I see birches bend to left and right
> Across the lines of straighter darker trees . . .

Because of Western Music's love affair with two-, four- and eight-bar phrases, the standard lines of lyric are usually tetrameter (four strong stresses) and trimeter (three strong stresses). The typical song lyric is built either on common metre ('Mary Had a Little Lamb') such as Bob Dylan's 'Tangled Up in Blue':

She was wórkin' ín a tópless pláce	(four stresses)
And I stópped in fór a béer,	(three stresses)
I júst kept lóokin' at the síde of her fáce	(four stresses)
In the spótlíght so cléar.	(three stresses)

or on matched tetrameter couplets ('Eenie Meenie Miney Mo') such as these lines from Sting's 'Stolen Car':

Láte at níght in súmmer héat.	(four stresses)
Expénsive cár, émpty stréet	(four stresses)
There's a wíre in my jácket. Thís is my tráde	(four stresses)

The only lyric form consistently employing five-stress lines is blues:

My báby léft me, I'm só alóne and blúe	(five stresses)
Yes, báby léft me, I'm só alóne and blúe	(five stresses)
I crý all níght, I dón't know whát to dó	(five stresses)

For the lyric's line lengths, musical considerations drive the bus. The two-bar building block of western music creates the format for the lyric: since two bars of 4/4 time contain a total of four stressed positions, the lyric relies on a heavy diet of four-stress and three-stress lines, adjusting to the confines of the two-bar phrase. The five-stress lines of blues live in four-bar phrases.

There are other differences between song lyrics and poetry, but this ought to suffice to put the stink on the often-heard claim, 'Her lyrics are pure poetry'. No, they are not, although those making this claim are probably responding to lyrics written in fresh, interesting language; language using provocative images and startling metaphor; lyrics containing some remarkable insight into the human condition. That is, 'Her lyrics are pure poetry' typically responds to *what is being said* – *to meaning*, certainly something that great poetry and great lyrics share in common.

Robert Frost wryly defines poetry as 'that which is lost in translation'. Meaning, images and metaphor can generally be translated accurately. The specific rhythms of a poem cannot. The poem's specific arrangement of sounds and rhymes cannot. The counter-pointing of line and phrase cannot. And these are the elements that give poetry its depth – its identity as a complete use of the language. These elements create the music that underlies great poetry. These are the elements that lyrics do not contain by themselves; they depend on melody, harmony and the rhythm of music to create it for them.

A great poem, like a great symphony, stands its own ground. It contains everything it needs. It doesn't require music, since it brings its own along.

While a great song also stands its own ground, a great lyric, by itself, does not. Lyrics are made to be married. As in an earlier age, there is a division of labour: one partner learns to cook, sew and raise the children. The other ploughs, hunts and builds shelters. Together, the team survives quite nicely. Apart, they usually create defective poetry, and muzak.

Poetry is made for the eye. Lyrics are made for the ear.

Discuss. ☺

Notes

1. A version of this chapter originally appeared in Charlotte Pence (ed.) (2012), *The Poetics of American Song Lyrics*, Jackson: University Press of Mississippi.
2. Reprinted with the permission of Scribner, a Division of Simon & Schuster, Inc., from *Collected Poems* by William Butler Yeats. Copyright © 1933 by The Macmillan Company, renewed 1961 by Bertha Georgie Yeats. All rights reserved.

References

Dylan, Bob (1975), 'Tangled Up in Blue', music and lyrics by Bob Dylan. *Blood on the Tracks*, Columbia Records.

Frost, Robert (1972), 'Birches' in Edward Connery Lathem and Lawrance Thompson (eds), *Robert Frost Poetry and Prose*, New York: Holt, Rhinehart and Winston.

Greenwood, Lee (1994), 'I Still Believe', music and lyrics by Doug Johnson. *God Bless the USA*, UMG Recordings, Inc.

Keats, John (2006), 'Ode on a Grecian Urn' in Richard Matlak and Anne Mellor (eds), *British Literature 1780–1832*, Boston: Heinle.

Shelley, Percy Bysshe (2006), 'Ode to the West Wind' in Richard Matlak and Anne Mellor (eds), *British Literature 1780–1832*. Boston: Heinle.

Sting (2003), 'Stolen Car', music and lyrics by Carl Terrell Mitchell and Gordon Matthew Sumner. *Sacred Love*, A&M Records.

The Teen Queens (1956), 'Eddie My Love', music and lyrics by Aaron Collins, Maxwell Davis and Sam Ling. *Eddie My Love*, RPM Records.

The Temptations (1964), 'My Girl', music and lyrics by William 'Smokey' Robinson and Donald A. White. *The Temptations Sing Smokey*, Motown.

Whiteman, Paul (1924), 'What'll I Do?', music and lyrics by Irving Berlin.

Yeats, William Butler (1996), 'After Long Silence', *The Collected Poems of W. B. Yeats*, New York: Simon & Schuster Inc.

30

Flash Fiction

Tony Williams

Flash fiction has established itself as a significant global genre. Many short-story writers had previously written very short stories on occasion, but the last decades of the twentieth century saw the increasing emergence of writers specialising in stories of that length and of magazines, anthologies and competitions dedicated to it. There was also an increasing critical and editorial apparatus that recognised that these were not simply shorter stories than usual, but constituted a distinct genre in its own right.

The reasons for the rise of flash fiction are unclear. There are various arguments about changing lifestyles and attention spans, desire for instant gratification, and the influence of technology and new media on our reading habits and preferences. These may be more or less convincing, but it is certainly true that one of the peculiarities of flash is the way whole stories can be read quickly, often in much less than a minute. This allows great beauty and intensity of effect, but it also poses fiendish problems for the writer.

Writing flash fiction is, in one sense, easy. In comparison with the daunting prospect of writing tens of thousands of words for a novel, writing a few hundred for a flash fiction might seem like a piece of cake. It will probably take you a lot less time than a novel, anyway. But of course, it isn't as simple as that. Anything worth doing is difficult: in this case, the problem is not writing enough words, it's making a story work without writing too many. Producing a fiction which satisfies the reader in, say, 300 words rather than 3,000 is a project which brings its own problems. There is simply not room to develop character, setting and plot so expansively. Novelists and short-story writers like to say that every word must earn its keep, but flash fiction writers know that both are far too lenient. Meeting these distinctive formal constraints produces solutions which are themselves distinctive – this is why flash fiction is its own genre, because stories of this length work and feel differently to longer ones.

Not everyone will enjoy reading and writing flash fiction, but I think every prose writer should try their hand at it. Learning to fit a story into a very small space demands tremendous discipline which will serve you well in your longer projects. And you may find – as I did, to my surprise, when I started writing flash – that the genre suits you and helps you to unlock ways of writing that you never suspected were at hand.

Definition of the genre

'Flash fiction' has become the widely accepted term for very short stories, though others are in use – 'short-short story', 'microfiction', 'nanofiction' and 'sudden fiction' being the most popular. Perhaps inevitably for such a young genre, the terminology can be confusing. Sometimes these terms are used interchangeably, and sometimes they are used to differentiate between flash fictions of different lengths. Editors, competitions and critics disagree about the length such stories should be. I have seen the cap set as high as 1,000 words and as low as 6, and pretty much every length in between; 150 words, 300 words, 500 words and 750 words seem to be popular, if arbitrary, limits. We won't worry here about exact terms and definitions. For the purposes of this chapter, we'll work on the basis that we are talking about any story under 750 words. But when writing and submitting flash fictions to magazines and competitions, make sure you pay attention to the word limit. Yours may be the best story they receive, but if it's a 600-worder then a magazine that only takes 100-word stories is going to reject it out of hand!

In general, stories under 750 words tend to 'feel' like flash fiction, 750–1,000 words is a grey area, and anything over 1,000 words starts to feel more like a conventional short story. By feel, I mean something to do with tone, pace, structure and cadence. If you read a lot of flash fiction you will start to notice that there *is* something distinctive about very short stories – that is what makes them into a distinct genre.

Reading flash fiction

You should, of course, read some flash fiction to familiarise yourself with it.

The genre's beginnings lie in Latin America and the USA, and a good start for English-speaking readers would be the landmark early anthology *Flash Fiction: 72 Very Short Stories*, edited by James Thomas, Denise Thomas and Tom Hazuka; the later *Flash Fiction Forward: 80 Very Short Stories*, edited by James Thomas and Robert Shapard; or, representing the Latin American tradition, *Sudden Fiction Latino: Short-Short Stories from the United States and Latin America*, edited by Robert Shapard, James Thomas and Ray Gonzalez.

Beginning with an anthology, apart from giving you a wide range of work to taste, will also bring out a strange feature of the reading of flash fiction: because each story takes so little time to read, it is possible to read an enormous number of them in a short space of time. This can be either absorbing or exhausting, sometimes both at the same time. As a reader, you may come to prefer reading just a few or even one at a time, and give the stories time and space to resonate. They often don't work quite so well if you churn through them like you would a novel. As a writer, you should learn from this and try to keep finding new ways to make your stories succeed. Originality is particularly prized in flash fiction, because of the way it is consumed.

As well as anthologies, you might try specialist flash fiction magazines, and whole collections by single authors. The best UK magazine is *Flash: The International Short-Short Story Magazine*, published by the University of Chester in the UK, which also maintains an excellent bibliography of flash fiction materials on its website (www.chester.ac.uk/flash.magazine/bibliography). There are many other specialist magazines, many of them web-based and international in scope. For single-author collections, you might try work by Lydia Davis, Etgar Keret, David Gaffney, Dan Rhodes, Donald Barthelme, Jennifer Egan, Dave Eggers, Tania Hershman and many, many others. Follow up on authors whose work you like in anthologies and magazines. And remember that many short-story writers produce flash fiction some of the time even if they are not recognised as 'specialists' in the genre.

Writing flash

Flash fiction covers a range of styles. It is often funny, although it should generally add up to more than just a joke. It can be strange or enigmatic in effect, perhaps because there is not room to explain anything. For the same reason, you should as a rule expect a single storyline and a very small number of characters. (So, no subplots, although the odd hint of a wider and richer world can be very effective.) At bottom is the requirement for narrative: this is flash *fiction*, and most or all examples of the genre offer something in the way of story.

Quite how much story, or how discernible that story should be, varies a lot. At one extreme flash fictions may be indistinguishable from prose poems, while at the other all the elements of narrative – character, motivation, obstacles, resolution – may be clearly present. Either way is fine. It doesn't really matter whether you are writing flash fiction or prose poetry so long as what you are writing is good. Most stories, anyway, will be somewhere between these two extremes: they will have some elements of narrative (they will be or feel like stories!), but perhaps not all of them. Simply because of the brevity of the form, flash fictions rarely present the whole of a story. Much more often, they present a single scene from which the reader must extrapolate.

If you come to writing flash with previous experience of prose fiction, you will find that it has much in common with longer genres. In particular, and obviously, it bears similarities with the short story. In fact, much of the advice that people give about writing short stories is applicable to flash: make every word count; only put in what needs to be there; start late and get out early. What is different is that with the even more draconian word limits of flash, these principles need to be applied more strictly.

What's the story?

The central requirement, then, is *story*. Your flash must do enough storytelling to satisfy the reader. (It's true that different readers will be satisfied by more or less, but let's not worry about that for now.) It probably won't tell the story as lavishly as a short story or, even more, a novel would: we will not get to see as big a slice of the action, or in as much detail. But it must be *complete* as a story, even if much is left implicit. Lots of failed flash fictions fail because really they are no more than story fragments; the reader does not get to see enough of the narrative arc to work out what is going on or how things might be resolved. That is not to say you need to explain everything, but you cannot just break off when you run out of words either.

Although you probably won't think in these terms each time you write a flash fiction, it is worth considering the elements of story and how they tend to appear in flash. I like to think about story in terms of character, because that is a particularly useful model for flash fiction.

A story needs a 'protagonist' who is 'motivated' to achieve something but is prevented from doing so by 'obstacles'. They take certain 'actions' to overcome those obstacles, and ultimately, whether they succeed or fail, are 'changed' as a result.

Your story is the actions the protagonist takes to achieve their goal.

Less is more

That model of a story, uninspiring as it looks, serves a useful purpose in showing you how most flash fictions ought to line up. In particular, notice what it doesn't contain: sub-plots, or lists of secondary characters.

As a general rule, your story should contain only the main story. Whereas in longer forms we may add in details and sub-plots in order to enrich and complicate, flash must achieve its purposes via a single line of thought, and is usually weakened by transitions, fresh starts, 'meanwhile's and 'also's. Of course that single line of thought can be complicated, and unexpected details and events can be vital, but the key to writing flash is to identify the right details. Do not leave that great piece of dialogue in just because it's good: it needs to be good *and* reveal character *and* move the story on.

Similarly, notice how many characters there are in the model: one – the protagonist. Any others need a very strong reason to appear. Lots of flashes contain only one character, and very many others have a second one. Stories may well *need* a second character in order to work: anything about relationships, for example. But after that there's a sudden drop-off. You really don't need a third or fourth or fifth character very often. If you do, if you really do, that is fine. But as soon as you add extra characters things get very busy, and you have to do lots of work establishing who they are and what they are doing. And remember, just because someone is in a story does not mean they have to appear, actually doing stuff: maybe a single reference to 'he' or 'she' is enough to give the reader the context for what happens.

A slice of the action

The Latin poet Horace said that narratives should start *in medias res* ('in the middle of things'), sometimes expressed in scriptwriting as 'start late, get out early', which is to say that you should cut the preamble and start at an exciting point, and then stop as soon as all the interesting stuff has finished. No prologues, introductions, scenes where we get to know the characters. Boring! Get on with it. And, when you get to the end, no epilogues, no tidying up of loose ends, or 'what happened to Harry, Ron and Hermione in later life'. (You can do that at the end of the most successful film franchise in history; you can't do it in a 750-word story.) A huge number of flash fiction stories can be improved at the draft stage simply by removing the first paragraph (or even more). The reader simply doesn't need to know what the writer is telling them in it.

That may seem unbearable. Maybe you like your opening paragraph: maybe you think it 'sets the scene'. There is no time for that. In flash fiction everything has to happen all at once. You have to set the scene at the same time as you are having the protagonist clambering over the obstacles – the same sentences must do more than one job. In other words, if in novels and short stories every word has to earn its keep, in flash fiction it also needs to work evenings and weekends.

Look at this opening sentence, from a story by Tania Hershman. We join the action well after the beginning of the events. We are efficiently made to understand that the protagonist has some illness with a poor prognosis; both past and future are implied clearly, but the action itself is focused on a specific and concrete present:

> 'I am a camera', she whispered to herself in the shower, sliding her fingers along the rail already installed for the day when she wouldn't be able to find her way out. (Hershman 2008: 25)

If you start late enough and get out early enough, you can probably get your story down to a single scene. A large number of flash fiction stories contain only one scene. The gains are tremendous: you do not have to do as much work helping the reader imagine the setting and action, and you do not have to work out how to move between scenes. It is usually more elegant, too: there just isn't room for lots of scenes and events in a story of this length. And remember that 'start late, get out early' applies not just to the story as a whole: it applies to each scene within that story as well. So your whole story might well boil down to a single scene, and that scene boils down to the key moment, or movement, which is the nub of the story. Maybe all the reader gets to see is somebody opening the boot of their car and sighing. But because of the weight of nuance and implication, the deft nudges and winks that you use in describing this scene, you manage to imply what comes before and after, and the reader smiles and says, 'Aha!' to herself because she grasps the significance of all the boot-opening and sighing. The most mundane details can be used to suggest characters, their relationships and attitudes to one another:

> I take my place at the till and you tell me how much you're looking forward to X Factor (Selzter 2011: 31)

Flash fiction is about implication, teasing and trust. Almost all flashes demand that the reader imagine parts of the story that are not supplied. Readers are good at this, provided they are given the right kind of clues. Trust them. Practise the most sly and scrupulous tact. And be glad, or at least accepting, when they interpret things differently from how you envisaged them.

Two ways to skin a cat

There are fundamentally two ways to write a story of 750 words or fewer. You can write a longer story and edit it down. This seems to be popular with lots of very good writers of flash fiction. It has the advantage that you get to think through the larger context of your story, imagine things in detail, and work out the best places to start and finish. It is a bit like mixing concrete to make a big block, and then whittling it down again into an egg cup. In that sense it is labour-intensive, but if it leads to a better story then such considerations are irrelevant. You end up with a hell of an egg cup.

The disadvantage of writing long drafts and then editing them down, for me, is that I cannot make it work. Once I have an idea for a story in my head, it seems to arrive on the page in a very small number of words. It would feel false to add more words just so I can cut them out again later. Mine is probably a more hit-and-miss method, and a dangerously attractive one for lazy writers. You should try both, learn from both, and find out what works for you.

Keeping notes

In general, story ideas can be fragile things. Once you have expressed them in one way, even in note form, they can dissipate, leaving you unable to make them come to life in another form. This is especially dangerous with flash fiction, where a one-paragraph synopsis might be almost as long as the story you want to tell. A flash *is* a synopsis, done stylishly. On the other hand, if you don't record ideas, you forget them anyway. My own practice, which you might as well have a go at, is to keep a single sheet of paper on which I jot down ideas – usually just a single word or phrase per story, something to jog my memory about what the story might be. Sometimes this phrase ends up as the story's title. When I am ready to write, I sit down and pick ideas from the list which appeal to me. Some succeed; some fail. Some never get written. But having a sheet of short prompts is a useful way of keeping ideas warm at the right stage of development.

Multitasking

We've already seen that each sentence has to do more than one job. You can't waste a paragraph on just setting the scene or establishing your protagonist. Always, always advance the story too. Writing flash is like spinning plates – in order to fit a whole story in, you need to get everything moving at once. Above all, be brief: no whole paragraphs of beautifully observed description (but see 'Pace' below); make one single detail stand for the whole.

Don't write: *The quiet of the library was oppressive. The almost-silent fans whirred in the brightly lit roof. The smell of books was drowned out by the smell of cleaning fluids and IT equipment. I fancied the librarian who kept shushing me.*

Write: *She's so wonderfully stern, looking over the top of her black-rimmed glasses when she shushes me.*

Remember that character and story are interchangeable: by telling the story, you also reveal character, and vice versa. After all, character is at bottom how we behave, not what we look like or how we feel. By describing what happens, you automatically help the reader to imagine the character. Or, to put it the other way round, by revealing character effectively, you will automatically tell the story.

Pace

Because it is so important to keep the story moving, there is always a temptation in flash fiction to keep up a frenetic pace. Resist it. All fiction benefits from variations in pace – sometimes slowing things down to add contrast or tension or to create space in which ideas, events and images can resonate – and the same is true of flash. If you keep everything whizzing along quickly, it will come to seem like a speeded-up film; and it is hard to *care* about the people we see in speeded-up films. They just look a bit ridiculous. So do not be afraid of slowing things down every now and then, so that the reader can perceive and enjoy the significance and nuance of events. Done at the right moment, that *is* moving the story forwards.

Voice and narration

You can tell your stories in any way you like, but certain approaches to narration are more popular than others, and for good reason. There are relatively few flash fictions which use omniscient third-person narration, probably because most flashes simply don't contain enough characters for it to make sense popping inside their heads. And switching between characters is difficult to manage gracefully in such a small space.

It is much more common to focalise and vocalise the story through one character, whether directly through first-person narration or indirectly through third-person narration. There are several benefits of doing this. For one thing, telling only one side of a story usually takes up less space and creates more opportunities for doubt, implication and nuance – the stock-in-trade of the flash-fiction writer. And, perhaps more importantly, in these forms of narration the voice of the narration is often also the voice of the protagonist. The way you tell the story, the language you use, becomes part of the setting, and an expression of the protagonist's character: it tells the story for you. The more precisely and evocatively you can render the protagonist's voice, the better and more efficiently you will tell the story. Multitasking, again. Voice is everything. In this example from David Gaffney, voice, tone, character and setting are perfectly in tune:

> I didn't want to be known as Big Jan, like some bull dyke prisoner. Harriet tried to reassure me; the new Janet was Little Jan, but I would always be Jan. But they might as well write fat cow on my forehead for all the difference that made. So-called Little Jan is a 12 at least, and not TopShop, more like Marks. (Gaffney 2006: 42)

Something else

Now things get frustrating. Everything I have told you so far is true, but it doesn't add up to a recipe for writing flash fiction. As we know, all writing rules are meant to be broken, and somewhere along the line you usually do have to break a rule in order to succeed.

The thing about flash fiction is that the difficulty of squeezing a whole story into a short space can seem so overriding, that in achieving it we also squeeze the life and potential out of our story. The obvious solution would be to relax the generic constraint and allow ourselves a few extra words to play with. But the best solution is – paradoxically – to make things more difficult, not less. To put yourself under more pressure, and see what happens. One reason for this is the need for originality. Remember I said flash fiction can get boring when you read a lot of it? In order to avoid being boring, you need to change the game. The exercises given below are all fundamentally ways of finding a new angle on writing, a different kind of pressure on yourself.

All good flashes have a kink in them, a place where things start moving in a different direction. In this sense they are like sonnets, which need a volta to be dynamic and interesting. Or they are like jokes, in that they set up expectations in the reader and then confound them. (Sometimes they do this by making the reader look for a change in direction which never comes.) Some of the best flashes have two such kinks, a double whammy of surprise. Many failed attempts fail because they do not have a kink. When your draft is not working, chuck in a new complication or a change in direction. Do something to surprise yourself and the reader, and see what happens. Chase the story, if you didn't find it where you thought you would.

Exercises

- Try making the story even shorter – if a piece isn't working, try making it fit in half the number of words.
- Try fitting in much more of the story – instead of starting late and getting out early, start early and get out late. How can you fit twenty years of narrative into 750 words?
- Try writing a story with fifteen named characters, each with a fully fledged motivation of their own.
- David Gaffney recommends putting the end of your story halfway through, and using the second half as a space in which the ending can resonate.

- As a variation on that, try ending your storyline half way through and then starting another one in the same piece, and see where it leads.
- Or try telling two stories – or perhaps one and a half – simultaneously. One on its own can be dull, but if you make the reader keep track of two at once, and think about how they interact, that can be magic.
- Think small: car chases, big explosions and grisly murders tend not to work well in flash, because there isn't room to ramp up tension or establish why they matter to characters. Find small actions and images that really matter. Small does not have to mean trivial.
- Now try writing a flash about a car chase, a big explosion or a grisly murder . . .
- Voice is everything – except when it isn't.
- Try writing flash in the style of a nineteenth-century novel.
- Have a look at all the short texts there are around you. Try writing a flash in the form of a shopping list, a memo, a book's blurb, an email or letter, a set of instructions.
- Add more: more story, more problems for yourself, more pressure. Pressure is what leads to imaginative solutions.
- Try writing something which doesn't seem to be in the form of a story at all. What can you do in a few hundred words that hasn't been done before?
- Off camera: maybe the story you've written isn't focused right. Imagine all the important stuff happening off camera, or before your narrative begins, and then write the story of your characters reacting to it.

Beyond flash

Wonderful as it is, flash fiction can (unsurprisingly) feel constricting. Most people would not want to read it, or write it, all the time. Most of the 'specialist' flash fiction names also write longer stories, or novels, or other things, and that is perfectly healthy. Severe word limits enable you to do things you could not otherwise achieve, but they also make other things impossible. You might write flash for a while and then move on to other genres, and look back on it as a training ground. Even if you stick with it, you will probably fool around with other genres too.

What does flash teach us about the construction of longer texts? Well, many or all of the techniques for writing flash are similar to the ones you would use to write any fiction, so a grounding in flash should equip you with good command of story, pace, momentum, character, narration and so on. You will have a brisk attitude to scenes. You might need a bit of calibration when faced with the gaping expanse and opportunity of a 5,000-word limit ('how could anyone *need* that many?'), but once you've got to grips with it, your ability to work at a tiny scale should help you to become a dynamic writer.

Very often, longer texts are made up of lots of short ones, whether these are the scenes or sections of a short story or the chapters of a novel. It is important to see these component texts as formal units in their own right. Mastering flash will put you in a good position to construct such units, paying attention to the little narrative arcs, even while another part of you is eyeing the grand novelistic vista. And you might like to consider the flash sequence – a number of flash fictions not loosely strung together as a collection but constructed deliberately to form a more-or-less unified whole, such as Gemma Seltzer's *Speak to Strangers* or Roberto Bolaño's *Antwerp*.

References

Bolaño, Roberto (2011), *Antwerp*, London: Picador.

Gaffney, David (2006), *Sawn-off Tales*, Cambridge: Salt Publishing.

Hershman, Tania (2008), *The White Road and Other Stories*, Cambridge: Salt Publishing.

Seltzer, Gemma (2011), *Speak to Strangers*, London: Penned in the Margins.

Shapard, Robert, James Thomas, and Ray Gonzalez (eds) (2010), *Sudden Fiction Latino: Short-Short Stories from the United States and Latin America*, New York and London: W. W. Norton.

Thomas, James, Denise Thomas and Tom Hazuka (eds) (1992), *Flash Fiction: 72 Very Short Stories*, New York and London: W. W. Norton.

Thomas, James and Robert Shapard (eds) (2006), *Flash Fiction Forward: 80 Very Short Stories*, New York and London: W. W. Norton.

31

Writing as Experimental Practice

Thalia Field

My husband and I make 'experimental dinners': we open the cabinets and create something from whatever we find. We never know what's going to come of it and often we don't even know what to call the results other than 'tasty' or 'barely edible'. It doesn't hurt that we have experience with traditional cooking, we know what to expect with foods or how to take a shortcut when needed. But when it comes down to it we enjoy the challenge and surprise of meeting the kitchen head-on. When I was asked to think about experimental writing, this is what immediately came to mind.

When it comes to writing, I often wonder if designating something 'experimental' is more a public, critical or personal act? Most attempts at defining 'experimental' dead-end into 'you know it when you see it' tautologies, or result in descriptive catch-all-isms where 'experimental' means 'non-traditional'. Tradition in this context mostly implies formally recognisable poetry and fiction oriented toward epiphany, closure, and a neat and tidy naturalism where visual details correlate to psychological ones and the author and characters are clear and coherent. In the opposite corner and equally generalised, the qualities of experimental writing include writing which is polysemous, indeterminate, polyphonic, multi-genre, documentary, meditative and puts the reader in an unstable position *vis-à-vis* the work's meanings. Of course these only describe a spectrum, and most writing exists somewhere in between these extremes. Still, lists of attributes tell us more about the past than the present, so is there a less forensic and more useful way to determine a literary experiment? Are there material differences between experimental and other writing practices in terms of creative process? Let's get back to this in a minute.

Looking historically, there have certainly been normative aesthetic traditions against which various experimental avant-gardes positioned themselves. Staging innovative literature as a critique of dominant art practice, and by analogy a critique of dominant culture, requires faith that language takes action, that writing functions as a privileged social gest, or mirror. In this way the history of aesthetic forms can be read as the dialectical content of history and formal evo/revolutions as evidence of culture's mutability. The revelation that no aesthetic attribute is ontologically fixed or sanctioned by God or King was an eye-opener of the early modern period, leading individual artists to work outside the patronage system to display other 'knowledges' and experience.

Meanwhile, the term 'experimental writing' emerged from the scientific work of French physiologists in Second-Empire Paris. The new laboratory science positioned 'experimental' medicine in opposition to the reigning paradigm of medicine as intuitive, quasi-religious art. The introduction of 'scientific method' was useful for debunking non-empirically tested beliefs about disease and treatment. Through the new experimental approach, knowledge emerged based on testing hypotheses in controlled laboratory conditions and 'going on the evidence'. This was a stricter method in which one's ideologies take a backseat to the experiment's ongoing results. The experimental, in this idealised form, asks a practitioner to shed all notion of what 'should happen' in favour of a blunt realism, a moving aside of ego for the sake of the work. This so-called objectivity, this 'materialism', challenged prevailing (mostly religious) systems wherein long-dominant norms determined *a priori* what one would 'find' in practice. Nowadays the 'objective' ideals of scientific method have been rightly problematised, but in the late nineteenth century Émile Zola took up the charge for an 'experimental literature' which could translate the scientists' realist vision into a more materialist literature, a hard core presentation of life's facts without a moralising or transcendental lens. Of course escaping the lens of one's own ideas proves difficult, and realism atrophied into naturalism, becoming a style all its own. But perhaps what is most important is that experimental writing began as oppositional and radical, self-consciously construed as a methodological way out of a prevailing symbolism, idealism and absolutism.

To show unadulterated 'truth', artists paid attention to presenting 'what is' rather than what 'should be' thereby opening the way for literature to follow the visual arts into an allegiance to perception over ideas and phenomenological (temporal) process over static ahistoric objects. That social issues could also be addressed through a materialist/realist/phenomenological language came from the modernist belief that structures of representation reveal the 'unconscious fantasies' of the cultural psyche and therefore making new forms is tantamount to remaking the inheritance of old ways of thinking. Metaphors and discourses of science, from relativity theory, chaos theory, quantum theory and information theory, have continued to find strong affinities and provide analogies for the experimental arts. That models of self and world are represented in culturally constructed (rather than 'natural') forms, that artistic expression is not 'innocent' of individual perspective, allows any writer to create agency (and share this with readers) using the same tools (language, narrative, discourse, performance) as the cultural mainstream.

It might therefore be argued that experimental writing has played a dominant, even essential part in the modern industrial/democratising period, as integral to its character as it can seem oppositional within it. In this way one could say that the history of modern European/American art is the history of experimental artists breaking down familiar dichotomies between museums and streets, 'high' culture and 'pop' culture, masterpieces and Xeroxes, noise and music, thought and event, performance and object, process and product, author and audience. The list goes on to include the total hybridisation of established genres and the larger imperative that no matter what else one does, one should address the audience's perception, 'make it new' or 'make it strange'. This basic commitment to the practices of defamiliarisation (a concept popularised by the Russian Formalists but expanded across a range of avant-gardes) shows that artistic devices (formal structures) represent the life of the artwork in history. Art forms must change so that a distance between art and 'everyday' perception can be maintained or revived, renewing the audience's sense of themselves as citizens of their time and agents of personal and collective history.

If artwork thus made 'strange' was also challenging for the audience, this slowed or difficult reading was a sign of poetic potency, a measure of its distance from the commonalities which are useful in social interaction but deadening in art. This formulation of aesthetic revival through fresh language reveals a link between experimentalism and romanticism. When the critique is made that experimental writing feels perfunctory or empty of felt experience, this indicates both the critic's longing for this romantic aspect as well as what may be the writer's allegiance to form over practice. Bad experimental writing, like bad writing generally, fails to create the sublime shock of something surprisingly and suddenly true.

I introduce the word 'true' as a gamble, a provocation. Though experimental literature has been aligned with post-structuralism and often foregrounds the non-essentialism of identity or the complex features of post-colonial cultures, its practitioners put forth the possibility that theirs is a more genuine literature in the sense of 'filled with the shock of truth' even if that truth presents itself as non-sense or new-sense. That experimental practice engages the complex, multifarious, non-generic world does not necessarily exclude the role of radical subjectivity. In fact, bringing together a writer's unique experimental process with the material givens of the world results in what Gertrude Stein called the 'continuous contemporary'. In this condition, an and/both phenomenon occurs between self and world relieving the pressure of previously intractable binaries into a new and productive interdependent space and time.

So now we may ask again: what makes experimental practice different from other habits of writing? Certainly many writers confront the infinite and open possibilities of their art and world. Still, traditional writers take their discoveries only as far as normative limits of form or material allow. Where a poem reaches some sort of crisis, a more experimental practitioner makes an important swerve away from the habitual approaches to material and toward a radical 'not knowing', allowing the work to stay open, to be completed in the encounter with a reader. So perhaps what makes a writing practice 'experimental' is the intention of the writer to continually re-open their ways of proceeding, their habits, as they encounter the world. A text held open may go beyond the parameters of both familiar forms and habitual creative process. The results do not necessarily have to be complex or difficult, but they are surprising.

The blank page has been the location of much excitement or trepidation. Fear of it can result in a writer's retreat into stale and prefabricated choices. Confronting the blank page in a traditional practice is just as challenging as for the experimentalist, and yet I think the traditional writer fills in the blank page as though it were a pre-formatted space awaiting content. A sentence makes sense. A character emerges in a situation. A concrete detail, a situation to describe ('the objective correlative'). Pretty soon, one finds oneself in a conventional fiction or poem, a single human protagonist described in adjectival prose, 'life like' against a scenic (cinematic) backdrop. The frame of the camera's view provides the scale and time of the action, an antagonist will be there, a tragic flaw. The conflict will take the hero into some revelations, the resolution will provide a catharsis from the event. Language is only that which delivers this content in a clear and descriptive way from author to reader with a minimum of confusion. There is a tidiness to the symbolism, the events, and no messy confusion for a reader to grapple with. Language does not intrude upon the telling, but stays grammatical and 'transparent' to the intention of the author. Formally there are paragraphs or line breaks and type left-justified between wide margins. There is dialogue and there is plenty of visual and psychological description. Characters, plots, language remain stable and constant throughout the piece. You need to dream up the specifics, which constitutes the main writing practice. Perhaps you brainstorm on the blank page, troll for details and clues as you 'discover' the piece, even your 'voice' (your

style within the larger constraints of this overall style) and probably your characters, conflicts or themes. This describes the sort of psychological naturalism prevalent in our time.
Yet many writers spend a lot of hard work and joyous exploration in the brainstorming/
dreaming practice of this form. So why isn't that experimental?

I think the blank page for the experimentalist doesn't exist to be 'filled in' in the same
way. Because form and content are indistinct, one does not conjure the work from the
imagination as though it was something detached from the world it emerges into. There
is never 'silence' or 'emptiness' (or perhaps even a blank page) in the laboratory sense of
a Newtonian idealised world in which art exists coherently and untroubled, to be looked
in on as though from outside. Writing as an experimental practice assumes no convenient
originating vantage, no way to present tidy geometries of symbol, culture or identity. And
with the blank page troubled by the shadows and sounds of a world always already moving
around it, there is material already present at hand. Writing in this sense is a finding, a
following, a listening, and not only in the sense of going along with what's in one's mind.
The many ways one enters the conversation with the world's shadows and sounds provide
the myriad of forms experimental writing takes. Finding content is never other than
finding form. In what has been called an 'organicist' or ecological encounter, the fullness
of the blank page becomes, then, a way of waking mindfully into an inseparable world.
Experimental practice and the project of deep ecology come together where writers relate
not to landscapes but to 'being worldbound'. This awareness of a different definition of
subject, object and action, results in work where the normative human-hero-centered
conventions of representation are replaced by more polycentric, polyrhythmic, or stochas-
tic processes. Whether these are mental or environmental, the very notion of 'event' and
'character' may reflect the collapse of distinctions such as those between nature/culture
and media/message.

So now let's look at some specific ways one might proceed 'experimentally' in practice.
These categories are intended to provide a few of the infinite approaches a writer might
take as you move away from habitual strategies toward the play of the unknown. It is
paradoxical to sketch examples as an invitation to ignore them and go on your own, but
here we go.

Mixed media, mixed genre

To some, writing in conventional forms feels insufficient to express the fullness of creative
energy, and though the usual print genres have their potency, an abundance of other
resources gets overlooked. For example, could a story be written from an array of digital
sounds? How about poetry as radio play, CD-Rom or site-specific installation? Experimental
practice has long embraced multiple genres within a given work: photography and poetry
create visual and aural images that abut, collide, overlap, or sculptural writing moves text
away from two-dimensional pages and the conventions of the book form and brings print
into social space and time. Perhaps a short story could gain poignancy by being printed on
a length of fabric and read by being gathered in one's arms or sorted through in piles, like
laundry. Perhaps there is a piece in which writing and digital images are alternately pro-
jected on a dancing body. Any inter-genre experiment proceeds through a variety of drafts
in which the expressive material takes different forms. These expansive gestures entice an
audience to consider the act of 'reading' in surprising and poignant ways. As technology
and new media increasingly impact cultural production and as questions of performativity become prevalent, one can see artists foregrounding how poetry or storytelling retain

vitality in the face of new language or image practices. Consider this an area as open and complex as life itself: make a piece of work which uses different methods of creative expression – mix traditional print or writing with some other art or media.

Other languages

Related to mixed genre writing is the use of discourses or languages traditionally considered unsuitable or incompatible with 'creative writing'. The paradigm of the writer squirreled away with only their mind, dreams and imagination as resource and muse does not easily give way to writing which incorporates multiple languages or vocabulary and discourse methods from other disciplines (such as television, sports, religion, science, etc.). Though the history of the novel began with an approach to the book flexible enough to contain letters, found texts, dialogues, treatises, etc. – this openness receded with the rise of the naturalist psychological novel and the convention of the 'invisible' author and seamless narrative. Instead, try playing with a collage of three or four distinct languages or texts. Don't smooth them over into one whole but let the braided edges and untranslated parts create fortuitous connections. Another experiment might be to take one form of writing and try filling it in entirely with another such that the so-called form of one and the so-called content of the other make new meanings apparent in both. Another approach is through translation. Translate a text from English to English only by the sounds of words (homophonic), or do a translation from a language you don't know by following what you think is the sense. You could try translating a piece by substituting words by other words which appear near them in the dictionary (a procedural approach) or by words that appear in the same place in a second text. Perhaps you could translate a very private text by asking a random sample of people what word comes to mind when they hear certain words and then make a number of these public 'translations' done by strangers. You might even collage different languages together to make something which is entirely unreadable in only one language. In a globalising world with ongoing local concerns, there is something potentially rich about these experiments in multi-lingual form. Related to some of the above are writing practices often called 'documentary poetics' or lyric essay which contain a high degree of researched material or 'outside' sources of information, current events or news. Work which uses these alternative sources (without subsuming them into a hermetic authorial style) again challenge the process model of the writer alone with their work, and allow historical or cultural materials to be redeployed and often defamiliarised by new context.

Confound, invert, 'make strange' traditional genre expectations

There is a long history of writers combining poetry and prose forms, and functionally this hybrid comprises a tradition in itself. Prose poetry, sudden fiction, so-called 'new narrative', even L=A=N=G=U=A=G=E poetry all consist of renewing the uses of the prose sentence and non-lineated form. As an exercise, a writer might ask oneself what they think is the limit of what can be called a story or a poem. Must it be written down? Must it have words? Must it have a character? Then ask yourself what exists on the other side of your own limits? Write something which is definitely not a story, according to you. Or definitely not a poem. The message on the answering machine? A grocery receipt? A single word? A scream? A gesture? A joke? Now find a way to make stories and poems from these things without turning them into traditional poem or short story forms. Then, for fun, find writing in the world which is not intended to be either a story or a poem but which could be, and find a way to 'publish' this on a page. Another set of potential experiments might come from asking oneself what the parts and pieces of genres are, and examining what happens if these are radically altered or removed. Let's say you feel a story must have at least one character. Try writing a story in which there is nothing that could conventionally be called a character. Or a story with at least a million characters. Do you think a poem must contain at least one image? Try a poem which has only sound. Any of these experiments would, through association to common understanding of aesthetic expectations, make visible a rupture in the expectations for that form. Rather than being merely oppositional, this rupture can provide a point of awareness, a way to reveal the habits of our story- and meaning-making culture.

Meditative poetics, automatic writing

A different lineage of experimental writing has emphasised what happens when the author applies contemplative or meditative practices to writing in an attempt to trouble authorial ownership (re: the ego) and habitual mind. These are strategies which foreground the cultivation of awareness without conceptual or intellectual filtering. Writing which is a record of these practices reveals relationships and qualities of things unseen when names (nouns) and other habits of mind constrain the open field of perceptual possibility. If you imagine writing in which you do nothing but transcribe bare awareness, allowing it to emerge unforced and without fabrication, you can see how different this is than writing which is modelled on what you 'think' about something, content conceived in conceptual terms. That a writer thinks of a specific tree and then transcribes that thinking as the general word 'tree' is diametrically opposed to writing that functions as thinking itself, a mind getting out of the way so that the tree is described from the 'pure' perception of it without ever using the concept-name 'tree' at all. There are several ways to try this, including the 'automatic writing' or 'free writing' approaches where you do not stop moving your pen for a certain length of time. This practice doesn't allow you to stop and think and then write what you think, but keeps the writing and thinking moving apace. Historically, automatic writing was considered vital for revealing hidden aspects of the unconscious or intuitive associations between thoughts, images, etc. Meditative poetics functions slightly differently in the sense that one does not merely fill space with words but tries to employ the meditative equipoise of awareness to allow perceptions to pass unfiltered, recording those that seem particularly insightful or genuine. It is helpful for these if the writer also has a meditation practice, but not essential.

Page and performance dynamics

The book form has its own conventions: print must be durable, legible, reproducible, non-ephemeral, able to fit on a bookstore shelf or held in the hand, the writing should be on pages which turn, and so on. What about writing for a different set of assumptions: writing using perishable materials, or 'published' as a sculpture or across a piece of architecture. Can you enhance the inherent performance qualities of text through spacing across the page or through a book? Can a piece put the issue of legibility at stake? How can secrets, lies, and other forms of human language behaviour be translated to a book form? Can a moment of time, in all its performative richness, be captured through a series of pages? What about using pages 'unbound' – that is, flyers, broadsides, posters, postcards, business cards, stamps? What about a piece which gets sent through the mail? Or is performed by actors at a particular time in the same spot every day?

Procedural writing

Perhaps a writer decides they will take the first word they hear every day when they step onto the subway and use it as the first word of each sentence of a story. When a proper name is heard, that character appears until the next proper name is heard. This experiment in storytelling becomes a combination of intention and accident in such a way that language from the world interpenetrates the writer's language (habits of vocabulary, preferences of style) to create a new form of narrative, certainly indeterminate regarding outcome. This is a simple example of procedural writing, a form of experimentation which yields surprising and often riveting work. A writer might investigate a method such as this because they have a suspicion that 'found language' from the subway is integral to a narrative able to enact the experience of a crowded and anonymous world. How this writer 'marks' the found language (the procedural constraint) so that the reader can participate in the 'game' is one of the challenges of procedural writing. Allowing constraint to impact the writing not only challenges the notion of the writer as unfettered genius, but exploits the richness of accidents and obstructions, non-intention and rule-based practices, which represent the contours of freedom. In procedural writing, the initial constraint (in which the writer sets up the material and the 'way of proceeding') forms a large part of the meaning and impact of the piece, the 'how' which matters to the reader as much as the 'what'.

Alternative forms of authorship; collaborations

From procedural work come other creative practices where the traditional role of the writer as sole creator/genius is troubled or redefined. Collage or cut-ups present the writer with a different role, as do collaborations and collective forms of writing. With a group of artists, come up with a project in which all can participate fully without constraining the outcome or impeding one another. This writing 'jazz' or indeterminate ensemble can produce performance work which is different every time or else create a print form which re-enacts the trace of the collaboration for readers. What's most important is that the work remains beyond a single person's vision and thus models a different kind of world.

These approaches to writing practice are only experimental insofar as they are about a writer at play with the givens of their world, willing to forego attachment to outcome for the sake of following the material. In writing this I realised that both the history of experimental writing and these suggested exercises are totally up for grabs and there are certainly experimentalists who would ask other questions, public, private and critical versions of an unsolved riddle. Perhaps what ultimately comes from writing as experimental practice is the surprise of presenting yourself and your world as you hadn't imagined them, and yet are shocked to recognise.

32

Creative–Critical Hybrids

Hazel Smith

Critical writing and creative writing are often considered to be separate and contrasting activities. The distinction between the two, which this chapter will unpick, rests on the assumption that creative writing is an imaginative and subjective activity, while critical writing is an interpretive, discursive and more objective activity. Historically, authors tended to identify primarily either as critics or creative writers. Even when they were both, they usually produced texts that were designed, in each case, to be either critical or creative in direction.

Creative–critical hybrids collapse this polarisation of the critical and creative, and meld the two together in the same text. Such hybrid works contest the idea that creative work is only imaginative, and critical work only interpretive and discursive, and point to their symbiosis. They highlight the intellectual work that creative writing undertakes, and the way it engages with philosophical, cultural and political systems of thought. At the same time they suggest ways in which critical writing can break out of its conventions, and be enlivened through the adoption of creative writing techniques.

Both critical studies and creative practice are very broad areas that give rise to many different approaches to writing. Historically, the term critical writing has tended to suggest the analysis of literary texts, but it is also employed much more widely to refer to writing that engages intensively with literary or cultural theory, with cultural analysis, or with a range of disciplines such as politics, philosophy and the sciences. Creative writing is also various: it can take the form of fiction, poetry and drama, or it can spring from the cross-fertilisation of genres. Creative–critical hybrids constitute a type of cross-genre writing that transgresses the boundaries between different kinds of writing (Smith 2005b).

To some extent, literature has always fused the critical and creative. All literary texts harbour ideas that are informed by other philosophical, sociological, psychological or political systems and texts. George Eliot, for example, was steeped in philosophy, and the work of Spinoza and Feuerbach resonates throughout her work. The difference with creative–critical hybrids, or 'hybridised writing' as Amanda Nettlebeck calls it (Kerr and Nettelbeck 1998: 3), is that the critical component may be more overt and direct, and less subsumed in poetical or fictional modes of expression. In a novel, for example, dialogue that develops character and plot may also be employed as a means to debate a particular set of ideas. However in creative–critical hybrids such ideas can be presented and discussed, if required, without dramatic or fictional mediation. In this sense hybrids often subvert the well-known creative writing maxim 'show not tell'. While this maxim may convey useful advice in terms of fully realising character and plot in a realist novel, it may be unhelpful for writing a piece that interweaves a more discursive style with narrative or poetic elements.

The rise of the hybrid; fictocriticism

An increased desire to fuse the creative and the critical has arisen partly as a response to changes within the university environment. In the academy, literature as a discipline now has two main trajectories, critical studies and creative writing. In the past, teachers and researchers within the university have often positioned themselves – or have been positioned by others – as either a scholar or a creative writer, but involvement in both areas at once is strongly increasing. Consequently, since creative writing became a force in the universities during the latter part of the twentieth century, some scholar/practitioners have been trying to develop forms of writing that mesh together creative and critical strategies. This evolution in writing relates to broader, topical issues about the relationship between creative practice and academic research, and the advantages of intertwining them (see Smith and Dean 2009). However, a wish to create synergies between criticism and creative practice is not restricted to academics, but has become increasingly important to writers and intellectuals more generally.

At the same time many writers have grown impatient with the conventions of the scholarly essay. The characteristics of the scholarly style in its purest form are a clear introduction, middle and conclusion, a logical argument, fairly formal language and a degree of objectivity and impersonality. A grasp of these conventions, particularly the ability to pursue a convincing argument, is indispensible in academic writing, and employing them is the most effective way of conveying some kinds of research insights. However, a sophisticated writer will tend to play with the conventions a little to make the text a more enticing 'read'. It is now considered quite normal to inhabit the first person in an academic essay, to employ colloquial and informal language, to construct new terms for new concepts, or to open the essay with a preamble rather than a thesis statement that summarises the argument.

But some authors have been committed to freeing up the essay form even further, introducing personal anecdote, narratives, poems or digressions into the essay with a view to making it more personalised, more relevant to everyday life. One of the ideals of such writing is to make intellectual activity multidimensional, that is, responsive to a number of different levels of experience: mental, emotional and sensual. Such an approach also ensures that topics such as gender, ethnicity or disability are presented in a way that unites thinking and feeling. On the one hand, such an essay may still propel a tenacious argument, but use literary techniques to amplify or reinforce it. On the other hand, the essay may take shape as a multi-voiced experiment which, rather than promoting a single argument, disseminates several points of view that contradict each other. Writers who want to perturb the traditional essay form often embrace a fragmented, segmented style that courts juxtaposition, rather than logical continuity, as its main dynamic. The author may circle round an idea, re-entering it from an array of angles, rather than progressing methodically through an ordered succession of points.

The desire to break out of the conventions of essay writing is apparent in the work of a range of twentieth- and twenty-first-century essayists, both academic and non-academic. Joan Didion's 'The White Album' (Didion 1979) is an extremely resonant essay that is, nevertheless, unconventional in the way it juxtaposes personal and political history

(Didion's putative psychological breakdown and the political chaos of the 1960s). It includes many different genres – a packing list, excerpts from newspaper reports, a doctor's diagnosis, transcripts from criminal trials and song lyrics. It raises questions about social issues, not abstractly through enunciation and argument but by juxtaposing (sometimes with abrupt transitions) numerous short narratives and anecdotes that resonate with each other. The result is a profound meditation on the 60s, in particular what political activism can and cannot achieve. Susan Sontag's 'Notes on Camp' (Sontag 2001), originally published in 1964, invents a notes structure to talk about camp, a concept that has been highly influential but, she suggests, is difficult to pin down. In the notes she does not so much run an argument about camp as give an impression of a range of attitudes and behaviours that exemplify it. The unusual style and subject matter of Lydia Davis's 'Foucault and Pencil'(Davis 2010: 149–50) stretches gracefully and humorously across the boundaries of short story, short prose and essay. It is about the process of reading a theoretical work by Foucault, and the struggle to understand it: 'Short sentences easier to understand than long ones. Certain long ones understandable part by part, but so long, forgot beginning before reaching end'(149). Written in the compressed style characteristic of note-form, and with deprecating self-irony, it is not about the content of Foucault's essay, but about how the author attempted (with difficulty) to follow his argument.

At the high theory and more academic end, the work of poststructuralist theorists, such as Derrida, Barthes, Deleuze and Guattari and others, modified the essay form to embrace experimental creative-writing techniques. Derrida habitually engaged in linguistic play (for example in his construction of the word '*différance*' to bring together the words differ and defer) to conjure new concepts. His influential work, *Glas*, juxtaposes the literary and the philosophical: it is written in two columns with different font sizes; one column is a reading of Hegel's philosophical works, and the other a dialogue with Genet's autobiographical writing; both columns are interspersed with numerous quotations and supplementary comments (Derrida 1986). Another loosening up of the essay form came through the development of autoethnography. Autoethnography is an intervention in ethnography that allows for a more personalised and informal approach to writing (see for example Bochner and Ellis 2002). It embraces the personal experience of the researcher and meshes it with the empirical approach characteristic of the social sciences.

Creative–critical hybrids vary from place to place and within different cultural contexts. Australia has been distinctive in developing a term for such hybrids: fictocriticism, a word that has been used in an inclusive sense, even if it seems initially to privilege fiction over poetry. Fictocriticism, which often contains autoethnographic elements, arose in the 1980s and 90s in the university environment in tandem with the growth of creative-writing programmes, the rise of postmodern and poststructuralist theory, and the wish to find alternatives or supplements to 'straight' academic writing. For essays on fictocriticism, or samples of fictocritical work, see Brewster 1996, Deane 2010, Smith 2005b, Azul 2011, Dawson 2004, Kerr and Nettelbeck 1998 and Bartlett 2009, as well as other examples in this chapter.

In America and the UK, many experimental poets have also been astute theorists and critics, and have sought to integrate the poetic and critical, often through what I call the poem-essay. Here the work of the American language poets and theorists Charles Bernstein, Ron Silliman, Bob Perelman and Lyn Hejinian from the 1970s onwards – and their counterparts in England, such as Peter Middleton – have been very influential. Many of the concepts in Charles Bernstein's poem-essays, have become widely cited as criticism.

Peter Middleton's stimulating volume *Distant Reading* (Middleton 2005) includes a poem-essay with highly disrupted syntax, 'The Line-Break in Everyday Life' (124–36); a prolonged critical engagement in non-linear sections 'Dirigibles'(160–98); and a polyphonic text arranged in two columns, 'Eat Write'(199–220).

These hybrid interventions, then, do not emanate only from critics, but just as much from creative writers impelled towards criticism and theory. Coetzee is probably one of the most notable fiction writers whose work has also overtly interwoven the creative and critical: his novel *Elizabeth Costello* (Coetzee 2004) interleaves essay-like sections with a narrative in ways that are somewhat fictocritical but are strongly rooted in the genre of the novel. The essays take the form of lectures given by the main character, writer Elizabeth Costello.

The art of partnering

Creative–critical hybrids appear in many different guises. One of the excitements of operating in this area is the almost infinite opportunity for new types of exploration, and the way in which any kind of creative and critical writing can be intermingled. Below I delineate some possible approaches; however, there are many other potential ones. In addition, any single work may draw on several of the techniques outlined.

The poem-essay

The poem-essay is a fusion of essay and poem. Some of the poetic features that tend to distinguish it are line breaks, extensive use of metaphor, and disjunctiveness (switching from one topic to another abruptly rather than by means of smooth transitions). These poetic features are usually grafted together with the more prosaic and argumentative style we associate with an essay.

One of the past masters of the poem-essay is Charles Bernstein. His 'Thelonious Monk and the Performance of Poetry' (Bernstein 1999: 18–24), for example, is about the reading and performance of poetry. Here is the opening:

> What is the status of performance
> in poetry? This statically
> worded question will not likely lead me
> to a discussion of Thelonius Monk.
> But you start where you can,
> where mood flings you, like an old dish
> towel drying in the rain. (18)

After outlining some of the reasons why he used to feel that the page was the primary outlet for his poetry, and that performance of the work was less important, Bernstein begins to outline his argument:

> Nonetheless, I've come to feel
> that the idea of the written
> document as primary makes for an unwarranted
> or anyway unwanted
> Hierarchy; hearing

work performed is in no way inferior to
reading it yourself. Rather, these are two competing
realizations of the work, each
with its own set of advantages &
limitations. Moreover
all reading is performative
& a reader has in some ways to supply the performative
element when reading –
not silently before a page but out
loud & with a beat. (19)

This poem-essay produces an argument with several components: that the written aspect of a poem is not definitive, that its performative aspect is also its social aspect, that all readings are performative, and that poetry in performance comes close to the condition of music. It also sets up a context for the argument by taking issue with various ideological stances about performance and poetry that poets and audiences tend to endorse, for example the idea that a reading of a poem brings out a poet's authentic voice. It includes conjunctions that are quite prosaic – 'of course', 'nonetheless', 'moreover' – to further the argument, and is less syntactically complex and compressed than much poetry. At the same time, it draws on the resources of poetry to make its points. It employs the line break to generate rhythm and to accentuate (sometimes unpredictable) words. It embraces metaphor – 'an old dish /towel drying in the rain' – including the overarching metaphor of jazz piano playing; associative sound patterns – 'hierarchy', 'hearing'; and the non-sequiturs characteristic of experimental poetry. Bernstein's poem-essay also embodies its content as form. It talks about performance but is itself performative, exploiting rhythmic propulsion as a form of rhetorical persuasion. In addition, it starts with a question addressed to the audience, and adopts a talking style, personalised interventions and spoken language to reinforce its performative dimension.

Dialoguing, commentary

Creative–critical hybrids tend to be intertexual, often dialoguing with other texts by commenting on or quoting from them. This kind of critical engagement is typical of the work of Rachel Blau DuPlessis who, like Bernstein, is an impressive exponent of the poem-essay, though her work looks very different from his. DuPlessis is a distinguished academic as well as a poet. Her long poem essay *Drafts* (DuPlessis 2004) – already in two volumes and ongoing – displays the characteristics and advantages of poetry, but converses energetically with critical and theoretical texts.

In 'Draft 52: Midrash'(DuPlessis 2004: 141–57), DuPlessis uses the famous quote by Adorno, 'To write poetry after Auschwitz is barbaric', and subjects it to intensive enquiry in poetic form. Here Du Plessis adopts what she calls midrash, an approach that is fundamental to her work. Midrash is a Hebrew term for a method of interpreting and commenting on a biblical text. DuPlessis's poems are midrashic in the sense that they incorporate meditations, interpretations and commentaries on other poems or texts. The opening of this section begins:

Poetry/Auschwitz/barbaric.
Oblique triangle.

Also
human litter
has not ceased /to be/ created. (141)

Throughout 'Draft 52: Midrash', DuPlessis enters Adorno's quotation from a number of points of view, showing how it can be read in alternative ways. She raises questions such as why did Adorno choose poetry (as opposed to painting or music), and also rehearses what he meant by 'barbaric'. To subject his words to critical scrutiny, she weaves in the work of critics or theorists who have discussed Adorno's words, and gives detailed documentation of these sources in accompanying notes. She does not so much construct an argument as approach the material from different, sometimes opposing, angles and employs provisional turns of phrase such as 'perhaps his issue is metaphor, imagery'(147). She does not strive to capture exactly what Adorno meant, but to elaborate on the interpretive possibilities of what he said. She introduces quotations extensively, but also sometimes transforms them (for example when she remakes a quotation from Adorno by interjecting line breaks and placing each component in inverted commas):

'perspectives must be fashioned'
'that displace and estrange'
'the world, reveal it'
'to be, with its rifts'
'& crevices,'
'as indigent and distorted'
'as it will appear one day'
'in the messianic light.' (154)

Stealing and subversion

Some writers extract features of the academic essay, but subvert them as part of the project of creative writing. A good example of this strategy is Jenny Boully's 'The Body' (Boully 2003). In this piece Boully produces a text that is only footnotes but has no 'body', so the upper half of the page remains blank. This throws up intriguing questions about what the function of the footnote is, and its reliability as a source of information. Although advice from academic journals is usually to minimise them, footnotes often comprise an engrossing aspect of an academic essay: they contain information that does not fit into the main text but supplements it, they reveal the sources of the research and provide tangents for further enquiry. However, normally footnotes are not an independent entity, they are parasitic on the main text.

Boully's footnotes range from jottings about personal feelings (unusual in academic footnotes) to biblical quotations, allusions to theoretical discourse, and almost encyclopaedic entries. They point in numerous – and sometimes seemingly contradictory – directions, so that we are constantly wondering what the subject of the missing main text might be. Our curiosity is further heightened by the many ambiguities, gaps and incongruities within them. For example, Jenny Boully has multiple identities: as the compiler of the footnotes, the subject of some of them, and lover of 'the great poet' who is also a focus of the main text; similarly there is slippage between poetry, theatre and film as the principal object of attention (Boully 2003).

The sandwich effect

Many hybrids grow out of a segmented or fragmented structure that facilitates the ability to enter a topic, or set of topics, from a multiplicity of angles. In some cases this may involve an alternation between the creative and critical, with narrative or poetic segments sandwiched between more discursive sections. In my collaborations with Anne Brewster (Brewster and Smith 2002; Brewster and Smith 2003) – which we refer to as fictocritical – critical sections tend to alternate with sections of creative writing. However, this distinction is not systematic or clear-cut: sometimes the theoretical sections are coloured by metaphorical or narrative elements, and the poems and narrative fragments are often triggered by critical ideas.

Alternation is also one of the dynamics of Anne Brewster's fictocritical text, 'Beachcombing: A Fossicker's Guide to Whiteness and Indigenous Sovereignty' (Brewster 2009). This essay promotes a complex argument about what Brewster calls the 'contrapuntal' relationship between creative practice and research (130). Her particular interest is the use of autobiographical writing in critical whiteness studies, an area that focuses on indigenous history and culture, but problematises the role of the white researcher. In the essay, the contrapuntal aspect takes the form of a sandwich structure. The more scholarly and theoretical writing is broken up with passages about strolling and fossicking on the beach, and reflections upon the beach as the historical site of colonial encounter. The critical and creative writing interrelate thematically through their emphasis on the significance of the body in writing, and the idea of fossicking as a metaphor for writing and research. The essay not only puts forward an argument about the relationship between creative practice and research, but also embodies that relationship through its own adroit juxtapositions.

Segmentation, and a non-linear structure, is a feature of Stephen Muecke's 'The Fall' (Muecke 2002). Like the Brewster essay, this piece is self-referential in that it refers to, but also demonstrates, the process of fictocriticism. Muecke draws on Deleuze's distinction between the concept and the percept to characterise the way fictocriticism fuses thinking and feeling:

> Criticism uses concepts and fiction percepts. Philosophy, according to Deleuze, is about the invention of new concepts which have the abstraction and flexibility to be taken up by others and used. Art, on the other hand, invents percepts, monumental perceptions if you like, which are just there, either they work or they don't. They can stand alone. You can use someone else's percept, but it will be an imitation. And percepts and concepts chase each other around successively masking and unmasking. (109)

'The Fall' alludes informally and anecdotally to the author's encounter with a woman he finds attractive, and to ideas generated through his university teaching and research. The piece alternates between the personal and the critical/theoretical, but this alternation is not necessarily delineated through sectionalisation, and the main dynamic is the interlacing of the two. In some sections critical and theoretical ideas flow into the apparently autobiographical passages or vice versa. In section three, for example, the author moves from 'You smile at me like a flower opening brightly . . .' into alluding to this as an example of a percept: 'The smile is a percept, it is not in you or at me'. Similarly, 'I invite you to the cinema but you say you cannot come' leads into a meditation on Hitchcock's *Vertigo*, a film that is concerned not only with falling in love but also with physically falling.

Throughout 'The Fall', a plethora of metaphors – principally the notion of the fall with its connotations of falling in love, falling into the text, insects falling into pitcher flowers, the fall of criticism and creative writing as separate disciplines – blend the personalised and intellectual aspects of the text together, but also present in several different modalities the relationship between percept and concept. By the end, a point about precept/concept and its relationship to hybrid writing has been made, but also actualised through the writing.

Coda

Creative–critical hybrids can, therefore, take many different forms: sometimes they may seem more like works of criticism or theory, sometimes more like creative works that have a critical or theoretical aspect: whichever, they disrupt any clear distinction between the two. The relationship between the creative and the critical in any given text can be very overt, but sometimes it may be more covert. In my own work, I often use theoretical texts as a mode of inspiration for creative works. Sometimes this relationship becomes part of the text: for example, my poem 'The Idea of Elegy' (Smith 2008: 49–51) alludes to William Watkin's work on elegy (Watkin 2004). Sometimes the relationship is not explicit: the influence of Elizabeth Grosz's *The Nick of Time* (Grosz 2004) on my poem and multimedia work 'Time, The Magician' (Smith 2008: 10–13) only becomes apparent through an accompanying note.

Finally, hybrid works do not always have to be page-based. They can also appear in performance and new media forms. As mentioned earlier, such works often have a performative aspect because they are multi-voiced; some, even if written for the page, may deliberately adopt a performance style (Deane 2010). The feminist theorist Hélène Cixous realised many of her ideas in the theatre. The philosopher Alfonso Lingis gives performances that straddle the lecture/performance line. I have constructed the term 'performative fictocriticism' for performance works that might have some overt critical or theoretical elements, including my own 'The Erotics of Gossip' (Smith 2005a).

Similarly, new media writing projects lend themselves particularly well to the fusion of the critical and the creative because of the dynamic technical apparatus of new media. This makes it easy to juxtapose the creative and critical by splitting or sectionalising the screen, interlinking textual fragments, or morphing one into another. There are a number of new media practitioners, such as Talan Memmott, Maria Mencia, Mark Amerika and John Cayley, who are influenced by theory, who write theoretical essays (sometimes in an unconventional form), and whose work sometimes contains elements of theory. One new media writing project that mashes together theory, criticism and creative writing is Mark Amerika's *remixthebook* (Amerika [ongoing]). My fictocritical collaborations with Anne Brewster, mentioned earlier, both appeared subsequently as multimedia projects. They were transformed through programming input and sound from Roger Dean; 'Affections: friendship, community, bodies' in the multimedia version became *SoundAFFECTs*. Both works retain their critical-creative juxtapositions in the multimedia form (Dean et al. 2004; Dean et al. 2009).

Exercises

You might like to try some of the following exercises:
1. Take an essay you have written that has critical or theoretical content, and rewrite it so that it includes autobiographical, narrative or poetic material. Create interplay between

the critical writing and the creative writing, so that each transforms the other. It may be helpful to fragment, sectionalise and rearrange the critical material and to rewrite passages. You may also wish to develop metaphors that relate to both types of material.

2. Write a poem-essay on a topic that interests you. Play and experiment with line breaks, with metaphor and with abrupt and smooth transitions.

3. Take a topic such as memory, the body, disability or ethnicity, and write a text in sections, some of which are more concerned with pre-existent critical or theoretical writing, and some of which are your own creative writing. For example, if the subject is memory, you might include actual memories in some sections, and then in other sections, explicate, discuss or critique ideas that critics, theorists, psychologists or historians hold about memory. If you don't know much about the topic then undertake some research on it: for example, search for relevant articles in Google Scholar, read the articles and allow them to trigger ideas.

4. Make a collage from the work of a theorist or several theorists who interest you. That is, take fragments of their writing either on one topic or several different ones. Intersperse your own creative writing into the collage, using ideas from the theorists as triggers. If you wish, also make this a visual collage, for example spacing out the fragments in boxes, and/or at different angles, to create a spatial design on the page. (You will find more advice on making collages in *The Writing Experiment* [Smith 2005b: 67–77]).

5. Divide the page vertically into two columns with critical writing down one column and creative writing down the other. What relationship do you find you have created between the critical and creative writing? Do you want to change that relationship by rewriting or rearrangement? Can you make these two columns speak to each other?

6. Take a formal feature of the critical essay and use it as the basis for a piece of creative writing.

References

Amerika, Mark (ongoing), *remixthebook*, http://markamerika.com/news/remixthebook (accessed 6 August 2013).

Azul, David (2011), 'Gramophony of an application for "Recognition of a condition of permanent desire": A Performative Exploration of the Relationship between Notions of Subject, Voice and Writing', *Qualitative Research Journal*, 11, 13–33.

Bartlett, Alison (2009), 'On Fictocriticism' (whole issue edited by Alison Bartlett and featuring fictocritical work by Anne Brewster, Moya Costello, Majena Mafe, Rosslyn Prosser and Barbara Brooks), *Outskirts*, 20, http://www.outskirts.arts.uwa.edu.au/volumes/volume-20 (accessed 6 August 2013).

Bernstein, Charles (1999), *My Way: Speeches and Poems*, Chicago: The University of Chicago Press.

Bochner, Arthur P. and Carolyn Ellis (eds) (2002), *Ethnographically Speaking: Autoethnography, Literature, and Aesthetics*, Walnut Creek, CA: AltaMira Press.

Boully, Jenny (2003), 'The Body', in John D'Agata (ed.), *The Next American Essay*, Minneapolis: Graywolf Press, 435–66.

Brewster, Anne (1996), 'Fictocriticism: Undisciplined Writing', in Jan Hutchinson and Graham Williams (eds), *First Conference of the Association of University Writing Programs*, Sydney: University of Technology, Sydney, 29–32.

Brewster, Anne (2009), 'Beachcombing: A Fossicker's Guide to Whiteness and Indigenous

Sovereignty', in Hazel Smith and Roger Dean (eds), *Practice-led Research, Research-led Practice in the Creative Arts*, Edinburgh: Edinburgh University Press.

Brewster, Anne and Hazel Smith (2002), 'ProseThetic Memories', in Terri-ann White (ed.), *Salt. v16. An International Journal of Poetry and Poetics: Memory Writing*, Applecross, Western Australia: Salt Publishing, 199–211.

Brewster, Anne and Hazel Smith (2003), 'AFFECTions: friendship, community, bodies', *Text*, 7, http://www.textjournal.com.au/oct03/brewstersmith.htm (accessed 6 August 2013).

Coetzee, J. M. (2004), *Elizabeth Costello*, London: Penguin.

Davis, Lydia (2010), *The Collected Stories of Lydia Davis*, London: Hamish Hamilton.

Dawson, Paul (2004), *Creative Writing and the New Humanities*, London: Routledge.

Dean, Roger, Brewster, Anne, and Hazel Smith (2004), 'soundAFFECTs', *Text*, 8, http://www.text-journal.com.au/oct04/content.htm (accessed 6 August 2013).

Dean, Roger, Brewster, Anne, and Hazel Smith (2009), 'ProseThetic Memories'. SoundsRite, 1, http://soundsrite.uws.edu.au/soundsRiteContent/volume1/prsthinf.html (accessed 6 August 2013).

Deane, Laura (2010), 'Theorising the madwoman: fictocritical incursions – a performance', *Text*, 14, http://www.textjournal.com.au/oct10/deane.htm (accessed 6 August 2013).

Derrida, Jacques (1986), *Glas*, Lincoln, NE: University of Nebraska Press.

Didion, Joan (1979), *The White Album*, New York: Farrar, Straus and Giroux.

DuPlessis, Rachel B. (2004), *Drafts 39–57, Pledge, with Draft, unnumbered, Précis*, Cambridge: Salt.

Grosz, Elizabeth (2004), *The Nick of Time: Politics, Evolution and the Untimely*, Sydney: Allen and Unwin.

Kerr, Heather and Amanda Nettelbeck (1998), *The Space Between: Australian Women Writing Fictocriticism*, Perth: University of Western Australia Press.

Middleton, Peter (2005), *Distant Reading: Performance, Readership and Consumption in Contemporary Poetry*, Tuscaloosa: University of Alabama Press.

Muecke, Stephen (2002), 'The fall: fictocritical writing', *Parallax*, 8, 108–12.

Smith, Hazel (2005a), 'The Erotics of Gossip: Fictocriticism, Performativity, Technology', *Continuum*, 19, 403–12. Republished in *Textual Practice*, 2009.

Smith, Hazel (2005b), *The Writing Experiment: Strategies for Innovative Creative Writing*, Sydney: Allen and Unwin.

Smith, Hazel (2008), *The Erotics of Geography*, book and CD-Rom, Kāne'ohe, HI: Tinfish Press.

Smith, Hazel and Roger Dean (eds) (2009), *Practice-led Research, Research-led Practice in the Creative Arts*, Edinburgh: Edinburgh University Press.

Sontag, Susan (2001), *Against Interpretation and Other Essays*, New York: Picador.

Watkin, William (2004), *On Mourning: Theories of Loss in Modern Literature*, Edinburgh: Edinburgh University Press.

33

Writing as 'Therapy'

Fiona Sampson

Over the last two decades, creative writing in British health and social care has developed as a publicly-funded practice. It's one which, though studied and imitated elsewhere in the world, has its roots in the particular British context of arts access thinking and policy since the 1970s (European projects on the British model include poetry-reading groups in a hospice in Lund, Sweden and writing projects with children in integrated day centres across Macedonia [Sampson 2004]). Teasing out the strands of this thinking a little can allow us to see exactly what's going on when, for example, a poet leads a workshop with stroke patients in rehab; or a writer and a clinician co-run a psychotherapy group for people with dependency problems. And this, in turn, is important for the thinking about writing as 'therapy' which might go on in our individual practice as writers, students and teachers of creative writing.

If, for example, work in health care suggested that certain ways of writing are always beneficial, or that the process of writing created a special kind of context in which particular beneficial interventions could be achieved, there would be a number of possible implications for individual writing practice. These might include:

- The usefulness of open-ended, process-led writing techniques, such as free-writing, for an individual's personal development
- Or conversely, the significance of achieving narrative form, or meaning-making, in personal development
- The resonance of certain forms or discourses, such as the heightened language of elegy, with significant human experience
- Or conversely, the significance of the imaginary as a way of escaping the limits of immediate experience
- Engagement in the writing process as a way either of reinforcing the individual self – their Subjectivity, their belief in the value of their own world-view – or of loosening up that self, making its boundaries more flexible and able to negotiate change or accommodate new approaches
- A particular link between personal and writerly development – as if they might go in the same direction
- A particular sense of what not only writing practice but written texts might be for: such as the idea that good or important fiction or poetry speaks from the best in

human nature and does not embrace, by exploring, such aspects of the human psyche as intolerance.

Some of these are large claims indeed; and this chapter will not be making very many of them. This does not mean, however, that they have not been made elsewhere: not necessarily by practitioners within the field of writing and health care but in a variety of literary critical discourses and approaches to the teaching of creative writing. I will refer to some of these sources later, when I suggest certain links which may nevertheless exist between writing – practice and product – and the importance of agency in sustaining a sense of the human self, especially when that self is under pressure. Particular contexts, such as health care or political orthodoxy, may bear down on the very individual they have, at least in theory, been instituted to help; in particular by 'knowing better than' him or her. This chapter looks both at writing in health and social care and at the wider significance of writing as a form of resistance; of individuation of approach and voice rather than necessarily through exploration of the writer's own physical or mental health. 'Writing as therapy' may be seen here to refer to what John Keats calls its 'salubrious' effects within the shared world of the reading and writing community rather than simply to 'privatised' benefits experienced by writing individuals (Keats 1973: 781).

In a recent essay, the Australian poet John Kinsella articulates his belief in the importance of writing which refuses to let the reader be lulled: and therefore to be accepting, conservative (Kinsella 2006). Since reading, like writing, is a form of thought, this means challenging the reader to *think* in a way that isn't conservative; to read the world as well as the text in new, questioning ways. But Kinsella isn't talking about writing essays on political or critical theory – but about the way an unexpected line break wakes the ear up and makes reading a poem suddenly much more 'polymorphous' than being guided by a seductive 'lyrical' music would be. In other words, the *text* can affect the *experience* of an individual reader.

There's nothing new in this insight, of course. Contemporary debate about censorship, or the nine o'clock watershed on broadcast media, reproduce arguments about the ability of a written or performed text to affect its audience which go back to the origins of tragedy in ritualised catharsis; or the arguments Plato makes for banning poetry from his ideal *Republic*:

> Poetry has the same effect on us when it represents sex and anger, and the other desires and feelings of pleasure and pain which normally accompany our actions. It feeds them when they ought to be starved, and makes them control us when we ought, in the interests of our own welfare and happiness, to control them. (Plato 1955: 384)

What *is* distinctive is Kinsella's point that, while responsibility for (some of) a text's effects must lie with its author, these effects need not originate solely from programmatic authorial intent – for example using rhetorical devices, such as 'accessible style' or sentiment, to persuade the reader of a particular argument – but may instead transcend the piece's particular content, releasing the reader not only from any particular reading of it; but into reading other texts and experiences altogether. A familiar example of this is T. S. Eliot's argument, in 'Tradition and the Individual Talent', that the new poet comes to his (sic) own writing through a feeling of intimate recognition of the pre-existing *oeuvre* of an earlier poet (Eliot 1951). That earlier writer didn't produce his poems *in order to* generate the work of his successor; yet, far from being a distortion or appropriation, this is a reinforcement of the original.

I experience something similar when, in writing this chapter, I feel my training in Anglo–American philosophy 'speak through' me. What we study, which is to say read, can *inform* our thoughts to such an extent it might be said to *form* them. 'Creative writing' – that literary, inventive practice of which poetry is a useful paradigm – has regularly been cited by its exponents as a way of thinking which offers methodological insights, as well as the insights of particular content (such as those of a poem which concludes that myths of women are cultural conspiracies to keep the lid on the Pandora's Box of their energy and talents [Jamie 1994: 9–11]), into the world of our experience. For Keats, poetry teaches us to be 'capable of being in uncertainties, Mysteries, doubts, without any irritable reaching after fact and reason' (Keats 1973: 768); for Romantic poets like Shelley its avowed Subjectivity makes it a model of individual self-governance (Shelley 2004): for Imagists like Ezra Pound it helps us bring thought out of abstraction into the immediacy of concrete experience – through what is elsewhere known as the 'pathetic fallacy' (the term is John Ruskin's in *Modern Painters* [1856]); while for Celan – as, paradoxically, for Heidegger – it shows us the limits of language as a realist project (Celan 2001; Heidegger 1975). As models and – in being written and read – as mental experiences, poems have been widely held to help us think in 'salubrious' ways.

If we look more closely, we see that these models of thinking cluster particularly around forms of agency. Poetry is associated with, respectively: the ability to 'hold a line' and not join one camp or another; thinking for oneself; having more fully-realised thoughts – and knowing their limits. The poetry writer or reader practises being not simply responsive, but responsible. This is some distance from the notion of poetry as 'self-expression', a somehow unmediated movement from the 'inside' outward, which we might associate with 'writing as therapy' (reflected in the name of the national organisation representing the field. LAPIDUS supports the 'Literary Arts and Personal Development').

What the contemporary British poet Don Paterson calls 'the sin of *expression*' is something other than the work of a poem or piece of music (Paterson 2004: 33). We do not write fiction or poetry when we simply discharge emotion onto the page. What we do instead is complete what the art therapist Joy Schaverein calls a 'scapegoat transference': the text 'takes on' our emotion for us and we feel better as a result (Schaverein 1999). Our own relationship with such a text is based on its emotional role rather than intrinsic literary qualities. We may have an exaggerated view of its literary value because it is 'emotionally true'; or conversely – as with what we could call 'teenage diary syndrome' – we may be mortified at the idea of our grotesque emotions being revealed. In therapy sessions, the image or text and the paper they're on may be treated in a quasi-symbolic way – the touching emotions of grief stored away in a special box, the 'bad' emotions of anger torn up or set light to – or they may be analysed as symptoms. An art therapist won't 'read' a series of strong marks (we might use the analogy, in writing, of a high register language or of imagery) as an aesthetic *choice*, but as a *sign* of an emotional experience such as anger.

Analysis of an achieved literary text from within a psychoanalytic framework – when Susan Kavaler-Adler reads Sylvia Plath, for example – runs the risk of failing to move out of this therapeutic approach, in which writing is a symptom, into a literary one, in which writing is part of a professional cultural practice (Kavaler-Adler 1993). Kavaler-Adler cites Plath's work as an example of 'repetition rather than reparation' because, she says, the poems describe unhappiness rather than attempt to resolve it. A poem such as Plath's furious lament for her father, 'Daddy', represents an inability to 'move on' (Plath 1981:

183–4). But in fact this is a reading not of the words on the page but of a conjectured motivation for those words. It misses the fact that writers may explore dark emotional material in order to produce a more interesting text. From the gothic novel to the finely-drawn psychodramas of Henry James; from Angela Carter's dark fairy-tales to contemporary writing for teenagers, much writing plainly draws on unconscious and emotional experience. It does so because, as the Japanese poet Yasuhiro Yasumoto has said of poetry, each work 'needs to include a little element of viciousness' (Yasumoto 2005).

A key idea here might be that of *exploration*. Rather than a passive re-experiencing of involuntary emotion, the writer actively engages with their material in order to shape a text. Instead of repeating an emotional experience already achieved, they are conducting a process of discovering its resources and dimensions. This is not to say that writing is simply 'going on a journey', that famously 'therapeutic' phrase, towards the destination of conclusive insight. Creative writing – as opposed to, say, diary keeping or email flirtation – is explicitly concerned with making as much as with preparing to make; with product as much as with process. Mental experience is shaped and developed through a series of thoughts which are had by writer and (subsequently) by reader. Looked at this way, we could say that writing is shared thinking.

Writing, in other words, may help us to think – for ourselves. Our mental worlds can be inflected by both reading and writing. Political theory has understood this for a long time. Richard Hoggart's *The Uses of Literacy* argued that literacy was what freed people not only into greater job opportunities but into a wide-ranging, reflexive awareness of the society and world they lived in (Hoggart 1992). This awareness was the first step in granting working-class individuals agency. Through having more sophisticated ideas than we could come up with by ourselves we are developed to that point of rational decision-making which fits us to be citizens. Raymond Williams's later *Marxism and Literature* argues, rather like Keats in his talk of 'soul-making', that 'literary production then is "creative" . . . in the material sense of a specific practice of self-making . . .: self-composition' (Williams 1977: 210). Both Hoggart and Williams worked within the British socialist tradition; their theories echoed and were echoed by the practices of, for example, Miners' Institutes in the Welsh Valleys (a gas-lit version of the world of the working-class auto-didact is evoked by miner's son D. H. Lawrence in *Sons and Lovers* [Lawrence 1998]). In his *Politics*, Aristotle argues that education is important because 'A city can be excellent only when the citizens who have a share in government are excellent' (Aristotle 1990: 175). Education has traditionally been withheld from groups, such as women, slaves or peasants, who must not be allowed self-determination.

The contemporary educationalist Jane Mace writes about how literacy is always a joint practice (Mace 2002). We all have textual questions we have to ask: whether because language changes fast to accommodate slang and loan words we don't know how to spell, or when we don't know the punctuation house style of a particular publication. Writing and thinking are also joint practices. So writing is socially beneficial – 'salubrious' – not only because it gives individuals in a society skills but because it is in itself a social, collective practice.

Thinking along these lines seems to suggest all writing is persuasive and tendentious, consciously shaping the reader. Yet one of the rules taught in creative writing is that the polemical does not make good literature, because it is already programmatic. There's nothing exploratory about a piece which already knows what it wants to say. This is not of course to say that standpoint writing – especially committed or political writing – must fail as literature: and this distinction is an important one for writing in health and social care. But committed writing – whether the novels of J. M. Coetzee or the prose of John Berger – works when it doesn't simply rehearse an argument but explores the world of a particular standpoint. Charles Dickens's novels showed their middle-class readership the life of the Victorian poor in vivid detail – but did so within narrative-driven stories of loss or belonging; the Granta school of 'dirty realism' brought British 'cool' diction of the 1980s and 90s together with an essayistic, travel-writing sensibility to create highly-achieved literary forms. Writing which seems to adopt an overtly 'political' standpoint is in fact only doing what all good writing does, which is to offer the reader an author's-eye view of the world. Even the Aga-Saga, and its baby sister chick-lit, write from a specific social and therefore political standpoint: it's just that theirs is a conservative, socially-disengaged one. Helen Fielding's *Bridget Jones' Diary* works because it's a small masterpiece of characterisation of the self-referential world of a young single woman in a society which sees that as a mark of failure (Fielding 2001). George Orwell's *Keep the Aspidistra Flying*, first published in 1935, is the similarly claustrophobic story of Gordon Comstock, a young man who has chosen an anti-materialistic life, against the grain of contemporary society, and whose world contracts to small details of his daily struggle as a result (Orwell 2000). Awkward, dreary Comstock, progeny of the politicised Orwell, is a solipsist as fully-realised as the ditzy Bridget Jones.

He is also as real as the Schlegel sisters in E. M. Forster's earlier (1910) *Howards End* (Forster 2000). As Germans, these characters, too, are outsiders in English society. They illustrate their author's recurring theme of the importance of authenticity, something which for Forster is characteristically witnessed by the outsider. But Forster is a writer who sails close to the polemical wind. Both lapse, at times, over the line from the exploration of a standpoint into the repetition of an argument. In his short stories, and in the more schematic first novel *Where Angels Fear to Tread*, Forster repeats oppositions – between Apollonian and Dionysian, city and country, the British 'insider' and the foreign 'outsider' – which become formulaic (Forster 2001).

All writing, then, adopts a standpoint; but it is persuasive only when it works in literary terms. All writing – and reading – takes place in a context which is, by definition, social (for a fuller examination of the way the writing self brings their context into the authorial project, both deliberately and accidentally, see *Writing: Self and Reflexivity* [Hunt and Sampson 2006]). But as we write our context may also include, for example: our income and its consequences for the opportunities we have to write; a supportive or distractingly stressful personal life; our professional status and the career implications of what we're writing; states of mental and physical health. We may consciously adopt some of these contextual elements into our text – at which point they become authorial concerns and contribute to textual standpoint. However, all of them contribute to the writerly context in which that standpoint is developed. We can think of them as comprising a kind of unconscious or prehistory of the text.

When we write from a particular social and experiential standpoint such as, let us say, a newly-acquired disability – whether or not we intend to explore a particular aspect of that position – we bring the world of that experience into the world of the text in a number of ways:

- By exploring the 'inner' world of our own experience of a situation; for example in examining or metaphorising feelings of loss
- By exploring the 'outer' world of a situation of which we have first-hand knowledge: for example a narrative full of the fine details of legal wrangling

- In bringing our thinking selves to bear as we write and so bringing the world of our experience to bear in each textual choice, both consciously and unconsciously; for example it might not occur to us to write a fiction in which every character is able-bodied
- When our writing, with its freight of ideas and perspectives generated by our own context, joins the 'world' of published texts available to readers and modifies that experiential world to some – perhaps incalculably small – degree. For example, a reader lacking direct experience of disability reads a novel with a fully-rounded disabled protagonist for the first time.

In other words, when we write from our own experience, which we always do – even in imaginative engagement with the other we have to do so as ourselves – we not only have the space to explore our own thoughts, including images, whether or not they relate to that experience; in speaking *from* our standpoint we act as a kind of indirect witness in the discursive choir.

Health problems are always both 'inner' and 'outer' experiences. 'Internally', they may make us feel weak, tired, irritated, distracted, afraid; leave us nauseous or in pain. But they also set up a series of relationships and parameters in the 'outer' world around us. We may become known as the guest who never drinks because wine sets off migraine; may develop a chatty relationship with the physiotherapist who works on our slipped disc; or may structure our life around the weekly pain relief her sessions offer. Undergoing chemotherapy, we may hate people's pitying attitude when we lose our hair. We may be precipitated into poverty by a long-term illness. While on crutches after a car accident we may find ourselves stuck at home, unable to use even public transport. The French philosopher Michel Foucault argued that society constructs 'madness' (and indeed sexuality) by defining – and confining – it (Foucault 1967).

Foucault's model can be applied to physical as much as to mental health: think of the medicalisation of interventions for weight problems, or of plastic surgery to help with issues of self-esteem. Society not only defines health – we often only need to change countries to acquire a new diagnosis or treatment – it responds to health and illness. Patients are not, traditionally, agents in their own recovery but passively bear the treatment offered to them. Patients also 'bear' prejudice, assumptions, pity. In having their agency removed, they have been dehumanised. This connection between agency and humanity – and what that entails of rights and dignity – was from Romanticism until postmodernity carried in the idea of the Subject, whose reflexive human consciousness was what made her, or often more often him, not only a locus of decision-making but of meaning-making.

Writing decisions are clearly connected to meaning-making. We can choose the moral of the story; we choose what we record and explore. Writing, therefore, celebrates and records the writer's agency. This is particularly striking in writing from within institutions such as prisons and hospitals. If totalitarian regimes often imprison influential writers because their practice itself declares the importance and the enduring fact of individual agency, regardless of their writing's actual content, their writing from within prison acquires symbolic and cultural importance for the same reasons. Mandelstam's late great poems, memorised by friends in a form of distribution prior even to *samizdat* publication; Wole Soyinka's execution; the trial of Orhan Pamuk by Turkish authorities who accuse the writer of misrepresenting his country: these are celebrated examples of the way writing from within confinement is important not only as witness but as a reinstatement of agency within a national culture. Although the tragic biographies of writers like John Clare, incarcerated in the asylum at Northampton, are famous, a writing context of physical ill-health may not be thought to have an equivalent bearing on the poetry and fiction being produced. Flannery O'Conner's lupus, for example, may be seen as cutting short her output but not as a presiding condition of the work. And yet we could conjecture that the confinement of serious illness informs the claustrophobic texture of her writing as well as her choice of short story genre.

Such conjecture is itself a wilful meaning-making: it is not necessarily *true* but reminds us that we might think about the writer's agency; their ability to make choices including the choice to write despite their context. This is very far from thinking about such a person as a passive patient: in fact it turns our relationship with the speaker inside out. This is why writing projects in health and social care settings are powerful, particularly when delivered as part of the ever-increasing model of person-centred care, in which people are involved in the decision making about their own treatment and care (person-centred care was a plank in the British Government's 2000 *NHS Plan* [British Government 2000]). Writing in health care in the UK arose from public arts provision on the 1970s community arts model, in which all members of society should have access to the arts as part of their common culture, and outreach to groups for whom institutional and social barriers to this access are operating is therefore socially 'healthy'. In his survey of the state of contemporary British poetry, Sean O'Brien examines the way social 'deregulation' has weakened the social role of a poetry which is increasingly concerned with small personal themes (O'Brien 1998). Community practice puts an emphasis on the participatory because, since the disadvantaged groups it works with have had limited access to the arts, they will have had correspondingly little chance to become arts practitioners. This is limiting both for them and for the arts, which lack their voices as a result. Writing in health care, then – which has developed since the late 1980s – has always carried with it an understanding of the importance of *writing from* a specific experience or social viewpoint (Hunt and Sampson 1998).

This is healthy for society – but is it healthy for the individual? As we have seen, to write is to articulate and develop the thinking self. It is to claim agency in the teeth of whatever educational, social, emotional or physical context we write from. It may even be said that we write against the grain of the pressures, both internal and external, associated with the ill-health we experience; as perhaps to some extent we must always write against the grain of the limits and discomforts of embodiment. Writing, and the *move into form* of our thinking, teaches us about our rights and responsibilities as thinking agents; it records our individuality. Without these things, we cannot achieve insights and changes which we might call therapeutic. However, writing itself is not therapy. As we have seen, writing achieves what it does because it is built out of both process and product, in continual dialectic. Writing is a process leading towards and led by text, and whose outcomes are defined in textual terms. Participating in the practice, as reader or writer, is beneficial because it helps shape the way we think. These benefits, however, may not be extra-textual. They may simply feed back into writing. Or, to put it another way, the chief benefit of writing may be that practising it helps us to write better – with all the personal and social consequences that may have.

References

Aristotle (1990), *The Politics*, Stephen Everson, ed., Cambridge: Cambridge University Press.

British Government, The (2000), *The NHS Plan: A Plan for Investment. A Plan for Reform*, London: The Department of Health.

Celan, Paul (2001), *Selected Poems and Prose of Paul Celan*, trans. John Felstiner, New York: W. W. Norton.

Eliot, T. S. (1951), 'Tradition and the Individual Talent' in *Selected Essays*, London: Faber.

Fielding, Helen (2001), *Bridget Jones' Diary*, London: Picador.

Forster, E. M. (2000), *Howards End*, Harmondsworth: Penguin.

Forster, E. M. (2001), *Where Angels Fear to Tread*, Harmondsworth: Penguin.

Foucault, Michel (1967), *Madness and Civilisation*, trans. Richard Howard, London: Tavistock.

Heidegger, Martin (1975), *Poetry, Language, Thought*, trans. Albert Hofstadter, New York: Harper & Row.

Hoggart, Richard (1992), *The Uses of Literacy*, Harmondsworth: Penguin.

Hunt, Celia and Fiona Sampson (eds) (1998), *The Self on Page: Theory and Practice of Creative Writing in Personal Development*, London: Jessica Kingsley.

Hunt, Celia and Fiona Sampson (2006), *Writing: Self and Reflexivity*, London: Palgrave.

Jamie, Kathleen (1994), 'The Queen of Sheba' in *The Queen of Sheba*, Newcastle upon Tyne: Bloodaxe.

Kavaler-Adler, Susan (1993), *The Compulsion to Create: A Psychoanalytic Study of Women Artists*, London: Routledge.

Keats, John (1973), 'Letter to George and Tom Keats, 21/?27 December 1817' in Kermode et al. (eds), *The Oxford Anthology of English Literature Volume II*, New York: Oxford University Press.

Kinsella, John (2005/6), 'Line breaks and back-draft: not a defence of a poem' in *Poetry Review* 95:4 (Winter), 70–8.

Lawrence, D. H. (1998), *Sons and Lovers*, Oxford: Oxford University Press.

Mace, Jane (2002), *The Give and Take of Writing*, London: National Institute of Adult Continuing Education.

O'Brien, Sean (1998), *The Deregulated Muse*, Newcastle upon Tyne: Bloodaxe.

Orwell, George (2000), *Keep the Aspidistra Flying*, Harmondsworth: Penguin.

Paterson, Don (2004), *The Book of Shadows*, London: Picador.

Path, Sylvia (1981), *Collected Poems*, London: Faber.

Plato, *The Republic* (1955), trans. H. D. P. Lee, Harmondsworth: Penguin.

Sampson, Fiona (ed.) (2004), *Creative Writing in Health and Social Care*, London: Jessica Kingsley.

Schaverien, Joy (1999), *The Revealing Image: Analytic Art Psychotherapy in Theory and Practice*, London: Jessica Kingsley.

Shelley, P. B. (2004), 'Defence of poetry' in *Defence of Poetry and Other Essays*, New York: R. A. Kessinger.

Williams, Raymond (1977), *Marxism and Literature*, Oxford: Oxford University Press.

Yasumoto, Yasuhiro, in conversation with the author, 9 November 2005.

34

Writing in the Community

Linda Sargent

We seem to be primed to tell stories wherever we are. You have only got to sit on a train, stand at a bus stop, listen in on other people's lives and it's there, this push to share, to say we matter, we have a place and that, more often than not, want to tell people about it. Those of us who write usually crave readers; just as a storyteller craves listeners, just as I am sure those early cave painters who left their handprints and other pictures of life as they saw it, were making a vivid and enduring statement to show that they, like us, were once here and wanted to say something about the experience. I often think of them as the first writers in the community, sharing their lives amongst their own social group, their own tribe. Working with people in our communities who want to write is a way of enabling them to have and develop their own voice, to make their mark in the way of those early ancestors.

This chapter will offer ideas on how to set up and run groups, based on case studies, with examples of work, as well as a general guide to running a workshop in a community setting.

Contacts and setting up groups

As a writer who is interested in working with groups in this field a useful starting point is to find out what is and has been happening in the area. Much of the work discussed below arose from outreach activity and contacts in local adult and community education. Outreach workers in other organisations such as museums, archives and galleries, as well as arts bodies and those attached to educational institutions, are likely to be invaluable sources of knowledge here. They are the people who – by definition – will know what is going on at grass roots level within their community. The nature of projects and audiences can range from:

- Those who join a creative writing group as part of an adult education programme
- Older people living independently in the community or in a variety of 'sheltered' environments, for example housing association complexes, residential or daycentres, health care settings
- Members of the travelling community, such as in Britain, the Irish (and other) Travellers, fairground workers and other itinerant workers
- Intergenerational work linking adults and children

- People with disabilities who may want to explore personal issues relating to disability through writing
- Others who hold common experiences, such as homelessness, unemployment, mental health needs, anything that can sometimes seemingly exclude people from mainstream activities and that may find an expression through the shared process of writing creatively.

Case studies

Most of the examples discussed here sprang from my work as an outreach organiser for community education in Oxfordshire UK from 1989–2002. During this period I worked with a variety of groups, from older writers, to Irish Travellers, people with mental health needs and those in residential care. The example below is from a group of writers who met in the public library of a small village.

The group, called Tell the Tale, was established in 1990 and they ran it themselves until 2005 when it came to a natural end. Their initial impetus was to share and tell their stories. Over this period they made tapes of their work, published booklets containing stories and poetry, talked to other groups and participated in the storytime sessions in the library where they met and, more recently, they produced work for a Training Guide in Creative Reminiscence Work. They also had visits from a range of professional writers. During the group's early days and in order to encourage them to begin to stand outside of themselves and look at the possibilities of fictionalising their lives, I asked them to re-write some of their childhood memories in the form of children's stories. Prior to this we had shared extracts from favourite personal examples of the latter to establish a tone and mood. One member, then in her eighties, wrote of her childhood on the edge of Oxford City. Her particularly evocative piece is called 'Dolly Remembers':

> In the spinney was a little dip and in the dip was a pond. It was a pretty place, but a very sad thing happened there. Nanny Martin had come wooding one evening with her young son, and while she was busy collecting wood the boy fell in to the pond and was drowned. The children of the Quarry knew this story and the sad memory of Nanny Martin seemed to haunt the place. Among the children there was the belief that if you came to the spinney at a certain time in the evening you might meet the ghost of Nanny Martin, seeking and grieving for her lost son. Dolly remembers that when she and her friend Bessie went walking in the lanes and fields after school, they always avoided passing the spinney, but it and the ghost did have a sort of fascination for them and one of the dares to prove that you were very brave, was 'All right then, run past Nanny Martin's spinney – dare you!' On those days Dolly and Bessie were very pleased to have Stella and Jean with them – although Stella and Jean were afraid of the spinney. They used to all catch hands very tightly and race!
> (Horwood 1995: 6; Stella and Jean were Dolly and Bessie's imaginary friends.)

This process of fictionalising real memories served to free the writers to explore their own creative potential and is often a productive way into this process for those who are new to writing narrative fiction. They were an extremely open-minded group and wrote poetry, more children's stories, short stories, and were at one period involved in a community radio play, having input into the script as well as taking part. The play was broadcast on local radio. They also took part in trial co-operative creative writing sessions linking with another group of older learners, to produce material to form part of a training guide in creative reminiscence work. During these sessions objects from a rural life museum, with a text extract from Flora Thompson's *Lark Rise to Candleford* (1974) were used to stimulate creative writing. The following account of this exercise illustrates the potential of such an approach.

Initially the two groups met separately to look at the objects and brainstorm some ideas and this proved easier for the more experienced Tell the Tale. Members of the second group were not from a creative writing background, although some people had recently been involved in an apparently more straightforward and intergenerational reminiscence project. They sportingly responded to the call from their organiser to undertake the same exercise that Tell the Tale had tried. And really it was the energy and enthusiasm of this organiser who helped to produce such a successful outcome. When she advertised it to her members she entitled it Country Cousins and invited them to: 'Come and join us for an afternoon of reminiscence work, looking at mystery objects from the Oxfordshire Museum Store, sharing the memories they evoke and writing stories about the people who used and treasured them'. The experimental nature of the project was also made clear.

Workshop sessions

For the first session, the organiser and one of her members came along to observe and in order to take notes for use with her group in the second session. Both sessions followed roughly the same format. The main difference was that the Museum Project Officer and the Reminiscence Worker led the first session, whereas their organiser led the second group. The Museum Project Officer gave some detail on the project and explained that eventually both groups would meet up at Farm Museum to share this experience and samples of their work. She then went on to tell us about the *Eagle of the Ninth*, a children's historical novel by Rosemary Sutcliff and the museum object that inspired this novel. She also talked about the objects being used so that we didn't spend time in guessing games, but got to the point of the exercise.

The session continued with us looking at and handling the objects, followed by people brainstorming associated and connected words and phrases, thinking about the people behind the objects. There was much discussion and reminiscing. The phrase 'They never flinched' from Flora Thompson's *Lark Rise to Candleford* was given to the group as a theme to build their pieces around. People were asked to choose some of the brainstormed words as well as this suggested theme in order to write a creative piece on the people behind one or several of the objects. Tell the Tale did this for their homework and posted their pieces to the Reminiscence Worker.

I think it is probably true to reflect that both groups found the exercise challenging. Although Tell the Tale were initially less daunted by the idea of 'creative' writing for obvious reasons, it does seem that the objects themselves almost presented an obstacle. Real objects were once used by real people and therefore there was a certain amount of respect for them and, I think, a feeling that entering them into a piece of fiction might somehow be dishonourable or untrue. Certainly the second group had a strong debate on this aspect of the exercise and it is interesting to note that they felt that perhaps some time on warm-up exercises might have been valuable. Again, the Rosemary Sutcliff example mentioned above might have been helpful here too, as might other writing similarly inspired. However, what is worth noting is that in spite of the struggles mentioned, people produced some good, inspiring and sometimes moving writing. If a longer project was planned then indeed this exercise could in itself been the basis of the required warm-up.

The final sharing and meeting at the Farm Museum proved to be especially helpful. (And made possible by the provision of transport.) This meeting began with a guided tour of the barns and farm house, with the added bonus of passing through the kitchen just as Welsh teacakes had come warm from the oven. It seemed people felt the closeness of the occupants of the place and immediately started to speculate and imagine the lives lived out there.

Back in the café afterwards, we shared some of the work out between the groups and there was a real buzz of shared achievement and praise. The discussion and short feedback session that followed again raised the truth/fact debate and we talked about the continuum along which truth, creativity, imagination, fact lie. One example given was the idea that we don't necessarily believe (for good reason) all that we read in the press now so why should it be any truer because the newspaper is, for example, dated 1895? We shared an extract from Keats's 'Ode on a Grecian Urn' and there was a lot of nodding and smiling as this touched a real chord with people.

But maybe the best part of this session was the fact of the two groups who had never met before, coming together to share some of their creative work. Both parted feeling they would like some kind of follow-up to this 'experiment'! This is a good example of the kind of work that can develop when working in the community, not only in terms of the outcome for the individuals and the project, but also in respect of the partnership. When setting out to work in this kind of environment such co-operation can produce satisfying and useful results for all concerned.

The last word on the value and endurance of such a community writers' group is best summed up by one of the members who recently compiled another collection of their work and which gives insight into the process from a participant's viewpoint:

> Our very first meeting was held on a Saturday afternoon in a room in the old stable block of a local senior school where it attracted fifteen people who had seen the notices in the local villages, or in the mobile library van, asking Have You a Tale to Tell? We met the Outreach Worker who started the ball rolling. After introductions we were asked to go off in pairs and talk about our lives and soon the words were flowing freely. We then had to relay to the others what we had learned about each other and soon friendships were formed.
>
> It became apparent that the stable block was not the ideal meeting place as the bell clanged overhead every few minutes and would have been very distracting, also (since the school is out of the village centre) it would have been difficult for those without transport. The Outreach Worker organised for us to use the village library as our venue when it would not be open to the public and the group began on 10 May 1990.
>
> Our first assignment was to write a piece on Old Age. It seemed a grim title but some very good pieces of writing evolved from it, some in poetic form. In the beginning we met weekly on Thursday mornings (this later changed to every two weeks) and different topics were given to us for our 'homework'. In 1994 we selected some of our material to self-publish our first booklet which we called Ripples, with the help of community education for typing and finance. About sixty books were printed and some were sold locally to help defray costs. After three years, the group began to run itself and continues to do so, still producing booklets and taking part in other arts projects when invited.

Working with other artists

The above case study gives an insight into how a group can be sustained long-term using its own resources as well as working in partnership. Often this partnership can involve a writer/facilitator combining with another artist. For example, I sometimes work on projects with visual artists. This can produce stimulating and inspiring results such as in one instance, a textile map made by a group of young women from the Traveller community depicting their life and culture with accompanying written comments. This toured local schools and other venues. Similarly, when working alongside a professional musician at a day centre for older people, their recollections were transformed into song. Yet another project combined writing with music where children from a junior school composed songs based on the lives and memories of people attending a day centre at a hospital. In order to form a contact between the older people in the day centre and the children in the junior school, we talked about hands; we drew round the older and younger hands and shared memories about them. Before the two groups met in reality they shared these visual hand histories and ultimately the children wrote a song (in consultation with the older group) to encapsulate this exercise, the chorus of one song acknowledged the joint process:

> From age to age we all have hands
> Unique but all the same
> With big hands, small hands, old and young,
> We all can play the game.

Creative partners can produce creative results.

Conclusion

In conclusion the following points are intended to provide some general practical guidelines for those aiming to embark on writing in the community.

Aims

Once the workshop has been set up, with a suitable time and venue, establish its aims, who it is for, what the needs of the group are. Choose a theme or themes to focus activities. Number of participants – a maximum of ten is workable if there is only one leader. Decide on the length of session – an hour and a half is often a useful time scale. If working with a co-leader, meet and plan individual/joint aspects of the workshop in advance. Such preparation means that the facilitator(s) are in the best position to respond to unexpected reactions or demands from the group; this is not to tie down every detail but to enable an atmosphere of easy, yet confident, flexibility – one of shared rather than imposed learning.

Setting and resources

Prepare the setting as much as is possible, with chairs set in a circle around a table or tables, depending on what's available; check heating, ventilation and physical access. Make sure you have all the equipment, notes, copies of poems, pictures, flipcharts and so on before you start. Bring a few extra resources along, poems, pictures, songs, (bubbles!) whatever is appropriate to the theme, a bit of creative back-up that inspires you, the facilitator. When such opportunities arise in a group it can help to foster and strengthen feelings of safety, and members soon realise that their needs and interests are important to the leader, plus it re-enforces the notion that individual creativity can feed into the collective group 'pot'.

Introductions and objectives

Once the group is assembled, allow a short settling moment or two. Assuming this is the first meeting, introduce everyone, starting with group leader(s). The method you adopt here might be dependent on the nature of the session, if, for example, the aim includes the role of memory in writing, this could be reflected in the manner of introduction; the facilitator will begin with 'I'm . . . and I was named after my great aunt . . . and I prefer to be called . . .'. A name biography game might work in this instance. Allow everyone time for this and acknowledge people by thanking them using the name they state they prefer to be called. Make a note of this. Don't try and force people to make links and connections regarding their names if they don't wish to, in order to have the opportunity to produce their best work they need to feel safe.

Explain what it is hoped will be achieved by the group 'us' by the end of the session, and although this should not necessarily be prescribed in great detail be clear, for example you might say we will have all produced and be willing to share one piece of creative work with the group, or if the aim is to work on a group exercise then we shall have made our own poem, scene, story, or whatever is being explored in the session. Alternatively, if the group has come together for the purpose of – say – learning how to use creative writing as a way of working in the field of reminiscence, the facilitator might tell the group that by the end of the session we shall all have explored, and have a better understanding of the value of creative writing as a tool in this field, as well as some methods to apply.

Ground rules – facilitator's role

As well as general goals connected to the specifics of the work, it is also advisable to set out some ground rules. Let people know how they will be working, that some of the exercises will happen in pairs, that not all of the work will be read aloud to the whole group, that timings will be made clear, also underline the confidentiality aspects of the work, if – for example – you wish to record the session in some way, ask the group's permission and make sure that people understand that anything that comes up belongs to them, emphasising that all members must respect what is written and shared as contained and private to the group. As a facilitator include yourself in the group 'we' – this underlines the shared aspects of the learning. It is also important that the facilitator(s) judge when or whether if it is appropriate to introduce their own material.

In terms of publication, the leader may direct people towards information or suitable local outlets; alternatively, the group might wish to self-publish or exhibit their work.

Set the first exercise, with aims, guidance on timing and how it will be shared; often if people are new to this kind of activity it is helpful to allow them to work in pairs with initial feedback to the main group as a pair. This will depend on the group and the extent of people's experience, but can provide an initial safety net if there is fear of exposure. It also enables individuals a means of getting to know one another, and a variety of pairing should be encouraged. If there are two leaders it can be helpful for them to take it in turns to work in partnership with group members.

When people read their pieces to the group, make it clear beforehand what is expected; the length of the extract, if it is a page then keep to a page, some people will always bring or do more, but encourage everyone to respect this rule otherwise it can mean less time for others. Be prepared to impose this on the group although it may be difficult in the face of pressure. Make it clear from the outset, however, be open to offering to look at the rest of the work at some later point, or if someone has written two pages instead of the requested one, suggest they read the second page only. Clarify the type of feedback that people will give and be given, stress the importance of putting the emphasis on the work and not the person, and also encourage members, by example, to take responsibility for their feedback comment: '. . . this makes me feel . . . I could visualise . . . I could hear . . . I was moved . . . I struggled with . . . I would have liked more . . . ' As a facilitator, when feeding back on work, bear in mind whether pieces were produced in or outside of the session.

If the group develops trust and cohesion, then moments of conflict or pain can be dealt with safely and securely and good creative work can ensue. The facilitator is there to provide this holding place by providing a channel for the group's activity or work.

Evaluation

At the end of the session celebrate and honour what has been produced and mark the finishing point by referring back to what was hoped for at the beginning. Give everyone space to evaluate their experience.

The facilitator should assess their own learning after the session has finished and evaluate what has occurred.

Writing in the community is going to be as rich and varied as those inhabitants contained in that community and will be as revealing, exciting and inspirational for the facilitator as for the participants. Everyone has a story to tell . . . a 'handprint' to leave . . . getting involved in this kind of work means that you can help to make it happen.

References and recommended reading

Crimmens, Paula (1998), *Storymaking and Creative Groupwork with Older People*, London: Jessica Kingsley.

Horwood, Dolly (1995), 'Dolly Remembers', in *Ripples: A Collection of Writing by the Tell the Tale Writers' Group*: Limited Edition Self-Publication.

Hunt, Celia and Fiona Sampson (eds) (1998), *The Self on the Page: Theory and Practice of Creative Writing in Personal Development*, London: Jessica Kingsley.

Moskowitz, C. (2001), *Playing with Poetry*, London: The Arts Council.

Sutcliff, Rosemary (1970), *The Eagle of the Ninth*, Oxford: Oxford University Press.

Thompson, Flora. (1974), *Lark Rise to Candleford*, London: Penguin Books.

Thompson, J. (2002), *Bread and Roses*, Leicester: National Institute of Adult and Continuing Education (NIACE).

35

Writing for the Web

James Sheard

The web appears to offer a great deal to the writer. Some writers are attracted by the apparent ease of publication and distribution it seems to offer; others by specific web technologies which offer alternatives to, or enhancements of, the text. The enthusiasm of creative writers for the Internet resulted in an explosion of individual and group websites throughout the 1990s – webzines, showcase sites, individual and group web pages, forums for feedback and critique and attempts to exploit the possibilities of sound, image, animation and text effects in poetry and prose. This explosion has shown little sign of diminishing in recent years. This chapter will touch only briefly on the topics of social media and recent developments in self-publishing, both of which are covered fully in other chapters.

For the reader, it is too easy to feel overwhelmed by the sheer quantity of writing available on the web, while being underwhelmed by the quality of much of that writing. For the writer, it is too easy to proceed from a rush of enthusiasm and a little knowledge to yet another abandoned website gathering virtual dust in an unvisited corner of the web. Above all, the writer seeking to exploit the web needs a strategy, and the strategy requires some understanding of the demands and opportunities of the medium, as well as some clear thinking about how to work most effectively within it.

The Internet is not so much a publication system as a distribution system. The bleak metaphor most often used for web 'publication' – for online literary magazines and personal sites alike – is that of handing out copies of the work, typically at no charge, on a street corner. The street corner is usually envisaged as having, by default, no – or, at best, very few – passers-by. The hawker of literary wares is delighted and grateful when a copy is taken. Before considering how the medium of the web shapes our writing, it is worth spending some time understanding how to make the distribution system work.

As in the real world, reputation is the key to acquiring readership. For writers and publishers with established reputations, it may be sufficient to rely on the potential reader's curiosity about whether the *London Review of Books* has an online version, or whether a particular writer has a website. The search engine (for example, Google) provides the answer and draws readers to the site. For the unknown, or relatively unknown, however, an online reputation must be acquired, and for these, reputation is initially bought with the currency of the literary web – feedback, critique and engagement in the work of other writers. Awareness of one's existence as a writer can also be achieved by use of social media such as Twitter and Facebook.

The Internet has many forums where writers post their draft work for comments and critique, and the web writer is well advised to get involved in one or more of these (search terms: writing forum; poetry forum, etc.). Finding a forum which contains at least some good writing and genuine critique (that is, beyond 'This is great, thanks for sharing') can take time, but it is worth the effort to find those online writers' communities which are serious in purpose, populated with writing and critique of a good standard and have a large user base. Once you have found one, the best advice is: first, 'lurk' (read without posting) for a couple of weeks, to gain some understanding of the prevailing culture and personalities of the forum; then introduce yourself; then concentrate on giving workshop-style critique for a while, rather than posting your own work too often. A reputation as a competent commentator who gives time generously is worth a great deal in such forums, and such a reputation will gradually draw a readership for your own work, career and online projects. Two warning notes should be sounded at this point: first, such forums – free as they are from the moderating influence of the face-to-face meeting – can be forthright, even brutal places for the thin-skinned writer; and, whilst it is acceptable practice gently to make readers aware of your off-forum online presence (by way of a link to your website at the bottom of your messages, for example, or occasional mentions of specific updates and events), overt self-promotion and advertising is often deemed to be 'spamming' (unsolic-ited and irritating advertising).

Offering feedback on the work of other writers is not limited to forums and discussion groups. Internet writers often have websites of their own, offering their work on their own street corner, and hoping to catch the interest and comment of passers-by. Engaging with these fellow-writers via commenting systems on their websites or email can yield reciprocal visits and links to your own work and the development of groups of writers who help to build your reputation as someone worth paying attention to.

Such reputation-building can be effectively enhanced by the use of social media. Writers have taken to Facebook and Twitter in particular, establishing themselves in these forms of Internet media for the purposes of, variously, communication with other writers; brand-building; dissemination of information about literary events and publications; and to put a friendly public face on one's writing. When considering a strategy for using these media in the context described so far in this chapter, it can be helpful to consider what kind of participant in these fast-moving and open spaces one wishes to be. For some writers, it is largely about a personal presence, to which information about one's writing and writerly activities is subtly attached. For others, it is about building networks and groups of writers/readers for mutual benefit. Other roles can include the literary equivalent of 'clicktivism' – sharing and promoting events and news from other writers, in the hope of mutual appre-ciation and back-scratching; 'curating' literary and artistic texts, news and oddities to draw and maintain the interest of potential readers; or for outright marketing purposes. All of these are legitimate, and all have benefits and pitfalls. The writer on the web should think carefully about which role suits her/his character best.

Alongside the acquisition of a reputation and a potential readership comes the respon-sibility of using the web as a medium for distributing or disseminating your work. This might involve seeking online publications which might be suitable for your writing, creating your own web presence (a website), or both. Online publications fall into two categories: web versions of print publications and web-only publications. The former usually – but not always – draw their content from the print version. The quality and purpose of online-only publications varies wildly, from poorly thought-out and designed vanity projects to serious and well-respected contenders in the literary periodicals market.

Recognising the better end of this spectrum requires a little time spent browsing current and previous issues, and the clues are similar to those found in the print world: evidence of rigour in the submissions guidelines and editorial process; perhaps an ISSN number; a continuous publication history; writing of consistent standard; some known names; design values which are appropriate to the medium. As always, submission guidelines should be read carefully and adhered to. As in the print world, it may also be worth gambling on new online literary publications which seem to have a genuine desire to occupy the better end of the spectrum. It is also worth considering, if your experience of providing critique and feedback in more informal web settings has proved successful, offering yourself as a reviewer to web publications which have reviews of books and literary publications as part of their content.

As a literary medium, the web has always seemed most hospitable to short forms in plain text at one extreme, and experimental uses of web technology to deliver 'alternatives to text' at the other. Poetry, journalism and neo-journalism, and shorter prose forms have flourished, as have multimedia combinations of visual and aural effects around a central creative text. This is not to say that longer forms cannot be delivered via the web, but that decisions about the delivery of creative texts via the web should bear in mind the natural fit between screen reading and discrete shorter chunks of readable material.

In the 1980s and 1990s, creating a website of writing invariably involved a knowledge of HTML and sufficient knowledge to create – at the most basic level – a website of linked pages and a navigation system for the reader to work through. Whilst this is still an option for those wishing complete control over the design of a website, the demands of amateur/ non-mainstream journalism have created a range of web 'tools' (typically a set of php scripts; search terms: *opensourcecms*; *blogging software*) which allow a writer to add content to their own website in a more direct way, effectively using a web browser as a word proces- sor. Variously known as 'blogs', 'content management systems' and 'portals', depending on their complexity and functionality, these tools can easily be co-opted for the creative writ- er's requirements. Whether designing a website oneself, or opting to work with a writing tool of the kind described, you will need an Internet account which includes webspace, or a web server from which the site can be delivered to the Internet. Alternatively, services such as WordPress offer a standardised 'writing presence' which requires only a connection to the Internet and a web browser to create a blog (an online journal with tools to link and interact with other bloggers).

The most critical design consideration for the 'plain text' web writer is 'usability' (the ease and clarity with which text can be accessed and read by the website visitor; search terms: *jakob nielsen*; *web usability*; *jukka korpela*). This emphasis on text as prime content is best achieved by relatively unadorned layout and navigation; an unfussy typeface choice (sans-serif fonts work well for on-screen reading) at the default point size for browsers (typically 13–14 pt; better still, an unspecified point size in a web document will render at the default size in the reader's web browser); and, perhaps, a downloadable print copy (*.pdf – Portable Document Format is a better choice here than *.doc – Word Document).

For the writer who wishes to explore the opportunities offered by web technologies to enhance, or even replace, text with some form of multimedia, design and delivery consid- erations become much more complex and individual. For some web purists, questions of usability outweigh the attractions of delivering such 'fripperies' as animations, sound files and video. It is worth pointing out, however, that the core idea of the Web – the HTML in which web pages are written – was designed to be an enhanced form of text: it was envisaged that (primarily academic) texts would contain hyperlinks to other documents and references. Creative writers quickly saw opportunities to exploit this key technology to artistic ends (search terms: *hypertext creative writing*; alternatively *hypertext poetry*, etc.) A similar co-opting of core HTML functions to serve creative ends can also be seen in the uses of a web page's ability to display images, simple animations (the *.gif format) and 'image maps' (images containing defined areas which are clickable hyperlinks). (Search terms: *interactive poetry*; alternatively *interactive stories*, etc.) The use of varying fonts, colours and point size to 'enhance' text can also be found. While the success of such experiments is as varied as the quality of the writing they enhance (or, in some cases, thrown into unpleasantly stark relief), it is undeniably the case that interesting and sometimes fascinating uses of basic web technologies by writers can be found all over the web.

When considering the extent to which one intends to make use of these methods of enhancing text, it is important to consider the reputation, presence and audience one wishes to construct as a web writer. Plain text purists and new media artists are different breeds, cluster in different places and have very different notions of how the web should be used to deliver writing. Building a reputation as a competent commentator who is generous with their time in a forum where participants are vocal in their suspicion of anything beyond the literary quality of the text will be inevitably undermined by a New Media-oriented web presence, and vice versa. It is also worth bearing in mind that many New Media artists are highly skilled in the technology itself, and while a naïve use of the technology can be interesting, it can also detract, for certain communities on the web, from the underlying text. This latter point also prompts a key consideration for writers who are interested in delivering digitally-enhanced versions of their writing: being clear and certain that the enhancement genuinely serves the text, rather than merely adding noise, and that the intention of the writer is matched by skill of the 'surrounding' artistic work. For the inexperienced web-media writer, these considerations are best engaged with through participation in relevant discussion forums and – often very successfully – through collaborations with technically-proficient digital artists (search term: *new media literature*).

It is probably fair to say that creative writers build a readership most effectively through a combination of participation in an online writing community and mixing their creative work with comment and neo-journalism on a blog-type site of their own. Online writing communities and blogs are, to some extent, being superseded by social media sites and technologies, and an awareness of this should be built into a strategy. Static, showcase-style websites tend to be visited more rarely than dynamic ones, and the writer is well-advised to develop changing content in a related writing genre (reviews, for example) to draw regular visits from the readership he or she is building.

Writers approaching the Internet for the first time often have concerns and questions about copyright, protection of their work and – in some optimistic cases – payment. A common first post to a writing forum might be 'I would like to post my work here for comment – but how do I know it won't be stolen?' (The typical answer: 'Why on earth would anyone want to steal it?' serves as both a call for clearer thinking and an introduction to the often hard-faced world of online discussion). Copyright is a complicated area in a medium as global as the web, but some simple facts should be borne in mind (see the chapter on 'Copyright' in this book; links: www.benedict.com; www.wipo.org). A writer's claim to their work is established by the creation of the work itself. No further copyright action is required. As in the print world, breaches of copyright need to be noticed, pursued and established. A writer's original work, posted on the Internet, is not in the public domain unless it is specifically stated as being in the public domain. It is possible in most countries to take the additional step of registering one's copyright – at a cost – to a particular work with the relevant national authorities; this does not strengthen the rights to a work, but allows for greater damages to be claimed if a breach of copyright is established. The Internet is, as has been mentioned, a distribution system and, as with a widely-distributed print publication, copies might be made and anything legal or otherwise might be done with those copies. It is effectively impossible to prevent this in a way which cannot be circumvented, on the web or in print, but this does not affect a writer's claim to his or her work, nor does it affect the ability to pursue breaches of copyright.

New web writers also wonder about publication rights, and what impact putting work on the web might have on future acceptance of work by publishers. There is no clear-cut answer on this; current or future editors or publishers of one's work are entitled to take whatever view they wish of a prior appearance of the work on the web. As a rough rule of thumb, the writer might take the view that work posted to forums for feedback need not be the concern of an editor; work placed on a personal website, if removed when accepted for publication, might also be glossed over, although a careful reading of any contract is recommended; work placed with an online publication of any sort is equivalent to prior publication in a print journal, requiring – at a minimum – an acknowledgement.

The street corner hawker of literature mentioned at the beginning of this chapter is unlikely to be selling copies of their work for a price. It has proved difficult for even well-established writers and publishers to charge for online (that is, digital) content – except, perhaps, in cases where the existing print version is an established journal or periodical. As a result, web-based writers have traditionally offered print versions of their work (whether self-published or as a means of selling copies of published pamphlets or author's copies of books), or adopted the web version of the passed-around hat: online donations. In either case, the ability to accept small payments online via a secure third-party payment service (such as PayPal www.paypal.com) can be useful. It is also worth noting that using the web as a way of marketing one's print publication has some advantages, not least the ability to provide sample work for the potential purchaser to judge.

Writing for the web requires some planning, a certain amount of strategic effort and, above all, participation in the engine that drives it: interactive communities. The benefits of direct communication with a readership, and the consequent (or subsequent) interest in the writer's offline career is well worth the effort.

References to websites

Copyright Website: www.benedict.com
PayPal: www.paypal.com
WordPress: wordpress.com
World Intellectual Property Organisation: www.wipo.org

36

The Role of the Critical Essay

Scott McCracken

The relationship between writers and critics has never been an easy one. Despite the fact that most writing programmes are housed in English departments, where the main activity is literary criticism, many writing students are reluctant to engage in criticism and some can be downright hostile to literary theory. The complaint that the student came on the course to learn how to write, not to 'theorise', is not uncommon. For many the 'isms' (Marxism, feminism, poststructuralism, postmodernism) distract from the practical activity of writing. Ideas such as the 'death of the author', which can seem fresh and exciting in a third year undergraduate seminar on a traditional English degree, can appear absurd in a room full of struggling novelists; and their derision is hardly likely to be contradicted by a creative writing tutor who writes to live.

In this chapter I will look at: the relationship between writing and criticism; how it differs at undergraduate and postgraduate levels; the importance of the institutional context; the different public spheres addressed by writers and academics; and finally as a way of addressing all these points, I will examine in detail a specific module in a specific institution, where the critical essay is used as part of the assessment. 'What is Contemporary?' is the core module in the MA Writing at Sheffield Hallam and its development and evolution addresses many of the key concerns raised in this chapter.

Despite the fraught relationship between writing and criticism, most writers have also been, in one form or another, critics; and criticism plays an important role in the creative process. The creative writing workshop, the basic pedagogic tool of the writing course, is designed to enable constructive criticism in a supportive environment. Thus the contradiction between writing and criticism lies at the heart of teaching creative writing. The creative writing tutor has to tread a fine line between support and criticism. Often, in a way that sometimes perplexes students, the tutor must first support and then criticise. The warm and friendly community of writers students enter at the beginning of the course, must eventually become one in which they are assessed and judged – a process that is part of the painful preparation for the judgements and rejections that being a professional writer entails.

If not handled carefully, this can lead to confusing messages being sent to the students. On the one hand, a supportive environment is needed to encourage student writers and to give them the confidence to write. On the other, the workshop encourages students to reflect on their own work and that of their fellow students. This process of reflection is not just a necessary precondition for criticism, it is itself a form of criticism, which is often formalised as a 'reflective statement', presented as an accompaniment to assessed work. Yet students with no formal critical training may not possess the analytical tools that equip them to give or receive criticism effectively. The inability to formulate a critical judgement will reduce the effectiveness of a workshop; but the capacity to receive criticism is as important as the capacity to give it. Thus, some training in critical techniques and methodologies can greatly enhance a student's capacity to benefit from a writing course.

The relationship between creative writing and criticism differs at undergraduate and postgraduate levels. Undergraduate courses in creative writing are usually combined with the study of literature, language or both. This is partly because, historically, creative writing programmes in Britain have been appended to degrees in English Studies. But some teachers of creative writing oppose the idea of a single honours BA in creative writing. They argue that undergraduate students need the rigour of an academic discipline. A student who only studies creative writing lacks a knowledge of history and context and, as a consequence, has only an inadequate understanding of language and literary form. The writing that this produces is characterised by a narrow sense of literature as 'self-expression', leading to derivative and confessional work.

At MA level, the issues are somewhat different. Students tend to be older. Many courses in fact discourage applications from younger students, suggesting that promising younger writers spend a few years living before doing a higher degree. Thus, MA students bring a more varied life experience to their writing. This means that, in the workshop situation, critical interaction is more varied and draws on a wider range of experience and reading. Discussion of influences and inspirations will be an important starting point for both tutor and students. The problem here is establishing a common set of reference points.

The quickest and most practical way to bring the group together is through a readings list. Students beginning a novel workshop, for example, are likely to be set a list of novels to read by the tutor. The list then acts as a common resource, allowing students to situate their work in relation to a wider field, as well as offering examples of technique, style and form. The process of contextualisation initiates a critical process that the critical essay can enhance, but only if its role remains clearly relevant to the workshop situation. It takes its place in relation to other forms of critical reflection, such as the 'reflective statement' that accompanies submitted work. In this respect, it can help to prepare students for the process of review that is an inevitable part of getting published, cultivating the necessary distancing required for such practical tasks as: writing a covering letter; constructing a synopsis; or choosing exemplary chapters. It can also prepare students, who are often idealistic and sometimes naïve about the brutal realities of publishing and the book trade, for the process of criticism and editing to which all submitted manuscripts are subject by agents and publishers, as well as the later (hoped-for) reviews in newspapers and literary journals.

There is, then, no practical reason why the inclusion of the critical essay or critical module need be viewed with suspicion by students. But there is a more practical problem that concerns the nature of the institutions within which creative writing is taught or, more precisely, the different relationships to those institutions as experienced by professional academics and professional writers. Professional academics usually work full-time in universities. They present and discuss their work to and with other academics. They write for disciplinary-specific journals and edited collections published by academic presses. Career progression is tied to specialist publication and 'esteem indicators' such as invited lectures at international conferences. Even in the discipline of English Studies there is little interaction with living poets, dramatists and novelists and little attempt to reach out to a non-specialist audience.

Writers, on the other hand, are less dependent on the academy. They are often engaged in discussions, formal and informal with other writers, but they also have another audience: the reading public. They communicate with that public through public readings and other literary media: newspapers; literary reviews; specialist publications for writers; little magazines; and arts programming. Writers and academics in other words speak to two different, albeit overlapping, public spheres. Even where they are ostensibly talking about the same thing, their different audiences demand different critical languages: languages that may even use the same terms, but which often use them in different ways.

As with all translation, this can lead to misunderstandings. Foisting a critical essay on students without being aware of the potential incomprehension that may ensue can be counterproductive. In order to make the exercise work, three things must be borne in mind: first, the institutional context; second, the pedagogical context; and finally pedagogic practice. As it is impossible to discuss such things outside concrete examples, in what follows I draw heavily on my experience of the core module of the MA Writing at Sheffield Hallam University: 'What Is Contemporary?' The experience of that course was that a productive dialogue can be established between the practical elements of an MA in creative writing and academic criticism. I am not suggesting it as a model, but rather as a case study that highlights the problems and the opportunities likely to be encountered.

The 'What is Contemporary?' (WIC) module was originally set up by the poet E. A. Markham and reflects the philosophy behind the MA Writing at Sheffield Hallam. One of its distinctive elements is that it encourages students to think about their own work in relation to other forms of writing as well as the broader culture in which they live and work. Most students study more than one genre (from: the novel, short story; script or poetry), while, as the core module, 'What is Contemporary?' has two key aims: first, to encourage students to think about their own work in relation to contemporary culture, leaving definitions of the contemporary open to debate and discussion; second, to allow students to develop analytical skills that incorporate some of the critical and theoretical concepts in use in academic criticism. It is always co-taught by one writer and one academic critic, who is usually also the Course Leader for the MA. The module runs in both semesters, the academic critic appearing twice a year, with a different writer in each semester.

The MA Writing at Hallam is taught within the English Department, but in an institutional context where, as with most English departments, there are limited opportunities for exchange between full-time academic critics and the (mostly) part-time writers. Thus opportunities and structures where dialogue between the groups could take place had to be created. The Course Leader had therefore not only to act as an intermediary between the writer-teachers and the institution, but to bridge the gap between the writers and the academic critics. Co-teaching – the pedagogic context – set up a structure designed to enable dialogues and if necessary to clarify points of disagreement between two positions. Students were encouraged to take up positions within that context, and to develop their own arguments. To create a common point of departure, students studied three set texts: a novel; a collection of poetry; and an example of script, usually a film. Critical reading at first consisted of an anthology of cultural theory, but this was later modified to also include specific essays for discussion, each chosen by one of the tutors. The module spanned twelve weekly two-hour sessions, each divided equally between the tutors and students. The first week consisted of introductory business and a presentation from one of the tutors on theories of the contemporary. The following four to five weeks would begin with an hour where students read from their own work and then took supportive, but critical responses. In the second hour, the tutors took turns to present for twenty minutes on an aspect of contemporary culture, drawing on their own interests and work. Topics included translating poetic drama; the culture of work; religion and poetry; as well as introductory presentations on the chosen texts and essays. Unlike a standard academic module, the presentations were never the same as the year before and were designed to provoke dialogue and debate.

In the second half of the semester, students gave their own presentations on an aspect of contemporary culture previously agreed in a short one-to-one session with one of the tutors. The presentation was marked both on its own merits and in terms of the discussion it provoked. At the end of the module, students were required to produce two pieces of written work. The first was a relatively short (2000 words) critical response to one of the presentations and/or the discussion to which it gave rise. The second was a full-length critical essay (3,500 words), usually a development of the student's original presentation given in class. This was marked both for its level of analysis and its use of critical concepts and theoretical ideas and had to be presented at an academic standard with proper referencing and a full bibliography.

The essay thus took its place in a context and structure designed to engender and develop dialogue and discussion between academic criticism and the practising writer. As an MA in Writing inevitably attracts a heterogeneous group of students, the module was designed to offer several points of entry. Students with little or no academic background could begin from their own experience, but were encouraged to relate that experience to the ideas they encountered on the course. The early one-to-one tutorial functioned to recommend further reading that would develop the student's ideas. Other students began with one of the set texts or used their own material. This meant that the presentations were unusually wide-ranging. There were no restrictions on content. Examples included a presentation on Huddersfield Town Rugby League Club, where the decline in interest of the student's elderly father coincided with the League adoption by Rupert Murdoch's Sky television. One student gave a historical view of the decline in the influence of feminism, using popular women's magazines to illustrate the point. Approaches ranged from the autobiographical to the formally critical. One student, for example, made an argument for difficulty in poetry. Another began by asking everyone in the seminar (including the tutors) to fill out a questionnaire on their contribution to domestic labour before delivering a presentation on the cultural phenomenon of what she called 'Quiche Man' (a new example of masculinity: the man who can cook a quiche, but contributes very little else to the domestic economy) and the new gender relations.

Successful presentations tended to combine a passionate interest in the subject matter with an ability to make a critical judgement on its broader meaning. Less successful presentations tended to be more descriptive than analytical. A topic might succeed in gaining the interest in the group, but if the student was not able to offer a structure in which critical debate could take place, then discussion tended to become anecdotal. Thus the presentations acted as good indicator of the kinds of intervention the tutors needed to make in order to advise on preparing the critical essay. A second one-to-one tutorial delivered marks and feedback on the presentation to allow the student to plan the essay in the light of the tutor's comments.

The set texts had an important role to play in setting the tone of the sessions. These were chosen for their capacity to provoke debate or because they called for a productive dialogue between form and criticism. Jonathan Franzen's novel, *The Corrections*, was a typical example. The novel has great strengths and moments of comic observation that make it a hugely enjoyable read, but it straddles a fine line between the literary novel and popular fiction. Its uncertain position as both bestseller and a stab at 'the great American novel' made it an ideal text, but this was enhanced by the debate surrounding the book in the US. Jonathan Franzen was, to use his own word, 'disinvited' from the Oprah Winfrey show, where his book was due to be discussed, after he publicly discussed his qualms about having his book associated with her 'Book Club', through the imprint of its logo on the cover (see Franzen 2000).

In class, the writer and the critic took very different views on the spat, views that reflected their different professional interests and the different public spheres in which each operated. The writer saw Franzen as taking a stand against the misrepresentations artists suffer in the media. The critic denounced Franzen as a 'literary snob', claiming that his discomfort came from the novel's own ambivalent status as part literary fiction and part family saga. His objection, the critic claimed, was a hypocritical one: to an association with the middle-brow (and mid-West, Winfrey's show is recorded in Chicago) audience the novel had successfully courted. In the piece Franzen wrote for the *Guardian*, he expressed his unhappiness with having been filmed in his home town and related how he asked to be filmed in New York: where his status as metropolitan sophisticate might be more obvious. Of course, you are getting the critic's side of the story here; but my partiality is part of the point. The effect of such disagreements in the classroom was always productive. In fact, students seemed to enjoy it so much when the tutors crossed swords that such debates started to become a partially staged feature of the seminars. In this case, the debate led to a discussion about the relationships between literary and popular fiction and the author and the media to which everyone contributed.

In another discussion, this time of J. M. Coetzee's *Elizabeth Costello*, the tutors lined up together in defence of an experimental novel, written by a writer who is also an academic critic. The majority of the students disliked the book, some claiming that it wasn't a novel at all. In some ways, such situations were trickier than disagreement between the tutors, who had to be careful not to use their authority as teachers (for example, 'we are right and you are wrong') rather than critical argument to make their points. But the discussions about what a novel is and the importance of academic knowledge, for example Coetzee's relationship to Franz Kafka, were again very fruitful.

Essays tended to be most successful when they brought a degree of critical analysis to a topic that had already provoked debate. In order to enable students to achieve the necessary level of analysis, proper guidance and support has to be given about what is meant by academic rigour and the technicalities of referencing and bibliographies. As stated above, the early experiment with an anthology of cultural theory had been only partially successful. Supplementing the anthology with critical essays that were discussed in class gave an opportunity to look closely at argument and evidence. Style, referencing and bibliographies, often difficult to teach in an interesting way, could be made relevant to creative writing students in the context of teaching different modes of literary editing. It is essential to provide supporting materials on the basic requirements. Examples can be found in most undergraduate course handbooks in English Literature or on the websites for academic journals and publishers.[1]

In conclusion, the relationship between writing and criticism can be constructive. There are tensions, naturally, but these should be productive. The key to the successful critical essay on a creative writing course is that its role is clear in relation to the overall aim of the course: that is, teaching writers to write. If criticism is understood in relation to the role of feedback and commentary in the classroom and in the context of the kinds of responses a writer is likely to get from publishers, agents and editor, the critical essay will be accepted and welcomed by students. But the benefits of discussing literature in an academic context can and should be broader than that. Opening up areas of literary history, introducing ways of reading and points of debate unknown to students can generate dividends in their creative work. Once again it is the institutional and pedagogic contexts that are all important. Only where dialogues between writers and critics are facilitated by modules, courses and institutional structures will a dialogue between writing and criticism be successfully achieved.

Notes

1. See for example that for English Literature at Keele University: www.keele.ac.uk/depts/en/STUDHBK.2056.doc; or there is a useful style sheet given by the journal *new formations*: www.newformations.co.uk; see also the Manchester University Press website: www.manchesteruniversitypress.co.uk/information_areas/authors/guidelines.htm

References

Franzen, Jonathan (2002), 'Ducking Out', *Guardian*, Saturday, 6 March, http://books.guardian.co.uk/departments/generalfiction/story/0,,667209,00.html

37

Translation

Susan Bassnett

Translating and writing

The relationship between translation and creative writing is a vexed one: many writers translate, though often their translations have received less critical attention than the rest of their work, since translation does not enjoy the same status as what is termed creative writing, particularly in the English-speaking world. Translation is often despised as some kind of secondary activity. Robert Frost announced that poetry was what got lost in translation, while Nabokov, in his 'On Translating Eugene Onegin' wrote:

> What is translation? On a platter
> A poet's pale and glaring head,
> A parrot's screech, a monkey's chatter,
> And profanation of the dead.
> (Pushkin 1991: 1)

Nabokov's cynical view of translation as an act that involves the destruction of the author by lesser talents is a powerful one, but more helpful for writers is the view expressed by Octavio Paz who, like Nabokov, knew several languages and also understood the implications of translating. In a famous essay on translation, Paz argues that translation is inevitable and important, for it is through translation that we can come to know more about the world we inhabit and understand more about the discourses we employ:

> Thanks to translation, we become aware that our neighbours do not speak and think as we do. One the one hand, the world is presented to us as a collection of similarities; on the other as a growing heap of texts, each slightly different from the one that came before it: translations of translations of translations. Each text is unique, yet at the same time it is the translation of another text. (Paz, in Schulte and Biguenet 1992: 154)

In the medieval world, the importance of translation as a means of training individuals to write well was fully recognised. Translation and imitation were cornerstones in the teaching of medieval rhetoric, and students undertook translation as a way of engaging with the language and thought of other writers. Cicero had recognised the importance of translation as a key to greater understanding of texts produced in different cultures and simultaneously as a means of expanding one's own literary vocabulary. For centuries, translation played an important part in the education system of Europe, starting to decline only after the advent of printing and the emergence of the idea that originality, however defined, should be seen as more important than a literary activity that involved transposing work produced by other writers. With the advent of copyright, the status of translation declined still further, and today we have the uncomfortable situation whereby often the name of a translator is given far less prominence (at times omitted altogether) than the name of an original author. The irony is, of course, that without translators, texts written in languages of which readers have no knowledge would remain unknown and unread.

The emergence of the field of study known as Translation Studies in the late twentieth century has led to a reconsideration of the importance of translation. It is now increasingly acknowledged that translation is a means of ensuring the survival of a text, and as Walter Benjamin pointed out, it is a way of regenerating writing from earlier times that would otherwise cease to exist (Benjamin, in Schulte and Biguenet 1992). The fact that so many contemporary writers draw upon the work of ancient Greek poets and playwrights, for example, is due to the skill of translators who have consistently engaged with their works, despite a decline in knowledge of classical languages that has become universal. Highlighting the role of translation in preserving the best of ancient writing changes perception of translations as a secondary, lesser literary activity.

Translation and power relations

Translation has also come to be reassessed from a post-colonial perspective. Much of the older discussion of translation concentrated on the issue of loss: translation, it was held, involved the loss or destruction of important elements of the source text, and the end product was an enfeebled piece of writing. Another way of looking at translation, however, involves challenging the view that the task of the translator is to try and reproduce exactly what the original author wrote and recognising the creativity of the translator. The Brazilian poet and critic, Haroldo de Campos, formulated a theory of translation that involved the 'cannibalisation' of the original, whereby the translator in the New World could feel sufficiently empowered to devour the source:

> Any past which is an 'other' for us deserves to be negated. We could say that it deserves to be eaten, devoured . . . the cannibal . . . devoured only the enemies he considered strong, to take from them the marrow and protein to fortify and renew his own natural energies. (De Campos, in Vieira 1999: 103)

De Campos' theory of translation is transgressive, in that it pays no heed to the status of the original and consciously rejects any idea of trying to reproduce something written by somebody else. What he proposes is a translation strategy that will absorb those elements of the original that are deemed important and necessary, and render them in a new, exciting way for a completely new readership. The power exerted by the original is subverted, and the translator is seen as a creative writer in his or her own right.

The question of power relations is fundamental to any thinking about translation. Unlike other forms of writing, the translator already has a text when he or she starts the process of translating and has to negotiate with that pre-existing work. The negotiations that the translator has to engage in vary considerably. At different points in time, the relationship between the translator and that original text has been viewed in very different ways: at one extreme, the translator has been seen as the servant of the original, whose role is faithfully to follow its content and structure, while at the other extreme, the translator has been seen as a kind of thief, stealing someone else's text and appropriating it. These different attitudes have led to different strategies on the part of translators, with some keeping close to the source and others moving a long way away from it. Some translators have advocated the deliberate use of foreignisms in a translation, so as to signal to readers that the text belongs to another culture, while others have sought to create a text that carries no trace of otherness at all. The old dichotomy that has existed since Roman times between word-for-word and sense-for-sense translation is still in evidence today, even though the prevailing trend in the English-speaking world is for translations to read like original works.

Reading and writing

What distinguishes translation from other forms of writing is that the translator first has to read a text written in another language. That reading gives the translator clues as to how then to proceed to transpose that text. On the most basic level, the translator has to understand what the text says, then take a series of decisions about what can and cannot be translated. Since no two languages are the same, it follows that no translation will ever be identical to the original. Moreover, since different cultures have different world-views, it follows also that such differences will also be encoded in language. The translator must decide not only what can be done on a linguistic level, but also the extent to which cultural differences can be translated.

The best way for any writing student to begin learning about translation would obviously be to learn another language so as to understand just how complex translation actually is. Since that is unlikely to be feasible, the next best thing to do is to look at several translations of the same piece of writing. It is a fact that just as no two readings are ever identical, because each reader brings a unique set of skills and experiences to his or her reading, so no two translations are ever identical. Besides, translations give a very clear way of understanding prevailing literary norms, so comparing translations has both an historical and a stylistic dimension. One of the most useful books to read is by the poet and translator Eliot Weinberger and Octavio Paz, entitled *Nineteen Ways of Looking at Wang Wei*. Starting with the statement of principle 'Poetry is that which is worth translating', Weinberger and Paz have assembled nineteen variations of a single four-line poem by the eighth-century Chinese master poet, Wang Wei (Weinberger and Paz 1987: 1). Each variation is laid out on a single page, and the editors comment on each one on the facing page, showing what the translators have done, questioning the success of each version and pointing to the discrepancies and variations. The book is an important resource, not only for anyone with a specialist interest in Chinese poetry but for anyone wanting to understand more about why translations differ so much from one another.

Ancient or modern?

One crucial decision that a translator has to take is whether to bring a text from the past into the contemporary world, or whether to try and take the contemporary reader backwards in time. Ezra Pound summed up the issue when he asserted: 'The devil of translating medieval poetry into English is that it is very hard to decide HOW you are to render work done with one set of criteria in a language NOW subject to different criteria' (Pound 1954:

203). In the nineteenth century, translators favoured historical reconstruction, so that archaising was a favoured device, and translators of ancient or medieval texts used a form of Olde English, with 'thee' and 'thou' and 'prithee' and similar turns of phrase. Today, this kind of writing is unacceptable: poet-translators like Tony Harrison, Ted Hughes and Josephine Balmer use modern English, often in colloquial or dialect forms.

Edwin Morgan, the Scottish poet, often translates into Scots. Some of his versions of the poetry of Vladimir Mayakowsky, for example, use down-to-earth colloquial Glaswegian, as in these opening lines of 'War declarit':

> 'Eenin pa-pur! Eeenin pa-pur! Eenin pa-pur!
> Ger-many! Au-stria ! It-aly'
> And a burn o purpy bluid cam wor-
> ryin through the squerr, aa black-bordit and drubbly.
> (Morgan 1996: 112)

Morgan explains that in his view Scottish literature has a line of fantastical satire that comes closer to accommodating Mayakowsky's black Russian humour than anything in English verse. What he has done is to read Mayakowsky carefully and find an equivalent register, drawing upon two literary traditions, the English and the Scots and opting for the one he feels is closest in mood and tone to the Russian. Similarly, translating the *Oresteia* for the National Theatre, Tony Harrison deliberately used Northern variants of English and when challenged explained his decision: 'One critic wrote that the chorus sounded like fifteen Arthur Scargills! I make no apologies. There's no earthly reason why a Greek chorus should sound like well-bred ladies from Cheltenham' (Harrison 1991: 437).

Harrison is here challenging accepted conventions of linguistic and social register. Ancient Greek texts were traditionally rendered into Standard English and usually performed by well-trained actors using Received Pronunciation to highlight the status of the work. Harrison argues that a proper equivalent is to be found in the living language of regional speakers, not in a restricted more elitist language that has no roots in the community.

Finding a suitable equivalent is the principle task of the translator. E.V. Rieu, who translated Homer's *Iliad* and *Odyssey* for the Penguin classics series in the 1940s, proposed the radical view that ancient Greek verse should be transposed into English prose, since the contemporary equivalent of the epic poem was the novel. His flat prose versions probably introduced more readers to Homer than any other English translations, but the result is that Homer's epics are no longer read as poetry, but simply as stories. The shift from poetry to prose changes the emphasis. On the other hand, the inability of translators to render Icelandic sagas into a readable English form means that these great epic texts are still relatively unknown in English. No Icelandic translator had the courage to emulate Rieu and address the challenge of translating a genre that has ceased to exist in any meaningful way.

Poetic form and freedom

What is instantly striking about any comparison of translations of the same text are the formal variations. To an extent, these variations reflect the taste of a particular age: when rhyme was in vogue, translators tended to produce rhymed translations, adapting the text to the predominant rhyme scheme of the day. So French alexandrines have often been rendered into English in rhyming couplets, while Germanic epics have been transposed into blank verse. Occasionally, as with the Petrarchan sonnet, a verse form has been successfully translated and then adapted in the new context. The traditional Petrarchan sonnet was divided into two sections, one of eight lines, often subdivided into two stanzas and one of six, again often subdivided into two sets of three lines. In English, though the basic fourteen line pattern is retained, there was a shift to three sets of four line units followed by a final couplet, which is the basis of the Shakespearean sonnet. What this formal variation does is to focus attention on that final couplet, which then becomes the culmination of the whole poem. Shakespeare's ironic endings were made possible by a simple metrical variation to the basic Italian form. Later, when *ottava rima* was introduced into English through translation, it was taken and developed by Byron in his *Don Juan* into a supremely comic verse form.

Translation can be a source of revitalisation of a literature through the introduction of new ideas and of new forms and genres. A classic example of this in English literature is Ezra Pound's *Cathay*, which came out in 1915. Pound had worked with literal translations of Chinese poetry to produce his own versions, but the combination of subject matter and startlingly innovative imagery effectively created a new genre of English–Chinese poetry, so powerful that it dominated twentieth-century translation from that language. Moreover, the timing of the publication of *Cathay* meant that readers were approaching the poems from the perspective of a society gripped by the horrors of the First World War. The sense of loss and despair in many of the poems found a resonance in wartime England, and it is now generally felt that Pound's translations not only affected subsequent attempts to transpose Chinese poetry into English, but also influenced the work of the emerging war-poets. Imagism came into English literature through translation.

Letting in light

In the translators' preface to the 1611 version of the King James Bible, the translators use a string of powerful images to describe their work:

> Translation it is that openeth the window, to let in the light; that breaketh the shell, that we may eat the kernel; that putteth aside the curtaine, that we may look in to the most Holy place; that remooveth the cover of the well, that we may come by the water. (A. V. Bible Preface 6.8)

These images stress the hermeneutic dimension of translation: as the meaning of a text written in another language is revealed, so readers are enabled to see that which has previously been hidden from them. The issue, of course, which was particularly felt by Bible translators, who could face the death penalty for heretical interpretation of a sacred text, is that what is revealed is not an absolute truth but rather the interpretation of the person who has undertaken the translation. William Tyndale, who was savagely attacked for misinterpreting the Scriptures by Sir Thomas More, was one of the great Bible translators of the English Reformation, but was executed for heresy in 1536.

Translation always involves a first stage of reading and in consequence involves interpretation before the process of rewriting can take place. Ezra Pound has an enigmatic but interesting piece of advice for writers. He argues that it is useful for writers to try and write good prose, adding, 'Translation is likewise good training, if you find that your original matter "wobbles" when you try to rewrite it. The meaning of the poem to be translated can not "wobble"' (Pound 1954: 7).

What Pound means by 'wobbling' is a failure to understand fully what is going on in a piece of writing. Mistranslation occurs when a translator fails to understand the linguistic content of a text and simply does not understand what the words are doing; what Pound is getting at here is what happens when the translator is not quite sure what is going on in a text, despite having apparently understood what the words signify. This can be as straight-forward as failing to grasp the foregrounding system in a poem. Often translators will reproduce the punctuation system and patterns of foregrounding of the original, without reflecting on whether they work in English. Usually, they do not work, or certainly not in the same way, because word order differs between languages and there are different conventions of beginning and ending lines. One good way to test this is to take a translated text and change the word order, experimenting with different ways of rewriting it to explore different results. A good translation will often be resistant to such experiments, while a weaker translation may well be improved.

Co-translation is an interesting way of working. When Ted Hughes translated the poetry of Janos Pilinszky, he worked with a Hungarian native speaker, János Csokits. What came out of this collaboration was Csokits' recognition that while he produced versions in good basic English, Hughes would then work to deconstruct them, opting for a process of defamiliarisation. When I worked with Piotr Kuhiwczak on an anthology of Polish women poets, I discovered that we were working in a similar way: he would bring me versions in standard English, which I would then play around with, trying to remove the smoothness of his sentences. I was helped in this by going back to the originals. Despite not being able to understand much in them, what could clearly be seen were patterns of repetition, clusters of words and sounds, occasional rhymes, all of which were missing from the literal transla-tions. For a writer to work with a native speaker from another culture is very rewarding: you start to discover the other text and at the same time are forced to think strategically about how best to bring your discoveries to your readers.

What is a good translation?

The acid test of translation quality is whether the version works for a new set of readers or whether they have difficulty appreciating it. This is not primarily a question of understand-ing, rather it is a question of adequacy on the part of the translator as writer. A translator can be an excellent, clear-minded reader and know everything about the original but then fail in rendering the text into his or her own language because of inadequacies as a writer. Sometimes this is due to a desire on the translator's part to try and ensure that as much as possible is included in the translation. So, for example, where there are words or ideas that simply do not exist outside the source culture, the translator may feel that he or she has to add an explanatory phrase or two to make the meaning clearer. This can work, of course, but more often it tends to disrupt the flow of the text and ultimately it is patronising to readers. Significantly, many writers from Africa or India who use English as their medium include in their works words and phrases from other languages that are not glossed or explained, a deliberate strategy to remind readers that there is a universe of discourse beyond the familiar.

Some translators make radical cuts. Ted Hughes did this in his version of Seneca's *Oedipus*, for example, and in his award-winning *Tales from Ovid*. The thinking behind this strategy is that not everything can be rendered adequately into another language, and therefore it is the responsibility of the translator to ensure that what is translated will work as well as the original for the new readers.

Translation always involves a balancing act. In the figurative language that translators use to describe what they actually do, predominant metaphors return again and again to ideas of inbetweenness, to no-man's-land, to bridging between cultures, to juggling plates.

The translator is reader, editor and (re)writer, someone with a dual responsibility, both to the original author and original culture and to a new group of readers who are dependent on translation if they have no knowledge of another language. For these reasons, translation has been seen as a significant instrument in the training of writers, and as a way for many writers to expand the parameters of their own work.

The power that translations can exert within a literature should not be forgotten either. Edward Fitzgerald's *The Rubáiyát of Omar Khayyam* came to acquire such a significant place in the English literary canon that it has remained the pre-eminent translation, despite evidence that shows that it seriously mistranslated the original Persian and an attempt by Robert Graves to produce a new version that rectified Fitzgerald's errors. Keats' sonnet 'On First Looking into Chapman's Homer' is the most explicit statement about the impact that a good translation can have. Keats acknowledges that he already had some acquaintance with Homer, 'yet never did I breathe its pure serene/Till I heard Chapman speak out loud and bold'. In the last six lines of the sonnet, he compares his feelings of discovery with those of an astronomer seeing a new planet for the first time, or those of Cortez when he first looked out over the Pacific Ocean. Translation is a complex, multi-layered literary activity that has not received the critical attention it deserves, but it is the means whereby readers can move beyond the confines of their own language and literature and encounter other worlds.

References and suggested further reading

A. V. Bible Preface: www.jesus-is-lord.com/pref1611.htm (accessed 23 July 2006).

Bassnett, Susan (2002), *Translation Studies*, 3rd edn, London: Routledge.

Bassnett, Susan (2002), *Exchanging Lives. Poems and Translations*, Leeds: Peepal Tree.

Bassnett, Susan and Piotr Kuhiwczak (trans.) (1986), *Ariadne's Thread. Polish Women Poets*, London: Forrest Books.

Benjamin, Walter (1992), 'The task of the translator', trans. Harry Zohn, in Rainer Schulte and John Biguenet (eds), *Theories of Translation. An Anthology of Essays from Dryden to Derrida*, pp. 71–82 Chicago: University of Chicago Press.

De Campos, Haroldo (1999), cited in Else Ribeiro Pires Vieira, 'Liberating Calibans: readings of *Antropofagia* and Haroldo de Campos' poetics of transcreation', Susan Bassnett and Harish Trivedi (eds), *Post-Colonial Translation. Theory and Practice*, pp. 95–114, London: Routledge.

Fitzgerald, Edward (trans.) (1997), *The Rubáiyát of Omar Khayyam*, Ware: Wordsworth.

Harrison, Tony (1991), 'Facing up to the Muses' in Neil Astley (ed.), *Tony Harrison*, pp. 429–54, Newcastle: Bloodaxe.

Hughes, Ted (1976), *Selected Poems of Janos Pilinszky*, Manchester: Carcanet.

Keats, John (1995), 'On first looking into Chapman's Homer' in *Romanticism, An Anthology*, Duncan Wu (ed.), Oxford: Blackwell.

Morgan, Edwin (1996), *Collected Translations*, Manchester: Carcanet.

Paz, Octavio (1992), 'Translation: literature and letters', trans. Irene del Corral, in Rainer Schulte and John Biguenet (eds), *Theories of Translation. An Anthology of Essays from Dryden to Derrida*, pp. 152–62, Chicago: University of Chicago Press.

Pound, Ezra (1954), *Literary Essays of Ezra Pound, Edited with an Introduction by T. S. Eliot*, London: Faber.

Pushkin, Aleksandr (1991), *Eugene Onegin: A Novel in Verse*, trans. Vladimir Nabokov, Princeton: Princeton University Press.

Weinberger, Eliot and Octavio Paz (1987), *Nineteen Ways of Looking at Wang Wei. How a Chinese Poem is Translated*, Mt Kisco, New York: Moyer Bell.

38

Collaboration in the Theatre

Timothy Braun

Art takes a team of people to find problems, but not to solve them. If this makes complete and total sense to you, then you might want to move on to the next chapter in this book. Art, to me, is nothing more than finding problems, discussing these problems, exploring these problems, and doing these things over and over again until it is time for a sandwiches. Just look at the history of the arts, specifically theatre. It is important to think about and analyse the past to know where we have been. (I was once working with a young playwright in Ireland who insisted he didn't want to read Samuel Beckett because he didn't want know about the past as he was all about creating the future – which would be a noble idea if it wasn't shockingly stupid.)

Exercise
Make a list of problems you want to explore, problems you want to find on and in the stage. Have strong ideas on what you want to do before you start writing plays.

Everything I learned in school about succeeding in theatre, and as an artist, is worthless, and I couldn't be happier about that. I started doing theatre in the early 1990s. That was a very different time. There was the Internet, but it wasn't widespread and it was a rather slow beast. Only rich people had cellphones, and those cellphones were the size of bricks. At that time we would publicise performances by using sidewalk chalk and hammering posters to telephone poles. I have not had a poster, a physical paper poster, made for a show in at least five years. In that time everything was clean, clear, simple and straightforward on how to develop a show. However, we need to unlearn those muscles and look for problems to discuss. The way I would approach building a play today is a problem that I would not approach the same way years ago. If I were to adapt *The Seagull* today, I would be facing different problems to find from those I would have had last year. This is part of the idea of finding problems.

Exercise
Look at Anton Chekhov's *The Seagull* and make a list of problems you believe he explored. What are problems that he negotiated and brought to the story? There are so many problems he faced with that play. Why do you think this is? Why did he do so? See if you can 'negotiate' these questions from only the *text* of the play.

The basics that we understand in Western storytelling, and not just in theatre, are all laid out for you by the Greeks. They loved finding problems. The Greeks were experts in this. Most of the stuff we know and understand is centred on their ideas, and the term 'centred' is important. It doesn't matter how much spectacle a show has – with no core story, with no core idea, without characters the audience can follow for more than a few minutes, you will have a problem, and not the good kind. In any kind of collaboration, you need to be sure of your own art and what you want to achieve. In the theatre, when preparing a play and collaborating and negotiating, you need to be sure yourself of the basic elements of your play. Without knowing your story (can you sum up what this whole thing is about in one sentence?), plot (how does this story break down moment by moment?) and character (who are we following, and why are we following them?), you will struggle to retain your voice (and see later in this chapter for 'voice').

Let us establish a few ground rules: there is no such thing as original art, or, for these purposes, original theatre. None of the classical Greek plays was original. They were all based on earlier plays and myths. None of William Shakespeare's plays was original. They are all taken from earlier works. *As You Like It* is taken from a novel by Thomas Lodge. Chunks of *Antony and Cleopatra* are taken from a contemporary translation of Plutarch's *Lives*. Bertolt Brecht's *Caucasian Chalk Circle* is taken from a play by Klabund, of which Brecht served as dramaturg in 1926; and Klabund had taken his play from an early Chinese play. All of the aforementioned artists were looking to find problems, storytelling problems, and looking to find the most appropriate method to translate these problems in their 'modern age'.

Sometimes artists steal stories, ideas, images, even conversations from their friends and family and call this original. Sometimes some of us write about our own innermost lives, believing that, then, we have written something truly original and unique. But, of course, the culture writes us first and then we write our stories. I write a lot about my dog, who is currently sitting on my foot. When we look at a painting of soup cans by Andy Warhol, we recognise that it is a product of its time and place. We see that it has been derived from, and written by, the culture that produced it. So, whether we mean to or not, the work we do is both received and created, both an adaptation and an original, at the same time. Not much of what I just wrote is original. I paraphrased some of this from conversations I have had with my friend, playwright Chuck Mee, at The Flea Theater, New York City, in June 2005.

It is fun to say 'there are no rules', but there kind of, sort of, are rules: story, plot and character

In many cases, especially in the United States, we have placed theatre in the context of 'jobs', categories, and subcategories. This can be helpful, to a degree – without sub-designation we can get lost in exactly why we are in the room, and what portion of artistic problem solving we are expected to do. We get confused and encounter a great deal of miscommunication when we do not have a solid idea of what we are doing. In the United States, I am a playwright, I am the guy who is responsible for the words that come out of the actor's mouths. Without a solid story in place before I begin, I could find myself in trouble.

Story

Can you sum up the 'story' you are attempting to tell in one sentence? This might sound small, but it is important. When dealing with the various aspects of theatre you are looking at the context of *horizontalism*, meaning many different elements and collaborators coming together to work on a project. *Hamlet* is a very complicated and well-written play that has been dissected over the years. Is the title character crazy or sane? What about his relationship with his mother? I have yet to even mention the other characters. However, the story of that play is this:

> *Gloomy Dane seeks revenge for his father's death.*

If I'm pulling together a team of artists to build an interpretation of *Hamlet*, I think that sentence is what I share with everyone. Regardless of what direction we go with, style, or tone, we have a sounding board to return to on a consistent basis. A few other aspects of story to help you along:

- You need to keep in mind what's interesting to you as an audience member, not what's fun to do as a writer. Those can be very different things.
- Simplify the story, and allow the details of the characters to grow from there.
- Try this as an exercise: Once upon a time there was ___. Every day, ___. One day, ___. Because of that, ___. Because of that, ___. Until finally, ___.
- When you do this exercise, discount the first thing that comes to mind. And the second, third, fourth, and fifth thing as well. Get the obvious out of the way.
- Now, to help understand the aspects of 'story', pull apart the stories you like. What you like in them is a part of you; you've got to recognise it before you can use it. This leads to . . .

Plot

Dinosaur Bones. Think about a dinosaur for a moment. What does it look like, what does it sound like, and how do you know you are right in this? Chances are, you aren't perfect in your idea of what a dinosaur looks like. We have some idea, some representation, by looking at dinosaur bones. Take the Tyrannosaurus Rex. This animal was more than likely a gigantic hunting machine. How do we know? How do we know the creature was not a scavenger? Well, the monster had tiny hands and huge legs. Thus, with our basic knowledge of the circulatory system we know that the heart has to pump blood all over an animal's body, and if it had small hands more blood could be used towards the legs, the 'chasing' portion of the creature. Now I could go on and on about this, but what does the T-Rex look like? What colour was it? Was it covered in scales or feathers? To the best of my knowledge no one is 100% certain on this. However, with bones we can get very good ideas of what dinosaurs looked like. We can also do this with plays. Try this exercise:

Fill in the blanks:
1. This is a story about ___.
2. It begins when ___ does ___.
3. ___ wants ___.
4. It ends when ___ . . . *well* . . .___.

This is similar to an exercise I showed you in the 'story' section of this chapter. However, this time I want you to write these questions and 'blanks' at the top of four different sheets of paper. Now, can you fill the pieces of paper with the 'plots', the structure, the moment-by-moment happenings of these famous plays?

> *Oedipus Rex*
> *Hamlet*
> *Three Sisters*
> *Waiting For Godot*

The key to this is to do these four plays only by *memory*: do not look at the actual scripts or wiki pages, write only from what you recall by memory. The important matters of these plays from *your perspective* will rise to the top. I did this with *Hamlet* once and I left out the gravedigger scene when I constructed the plot from memory. Odd, right? Maybe one of the most memorable scenes in all of world theatre and I had forgotten about it. In fairness, the scene just doesn't resonate with me in my context of how I see the Hamlet story: *Gloomy Dane seeks revenge for his father's death*. This is how you are able to build from 'story' to 'plot'; or another way to think of it is a roadmap for the piece. If you are driving from Paris to Berlin there are many different winding roads you can take, and several towns and villages to visit. Which ones are important to you? You might skip over a town like Cologne (which would be a shame, because Cologne is lovely) but this is the way you have decided to construct, or interrupt, the journey. This is another way of finding problems, and this is the difference between *your* way of telling the story, and another artist's. Now, try the 'plot' exercise with these plays:

Richard Foreman's *King Cowboy Rufus Rules the Universe!*
Sarah Kane's *4.48 Psychosis*
Mark Ravenhill's *Mother Clap's Molly House*

Now, when doing this with your own work, try to keep a few of these ideas in mind:

- When you're stuck, make a list of what would not happen next. This might help in making the piece as problematic as you can, and that is drama.
- Trying for theme is important, but you won't see what the story is about until you're at the end of it. That stuff on paper four? Perhaps you should 'start' your project there. Come up with your ending before you figure out your middle. Endings are hard, get yours working, and it will inform you on what happens in the middle.
- What are the stakes? Give us reasons to root for the character. What happens if they don't succeed? Stack the odds against.
- Coincidences to get characters into trouble are great; coincidences to get them out of it are cheating.
- Now rewrite everything you just did from memory.

Character

I have no good advice on characters, and I have seen and heard little to provide help in this area. Here are some ideas for you:

- No one thinks they are the bad guy, and the best bad guys don't know they are villains. The best villains think they are right, or at least justified in their behaviour. Iago does bad things in *Othello*, but he believes he has earned the right to behave the way he does because of the way his father has treated him.

- You admire a character for trying more than for their successes. Many great characters fall short, but they tried.
- What is your character good at, or comfortable with? Throw the opposite at them. Challenge them. How do they deal? In that respect, what are you good at, comfortable with, and what is the opposite and why? If you can relate to your characters, even in the most esoteric ways, it can help as you write.
- Give your characters opinions. Passive and malleable might seem likeable to you as you write, but it's poison to the audience. Think about what is dramatic.
- If you were your character, in this situation, how would you feel? Honesty lends credibility to unbelievable situations.

Thoughts on collaboration: there is only one rule.

For some reason, and I have no idea as to why, most people discuss collaboration in the theatre using personal stories, most of them revolving around something the author had learned about themselves and the arts. As far as my research has taken me, there are no good statistics, or even raw data, on collaborations. So I will suggest that if collaboration is something you are deeply interested in, find the books by Anne Bogart – specifically the section known as 'Collaboration' in *Viewpoints* – and if you are not interested in collaborating you might want to abandon the performing arts altogether. At some point in the context of being a creative writer for the stage, you will need to 'give up' your works to others.

As I have researched collaborations it appears most people have some positive story, that might involve a struggle in the middle of said story, and then everyone gets along at the end. I am afraid I don't have any of those stories for you, but I would like to discuss my latest collaboration and how it went terribly wrong. Without any statistics, or even reasonability in writing this, I'll just guess that most collaborations I have come across have not gone as well as they could have, and I might even say that around one in ten collaborations do not go the way people want them to. But in theatre you will need to collaborate, you will need to give up something of your work, a give-and-take with actors and designers and directors, otherwise why don't you just write a blog?

In the past year I was asked to adapt *Three Sisters* by a young theatre director and producer. He had taken note that I adapt classic work and apply modern context to the story (what would the sisters do in the age of social media and how would it fill their longing?) and I agreed to create a new play, a new adaptation from scratch for him. Unfortunately the communication became extremely poor. From my perspective it appeared as though this guy didn't really know what he wanted, or how to approach the script. He would ask for multimedia, then cut that and ask for a dance scene, then cut that, and so on, and so on, and so on. We would often clash and when we tried to have discussions about art and vision for the project he felt slighted and would respond by telling me that he felt as though he didn't need to show me his resumé. This young director I write of lacked confidence, but he had a tremendous ego. Behind his back, I began to have meetings with actors he had worked with in the past, to see if I could find a way to communicate better with him. Every single actor I spoke with said 'he doesn't know what he wants' and 'he only cares about what his name looks like on the poster, what his biography looks like in the programme'. As I listened to people talk about this director it hit me: he was approaching me as a person with all these answers to questions he didn't know how to ask.

A playwright is not better than anyone else on the team. We do not have all the answers. We are just another form of life, like the person who is sitting next us in rehearsal is another form of life. We are not perfect, we are people, people who usually live inside their own heads, and often to one side of those heads. Now look at those quotes in the last paragraph again. How often can you attribute them to yourself? How often do we know what we want to get out of collaboration? How often do we really know what we 'want' from our experience? The director I worked with on this project was arguably one of the worst directors I have ever worked with, but he is a nice guy and he is concerned about what his name looks like on the poster and in the programme because he wants the world to know that he was here. I think we all want that. Perhaps if we had a better understanding as to why we wanted to do theatre from the start, we would have had a better show. When the time was right I gave the director my resumé and he wrote the 100-word biography of mine for the programme, and I will tell you it was the best biography I have ever had.

I could have told you just about any story on collaboration; this is just one of many that went in a similar way, and I selected this one because it is still fresh in my mind. If I could do it all over again with this director I would have done what I will suggest to you right now. Ask each person, from actors, to designers, to directors, to make a list of ten things they wish to achieve with this collaboration. Share them openly, take all the similar things and make a word cloud with them. Do this in the first rehearsal and get everyone on the same page as quickly as you can. What do you all have in common, what can we understand about each other? Find these things and build off that. Then, take your original list of ten things you want and privately circle one thing that you refuse to compromise on. Collaboration is a matter of give and take, but I made a mistake when I worked with that young director. I forgot not to compromise on that one thing – I did, and in the end I invited not a single person to the play. I spent a year of my life working on that script, and in surrendering everything I had nothing left to call my own.

There are many rules to collaboration. You need to listen to each other, be kind to each other, give and take with one another. But you can read that elsewhere. The only rule of collaboration I want you to know is to not surrender yourself, or you may not invite people to see that 100-word biography of yours in the programme.

A few concepts to 'negotiate' with

Putting it on paper (not a computer) lets you start fixing it. A computer gives you the illusion that it is perfect. Your work is not. It needs to be fixed. And, regardless of this idea, if it stays in your head, a perfect idea, you will never share it with anyone. Take a movie you dislike. How would you rearrange it into what you do like? Staying with the dinosaur theme, *Jurassic Park III* is a movie I hate, because it had so much potential but was not good. The 'story' was there, but 'plot' failed, and the 'characters' suffered because of this. The three aspects don't work separately, they inform each other of themselves. Take a movie, or a play you see potential in, and re-write. As you do so, always ask 'why' before you make an edit to the original.

As I write this chapter, I am working on a multimedia adaptation of Chekhov's *Three Sisters* at The Off-Center in Austin, Texas. During downtime with the actors, we joked about what if Chekhov were writing today. Would he have written *Fight Club*, and what would be the rules? We came up with this: 1st rule of Chekhov's Fight Club – every element in a narrative is to be necessary and irreplaceable, everything else to be removed; 2nd Rule of Chekhov's fight Club – every element in a narrative is to be necessary and irreplaceable, everything else to be removed!

Conclusion: your voice, collaboration, get a dog

I never expected to find myself giving advice to people on being creative. I was a shockingly bad student and have no idea why you would sit through this chapter, a chapter I originally called 'The Rules', when I simply don't believe in many rules. How silly, because if you don't know it's impossible, if you don't know these 'rules', writing is easier to do, art is easier to do – so don't let those rules bring you down. Just because nobody has done it before, they haven't made up rules to stop anyone doing that again, yet. When you start off, you have to deal with the problems of failure. You need to be thick-skinned, to learn that not every project will last, and you learn what works for you and what does not. Everyone should do a little failing. Every now and again, I forget that rule.

Exercise
Make a list of the things you HATE, things you HATE to see on stage, and write a ten-minute play based on that. Produce this ten-minute play in one week, get anyone you can to help you, invite everyone you know to 'The Worst Ten-Minute Play Ever Written', buy them pizza and drinks, and talk about it afterwards. Find out what you 'hate' and when you find out what you hate, then ask yourself 'why?' Why do you hate this, why does it make you feel a certain way, and learn from it?

Make mistakes. If you're making mistakes, it means you're out there doing something, and doing it with guts. You can't teach guts. The urge, starting out, is to copy, or as I have said in this chapter, 'to steal', but that can show a lack of guts, of courage. Most of us only find our own voices after we've sounded like a lot of other people. The one thing that you have that nobody else has is *you*. I call my voice, my style, American Baroque. I take a realistic world and stretch it as if it is in a funhouse mirror. I get this from reading classic texts, some of those texts I mentioned earlier, and mixing the themes and ideas with a great many modern cartoons.

Exercise
What is your style? Can you describe it in one hundred words or less?

The things I've done that worked the best were the things I was the least certain about, the stories where I was sure they would either work, or more likely be the kinds of embarrassing failures people would make fun of me about, for years to come. But I gain my courage, my confidence, my guts, and my voice by making my rules.

So, make up your own rules.

Shockingly random things that I just want you to know

Show and Tell. Most people say, 'Show, don't tell', but that is silly, because when writers put their work out into the world they are like kids bringing teddy bears, and Transformers and dolls into class in the hope that someone else will love them as much as they do. Your play is like your toy: show us and tell us about it. Why is it special to you? If it is not special to you, why should I spend my time with it?

Do not go searching for a subject; let your subject find you. You cannot rush inspiration. Whether it's an account of a serial killer, a jungle adventure or a colourful Russian family of sisters, you cannot force your subject. Sam Shepard used to try and write a really cool world, but never got the attention he has now until he wrote about his father. Once your subject finds you, it's like having an itch you can't scratch. Shepard keeps writing about his father. It will be your constant companion, whether you like it or not. When this happens, don't be afraid. You might have the play of a lifetime on your hands. Which leads into:

> Write what you know. All art is autobiographical. The pearl is the oyster's autobiography. How do you make art from your everyday happenings into a play? Listen to your heart. Ask your heart, 'Is it true to me?'
>
> Be concise. Ernest Hemingway once wrote a six-word story. 'Baby shoes. For sale. Never worn'. What more do you need to know? What more did he need to write? Nothing. This leads to: What isn't said is as important as what is said. In many classic plays the real action occurs in the subtext and the silence.

Exercise
Simply let this thought guide your every word: 'Something is wrong – can you guess what it is?' as you write dialogue.

Revise, revise, and revise. Writing is not writing. Writing is rewriting. This chapter, at one point in time, was 10,000 words long. It is now 5,000. Revision is when you do what you should have done the first time, but didn't. It's like washing the dishes two days later instead of right after you finish eating. Remove a comma, move a monologue, shake your play up.

There are no rules. Only a fool would tell you there are. If everyone jumped off a bridge, would you do it? There are no rules except the ones you learned during your school days. Have fun. Be nice. If someone doesn't want to be friends with you, they're not worth being friends with. Most of all just be yourself.

Exercise
Make your own rules. Then systematically break those rules. May I suggest 'Get a dog' be one of them? And may I suggest that be the only rule you don't break?

Get a dog. When you have a good day, when the writing goes well, and you get grants, and the reviews are good, the dog doesn't care. The dog wants to go outside, smell things, poop, play with you, lick you, eat some peanut butter, and snuggle in bed with you, because you are the dog's best friend. When you have a bad day, when you know the play you are writing is bad, is never gonna get produced, when you get rejection letters, or – my personal favourite in this economy – get a phone call from your granter informing that they can't give you the money you were awarded because times are tough, the dog doesn't care. The dog wants to go outside, smell things, poop, play with you, lick you, eat some peanut butter, and snuggle in bed with you, because you are the dog's best friend. A dog keeps you grounded.

Now go, and make mistakes, break your rules, break my rules, and put your voice out in to this world. Find your team of people, your team of problem finders and make this a more interesting place to be in. Make me want to tell my dog to get off my foot so I can leave the house, or dog park, and go see your play. I have read many books dealing with the construction of art, many of which have been nominally helpful and interesting, but none has provided a singular answer on 'what is art?', 'what is it for?', and 'how do we make this thing we call art?', and not a single one of them has ever said this: honesty always trumps clever. Be honest with your mistakes, your rule breaking and your art. You can't 'negotiate' honesty: it is a dog, sitting on your foot, begging for treats. Give them honesty and see what happens.

References

Beckett, Samuel (1965), *Waiting for Godot*, London: Faber.
Bogart, Anne (1995), *Viewpoints*, Portland, ME: Smith & Kraus.
Chekov, Anton (2002), *Plays*, London: Penguin.
Kane, Sarah (2000), *4.48 Psychosis*, London: Methuen.
Ravenhill, Mark (2001), *Mother Clap's Molly House*, London: Methuen.

39

Creative Writing Doctorates

Graeme Harper

Creative evolution

Doctorates in creative writing: dubious academic 'intrusion', or a legitimate higher education activity? It is fair to say this question has not yet been answered to everyone's satisfaction. There are those who believe that Doctoral work in creative writing is still worthy of a modicum of scepticism despite – or perhaps even 'because of' – a now well-established history of these degrees in Britain and Australia, a history twice as long in North America, and a developing history of them elsewhere.

To a large extent, such scepticism revolves around notions of how creative writing might best be taught, or even whether it can be taught. It draws occasionally on examples of successful creative writers who have had little to do with formal higher education. And it connects, in part, to often strongly-voiced concerns about such things as 'publishability' and 'talent', as well as to anxious commentaries about academe's relationship with creative endeavour; in this case, such an 'intrusion' is even said to be threatening to cause the 'institutionalisation of creative writing'.

How, then, to respond? Perhaps, simply, with this chapter itself. But it is also worth recording that even though such scepticism is relatively limited it does reflect a continued need among creative writers, and particularly among those who work in and around universities and colleges, to clarify aspects of the activity's history, practices and approaches. Creative writing has always existed in some form in and around universities and colleges. Its modes of investigating the world have been in tune with the concepts of higher learning that resulted in the formation of universities; and its open attitude to communication with other subjects found in universities has guaranteed the success of creative writing's long term partnership with higher education. That said, if general opinion equates much of academe with 'the intellectual', this would place creative writing at odds with it – at least using the description of the intellect coined by philosopher and Nobel Laureate Henri Bergson.

In *Creative Evolution* (1911), one of his most well-known books, Bergson talks about the intellect as starting 'from immobility, as if it were the ultimate reality' so that 'when it tries to form an idea of movement, it does so by constructing movement out of immobilities put together' (Bergson 1998: 155). In its attempt to analyse and classify the world, Bergson says, the intellect spatialises thought, creates discrete units and compartmentalises.

Because of this, the intellect ultimately is 'characterized by a natural inability to comprehend life' (165).

On the other hand, 'intelligence', as Bergson describes it, is connected with what he called 'intuition'. By intuition, Bergson means 'instinct that has become disinterested, self-conscious, capable of reflecting upon its object and of enlarging it indefinitely' (176). This is a definition well worth recalling when considering the responsive understanding that forms the basis of creative writing Doctoral study.

Intelligence, in Bergson's analysis, displays methods of engagement with the world that show sympathy with its actual events and structures. The modes of engagement of the intelligence are fluid and dynamic, and are said by Bergson to be better able than the intellect to approach a true sense of the physical and the metaphysical with which we associate life. Bergson's work relates this to an investigation of the nature of knowledge, as well as to his consideration of the true composition and constitution of time.

It is important, of course, to approach the terms used by Bergson with due regard to the manner in which he intended them; and yet, even casual reference to his analysis of 'consciousness', 'duration' (*durée*), 'memory', 'thought', 'illusion' and the order of nature give some indication of how his work might reflect on creative writing, its modes and methods, and its place within a community of Doctoral candidates.

Points of graduation

The English word 'graduate' comes from the Latin *gradus*, meaning 'step'. Not surprisingly, then, the naming of degrees – Bachelor, Master, Doctor – has today come to reflect different levels of achievement, even though initially the terms reflected more the subject of study, or the degree's country of origin, rather than a hierarchy. Today, the notion of the Bachelor's degree graduate as having taken one step toward recognised expertise in their subject is strong. The Master's degree represents the next step, and the Doctoral degree the final step.

Thus we strike one of the most complex notes in considering the nature and intention of Doctoral degrees in creative writing. If a Doctoral degree is the highest level of achievement – that is, if it represents the most 'steps' confirmed toward expertise – in what has the Doctoral graduate in creative writing achieved the highest university qualification, in what have they 'stepped furthest'?

The answer to this question is not as obvious as it might first appear. It is additionally complicated by important historical, and what might well be considered 'national', conditions.

In the UK, historically, the Masters degree in creative writing has had a high public profile. This is largely because of some initial publishing successes emerging from the early MA programmes of the 1970s. It relates also to the intentions behind the creation of those programmes, connected as they were to individual programme creator's/course director's ideas about 'what a creative writer needs'. The expansion of Masters (or M-level) programmes in the UK during the 1980s quite often had its origins in the idea of a creative writer 'taking time out of other things to work on his/her writing'. A creative writing Masters course would allow a writer of 'recognisable talent' – most likely one who had studied for a first degree, and most importantly one who could submit pieces of creative writing that would identify them as 'a writer of potential' – the time and good guidance to bring her or him to up to publishable or performable level.

And yet this comment is a little misleading because it suggests universality. If there is one thing that has pervaded the teaching of creative writing in UK universities it is that there has not been any identifiable standard-setting or 'benchmarking', as it is sometimes called in the UK, beyond that seen in the process of 'external examining' of courses by individual examiners, or that undertaken on a relatively irregular basis by organisations not directly, or solely, concerned with creative writing – for example: the English Subject Centre, the Council for Graduate Education and, most recently, the Arts and Humanities Research Council (AHRC) (www.english.heacademy.ac.uk; www.ukcge.ac.uk; www.ahrc.ac.uk).

In that way, early UK Masters courses in creative writing often emerged not from a sense of progression from Bachelor onwards to Doctor, but from a particular version of an 'artist-at-work' ideal, often built on entirely local and personal interpretations of what this might entail. This is far from a criticism, because it can be shown that within the university creative writing is far more person- and project- specific than a great many other subjects. In fact, creative writing tends to emphasise, particularly at Masters and Doctoral level, a close investigation and employment of individual human intentions and dispositions; and at least builds upon, if not exclusively, a very individual approach to emotions, behaviour patterns and personal acts. It is hardly surprising that the history of postgraduate work in creative writing has reflected this emphasis. This is the case whether in the UK, US or elsewhere.

History records that as Masters level work became more established in the UK, courses began to emerge with a different sense of purpose or result, and a different sense of their potential students. By the early 1990s, with several handfuls of Masters programmes operating, what M-level work in creative writing meant was similar, but potentially different, between a considerable range of institutions. The public face that had highlighted the earlier 'artist-at-work' ideal still existed, but the notion of a Masters degree in creative writing had taken on a number of other complexions, including that connected with 'creative-critical writing', 'English combined with creative practice', the 'teaching and learning of creative writing', 'creative writing in health care or in education', and any number of genre-specific sub-programmes. This largely determined where, and when, UK Doctoral programmes would emerge.

Historical and national differences

It could be said that the initial development of creative writing Doctoral degrees in the UK was made more and less possible because of the strong growth of creative writing Masters degrees. More possible because MA development gave general credence to the idea that the creation of Doctoral degrees was the next natural 'step'. Less possible, because of the intention of a number of the original Masters degrees to provide an avenue for talented emerging creative writers to take a short break from their day-to-day working lives. The idea of undertaking a Doctoral degree was frequently based on a completely different premise.

Whereas the early Masters degree picked up on the 'artist-at-work' notion, linked to individual work in the creative industries – a term now frequently used in the UK and Australia and including such activities as book publishing, film and media production, drama and performance – the Doctoral degree arrived with entirely the wrong timings to be a period of artistic 'escape', and perhaps even had the wrong title. The idea of a Doctoral degree seemed immediately to suggest an academic career and, at the time of the introduction of these degrees into the UK and Australia, the vast majority of creative writers working in academe had not arrived there via formal study.

It is at this point that the difference between the US and British situations needs to be raised. It introduces a further complication and, perhaps, a point of speculation with regard to creative writing Doctorates.

In North America, the primary organisation representing creative writers who work in academe is the Association of Writers and Writing Programs (AWP – www.awpwriter. org). The AWP has favoured as the 'terminal degree' for creative writers who want to work in academe the Master of Fine Arts (MFA) degree. The MFA in Creative Writing is not an MA. These also exist in North America, but in much smaller number. The MFA usually takes longer to complete than an MA, and is promoted as a 'studio degree', meaning that it is very largely about the production of original creative output referencing a 'studio' setting (in creative writing terms most often the writing workshop). The MFA is fundamentally not about a developed and articulated critical response to creative output in the way that a creative writing Doctorate in Britain (and Australia, for that matter) promotes.

In other words, the MFA differentiates itself from Doctoral study by de-emphasising a formalised critical response, emphasising that it is a degree focused on creative activity. The Doctoral degree in Britain has tended to combine both creative and critical work, the creative most often being the far greater proportion, and the critical component (most often referred to as the thesis, the critical response, the dissertation or, in Australasia, as the exegesis) responding and further articulating the nature of the explorations undertaken in the creative work.

This becomes significant because Doctoral study in creative writing does exist in North America so, while the AWP favours the 'terminal' MFA, and has made this plain for some years, North American creative writing Doctorates are being awarded. Issues are raised, therefore, about the professional standing, possibilities for tenure (if that is what is sought) and, ultimately, confusion of the international communities about the similarities and differences between the MFA and Doctoral degrees: Doctor of Philosophy (PhD or DPhil), Doctor of Arts (DA or ArtsD), or Doctor of Creative Arts (DCA), among others. How accurate this distinction been MFA and Doctorate, given the substantial development of Doctoral study in creative writing, is open to debate. Regardless, any creative writing degree that includes little formal critical response stirs opposing thoughts. On the positive side it could be said to focus attention on the primary outputs of creative writers; while, on the negative side, it might be said to be largely superfluous to a writer simply aiming to write creatively, whether within or outside of academe.

The historical and national profiles of Masters and Doctoral work in creative writing relate directly to how the research/practice-based-research that is undertaken within the context of Doctoral study in creative writing is orchestrated. The support of outside agencies for creative writers to undertake writing projects – the support of Arts Councils and Literature Boards, the public monies of national or regional governments – adds weight to the argument that Doctoral study in creative writing cannot merely be seen as a way of completing a writing project. A Doctoral degree in creative writing has a more detailed and university 'site-specific' purpose, or set of purposes, and specific intentions.

Titles and descriptions

How many ways are there to describe Doctoral work in creative writing? While this might seem a rhetorical question, it could just as easily be a plea for information. In recent years the ground has been constantly shifting. A PhD in Creative Writing, a DCA in Creative and Critical Writing, a Doctorate in English with creative dissertation, classes in creative writing counting toward PhD coursework, a research-through-practice Doctorate, an ArtsD. Degree titles and short prospectus descriptions don't assist particularly in making comparisons and, in some cases, actually hide similarities or differences. Likewise, outlines of approach only touch the surface of what individual Doctoral programmes might offer any one creative writer, or a group of creative writers meeting within an academic programme. In some cases, individual institutions and, in essence, individual 'programme creators/course directors' have defined the nature of these degrees, and not necessarily by referencing a particularly wide set of comparative approaches.

In the US, creative writing Doctoral work distinguishes itself from MFA work most often by its greater emphasis on coursework in literature or history and culture or theory. In the UK, and in Australia, Doctoral study often does appear much like a lengthier version of research-orientated MA study in creative writing. However, given that the origins and intentions of M-level study in the UK can be quite different to those of Doctoral study, there are issues to track here, not least in relation to approaches and intentions. Notably, creative writing Doctorates in the UK draw more strongly on the discourses of research in English Literature. In Australia the range of 'inter-disciplinary' influences is wider. This difference no doubt has some connection with England's imperial history and Australia's colonial one.

Incidentally, 'length of submission' is one of the ongoing creative writing debates, particularly for those institutions and directors of studies involved in creative writing Doctorates. When assessing for the award of a degree, it might legitimately be asked how anyone can compare the submission of a short collection of poetry with the submission of an epic historical novel? Answers follow a little later.

Issues of the size and shape of submitted work put momentarily to one side, a Doctorate in creative writing might be undertaken for a variety of reasons. While among these is most certainly some link to thoughts of academic employment this is frequently not the sole reason. Included among the other reasons – and these are entirely anecdotal evidence – are a desire by an experienced writer to explore new forms and styles, not necessarily leading to publication; an interest in critical and theoretical investigation of writing product and process; setting in motion an investigation of the learning and teaching connected with creative writing; developing for publication a project involving considerable empirical research in the fields of history and psychology; applying philosophic, cultural and political ideas of various kinds to the production of fiction; investigating the ways in which a collection of poetry might be 'held together'; working from personal, family history toward broader cultural and historical investigation through prose and poetry; adapting and adopting ideas about narrative to the construction of new forms of digital film script.

The number of potential reference points is even greater than the examples above suggest. This is logical because, as noted, creative writing Doctorates tend to be more person- and project- specific than those in many other subjects. Likewise, creative writing is not an intellectual enterprise; rather, noting Bergson's definition, creative writing is an intelligent enterprise, not bound by compartments of thought or, indeed, by the maintenance of discrete units of investigation. Creative writing is fundamentally dynamic, fluid, based on process and a sense of sympathy with the world in that manner Bergson once described as 'intuition'. Well-known, even somewhat legendary turns of phrase reflect examples of this: the concept, to relate one instance, of a piece of writing being 'abandoned' rather than finished; the frequently recalled importance of 'drafting'; the concern with writer–reader relationships; even the pervasive notion of some form of exchange through publication or performance. Each of these relates to the dynamism and 'intuition' that lies at the core of creative writing.

With this in mind – and despite the most common location of Doctoral work in creative writing being university English Departments – there is very little evidence to suggest that modes of literary analysis provide the *only* modes of engagement with creative writing. Indeed, not even perhaps that they provide the best modes of engagement. Naturally, this is in part dependent on genre – the screenwriters are probably already nodding their heads in agreement. But the point goes well beyond genre considerations.

Because Doctoral work in creative writing is notably person- and project- specific, each creative writing Doctoral student is to be encouraged to find the modes of engagement that best provide for, and articulate, their aims and intentions. These might not be literary – they *might* be, but they might not be – any more than they might be filmic, performative, aesthetic, communicative, or any other mode. There is no reason to believe that any one mode is preferential to the operations of the intelligence, or that any one mode is the right one for setting such dynamic research in motion. However, there is every reason to believe that any one creative writer's response to creative writing will be generated by a set of actions, events, processes, personal histories, personal psychology/physiology, contemporary circumstances, social wholes, structures and functions, and cultural influences. Defining 'action' and 'reaction' – that is 'creative practice' and 'the mode of display of responsive understanding' – is a key element of creative writing Doctoral study.

For this reason, creative writing Doctorates are by nature more investigative than MA or even MFA study, and relatively 'surface level' considerations such as 'length of submission' shouldn't detract from this fact. That said, length of submission has preoccupied many, and perhaps it is best here to put to rest the notion that resolving this issue is impossible. Simply, creative writing research/research-through-practice can be judged according to a sense of 'equivalence'. This is not solely defined by length; nor, indeed, is length unimportant. However, it is possible, commonsense prevailing, to evaluate and compare the submission of a collection of poetry with the submission of a novel, or the submission of a screenplay with the submission of a collection of short stories. This assessment of equivalent standard is doubly confirmed if, as is the case in a vast number of programmes, the creative writer submits a 'package' of material including, most importantly, a responsive critical component that assists in defining and confirming their understanding and their contribution to the site of knowledge in their field.

Responsive understanding

The conceptual thrust of creative writing Doctorates is such that they encourage a writer to delve more widely and deeply into knowledge of their field, and to show this clearly. Their intention is to contribute both to the development of the individual writer and to the holistic site of knowledge and engagement with the world that is defined by the term 'creative writing'. The primary word here is 'understanding', and the primary intention is both creation and articulation. That the knowledge created can be, and often is, the result of creative practice does not alter this key fact. However, it is sometimes the case that confusion has crept into the discussion of Doctoral research in this field because creative writing frequently has found itself referred to in universities on the basis of market outputs. A primary aspect of this confusion concerns the use of the word 'publishable'.

It has been the case that the success or failure of postgraduate study of creative writing has sometimes been said to ride on the word 'publishable', most often in an expression along the lines of 'the finished work should be of a publishable standard'. Expressions like this are often simply shorthand for a description of a piece of work that had reached a certain standard; however, the expression's inference is somewhat more elemental, and perturbing.

It is necessary to return to an earlier question. That is: ' If a Doctoral degree is the highest level of achievement, in what has the Doctoral graduate in creative writing achieved the highest university qualification, in what have they "stepped furthest"?' Is it the case that the Doctoral graduate in creative writing has stepped furthest in terms of the requirements of, say, the contemporary publishing, media or performance industries? Perhaps it is, but surely not solely. A sole emphasis here would be similar to saying that any Doctoral graduate has only made themselves 'useful' to industry; thus, in many ways chipping away at the universal ideal of Doctoral study involving 'an original contribution to knowledge'. University education, the concept of 'higher learning', has set it sights on something more than 'servicing' current commerce, something both related to and in some way advanced from the immediate demands of industry. More importantly still, the concept of 'publishability' most often touted in such descriptions is that linked to the birth of the modern book market. This concept is rarely considered in terms of whether it relates to creative writing itself or, in reality, to some more peripheral element connected to it.

Prior to the birth of the modern book market in the nineteenth century, published creative writing had value not in itself but for what it could do. In other words, its material worth was very limited; its ability to elicit a reaction, to do something, was what created its value. It was not until the development of copyright law – most importantly around the Statute of Anne of 1710 (see Woodmansee and Jaszi 1994: 32) – that creative writing began to gather 'item' value. Even then it was not creative writers who set forth to ensure this material value was recognised; rather, it was booksellers. Early copyright cases, in which the value of 'publishability' was attached to the material object in the form of a book or pamphlet, were to the benefit of booksellers, not for the purposes of deciding on the value that might be attached to the quality of the creative writing within them, if creative writing it happened to be.

Why then would creative writing – a practice that has been associated with universities since their founding, that therefore has a close connection with higher learning, and that can be judged in many more subject-specific ways – why then would creative writing be attached to a concept, often called 'publishability' but equating in reality more accurately to 'does this item have material value'? Such an equation makes neither historical nor conceptual sense.

This is not an argument for what might be called, often pejoratively: 'experimentation'. Nor is it an argument for a return to a kind of pre-mercantilist idyll. It is an argument – and an important one – about what someone studying for a Doctorate in creative writing is seeking to accomplish, or should be seeking to accomplish. That is, a level and display of understanding in relation to creative writing process, practice and product that can be seen by experts in the field to be equivalent to, though not the same as, the performance of Doctoral candidates in other fields (see Harper 2005).

A creative writing Doctorate begins with a desire to create and it depends on a desire to investigate what underpins the creation. There is no obligatory starting point for a Creative Writing Doctorate. Most candidates begin with a creative project, but this is not true of all candidates. Many have a relatively unformed idea of the understanding that underpins their creative work. But creative practice generates critical understanding. It is a natural process that various persons throughout time have commented upon (for example, Sigmund Freud linked it to the 'unconscious', Bergson, of course, linked it to his notion of 'intuition'). It can best be defined simply as 'response'. Responsive understanding is not necessarily self-reflective. It is generated by a process, action, event or object, and it produces an attached action, event or object.

In creative writing Doctorates the aim is to assist and heighten the responsive capabilities of the writer; that is, to assist the writer to develop, and to display, a considerable understanding of their subject. This is higher learning in the subject of creative writing, and creative writing Doctorates are, most importantly, evidence of higher learning.

References

Arts and Humanities Research Council (AHRC), www.ahrc.ac.uk

Bergson, Henri [1911] (1998), *Creative Evolution*, New York: Dover.

Council for Graduate Education: www.ukcge.ac.uk

English Subject Centre: www.english.heacademy.ac.uk

Harper, Graeme (2005), 'Buying or selling? Creative writing research in the university' in *New Writing: the International Journal for the Practice and Theory of Creative Writing* 2.1, Clevedon: Multilingual Matters.

Woodmansee, Martha and Peter Jaszi (eds) (1994), *The Construction of Authorship: Textual Appropriation in Law and Literature*, London: Duke University Press.

40

How to Start a Literary Magazine

Rebecca Wolff

In 1998, I founded a literary journal called *Fence*, which has been in continuous, regular publication ever since, and which has gone on to be quite successful and respected. In this chapter I will tell you, or at least imply to you, how I did this. For the purposes of this discussion, let's establish the premise that you, yourself, have decided to start a literary journal. I am going to put before you some of the questions that I, in the bright light of hindsight, would have liked to be asked at the beginning of my process.

But first, let's acknowledge the role that impulse, and fantasy, and recklessness have in the founding of a literary journal. It is quite possible that, had I been asked all of these questions, and made aware of all the ensuing issues, and barraged with prerequisites in the manner in which you will be here, that I might have come to my senses, thrown up my hands, and quit before I began. Many is the time that I have been standing in a group of young students of writing, perhaps during the break in a class, or after a reading has ended and the cigarettes have been lit, and overheard one student say to another: 'I'm starting my own journal. It's going to be called "Old Lettuce"'. Do I, you may wonder, upon hearing this, attach myself to the student and bedeck her with reality-checking questions about funding and distribution? No, I do not. Or at least I do not, anymore. Or at least, I do not until the student comes running to me, months later, in a panic over the price of printing or the difficulty of finding distribution for *Old Lettuce*.

It is a peculiarity of my own journal, and my own journal-founding process, that I troubled *myself* from the get-go with questions such as the ones that will follow. I had, you might say, a head for business, at least in this one instance. There is something about the industry of literary production that I have an appetite for – something that in what I will churlishly call 'real life' I have no appetite for at all. You might call this something 'the nitty-gritty'. I suggest, at the outset of this discussion, that if you yourself don't have an appetite for the nitty-gritty, you find someone who does, and attach them to your project immediately. Unless, of course, you find yourself answering certain of these questions in a certain manner.

So here, finally, is a question to ask yourself: just exactly what kind of writing are you interested in publishing? To say 'good writing' is generally not enough – hundreds of journals are published annually, each one claiming that what they are publishing is 'good'. What you ought to have in mind is a specific editorial vision of what distinguishes the good work you plan on publishing in your journal from that published by the teeming hundreds. Why, in short, does your journal demand to come into being?

Your answer to this question may evolve in terms of how you envision its audience: is your journal of specifically regional interest? Is your journal intended to speak, either by virtue of its aesthetic policies or of its format and distribution, to a very specific group of people, one almost exactly the size of your address book? Many worthy journals arise out of the publisher's desire to publish his or her own writing, as well as the writing of his or her friends and community, between handmade hemp covers, and to hand-deliver the results. (If this is the case, you may find the acquisition of a business manager unnecessary).

But whatever the case, it is necessary to know exactly what you want out of your journal.

Once you've settled on your journal's identity, it's important to be able to articulate it. Hence, the 'mission statement' – a concise, one- or two-sentence description of your journal's *raison d'être*. If your journal is to be run, as many are, as a nonprofit organisation, this is an absolute prerequisite, as every grant application will request a mission statement. If your journal is to be run by the skin of your teeth, out of your own back pocket, this is still a very good idea, as the question you will be asked most often, when you mention to a friend or an author that you are starting a journal, is: what kind of journal is this to be? Why, in effect, must there be another journal in this world?

Necessarily, you have come upon the answer to this question after having immersed yourself in a sampling of what is already being published by other optimistic, creative, hardworking publishers like the one you hope to become. I say necessarily because it *is* necessary, in order to publish a journal worth the paper (or potato sack, or toilet roll) it's printed on, to understand the context you are entering, the field onto which your entry will march. Ideally, you have even spent some few months or even years working on an already existing literary journal. This will not only help you to understand the time and energy necessary for the project, but it may even dissuade you from proceeding.

But once you have determined that your journal simply *must be*, there are a few more questions to be answered.

Planning

How often shall *Old Lettuce* come out? Depending on your answers to some of the following questions, the usual frequencies are one, two, three, and four times a year. How high shall *Old Lettuce*'s production values be? It could be photocopied and stapled, printed on an antique, hand-cranked letterpress and hand-sewn, or professionally offset-printed and machine-bound with what is known as a 'perfect binding'. (Virtually all commercially distributed publications are perfect-bound, that is, they have a flat spine on which can be printed the title, name of the publisher, and so on). How many people shall I involve in *Old Lettuce*? Do I want total editorial control or do I like the idea of a more collaborative effort? And could I do this on my own, even if I wanted to? A big question: Is there a sponsoring institution available to me, such as a community centre, arts organisation, or even a university? An even bigger question: Do I wish to incorporate as a nonprofit organisation, so that I may apply for grants and solicit donations from private foundations and individuals? Or perhaps I will be able to finance this journal myself, as I have lots of money. Or perhaps I will attempt to support it by means of advertising sales, subscriptions, and the occasional fundraising event.

For the purposes of this discussion, I will jump to some conclusions and assume that *Old Lettuce*, soon to be renamed something more promising, like 'Thunderclap', or 'The Holy Grail', is to be a professionally printed, perfect-bound, regularly published and nationally distributed journal.

But for the purposes of a diversion, I will briefly and tangentially entertain the notion that your goals for *Old Lettuce* are more modest, or more community-bound, and that your romantic imagination is captured by pre-industrial means of literary production, such as the photocopier and stapler, while your aesthetic inclinations lead you, for a variety of possible reasons, toward the 'coterie' approach to publishing. There are a few good arguments for running this kind of shop, that is, a journal whose purview is self-limiting, and which aims to represent a very special slice of the literary landscape (your own backyard). You get to publish your friends, without too much bother about whether their works are quite up to par. You get to work with your hands, which, as everyone knows, is good for body *and* soul. You are free to ignore the potentially quite stressful issues of circulation ('How do I get my journal into somebody's hands so that they might read it?') and funding ('How do I convince some person or institution that my journal is worthy of their support?'). In the best of cases, as with certain famous journals of the past such as *Locus Solus*, or *The Little Review*, your friends are geniuses, and with your scantily-clad journal you are creating literary history on a scale to be known only by readers of the future.

Finances

Many journals, like the one I edit, *Fence*, acquire nonprofit status. This route, much like the decision to start a journal in the first place, is not to be taken lightly nor for granted (no pun intended). The 501(c) (3) moniker means that you offer a public service worthy of support by charitable institutions, and even possibly by the government. If you are a nonprofit you spend an awful lot of time providing evidence of your worthiness of this support, in the form of grant proposals and financial reports. Nonprofits are also required to form a Board of Directors, a group of interested (and, ideally, affluent) people who will help maintain organisational and financial stability. The Board has both legal and financial responsibility for that organisation, and can make decisions without any input from The Editor. (It also has the power to put a new editor in place at any time.) The process of attaining a 501(c) (3) is lengthy and full of paper, and should ideally be performed for you by a lawyer.

Many journals, both nonprofit and otherwise, have what is known as a patron, or sometimes, 'The Publisher'. These lucky journals are supported in large part by wealthy individuals, or private foundations endowed by individuals. The degree of editorial involvement desired by this publisher or benefactor will vary considerably from journal to journal – if the benevolent publisher is you, then this will never pose a problem. If, on the other hand, you find yourself in a relationship of dependency with a patron, issues can arise – most notably: what exactly does the patron want in return? Editorial input? Social prestige? To be published in your journal, or to publish his or her friends? In the best instance your patron will be one who wishes to use his or her wealth to good end, and has decided that your journal is a great end, and looks forward to being in the company of like-minded souls.

If you plan to raise money for your journal, on whatever scale, the first thing you ought to prepare yourself to do is to become an Event Planner. Readings, either singly or in series; launch parties; parties with readings; benefit readings with wine and cheese; fancy fundraisers with famous writers; and so on. *Fence* funded its entire first print run with a benefit reading featuring four wonderful poets and a novelist. Event planners are resourceful people: you will wrack your brain for what are called, in any industry, your 'connections': people or organisations you have access to who can provide you with or help you locate free stuff: free venues, free wine, free catering, free printing of your invitations, free mailing lists to which to send your invitations, and so on. The more connections you have, the easier it will be for you to get free stuff and therefore to have successful events and to accomplish your fundraising goals. If you are a nonprofit your Board of Directors should be helping you to accomplish some of this, either by throwing the fancy parties or by locating potential funders.

But you should plan on putting up a lot of your own money, be ye rich or poor, at first. With any luck you will be able to reimburse yourself within a few years.

Submissions

Writers love to be solicited. For your first issue, go wild with invitations. Invite everyone you've ever admired, or fantasised about publishing, including former teachers. Depending on your structural decisions concerning your audience, you may wish to include lots of well-known, even famous writers (read: big draws, names to put on the back of *Thunderclap* so that people in bookstores will pick it up and not put it down immediately), or you may wish to entirely avoid such names and exclusively present the work of writers known only to you and your immediate circle. The thing to do is to know what you want, and why you want it, and to understand the consequences. A journal that does not feature any or many well-known authors, whatever the realm of their notoriety, will not sell on the newsstand, and will have difficulty finding distribution. More about this later.

After your first issue has come out, you will swiftly begin receiving unsolicited submissions. Again, depending on your desires, you may want to list *The Golden Fleece* in such venues as The Poets Market, and so on. Be aware that if you do this, *The Holy Grail* will soon receive such a tidal wave, a tsunami, even, of unsolicited and mostly inappropriate submissions as to render your editorial staff completely immobile. More effective, perhaps, is to circulate complimentary copies of your new magazine to writers and other significant figures you wish to know about it, in the certainty that they will pass the word on and in the probability that they will soon send work themselves.

Handling mail

While many journals employ interns to open and sort through mail, opening your own mail, at least at the beginning, while it is still manageable, is a really good way to keep tabs on operations, both editorial and financial. Bills will get paid on time, promotional opportunities such as conferences and readings will be duly considered, and most importantly you will know what kinds of readers *The Golden Grail* is reaching. I have always considered it a pleasure and a duty to actually read the entire slush pile (an unflattering term for unsolicited submissions), or at least to divide it between *Fence*'s editors, rather than to allow interns to read and reject, read and reject, as many journals do. This is because it is inherent to *Fence*'s mission that we publish a significant amount of work by writers who are not part of any particularly prominent circles, scenes, or cultures. Our interns may miss some of the genuinely original, sometimes-difficult-to-recognise writing that comes in from inauspicious corners.

For a very long time, from January of 1998 until April of 2006, to be exact, *Fence* had in place the following procedures, concerning poetry submissions. We have four poetry editors. About every four months, the stack of submissions was divided between us according first to whom they were addressed and then second to whose pile was biggest (we try to even them out). Each editor read his or her pile and rejected what he or she felt comfortable rejecting, then made copies of the work he or she was interested in publishing or at least discussing with fellow editors. Each editor mailed these copies to the other three editors about two weeks in advance of the date set for the editorial meeting. At the meeting the editor then employed a highly sophisticated system of cajolement, seduction, and harassment in order to try to convince the other three editors of the value of his or her favourite poems. The resulting *mélange* of accepted work is generally successful at representing the mélange of our editors' actual tastes and concerns. In April of 2006, *Fence* went exclusively digital; we now accept only online submissions. This is a slightly sad development, in that we will miss the excitement of opening real mail in search of the unexpectedly brilliant submission from a complete unknown; on the other hand, the ratio of submission to accepted work had grown insupportable, as is perhaps inevitable with a journal that aims to be recognised on a national level, and we could no longer manage the simple bulk of paper in our tiny little basement office.

Fence operates with a publishing backlog, at this point, of at least a year, which allows us to use a bit of hindsight in curating the issues; we attempt to create an even gender ratio – that is our only demographic concern aside from an abiding desire to publish writing we like by writers of colour as often as it comes our way. Because our response time has lengthened from four to sometimes as many as twelve months, we welcome simultaneous submissions; it's only fair.

Copyright and contracts, author fees

Most journals obtain Serial Rights, which means that they have the right to publish the work first and that the rights revert back to the author upon publication. If the poem or story is subsequently anthologised or published as part of a collection, *The Holy Fleece* must be acknowledged in the copyright or acknowledgements page.

A contract is a good idea, as it will help to avoid any future confusion as to what exactly has been agreed to by the author. This document can easily be mailed out as part of your acceptance letter. Contractual considerations for the publisher include: Do you wish to obtain permission to post the work on your website, if you have one? Do you wish to be able to reprint the work in any anthology you may publish later, that is, *The Best of 'The Goose'*? At the very least your contract should ask for a current correct address for the contributor, including email address, and a signature assigning first serial rights. The contract should also state that the author must provide *The Goose* with a digital file of the work and a biographical statement, within a certain time, and delivered in its preferred mode (by e-mail, in the mail on a disk, and so on). If *The Goose* is lucky enough to be able to pay its authors, the contract should state its rate of payment and when the author can expect to receive this payment.

Production

Desktop publishing has changed the literary landscape possibly more even than *Thunderclap* will. It is now feasible, even quite easy, for one person to edit, design, and lay out for production an entire book or journal. To do this requires many different 'skill sets', as they're called, most of which I personally have acquired on the fly, so to speak. If you are design-savvy, and handy with such programmes as Quark, PageMaker, InDesign, Photoshop, and so on, then you will be many steps ahead of the game. If you are savvy, but not handy, then you will need to either take a course or to find someone who is handy: a Production

Editor, who can work with you on the design of the magazine and then lay it out. If you are neither savvy nor handy, you will need to hire a Designer. This designer will come up with some ideas for the look of the magazine ('trim size' – width x height; what the pages will look like – fonts, text styles, and so on; a title design or logo) and work with you on arriving at a final accord.

A word about titles. Think carefully about how you want your journal's title to resonate in the mind's ear of your reader. Is your journal intended to have a slightly goofy tenor, and therefore might appropriately be titled *Old Lettuce*, *The Duck's Cracked Egg*, *Four Bent Fingers*, *Up in the Attic*, *Crocheted Plasma Afghan*, or some such thing? At the opposite end of the spectrum, pause for more than a few minutes before burdening your journal with a completely boring title like *The Poetry Review*, or *Writing Quarterly*, or *Journal of Poetry and Fiction*. Something like *Thunderclap* is safely middle-of-the-road, and as that, it runs the risk of driving in one ear and out the other. A good title is hard to come by, but ideally it will occur to you as part of your original desire to start your own journal, much in the same way that a good poem or story's title will seem to be of a piece with the actual text itself.

Similarly, the look of the journal should be considered carefully as a reflection of the kind of aesthetic statement you wish the journal to make – a very plain, convoluted, or unconsidered design may indicate to potential readers that the editor is not sufficiently engaged with the sensual world to be able to recognise interesting writing as a feature of this world. In beginning *Fence* I first came up with the title; for reasons I hope are obvious, the image of a fence, and those who sit upon it, was correlative with my goals as an editor. Hot on the heels of this title came a design imperative: I wanted *Fence* to be beautiful. I wanted readers to be attracted to its size and the image on the cover, to wish to hold it in their hand and look inside, and to be moved by the clarity and confidence of its interior layout as it serves to present the writing, confidently and clearly.

Generally, your production schedule for *Birch Bark* goes something like this: for an issue that you want to come out in, say, early May, your editorial deadline should be in early February. That's right, February. This means that by 5 February, all contracts have been mailed out and received back from the authors along with the works in digital form, ready to be poured into your template. First, you must decide in which order the work will appear in the journal, and inform your designer. The designer (or you, if you're handy) will pour everything in and, within a week or so, provide you with a version that is ready for you to start proofreading. This could either be an actual hard copy or a PDF file for you to print out yourself, depending on the benevolence of your designer. You proofread this 'first pass', using your copies of the original submitted work to make sure that errors in formatting have not occurred in the translation into digital information. You make your corrections, as well as any changes in formatting you would like to make, such as last-minute switches in the order, or the decision to move a poem into the middle of the page instead of justifying it against the left margin, and return the pages to the designer, who inputs the changes and prints it out again and returns it to you: The second pass. It is now approximately 10 March. It is wise to bring in at least one set of fresh eyes for the second pass, as they will invariably catch errors you have missed. Once you have retrieved these changes from Fresh Eyes, passed the changes on to your designer, and received a fresh printout, (15 March) it is time to check all the changes you have requested (the foul copy) against the new copy. The third pass. At this point it is extremely wise to ask your designer to create individual PDF files of the poems and stories and email them off to your contributors with a note requesting that they get back to you with any corrections (*not* revisions – the time is long past for such things) in a few days, that is, by 1 April. Then these changes must be entered and a fresh copy printed out. When you have ascertained that everything is as it should be, it's time to get the thing together on a disk and ship it off to the printer: It is now 5 April.

Printing

Regardless of your chosen format, you will need to find a printer. Perhaps the local copy shop will be your printer, if you are going low budget; perhaps you will seek out the services of a local artisan with a letterpress in his or her barn. But if, as we are assuming for the purposes of this discussion, you are intent on creating a journal that can be distributed nationally, that is, by a distributor, you will need to find a printer who can produce a perfect-bound journal.

Most printers now have electronic quote forms on their websites, wherein you submit your 'specs', that is, trim size, print run, colour/black and white pages, shipping information, and they in turn submit to you an estimated cost. Undoubtedly, you will want to receive at least three bids on your job. It is not always wise to go with the lowest bid; you'll want to see samples of their work and make a choice based on quality, rather than budget.

Your chosen printer will get what is called a 'proof' back to you within two to four weeks (19–25 April), depending on the size of the company and their busy-ness. This proof stage is crucial in terms of your ability to get *Birch Bark* out on time. You must check over these proofs (it's your last chance to fix errors; it will cost you something per every page that must be corrected) quickly and get them back to the printer as fast as possible. Once they receive the proofs and make any corrections necessary, they will begin to run the job, and *Birch Bark* should be ready to ship sometime around 5–15 May.

Distribution and promotion

Only you will be able to judge how important these last two subjects are for the success of your magazine. It all depends on your mission: some journals, as I remarked before, are distributed by hand. Some are distributed only by post, publisher to subscriber. Many of the larger distributors are more accustomed to dealing with larger periodicals, and will have difficulty understanding that when they fax you a print order, they are reaching your home telephone. Similarly they will have difficulty understanding the care and attention that *Birch Bark* requires in order to ensure that it reaches its audience. I have personally discovered that in this instance as in most others, it is useful to be a squeaky wheel. I have developed a friendly telephone relationship with my account representative, over at my distribution centre, and have been able to effect many changes for the better with regards to the actual destination of those precious 770 copies of *Fence* that are distributed between four hundred or so bookstores and newsstands all across the US.

It can be very difficult to get a new journal distributed. Your chosen periodicals distributor will ask you to fill out an application form providing information about your journal such as the trim size, frequency of publication, and category of contents (literary, romance, gardening, etc.). They will also request that you send ten or fourteen sample copies of the current issue of the magazine, which they will cleverly deposit in a few of their stores. If they sell an acceptable number of copies within an acceptable time limit, they will accept your journal for distribution. Note that it is virtually impossible to find distribution for a journal before it has published at least one issue.

Fence was conceived with active promotion (or publicity, or marketing) as a prerequisite of its success. I wanted to reach as many readers as possible. This is what I desire for the writing we publish; this is what I see as the *raison d'être* of this particular journal: not to be known and read only by a lucky band of insiders, but to become part of a very large conversation, or dialogue, between the many different writing communities at play in the fields of the Writing Lord.

With this in mind, we have coordinated and participated in as many readings, conferences, panel discussions, talks, festivals, and other gatherings of live bodies as possible. I highly recommend this as *Birch Bark*'s best means of promotion: there is nothing like actually meeting people and talking about your magazine to help create a sense of excitement and actuality about it. Other, more expensive and less friendly means of promotion include: advertising, which I also highly recommend if you can afford it; Press releases, which are only as effective as your mailing lists; and email announcement lists, which are not actually expensive but which can be very time-consuming to create and maintain, and which often annoy people if they are used injudiciously.

While the initial impulse to found a new journal is a joyful one, it is one that is wisely tempered by a dose of pragmatic realism. Long live *Birch Bark*!

Section Three

The Writer's Life

41

How to be a Writer

John Milne

'How to be a writer' is a title worthy of a Cicero or an Orwell, and I am aware I'm a poor substitute. However, I have made my living exclusively as a writer for well over twenty years. Though this might surprise and even console my old schoolmasters, were they still alive, it is some sort of qualification.

My main writing experience has been in fiction; specifically in the fields of novel and scriptwriting. Therefore the nominal writer to whom this article is addressed is a writer of fiction. Though some of the things I write may be useful to journalists or poets, I won't try to address my thoughts directly to them. I am as keen a reader of newspapers and poetry as the next man, but everyone's sphere of competence has to end somewhere.

In 'Why I Write' Orwell draws up four reasons for writing. They are (1) Egoism (2) Aesthetic enthusiasm (for one perceived form or another) (3) Historical impulse (to set things down for the benefit of history) (4) Political purpose (by which Orwell says he means the need to drive the world in one direction or another) (Orwell 1968: 3–4). This last, to modern eyes, is laughable. Leaving aside the great religious tomes of the dark ages, why would a book drive the world in one direction or another? Perhaps the last real attempt to do this was Mao's Little Red Book. The ignored copies must run close to a billion. I can't think of a contemporary work of fiction which attempts, leave alone achieves a political purpose. The historical impulse exists but is really a minor influence on contemporary novelists. The constant din of twenty-four hour rolling news current affairs has all but drowned it out. Instead people turn to 'life writing', a kind of withdrawal into the domestic and private which has its strengths and attractions. Aesthetic enthusiasm exists of course. We all enjoy one form of writing above others, whether that's style or storytelling form. Perhaps we prefer books printed this way or that. I don't really believe though that any writer is drawn to write just by form.

I'm afraid we write for egoism. We write because we want to find a voice and utter something through it. As American painter Barnett Newman put it, 'Original man, shouting his consonants, did so in yells of awe and anger at his tragic state, at his own self-awareness and at his own helplessness before the void' (Newman 1947). Writing, like speaking, is existential. But is what we write about? Are we simply to exist as writers, to label ourselves as such and then expect something to happen? To be a writer you have to act.

The old saw goes, 'everyone has a novel in him'. And she may. However, it is not in publishing a novel that a writer is made, nor in having a play staged, nor a screenplay filmed. If writing is to be your business, those are just beginnings. Readers of this chapter are likely to be already familiar with that feeling, a sort of breath-taking, heady mixture of fear, pleasure and stomach-upset as we reach the end of writing our first substantial work. I will write as if it's your first drama or novel, but what follows will be true I'm sure whether your project is a collection of *belles-lettres* or a car maintenance manual. For many of us the journey will have been incremental, with shorter works written first. The completion of that substantial text is like stepping onto a sunlit upland. It is a pleasant contrast from the months the writer has spent condemned to the garden shed or the back bedroom or worse yet, trapped next to a wheezy tramp in the reading room of the local library. Writing sometimes brings unexpected physical demands.

Perhaps the work finds a publisher or producer, perhaps it doesn't. Some real drivel has been published or staged, so it can't be the process of publishing or staging which makes a writer. What does? If we look around ourselves we can see that repetition plays a large part in professionalising any activity. Putting in a tap does not make a plumber. Writing a letter does not make a lawyer. Handing out aspirin does not make a nurse. Having a practice, where these or similar activities are repeated in a more or less rational and professional way, does. The skills learned in one tap-fitting inform the next. The painful lessons of writing the first novel or screenplay will inform the second. There is a difference though. The plumbers', lawyers' and nurses' activities have boundaries and carry prescriptive rules for success and failure. The sink clears, you win your case, the patient walks out; job done. Fiction writers (like me, probably like you) can only dream of prescriptive rules which not only identify what is achievement in fiction but draw a map of how to achieve. Does the work have to be published? Not necessarily. Should I have an agent? Not necessarily. Does the work need to be bound? Not at all. Does it have to run in chronological order? Obviously not. Should it follow a three-act form? Sometimes, unless it would be better to use four, five or none. Is it bound by rules of good taste? Probably not. Should it have one author? Not necessarily. Should it be written in the first person? Third person? I don't know. You try the second person then you tell me.

At the end of each completed bout of writing it seems the fiction writer – instead of arriving on solid ground – has no choice but to begin again. A work of fiction defines the form, then immediately demonstrates how temporary that definition is. It's as if the work says 'if and only if this fiction is the world then this form is the way to do fiction'. At each sally into the field of fiction-making the writer has to confront and examine what the form is and what it could be. The equivalent would be if the lawyer had to start each day wondering what tort is or as if a plumber spent his day wondering whether a plastic bag or a tin can wouldn't do as well for a radiator. 'Briefly' would be the answer. No such certainty is available in fiction. No wonder writers get depressed.

Take heart. If the irony of the fiction form is that it forces you constantly to consider, 'What can this be?' its strength is its formal inclusiveness. A leaky water system is hardly a system at all, but fiction is fiction as soon as Picasso's 'lie that lets us realise the truth'[1] is uttered. If writing is a craft, all fiction at least aspires to be art of some sort. Sometimes it succeeds. Crude carving can be beautiful and great paintings sometimes sit on flaking gesso, so in the same way a faulty novel may be a very good novel indeed. Think about the novels of Daniel Defoe; a modern editor would have a lot of notes, but no one suggests they're not novels.

Having stepped blinking into the sunshine it seems the writer has no choice but to go back into the shed and try again. This is true no matter how successful in publishing, staging and financial terms the writer has become. Jo Rowling has the same problem as Joe

Schmo, or me or you. Repeating the performance, having an ongoing practice as a writer, just as a doctor or an engineer or a solicitor has a practice, is the real difference between a professional and an amateur. What's more this is true whether you are published or not. If earning your main living from writing was the test of professionalism there would be few of us indeed. If the first and obvious rule of how to be a writer is 'write something', the second and possibly less obvious rule is, 'do it again'.

But how to do it again? The first substantial work of fiction by any writer may well contain some element of autobiography.[2] It may be that to tell a story over sixty or so thousand words or to hold the viewer's attention for sixty or ninety minutes is at first too much for us. Large scale, sustained storytelling in book-length form may be so difficult we have to compartmentalise the acquisition of the skills surrounding it. Starting from what you know, extemporising on a story which is familiar, takes part of the burden off your shoulders. But if you are going to go on and be a professional writer, however commercial or literary your definition of that activity, you are going to have to devise an ongoing way of working. You may well have 'a novel in you', in story terms. But do you have a dozen novels in you? I doubt it. And if you do, as Gore Vidal argues, 'write what you know will always be excellent advice to those who ought not to write at all' (Vidal 1983). You will have to devise other storytelling strategies to go on writing. That probably means not just relying on the incidents in your own life or those close to you but inventing. This brings me to the third rule, though it may well have been the first core skill a writer acquired. To write you need to read. The third rule of how to be a writer is, 'read'.

It's surprising how many people who want to be a writer read little, or read in a very narrow band. You can't write novels unless you read them. You can't write TV or film scripts unless you read them, though they are perhaps a little more difficult to come by. You can't solve every problem by brute force of your intellect, no matter how clever you are. You can't constantly stay in a positive frame of mind. Even the most upbeat writer's confidence will flag at some point. Reading good fiction, whether prose or drama, renews the spirit of optimism, refreshes the writer's mind, opens out a palette of possibilities. The professional writer has probably trained him or herself with a lifetime's reading before setting pen to paper. I did. I've never kept a note of the books I have read but I sometimes wish I had. Even the rubbish, even the drivel lays something down. The good stuff, the Dickens, Shakespeare, Zola, Austen (name your poison) sustains, exemplifies, reinforces . . . it just helps you.

Serendipity plays an important role in the writing process. You are not necessarily reading in hope of discovering direct formal answers to your problems – though sometimes you will find them. Rather, you read because if you are in the right literary soup the ingredients you need may just float by. The only thing we can say for certain is that if you are not in the literary soup they will never float by and you will have made things harder for yourself. As writers we stand on each other's shoulders (on the shoulders of giants, I would have written had a politician not bankrupted that rather nice phrase a few years ago). There is no formal problem in fiction which hasn't been examined and likely resolved by another writer, even if they are writing in another period or another language. Answers you may not have imagined will emerge from the other works. Maybe even questions you might not have thought existed will be presented in the course of reading these other works. Here are some examples. If you can't pace your story, read Bashevis Singer's 'The Slave'. The psychological turns in the story are perfectly paced. If crime writing looks formally dull and formulaic read Derek Raymond or Nicolas Freeling. If you find it hard to visualise your story read Elmore Leonard. If a camera could write the scene unfolding before it, Leonard would be the result. If you are anxious about writing jump-cuts in a drama script read Shakespeare, especially *Henry V* or *The Tempest*. There is no doubt that reading other fiction with your 'writer's eye' will allow you to see the formal problems and formal solutions the other writer has found. If these examples – which after all are my prejudice – don't suit you, keep reading. You will find your own.

Wanting to write and wanting to be a writer are different things. You become a writer because you write, not vice versa. I don't know any really good writers who have entered the profession wanting to be a writer. It would be a peculiar and frankly masochistic ambition. You might as well form the ambition to sit in a room on your own most of the time and be ignored, for that is what will happen to even the most successful writers, most of the time. This leads me on to another, often ignored rule for writers. Observance of it leads towards greater professionalism. Rule (4) respect your own time. Few writers manage to do this, but I'll explain what I mean.

Imagine you are in the running to be commissioned to write, say a single two-hour TV drama called 'Capabar'. The drama *Capabar* may cost, say, £1.5 million at 2006 prices. Do you think the producer is going to commission you at random to write it? Of course not. Who'd be mad enough to allow someone they know nothing about to play with a £1.5 million toy? The producers will go through a whole rigmarole with agents, ringing different ones, inviting them to put forward their clients as a sort of literary beauty parade, calling for examples of previous scripts which are enough like *Capabar* to prove you can do it, while all the time demonstrating your ability to take on the powerful and unique vision which is the producer's *Capabar*. They'll want to see you, to hear you explain why they should commission you. You'll have to explain your unique view on the project. You'll have to prove the project is important to you. You must be able to put your hand on your heart and lie, saying that you have no other irons in the fire and you will not be doing any re-writes to the last thing you wrote while you're writing *Capabar*, nor will you be taking meetings with other producers to discuss other projects while you are writing *Capabar*. Then you'll have to write a little document, a sort of 'premise' as to what the film could be, something not too long and carrying a huge amount of selling detail in a few punchy paragraphs. The premise is like an abstract of something yet to be written prepared for a busy and rather tetchy reader. Many years ago a script editor gave the game away to me. 'The first couple of lines have to work', she said, 'otherwise he's too impatient to read on'. I felt like saying, 'Just how crass is this man?' but resisted. After all, the woman had merely confirmed something I knew existed. Why blame her?

If the premise works, the producer will commission a 'treatment', a ten or twenty page document outlining *Capabar* the story (so far they only had *Capabar* the pitch – it's as if Alan Sugar sold dummy boxes to retailers on the basis he would find someone capable of thinking of something to put in the box later). The premise may have passed because it was a good brief read which avoided tackling any embarrassing detail. The treatment won't be afforded the same lenient view. Suddenly the producer becomes a cross between a dentist and a VAT inspector. The producer has a view, the executive producer has a view, you have a view, the script editor has a view . . . how can this one little document written by you be the container for all these views of *Capabar*? If the discordance between the views is gross or if the story you have written is lacking in some technical way they may ask you in to fix the problem. This means a meeting with a producer and script editor or if you're unlucky, a script editor alone (script editors vary between those who are experienced and bitter and those who are so in awe of their producer they may well be better replaced by a telephone answering machine – neither is much use to a writer and their role is usually a convenience for producers who can't be bothered to take the meetings themselves).

To fix the treatment the two or three of you might prepare a 'beat document', where you write down all the main beats of the story, whether they are acted out on screen or not. 'This is where she decides she doesn't love him. This is where the doctor says she's pregnant. This is where Charlie is found nailed to the floor'. You get my drift. You'll try to figure out what you can do to make this story really satisfying, with enough twists and turns and ups and downs, with enough revelations (reveals, they are called in TV) to keep the viewer entertained and to keep their appetite for the drama whetted. Then you the writer will go away again and write a scene breakdown, a sort of bulleted list of the scenes you intend to write. It never really manages to encompass all the things you will write, but everyone is aware of that. Sometimes you meet an over-enthusiastic and inexperienced script editor who will want the scene breakdown to have all of the film except the dialogue in it. You explain. They take umbrage. Things will never be the same between you again. But hey, who cares? There is some arrogance in being a writer. Just don't look down.

By this stage you may have had feedback (as people like to call it) from one or two executive producers, a producer, one or two script editors, your wife, your cat, your agent and whoever was sitting next to you in the library when you started to cry about the project. Then you begin to write. What's the point of this detailed description? Remember at the beginning I wrote that you should respect your time. If the TV producer wants to see a premise, a treatment, a beat document, and a scene breakdown before he (or more likely she) will let you loose on their £1.5 million toy, how come you can't count your own time and your own work just as expensive and just as important when you set yourself loose on your own novel?

Beginners usually do 'have a novel in them' and manage somehow to stagger to a conclusion, making it up as they go, listening to the voices in their head, allowing the characters and the action to simply unfold. It may work. It may even work for a second novel. But surely after that you must have some respect for your time and fall back on making a plan. I've heard novelists say they want to write as if they just step off a cliff. I can imagine just stepping off a cliff is exhilarating. People say they want to take their writing into a place where anything can happen. That sounds exhilarating too, though at that stage something should nag at the back of your mind. In a place where anything can happen one of the 'anythings' is nothing. Respect your own time in your only life. Make a plan when you write. Be professional. No one else will be professional for you.

Rule (5) is, Whatever you are writing, start each scene late. This is strictly for fiction writers and is strictly a writing rule, rather than how to be a writer. Yet the tightness and absence of bagginess (shoe leather, sometimes directors call it) in fiction scenes is a sure sign of a professional writer. The point of coming in 'late', rather than starting each scene with some sort of preamble is that in so doing your writing keeps up a sense of urgency. It doesn't try the reader or viewer's patience. Starting scenes, whether in drama or prose, too early or too slowly is disruptive for the 'suspension of disbelief' bargain the writer and audience have struck. I suppose another way of expressing this is, 'have a bit of discipline, don't be a bore, cut to the chase'. Just because you have fallen in love with your ability to string words one after another, don't presume everyone else has.

Rule (6), Be feminine. I'll quote the explanation for this from Nicholas Freeling's *Apologia pro sua vita*, 'the traditional male qualities of logic, reason and structure are hostile to a world that defies analysis . . . women are much better at metaphysical exploration, a fact vexatious to most men' (Freeling 1994). There's another way of putting this. As a writer, be anything you want, but be *good*. All the planning in the world crumbles before this simple imperative, yet men (or rather the male, because here Freeling was writing about characteristics strictly rather than gender) tend to want to make a plan and stick to it. Actually, a writer needs to be a person who will make a plan and then not stick to it, and the willingness to engage with and the ability to choose the timing of the engagement with the irrational are characteristically feminine skills. Acquire them.

If Orwell's attempt at deriving rules as to why people write is time-expired, his style rules on 'how to write' are so powerful and useful that I would bring them to your attention. So to my own, eccentric, self-generated 'how to be a writer' rules:

> Write something.
> Do it again.
> Read and continue to read.
> Respect your own time.
> Whatever you are writing, start each scene late.
> Be feminine.
> Don't despair (OK I sneaked this in, but it's very important).

I would add these, from 'Politics and the English Language':

> Never use a metaphor, simile or other figure of speech you are used to seeing in print.
> Never use a long word when a short one will do.
> If it is possible to cut a word out, always cut it out.
> Never use the passive when you can use the active.
> Never use a foreign phrase, a scientific word or jargon word if you can think of an everyday English equivalent.
> Break any of these rules sooner than say anything outright barbarous.
> (Orwell)

I first read these words thirty years ago, long before I began to write seriously. At the time I was a factory worker, reading Orwell in my breaks. I still think of them as going to the very core of what it is to be a writer. If you want to be a writer, you've got to have style.

Notes

1. We all know that Art is not truth. Art is a lie that makes us realise truth, at least the truth that is given us to understand. The artist must know the manner whereby to convince others of the truthfulness of his lies. If he only shows in his work that he has searched, and re-searched, for the way to put over lies, he would never accomplish anything'. (Picasso to Marius de Zayas, in Barr 1980)
2. I'll admit my own first novel (*Tyro*, Hamish Hamilton 1982) wasn't autobiographical but it was the fictionalised story of someone I had known very well.

References

Barr, Alfred H. (1980), *Picasso: Fifty Years of His Art*, Boston: Museum of Modern Art.

Freeling, Nicolas (1994), *Criminal Convictions*, Boston: David R. Godine.

Newman, Barnett (1947), 'The first man was an artist', October, *Tiger's Eye*.

Orwell, George (1968), 'Why I write' in *The Collected Essays, Journalism and Letters of George Orwell. Volume 1. An Age Like This 1920–40*, pp. 1–6, London: Secker and Warburg.

Vidal, Gore (1983), *The Second American Revolution and Other Essays (1976–82)*, New York: Vintage.

42

How to Present Yourself as a Writer

Alison Baverstock

The premise for this chapter

This chapter is based on a single assumption: that you want to achieve a wider audience for your work, most usually through publication and dissemination.

Not every writer aspires to do this. You may be happy writing a family history for your relations to enjoy in the future, and these days it is possible to assemble a range of task-specific resources from publishing services companies, often the very same ones who work for professional publishers, and to turn your material into a worthwhile and lasting publication. Writing about how you feel is an excellent way of coming to terms with complicated emotions or key issues – perhaps redundancy or retirement; the serious illness or the death of a close family member or friend. It may be inappropriate to share these personal feelings with anyone other than the addressee of a letter – and you don't even have to send what you write. Alternatively, you may decide to form a small writers' circle, or research group, circulating information between yourselves and receiving feedback, which further fuels the creative process – and may lead to a formal output in due course. Many thoroughly worthwhile writing projects begin as personal commitments that turn into content you later want to share. This chapter is however presented for the specific benefit of those who are actively seeking to achieve a wider audience for their work in the short term.

Why do you want to be published?

It's a good idea to think about this before proceeding further. If you are specific about your goals then it's easier to harness motivation and recognise success – which can be built upon in future.

Some people publish for professional advancement; this is routine in universities, where an individual's academic publication record is crucial to their career prospects. Similarly, business consultants or trainers may find that a publication enables them to offer a summary of their competence in reassuring detail – a 'book as business card' which promotes their value and justifies a higher than market-average price. Others write because it improves their visibility; celebrity autobiographies, whether ghosted or not, help to prolong a media shelf life, or can capitalise on former fame for future financial benefit. Others write simply because they want to be read. It follows that if you are clear about what you want to achieve, you will make a better choice about whom to work with, and which publishing means to pursue as you seek to present your writing to a wider audience.

An uncomfortable starting point

One important caveat before we begin. You may not like the process of getting better known; it may seem trivial, intrusive – or both.

Most published writers have experienced a struggle to get their work accepted. If a writer tells you they have never been rejected, they are probably either being economical with the truth – or are exceptionally talented/lucky. There are so many hurdles along the way: rejection letters; lost manuscripts; overly dismissive commissioning editors; the dispiriting effects of the not-particularly-talented getting huge advances whilst you remain unpublished; the fear that each title will be your last (either you won't be able to do it again or public taste will turn against you). What keeps many authors motivated during this process is their sense of themselves as a writer; of writing as something they have to do, and with which they will continue, even if it means working alone.

Yet if your work is to achieve any kind of recognition, you must now look at yourself objectively and decide why the world should take notice. You need to consider adopting a different kind of writing style when describing yourself – however strong your preference for polysyllables, promotional copy is best written in short words – and be absolutely unsqueamish about benefiting from marketing opportunities (see Baverstock 2007).

For some this is remarkably difficult. You may feel very uncomfortable writing puff about yourself and the process may feel like bad luck; that by describing yourself in these terms you somehow reduce the chances of it becoming a reality. Others may feel that the whole business of marketing is inappropriate or even distasteful, that if the work were any good, it would sell without advertising. But in recent years we have witnessed both a fragmentation of existing media and a huge rise in the number of outlets through which information may be circulated, and there has been an equally dramatic increase in new ways of communicating through social media. It is very difficult for publishers to know how to reach the market for writers they invest in, and the author is almost inevitably brought in to guide, assist and support.

There has also been a blurring of boundaries. No longer does the reading public tend to observe a respectful distance from the author. Literary festivals offer them the opportunity to meet face-to-face and authors using digital communication (e.g. websites) or social media (blogging, Tweeting, etc.) can find their readership gets to know them very well. The boundary between where the book ends and the author starts is not precisely drawn; the identity of the author is part of the product the reader buys and so what is marketed tends to be author and work, not just work alone. And given the huge amount of reading material available, it follows that in order to get your idea noticed, you may have to compromise your view of yourself as a person who is mainly significant for their writing.

Your marital circumstances, for instance, or where you live, may temporarily capture the reading public's imagination more than your literary merit of your work. Your audience may be similarly fascinated by a simple human situation identified in your work that, while it is a tiny part of your extensive research, may spark the readership's interest. For example, I have heard biographer Anne Sebba hold audiences spellbound as she describes the impact which eighteenth- and nineteenth-century underwear had on adultery – the forward planning it necessitated.

Some writers mark this down to expedience; others feel frustrated and diminished. Why should a writer, who is known for writing, be equally effective in spoken communication? The reality is that if you want to get your work better known you will have to think seriously about making yourself sound interesting to the media, and this is best achieved by a positive attitude to the process – along with the journalists, publications and wider broadcasting opportunities that make it possible.

What you need to know about traditional agents and publishers

They have *lots of material to choose between*. One agent I know receives thirty to fifty unsolicited manuscripts every day. She takes on about five new writers a year, so she is looking for reasons to say 'no' rather than 'yes'. Writing competitions attract large numbers of entries and surveys have shown that to be published is a consistently common ambition. The MA in Creative Writing at Kingston University was set up in 2004 and within one year became the largest MA programme in the university.

They need to know *where your book will sit*, both within individual publishers' lists and within retailers' mechanisms. What kind of product is this, briefly, and what else has sold well in this category? What can it be compared with?

They would like you to *prove the size of a market* or specialist interest, maybe by quoting audience figures for relevant programmes on television, readership of a relevant specialist magazine or attendance at a relevant event. For example, if you were writing a novel based on attendance at a slimming club, it would be helpful to know how many people attend them regularly. Are they men or women? For what length of time do they belong, and how much does it cost them to join and go? If you have established interest in your material through self-publishing – releasing a few chapters or the whole work – or discussed the subject matter over social media, you may be in a strong position to prove likely demand.

They want to know *why you are best placed to represent this group*. This is an opportunity to air your brief, relevant – and interesting – history, not tell them what grades you achieved at school or the long route you travelled to this point. Publishers want to know what's *promotable* about you. Have you given press interviews in the past, done anything interesting in your holidays/youth/former career? Do you have an unusual hobby or nickname? What is the funniest thing that has ever happened to you? If you had ten seconds to attract the attention of a daytime television show host (and there's nothing better for getting a popular book noted), what would you say? They will also want to know how connected you are; how many followers you have on Twitter and whether or not you blog regularly. Do you have a website that could help promote the work to be made available?

They *don't require you to give up the day job* in order to sound serious about your writing. Fitting writing around other commitments shows determination, and there are many successful writers who held down full-time jobs before making the transition to full-time writer. Nick Hornby and Roddy Doyle were both teachers, Michael Ridpath was a banker. Indeed, agents often say they like to take on those who have been successful in another field before coming to writing, as they have a wider range of experiences to draw on, and have sufficient motivation for writing to have chosen to make a change – and perhaps also have an established income or the option of part-time work to fund their writing. Publishers and agents get a little nervous when writers assume they will make enough from their work to live on, or support others, straight away.

They *need a title*. What is your writing idea called? The title you come up with matters hugely. It's not something to think about later; it's a key part of the pitch you make to those you are hoping will invest in you. Get your friends, relations and colleagues thinking about this too. Many people will buy a book on the grounds that it simply appeals – and now that so much buying is done online, an attention-grabbing or evocative title can draw followers. As personal evidence I have bought, as presents, many copies of *Fifty is not a Four-letter Word* (Linda Kelsey) and *Revenge of the Middle-aged Woman* (Elizabeth Buchan).

They want you to *pay attention to the instructions they give*. Many publishing houses now offer information to authors on their websites on how to submit material. They may want the first three chapters rather than the whole manuscript, as email attachments or as a printout. It is folly not to pay attention to their requests. If they say 'no unsolicited submissions' but you feel what you have is a particularly good match for their general list, then you could try sending an email outlining your rationale and asking them to take a look. Remember that publishers and agents need a range of material to offer to their market (because people seldom buy the same book more than once) and so you could interpret this as 'no ill-considered submissions'. Above all, bear in mind that they are wordsmiths and a badly presented text will instantly repel.

They will appreciate you sending *a good covering letter/email* with what you suggest. Ensure you look at yourself from *their* point of view rather than *yours*. They are more interested in knowing that other people want to read what you have written than how much you want to write it. They want to hear that people have already enjoyed your writing and that similar markets are contactable (if so – where, when and how?), not be told that their existing customers 'will love it'. As a guide to how to do this, if you can say 'So what?' to any statement you make about yourself and your writing, and not come up with a good answer, then you are not adding to your argument for publication. Add any endorsements you can secure. These need not be from the famous, just the believable. For example, a new novel would benefit from a testimonial from an enthusiastic reader or local librarian; a children's book from a reader of the right age – or their parent, on how their child had been hooked.

They need you to *guide them around the market* you know better than they can ever do. Authors are frequently astonished that publishers are not expert in all the fields in which they publish – but that is why they need authors. For example, as they have full-time jobs, they can't watch daytime television, so they may need to be told which programme is most important to the prospects of your book. The media is in any case so fragmented these days, with many more commercial radio stations and options for the viewer/listener, so keeping track of all the possible outlets may be difficult. Similarly, the more specialised the field, the more they need the help of the author to help them find the right outlet for coverage.

They are human. Sending in a casually presented or physically battered manuscript makes it look as if you do not care to make a good impression or have already been rejected many times. In your accompanying note, explain why you want *their* publishing house to produce your book. Publishers are looking for a connection between their titles, in order to 'cross-sell' and increase the size of the customer's overall order, so if your book would expand their offering, do let them know.

How to increase your profile as a writer

The best advice is to be proactive, to see your writing as the product, and to put yourself in another – and entirely objective – mindset when writing about your writing.

When people ask you what you do, *say that you write*. Who knows who may be listening and could pass on your information? Some people even see knowing a writer as an enhancement of themselves; they may boast about their 'friend who writes'. Making the transition to describing yourself as a writer is difficult for many, but in the long run I think taking yourself seriously is a crucial step to having the rest of the world do the same.

Be flexible. You may have a long-term objective to write a series of saga novels set in a specific location, and have planned the lifestyle to support this, but getting published is usually achieved in small steps. Writing for a website, or for a school or parish magazine, helps you build up a portfolio of examples and your sense of yourself as a writer. Local papers and online groups can be an excellent way of getting your ideas noticed, so find out what publications or organisations might include information on your work (parish/school/parent–teachers association/relevant association/special interest group).

Social media can help you circulate a message very quickly, but there are associated dangers. The first is that you share too soon – and feel your ideas shrivel through too-early analysis or negative feedback. You may also turn yourself from a writer who blogs occasionally into a full-time blogger, as setting up and maintaining a blog is a lot of work. An alternative might be to target a blog you read, and ask if they would accept a guest contribution from you. Twitter is widely used by writers and journalists and can help drive traffic to what you have written. But people jostle for attention online, and the need to get noticed may tempt you to offer more eye-catching material. You should be aware that while the more personal the information you offer about yourself, the more likely you are to attract interest, there is a big difference between attention and approval. Once a story is out there, it cannot be recalled and material you find uncomfortable, along with other people's comments, can go viral just as quickly as positive publicity. Mae West may have said that 'There is no such thing as bad publicity' but it requires a strong personality to withstand both invasion and ongoing negative coverage (see Baverstock 2011, chapter 19 on using social media and chapter 20 on marketing).

Get involved with writing communities, both online and offline. You could offer to deliver a presentation to a local organisation; give a talk to a local book group; give a workshop or reading in a school to coincide with national book events; or help judge a writing competition. You could suggest a feature to your local paper on local writers and offer to be interviewed (local papers love stories about local people); write to the letters page; get yourself interviewed on local radio; offer to do a reading in a local bookshop (many have the equivalent of 'open-mike' sessions); offer to do a session for your library's regular story-time session.

Send your CV to the local media that might interview you. Many media careers start with pro-activity on the part of the interviewee; courting the relevant programmes, sending in a CV in and then following up. Bear in mind that the relationship between the media and writers is entirely symbiotic; they need content as much as you need publicity, but they won't know about you unless you send information to them. Activity here is also an investment in your future; a series of links to previous press coverage and relevant blogs will impress any potential agent or publisher.

Be imaginative about what you submit. Newspapers are inundated with images of people standing in line holding drinks, so try to think more creatively. For example, author Catherine Charley writes about exploring dangerous places and when one of her children's books was being published, she got a husky farm in Northern Ireland to supply dogs and a sled to drag her through the centre of Belfast, to present a copy of the new book to Waterstones. The dog farm was delighted with the publicity, the Northern Ireland Tourist Board similarly so, and the police and city council were happy to co-operate. She dressed up for the occasion in a parka and images of dogs, book and author appeared everywhere. Large sales followed.

Build the relationship with your publisher or agent. Publishing is a collaborative venture, so once you have acquired a publisher, make sure to work with them to grow your shared commitment. Try to understand their working environment. Marketing books is a very inexact science. Budgets are low and the audience – the public – unpredictable. Some books will take off in huge numbers, because word of mouth gets behind them, others will sink without trace despite the publisher's best efforts. Media coverage is hard to achieve and never guaranteed. Sometimes sending out a simple press release will have the entire press corps beating a path to your door, while at other times extensive circulation of journalists may yield nothing. Promotional coverage achieved is not a mark of the amount of effort put in.

Most publishing houses produce an Author Publicity Form (the name may vary from house to house), which they send out to authors to complete when a book is commissioned (signed up and you receive your first payment). It asks a lot of very basic questions that you might assume they already know the answer to (for example, who is this title for, why was it written, where is the market, who should review it?). This is a crucial marketing platform, so please put aside any temporary frustration that they should be asking you such basic questions. Devote enough time to filling it out completely and legibly, preferably online. There is always something extra that can be done for a title, and if you have given more useable information, you may be the beneficiary of a little extra effort. So, if you recommend a conference at which your title could be displayed, spell out its full name (not initials or acronyms unless very well known) and the organiser's full details. Do not write (as I have seen on such forms) *?Milan – 2014/15*. Be specific: if you help save your publishers time, they may pursue the lead, whereas if you leave them more work to do, they may not take up the opportunity.

Resist the temptation to give sarcastic answers to basic questions; and on all accounts, avoid referring them back to their internal organisation ('I have already told your editorial director, ask her'). If you are asked who is the target audience, tell them, rather than giving them a succinct debrief on the extent of their ignorance. And be helpful. Describe your career to date in objective terms, without excessive modesty or assuming they know things they may not. Just because your recent humanitarian expedition to Bosnia was widely reported in the press does not mean the marketing executive saw it too – she may have been taking her finals at the time. Don't crow or sneer; explain.

Remember that publishers are dealing with many titles, not just yours. An average marketing person may be handling thirty titles a month; it's most unlikely that the work of a single new writer would be their only job. So be helpful, feed them the right information at the right time, don't wait until publication to tell them you know the Features Editor of *Good Housekeeping*, refrain from keeping a grudge list of what they should be asking you for and don't yet know as a result.

Timing is very important. Amalgamate your information/helpful hints and provide it early (at least six months pre-publication). Ringing up with ideas just before publication is immensely frustrating; by then it may be too late to do anything (lead times in the press are long – a woman's magazine will be working four to six months ahead of the cover date). There is a strong emphasis on looking at what is new, both within the media and the book trade, and it can be very difficult to revive the fortunes of titles that do not get noticed on publication.

Say 'thank you' if things go well (and maybe even if not, but you feel they have done their best). Nothing is better calculated to make publishers try harder for you in future.

Self-publishing is featured elsewhere in this publication, but all the same processes and stages apply – the difference is that it's up to the author to arrange them. Recent research has revealed that far from requiring you to do it all yourself, many self-publishers are operating in teams, accessing a pool of freelance services or arranging for a single supplier to provide a complete service (Baverstock and Steinitz 2013) – or, as one such firm elegantly dubs it, 'professional publishing for the self-funding author' (SilverWood Books 2013: home page). In the process they may accumulate sufficient 'proof of concept' to convince the traditional investors (professional agents and publishers) that this is a market they should investigate on their behalf – or acquire the energy and market knowledge to further publish themselves.

A final word of advice

I often give talks to groups of writers. Talking to them about their need to get involved in marketing seldom produces a uniformly positive response. The majority now appreciate that those they hope will invest in their work, whether through time or financial resources, will be interested in *them* too – and that in order to get their work noticed it helps if they are cooperative. But there are always those who feel it is the publisher's or agent's job to be utterly objective; to look for the best writing and publish that, rather than get distracted by the knowledge that one author would interview better than another.

I am afraid my response is pragmatic. I have been a publisher as well as an author. Publishers are not the taste police; they are on the lookout for writing for which there will be demand, and which can in turn subsidise other fledgling ventures. In any case, the market for writing does not consist of a single group of consumers, any more than one book would meet all their needs. The reading public is whimsical and distracted, fickle in its tastes and disloyal to publishers, imprints and even long-term favourite authors. Publishers are trying to meet both current and anticipated needs, and yet the development and production time for a book is protracted and not instantly replicable. Ebooks may be disseminated much more quickly but still need all the same careful stages of manuscript preparation and careful delivery as more traditional formats. Authors may take longer than they have promised to deliver their book and they may not deliver what was expected. It is a difficult business to get right – they say the way to make a small fortune in publishing is to start off with a big one. Faced with so many potential suppliers, it is not surprising that most agents and publishers will look for good writing *and* a promotable author behind the package. The enigmatic stance of 'my writing says it all' is getting harder and harder to achieve.

Whether you decide to keep your writing to yourself, or ease its path to publication by working yourself into the equation, I wish you the best of luck.

References

Baverstock, Alison (2007), *Marketing Your Book: An Author's Guide*, London: Bloomsbury.

Baverstock, Alison (2011), *The Naked Author*, London: Bloomsbury.

Baverstock, Alison and Jackie Steinitz (July 2013), 'Who are the self-publishers?', *Learned Publishing*, 26:3, 211–23.

Buchan, Elizabeth (2002), *Revenge of the Middle-aged Woman*, Harmondsworth: Penguin.

Charley, Catherine (2000), *The Big Freeze*, Harmondsworth: Puffin.

Kelsey, Linda (2007), *Fifty is not a Four-letter Word*, London: Hodder.

SilverWood Books (2013), http://www.silverwoodbooks.co.uk/ (accessed 4 September 2013).

43

Meet Your Public: Creative Writing and Social Media

Lou Treleaven

Social media offers the creative writer multiple opportunities to engage with readers, other writers and the world in general. Whether you are published or trying to get published or self-published, a creative use of social networking can turn the general public into your public.

What is meant by social media?

Social media is the name given to Internet websites which combine a high amount of user-generated content with the opportunity to make connections with other users. (The term social networking is sometimes used in place of social media, but more accurately it describes websites that typically involve having your own page within the site while visiting, commenting and sharing with others on the same site – for example, Facebook.) Social media can take a variety of forms.

Types of social media

Forums

These are noticeboard-style text-based discussion sites, usually centred around a common interest. They are often part of a wider website, encouraging regular visitors to stay and debate or chat. Popular forums for writers include the writers' discussion site Absolute Write, self-help forums for e-publishers and forums on fan fiction sites where the fiction is posted into the forum itself. Joining a new forum can be daunting; everyone seems to know each other and there are a lot of in-jokes and indecipherable references. However, regular visitors who leave polite and thoughtful comments will soon be welcomed. A writers' forum can be a very supportive place. It is also an ideal arena to ask questions.

Forum posts can be public or private depending on the settings of the thread (the particular conversation), so check this out by looking at the thread description before sharing anything personal.

Microblogging

Microblogging services allow users to share updates, links or reactions to current events using a limited number of characters, usually less than two hundred. Microblogging is dominated by Twitter but there are other sites that offer a similar service or specialise in a niche area, such as sharing your mood or rating your day. Other social media sites may also incorporate a microblogging element such as a status update. Twitter is a useful way to connect with authors, agents or publishers that you don't have a real life relationship with, as it is acceptable to 'follow' people you don't know. Find the relevant people or companies that will allow you to keep up to date in your field.

Social networks

Social networking sites include Facebook, Google+, LinkedIn and MySpace. Users create a profile page and share information and updates with other people – normally existing friends, colleagues or online contacts. Your profile page can act as a mini-website for you and you should include and promote your achievements. Some writers prefer to have a separate writer page and keep their profile personal. A writer page or dedicated page for your book will allow people you may not know personally to visit and 'like' your activities (see Promotion).

Common-interest communities

Users within a community can interact with each other by befriending, reviewing and commenting and so this can also be classed as a form of social media. Steam, for example, is a website for purchasing, downloading, storing and playing games but also involves user interaction and friendship. A pertinent site for writers is Goodreads, which allows members to record, review and categorise virtual bookshelves, create book groups and discuss current reads through forums.

Media sharing

Interaction on media-sharing sites is based around posting photos or videos, sharing, rating and commenting. Popular sites include YouTube for video and Flickr, Photobucket and Instagram for photos. Pinterest is a particular favourite among the crafting community. Members can create noticeboard-style pages using their own photos or any images found on the web. The latter link back to the original source and can be 'repinned' by others on their own boards. Creating relevant Pinterest boards may draw people to your website.

Blogs

The word 'blog' originates from a shortening of 'web log' and is a diary-format website, usually updated frequently and used for a variety of purposes. Blogs can have single or multiple authors and can be free or paid for. Well-known free blogging platforms include WordPress.com, Blogger and Tumblr. A blog is an attractive tool for a writer for obvious reasons and an ideal starting point for social media interaction. Finding like-minded people and visiting and commenting on their blogs can create a feeling of community and support. Regular blogging is an excellent way to show off your writing skills. If you are unsure how to start or what to write about, try how-to articles about the writing process, interviewing other writers or reviewing books.

Discussion groups

A discussion group is a cross between a forum and a mailing list. You can start your own group and control who can join. A discussion group hosted by Yahoo Groups or Google Groups is a good choice for a reading group or writers' circle who wish to communicate with a number of members at a time without having to set up a public website or personal mailing list. Groups can be public or private and you can search for one that matches your interests – for example, a Yahoo Group for women's magazine fiction writers.

Chat rooms

Chat rooms can sometimes be attached to forums. They allow members to communicate in a group by typing to each other in real time. Abbreviations, acronyms and slang words are often used and, like forums, there are usually etiquette rules to follow.

Virtual worlds

Online games such as Second Life or World of Warcraft contain whole communities who interact with each other using avatars (in-game characters that represent the players). Identities may never be revealed, but some products and services use the virtual infrastructure as an opportunity to advertise, provide monetised services and even conduct job interviews.

Social news

Social news sites allow users to post text or links to existing web content in a bulletin board-style format. The posts can be commented on and voted up or down. Social news sites allow mass discussion on any topic and indulge niche interests as well as being used to drum up support for various causes. Reddit and Delicious are two such sites. Visiting social news sites will give you a snapshot of current 'hot topics'.

A website may contain a number of different social media features such as a blog, a forum and a chatroom.

Why use social media?

As a writer, there are three main reasons for you to engage with social media: to promote yourself and your work, to share your writing and express yourself creatively, and to enjoy the support and advice of other writers.

Promotion

Published writers are expected to take an active part in promoting themselves and their work, while self-published writers need to market themselves effectively in order to sell books. Even an unpublished writer will usually be expected to have some sort of online presence. In the case of non-fiction, a book proposal is much more likely to be successful if the author can point to a ready-made market of potential readers on the web who are already interested in their work.

Most established authors are likely to have a website which they may or may not get involved in personally. Authors who enjoy engaging more actively with their readers may also have a separate blog, a Twitter account and a social networking page, for example on Facebook. (At a certain level of fame unofficial fan sites and forums also spring up, over which the author has no control.)

Here are some other suggestions of how to use social media to promote your book:

- For most authors starting out, a simple blog is a good place to make a home on the web (see Getting Started). It's quick, easy and free, and ready-made templates will give your blog a professional look in minutes. Make sure it includes a page about you and your writing, contact details and information about where to buy your books.
- Make a book trailer. This sounds daunting but you don't need to hire a director to make your own trailer. If you are on a budget, a simple slideshow of photos, some text and a soundtrack may be all you need, using Movie Maker or a similar program to bring it together. You can even use PowerPoint to make a slideshow and convert it into a movie. Upload to YouTube or another video-sharing service and make it public. Don't forget to provide a link to your site. You can also embed the trailer into your website or blog.
- Make a social networking page for your book. This should be separate from any personal account and is more similar to a fan page where visitors can 'like' you and get updates on your writing activities. In Facebook you can create events and invite people to your book launch or other promotional activities.
- Join relevant communities. If your book is about pastry making, for example, see if there are forums or groups based around baking. Become involved – but don't push your book on to people with every post. A gentle approach is best.
- Create collections. For non-fiction writers, Pinterest boards are ideal for collecting relevant images that tie in with your book. Fiction writers could make a collection of their book covers or anthologies they have appeared in, or websites they have been published on. Ensure you link back to your website or blog.
- Post extracts. You can post short extracts on Twitter or longer extracts as blog posts. (Check with your publisher how much they agree you can quote.)
- Have a virtual launch party. This can be done on social networking or microblogging sites. Pick a day, invite friends and pop some virtual champagne corks. Play games, run competitions and make the experience fun.
- Go on a blog tour. This is an author tour from the comfort of your armchair. Ask fellow bloggers or writers if they will interview you or allow you to guest post. Make a schedule of where you are going to 'visit' and publish it.
- Encourage others to spread the word. If you are getting positive feedback on your book, is this reaching the general public? Consider asking people who have liked your book to Tweet or 'like' on Facebook or go a step further and write a review on Amazon or Goodreads, or even a blog post.

Creativity

It is easy to forget that social media is not just for networking: it can also be an end in itself. Everything that we type into blogs, forums and social networking sites is regarded as published. In fact social media is the ultimate in do-it-yourself publishing, requiring minimal effort but having the potential to garner maximum readership. This has its advantages and disadvantages. Work you posted on a private forum for critique may be ineligible to enter for a competition because it is considered published. Words you have written years ago may give you cause for regret. You must be able to stand by every word you say, or at least be prepared to backtrack and apologise.

On the positive side, social media is a personal publishing platform where we can write whatever we like without being influenced by market trends or commerciality. A thriving example of this is the fan fiction community where readers post stories based on their favourite books, films or television series, often using a forum format to do so. Writers can indulge their fantasies or simply flex their writing muscles while sharing their work with an eager audience. Some of these stories gain momentum and go on to be published as books in their own right.

So what are the different ways you, as a writer, can express yourself creatively within social media sites? Here are a few ideas:

- A blog is so much more than an online diary. Try writing a fictional diary, perhaps based on one of your main characters or from a historical viewpoint. How would Pepys write a modern-day diary?
- Blogs have the ideal format for an episodic story. Try writing a chapter a month, or a collection of short stories or poems. How about an interactive story where users suggest what's going to happen next? This can be done either by embedding a poll into your post and offering a choice of events, or by encouraging suggestions in the form of comments. Remember to have a summary page where readers can catch up with previous instalments.
- Blogs can have multiple authors. Could you set up a blog with writer friends and take turns to post short work? Could you work together on a shared work or create a shared world?
- The next step from a shared blog is a blog open to submissions – in other words, your blog becomes an e-zine. Put out a call for submissions, stating word count and subject matter. Remind people that this will count as published work even though they won't be paid. Be prepared to edit entries and spend time responding to queries. Don't forget to include some of your own work too, or links back to your personal site, if you have one.
- A limit of 140 characters on a microblogging site like Twitter lends itself to pithy remarks or quotations, but how about letting your main character or villain have a say on current events? How would a historical character react to a modern political event? How would your hero and heroine talk to each other on Twitter? What sort of viewpoint would a minor character in your story have? Explore the site and find some popular parody accounts to see how microblogging can be used in character.
- Microblogging is also the perfect vehicle for haikus and other short poetry forms. How about challenging friends or followers to a poetry contest?
- Could you write a short story in 140 characters, or sum up a classic in just a few words? Restrictions on length can spark unexpected creativity.
- Facebook pages are like character profile pages – they store a lot of personal information, life events, and likes and dislikes. Could you set up a Facebook page for a character? What TV programmes would they watch? Who would they be a fan of? Would they be a friend of yours and if so, how would you interact with them as their creator? If you don't

want to unleash your character on the world just yet, keep their details private and use the page as an ideas bank.

- Some forum members love to play word games – everything from word association to Consequences to full-on role-playing or short story compositions. As well as being a good way to warm up and have fun, this is an interesting and unpredictable method of creating work. How about starting a story where each new sentence has to begin with a consecutive letter of the alphabet? Or retelling an event in rhyming couplets?

Support and advice

Everyone knows a writer's life can be, by necessity, a solitary one. Social media can provide valuable moral support and friendship to help keep you motivated and on track. Who better than other writers to understand the crashing disappointment of another rejection, or the crazy high of a full manuscript request? You can meet people through forums dedicated to writing or to a particular author's work or genre. You can also join critique groups and share work with others. This will involve time as you will be expected to analyse others' work, so be prepared to put the hours in.

Having a support network is also useful when it comes to asking questions or carrying out research. Got a query about a contract or want to check out a dodgy publisher? Someone is bound to know the answer, or direct you to the right website. Want to know how to hold a sheep while shearing, or what it's like to abseil down a mountain? Someone will have done it or know of an expert who can help. Sites like Pinterest can be useful for organising research material such as location photos.

Getting started

The amount and variety of social media sites can be overwhelming to a new user. Before you plunge in, it is worth calculating how much time and energy you have to invest in online activities. Joining a site such as a forum or critique group in which you don't have time to participate regularly can damage your profile and alienate other users. If you do not think you can put much into a social media site, there is little point in joining.

The writer's blog

If time is limited but you do want to establish yourself online, a free blog is probably the best option. It gives you a presence, allows you to communicate with potential readers and other writers, showcases your work and puts your name into search engines. Updating it regularly with new content is imperative, but this does not have to be a daily chore. Once a week is ideal, but even once a month is acceptable as long as it is regular. Fresh content keeps your blog in the search engines, attracts followers and shows publishers and agents that you are active.

A well-known free blogging platform such as Wordpress.com, Blogger or Tumblr is a good bet for your first blog. You will be quickly picked up by search engines and people are more likely to follow you and leave comments if they have the same type of blog. Once you have created an account you can choose a template and start blogging straight away. Each blog entry is called a post and these will by default be displayed on the front page of your blog in date order, with your most recent post at the top. Post regularly to keep your site looking fresh. Blogs can also have pages of fixed content. These usually sit 'behind' your blog page, accessible through the menu, and contain information such as contact details, list of books or articles written by the author, or samples of work. (An easy option to make a website instead of a blog is to set up a blog using only fixed pages – or put your blogging posts behind a fixed front page.)

An 'about me' fixed page is an opportunity for you to list your achievements as well as contact details and where to buy your books. As mentioned earlier, consider also putting this information onto side bars which will appear on all your pages. It should also be obvious to readers how to sign up to your blog and you should place a sign-up box in your sidebar in a prime position.

An important part of blogging is using categories and tags. Categories enable you or your reader to sort your blog content into easily identifiable topics, almost like chapter headings. Tags are more specific, like an index. So if your blog is about reading, a book review might have the category of 'review' and be tagged with the name of the book and the author. Categories and tags are an essential part of getting your blog posts into search engines and, used accurately, will widen your reach.

Tips for blogging

- Respond to comments. Replying keeps your blog relevant and reinforces the idea of you as a person at the other end. If you have set your blog so that you have to approve comments then do so promptly.
- Visit others. Find people who are doing what you do. Mutual respect is a good basis for an online friendship.
- Consider guest blogging or interviewing other bloggers. Shared traffic is a boost to both parties.
- Create content that fulfils a need. If you have had trouble researching something, the chances are others have too. Write a blog post that can help people.
- Be generous with information. That competition you want to enter may have more entrants if you publicise it, thus decreasing the odds of your winning; but equally it has more chance of running again next year if it has some healthy interest this year.
- Keep popular blog posts up to date. If your stats show certain old posts are still pulling visitors in, consider keeping them relevant with new information, or reporting again on the same subject. Create a menu that links to them from your main page.
- Spend time and effort on your posts. Your blog, your social networking page, even your Twitter account – they are your business card. You never know who might come calling.

Your public

Social media is all about reaching out and making connections, and within that melting pot of online personas is a very special group of people: your followers. These are the people who made that extra effort and clicked on a button to ally themselves to your cause. They like you. They want to hear more from you. Having followers is a great ego boost. But it is also a responsibility, because once people have signed up to follow your posts you owe them some sort of return. These are your future readers, your potential fans, and they are precious. If they have signed up to your blog, give them a blog worth signing up for. Keep posts regular, informative and entertaining. If they follow you on Twitter, don't bombard them with sales pitches. One in ten tweets mentioning your book will be plenty. Comments or replies to your posts should be approved quickly and responded to promptly and politely. If you cannot spare the time to reply to individual comments, a blanket response thanking people for discussing a particular point may suffice. And finally, try to visit the people who visit you. You might find that you become a follower, too.

Being a follower

Social media isn't all about gaining followers and fans, it's about being a fan too. Keeping abreast of your favourite author's activities and being able to comment on and interact with their posts is an enjoyable way to feel part of the writing world. Twitter is a good place to find writers to follow, and there is something fascinating about watching famous authors trade witty remarks with one another – much like a modern version of the old literary salons. A personal reply to a comment made to your favourite author is something to treasure, and remembering this feeling of being singled out is useful when considering how to interact with your own followers.

Staying safe

Staying safe online involves not only keeping your device safe from viruses and malicious software, but also keeping you safe personally. Always make sure you have up-to-date anti-virus, anti-spyware and firewall protection. Some operating systems have their own all-in-one security programs included, such as Microsoft Security Essentials. Free and paid-for anti-virus and anti-spyware programs are available to download on the Internet or they may come with your PC. Keep your computer operating system up-to-date as well, to give these programs the best chance of working.

Use secure passwords – combinations of letters and numbers are best, including capitals – and change them regularly. Avoid obvious choices like pet names or birthdays. Keep personal information such as your address, phone number and date of birth hidden from public view. If you are not sure what others can see, log out of the site and try to view your profile as an outsider. Some sites have a 'view as' function which allows you to do this without logging out. Avoid giving away details of your routine such as what time you leave for work, or when you go on holiday.

If you decide to meet up with friends you have made online, follow a few simple rules to stay safe. Meet in a public place – a café is ideal – and always let someone else know where you are going. Keep things light and avoid giving away too much personal information.

Personal versus professional persona

It is a good idea to keep your author activities separate from your personal accounts. If you are trying to attract the attention of an agent or publisher you will want to have a smart, professional-looking website or blog rather than one filled with your holiday photos and anecdotes about your pet. The exception to this would be if you are marketing yourself as a columnist who writes about his or her own life; in this case a well put together and entertaining blog about your daily life might just be the perfect calling card. (But do remember to protect the identity of other people you might refer to. Don't post pictures of others online without their permission and do use false names if you think people might be hurt or misrepresented by what you are writing.)

If you have a personal Facebook or other social networking account, set up a separate author page for all your writing news. You can advertise it and link to it from your own page as much as you want and the page will act as a mini-website for you.

Even if you do keep your personal life and writing life separate, inevitably there will be overlaps and people searching for you as an author may well come across the 'real' you as well. With this in mind, consider what you post or share as yourself, even if you write under a pseudonym. If it could be harmful to your writing career, is it worth the risk? If you write for children, is your online identify suitable for family viewing? Go on to a search engine and look up your name (in double quotation marks) to find out what other people might see.

Creating a brand

It's a good idea when promoting yourself as a writer to keep your image consistent. Even though you may be using quite a few different types of social media, you can create a brand identity which will link these different communications together. Start off by using the same photograph. A simple headshot will look professional, particularly if it's black and white. Use the same usernames if you can and try to use your author name rather than a nickname (unless you are trying to visit a forum anonymously). In your personal profiles, make sure you always link back to your website or blog. Think about your various accounts as a multi-pronged approach and consider how to use each to complement the other. For example, you might write a detailed entry on your blog about a new writing competition you have heard about, including closing date, entry fee, website link and other details. Twitter would be the place to broadcast the headline with a link to your blog. On Facebook or Google+ you might share the fact that you have updated your blog with some competition news, while on a writing forum you could start a thread asking who else is considering entering which also includes a link to your blog for the details. Even though you have used various different social media, they all point back to your blog, which advertises you and your writing.

Think about what your brand is and search out people, groups or companies in your field. For example, if you write picture books, follow authors on Twitter, 'like' a publisher's Facebook page and join a LinkedIn group for picture book writers. All this activity will show up on your profile and reinforce your brand identity. The content you post should also fit in with your brand and be of interest to others in the same area. This will attract followers who are relevant to you and your writing.

Juggling

Once you are active on several social media sites you will have to master the art of juggling between them and tailoring your content accordingly. If you want the feel of having all your accounts in front of you and at your fingertips, you can sign up with a social media aggregator or dashboard, a site that manages your social media accounts by displaying them in one place and allowing you to update several simultaneously. Or concentrate on the sites you enjoy the most.

Time management (don't forget to write)

Time spent networking, sharing and collaborating online can easily expand to fill the precious hours you have put aside for writing. If you find this is happening to you, try to limit your social networking activities to a certain time in the day or restrict yourself to short bursts using a timer. In extreme cases you can download software that restricts your Internet use. Try to aim to do more writing than social networking, or match your time hour for hour. Unless, of course, you are writing creative content for its own sake!

Etiquette

Each social media site seems to have its own etiquette rules which can be confusing to a new user. Take the time to read any FAQs (Frequently Asked Questions) before starting to post and keep in mind the following general etiquette advice:

- Avoid using capitals throughout a sentence: this can be interpreted as shouting and looks aggressive.
- Read over everything you write before posting to make sure it can't be misunderstood or misinterpreted.
- Never post in the heat of the moment.
- If you have to argue, debate with imagination and intelligence. Don't trade insults.
- Consider using your writing name rather than a nickname. It ensures you act in a way which protects your professional reputation.
- Be active. A non-participating member of a forum who reads but does not comment is called a 'lurker'. Get engaged.
- Use the ratio of 10% promotion to 90% general interaction. Any more can look pushy.
- Stay on topic. If you are on a forum, keep to the thread topic or start a new one if you want to talk about something else. If you are visiting a blog, participate in the blog topic.
- Be helpful to others and seek help in your turn.
- Maintain a professional persona. You are your brand. Be an ambassador for yourself.

44

Publishing Fiction

Mary Mount

The person with whom the writer wants to be in touch is his reader: if he could speak to him directly, without a middleman, that is what he would do. The publisher exists only because turning someone's written words into a book (or rather, into several thousand books) is a complicated and expensive undertaking, and so is distributing the books, once made, to booksellers and libraries. From the writer's viewpoint, what a mortifying necessity this is: that the thing which is probably more important to him than anything else – the thing which he has spun out of his own guts over many months, sometimes with much pain and anxiety – should be denied its life unless he can find a middleman to give it physical existence. (Athill 2000: 132)

There are very few rules in literary publishing. Editors turn down novels that win Booker prizes; one literary novelist might get reviewed everywhere, win prizes, sell hundreds of thousands of copies, while another, equally brilliant will sell five hundred copies, live in penury and be reviewed in one local newspaper. Edith Wharton showed Henry James a motor car and said this is what her latest bestseller had earned her; Henry James pointed to his wheelbarrow and said that was what he had got out of his latest book. Some writers receive the best reviews in the world and sell nothing, some writers get no reviews and sell millions. On a book tour a writer might have an audience of hundreds in one town and a bookseller and a stray dog at the next.[1] Some authors will write six novels before any of them are commercially successful, some novelists will write one book that is truly great. Some authors look like models, many don't; some do endless publicity, others go to a foreign country on publication day. The nicest thing about the publishing world is that nothing is certain. This may not be very helpful at the beginning of a chapter on acquiring and editing literary novels[2] but it can be a comfort to anxious writers and their editors.

The editor and the writer

Where do editors find writers?

Most editors working for a literary imprint will receive about three to five submissions a week. This varies a little depending on the time of year: during February and March editors' in-trays tend to fill up at a greater pace as agents try to sell books in advance of the London

Book Fair, and again, in the autumn agents and publishers will try to sell rights in advance of the Frankfurt Book Fair in October.

Editors receive manuscripts from a wide range of sources:

- From literary agents
- From publishers seeking to sell rights abroad
- From foreign language publishers trying to sell English language rights
- Directly from members of the public (although many publishers do not accept unsolicited material)
- From friends of authors whom the editor already publishes
- From friends of friends
- From creative writing schools following visits.

Editors also seek out writers from magazines, the web, newspapers, journals and competitions. This doesn't necessarily mean that an editor will be the only one to see that writer's work when it is ready for submission but at least it means the editor has established interest with the writer and has got a headstart on other publishers.

How does an editor decide what to read first?

Editors tend not to read new submissions in the office, unless they are very urgent, but spend their working day talking to authors and agents, editing, writing blurbs for hardbacks, briefing covers, presenting at marketing and sales meetings. They take home manuscripts to read in the evenings and at weekends. The best way to think about how editors make decisions is to think about the way most readers buy and read new novels. You may decide to buy a new novel in a bookshop because of the cover, the blurb, the first page. Perhaps you've read the author already in magazines or newspapers. Maybe the novel has been personally recommended or it has been well reviewed.[3]

Editors, on the other hand, will often be reading first drafts, there will be no blurb (apart from the agent's covering letter which is, for obvious reasons, often a little too subjective), there will be no impartial, personal recommendation, the editor will not know very much about the author at all. However, editors, like readers, do subconsciously look for signals to help them decide which novel should be read first from their pile, which ones to carry on with to the end, which ones to acquire for the list. Here are some of the ways in which an editor is influenced in his or her decisions:

- If the first few pages indicate writing of quality (it could be that the first paragraph isn't brilliant but that the writing has something special about it – you must remember that the editor is reading it with an eye to being able to edit it, but is also looking out for something special, something that will stand out from the crowd).
- If the author has a track record: of journalism; has appeared in anthologies; has been to a writing school with a particularly good reputation.
- If the author is represented by an agent with a very good list, an agent who submits very little and who shares the same tastes as the editor (similar to a recommendation by a friend but with a little more vested interest involved!). The longer an editor works in publishing the more he or she will be in tune with certain agents.
- If the author comes with a recommendation from another writer.

Do editors always finish every manuscript they read?

Again, editors will, of course, react in a similar way to readers – they wouldn't be any good at their jobs if they didn't. Just as you as a reader need a good plot, good prose style, originality, and many other things to feel compelled to finish a novel, so too does an editor. It may come as a shock to you that editors do not read all their submissions to the end. This would be impossible given the number they receive and is also impractical as most people can tell if they really don't like a book after reading a hundred pages. Without going into an exploration of what makes good writing, there are some basic things that we all notice as readers and that makes us decide whether or not to continue with a book. The style may be too self-conscious, the characters may not come alive, the plot might seem predictable, the narrative voice may not be compelling, the themes may seem hackneyed. All of this would stop you as a reader from finishing a novel and it will have the same effect on an editor. An editor will read a substantial amount of a novel and, if the book really isn't grabbing her then she won't continue. However, there are two essential differences between the way an editor reads a manuscript and the way most readers read novels. First, an editor is reading a manuscript in the knowledge that it is a first draft. If the novel is special enough the editor may well commission it with the proviso that some editorial work will be done. The other difference is that an editor might enjoy a novel but may not feel strongly enough about it to make an offer for it. Editors need to feel very strongly about a book in order to be able to publish it, just as you as a reader might finish a novel but you would need to feel very strongly about it in order to be able to recommend it to a friend.

How does an editor decide?

This may seem an obvious question: surely if an editor likes a novel then she'll want to publish it? However, as an editor, deciding whether you want to publish a novel is rather like how you do or don't recommend books to friends. We have all read novels that we've liked but not loved, novels that are OK but nothing special. From an editor's point of view the hardest decision we make is to reject a novel that we *quite* like. We read many manuscripts that have some good qualities but are forgettable, or as editors often put it, 'too quiet'. Those novels are the hardest to reject and also the hardest to publish. They may depict a situation well, or they may be good at character, but they are just not exceptional – they are interesting but not thought-provoking, they might mildly amuse but won't make you laugh out loud, they may be superficially moving but ultimately don't really touch you deeply. If an editor does not feel utterly convinced by a novel, she won't publish it convincingly. Just as, if you read a novel that is ultimately unsatisfying, you wouldn't recommend it to a friend. This is probably the most subjective area of the editor's job – when it isn't a choice between bad or good writing but the book's overall *effect*.

In the end, in terms of literary fiction, as a reader you are looking for something special. And the same is true of editors, except they have to be able to convince more than one reader. As opposed to the agent who only has to sell the book to an editor, the editor has to convince the sales people in the building of its merits, the publicist has to convince the literary editors that they should review it and has to have confidence in the reviews it's going to get, the sales people have to convince the booksellers to stock it, the booksellers have to convince readers to buy it and then the readers have to like it enough to finish it and tell other people to read it. Editors have to have this in the back of their minds when they finish a novel and are trying to decide what to do. A book that really works is one that the editor will finish and will rush in to the office the next day and say, 'We have to publish this!' Unfortunately for the editor, there are probably four or five other editors at other houses doing and thinking exactly the same thing . . .

The editor and the agent

How do editors acquire books for their list? What is a book auction?

In *Stet*, Diana Athill's wonderful book about her life as a book editor, the author describes how she felt when she read Norman Mailer's first novel, *The Naked and the Dead* in manuscript. She remembers how it 'genuinely expanded the range of my imagination' (2000: 32). This is a reaction that every editor dreams about when they start the first sentence of a manuscript, sitting in their front room on a Monday evening. However, these days there are a few more hoops to get through before the editor will be united with the book of her dreams.

Agents work in many different ways: some will auction a book to as many publishers as possible. This means they will send out a submission to all the literary houses and then try to get editors to bid against each other. In this scenario the highest advance usually wins (although, when it gets very heated, publishers do offer other incentives like marketing plans or strange gifts with some connection to the content of the novel), often combined with the prestige of the house and the way the editor and author respond to each other on editorial questions.

Other agents will be quite clear about which houses or editors they want for their authors' work and will limit their submissions to only a few editors. This means that they have more control over how the book is published (that is, that they don't find themselves selling a book to a publisher who isn't very good at publishing a certain sort of novel but are forced to do so for financial reasons).

Agents on some occasions will send books exclusively for a limited period to a single editor. This may be because that editor has had a great deal of success in a particular area, or that the publisher knows the author very well or the agent feels that at the right price the company will do the best job for this author and his or her novel.

From an editor's point of view the best agent is the one who is thinking all the time about how a book is being published, what is right and sensible for the author. The best agent will continue to work long after the deal has been struck, badgering the editor (if the editor needs it!) but also offering good advice to an author, calming their nerves, explaining the process, keeping relations between editor and author as clear and positive as possible. A good agent will also work hard to get the author journalism or reviewing work (if they seek it) and generally contribute to helping both author and publisher get the best for the book. Some agents do editorial work long before the book is submitted, thereby giving it a greater chance of finding a publisher. (And this is not uncommon given most agents were publishers and/or editors at one time.)

Agents, if submitting material by email should always contact the editor beforehand either by telephone or by a preliminary email explaining what the book is and checking whether it is OK for it to be sent by email. Agents, particularly those who operate in the same country as the primary market for their books, who send out manuscripts of new writers via email with no prior warning, are not giving a good service to their author. If the agent is half-hearted about a submission then an editor will be half-hearted in their response.

Reading the papers these days one would think that writers are constantly receiving millions of pounds in exchange for their work. The reality is very different. First, most publishers only pay advances in quarters (on signature, delivery of manuscript, first and second publication). Given that there is often a year between delivery and first publication and a year between first and second publication it usually takes two years minimum for an author to receive all of his or her advance, and it can often take longer. Also bear in mind that an agent will take 10 percent or 15 percent for a local sale and 20 percent for a foreign sale as well as often charge for photocopying before the book has even been acquired by a publisher. If you think that the majority of writers receive less than £40,000 advance set against royalties then the garret doesn't seem very far away.

The editor and editing

In literary publishing the ideal is that a perfect, fully-formed manuscript lands on your desk. More often than not, and particularly in the case of debut fiction, some editorial intervention is required and is usually welcomed by the author. I have never come across an editor who doesn't edit. The editor is usually tentative in his or her remarks: 'I'm not sure that this paragraph works' for example, rather than bullying. The author does not usually resent suggestions (and, in fact, given that he or she will probably have been sitting alone in a room with their work for a long time they are often pleased to be able to discuss their work with someone who has read it closely). No changes are made without an author's approval and disagreements on issues of the text tend to be rare.

In most publishing houses editors and copy-editors perform two different roles. The editor will be responsible for finding authors, acquiring the rights to publish their novel, editing the book (in broad terms – usually giving advice about structure, characters, endings, dialogue), presenting it to colleagues in-house, briefing the jacket, writing the blurb, garnering quotes, being the main port of call for the author. Copy-editors, often freelance and working out of house, will check facts, look for consistency in dates, timing, tidy up grammar and correct spelling.

The editor and the market

Book-chains now dominate the market and increasingly books are ordered centrally, whereas in the past sales reps would visit individual shops and handsell a literary list to the fiction buyer of that particular shop. These days the big chains sell many more copies of a single title: most readers will be familiar with piles of the same title piled up at the front of a large bookshop. This way of selling means that the range of titles is reduced and space in bookshops is increasingly competitive. People now tend to use the Internet to search for more obscure titles. The depressing fact is that on occasion a major chain may decide not to stock a first novel in hardback at all. Faced with this situation publishers have to work harder to set up a platform long in advance of publication. Jackets have to be ready seven months in advance, endorsement quotes are needed not just to sell to readers but to convince bookshops to stock the book in the first place (which means getting quotes for books at least six months before the book is published). There's no point in getting an amazing endorsement quote if the book isn't available in the shop. Increasingly publishers need to show that a book has a platform in order for a chain to stock it (maybe a confirmed interview in a national newspaper, radio serialisation, bestseller status in another country, previews in newspapers). In this way, an editor is not just buying and editing a book but continues to work right up to publication to ensure that the book will be stocked and will get the attention at the front of the bookshop. The change in the way books are sold has affected publishing enormously. You will notice that lists are much smaller and even within these smaller lists publishers will spend most of the marketing money on a smaller proportion of titles.

Authors also need to be aware that when a book-chain decides to promote a title the publisher is asked to pay for that promotion. Most marketing spend in the booktrade is spent on these crucial promotions. The most important thing for publishers is that a book is stocked and displayed in a prominent position in the shops.

Price promotions like 'summer reading', 'book of the month', 'three for two' are all seen as fundamental to a novel's potential sales life. This means, in turn, that covers, particularly in paperback, play a significant role and booksellers have been known to refuse to stock a book if they don't like the jacket. Book clubs, particularly televised ones like *Richard & Judy*, can transform the sales pattern of a new novel.

This information about the book trade is not there to make you feel despondent but just to give an insight into the pressure that each literary imprint is under. Why should a literary editor review a first novel by a completely unknown writer? Why should a book-chain stock a hardback novel by a completely unknown writer? Why should a reader buy a novel for £14.99 by someone they've never read? It is the editor's job to get over all these hurdles – to show complete faith in the writers they publish and to transmit that faith to critics, booksellers and readers.

And every year jaded publishers and booksellers are taken by surprise. It's as true now as it ever was that publishing is not an exact science. Every year there is disappointment and every year an exciting new writer gets the attention he or she deserves. Editors may rely on good writing and good judgement but they also rely heavily on good jackets, good titles, good distribution, good timing and, most important of all, good luck.

Final dos and don'ts

Don't send an unsolicited manuscript to an agent or publisher by email with no warning: why should a complete stranger print out a copy of your manuscript and take it home if you won't spend time printing it out, writing a covering letter and sending it by post?

Don't argue with a turn down. You are right, editors are not geniuses, they may have got it completely wrong and you may be the next Proust but, like you, if they don't like a book, whatever you say is not going to change their minds. If they really are incompetent they won't last long in their job anyway (if that is a comfort!).

Don't send a revised manuscript that the editor has already turned down unless you've been asked to. It is very difficult to feel enthusiastic about a novel if you didn't like it the first time you read it.

Don't expect fame and money! There are easier and quicker ways to get rich and famous.

Don't hurry. If an editor has made some suggestions and wants to see your work again then think about the suggestions carefully, mull over them. In your keenness to get published don't do some quick fixes and send back the manuscript but sit back and look at your script after a bit of a break. It will be better for it.

Don't be despondent – editors often get it wrong and if your writing is good, it will find a way to reach readers. Also remember that many established writers still have their first novels in a bottom drawer, unpublished. Many well-known writers often find they have to abandon a novel half way through because it just isn't working. *The Curious Incident of the Dog in the Night-time* was Mark Haddon's second adult novel: the first was unpublished. On the other hand, if someone is trying to tell you that publication is unlikely (and you want to get published, of course there are many people who write just for the pure pleasure of it and not for publication) then don't decide the world is conspiring against you. Maybe think about doing something else.

Do make sure you feel as satisfied as possible with your work before you send it. It will simply stand a much better chance if it is as polished as possible.

Do check for spelling and typos! This may sound obvious but if a script is littered with typos and spelling mistakes then that will lessen the impact of the work.

Do a bit of research before you write to agents. Look at the *Writers' and Artists' Yearbook* or *The Writer's Handbook*, edited by Barry Turner (both are updated every year so make sure you get the most recent issue as companies move and change often) to see which authors each agent represents and work out if they match your tastes (it may be that your writing isn't like the authors they represent but chances are that if you like their authors then you will share a sensibility).

Do send more work if you're asked to. If an editor doesn't take your book on but expresses interest in seeing what you write in the future then take them up on it! They won't ask to see your work again if they don't want to.

Do think about criticism. If someone you trust makes suggestions about your work then take them seriously. Criticism is very healthy and even if you disagree, think about why they might have responded to your work as they have.

Do read, read, read. A professor in charge of a creative writing course at an American university said, 'It's not so much that we're teaching them how to write, but that we're teaching them to read'. Reading really is the best way to improve your writing.

> It is advantageous to an author that his book should be attacked as well as praised. Fame is a shuttlecock. If it be struck at only one end of the room, it will soon fall to the ground. To keep it up, it must be struck at both ends. (Samuel Johnson)

Notes

1. For more on the pain of public readings see the brilliant collection, *Mortification: Writers' Stories of Their Public Shame* (Robertson 2003).
2. I am restricting this discussion to literary fiction. Publishing non-fiction is perhaps more predictable: is the subject of current interest? Has it been written about before in book form? How long ago and how well? Will the subject still be of interest by the time the book is delivered and published (most non-fiction is commissioned on the basis of a proposal and sample material, unlike fiction which is commissioned usually on the basis of a finished script). Can the author pull it off? Fiction, on the other hand, seems a more subjective area and more unpredictable and perhaps needs more explaining . . .
3. One of the most common reasons for readers to buy a new novel in a bookshop, particularly in the chains, is when it is heavily discounted. For a discussion of promotions and discounting see section entitled 'The editor and the market' later in this chapter.

References

Athill, Diana (2000), *Stet*, London: Granta Publications.
Boswell, James (2004), *The Journal of a Tour to the Hebrides with Samuel Johnson, LL.D.*, Mississippi: Oxford.

Robertson, Robin (2003), *Mortification: Writers' Stories of Their Public Shame*, London: Fourth
    Estate.
Turner, Barry (annual), *The Writer's Handbook*, London: Macmillan.
Writers' & Artists' Yearbook (annual), London: A&C Black.

45

American PoBiz

Chase Twichell

There was a time, not so long ago, when independent small presses were the refuge of 'alternative voices' (poets likely to be rude, naughty, or overly ironic, or poets whose work had 'literary merit' but was unlikely to sell well enough to make any money for anyone). But since it is now possible to produce well-made books for a reasonable sum, and to publish, distribute and promote them through the Internet and elsewhere to a potentially huge audience, the entire economy of the publishing industry is undergoing seismic quakes. A small press – even a single individual – can reach national and even international audiences with a budget unimaginably modest only a dozen years ago. According to The Council for Literary Magazines and Presses, a not-for-profit organisation dedicated to furthering the interests of independent publishers, 98 per cent of poetry published in the US is currently published by independent presses. Some that started in a spare room are now among the most important publishers, for example City Lights, BOA Editions, Sarabande, Copper Canyon, Milkweed Editions, Graywolf, and Coffee House, just to name a few. Finalists for literary prizes such as the National Book Award, the National Book Critics Circle Award, and the Pulitzer are increasingly books from independent literary presses. The old systems of promotion and distribution have rusted and broken down, and the new ones are evolving faster than describable. We're back in the Wild West, a bucking bronco of an age, and it's the best thing that's happened to American poetry in decades.

In order to understand the politics of poetry publishing in the US, you have to understand its economics. Media magic has enabled a new generation of publishers to dance with the behemoths, the big old commercial houses like Random House, HarperCollins, Grove-Atlantic, Houghton-Mifflin, Knopf, Farrar Straus and Giroux, Simon and Schuster. These mighty publishers still have small poetry lists, with a mix of known names and newcomers, and they publish and promote their books perfectly well. But the behemoths are no longer free-ranging. An example: Rupert Murdoch 'acquired' Fox which 'acquired' two children, HarperCollins and Hyperion. Little fish swallows money; big fish swallows little fish. There are a few exceptions, but most of the once-independent commercial publishers are now subsidiaries of larger media corporations, the withered book arm of an octopus that has its other tentacles in music and entertainment, cable, satellite, cellular technology, major newspapers worldwide, and the magazines we flip through while waiting for the cashier to ring up our groceries. Even University presses, once a mainstay of poetry publishing in the US, often wince at the P-word these days. Here too there are exceptions, of course, but the reality is that the entire industry is in the throes of re-imagining itself, and it's all shook up.

Which is an excellent state of affairs for both independent publishers and poets. I consider the media revolution to be the biggest challenge to the status quo of American poetry since the Beats. A number of very intelligent and ambitious editors, publishers, and poets are out there producing, distributing and promoting poetry, and engaging in profound and passionate exchanges about human consciousness and literature, good and evil, politics, the future, etc. This ferment of activity is happening both online and on paper, and in both periodical media and books, and it means that there's a near-infinity of venues for poetry. I doubt that it has ever been easier to publish one's work. It means, however, that we must forsake our old notions of hierarchy, and be open to new authorities, champions, and seals of approval, and alert to new underminers and foes.

It's difficult to map this vast new territory, but that has always been part of the business-work of being a poet: to find out where you belong in the poetry universe. What's out there? The old line-up of venerable literary magazines is still very much intact. Print journals like *The New Yorker, The Atlantic, Paris Review, The Hudson Review, The Georgia Review, The Yale Review, Field, Ploughshares, Poetry, Kenyon Review, American Poetry Review, AGNI* and so forth continue to publish serious and important work. There's a multitude of others ranging from Establishment to Guerilla, decades-old to born yesterday, cotton bond to liquid crystal diode. Poems are displayed by municipal transit authorities in buses and subways; new blogs and e-zines light up the Internet. From where I'm sitting, it looks like an amusement park.

Yet the statistics are discouraging. I'm speaking as editor, teacher, and Battered Poet with enough rejection slips to paper two-point-five bathrooms, which I fully intend to do someday. If I limit my calculations to the thirty largest poetry presses as well as all contests resulting in publication, I'd hazard that about one in every 500 strong manuscripts is eventually published, one out of every several thousand poems. By 'strong' I mean intelligent, well-crafted work with something of genuine and pressing importance to say, and am not including the sort of manuscript that would get weeded out in the first go-round, for example lite, inspirational, or greeting card verse, teenaged haiku, and *The Complete Old Testament* retold in the voice of a donkey.

Each magazine or book publisher is powered and defined by a group of individuals, and editorial decision-making varies widely, from a single person to co-editorial boards of various sizes. Yet all editors are doing the same thing: looking for books that excite them. I'm looking for books I want to live with on a near-daily basis for a year and a half before they go off like fledglings into the world. Where do those manuscripts come from? How do they find their way to their future editor? What makes me pick up the telephone to call a poet? Why *that* particular manuscript? Why *those* poems?

Publication of individual poems in magazines (both print and web) is generally necessary before book publication, not just because it takes a long time to write a good book, but because it's a track record of the company you were keeping, and a history of influences. Editors note those things. If I love two poems with equal intensity, I'm going to take the one by the poet who's been sending me a batch of poems once a year or so for the last few years, whose work I always notice and have been following, rather than pluck the only lively puppy out of a litter sent by a poet new to me. Persistence is required. Rejection is the general rule. Over and over. If you can't stop yourself and have the stamina, you will continue to teach yourself to write better and better poems until you die, no matter whether anyone takes notice. You'll learn the Truth About Poetry, which is that the work of writing a poem is always and only the work of apprenticeship. There is nothing beyond apprenticeship. It's a Way of Life, though no one knows whether it's a curse or a calling, an addiction or a manifestation of pure will. (It's my own conviction that the life-long writing of poetry is never wholly voluntary, but that is outside the scope of this discussion, alas.) In any case, persistence is far rarer than talent. Most aspirants quit before they take the vows. Many, including some of great talent, have thus disappeared. (Those who thought the correct answer was *B, a LifeStyle*, this is your stop.)

It's unfortunate but true that in a very tight job market, most American colleges and universities require that candidates for entry-level jobs teaching creative writing have published a full-length collection. It's a shame that such jobs depend upon publications, but they do. I hope that there will someday be another way to measure the value of teach-ers, because some poets' most powerful gift is to teach the great poets of the future, though they do not themselves aspire to greatness. But for now, publishing one's work seems to be a necessary rite of passage for poets wanting to teach or do other work in the academic world. There's also the matter of contests, prizes, awards, fellowships, grants, and teaching and editorial positions. They're part of the landscape; ignore them as long as you can. But when it's time, here's some free advice on improving your chances of acceptance.

1. The writing of poems is more important than what happens to them afterwards. Write that on a slip of paper and tack it to the wall above your desk. If you're unconvinced, can we agree at least that before we hope to publish, we ought to be writing poems that are fully realised works of art? If your poems are profound works of art, they will reach other minds because those minds are out there looking for them: readers and editors with a great range of tastes and predilections, sensibilities, and personal preferences. Some will be drawn to your work; others will not. All you can do it put your poems out there and wait. It's like fishing. Use good bait.

2. Remember that there is no relationship whatsoever between our poems (good, bad or indifferent) and the business of submitting them to magazines and publishers, contests and prizes. That said, how good are your poems on a scale of one to infinity? That's the scale we have to keep in mind. One of the most career-damaging things a young poet can do is send out work that is immature, unfinished, not yet fully realised art. Practice-poems. To do so is to tell the editor that you are unaware of a higher standard, at which point she will stop reading. Ask yourself, 'What do you want from poems when you pick up a book? With whom are you in love?' If you're not in love, you're reading the wrong books. What gives you a feverish chill and what merely blows kisses your way? Do you want to write kiss-blowing poems? I'm going to assume you do not, but rather that you want your words to ride on the great river of the English language, maybe someday to snag on a branch or wash ashore where someone might find them.

3. Send out only your best efforts. Wait until you have a substantial body of work you con-sider unimprovable, either a book manuscript or enough poems – twenty to thirty – to be able to show an editor more than a few greatest hits.

4. Know to whom you are sending it. Editors declare their poetics in what they choose to publish. You'd be astonished at some of the things people send us. Gran-Gran's limericks (some of which were quite good), recipes for wholesome pet foods, a three-volume cross-species family saga in blank verse, etc. Thank you, but in my job as editor I'd rather not make a special trip to the Post Office returning manuscripts submitted from outer space or outside of our reading period. Many or even most poetry editors are poets themselves, devoting their time and probably money to give you the chance to have your work read

by serious eyes. That's a generous offer, is it not? There's a real live human being with a four o'clock dentist's appointment resting her elbows on a desk reading your poems. The editor's encounter with your work may be fleeting, or it may be prolonged and profound. You've sent your poems out in search of other life forms, and here is the first it encounters. Is that poem your best emissary? If not, then why have you made it your ambassador to the world? As Master Dogen would say, *These are important matters and should be studied carefully.*

5. Never, ever, submit the same poem to more than one magazine at a time. What you are offering is First North American Serial Rights to the work, and that's a legal contract. Besides, it's bad manners. Withdrawing a poem because it was taken elsewhere tells an editor (who's likely to have a memory like an elephant's) that you are unappreciative of the long hours she works on your behalf, or that you don't care. I know of poets who have seriously damaged their reputations by this practice. Some editors won't even read their work. Don't do it.

    For book-length manuscripts, it's perfectly acceptable to double-submit. As a courtesy, mention that you've done it in your cover letter.

6. For books, do not send an editor the same manuscript you sent last year, with a few new poems, a new title and reorganised sections. Wait until you can send a brand new better one.

7. Do not send more than one manuscript at a time. Send only your best work. Leave the rest behind. Yes, abandon it! Is it so precious? Move forward. Don't drag around the tail of your past efforts. It's heavy and will slow you down.

8. Don't forget that poems have nothing whatsoever to do with publishers and editors and contests and prizes and jobs.

An understanding of how books are made is useful information for a poet because it clarifies exactly what it is you are asking a publisher to consider doing when you submit a manuscript (I'm talking about books here, not magazines, the production of which is less mystifying). You should know who's on the other end, and what they do all day. The sequence of events is roughly the same whether the publisher is a giant like HarperCollins or a few-books-a-year 'indie' press dedicated to a niche market.

Here's what happens at Ausable Press. Once a contract is signed and the advance paid, work begins almost immediately. Publication is usually scheduled about eighteen months from acceptance, and there's a lot to do in between. For several months the editor and poet work together refining the manuscript (if necessary). Sometimes this amounts to little more than small queries and clarifications, standardisation of punctuation and so forth; at other times a profound conversation evolves concerning the book's structure, or the inclusion or exclusion of certain poems. Once the manuscript is finalised, it is set in type and the first set of galleys sent to the poet for proofreading. Meanwhile, the Art Director works on the cover. This involves numerous back-and-forths with the poet about possible images, negotiating and securing reproduction rights, getting estimates for the printing, scheduling the work and so on. The editor recruits blurbs, writes a press release and copy for the distributor's and for our own catalogue, website, and ads. ISBNs, barcodes, and Library of Congress numbers are assigned. At the same time, the Marketing Director is preparing the book for presentation to the distributor. Pre-sales and sales meetings are held to promote each book's unique qualities so that sales representatives travelling to various book stores will be able to describe it to its best advantage. He also begins working on setting up interviews and reviews, radio appearances and readings. When the book is published, the printer (in Michigan) ships the books to the distributor's warehouse (in Minnesota). The Managing Editor sends out hundreds of review copies and enters the book in all contests for which it is eligible; she mails announcements to our database, and follows up on inquiries and requests for desk copies, review copies, and orders. When the boxes arrive at the offices, we tear them open with delight and celebrate. The Editor updates the website and the book debuts.

Then, for a while, nothing happens. We wait for reviews, study sales patterns, work to get maximum exposure for the poet, and get back to work on the next season's books.

It's easy to forget that aside from being a labour of love, publishing is also a business – a commodity is produced, advertised, and sold. It's a poor sort of commerce, of course, since the chances of breaking even are negligible and of making a profit nonexistent, but then, none of us is in it for the money. The vast majority of independent presses are either not-for-profit corporations supported by grants and donations, or are privately funded in some other way. It costs roughly $10,000 to publish and market a book adequately, more to do it well, and that figure includes zero overhead. Ausable publishes four to six books each year with an operating budget of $150,000, and there's absolutely no fat in that figure. Office space is donated, and the editor takes no remuneration. Everyone else works for far less than they could make in almost any other business. But the small press world is one of cooperation and sharing of information, and the prevailing mood, in spite of the depressing Stock Market of Poetry, is one of excitement, revival, and hope.

Now that you know what you are proposing when you ask an editor to consider your work, here's the lowdown on the social rituals, etiquette and logistics of submission. It all boils down to common sense and manners.

I'm going to begin with submissions to magazines because publication in periodicals generally precedes book publication. I am writing with the assumption that you have read deeply and widely, have identified magazines of kindred spirit, and know their guidelines. A poet might send five or six poems, with a *very* short cover letter (if any), and include a self-addressed, stamped envelope for the response. Do not send reviews, nice things people have said about you, or cookies. Be patient. If you've heard nothing in three or four months, you can send a polite note to the editor asking when she might make a decision. Be certain to have a number of already-addressed envelopes and s.a.s.e's (self-addressed stamped envelopes) on hand so that the very moment the rejection comes back it can go out again without aforethought.

Among both magazines and presses, there's a very wide range of editorial policies, from a single editor to a panel of judges. Often there are 'first-readers' who winnow out the weaker submissions, so that the editor sees only a partial selection.

Other editors read everything themselves. Waste no time trying to second-guess which editor might like what poems. It changes the odds not a whit, and I know of not a single poet who can do it accurately. Just send them out and get to work on the next ones.

Forms of Rejection Slips, from lowest to highest:

1. A xerox or otherwise mass-produced slip of paper, neither signed nor initialled, saying a polite but firm no. We all get them. Ignore it.
2. Same as above but with a few personal words scribbled, perhaps 'Sorry' or 'Thanks for sending'. Neutral response, not an invitation. Send new poems in a year.
3. A personal note from an editor or other reader commenting on the work in some way and asking to see more. Editors don't say this to be polite. Send poems at least as strong as the first batch within a few months.

4. A note from an editor with a conditional acceptance, asking you if you would consider making changes. Congrats, but tough call. Don't dither about it; just follow your instincts. If the editor is wrong, thank them politely and withdraw it, and send some new poems in a few months. If you do make the suggested changes, and later conclude it was a mistake, you can always reinstate the original when the poem is published in a book.

For poets who do not yet have a full-length collection there are a few chapbook prizes worth considering. A useful magazine for keeping track of such things is *Poets & Writers Magazine* (www.pw.org), which publishes deadlines, guidelines, awards announcements, and all kinds of advice. It's PoBiz Central.

Poets who have a full-length collection have many options, from large commercial houses to self-publishing with the new print-on-demand technology, which allows you to publish a book – to produce, promote and sell it – on the web for an initial investment of under $1,000.00. In between, there are independent, university, for- and not-for-profit publishers of various sizes, and all manner of cyber-publishers colonizing the new frontier. Another option is contests, the ethics of which are being heatedly debated these days. This is a subject about which you must come to your own conclusions. The poet pays a fee (currently around $20.00) to submit a book to a competition sponsored by a publisher, to be judged by a Famous Poet or someone else with credentials. One manuscript is selected, published and touted. The controversy concerns fairness: what's to stop a judge from choosing a book by someone personally known to her, or worse, picking someone she knows and never even reading the others? Should judges always judge blind? How would that be possible, since the poetry world is quite small and most editors are likely to recognise poets they've read before? Contests are lucrative for the publisher. They bring books into the world. They range from the prestigious/impeccable to the probably-corrupt, and there are hundreds. If you figure it out, let me know.

Another element to bear in mind is graduate schools, which are also very profitable for their host institutions and thus are proliferating with abandon. They offer fellowships, teaching assistantships, stipends and so forth, all of which are valuable to poets, but they also produce literally thousands of 'publishable' manuscripts, the standard generally set for acceptance by the thesis committee. To my mind, graduate schools can be a useful formalisation of the first two or three years of serious apprenticeship, and that's how the thesis should be regarded: as an anthology of that apprenticeship, a showcase of its artefacts. Each year I see literally hundreds of manuscripts that are exactly that.

When your work begins to be accepted by magazines, and when you publish a first book, it's a heady time. What happens next? Well, actually, that's about it. What happens after publication is nothing much. It's all a big let-down. Poets are often surprised to find themselves a bit depressed. The readership for poetry in the US is small; most books sell under a thousand copies. But those readers and buyers are also passionate, devoted, hungry, and curious, and there's a rapidly increasing interest among younger people as they search for meaning in an increasingly fragmented and dangerous world. As has already happened in the music world, the boundaries between nations are eroding. More poetry in translation is appearing, and more presses are open to publishing work from outside the US. Nevertheless, the publication of a first book of poems is decidedly *not* like that of a debut CD.

I would be remiss if I did not mention the current political shadow. A chill and a pall have fallen over our land. Yes, there's energy and hope, but also profound caution and unease concerning free expression. These are dark times of war, gluttony, greed, deceit, and faithlessness of all kinds. We must remember why we write poems, and write them for that reason alone. I believe that human beings are uplifted by art, by words dedicated to truth, and that the act of publishing books is therefore necessary to our wellbeing as a species. Poetry should send all its bright arrows against war's narcotic dream of power. That's why this media earthquake is so important. I'm not exaggerating when I say that I believe the independent presses are the sole future refuge of American literary culture. Art is the highest expression of human consciousness, and it's being increasingly banished from the mainstream media. But on the new frontier of publishing, it's celebrated and flourishing.

46

Publishing Poetry in Britain

Sean O'Brien

Context

Poetry, it is said, is in crisis in Britain. Book sales are down, and despite the success of one or two anthologies, many readers never make the crossing from browsing among the work of many to purchasing and reading in detail the work of, say, five or six. Were they to do so, the figure would please the Poetry Book Society, the book club dedicated to poetry. The PBS also administers the T. S. Eliot Prize, which along with the Forward Prize, is the major award for poetry in Britain. These awards were instituted in order to draw attention to poetry as a whole, but latterly, as with fiction in the case of the Man Booker Prize, for reasons of convenience they have come to be treated by the media almost as poetry's *raison dêtre*. Why poetry has never made the breakthrough to wide popularity which was predicted in the 1990s (and several times before that) is open to debate. It is certainly connected to shifts in cultural taste which tend to emphasise qualities other than verbal richness or complexity. There is also an inclination to avoid and even deride art which requires the audience to engage with intellectually demanding material. Liberal capitalist democracy, as currently constituted, is not an especially healthy environment for the kind of seriousness poetry has to offer. Passivity and assertion, rather than engagement and argument, are notable characteristics of the contemporary audience and those who create its tastes. Hopes of a wider imaginative enfranchisement, nurtured since the 1960s, have been disappointed.

This being the case, the outlook for poetry and poets is not especially bright, if success is judged by sales numbers and media recognition. However, one of poetry's strongest characteristics is persistence: whatever the circumstances of the moment, it goes on being written, eventually finding the audience who know how to value it.

The poet who wants to publish her work needs some understanding of how poetry is published, and what the chances and protocols of publishing are. Few large commercial publishers still maintain poetry lists. At present, the leading commercial publishers of poetry are Faber and Faber, Picador, Jonathan Cape and Chatto and Windus. There are also a number of important specialist poetry presses receiving Arts Council subsidy, including Bloodaxe Books, Carcanet Press, Anvil Press, Seren Books, Arc and Enitharmon Press. Peterloo Poets has recently lost its Arts Council grant, while Salt Books is proudly independent. Small publishers are of vital importance, since they can – at least to some extent

– publish work of merit which is unlikely to sell in large quantities. There also exist several significant smaller publishers, also subsidized, often with a strong regional basis, including Flambard, Iron Press, Smith Doorstop and Shoestring. Beyond this lies a wealth of smaller imprints. These are often heroic one-person operations. However, there are never enough outlets to satisfy the demand for publication. While poetry appears short of readers, it never wants for practitioners, and the demand for publication appears even stronger among poets than writers of prose fiction. As was observed in the introductory essay on poetry, in many cases publication will have to be its own reward.

Alongside printed publications, the Internet is assuming an increasing importance as an outlet for poetry. In poetry, as in every other matter, the output is unregulated, so that, for example, traditional distinctions between professional and amateur work are eroded by the democracy of the medium itself. In other areas – the political blog, for example – the Internet is having an influence on print media. It remains to be seen whether anything comparable will happen in poetry.

At the moment, poetry on the Internet seems more like an extension of existing opportunity than an agent of change, though clearly the *potential* for large readerships exists. The Internet remains at present an open medium: time, commitment and a modest financial outlay enable anyone to participate. Surfing poetry sites reveals much of interest, but it can produce an effect akin to Balzac's description of nineteenth-century Paris as a city with no solid floor; on the web it is always possible to seek deeper levels of incompetence and ignorance, down among the cat-fetishists and the improving sentiments of latter-day Ella Wheeler Wilcoxes. There is also a good deal of piracy: the unlicensed reproduction of poems is commonplace, and the copyright situation on the web is largely unexplored territory. Some sites require the payment of a subscription. It is, more than ever, the task of the reader/user to navigate among the work on offer and find the sites which best suit his or her interests. New websites emerge and disappear rapidly, so that information soon becomes obsolete. The best approach is by careful and sceptical study.

A route to publication

Writing is sufficient activity in itself, until you seek publication, at which point a sustained injection of worldly practicality becomes advisable. The unworldly poet may simply get lucky and be discovered, but this is rare. More likely he will bestir himself in order to find out how the publishing of poetry actually works. The danger then, of course, is that a wholly commendable commitment to art for art's sake is replaced by the maddened pursuit of success, however that is to be defined. A proper balance is difficult to achieve, but necessary. Whatever happens is likely to take a long time.

There is no single route to publication for poets. The experiences of individuals differ widely, and the level of publication which individuals seek or will accept is also extremely various. Even the definition of 'publication' is not absolutely fixed. Self-publication can be a legitimate course under certain circumstances, perhaps as a response to an unsympathetic climate for your brand of seriousness. But as a rule of thumb, before considering such an act, publication is what happens when somebody other than yourself decides to publish your work. If money is to change hands, it must go from publisher to poet and not the other way round. If you pay towards the publication of your work, either directly or by agreeing to buy a number of copies as a condition of publication, this is vanity publishing. Vanity publishing will exclude you from serious consideration. There is a substantial industry of vanity publishers who exploit the ill-informed and the impatient. Vanity publications are characterized by transferring costs to the poet (for these books are not genuinely marketed for sale to the public) and by the absence of editorial standards. A richly comic account of the contrast between legitimate and vanity publishing can be found in Umberto Eco's novel *Foucault's Pendulum*.

The first place for a poet to seek publication is in a magazine or journal. Before sending anything, read the magazine you have in mind and take careful note of its submission guidelines. Does this magazine actually invite contributions? If so, it is best to send a small sample of work (no more than six poems) with a brief note asking that the work be considered for publication. The poems themselves should all carry your name and contact details. Unless a print magazine accepts email submissions (not yet generally the case for unsolicited submissions) you should remember always to supply a stamped addressed envelope for the return of your work. This fundamental courtesy is likely to ensure not only that your work is returned if unwanted, but also that it will actually be read in the first place. Overseas publications (for example in the US) will require an International Reply Coupon. Remember too that the writ of the Royal Mail does not extend to return posting from the Republic of Ireland.

Frustration and disappointment often arise from the failure to meet these basic requirements. Remember: you are the petitioner; the magazine knows there are plenty of other poets where you came from.

With magazine submissions it is discourteous to submit the same work to more than one publication at once. If you have not had a reply within three months, write or email to enquire about the progress of your submission, but bear in mind that magazine editing is an extremely time-and-labour intensive activity; that it is often carried out on a voluntary unpaid basis as one task among several; and that good magazines in particular are likely to be dealing with a substantial backlog of submissions. Poetry involves a good deal of waiting. The frustration of trying to achieve publication is one of the major incentives towards the founding of new magazines. Anguished victims of neglect, delay and rejection often decide to create an opportunity to publish the work of a group of the likeminded and thus free themselves of the constraints of the establishment, but while the decision to take control of the means of production may confer a novel sense of power it also entails reading all the material submitted to the revolutionary organ, thus inculcating an appreciation of the plight of editors as well as of poets.

What magazine to send work to, though? One way to begin looking is to examine the acknowledgements page in a collection of poems by a writer you admire. This page serves as a courtesy to the publications in which some of the poems first appeared.

Example 1
A list of publication credits taken from a first collection: *Orbis, Oxford Poetry, Poetry London, Poetry Review, The Rialto, Stand, Staple*.

This indicates a poet making a promising beginning to a publishing career, gathering a respectable array of credits in places including established 'small magazines' and more prestigious titles.

Example 2
The Guardian, London Review of Books, New Republic, New York Review of Books, New Yorker, Poetry London, Poetry Review, Times Literary Supplement.

In this case the poet is more experienced and established (this is a third collection), with work accepted in leading British publications and also in the US, and she is achieving a degree of prominence in the field.

The publications named here can for the most part be investigated individually via the Internet. In addition, the Poetry Library in London stocks many of them and has a website dedicated to poetry magazines (www.poetrymagazines.org.uk). The best course in submitting to magazines is to be ambitious and persistent, and not to be disheartened by rejection (inexplicable as this may seem at times).

As you begin to develop a body of work which you think is publishable (some of which is likely to have found its way into magazines), it may be time to seek to publish a small collection (up to, say, fifteen poems) in pamphlet form. The pamphlet is a useful staging-post on the way to full book publication. Pamphlets, it is worth adding, are often collectable objects in themselves and have proved popular with established poets seeking to showcase work from forthcoming full collections. The very simple pamphlets published by the magazine *The Honest Ulsterman* in the 1970s and 1980s, which included work by Seamus Heaney and Derek Mahon, have since become collectors' items. The same is true of work published by Turret Books, which included early poems by Carol Ann Duffy and Lavinia Greenlaw, among others. The importance of pamphlet publication has recently been recognized by the Poetry Book Society, which has created a pamphlet category among its quarterly Choices and Recommendations. Perhaps the most durable current pamphlet series is published by Smith Doorstop, the publishing affiliate of the magazine *The North*, which runs an annual competition whose winners have pamphlet collections published. One of the authors is then chosen for a book-length collection.

The ingenuity of Diamond Twig, a small Newcastle-based publisher with an eye to attractiveness and collectability, has produced a striking new list of carefully designed and branded small collections of poems (and short fiction) by women writers. The North East of England is a region traditionally rich in poetry publishing, and the diversity of material available can be sampled on the Literature North East website (www.literaturenortheast. co.uk). Not all regions are as well served in this regard, but the various regional branches of the Arts Council should be able to supply information on the available provision. Poetry may often and quite rightly be sceptical of administration, but it is important for poets seeking publication to take the trouble to understand the workings of their chosen sphere, to be on the lookout for opportunities and thus to practise responsible stewardship of their talents. Useful information about matters connected with poetry can be found on the Write Word site (www.writewords.org.uk) and the energetic one-man Poetry Kit (www. poetrykit.org), as well as on the site of The Poetry Society, the national body representing poetry in the UK (www.poetrysociety.org.uk).

A poet with some magazine credits and perhaps a pamphlet under her belt may begin to look for recognition and encouragement in the form of grants, awards and, perhaps, residential writers' centres. For poets under thirty years of age, the Gregory Award is a long-established marker of early recognition. It is administered by the Society of Authors (www.societyofauthors.org) and judged by a panel of poets. A Gregory Award may serve as a calling card to possible publishers, as may financial awards such as those offered by regional branches of the Arts Council. Here again, provision varies. Arts Council regions may also provide subsidy for periods of intensive writing at centres such as Hawthornden Castle in Scotland or the Tyrone Guthrie Centre in Ireland.

Poetry readings could be treated as a separate subject, but in this context their obvious value is to enable the poet to contact an audience, to get a hearing for her work and to sell books. In the micro-economy of poetry the live reading is a significant event. A poet with a new book out may be required by a publisher to give readings. Such events publicize new work and help emergent poets to gain recognition and readers. It is worth taking the trouble to read well – that is, audibly, clearly and naturally, and to give thought to the order and variety of the work you will read. You may have no desire to be a performer, but listeners often comment that their understanding of poetry benefits from hearing it read aloud properly. Twenty years ago many poets did not serve their work well in public readings. The general standard is now much higher. Practise reading aloud. Get a friend to listen and to comment on your delivery.

Manuscript and submission

Assembly

Although, given the pressures of fashion, publishers and reviewers may sometimes feel inclined to dispute it, no two collections of poems are the same, and no set of advisory remarks will be entirely suited to each case. Common sense makes obvious most of what follows.

Let us suppose that you are intending to send out a manuscript of about thirty-five poems, making the proverbial 'slim volume'. There is no obligation for a collection of poems to have a unifying theme or narrative like Ted Hughes's *Crow* or Carol Ann Duffy's *Rapture*, but a book of poems needs somehow to be more than a random miscellany. It is likely that your work will have certain recurrent concerns, and it may be helpful to determine what these are and make initial groupings of poems accordingly. At the same time, there is no need to treat these divisions as binding on the order you eventually choose: what you are also seeking is a kind of arc, akin but not identical to narrative – an arc, that is, which conveys a sense of shape, momentum and completeness.

You may of course freely reject such a model, but there can be much to gain from laying the poems out on the living-room floor and seeing which handfuls of them seem drawn to keep each other's company and which clearly belong elsewhere in the book. The order towards which you are slowly working is designed to show your poems to best effect, and also to enable your manuscript to be read with a sense of unfolding purpose which will make it seem like a book waiting to be published rather than a small stack of typed pages. It is important to open the book strongly, not necessarily with the 'best' poem, but with a piece which invites the reader's interested attention. Likewise there needs to be a strong closing poem. In addition, if you are not inclined to divide the manuscript into sections, there should be peaks every half dozen poems or so, with a significant point of renewal between two thirds and three quarters of the way through the manuscript. Alternatively, section breaks can provide natural rests, followed by renewed stimulus.

This is of course an account of an ideal, Platonic manuscript, one capable of fulfilling a strategy of design which no actual collection of poems can truly satisfy, and one indeed for which actual poems were never intended. But a sense of timing, and the careful use of complement and contrast (of form as well as subject), can help to draw attention to a book's strengths, even though the reader may never actively turn to consider the matter of its organisation. A good publisher's editor is likely to take an active interest in the eventual ordering of the text: the form you arrive at provides, at the very least, a useful basis or further discussion if the work is accepted for publication. Lastly, although the author might not care to admit it, all books have weaknesses too, poems which, while perfectly competent, respectable and interesting in themselves, are not the work by which the book is going to live and die. This supporting cast needs to be carefully positioned in the manuscript. By this stage, the poet should be in a state of extreme alertness to the strengths and weaknesses of the work. The assembly of a manuscript can very easily (and probably should) become a further stage of revision. Be prepared to reconsider, to discard work, to decide to wait a while and write some more poems. Time spent like this is unlikely to be wasted.

Where to send the manuscript

Many poetry publishers and editors are constrained by being able to publish only a limited number of new books in a year – perhaps half a dozen or less, with some of these slots required by poets already on the publisher's books. The competition for the few spaces available is therefore intense. Disappointment is more likely than not, and, as with magazine submissions, there is likely to be a good deal of waiting around for a reply. Here again, you should check the publishers' submission guidelines (see websites and *The Writers' & Artists' Yearbook*). In some cases the sheer volume of work received has led publishers to stipulate that they will not consider unsolicited manuscripts. To act in ignorance of this fact would be a waste of your efforts and you might not even receive a reply. However, publishers of poetry are always interested in exciting new work. It is a significant part of what they live for. The poet, too, should make a careful study of work currently being published, not in order to adjust his or her poems to the dictates of fashion, but to try to assess the tastes of the individual editors in order to narrow the range of possible choices. To put it crudely, there would be little point in sending highly wrought poems in traditional forms to an editor committed to the avant garde and free verse.

Editors do take an interest in poems that appear in prominent magazines, as well as listening to recommendations from other poets and keeping an eye on writers emerging on postgraduate writing courses, and on competition winners and recipients of Gregory Awards. None of these factors will in itself secure publication, but they may help to put you in the frame of reference. Therefore it is a good idea, for example, to try to place your work in magazines which are likely to have a readership extending further than their own contributors. This way your name may not be wholly unfamiliar to the editor you choose to approach.

The way to approach an editor is the subject of debate. If the publishers accept unsolicited submissions a full manuscript will eventually be read (though it may not survive past an initial sampling of half a dozen poems if the work is not of a high enough standard, or if it fails to make an impact) but the time this takes will vary. Bloodaxe Books, for example, the largest independent poetry publisher in Britain, has indicated that it has a waiting list of two years. Bear in mind too that editors are not simply waiting for work to turn up. They may be seeking to add some already published poets to their lists, at the same time as cultivating newcomers whom they've spotted as possible future acquisitions. An unsolicited approach to a publisher might best be made, in the first instance, by sending a sample of work (up to a dozen poems) with a letter of introduction containing very brief relevant biographical information and an enquiry as to whether the editor would be willing to read a full manuscript.

The physical manuscript

Use good quality A4 white paper. The font you use should be clear (for example, Times New Roman or Garamond rather than anything distractingly eccentric) and not smaller than 12 point. Leave 1.5 or 2 spaces between lines and double this between stanzas. Put the titles of poems in bold. Number the pages. For security, include your name and contact details at the foot of each page of text as well as on the title page. After the title page, supply a table of contents with page numbers, and then a page of acknowledgements. Check spelling and punctuation meticulously. Bind the pages loosely with a treasury tag or in a spring (not a ring) binder. Package it securely, but not before ensuring that you enclose sufficient postage for the manuscript's return. If the manuscript is returned, give careful and realistic consideration to any comments the editor has made. Before sending the manuscript out again, examine its physical condition. It does not take long for it to become apparent that a manuscript has been unsuccessfully doing the rounds, so be prepared to print off a fresh copy to send out. You may in any case wish to reconsider the contents. When you are ready, send it and prepare to wait. In the meantime you can work on some new poems.

References

Eco, Umberto (1989), *Foucault's Pendulum*, London: Picador.

Literature North East: www.literaturenortheast.co.uk

Poetry Kit: www.poetrykit.org

The Poetry Library, website dedicated to poetry magazines: www.poetrymagazines.org.uk

The Poetry Society: www.poetrysociety.org.uk

Society of Authors: www.societyofauthors.org

Write Word: www.writewords.org.uk

Writers' & Artists' Yearbook (annual), London: A & C Black.

47

The Literary Agent (Novel)

David Smith

'Agents make books expensive'.

So I was once told by a senior editor from one of the major London publishing houses. I was fortunate enough to be her guest for lunch at the time, so I suppose she felt that any protest I might make would be restrained by a sense of courtesy and obligation. On the whole this was the case – but I did point out to her that agents cannot force publishers to buy books they don't want. The argument could have rumbled on for hours, so we agreed to differ.

But this exchange illustrates something significant about the world of book publishing in the UK: the commercial and competitive pressures on all parties are immense and everyone is convinced that those pressures are of someone else's making. Publishers will complain about the unfair leverage applied by agents when negotiating new contracts for best-selling authors; or seek to explain to an author why the disappointing sales of that promising debut novel is the result of the book trade's failure to support them. Agents will wring their hands over what they perceive as the publishers' marketing-driven conservatism in rejecting the work of dazzling new authors and by extension the bookshops' reductive view of what constitutes commercial potential. Booksellers will upbraid the publishers for flooding the market with far too many books and accuse them of failing to give the appropriate level of marketing support. Authors will minutely inspect the shelves of every bookshop they pass and discover appalling gaps in availability – some will tuck their disappointment away quietly, while others will fume and roar at their publisher or their agent.

The fact is that publishing is an imperfect business. But it is nevertheless a business, and if you are serious about getting into that business you ought to know what horrors, along with joys, you can expect to encounter. Like any business, it operates its own language, its own custom and practice, its own system of priorities; and like any business it is therefore a completely alien beast to anyone on the outside. This is the reason why agents exist and why you need one.

First I need to put the role of the agent in context. Book publishing in the UK is constantly evolving and adapting, in response to what is perceived as a perpetual crisis. The number of books published increases every year, but the number of debut novels is declining. Profitability too is falling – at least for publishers, authors and agents, all of whom share the burden of the inflated discounts demanded and won by the major book chains in return for access to in-store promotions and by the supermarkets simply for stocking the books in the first place. The majority of books published never make a profit at all. It's a grim place to try to make a living from writing.

Publishing is dominated by large corporate publishing houses, many of them owned by even larger foreign corporations. Within those houses a diversity of imprints divides up the huge range of books into classifiable sub-sections: for example, Random House (RH) publishes mass market fiction under the Century imprint, or possibly Hutchinson – or if it's more genre-based or humorous and going straight into paperback it might be Arrow. If it's literary fiction it may come under Chatto & Windus or Heinemann or Vintage and if it's foreign literary fiction it will probably bear the name of Harvill Press, an independent acquired by RH in 2001. RH also owns Transworld, which operates autonomously and has its own imprint structure.

This pattern is mirrored at all the major houses and they also share what is essentially the same approach to the acquisition of new books. As recently as the 1970s it was common for a commissioning editor to receive material from an agent, love it, acquire it, and then instruct the publicity department and the sales team to sell it. Today the process is very different. If an editor loves a book she will first have to share it with colleagues in the editorial department. If it gets their support she will then circulate material to colleagues in all the other departments: marketing, publicity, paperback, rights. If she can win over the support of everyone who has any influence on decision-making, then she can try to acquire the book. However, any of those senior colleagues, if their doubts are strong enough, whatever their department, has an effective veto. Every agent can tell stories of editors who fell in love with a novel but found themselves blocked at the acquisition meeting; every agent probably keeps a bitter store of emails and letters from editors almost apologising for the intransigence of their colleagues.

The truth is, no one knows what will sell. All we have in the industry is a collection of different people's instincts, experiences and prejudices. No one can predict spectacular success or dismal failure. Everyone in the publishing houses is agreed on one thing: every book published is intended to make money. That relatively few of them do so may be evidence that the current system does not work, or it may simply illustrate that the market for fiction is too wide, too unpredictable, too varied and too fickle to be manipulated by marketing, demographics or any other means into buying what it is told to buy. You can't even guarantee best-seller status by hurling money into advertising campaigns, or by securing short-listings for prestigious prizes. Television 'book clubs' may be a highly reliable method of promotion, but by their very nature these are available to only a miniscule fraction of the total number of novels published.

Into this chaos steps a gifted new author: perhaps you. And you need to find an agent. There's no shortage of us, but how do you find one who is even taking on new authors and then convince them to represent you? It's true that a lot of agencies will temporarily if not permanently draw down the shutters to new clients. This isn't through complacency – although agencies with a couple of dozen top-selling international authors probably don't need to expand their lists – but because they are being realistic about the amount of time and resources they can spare to launch new careers. It would be of no benefit to you if your agent simply didn't have the time to look after your interests. But there are also many agencies which as a matter of business principle, will never describe their lists as closed. This is true of my own small agency as well as others of all sizes right up to the biggest corporate animals. You simply have to find out: check the trade reference books, visit the agency websites, phone up and ask.

Whom should you approach? You can sometimes get a feeling from a website or even from a reference book entry whether your work would sit happily on an agency's client list. Or you may find agents thanked in the acknowledgements section of a book you admire. It isn't easy, but it can be done. It may be worth considering whether an agency is a member of the Association of Authors' Agents, which follows a straightforward code of practice, but I have to admit that some of the most successful agents have never bothered to join. You need to be sure that the agents you approach have the means to exploit all the rights in your work – US, translation, film and television rights – through either their own departments or specialist associates. These rights can provide valuable additional income if retained and sold independently.

How do you approach them? Opinions differ, but what you want to strike is a balance between satisfying the agency's stated preferences and displaying your work to its best advantage. I think it's better not to send a preliminary letter on its own, or even with a synopsis, because we really need to see the writing itself and there's a risk that an agent will respond poorly to an unsupported synopsis and you've missed your chance. My advice is, send your covering letter, your brief synopsis, and approximately the first 10,000 words. How long should the synopsis be? No more than 500 words and preferably less. What should it do? It should work in the manner of an extended book-jacket blurb, giving a strong sense of the novel's premise, flavour, tone and direction, but stopping well short of mapping out every turn of the story, and certainly not divulging the ending. It is a tool to get the attention and whet the appetite of the agent. It's the sample text that does the real work.

Does it have to be the first 10,000 words? I would say 'yes', except in very unusual circumstances. Writers often submit chapters from the middle of their novels, explaining that they are more representative of the whole, or that the novel doesn't really get going until Chapter 5. My answer is simple: go back and start again. If the first 100 words, let alone the first 10,000, are not representative you must rewrite them until they are. And if it doesn't get going until Chapter 5 then those first four chapters are dead weight that must be jettisoned or revised.

On the other hand, your covering letter is not something to agonise over. It simply needs to be business-like, giving a couple of sentences about your novel, explaining anything about yourself that may be pertinent (for example, an MA Creative Writing qualification, or a personal experience which qualifies you to write about some aspect of the story), stating whether the work is complete, and making clear whether you are submitting it to only one agent at a time or, if not, how many agents you have included.

Agents can be very swift in reading material and getting back to you – in days perhaps – but will often take weeks and sometimes months. The interests of existing clients simply have to take precedence, which means sometimes new material has to wait. But a polite enquiry after four weeks or so is a reasonable follow-up. I think most agents still prefer to receive material as hard copy, but if you enquire before sending you may find a willingness to accept email attachments, provided you can guarantee they will be virus-free.

If an agent is taken with your sample material she will ask to see the full script, and this may lead her to offer to represent you. If you have approached more than one agent at a time, be careful if you are stalling for time while waiting to hear from the others. An agent's view is that since you can have only one agent, and one of the ones you chose to approach has offered her services, why prevaricate? Are you holding out for another agent, because you think they will be better? If that's the truth then you shouldn't have approached the others. You're not auctioning your custom – you're seeking professional services.

Now that you have appointed your agent, the first thing she will tell you is that there are no guarantees, that your work is wonderful but plenty of wonderful novels go unpublished, and that you cannot plan to give up your day job. But she should also tell you what an immense thrill it is to see the alchemy of publishing turn your script into a published novel.

The chances are your novel is not quite ready for submission to publishers. You may think you have perfected it but it's quite likely that your agent will suggest revisions. These are not so much aesthetic considerations as responses based on her experience of whatever consensus or prejudice is at large within publishing. Remember that your agent is talking to editors all the time – finding out what they're buying, what they're not buying, what they love and what they hate – and this enables her to build a fairly reliable picture of how any new novel might be received. So if your agent advises you to simplify a split narrative into a single voice, it's probably because split narratives rarely find favour with publishers: those that do (a few) are written extremely well, those that do not (many) are uneven at best. Or if she suggests injecting more drama into the opening it's because she knows you can't keep publishers hanging around: a novel has to grab the reader from page one or it will soon be laid down and passed over.

This is the agent's editorial role, one which has evolved over the years as the demands on publishers' time has increased to such an extent that, whereas once they might have bought a book that was 75 per cent perfect with a kernel of brilliance but a lot of work to do, now and in the future they will be looking for something that is ninety per cent perfect or even more. An agent therefore plays a crucial part in preparing the script for submission by getting it as close as possible to perfection. This is not to say that agents see themselves as writers (although some are), but that we are able to share our knowledge of the commercial advisability of certain narrative techniques, plot developments and characterisation. At this problematic intersection between creativity and commerce we are trying to make the book 'better' not as a work of art but as a saleable commodity. Some agents are more willing and able to take on this role than others. Find someone who will.

What should you write? There are very few rules and some of those that do exist will often be broken – sometimes disastrously, sometimes triumphantly. But you need to start with the raw DNA of storytelling. What does every successful novel have in common, in some form, however mutant? The obvious elements are a gripping story; imaginative and distinctive writing; and enthralling characters. The story doesn't need to be heavy with plot, but it does have to hook from the first paragraph and keep you turning the pages. The writing doesn't have to emulate a literary giant, but it does need to have its own appropriate, attractive voice, avoiding verbal cliché at all costs. The characters need not be loveable or even likeable, but they must be people with whom you are very happy to spend time; strong, memorable and human.

Of course, an aspiring author really requires more than a desire to write and be published; she must need to write, whether she is published or not. And this obvious truth extends to the choice of material. An author must have a story to tell – not one that she has tried to construct for the sake of having something to write, and not one that is barely a story at all but simply a vehicle for ruminations on contemporary life or the human condition. These works are not novels. They are platforms for individuals to preach from. No one is interested – least of all publishers.

But if you have a story you are aching to tell – even if some parts of it are not clear in your mind until the writing is underway – then you have a sound start. What you need to do is to transport the reader to an unfamiliar place: that could be a foreign place, or a distant time, or in a more metaphysical sense it may be a setting or an experience that seems very close but which by your storytelling you make into something new and strange. Be surprising.

What about the narrative voice? In many ways the safest and most versatile voice is third person past tense. It allows you to shift viewpoints with omniscience and to choose what information to reveal and what to withhold, but all within the context of one narrative voice, which, if you're doing it right, is utterly compelling. First person is popular with writers and has many historical precedents, but is much more limiting since the reader can only know as much or as little as the narrating character knows. Multiple narratives are very risky. If an author is immensely skilled, careful and lucky, these can succeed, sometimes brilliantly. But the danger is that if you split your novel into two or more voices, one of them is likely to develop into a more compelling voice than the others, and a reader will start to grow impatient and only really be interested in the one that works best.

All of this might seem elementary, but it's surprising how much material from promising new writers falls into one of the traps I've tried to warn about. Be circumspect and rigorously self-critical. Join a writing group. Don't allow yourself to be lazy. If you know that something in your novel isn't working it needs to be fixed, because an agent or a publisher will spot it in an instant.

Once the novel is deemed ready – that is, it's as strong as the author and agent feel they can make it – the agent takes over and the author can really only wait. Your agent will have drawn up a list of commissioning editors that she judges will be the best fit for your novel. This judgement will be based on her knowledge of their tastes and of the profile and demands of their particular imprint. Some editors enjoy the freedom to publish across different imprints but it's still vitally important to get the novel in front of the right person, because the very first hurdle to jump is to find an editor who will fall in love with your book.

Submissions are made either exclusively or simultaneously. If an editor is given exclusive sight they understand that they are in a privileged position – the agent might have decided this is a book that has great potential but fears that only a few editors will really take to it with passion, and therefore singled out one person as a likely champion. But on the whole this approach has fallen out of favour and there's no doubt that auctioning a book amongst a number of interested editors will generate a higher advance and a better deal. A simultaneous multiple submission is designed to elicit competing bids and lead to an auction. Your agent will contact the editors she has selected for her first round of submissions – it might be four, five, six or many more – to introduce the concept of the book, gauge interest and make sure they are primed for it when it lands on their desk or in their email inbox.

Your agent will write a 'pitch' letter to accompany the manuscript. This is designed to pique the curiosity of the editor and encourage in them the appropriate expectations towards what they are about to read, as well as pre-empting any doubts or prejudices that may colour their reading. No pitch letter however good can sell a sub-standard novel – but it can prepare the terrain for a positive response.

Your agent may set a deadline, either for initial responses, or for offers. If she asks for offers by a certain date she really needs to enforce that deadline in order to treat all parties fairly. She may decide to refuse early offers and only agree to receive them on the date set – this is to avoid what is known as a 'pre-emptive bid'. A 'pre-emptive' is made when an editor has managed to gather enough support among colleagues quickly and wants to avoid competing in an auction – so she makes an offer which will be much higher than any opening bid, but the offer must remain confidential and must be accepted, usually within a certain time specified by the editor, or it will be withdrawn. Pre-emptives can be very attractive and if they are high enough are very likely to succeed: the agent will then accept the offer, tell the other editors what has happened, and then proceed to negotiate contractual terms with the pre-emptor. But if an agent feels the pre-emptive is not high enough, she may advise the author that it is worth gambling by rejecting the pre-emptive and waiting to see what an auction might throw up. This is obviously a dangerous game and requires utter conviction and strong nerves. What if a pre-emptive of £50,000 is rejected, the agent holds out for an auction and no one else offers? The £50,000 has been withdrawn and the editor who made the offer will have replaced it with an opening bid of, say, £10,000. In the absence of competition it's very unlikely that the agent would be able to lever much improvement out of him. But what if the agent and author are so convinced that the novel can sell for a more substantial advance? Settling for £50,000 might always feel like under-selling. They will never know the truth. There are many anecdotes on this subject, but my favourite is the agent who turned down a pre-emptive offer of £100,000 for world rights (UK, US and translation), proceeded to auction and finally sold the book (UK rights only) for £150,000 to the very same editor who had made the pre-emptive bid. The instinct was right.

If there are no pre-emptives but several interested parties then bidding will begin, with the agent organising this in rounds – every editor who wants to acquire the book will make an opening bid, but the highest one will not automatically win. The agent will then ask for improved bids. As this process continues, some editors will drop out, but if two or more are still fighting it out and there's no sign of a winner emerging the agent is likely at this point to ask for 'best offers'. This is a blind bid which represents the very most the editor is prepared to offer for the book. If an agent moves the auction to this level then she and the author are obliged to take whichever is the best offer. There's no law about it, but custom and practice in the industry expects it.

Of course, very often no one offers for the book. There are some wonderful unpublished novels on PCs or in drawers all over the world, which were evangelically supported by agents dedicated to their clients' success. But a combination of commercial, aesthetic and imponderable factors meant that no one would quite commit to publishing them. Do not get discouraged. Start again. Believe in yourself. And don't be bitter. It's no one's 'fault', it's simply the vicissitudes of business.

Equally, in many cases there will be only one offer. This robs an agent of the leverage of competing bids, but a good agent should often be able to negotiate some improvement even without competition. And provided the publisher is a good one, who understands the book, has sound marketing plans and can command the co-operation of the bookshops, there is no reason to think that your book is going to be sidelined. No publisher publishes a book for any reason other than to make money. Life-changing advances are of course the stuff of dreams, but they are infinitesimally rare, and for all those that are ultimately justified by the success of the book there are probably as many others which blight the promising career of new writers when the advance has to be written off by the publisher in the face of dismal sales.

Once the offer is accepted the rather duller but no less important business of contractual negotiation begins. While some issues will have been settled at the offer stage, there will be other matters such as subsidiary rights, options, delivery deadlines, author discounts, and artwork consultation over which the agent and the editor will argue for a while, before the contract is agreed and signed. Soon after, the first tranche of your advance – payable on signature – will be received, and, if the novel is deemed to be in a finished form you may receive the delivery advance as well. Other amounts will – depending on the contract – become payable on hardback publication and possibly also on paperback publication. But you the author are now on a new road, towards the final realisation of the dream. Inevitably errors will occur during the approach to publication – publicity slots that disappear, promotions that do not materialise – but throughout you should be able to rely on your agent to police this process, right up to and beyond publication. The relationship is a continuing one, despite the new relationship you will have developed with your editor. Remember that your agent is always there to lend assistance – even if it means playing the bad cop and banging the publisher's table so that you don't have to.

At its core, your relationship with your agent is a personal one. You have to get on, trust each other, like each other and respect each other. You have to be comfortable that you can ask or tell your agent anything. There will be as many ups and downs as there are frustrations and disappointments, but if you believe in each other then you can maintain a very successful and friendly business relationship. Being a good agent is about far more than making a living; expertise and experience, while vital, will only take an agent so far. It is the pride in a client's work, the excitement at a deal well done and the commitment to the development of a career which mark out the great from the good. And don't forget: your agent is on your side.

48

The Film Agent

Julian Friedmann

The chapters on television, radio and theatre agents, and on literary agents (novel), cover many aspects of being a writers' agent, whatever format a writer chooses. Most film agents also handle television, radio and theatre (in Britain there are not enough films made for most writers to earn a sufficient living writing only feature film scripts).

There are, however, significant differences between agenting writers in the film business from the others, notably the unpredictability and unreliability of the film business compared especially with television. Where television needs thousands of scripts a year (and produces thousands of episodes of drama, comedy, two-parters and so on in a year), there is a limited number of feature films made and therefore any career strategy restricted to feature films alone is a highly risky one.

Many independent producers have little or no development money. They need books or treatments or scripts in order to go out and raise the money to pay the writer (and themselves). So the frequency of the minimal or free option is increasing. This naturally impacts on the way film agents have to work.

While it is true that an independent producer optioning or commissioning a script for a television drama may have great problems finding finance from the broadcasters, the broadcasters do have an appetite for product and the finance to acquire it. An independent producer (in reality the most dependent producers of all) attempting to raise finance for a film faces a far more complex and difficult task, since most films are financed by bringing together multiple sources of finance, usually from more than one country.

Conventional sources of film finance include:
- Tax-based finance, including EIS investors (subject to the vicissitudes of the Treasury)
- Regional money (Lottery money in the UK, handed out by the regional 'branches' of the UK Film Council – a list can be found on the UKFC website)
- Co-producers either in the same country or more often from various countries
- The sale of rights to a sales agent or a distributor (usually called a minimum guarantee)
- Private investors or banks (usually in return for rights in the film as collateral)
- Deferments (usually from whoever the producer can persuade to take their payment later).

A moderately expensive film in Europe (£3–5m) could have as many as ten co-producers. This means that there are heavy legal costs involved as every co-producer needs to be tied in legally; there are also complex cultural implications on the creative development and casting of the project.

What has all this to do with film agents? It is not that common to sell and negotiate a deal for a feature film script by a client and then sit back and collect the payments as they fall due. For television writers it is fairly usual to sign off on a deal and then the main activity for the agent is to police and chase money that is late. So film agents can spend a considerable amount of time navigating between the mix of people who become involved in the financing of a film.

Most films lose money so there is not an obvious investment environment encouraging people to sink their hard-earned money into films. Agents for writers of film scripts spend a considerable amount of time negotiating *after* a deal has been agreed and signed than ever before. This is not because the contracts that were signed were not respectable and tight contracts. It is due mainly to the difficulties producers have in putting the deals together.

Agents also spend an increasing amount of time looking for sources of finance. In other words agents representing feature-film writers tend to become more involved in the whole process of raising the money and identifying potential co-producers than they do for writers of television drama.

In Hollywood (and less so the indie sector in New York) a film agent or lawyer is essential. Many production companies (and all the Studios) refuse to accept unsolicited scripts, partly because they don't want to be sued if they later make a film similar to the script you submitted. It actually makes little difference that it comes via an agent. But in part it is because they want to receive material that someone else has read and thought worth submitting, since writers don't always know how unproducible their scripts are.

Agents in California can only charge 10 per cent by law; however there are also managers, who take a more general over-view of their clients' careers than an American agent is likely to do (and can charge between 10 per cent and 20 per cent). In the UK good agents cover the work done by both in the States.

American agents, while admitting that British writers sometimes have class, are very rarely interested in representing them. For a start British writers are too far away to have a quick meet in the Polo Lounge, and they seldom write with the economy (or feel-good endings) of American writers. If you can write a script with the muscular economy of *Basic Instinct* – a great example of American scriptwriting – then go for it. If you are a British writer serious about writing American-style films for the American market move there for six months: everyone will meet you and you will give yourself the best chance of landing an agent even if you don't get a sale or commission. But get your calling card scripts and pitches into better shape than you would expect to for the European market.

It is also far more likely that a writer will get a feature-film break after they have had some success with either shorts (agents don't tend to get too involved as there is no, or so little, money in shorts) or television. Enabling a writer to get a feature break therefore often is the result of the agent and the writer (they should be seen as a double act, not as two separate players) getting credits for the writer on other types of productions and then moving the writer upwards.

For example, there are 'access' television shows, usually thirty-minute-long episodes, including soaps, that writers can get onto without having an agent at all. A writer who does is more likely to be attractive to a good agent than one who can't even manage that. Once on a television show the agent should start positioning them to get onto more desirable thirty-minute shows and then onto hour-long dramas.

It is easier to 'promote' a writer who is working than one who isn't, so while a writer is notching up early career credits, the film agent should be encouraging the client to develop treatments and pitches for feature film ideas. This should be a realistic exercise: the agent should be able to identify the writer's strengths and the ideas should also not be mega-budget films that could only be made by studios (although expansive ideas well-presented are important too).

For an agent it is easier and more effective pitching a writer's idea for a film while saying that they are busy writing for a TV series, than it is pitching them when they have not worked for six months. Confidence breeds confidence and if other producers want a writer they must be doing something right.

This is one reason why writers who have an offer to write episodes should think twice about not using an agent in order to save the commission, because if the agent is a good one he or she will be working away at the development of the career in the background all the time.

There is also a myth that the film industry is keen to find original voices. The film industry is conservative. Making a film written by an A-list writer is a huge risk; a script by an unknown writer can be an even bigger risk. Of course producers do make the mistake of presuming that a great writer with lots of credits will be a better bet, when a careful read of the scripts could show that the unknown writer's script is far more commercial.

The film industry, in contrast to the television industry, loves 'discovering' new directors. This encourages some writers to announce that they will direct their own work. A good agent will encourage this cautiously, in that too often the script may not have been through as rigorous a development process without the intervention of a second opinion, in the form of a director.

So into this unpredictable and messy business – sometimes called Development Hell – agents and writers march, often with very little real hope that the film will actually be made. More time and effort can go into raising the budget than went into getting the script into good shape. The end result – if the film is made – is often disappointing. Film writers (and to a lesser extent film agents) need to be more passionate and optimistic than television, radio or theatre writers. More often than not the script that gets commissioned from the lucky writer is not their idea, but an idea from the producer or investors. How does the writer get the gig? Usually because they, with their agent, have developed calling-card scripts and treatments.

The calling-card portfolio should demonstrate the range of the writer's craft skills: emotion (always the most important thing to show in a script), drama, action, comedy and so on. The writer should be encouraged to have 30- and 60- minute scripts in the portfolio, alongside 90- or 120- minute scripts.

When a producer is looking for a writer it helps to be able to offer a script demonstrating the qualities that the producer needs. A good agent will help ensure that their clients have this material to hand.

Calling-card scripts are so-called because they are written 'on spec', that is, speculatively, without any contract or payment. It is possible to sell calling-card scripts but it is not that common. What usually happens is that the agent submits the script to a producer looking for a certain type of material and if the producer likes the script, they then meet the writer and if the two of them get on, the producer either options the calling-card, or commissions a new script, based on an idea by the writer or by the producer. The commission may be to adapt a book or short story or magazine article.

I was once approached by a producer with a newspaper clipping about a foreigner murdered in the wrong part of Miami. It made a TV movie. The sources of ideas are another area where agents can be part of the double act. Agents should read the general press widely and also read the trade press. This means that while a serious feature-film writer would subscribe to *Screen International* and/or *Variety*, the agent should be reading several trades in order to have a broader sense of what is working and who is looking for what.

If a film suddenly takes off at the box-office, or is announced to be going into development from a major company, writers sometimes rush out similar ideas, and it is the sad job of a film agent to tell a client that it is at least two years too late to promote a similar idea. An agent can save clients a great deal of time developing projects which will have to compete with a similar one.

As has been mentioned in the other chapters on agents, the film agent needs to network extensively in the interests of their clients: there are apparently more film festivals around the world than there are films made, so agents can usefully swan off to Cannes, Venice, Berlin, Edinburgh and many others.

There are industry events that producers attend, organised by – for example – PACT (the producers' 'union' – Producers' Association for Cinema and Television); industry screenings at BAFTA and other venues, seminars and workshops. Agents frequent these in order to meet producers. The Frankfurt Book Fair now has a special section for the selling of film and television rights in books, where agents can meet producers.

They also have lunches and dinners and coffees and drinks with producers. Some film agents research local and international producers and pitch specific projects to them; others use the meetings as fishing expeditions, to find out what the producers are looking for, and then send them appropriate material.

One benefit film writers get from a busy and liked agent, who travels around, is that they will be doing deals with a range of companies and countries, and while writers are in competition with each other, a busy agent is more likely to hear of opportunities than one who sits in his or her office and doesn't mix.

It is important for agents to have a certain amount of integrity (I know that the frequent jokes about agents imply that this is a contradiction in terms), but if an agent sends inappropriate material to a producer, that producer will not look seriously at the agency's submissions. So if an agent does not wish to submit a script, either because it is – in the agent's opinion – not ready or because it is inappropriate, a writer should take some notice. Agents only get paid when the writer gets paid. If an agent is willing to read and edit a script numerous times, it is because the agent believes that it is getting better.

Which is not to say the agent is always right. But most good agents do a great deal of speculative work on their clients' treatments and scripts because they believe that this will result in a better deal (or maybe in any deal!). However, writers should be free to change agents if they do not feel that the agent is the right representative. This can be a fraught process for some writers, but all agents have been fired at some time or another: agents have a number of clients while writers have one career. It can still be galling to have helped a writer make steady progress only to find that they are lured to a bigger agency where they may indeed be well-served, or they may become smaller fish in a bigger pond. But the bigger agencies have proportionately as many defections as medium and smaller ones. It is a bit like a marriage. No one should go into it believing it won't work, but most marriages end in divorce so both parties should simply be elegant and civilised about it.

Apart from the creative input a good agent can provide to the ideas and stories a writer wishes to script, a good agent should be equally creative when it comes to deal points. Producers usually offer the least they think they can get away with. After all this is business and they should do deals that work for them. An agent can fall back on precedent ('I never accept less than X or Y', or 'I have never agreed to that before' carries some weight from a reputable agent). Alternatively agents can play with *quid pro quos*: we will agree to this if you agree to that.

Most writers do not study their contracts sufficiently; their agent should always be able to see trade-offs. If there is no option or only a small option payment, then there are various strategies to ensure that the deal is not unfavourable in too many respects for their client:

- Instead of a £1 option the agent (or a savvy writer) can argue for a £1000 option with the writer deferring £999 (if there is no possibility of a decent option payment and the writer really wants the deal). The deferred amount becomes due as soon as the producer enters into any agreement with a third party to co-produce the film or any third party financing agreement, especially if soft subsidy money is received.
- The option is usually renewable when a further sum (great, another £1!) is paid after twelve or eighteen months. A better deal is that this renewal is only possible if something else has happened, such as the second draft script has been commissioned (and that is sometimes easier to get money paid for), or upon material evidence of progress (difficult to define but it puts pressure on the producer to keep the writer and their agent in touch with what is happening). There is a bonus of say £5000 or more on the first day of principal photography. Sadly this day (abbreviated as 1stdpp) usually never comes.
- The first option is much shorter, and sometimes tied into the producer seeking finance from say two third parties only. If a deal is struck then the option is extendable and some money is paid to the writer. If no deal is struck then the script has not been widely shopped around.

Producers tend to work harder to safeguard an investment from their own pocket than they might if they have gathered free options on twenty projects all of which they are throwing at the wall in the hope that one might stick.

The agent can also fight for better reversion and turnaround terms than is usually offered voluntarily by producers. (For more information on negotiating and contracts see my book *How To Make Money Scriptwriting*, Intellect Press. And for an independent view of agents see the article by media lawyer Sean Egan in *ScriptWriter* magazine issue 6, or on the website www.scriptwritermagazine.com in the legal surgery section, under the title 'All you need to know about agreements with agents but were afraid to ask'.)

When the producer pays a substantial option and agrees to a high purchase price, it is more difficult to squeeze concessions. But there are a number of important concessions that can be obtained by the agent (or writer) through negotiation:

- Copyright should not pass until *both* the contract is signed *and* the purchase price payment has been received. This saves chasing for it since it is often late and a little leverage helps speed up the cash flow.
- The turnaround provisions can usually be improved: turnaround is what happens when a producer, having bought the rights, that is, paid the purchase price, fails to make the movie within the agreed five or seven years. They lose the right to make it but if you want to sell it to someone else then the first producer will often try to claw back the money they paid you, plus other money spent on development, plus interest, plus a charge against overheads. They do not always do this out of greed: it might be

because the money that they borrowed to pay you in the first place they could only borrow on these terms. This should be resisted if possible: after all, the producer buys an opportunity, he or she doesn't lend the writer money which has to be repaid plus interest when the producer fails. An agent is perhaps better placed to fight this battle than a writer.

A good agent makes sure that there are producers who trust the agent: it is then easier to get work by clients read and even commissioned on the strength of the agent/producer relationship, as the agent would not risk that relationship just to get one deal.

Some writers worry that their agents seem too close to producers. There may be occasions when this could be detrimental to a writer, but in general close relationships with producers benefits writers.

What writers should be aware of are the legal and financial obligations agents have: some of these are described in the chapter on Agents in *How To Make Money Scriptwriting*: Writers often ask about the importance of having contracts with their agents. The Association of Authors Agents [this, with the PMA is the other association of agents and is a good indicator when choosing an agent] advises that the business relationship between writer and agent should be formalised in a contract. It's the simplest and most effective way for each party to know what the other's obligations and responsibilities are.

Below are some of the key points which you should be aware of in the author/agency agreement used by members of the AAA.

- Should you wish to terminate the representation you should be able to do so at any time. The writer as principal must control their own career. It is normal however, to give thirty day's notice.
- All approaches regarding your work should be referred to the agent.
- The agent should not commit you to any agreement without your approval.
- You should warrant that you are the author and sole owner of the work you ask the agent to represent and that the works are original and contain nothing unlawful in content, do not violate the rights of any third party, are not an infringement of any existing copyright, contain no blasphemous, indecent, defamatory, libellous, objectionable or otherwise unlawful matter, and that all statements in your work which you say are facts are true. You will also have to indemnify the agent against loss, injury or damage caused by any breach of your warranty.

The agent's commission should be clearly stated. In The Blake Friedmann author/agency agreement it is described as:

> A percentage of the income arising from all contracts for the exploitation of works you create entered into during the period we represent you (and after that only to the extent mentioned in point seven below) at the following rates:
>
> | | |
> |---|---|
> | Books, serials and columns, UK | 15% |
> | Books, serials and columns, overseas | 20% |
> | Radio, television, film | 15% |
> | One-off journalism and short stories | 25% |
> | (journalism can be excluded) | |
> | Audio, abridged and unabridged, British | 15% |
> | Audio, abridged and unabridged, overseas | 20% |
>
> In Europe VAT must be added to the commission charged.

The agreement should state clearly that if there is anything contained in any such contract which the writer does not understand or does not wish to accept, it is their responsibility to make this clear before they sign the contract.

The representation will continue until terminated by either party giving not less than thirty days written notice to the other whereupon, unless both parties agree otherwise, the agency will cease to represent the writer but shall continue to be entitled to commission in respect of all income arising from contracts for the exploitation of your works entered into while they represented the writer and from all extensions and renewals of such contracts.

The writer should also remember that an agent has certain obligations to clients in common law. These can be summed up as follows (this is not an exhaustive list):

- An agent has legal and fiduciary obligations to clients.
- The rights and duties of Principal and Agent are to be determined in a contract between them. If there is no contract, then the fact that the relationship exists implies a contract.
- The primary duty of an agent is to carry out the business the agent has undertaken with the Principal, and to notify the Principal if he/she is unable to do it.
- The agent must always act in the best interests of a client. The agent must either follow the client's instructions, or if it not possible to obtain instructions, the interests of the client must guide the agent's actions.
- There is an obligation on the agent to keep proper accounts and to disclose them on reasonable demand to the client.
- The agent is obliged to disclose a conflict of interests.
- The agent must disclose any information gathered by the agency which is relevant to the client's interests.
- The agent must not receive any secret commission or bribe with regard to a client's contracts.
- The agent should not bind the client unless the agent has general or specific authority to do so.
- An agent should exercise skill, care and diligence in what they undertake to do on behalf of clients.

Being an agent can be great fun; helping writers realise their talent and ambitions is very fulfilling much of the time. But being a realist is necessary since many of the people who want to earn a living as writers do not feel it necessary to be completely professional about it.

Writing well is very difficult. A good relationship with a realistic film agent is likely to save a writer time and grief, even if that writer never gets a film made. In the end truly great scripts are few and far between. If you write one it will certainly get you an agent and almost certainly be made. Agents can help ensure that what their clients write is better edited and that a wayward director is watched carefully.

There can be no absolute protection, except abstinence

49

The Literary Agent:
Television, Radio and Theatre

Alan Brodie

Introduction

As William Goldman so eloquently puts it in his brilliant book, *Adventures In The Screen Trade*, agents are the catch-22 of the entertainment business in that everyone starting out desperately needs one and nobody starting out can possibly get one. He is commenting on artists working in Hollywood but that line, together with the perception of the heartless agent as a parasite always out to make a fast buck on the back of creative talent seems to be a common perception. I hope this chapter will show that this need not be true and that without agents, the industry would be very different and much more chaotic.

We are dealing here with the Literary Agent, that is the agent who represents writers. Within that generality, there are a group of agents who specialise in dramatists, that is, those writers who write words for actors to speak, which can be for any of the performing arts – film, television, theatre, radio and so called new media. There are agents who deal with actors, directors, technicians, composers – indeed there can be agents for anyone who attempts to earn money professionally from the entertainment industry. Whilst some of what follows applies to all agents particularly in dealing with personal management and career strategy, dealing with writers is very different mainly due to the laws of copyright.

The reason the job of the Literary Agent exists and the writer can make a living is because of the Law of Copyright. For that reason another (albeit old fashioned) name for the Literary Agent is a Copyright Agent. Without copyright, there would be no industry, there would be no incentive for creative talent to create and there would be no work for the agent!

The agent's primary job is to protect and exploit your copyright in such a way that you can make a living from your creative talent. However, it is important that the agent has a responsibility not only to you, his client, but also to the industry as a whole. A healthy industry benefits everyone and even in situations where it might be possible to squeeze more money out of a producer due to the laws of supply and demand, it can often backfire as that money has to come from somewhere and that could mean that the production values diminish to the detriment of the finished production. This is also a situation where to try to push fees up will not only cause bad feeling with the producer but could affect future work. It is the agent's role to understand this and see the bigger picture.

It follows then, that an agent does more than negotiate deals. In the following paragraphs I will go into more detail of an agent's role in the specific areas I am writing in. As space is limited, what follows is an overview of my views taken from my experience.

The first thing to note is that each client–agent relationship is different. No two agents are the same in the same way that no two writers are the same. Like in any personal relationship, you have to find your own way and you have to be clear about what you want to get out of it. In general terms what you will both be aiming for is to create the right climate for the writer to produce their best work. Once that work is created you will want your agent to exploit it round the world in as many different markets as possible so as you can make a living out of what you do. However one myth to burst immediately is the expectation that once you have an agent work will flow in. That is certainly not true. Of course it does happen and agents can guide you towards work and into certain areas; they can introduce you to key people in the industry but they can't write your script for you or guarantee you a job.

In developing your relationship with your agent, just how close it is will depend on personalities. Don't forget that most agencies have many clients and it will be impossible for an agent to have a close personal relationship with everyone. They should have a close professional relationship with all their clients or they have too many, but don't expect too much. Yes, an agent will provide many different services: dramaturgy, career strategy, PR and marketing adviser, creative consultant, legal, accountancy, analyst, social worker, friend. Some writers will use their agent to bounce ideas off but others will have their own 'creative' structure where they can run things by directors or others in the business that they trust. In that situation, the agent may not see the script until it is finished though that won't stop them making comments!

Do I need one and how do I get one?

If you are serious about a career as a writer and intend to interact with the professional world then you will at some stage need an agent. Not only will they help you in the manner described above, but in many cases, producers will not receive scripts from unagented writers. This is particularly true of film companies. It is also true that producers if they are honourable prefer the writers they are working with to be represented. They want to make sure that the writer will feel that he or she is fairly treated and perhaps more importantly to them, they don't want to discuss the dirty details of the deal with the same person that they need to have a constructive creative relationship with.

OK so you think you need an agent: it's really important to find the right one for you. A bad agent is no use to you. The wrong agent, no matter how good, is no use to you either. It is common sense that the more you do for yourself, the further along the track you get, the more choice you will have in seeking the right agent. Agencies come in all shapes and sizes: from small one man bands to the big American-run conglomerates. You need to decide what suits you best.

It is important to do your research properly in order to establish a short list of Agencies which might be right for you. This means seeking out those that specialise in the areas you want to work in. A useful starting point is *The Writers' & Artists' Yearbook* which is available at your local library. More importantly, seek out other writers and get their opinions. Talk to the people you work with in the business. No point in going to an agent who doesn't get along with your favourite producer. These days, Agencies are far more transparent with their client lists and often have websites. Check out your favourite writers and see who represents them.

When approaching an agent, find out who the right person in the agency is to contact. Call first and check how they prefer to be contacted. Not all agencies will respond to emails. Some will only take writers that come with a recommendation from someone they know so find out if anyone you have been working with is familiar with the agent you want and have them call ahead. Some will want a letter before they ask to see a script. Then, don't forget you are a writer so write a concise focused letter. Be confident but not boastful. You are seeking to make an immediate impression on an agent who hasn't read a word of your work but who gets many submissions each week. If you are bringing a potential deal with you then of course that can be helpful but it shouldn't be the be all and end all. Indeed if you feel that is the only reason why an agent might take you on then the warning bells should ring. Most good agents are looking for writers who have a long professional career ahead of them and who want to be part of that career. If you want someone to handle a one-off deal, then you are better using a lawyer.

The key thing of course is that the agent should like and engage with your writing. So you should send in your best script and the one that you feel best reflects your work. The script should be well presented, on one side of A4 paper with standard spacing and lettering. Don't try to save paper by squashing everything up! It's a false economy. An agent will have piles of scripts to read and you need to make it as easy for him as possible. It should always be an original script, not an adaptation and not a Treatment. Don't send in more than one or two scripts at the most. Ask for an acknowledgement if you would like one and then, be patient. An agent's primary focus will be on the clients he already has and clients' scripts will always take priority. You could try to establish how long it might take to read your script and if you haven't heard anything after about six weeks then a gentle enquiry might be in order. Don't nag them – if you are a pain now what would you be like as a client?!

If you are writing plays, then whilst there is nothing preventing you from sending the script in to the agent to read, far better to show initiative and have the play produced at one of the many small theatres (many linked to pubs) around the country. You can invite potential agents to performances and even if they don't come, it will be noticed that the play has been performed, particularly if it has been well reviewed.

If the agent likes your script he may call you in for an interview. The key thing to remember here is that this is a two-way interview. As I said above, no agent is better than the wrong agent so you need to make sure that your personalities are compatible. Not only must the agent be passionate about your work, the two of you must feel you are capable of reaching a mutual understanding of where your career might be heading. That means, feeling comfortable with each other. No point in being with an agent who terrifies you so much you are frightened to phone him. You must feel he is accessible and that the agency itself feels like a comfortable place to be. Don't be afraid to ask questions about the way the agency is run, about the clients and of course about the commission structure. Also, try to tease out from the agent how he sees an agent's place in the business. If it is all about money, then maybe he is not the right person for you.

When an agent offers representation, he is duty bound, under the Employment Agencies Act 2004, to send you a letter outlining the Company's terms of trade. In the UK (unlike the US) it is not common for there to be a binding contract between agent and client for a set period. Usually, there will be a Letter of Agreement sent out by the agent outlining his terms and method of operation. This usually allows the client or the agent to terminate the relationship at any time whilst setting out any obligations on termination. The letter will state the commissioning terms and how money collected is distributed. Usually the minimum commission will be 10 per cent but this can rise to 20 per cent in certain circumstances. You should certainly be clear with the agent what his commission rates are and take advice from a lawyer on the form if anything is unclear. You should check if the agency is a member of The Personal Managers Association. Agencies signing up to that organisation have to comply with a strict code of conduct which the agency concerned has to show you on commencement of the relationship. That would give you some comfort that you were being correctly treated.

The relationship will take time to develop and you must give it that time. You should learn how to use the agency in a way that suits you. Who is in the office? What does everyone do there? It helps to try to get to know the staff of the agency since they will be the ones offering day-to-day administrative support and at busy periods will know how best to reach your primary agent if you need to. Most of all, don't forget that a client–agent relationship is a partnership. Don't expect the agency to do everything for you. An agent has lots of clients and welcomes ideas and suggestions from them. So, communicate and discuss. You have to work at the relationship too!

However, always remember that you are paying the agent to do a job of work on your behalf, not the other way round. Agents should always be in the background and leave their own egos at home and should never forget that they are only as good as the talent they are representing. The legendary Lew Grade was once asked why he moved from the agency business to become a television executive: 'I was fed up with my clients taking 90 per cent of my income' was his retort. Agenting is not the right career for anyone with that attitude!

Television

If you are planning a career in television there will come a point when you will need representation. The fact is that television executives are much less likely to take unagented submissions seriously if only because they get so many scripts through their door that at least if it has come from a reputable agent there has already been some filtering. There are a number of writing courses run by the broadcasters from where new writers can emerge but even they now are, for the most part, considering writers who are already represented. Occasionally, scripts from the so-called 'slush' pile do get through but these are the exception rather than the rule.

In the UK the main commissioners of Drama are the BBC, ITV, Channel 4 and to a lesser extent Channel 5 and Sky. It is your agent's job to know the players and know how to get your scripts to them. This can take a number of forms: it may be that the scripts you have will never get made. That doesn't mean that they go into a drawer. They can be used as 'calling cards' which is a way of attracting the attention of a commissioner to you. Hopefully, they would like your script enough to want to meet you and listen to other ideas you might have or else they may have series that they are working on for which they are looking for writers. Writing an episode of a series is one way of breaking through. It's certainly not an easy option. It's hard work and you often have to put your own creative instincts to one side. This is particularly true with soaps. However there is no doubt that if you have the right temperament it can be very rewarding and very lucrative. But beware, once your career is on the move in this way it can be very hard to withdraw and I've seen some writers getting in so deep that it becomes difficult for them to tackle their own original work. All this should be constantly reviewed with your agent so that you are in control of your career rather than being swept along.

The key thing is to keep writing. Watch television, see what's out there and try to be objective. Even if you are writing episodes of series keep writing original work too. It was original work that would have attracted the agent and in turn the commissioning executive. Everyone is looking for that original voice. Be prepared to rewrite and rewrite and rewrite. As Neil Simon once said – a script isn't written, it's rewritten. Always listen to feedback but use your own instincts. If you give one script to five people you'll get six opinions. And don't rely on friends to tell you how good the script is. It's important too to create your own contacts where you can. Television doesn't owe you a living. An agent will unlock doors for you but it is up to you to push them open. There are no guarantees.

It's not just getting your script to the right person that is important. These days, with the advent of new media and the plethora of television channels across the terrestrial and digital networks, protecting your rights are absolutely vital and one of your agent's key roles will be to ensure contractual fairness. All the main broadcasters operate union-agreed minimum terms agreements: the BBC have a tripartite Writers Agreement with the Writers Guild of Great Britain and the Personal Managers Association. ITV have their own agreement with the Writers Guild as do PACT, the organisation operating on behalf of Independent producers. Writers are paid an upfront fee which is generally broken down to a payment on signature of the contract, a payment on delivery of the script and a payment on acceptance (though in the BBC's case the total fee is divided half on signature and half on acceptance). The Broadcaster/producer will have a certain amount of time in which to produce the programme. On the first day that principal photography takes place, the writer will receive another fee (usually 100 percent of his basic fee), which will be an advance against future worldwide sales and entitle the broadcaster to a certain number of repeats. The writer will continue to receive a residual payment from the sales of the programme after the advance has been paid off. An agent's job will be to collect whatever income is due to you; check the statements and make sure all is in order.

There are a number of important differences between the three agreements. Basically, the BBC operates under a system whereby they exclusively license the script for a number of years and from that flows all the rights that they are entitled to. The PACT agreement assigns the script to a producer which means that they can do anything they like with it unless specifically stated otherwise. ITV currently use a method where they only pay a script fee and no advance on principal photography. They do though pay residuals on sales from the first £ and therefore anything that sells really well could be of benefit to the writer.

In television, one of the most important things an agent will do is to listen to ideas and advise whether or not they are marketable. An agent will know which producers might be looking for projects or alternatively, the agents will be approached to suggest writers for particular projects. That is one reason why you need to know if your agent is right for you – will that agency be on the list of the broadcasters to call up in these situations? There is also in each drama department a considerable hierarchy of script editors, development executives, commissioning executives, heads of department, etc. who frequently change jobs and it is difficult to know how to get through the system. The agent will try to keep abreast of all this and advise you on what level to go in on. Of course, the higher up the chain you go the more chance you have of being commissioned. However, at whatever level you are, it is very important to treat everyone with the same respect from the most junior to the most senior. Today's junior script editor is tomorrow's commissioning executive and the next day's channel controller!

A question often asked is whether or not a writer should be putting ideas and scripts directly to a broadcaster (which in practical terms means the BBC as the other broadcasters require independent producers to produce any programmes they commission) or to an independent producer. As noted above independent producers operate through the PACT agreement, but ultimately, for the most part, the finance comes from the broadcaster. There are a number of strong advantages as to why you should work through an independent. It gives you time to create the relationship and develop the idea before it goes into a broadcaster. It gives you a producer known to you who will work with you in creating the best programme and someone who will work with the broadcasting organisation right through the production process. However, there are a large number of independent producers operating in the UK, all chasing a limited number of hours in the schedule. Some are better than others and, crucially, some have a much better chance of having programmes commissioned than others. If you are working in-house at the BBC you sometimes will have a more direct route to the commissioning executives and at least 50 per cent of the BBC's drama output must come from in-house production. Often it's down to personal relationships and who you feel most comfortable with. This is where your agent will play a key role in advising you.

Outside the UK, there is for some writers, the possibility of a lucrative career in the international television market. These days there are more and more international co-productions. In drama, this is not easy to achieve because of language and other cultural differences. Where the commissioners are the UK broadcasters then they will be the ones who will try to bring in finance by seeking co-production usually with one of the other English language broadcasters. The BBC have commonly worked with HBO and PBS in the US, along with other broadcasters in Canada and Australia. Occasionally, independent producers will commission scripts from writers and then go out internationally and put together finance. This is still rare as most of the time UK broadcasters prefer to be in right at the beginning of any script commission and will usually undertake the script development finance itself. However, I can certainly see that in the years ahead this form of commissioning will increase. There are also opportunities for a UK writer to be directly commissioned by an international broadcaster. German and Swedish Broadcasters use UK writers from time to time, as do Australian and Canadian broadcasters. A few agencies do specialise in these markets and many will know agencies in those territories who might be able to help.

It is very hard to sustain a dual career in more than one territory but the one territory that many television writers want to crack is the US market. It is also the most difficult. Many television writers in the UK would love to be commissioned to write an episode of *ER* or *West Wing*, but then so would almost every American writer! For the most part, any success that UK writers have in the US comes from major success in the UK first. I know of no case in my experience where scripts of ideas have gone direct from the UK into the US and come back with a commission. For an unknown writer to crack the US market, they would need, I think, to go and live in Los Angeles and work through the system there. Even for an established writer, selling ideas and scripts to the US is extremely difficult. It would be imperative to find an agent in Los Angeles who you could work with and who understands the complex commissioning system and knows what the networks (CBS, NBC, CBS, Fox) want. Your agent here may have relationships with US agents but to chase a US agent is usually counter-productive. It's better to wait until you are so established here that you will have US agents enquiring after you.

A common form of Television agenting particularly in the US is the 'Packaging Agent', which is where an agent will put together all the elements, often but not necessarily, from his own list: such as writer, actor, director and producer, and then seal the package to a network, taking his commission as a percentage taken from the budget. This kind of agenting is very different from the Literary Agent whose sole purpose is the development of the career of their writer client.

Theatre

Whilst all of the above can apply to an agent representing writers who are pursuing a playwriting career, there are further responsibilities incumbent on the Theatre Agent, or as they are more commonly called, The Play Agent. These days there are very few agencies which exclusively perform that role but many have agents or departments who specialise in theatre. It's important for anyone whose main ambition is to write for the stage or indeed have a parallel career between stage and television/film to make sure that the agency in question has considerable experience of the theatre. You need your agent to be able to be in contact with the producers throughout all the different sectors: commercial producers in London West End, the Fringe Theatres and the regional theatres.

A playwright earns his living primarily by his plays being successful at the box office. A writer can be commissioned by a producer and receive an up-front fee but this commonly is only between £4,000 and £10,000, which certainly does not offer a living wage when you consider it might take six months or longer to write. A system was therefore devised whereby the playwright would receive a royalty based on box-office receipts. This would usually be anywhere between 5 per cent and 10 per cent.

Theatre contracts are very different because for the most part playwrights licence their plays to producers for a short period of time. However, when a new play is commissioned, the producer will commonly 'participate' in the future success of the play. In the commercial theatre, producers will gear the royalty structure depending on the production cost and the weekly running costs. The traditional royalty structure has been eroded over the years and now commercial theatres use a system of royalty pooling, which involves all the royalty participants taking a minimum guaranteed fee and then they all share pro rata, in the weekly profits that a production will make. In the subsidised sector, there are union agreements which offer minimum terms. These are the 'TNC Agreement' operated by The National Theatre, Royal Shakespeare Company and The Royal Court, The TMA Agreement operated by the Theatre Management Association and covering in the main the UK Regional theatres and the 'ITC Agreement' (Independent Theatre Council) which covers many of the small scale fringe companies throughout the UK. These subsidised theatre contracts tend to have a royalty structure that is fixed but there is still a number of issues that need to be negotiated at the time of signing the contract.

One other contract that it is important to know about is the Approved Production Contract of the Dramatists Guild of America. This contract covers plays produced in North America. It is, as are the others, a minimum terms agreement. Anyone offered an 'APC' must take advice and this is where an agent specialising in theatre is vital. The contract has complicated provisions on the producers' rights to participation of future income and their rights in territories outside North America which will need to be amended or deleted at the time of signing.

Another major difference from film and television is that even after contracts are signed playwrights tend to have more control over the creative elements (whereas in film and television this tends to happen only to writers with clout). In their contracts, it will be commonly written in that the playwright has approval of the director and the cast of the play. There will also be a clause stating that nothing in the text can be changed without the playwright's permission. However, though these clauses are there for the writer's protection, use of them must be made wisely. Theatre is a collaborative medium and the best productions are generally borne out of the creative team working together in a constructive manner. Tensions are bound to arise – there may be a key element of the play which the actor involved is having trouble saying in the right manner; the playwright might disagree with the director's interpretation of a particular scene. It is here that the agent can perform a useful function by acting as the go-between, cooling tempers and trying to find a compromise.

So, the agent has read the various drafts of the play, found a producer, negotiated the contracts, advised on directors and casting, been on hand to offer help where necessary with publicity and then had the thrill of sitting in the auditorium watching the play, that one, two even three years ago was a mere idea, unfold on the stage. The reviews have come out, the congratulating or hand-holding has gone on depending on the success or otherwise of what can be very tense first nights. (It is one of the stranger functions of this business that the opening night of a play is played out in front of a group of critics on whom the success or failure of the play can often depend. Months and years of work can be ruined with the stroke of a pen.) The agent's job is over, right? Wrong. The job is actually just starting.

Whether the play is a success or not, it is incumbent on the agent to exploit the play in as many markets as is possible. This does not only mean film and television which though important, is rare, it really means seeking further productions around the world. A good play agent will have many contacts not just in English Speaking territories but also in the foreign language markets. There are certain foreign territories where there is a strong theatre tradition and it is the responsibility of the agent to seek these out. This is usually done through a network of foreign language agents, who are on the ground in particular countries and will buy plays, have them translated and sell them on to their local theatre companies. The major markets are Germany, Scandinavia, France, Holland and Japan. Some playwrights can have more success in foreign territories than in the UK so it's vital these rights are properly handled.

Depending on the nature of the first production of a play, there are a number of decisions that would need to be taken. If it is a play premiered in the regions, then should it come to London? If it is premiered in London, then how would it be best to have the rest of the country see it. And of course, what about New York? There are also other things to think about – who would be the right publisher for the play (now a very difficult market), how would it be best to exploit the amateur rights. Companies, such as Samuel French Ltd, will buy plays, paying some money in advance, publish acting editions and then licence amateur companies to produce the play. The playwright will receive a 'fee per performance' for these productions, less commission.

In North America there are a number of theatres which specialise in new writing and offer the UK playwright further opportunities, though it has to be said that nearly all American theatres will give precedence to the work of American writers unless that play has originally been performed in the UK. It is not uncommon for your agent in the UK to appoint, with your agreement, an agent in New York to look after your plays in North America. However many UK agents will deal directly with theatres on your behalf. Regional Theatres in North America are known as LORT Theatres.

The market in Australia for UK plays is likewise divided. There is a commercial sector mainly operating in Sydney and Melbourne which tend to produce musicals and the more commercial West End or Broadway play. Then there are the State Theatres in the capitals of the Australian States, which are subsidised and perform repertoires not unlike the National Theatre in London. Finally, there are a plethora of small fringe and touring companies which do new work and will produce the less well-known British play. Again, your agent will tend to work directly with this market rather than appoint an Australian agent.

It is worth pointing out here that as a playwright, your income comes from your plays being performed and this follows equally whether it is in the West End or a school. If the play is published there is a cautionary note inserted warning readers that the play cannot be performed without rights clearance. A typical note would be as follows:

> This play is fully protected by copyright throughout the world. All applications for professional performance should be made to [insert name of Agency] and any performance by amateurs to [insert name if different]. Applications should be made before rehearsals commence and no performance can be given until a licence is obtained.

You should note that this includes any performance of the play (or indeed an extract) even if there is no payment made to see it. A school play, where parents are invited would require a licence. Of course, in certain circumstances the agent might advise the playwright that the fee should be waived but that is entirely a matter for him or her.

As with television, a play agent will be looking for those writers able to sustain a career. They are looking beyond the one-off biographical play that many people write and then fail to deliver that crucial 'second' play. If you are trying to develop a parallel career in theatre and television then your agent will be crucial in advising how to do that. It's a fickle business and to disappear out of one genre or another for too long can be damaging so you need to work out how to balance the two.

Play writing is not an easy field to be a success in and making a living, even for the successful playwright is not guaranteed. However, it is extremely rewarding and can, if it is desired, be an excellent stepping stone for television, though my view is that continuing with the playwriting career can feed into television and film work in a really positive way.

Radio

Radio is one of the most underrated mediums for writers, mainly because it is the most unsung. And yet, it is, if you think about it, the purest writer's medium outside prose. Radio drama is all about the words and the imagination. There is less that gets in its way. It is also a fantastic way to make contacts, not merely with your director, but also with your cast, all of whom will be of excellent quality and many will be well-known faces. It is much more likely that your play will attract the great actors on radio where they have to give up only one week of potential film or television income than on stage where the commitment is so much longer. Your agent will help you follow up the contacts you meet and work with you on the possibilities for using the radio play as a taking-off point for the next step in your career.

Radio drama is dominated by the BBC. There are a number of independent companies who make radio programmes and this will grow so it is as well to keep up with who are the best players in this market. Your agent will advise you on this and also guide you through the various departments at the BBC in London and in the regions. If you live outside London, then it will almost certainly be best to go through your local regional drama department (the main ones are Birmingham, Manchester, Belfast, Glasgow and Edinburgh).

Radio can also be a terrific way of developing material and being noticed. A number of radio comedy series have been picked up by television of which *Little Britain* is just one. In other ways too, radio can help develop your career by improving your skills as a writer and help you be noticed. There can also be areas of further exploitation for radio plays through stage, film or television.

The BBC has recently entered into a major new Radio Drama Agreement which will improve the terms and conditions under which writers work. BBC Fees are currently a minimum of £59.20 per minute for new writers. There are considerably more contractual complexities with radio in the modern new media age. Internet streaming, pod casting, mobile phone use are only some of the ways audio broadcasts can be used and your agent will have a key role in making sure that your rights are protected and income collected.

Conclusion

I hope I have demonstrated that an agent's role is more than just doing the deal and collecting the money. Your agent will be a key person in your professional life and sometimes your personal life too. Good luck and keep writing!

Further reading and information

Goldman, William (2003), *Adventures in the Screen Trade*, London: Abacus.
The Dramatists Guild of America: www.dramaguild.com
The Guide to Selecting Plays for Performance (2006), London: Samuel French Ltd.
The Personal Managers Association: www.thepma.com
The Writers Guild of America: www.wga.org
The Writers' Guild of Great Britain: www.writersguild.org.uk
Writers' and Artists' Yearbook (annual), A&C Black.

50

Copyright

Shay Humphrey, with Lee Penhaligan

History

The 1709 Statute of Anne in England was the first law giving writers control over originally-authored works for a renewable fourteen-year period (UK Intellectual Property Office 2009). The first US copyright law was enacted in 1790, three years after its governing Constitution was adopted, which envisaged laws to 'promote the Progress of Science and the Useful Arts, by securing for limited Times to Authors and Inventors the exclusive right to their respective Writings and Discoveries' (Patry 2000). Registration, deposit and notice were central to all early copyright laws in the UK and the US.

International standards

Under the 1790 US Copyright Act, copyright protection was only available to US citizens. This led to importing of British and Australian works into the US without payment of copyright fees, which enabled US publishing companies to produce cheap copies for the American market (Allingham 2001). Canada similarly was able to import works cheaply from the US without paying copyright fees. Authors often suffered in their own countries where their works were more expensive to produce in their country of residence than in other English-speaking nations. The first attempt at international copyright protection and recognition was the Berne Convention which the UK signed at its inception in 1886 and brought into force in 1887 (WIPO Berne Convention 1886). Canada and Australia each signed the Berne Convention in 1928 but the US did not sign until 1989. The Berne Convention attempted to harmonise copyright laws on an international level and provide certain basic copyright guarantees in all countries. As you will see in this chapter, although each of the countries discussed is a Berne signatory, this does not mean that the copyright laws are identical in each country.

What is copyright?[1]

Copyright protects all original works including literary, dramatic, musical, artistic and broadcasts and sound recordings from unauthorised use (17 USC 101, *et seq.*; Canada Copyright Act, s3.1; Australia Copyright Act s31; Copyright Designs and Patents Act

[UK], s1). Copyright is a form of personal property and it may be inherited by will or passed on to heirs by statute (US Copyright Office: Cir. 1; Australian Copyright Council, Info. Sheet G084v04, page 4; Copyright Designs and Patents Act [UK], s90–93).

Works created or owned by the US government are not eligible for copyright protection (US Copyright Office: Cir. 1). In Australia, the UK and Canada there is Crown copyright, entitling the government to own and exploit its own copyright (Canada Copyright Act, s12; Australia Copyright Act, ss176–177; Copyright Designs and Patents Act [UK], s163).

What is not protected

Any concept, idea, discovery or method that is not or cannot be fixed in a hard copy, on paper or electronically, will not have copyright protection under the laws of any country. Titles, names, short phrases and slogans are not covered by copyright law but may be protected by trademark laws. Unlike copyright, trademarks can be protected in multiple countries simultaneously through the Madrid Protocol.[2] Works having no original content or ideas, like a form, certain compilations of facts or a reproduction of a work from the public domain will not be protected by copyright (US Copyright Office: Cir.1), although, in the UK tables or compilations are subject to copyright protection by statute (Copyright, Designs and Patents Act [UK], s3 (1)).

Moral rights

Canada, Australia and UK

Canada, Australia and UK provide moral rights (*droit morale*) of integrity and attribution to authors (Canadian Copyright Act, s14.1; Copyright Designs and Patents Act [UK], s77 and s80 (1); Australia Copyright Act ss193–195, 195AI). The right of integrity provides that, even if you sell or transfer your copyright, no one, including the copyright owner, is permitted to distort, mutilate or modify your work in a manner that disparages your honour or reputation. The right of attribution gives the author the right to be named as the author of the work whenever it is reproduced. Moral rights last for as long as the copyright and may be passed to heirs of the author even if the heirs do not own the copyright themselves (Canadian Copyright Act, s14.2; Copyright Designs and Patents Act [UK], s86; Australia Copyright Act ss195AM, 195AN).

Australia and the UK recognise an additional moral right for authors not to have their work falsely attributed to someone else or to have a work falsely attributed to them (Copyright Designs and Patents Act [UK], ss77 and 84; Australia Copyright Act s195AC). Authors in the UK must assert their right of attribution for it to apply but this is not necessary in Australia (Australia Copyright Council Information Sheet G043v13 Moral Rights, February 2012). In the UK, the moral right to not have a work falsely attributed to you lasts for twenty years after your death (Copyright, Designs and Patents Act [UK], s86). In Australia, moral rights continue for the length of the copyright duration in the underlying work (Australia Copyright Act, s195AM).

US

The US only provides statutory moral rights to visual artists, not to authors of written works. The US Congress claims that equivalent rights already exist in the US through other enacted laws, so no specific moral rights statute is needed to comply with the Berne Convention (Standler 1988, 'View of US Congress'). This is an overstatement. The US courts have recognised that the US has only a 'glimmer' of moral rights and lacks the respect for moral rights that Europe accords its authors (Eldred 2003: 260; Seshadri 1997: 803).

Public domain

Works in the 'public domain' are works that are not protected by copyright law either because copyright has expired, was not renewed, or no copyright protection was available. Anyone can use works that are in the public domain without permission but no one can own a work that is in the public domain (Stanford Univ. Lib 'Fair Use'). All works published in the US before 1923 are in the public domain. Due to recent copyright legislation in the US, no additional works will fall into the public domain due to copyright expiration until 2019, when copyright protection for works published in 1923 will terminate (US Copyright Office: Cir. 15a). Authors must exercise caution, however, for example the Grimm's fairy tale Cinderella has fallen into the public domain and anyone can use it, but Disney's 1950 version of the 'Cinderella' story is subject to copyright and cannot be reproduced without permission. Do not assume that works that are out of print or unpublished are in the public domain. These works may still be protected by copyright laws and you may not use them without permission of the author.

How to obtain copyright protection

US

In the US works created after 1977 are automatically protected from the moment of creation. However, registration of the work is required before an infringement suit may be filed in a US court (US Copyright Office: Cir. 1 'Copyright Registration'). The Copyright Office registers all properly submitted applications and does not search or compare a registration for similarity to other registered copyrights.

Online Application. The US Copyright Office now offers copyright registration for most literary works through its Electronic Copyright Office or 'eCo' Online System. The US Copyright Office home page has a link to eCo or you can go to the following URL where you will be asked to create an electronic account using an email address: https://eco.copyright.gov/eService_enu/start.swe?SWECmd=Start&SWEHo=eco.copyright.gov

The eCo System is designed to work with Microsoft Internet Explorer 6.0, Netscape Navigator 7.02 or FireFox 2.0. Safari and Google Chrome are not fully compatible with the eCo System. Pop-up blockers and third-party tool bars should also be disabled. To view and print documents with eCo, users must install Adobe Acrobat Reader on their computers (US Copyright Office: eCo Frequently Asked Questions).

The eCo copyright application template may be saved to a computer for future use, which is helpful for registering multiple copyrights for serial works. Draft applications can also be saved for submission at a later date by utilising the 'Save For Later' button. The eCo System is user friendly and uses red asterisks to note the required fields on each page. There is a detailed tutorial available at: http://www.copyright.gov/eco/eco-tutorial.pdf that gives page-by-page screen shots detailing each step of the eCo copyright application process.

Print Application. Print applications are still accepted and the forms are available online at: http://www.copyright.gov/forms/. For most literary works (that are not serials or derivative works), which have only one living author, short Form TX should be used (Ross 2002: 215). The Forms and Publications Hotline, which is available 24 hours a day, 7 days a week at (202) 707-9100, may be utilised to have print forms sent to you via regular US mail. You may also contact the Public Information Office at (202) 707-3000 or 1-877-476-0778 (toll free) to determine which form to file.

Fees. The application fee for an online application through eCo is $35 US, while print applications now cost $65 US. For print applications, fees must be paid by money order check in US dollars; however, for eCo, application fees may be paid by credit or debit card, electronic check, or US Copyright Office deposit account.

Processing Applications. For eCo applications, you will receive an email confirmation from the US Copyright Office acknowledging receipt of your applications and you can track your copyright applications and registrations online through your eCo account. No confirmation is sent for print applications, so it is recommended that print applications be sent by certified mail, return receipt requested. The processing time for eCo applications is generally 3 to 4½ months and for print applications it is longer, estimated at 5 to 8 months (US Copyright Office: I've Submitted My Application).

Preregistration. The US Copyright Office now offers preregistration for unpublished books that are in the process of being prepared for commercial distribution. The cost is $115 US and the preregistration is only available online through eCo. This preregistration is offered for works that are susceptible to infringement before they are released (US Copyright Office: Preregister Your Work).

Mandatory Deposit Requirement. The US has a mandatory deposit requirement for all works published in the US, whether or not the author seeks copyright registration (US Copyright Office: Cir. 1). Failure to make the deposit can result in fines but does not affect copyright protection (US Copyright Office: Cir. 7d). Unpublished works and works published only in electronic form may meet this deposit requirement by electronic upload through eCo after processing an online eCo application with payment of the required fee. Most authors choose to obtain copyright protection for their works prior to their publication, so the electronic upload should be able to be utilised by most authors of any new print or online works.

In a case where copyright protection is sought after publication, deposit of 2 copies of the best edition of the published work must be made with the Library of Congress within 3 months of publication. Certain works published in hardcopy formats may also qualify for electronic deposit but for those that do not, a user may still submit a copyright application through eCo; however, they will be prompted to print a shipping label that is specific to that electronic application to utilise for sending the deposit.

Mailing Address. The following is the address for mailing all print applications and all physical deposits:

> Library of Congress
> U.S. Copyright Office
> 101 Independence Avenue, S.E.
> Washington, D.C. 20559 USA

Due to enhanced security measures, delivery may be delayed for up to 5 days and to avoid damage CDs, DVDs, photographs and other similar fragile items should be sent in boxes rather than envelopes (US Copyright Office: 'Delivery of Mail to the US Copyright Office').

Canada

This is similar to the US in that copyright protection is automatic upon creation but deposit is required for works published in Canada. Registration of the work in Canada provides certain statutory benefits, although you may file an infringement suit in Canada without registering your copyright (Canadian Copyright Act, s34).

Online Application. Applications for registration of copyright submitted online are charged $50 Canadian and, if there are no deficiencies in the application, a registration will be issued within 5 business days. Payment online can be by credit card or deposit account. You will need to create a user name and password to file online, your browser must accept cookies and you must have JavaScript installed. The Canadian online copyright filing system can be accessed with Internet Explorer 7.0 or 8.0, Firefox 4.0 or 5.0 and Safari 5.1.2.

Print Application. For paper submissions, the fee is $65 Canadian and registration is issued within 7 business days. Payment by mail must be sent via cheque or money order made out to the Receiver General of Canada and must be accompanied by CIPO's Fee Payment Form. Print applications may be sent via facsimile to 819-953-2476 or by mail to:

> Copyright Office
> Canadian Intellectual Property Office
> Industry Canada
> Place du Portage I
> 50 Victoria Street
> Gatineau, QC K1A 0C9

You may file a request for accelerated processing for a $65 fee to receive your Registration Certificate by mail in 3 days. If an application is found 'in need', a report is sent to the applicant and a response is required within sixty days otherwise the application is deemed abandoned.

Mandatory Deposit Requirement. Unlike the US system, in Canada, the registration and deposit of works cannot be made simultaneously to the same location. For print publications, 2 copies of all publications must be deposited when 100 or more copies, in all formats, are produced. One deposit copy is required when between 4 and 99 copies of a work are produced. (Library and Archives of Canada: Legal Deposit) The work should be sent to the address below, along with a legal deposit form found at http://www.collectionscanada.gc.ca/legal-deposit/041008-0201-e.html:

> Library and Archives Canada Legal Deposit
> 395 Wellington Street
> Ottawa, ON K1A 0N4

For online publications, such as books, serials and annual reports, one copy of the work must be deposited. You can submit your online publication via a web submission form for files 200MB or less. To make arrangements to submit your publication by email, FTP or by post, you must contact the Published Heritage Digital Office at the following email address: epe@bac-lac.gc.ca. (Library and Archives of Canada: Online Publications)

If a work is published in multiple file formats, a deposit must be made for each format.

Australia and the UK

Copyright protection in Australia and the UK is automatic. There are no manda-tory registration or deposit systems, so no forms or fees are necessary. The Australian Copyright Council advises that to prove you are the author, you should keep dated drafts, outlines and research records and discuss the work with or show drafts to other people.[5] They note that sending a copy of the work to yourself as the author has no legal effect (Australian Copyright Council, January 2012, Info. Sheets G010v17 and G084v4). The UK Intellectual Property Office suggests that authors retain drafts of the work to prove authorship; deposit a copy of their work with a bank or solicitor; or send a copy of their work to themselves by special delivery (which gives a clear date stamp on the envelope). If the envelope is unopened, this will be evidence that the work was in their possession at the time of the mailing[6] (UK Intellectual Property Office: 'Automatic Right'). In the UK and Australia, there are private companies that offer services as unofficial copyright registers. For example, the UK Copyright Service (www.copyrightservice.co.uk) offers a voluntary registration service, with registrations available for five- or ten-year periods at a cost of £47 and £72 respectively. However, using these services is not absolute proof that you are the author of the work and may be no more effective than taking the other suggested actions (UK Intellectual Property Office: 'Copyright Registers').

Copyright notice

Copyright notice is no longer required in any Berne Convention country but it is still highly recommended and is part of standard publishing practice. The symbol © or the word 'Copyright', the year of first publication and the name of the owner of the copyright should be included as the copyright notice (that is, © 2014 Jamie Johnson or Copyright 2014 by Jamie Johnson). It is also recommended that the phrase 'All Rights Reserved' be placed in the copyright notice as it may be required in certain South American countries. It is also common practice, in the UK, to add a statment to the notice regarding unauthorised use, for example, 'Any unauthorised public performance, copying or adaptation will constitute an infringement of copyright'. The copyright notice can also be extended to allow for any permitted uses, but care should be taken to make clear precisely what is and is not permis-sible. For example, 'Permission is granted to reproduce for personal or educational use only. Commercial copying, hiring, lending is prohibited' (UK Copyright Service Factsheet P-03 2000-9: 'Using Copyright Notices').

Copyright duration

The following table details the duration of copyright for different types of works in each country. The US, Australia and the United Kingdom provide copyright protection for literary works for the life of the author plus seventy additional years whereas Canada only provides fifty additional years' protection after the author's death.

Copyright is computed as ending on 31 December of the year of expiration regardless of when copyright was obtained during that year. In the US and Canada, works submitted to the Copyright Office after 1 September get the following year's copyright date, which is considered desirable by most authors and publishers who do not want their work to look dated (Ross 2002: 184). For example, if you apply for a copyright in a published work on 2 September 2014 the work will have a 2015 copyright date.

	Type	Year Published	Term Duration
US	Literary Work	On or after 1/1/78	Life of author + 70 years
	Literary Work	Between 1964–77	95 years from date of publication
	Literary Work	Between 1923–63	95 years from date of publication only if copyright was renewed under the prior Copyright Act 1909
	Joint Authorship	On or after 1/1/78	Calculate from death of last author to die + 70 years
	Anonymous Work and Work for Hire (work made as an employee)		The shorter of 95 years from publication or 120 years from creation
	Unpublished Work Created in 1978 or after		Life of author + 70 years
	Unpublished Works Created before 1978 and published after 1977 but before 2003		Life of author + 70 years or 31 December 2047 whichever is later
Canada	Literary Work		Life of author + 50 years
	Work for Hire		Life of employee + 50 years
	Crown Copyright		50 years from publication
	Anonymous Work		The shorter of 50 years from publication or 75 years from creation
	Unpublished Work created in 1997 and published thereafter		Life of author + 50 years
	Unpublished work created before 1997 where author dies after 1936		50 years of additional protection from 1997 (that is, until 2047)
The UK	Literary Work	On or after 1 January 1996	Life of author + 70 years
	Joint Authorship	On or after 1 January 1996	Calculate from death of last author to die + 70 years
	Anonymous Works		70 years from the end of the calendar year in which the work is made or published
	Crown Copyright		125 years for all works but if published commercially in its first 75 years, protection only continues for an additional 50 years from publication
	Unpublished Work created before 1989 (never published)		Life of author + 70 years or 31 December 2039, whichever is later
	Unpublished Work created after 1989 (never published)		Life of author + 70 years
	Unpublished Work created before 1989 (author died before 1989 and Work published after author's death)	Before 1989	50 years after first published
		After 1989	Life of author + 70 years
	Unpublished Work created after 1989 (author died after 1989 and Work published after author's death)		Life of author + 70 years
	Unpublished Works (First to publish a work in which copyright has expired, gets a 'publication right')	On or after 1 December 1996	25 years from end of the year in which the work is first made available in European Economic Association
Australia	Literary Work	31 December 2004	If copyright was still in effect on 1 January 2005, term is extended as set forth below; otherwise copyrights expired (life of author + 50 years) were not revived
	Literary Work	1 January 2005	Life of author + 70 years
	Unpublished Work (never published)		Lasts forever, so long as the work remains unpublished
	Unpublished Work (published after author's death)		70 years after first published

Infringement

The use or reproduction of an author's entire work or a substantial or material portion of the work, without the author's permission, may be copyright infringement, which is an unlawful practice. It is important to realise that although use of an author's exact wording is infringement, the facts or ideas contained in the work may be freely utilised. Copyright is infringed where, without a licence, a work is reproduced, copies are distributed, a work is performed, displayed or published, or where a derivative work or adaptation is made. In the US, a 'derivative work' is a new work based on a pre-existing work, which new work includes original content that is copyrightable itself (US Copyright Office, Cir. 1). Only the owner of the copyright in the original work may prepare or permit someone else to create a derivative work or adapt a work. In the UK, authorising an infringing act, is itself a type of infringement (Copyright, Designs and Patents Act [UK], s16(2)).

Plagiarism, that is, copying another's work and claiming it as your own or including a substantial portion of another's work in your work without crediting the original author, is a form of infringement in countries that grant moral rights of attribution to the author, but is not always infringement in the US (CIPO, 'Fair Dealing and Exceptions').

The laws in all of the countries contain serious civil and criminal penalties for copyright infringement (17 USC 502–506; Canada Copyright Act, ss34–59; Australia Copyright Act ss114–135AK; Copyright Designs and Patents Act [UK], ss96–102). The UK and Canada each permit an infringement suit against a corporate director or officer if the person knew of and consented to the infringement engaged in by a corporation. Canada's Copyright Modernization Act reduces statutory damages if the infringement involved a private use rather than a commerical use.

Fair use and fair dealing

Each country allows the public certain uses of copyrighted material without permission, known as 'Fair Use' in the US and 'Fair Dealing' in the UK, Australia and Canada. Each country permits Fair Use/Dealing for incidental inclusion, criticism, comment, news report- ing, teaching, libraries, archives, research and copying for the blind (Copyright Designs and Patents Act [UK] ss28–76; Australia Copyright Act ss40–73; 17 USC 107–112; Canada Copyright Act, ss29–32.2). There are a few differences as to what each country deems to be Fair Use or Fair Dealing but the law on this has largely been harmonised in recent years.[7] To preserve the author's moral rights, Canada, the UK and Australia require that the author (and in Canada, the source) be credited in any Fair Dealing use (Canada Copyright Act ss29.21–32.2; Copyright Designs and Patents Act [UK], s77; Australia Copyright Act s195). In the US, several factors are looked at to determine whether the use of the copyrighted work is a Fair Use, including the amount used, the purpose and character of the use, the commercial nature of the work and the effect of the work that was of that use on the market (US Copyright Office: FL–102).

In the US, Fair Use has been extended by the courts to additional uses not expressly listed in the statute. Fair Dealing statutes have been broadened to include most of the same items deemed Fair Use in the US. For example, parody (spoofing or lampooning matters in the news or public figures) is regarded as Fair Use by US courts and is now considered Fair Dealing in Canada and Australia (Australian Copyright Council, Info. Sheet G083v04).

In the UK, an independent Report by Professor Ian Hargreaves commissioned by the Government (Hargreaves 2011) recommended various reforms to modernise UK copyright law for the digital era. The UK government subsequently consulted on proposals to make changes to *copyright exceptions* (permitting the use of copyright work without permission) and its full response was published on 20 December 2012 (UK Government, *Modernising Copyright: A Modern, Robust and Flexible Framework*). This response identified changes that the government intends to make in subsequent legislation, including extending permitted acts to allow copying content onto any medium or device the buyer owns, strictly for personal use (for example transferring ebooks to a tablet or mobile phone), a more general permission for quotation of copyright works for any purpose provided the use is Fair Dealing and the source acknowledged, limited copying on a Fair Dealing basis for parody, caricature and pastiche and the simplification of copyright licensing for the education sector. A technical review of proposed draft legislation (Intellectual Property Office, 2013, *Technical Review of Draft Legislation on Copyright Exceptions*) closed in September 2013.

Although it would perhaps be desirable, there is no prescribed number of words that may be used to guarantee that the use will be deemed fair. It is a question of quality, as well as quantity. In the US, it has been suggested that the use of up to 300 words from a book and 50 words from a magazine article may be Fair Use but these are estimates and not hard and fast rules (Ross 2002: 76). In Australia, Fair Dealing for the purposes of research and study will be found if 10 per cent of the number of pages or one chapter if the work is divided into chapters or 10 per cent of the number of words from an electronic work (Australian Copyright Council, Info. Sheet G053v08).

Permissions: assignments and licences

If you wish to use someone else's copyrighted material in your work, which is not covered by Fair Use/Dealing, you first must obtain permission. This involves: (1) locating the copyright owner; (2) identifying the rights needed (exclusivity, term, territory); (3) contacting the owner to negotiate payment or a copyright collective society to pay a licensing fee; and (4) getting written permission to use the work.

US

You can conduct your own search online at copyright.gov/records to see if a work has been registered with the copyright office and for the name of the owner in the Copyright Office records for works copyrighted after 1 January 1978 (US Copyright Office, Cir. 22). The Copyright Office will search its records for you at a cost of $165 per hour. If the work you want to use is protected by copyright, the next step should be to contact: RSI Copyright (www.icopyright.com) and the Copyright Clearance Center (www.copyright.com). They may be able to grant permissions in one or two days; however, most licences are not covered by these services and must be privately negotiated and obtained by contacting the author or publisher directly. It may, therefore, take several months to obtain permissions. Licensing societies and copyright collectives are not widely utilised in the US partly due to anti-trust restrictions and the reluctance of publishers to give up control over setting their own pricing scheme for licences.

Canada

A free search of Canada's copyright database is available at www.ic.gc.ca/app/opic-cipo/cpyrghts/dsplysrch.do?lang=eng for works registered after 1 October 1991. Canada's

Copyright Board sets royalties and tariffs for use of certain copyright material and arbitrates disputes between licensing bodies and third parties. If you cannot locate the author of a work, you may apply to the Copyright Board for permission to use the work and the fee is paid to the Copyright Board on behalf of the owner.

> Copyright Board of Canada
> 56 Sparks Street, Suite 800
> Ottawa, ON K1A 0C9
> Tel: (613) 952-8621
> Fax: (613) 952-8630
> Web: www.cb-cda.gc.ca

Canada also utilises 'collective societies', organisations that collect royalties on behalf of its members and determine the conditions of use. For example, Access Copyright (Canadian Copyright Licensing Agency) (www.accesscopyright.ca) grants licences to use copyrighted works and it collects and distributes fees on behalf of its members. The *Union des écrivaines et écrivains québécois* (COPIBEC) (www.copibec.qc.ca) provides the same function within Quebec (CIPO Circular No. 4). Most copyrights registered before that date, beginning in 1841, are available at the Client Service Center in Gatineau, Quebec.

The UK

The UK statute recognises licensing schemes to monitor copyright owners' rights to copy, rent, perform and communicate their copyright works (Copyright Designs and Patents Act [UK], s.116–117). A Copyright Tribunal exists to review the terms of any challenged licence schemes and to hear any dispute about refusal to grant a licence or a failure to grant one in a reasonable amount of time (UK Intellectual Property Office, 'About the Copyright Tribunal'). The UK has three associations that work together to regulate licensing of copyright. The Authors' Licensing and Collecting Society (ALCS) collects and distributes fees to writers whose works are copied, lent or rented under licence (www.alcs.co.uk). Membership is open to all writers (and those who inherit copyright rights) anywhere in the world on payment of a modest one-off fee and membership is required before the author can collect fees. Members of the The Society of Authors have reciprocal membership with ALCS without additional charge. The Copyright Licensing Agency (CLA) (www.cla.co.uk) is a reproduction rights' organisation that licenses businesses, education and government to make copies from books, journals, magazines and periodicals. CLA pays authors and publishers licence fees for copying and it may file suit for enforcement of the copyrights it oversees. The licences granted are usually blanket licences that are priced based on the number of users in the business or organisation requesting the licence. The Publishers Licensing Society (PLS) (www.pls.org.uk) organises a non-exclusive, voluntary licensing scheme and manages collective licensing for copying in the UK. Following Professor Ian Hargreaves' Report (Hargreaves 2011), the UK government also consulted on simplifying the licensing process, leading to the Enterprise & Regulatory Reform Act, which came into law on 25 April 2013, and includes changes to UK copyright law due to be implemented by April 2014. The Act confers power on the Secretary of State to issue rules providing for the grant of licences for *orphan works* (works where the copyright owner is unknown and cannot be found after a diligent search, and which could not previously be used without permission), and for voluntary extended collective licensing schemes. The draft rules will be subject to a public consultation before being finalised, and any rights holder who does not wish to be part of an extended collective licensing scheme will retain the ability to opt out.

Australia

The Australian Society of Authors (ASA) (http://asauthors.org/cgi-bin/asa/information.cgi) sets minimum rates of pay and conditions for authors and has a trust fund used to defend the rights of copyright holders. The Copyright Agency Ltd (www.copyright.com.au) represents authors and publishers and both collects and distributes statutory licensing fees and membership in the organisation is free.

Assignment and licences

An assignment transfers all or part of your copyright to someone else, often a publisher. You are essentially selling your rights to your work and you will not be able to renegotiate the terms later. You will retain only those rights reserved to you in the agreement or by statute. Licences can be exclusive (that is, only that one party can use the licence, this may even exclude use by the authors themselves) or non-exclusive (many users can be given the same licence). An exclusive licensee is treated as the owner of the work for the term of the licence. A licence is preferable for the author as the author retains copyright ownership but grants the right to use the copyright to another, which use is limited to the certain ways and times specified in the licence. Upon termination of the licence, all rights granted revert back to the author. Moral rights may not be assigned but may be waived and most publishers include a provision requiring this waiver in their standard form of contracts. Assignments and licences should be in writing and signed by the copyright holder to be given legal effect.

US

Assignments and exclusive licences may be registered by mail with the US Copyright Office for a fee of $80 US electronically and can be searched through the US Copyright Office. In the US, authors have a statutory right to terminate transfers of copyright ownership (assignments and licences) after forty years from date of transfer or thirty-five after the work is first published, whichever is earlier (17 USC 203). The author can serve notice of intent to terminate ten years before the date of termination.

Canada

Assignments and licences may be registered in the Copyright Office of Canada online, via facsimile or by mail by sending them a copy of the original agreement along with a fee of $65 Can. The same addresses may be utilised as for registering a work.

UK and Australia

There is no formal registration system for assignments and licences. In Australia, assignments and licences are governed by general contract principles. Assignments and exclusive licences must be in writing and signed by the copyright owner to be fully effective. (Australian Copyright Council, Info. Sheet G024v10). In the UK, to be valid, a copyright assignment has to be in writing and signed by the copyright owner (Copyright, Designs and Patents Act [UK], s90(3)). It is sensible for a licence also to be recorded in writing to avoid uncertainty regarding its terms.

Internet works

Copyright infringement happens every second on the Internet but this does not mean that the items on the Internet are not protected by copyright (Canadian Copyright Act, s27 (2.3)). Many people believe that works on the Internet are in the 'public domain' or are not subject to copyright because of ease of access, downloading and copying. This is a misconception and permission of the site owner or the author *is* required to utilise photographs, text, music or artwork posted online. Even the layout of a webpage may, if sufficiently original, attract copyright protection as a literary and/or artistic work. Canada now offers a 'making available right' to copyright owners, which is the exclusive right to control the release of copyrighted material on the internet. In the UK, it has been suggested that the new rules for the licensing of orphan works under The Enterprise and Regulatory Reform Act 2013 could legalise the taking of copyright material from the internet without paying copyright fees. As the rules will permit the use of internet material with no clear identifying metadata, photographers in particular are concerned that they will suffer financially if metadata identifying them as the copyright owner is stripped from their photographs which are then licensed and possibly sub-licensed without payment of a proper fee. However, the UK government has pointed out that the Act contains a number of protections for photographers and other creators and has stressed that a licence will be needed to use a work as an 'orphan', that applicants will be required to undertake a diligent search for the copyright owner, which will need to be independently verified, and will have to pay a fair price for the licence. It remains to be seen how fairly the rules will operate in practice.

Publishing contracts

Publishers have always had greater bargaining power and better financial resources than authors, who are often at the mercy of publishers and their standard book contracts (Copyright Society of the USA 2003: 426–7). Care should be taken in publishing agreements in relation to the following:

- Is this an Assignment or a Licence? (Remember that an assignment is equivalent to a sale of all copyright rights. Self-publishing companies are an alternative option that allow the author the ability to retain rights in the work in return for the authors coming forward with the funding to publish the work. [Levin 1988: 429]).
- Who will register and maintain the copyright and in which countries?
- Can the copyright be further assigned or sub-licensed to other parties?
- What territory can the publisher use the copyright in? Is it limited to the country of publication or is it a worldwide right? (In the US, the publishers will seek to acquire book rights in the US and Canada with the author retaining rights for the UK and Australia. [Levin 1988: 418]).
- What mediums can the publisher use the copyright in? Does the contract include both print and electronic formats? (The publishing contract will probably ask for grant of rights in all mediums or formats 'now known or hereafter invented' [Levin 1988: 417].

In the US, publishers only have the right to publish the works in the format provided for in the agreement. *NY Times v. Tasini*, at 506).

• What other rights to the work does the publisher obtain in the contract (that is, can the publisher make a movie based on the work, prepare a translation of the work or use the work in another collection)? Who can create derivative works or adaptations of the work and how will the author be paid for these other uses?[8]

Contact information

The following is important contact information and sources of information for each country:

US
Copyright is overseen by the US Copyright Office. You can obtain more information at their website: www.copyright.gov

Canada
The Canadian Intellectual Property Office administers copyrights in Canada. Their website is at: www.cipo.ic.gc.ca.

Australia
Information on Australian Copyright may be found at: Australian Copyright Council, PO Box 1986, Strawberry Hills NSW 2012 Australia (+61 2 8815 9777). Their website is: www. copyright.org.au. Most professional creators and arts organizations are eligible for free legal advice from the Australian Copyright Council. (Australian Copyright Council: Legal Advice). Legal enquiries are not accepted by phone or email but must be made online at: https://customer.copyright.org.au/register.php.

The UK
You can contact the UK Intellectual Property Office for copyright information and assistance at: Concept House, Cardiff Road, Newport, South Wales, NP10 8QQ, United Kingdom. Tel: 0300 300 2000 (UK callers only) +44 (0)1633 81400 (International callers) (www.ipo.gov.uk). Minicom (text phone): 0300 0200 015.

Notes

1. This chapter discusses registration and protection of written, literary works only. Copyright protection and registration requirements may be different for sound recordings, films and broadcasts and those works are not discussed in this chapter. See the heading 'Contact Information' to find out more about these other works from each country's copyright office.

2. For more information on obtaining trademark protection through the Madrid Protocol, see the WIPO website at: www.wipo.int/madrid/en/

3. A Deposit Account may be obtained at the US Copyright Office for frequent users of the eCo system as a reserve against which they can offset copyright fees. Each deposit into the Deposit Account must be for at least $450 and the account must be accessed at least twelve times a year. (US Copyright Office: Copyright Cir. 5)

4. In the US, this is inadvisable. US copyright owners should not disclose or show their work to others in the development stage or at least until copyright registration is sent into the US Copyright Office. As such, disclosure could lessen the commercial value of the work.

5. It is a widely-held misconception that this procedure, often called 'poor man's copyright' is effective, in the US, to establish copyright. This is inaccurate as registration is the proper method to secure copyright in the US.

6. Legal Advice. The material in this chapter addresses the general legal issue of copyright and is not legal advice and should not be relied on as such. The statements in this chapter may or may not be appropriate to your specific situation. Laws and procedures change frequently and are subject to differing interpretations. This chapter is not intended to substitute for obtaining legal advice from competent, independent, legal counsel in the relevant jurisdiction and your country of creation or publication. If you need legal advice or counsel on copyright laws or issues, please consult a lawyer.

References

Allingham, Philip V. (January 2001), 'Nineteenth-century British and American copyright law', The Victorian Web, www.victorianweb.org/authors/dickens/pva/pva74.html (accessed 24 July 2013).

Australia, *The Copyright Act 1968*, as amended.

Australian Copyright Council (January 2012), Information Sheet G010v17, 'An introduction to copyright in Australia', http://www.copyright.org.au/find-an-answer/browse-by-a-z/ (accessed 1 August 2013).

Australian Copyright Council (January 2012a), Information Sheet G024v10, 'Assigning and licensing rights', http://www.copyright.org.au/find-an-answer/browse-by-a-z/ (accessed 1 August 2013).

Australian Copyright Council (January 2012b), Information Sheet G053v08, 'Research or study', http://www.copyright.org.au/find-an-answer/browse-by-a-z/ (accessed 1 August 2013).

Australia Copyright Council (February 2012a), Information Sheet G043v13, 'Moral rights', http://www.copyright.org.au/find-an-answer/browse-by-a-z/ (accessed 1 August 2013).

Australian Copyright Council (February 2012b), Information Sheet G084v04, 'Protecting your copyright', http://www.copyright.org.au/find-an-answer/browse-by-a-z/ (accessed 1 August 2013).

Australian Copyright Council (February 2012), Information Sheet G83, 'Parodies, satires and jokes', http://www.copyright.org.au/find-an-answer/browse-by-a-z/ (accessed 1 August 2013).

Australian Copyright Council (2013), 'Legal Advice', http://copyright.org.au/legal-advice/ (accessed 1 August 2013).

Canada, *The Copyright Act*, R.S., c. C-30, s1, Chapter C-42.

Canadian Intellectual Property Office (CIPO) (May 2013), 'How your copyright application is processed', http://www.cipo.ic.gc.ca/eic/site/cipointernet-internetopic.nsf/eng/wr00039.html (accessed 1 August 2013).

Canadian Intellectual Property Office (CIPO) (July 2013) 'A guide to copyright' (section on 'Fair dealing and exceptions'), http://www.cipo.ic.gc.ca/eic/site/cipointernet-internetopic.nsf/eng/h_wr02281.html (accessed 1 August 2013).

Copyright Board of Canada (August 2010), Copyright collective societies', http://www.cb-cda.gc.ca/societies-societes/index-e.html (accessed 1 August 2013).

Copyright Society of the USA (2003), 'A brief history of author–publisher relations and the outlook for the 21st century', *Journal of the Copyright Society of the USA*, 50: 425.

Eldred v. Ashcroft, 537 US 186, 260 (2003) (dissenting opinion).

Fishman, Stephen (2004), The *Copyright Handbook: How to Protect and Use Written Works*, 8th edn, Berkeley: Nolo.

Hargreaves, Ian (2011), 'Digital opportunity: A review of intellectual property and growth', www.ipo.gov.uk/ipreview-finalreport.pdf (accessed 12 August 2013).

Levin, Martin P. (1988), 'A New Guide to Negotiating the Author–Publisher Contract', *Cardozo Arts and Entertainments Law Journal* 6: 411.

Library and Archives of Canada (June 2009), 'Guidelines for legal deposit of online publications', http://www.collectionscanada.gc.ca/electroniccollection/003008-1000-e.html (accessed 4 August 2013).

Library and Archives of Canada (October 2012), 'Legal deposit: preserving and providing access to Canada's published heritage', http://www.collectionscanada.gc.ca/legal-deposit/index-e.html#il (accessed 4 August 2013).

Patry, William F. (2000), 'Copyright law and practice', Bureau of National Affairs, Inc., http://digital-law-online.info/patry/ (accessed 24 July 2013).

Ross, Tom and Marilyn (2002), *The Complete Guide to Self-Publishing*, 4th edn, Cincinnati: Writer's Digest Books.

Seshadri v. Kasraian, 130 F.3d 798 (CA7, Wis, 1997).

Standler, Ronald B. (1998), 'Moral rights of authors in the USA', www.rbs2.com/moral.htm (accessed 24 July 2013).

Stanford University Libraries (2005–2013a), 'The basics of getting permission', http://fairuse.stanford.edu/introduction/getting-permission/ (accessed 24 July 2013).

Stanford University Libraries (2005–2013b), 'Fair use', http://fairuse.stanford.edu/ overview/fair-use/ (accessed 24 July 2013).

NY Times v. Tasini, 533 US 483 (US Supreme Court, 2001).

UK Copyright Service (August 2000; last amended 26 November 2009) Fact sheet P-03 'Using copyright notices', www.ukcopyrightservice.com/copyright/p03_copyright-notices (accessed 12 August 2013).

UK, HM Government (December 2012), 'Modernising copyright: a modern, robust and flexible framework, government response to consultation on copyright exceptions and clarifying copyright law', www.ipo.gov.uk/response-2011-copyright-final.pdf (accessed 12 August 2013).

UK, *The Copyright, Designs and Patents Act*, 1988.

UK, *The Enterprise and Regulatory Reform Act*, 2013.

UK Intellectual Property Office (November 2008), 'Automatic right', http://www.ipo.gov.uk/c-auto.htm (accessed 1 August 2013).

UK Intellectual Property Office (January 2009a), 'Copyright registers', http://www.ipo.gov.uk/c-register.htm (accessed 1 August 2013).

UK Intellectual Property Office (January 2009b), 'History of copyright', http://www.ipo.gov.uk/types/copy/c-about/c-history.htm (accessed 1 August 2013).

UK Intellectual Property Office Copyright Tribunal (June 2013), 'The copyright tribunal', http://www.ipo.gov.uk/ctribunal.htm (accessed 1 August 2013).

UK Intellectual Property Office (July 2013), 'Technical review on draft legislation on copyright exceptions', www.ipo.gov.uk/hargreaves-copyright-techreview (accessed 13 August 2013).

US, US Code, Title 17, Section 101, *et seq.*

US Copyright Office (February 2011a), 'Delivery of mail to the US Copyright Office', www.copyright.gov/mail.html (accessed 24 July 2013).

US Copyright Office (February 2011b), 'Preregister your work', http://copyright.gov/prereg/ (accessed 4 August 2013).

US Copyright Office (August 2011a), Circular 14, 'Copyright registration for derivative works', www.copyright.gov/circs/circ14.pdf (accessed 24 July 2013).

US Copyright Office (August 2011b), Circular 15a, 'Duration of copyright', www.copyright.gov/circs/circ15a.pdf (accessed 24 July 2013).

US Copyright Office (May 2012), Circular 1, 'Copyright basics', www.copyright.gov/circs/Circ01.pdf (accessed 24 July 2013).

US Copyright Office (June 2012), FL-102 Fact Sheet, 'Fair use', www.copyright.gov/fls/fl102.pdf (accessed 24 July 2013).

US Copyright Office (September 2012), Circular 7d, 'Mandatory deposit of copies or phonorecords for the Library of Congress', www.copyright.gov/circs/circ07d.pdf (accessed 24 July 2013).

US Copyright Office (2013), 'Welcome to the eCo (electronic copyright office) tutorial', http://www.copyright.gov/eco/eco-tutorial.pdf (accessed 4 August 2013).

US Copyright Office (February 2013a), Circular 5, 'How to open and maintain a Copyright Office deposit account', www.copyright.gov/circs/circ05.pdf (accessed 24 July 2013).

US Copyright Office (February 2013b), Circular 22, 'How to investigate the copyright status of a work', www.copyright.gov/circs/circ22.pdf (accessed 24 July 2013).

US Copyright Office (June 2013), 'I've submitted my application, fee, and copy of my work to the Copyright Office. Now what?', http://www.copyright.gov/help/faq/faq-what.html (accessed 4 August 2013).

US Copyright Office (August 2013), 'eCo frequently asked questions', http://www.copyright.gov/eco/faq.html (accessed 4 August 2013).

World Intellectual Property Organization (WIPO) (1886), Berne Convention for the Protection of Literary and Artistic Works, www.wipo.int/treaties/en/ip/berne/ (accessed 24 July 2013).

51

Self-Publishing and the Rise of the Indie Author

Jane Rowland

An introduction to self-publishing

As a writer it is likely that you have become increasingly aware of the concept of self-publishing and, even if you are not planning on taking this route yourself at the moment, it is still worth having a full understanding of how it works. Self-publishing is beginning to feel like a buzzword for writers. The term describes the process of an author electing to publish their book themselves, often paying to have their book published (as opposed to being signed up to a 'traditional' or 'mainstream' publishing deal, where the publishing firm takes the risk on bringing the book to market, rather than the author).

Some publishing purists have historically defined self-publishing as a process in which you, as the author, have literally done everything yourself; you have written the book, designed the cover, typeset it, purchased an ISBN (International Standard Book Number), arranged printing and you will distribute and market it yourself. This definition is too narrowly focused to represent modern self-publishing, however, as most authors outsource individual elements of the process or use a self-publishing services provider (a company that helps authors with some or all of the publishing processes) to help them with book production, printing or marketing. In addition, authors who are self-publishing in an ebook format often rely on the framework provided by distribution companies to get their ebook to the end users. This is true if you publish an ebook through Amazon's Kindle Direct Publishing (KDP), Kobo's Writing Life, Apple's iBooks Author or any other retailer's service that gives you a route to reach readers.

The development of self-publishing

Over the years, self-publishing has changed from something slightly unsavoury, lurking around the margins of respectability in publishing, to a growth area with some genuine and reputable players. The change has liberated authors, unleashing thousands of new writers onto the market and encouraging some key players in the publishing industry to change how they view self-publishing. But how did this revolution come about? Just ten or so years ago, authors funding the publication of their own book were generally thought to be dabbling in 'vanity' publishing . . . mostly considered to be without literary merit and done simply to boost the ego of the author. Vanity publishing had a bad reputation, largely as most companies that offered services in this area at best provided an expensive solution to a writer's needs, and at worst reeled in clients who thought they'd been spotted by a publisher, and then found themselves having to pay for overpriced services.

The publishing industry had little time for vanity publishing, writers' organisations warned against the practice and the costs to an author were usually high, with no hope of recouping the expense via sales. But times change and, with the advancement of new technology in the printing and publishing worlds, plus the proliferation of computers into everyday lives, we have seen a shift in perception towards authors publishing their own work. Vanity publishing morphed into self-publishing, bringing the emphasis back to the author and out of the hands of companies on the edge of respectability. Self-publishing is now one of the growing parts of the UK publishing market as each year new author services companies launch and more authors take the plunge.

It is difficult to offer definitive figures showing the percentage of books that are self-published today. If publishing through Amazon's KDP you don't need to use an ISBN, so many self-published ebooks are not recorded by the main data agencies that record the number of new publishers every year. To get an idea of numbers, we can look at the 2012 figures from Bowker (see Bowker 2012), which indicated that the number of self-published books in the United States had tripled to more than 235,000, an increase of 287% since 2006.

A more recent change within self-publishing is the reinvention from 'self' to 'indie', with many authors now disregarding the self-publishing label and instead referring to themselves and their works as 'indie' published. This shows how self-published authors have moved away from being, perhaps, embarrassed or ashamed to admit they had self-funded their book, to being proud that they have done so. The growth of self-publishing is sometimes compared by the new breed of indie authors to the music industry, where indie music was always considered to be cutting edge and offering something not found within the mainstream.

As within the music industry, changes in technology have made indie/self-publishing affordable, and in some cases possible, for many authors. One of the main game changers for self-publishing was the introduction of digital printing, and especially Print on Demand (POD) technology, which brought with it the possibility to print books one at a time, as required, with no stock having to be printed in advance and then stored. POD comes complete with a full distribution network, allowing authors to set discounts for the retail trade, but not to have to deal directly with retailers, as this is all taken care of within the POD distribution.

Today, ebooks are also a popular way to self-publish, with companies like Amazon, Kobo, Barnes & Noble and Apple putting tools for ebook publishing into the hands of their customers. For an author serious about targeting bookshops and retail sales, printing books up front for wider distribution is also still important and, in some cases, essential. It is also common to see a 'blended' approach, authors publishing both a printed book (for retail or POD distribution) and an ebook simultaneously.

Ebooks have become very popular as a format for self-publishing because the costs are typically less than for printing physical books and you can get your work out there very quickly. By allocating a competitively low Recommended Retail Price (RRP), you can reach new audiences, and the infrastructure for setting yourself up as a publisher and selling through the large online retailers is well established. In 2013, *The Bookseller* reported research from Bowker that indicated up to 12% of all ebook sales were for self-published books, with crime, sci-fi and romance the more popular genres (Farrington 2013). The same survey also showed that readers selected self-published books based on price rather than author brand, and found them while browsing online.

Self-publishing may have carried some of the stigma from the vanity publishing era into its new evolution, but this is rapidly dissipating as self-published authors become a fixture of the publishing world. The popularity of self-publishing has also had other consequences, with the rise of indie authors *wanting* to take charge of publishing their own books; mainstream publishers have to work harder to justify the value they add to a book in some self-publishing authors' eyes. Publishers may have been slow to react to these changes, but are now looking at other ways of working with authors outside the traditional models, ranging from simply monitoring the market and snapping up the rights to popular self-published books, to setting up their own self-publishing services to monetise their own slush pile.

In 2012 international publisher Pearson (who own Penguin and now Random House) purchased Author Solutions International (ASI), the US self-publishing services giant. In the press release announcing the purchase, Penguin group Chief Executive (John Makinson) is quoted as saying:

> Self-publishing has moved into the mainstream of our industry over the past three years. It has provided new outlets for professional writers, a huge increase in the range of books available to readers and an exciting source of content for publishers such as Penguin. (Penguin Group 2012)

This shows how a mainstream publisher like Penguin is starting to view the self-publishing world. In November 2012, Simon & Schuster launched Archway Publishing, a self-publishing service operated via ASI, effectively giving them a slice of the self-publishing pie too. We can expect to see other mainstream publishers looking to provide some form of self-publishing service in the future while the market continues to evolve – a move that is not without criticism from some writers' organisations who question the blending of a mainstream publisher with self-publishing services (Ross 2012).

In addition, mainstream publishers now regularly sign self-published authors. You will no doubt have read about the big-selling self-published authors such as Hugh Howey, whose self-published dystopian series *Wool* was published via Amazon's KDP before being taken on by Simon & Schuster, and Amanda Hocking, whose self-published paranormal ebooks earned her $2 million before she signed a mainstream publishing deal for the rest of her series (Pilkington 2012). There are plenty of other authors who have much more modest sales yet who get taken up by the mainstream after self-publishing, authors such as Barbara Mutch (*Karoo Plainsong*) and Sheila Jeffries (*Solomon's Tale*).

It's not just publishers looking to benefit from self-publishing either; literary agents have also started to use the model to maximise opportunities for their authors – from revitalising out-of-print titles to testing out debut writers. Agent Ed Victor (Ed Victor Literary Agency) launched Bedford Square Books, publishing (mainly) ebook versions of his clients' out-of-print books. Since launching, the imprint has also published some original fiction by new writers (Williams 2011). Curtis Brown Literary launched Curtis Brown Creative (see Curtis Brown 2012) and offers writing courses to aspiring authors with some self-publishing opportunities too. All of this shows how the publishing world is beginning to blend the traditional models with lessons learned from the self-publishing trend, demonstrating how self-publishers have become part of the publishing landscape rather than lurking on the fringes.

It's not just publishers and agents seeking to profit from self-published authors; there are now many companies that work exclusively with indie authors, from full service self-publishing firms assisting authors with every aspect of their book, to cover designers, editors, PR firms, all helping self-publishers produce, distribute and market a book. Some companies are highly recommended and reputable, others have less fulsome reputations, but with online author forums also in ascendance it is easier than ever for writers to connect to get the lowdown on any firm they may be thinking of using. In 2012 The Alliance of Independent Authors (ALLI) was formed to lobby on behalf of authors, and to bring indie authors together to share ideas and knowledge.

Two to three years ago, media stories about self-publishing were uncommon, yet now self-publishing news appears regularly in *The Bookseller*. The London Book Fair, *the* UK book trade event, now appears to have also embraced self-publishing and runs seminars and events aimed at self-publishers during the Fair when previously there was nothing.

So, why do authors self-publish?

Authors choose to self-publish for a wide variety of reasons. Historically it may have been because the author in question wanted, but could not get, a publisher to take on their work, and that is still one of the reasons some choose the self-publishing route. However, one important aspect of self-publishing is that the author retains control, and there is a growing band of entrepreneurial authors who self-publish specifically because they can do it their way. They network, learn and produce multiple books and create their own publishing brand. Many people come to self-publishing as the fulfilment of a hobby and for personal satisfaction, they love to write and the end result of their writing is that they want to produce a book or an ebook.

Some common reasons for self-publishing include:

- An author has access to the book's market and they want to maximise their profits – which means they want to sell direct to that market, cutting out the publisher .
- An author is targeting a niche market that won't turn enough profit for a traditional publisher to consider their work.
- An author wants to self-publish because they want to maintain control of every aspect of their work. One interesting recent case in point is Polly Courtney, who initially self-published, was signed up to Arrow on the back of her self-published sales, but who parted company with them as she preferred to maintain control of her own work in a way that her mainstream deal would not permit (see Courtney 2012).
- An author wants to publish a book as part of their business – books that are sold to boost the business's profile or at workshops, for example.
- It's also common for an author to have had a mainstream publishing deal and, at the end of their contract, opt to self-publish rather than pursue a new deal. They might also bring out-of-print books back to the market by self-publishing once the rights revert to them.
- Sometimes an author just wants books made available to family and friends, so they publish themselves. Publishing for personal vanity is still a valid reason for publishing as long as your expectations are realistic!

There are of course authors who still want a mainstream deal and, to prove that there is a market for their writing, they self-publish.

Why an author may self-publish leads us onto the question of how successful self-published authors are. The simple answer is that the project is successful if it meets the aims of the self-publishing author. If you self-publish to fulfil a hobby, having the book itself is often success enough. If you self-publish because you want to have a bestselling book or to become famous or to earn thousands . . . it is possible you will be disappointed if neither of these happens.

With all the media attention that self-publishing gets these days, it might be easy to assume that self-publishing is all about limitless success – but while popular, self-publishing your book or ebook is not necessarily going to make you rich. It is hard to give accurate figures, as most self-published sales don't pass through the tills of outlets that record sales data, but it has been estimated that many self-published authors will sell between 100 and 300 copies of their book (Finder 2012) and many authors will never make back the money they originally invested. On the other hand, few authors really self-publish to earn millions, and even in mainstream publishing few can afford a champagne lifestyle on their royalties alone!

The different routes to self-publishing

Back in the dark days of self-publishing, authors had very few options about how to self-publish. This was largely driven by the available technology – at the time, offset lithographic presses that only became economical if printing large numbers of books. Time and technology have moved on, and with the advent of digital printing, the market has opened up and continues to develop. The arrival of Amazon's Kindle and the standardisation of the ebook format to ePub across other platforms has also stabilised the ebook market and allowed companies and authors to come together. Another main change that has played into the hands of self-publishers is that the digital world has brought a new dimension to self-publishing – consumers are happy buying books online rather than only on the high street, and that model particularly suits the low-entry-cost POD and ebook methods that are popular with many self-publishers.

Many authors who wish to self-publish will use a self-publishing services firm, of which there are many, all offering different types of service. These range from services such as CreateSpace and Lulu, where you upload finished files yourself and what gets printed is based entirely on what you've input, through to full service companies like Matador, which offers a bespoke approach that includes full production, retail trade distribution and marketing. There are numerous other companies and individuals offering all sorts of variations, with the market changing often as players appear and disappear.

If you are looking to self-publish a printed book then a reputable firm should have the experience to produce books that are indistinguishable from any mainstream published book, and have the distribution systems to get that book into the retailers (and therefore to the readers). In addition, authors self-publishing ebooks need to rely on the sales and distribution services offered by the big ebook firms or retailers to have their books available for sale, so while they can do the formatting, cover design and editing of the book, they are still in a third party's hands for the delivery of those ebooks to customers' devices.

Some authors assume that self-publishing is synonymous with POD – and many self-publishing firms only offer POD options or packages. However, POD is just one method of printing and distribution available to self-publishing authors, not the only one, and sometimes not the best. POD is ideal for self-publishers who do not want to store inventory or take a financial risk by printing copies of a book up front, but it's not the ideal solution for an author who wants to sell lots of copies to bookshops. First, a POD book will cost the same to print for the first copy as it will for the five hundredth, so there are no economies of scale in the printing. Second, bricks-and-mortar bookshops often won't stock POD books – the customer pays for the printing of the book and if the bookshop has no customer specifically for that book, it won't take a risk on paying to print it to sell it. Despite these limitations, POD is a popular method of producing books for self-publishers, with the largest POD suppliers being CreateSpace and Lightning Source (who launched their own self-publishing service, IngramSpark, to authors in 2013 in response to the growing demand for the services they offer).

Self-publishers can also opt to use other methods of printing instead of POD – they can produce copies up front, which reduces the per copy price of each book, allowing the cover price to be set more competitively. This model of printing and publishing cannot rely on a POD firm's distribution network, so authors opting to print copies in advance need to be able to sell and distribute copies to the market. They are either assisted to do this by a self-publishing firm that has distribution arrangements in place already, or they have to be their own distributor.

Tips for publishing successfully

Self-publishers are publishing their book without the input of an editor or a marketing department and with no reference to the profit-based publishing model that the mainstream publishers use. This can be incredibly liberating as you are releasing your work to the world in the way you have chosen, but in the worst examples of self-publishing the books are error ridden, poorly produced and badly marketed. It is undeniable that there are many shoddy self-published books around – but importantly this does not mean that *all* self-published books are bad. It is also quite simple to make sure your self-published book is not poorly produced and full of errors, and to this end there are a few things you need to think of before you start the publishing process.

Just because you have read stories in your newspaper about authors making millions from uploading their vampire novel to the Kindle does not mean this is automatically the best route for you to follow. *The Self Publishing Magazine*, which I edit, has always encouraged authors to do their research before they start down any publication route or sign a contract with a self-publishing company. Make sure you understand what you are getting and that it matches what you need. For example, some self-publishing providers offer packages, essentially fixed price deals, which look great – but you may need something more bespoke for your book. Other firms are based outside the UK, and maybe you would prefer to work with a firm you can phone and visit more easily? Similarly, your route to self-publication should also depend on your aspirations for your book; if you want your local bookshop to stock it, then this cannot happen with an ebook and it is unlikely to happen with a POD title – you would need to print copies and have book distribution set up. It's incredibly easy to educate yourselves these days about how the book trade works: what an ISBN is, how you go about getting one, how to format barcodes for covers, ebooks and so on. You should certainly spend some time understanding the nuts and bolts of publishing before you begin.

The best way to self-publish an ebook, for example, also comes down to your understanding of the market. Are you happy to have the book available only on one platform, or do you want as wide a distribution available as possible? You can format your own ebook using programs like Microsoft Word or you can have the files formatted on your behalf by a self-publishing company who will often have the software and distribution links to get your ebook placed with a wide range of retailers. Some books, for example, are more suited to the ebook format than others – picture-heavy books might have to be produced as a fixed-format ebook, and have a more limited distribution as a result. Understanding limitations such as this will ensure your project runs to your expectations. The questions you need to ask yourself before you self-publish are:

- Is your book ready to self-publish?
- Do you have the skills to do all or part of the process yourself?
- Do you understand what you are signing up for if using a self-publishing firm?
- Have you understood the terms and conditions if using another company to sell, create or print your work in whatever format?

Nowadays there is no need for poorly produced books to exist at all. The main areas that cause problems for self-publishing authors include: assuming something about the service they have signed up for that was never part of the deal; publishing their book before it was ready and spotting errors later; using material that is copyrighted elsewhere without realising the implications; picking covers that are not commercial enough; not understanding the importance of metadata (bibliographic data) to push sales; not doing any marketing; or starting the marketing too late on in the process. All of these are entirely preventable errors, but surprisingly common.

The single most important piece of advice for anyone considering self-publishing is to do your research first. Clarify in your own mind why you are self-publishing, as often that will lead to the best method. Then consider whether you can do it all yourself, and whether you want to. Thoroughly research the market for companies to assist you. Recommendations from other authors who have been there are best, but there is a plethora of resources online offering independent advice on the good and bad service providers (the best is the online Independent Publishing Magazine's Publisher Services Index – see *The Independent Publishing Magazine* 2013). If you do decide to commission one or more companies to help you, ensure you know exactly what you are getting – never, ever *assume* that something is on offer.

Most people are very close to their work and cannot view it objectively. This generally becomes apparent when the book is being read and reviewed by a wider circle. Sometimes authors are not prepared for criticism or a negative review. Sales can be disappointing, especially for authors who launch the book and then watch the Amazon ratings, waiting for it to shoot up the charts. The hard work for a self-publishing author does not end when the book rolls off the press or goes live online as an ebook!

Part of the debate about self-publishing has to include a comment on the quality of self-published books. Some say that self-publishing is a liberating force and authors can publish what they want, while critics say that readers are turned off from exploring self-published books after poor reading experiences, or that the reading market is being saturated with inferior new titles (especially ebooks). There is undeniably a varying quality of self-published books; some should definitely have stayed unpublished, while others absolutely deserve as many readers as they can find. There is no quick fix for improving the quality of a self-published book – the tools to publish are now in the hands of the authors, which is all part of the evolution of self-publishing.

Despite the criticism levelled at self-publishers there is much to be celebrated. Self-publishers embrace change in the publishing industry and can react more quickly to markets. Many, indeed, are shedding the 'self' label and becoming 'indie', sloughing off the final shadows of vanity publishing and unashamedly publishing and promoting their own work.

The popularity of self-publishing also means that there are more companies offering services, more authors talking about self-publishing and more information available than ever before. All of this, when coupled with the ease of self-publishing and the increasing profile it gets in the media, ensures that self-publishing authors are now becoming a greater force in publishing. The indie author takes charge of their book, is proud to be indie published and, like the music industry, offers something outside the mainstream, or something that simply would not have seen the light of day under the gatekeeper model of traditional publishing. Maybe soon even the term self-publishing will be replaced by indie publishing in common usage, and a new chapter will begin. Whatever your view, self-publishing is definitely here to stay.

References and recommended reading

ALLi, a group to support and help indie authors. It also lobbies for self-publishers and brings authors together at events. http://allianceindependentauthors.org

Baverstock, Alison (2011), *The Naked Author – A Guide to Self-Publishing*, London: A & C Black.

Bowker (2012), www.bowker.com/en-US/aboutus/press_room/2012/pr_10242012.shtml (accessed 26 July 2013).

Courtney, Polly (2012), 'Walking out on Harper Collins', *The Self-Publishing Magazine*.

Curtis Brown (2012), www.curtisbrown.co.uk/curtis-brown-launches-a-digital-self-publishing-programme (accessed 23 July 2013).

Farrington, Joshua (2013), 'Bowker: self-published e-books 12% of sales', *The Bookseller*, http://www.thebookseller.com/news/bowker-self-published-e-books-12-sales.html (accessed 20 July 2013).

Finder, Alan (2012), 'The joys and hazards of self-publishing on the Web', *The New York Times*, www.nytimes.com/2012/08/16/technology/personaltech/ins-and-outs-of-publishing-your-book-via-the-web.html?pagewanted=all (accessed 20 July 2013).

Penguin Group (2012), press release, www.us.penguingroup.com/static/pages/aboutus/pressrelease/asi_071912.html (accessed 18 July 2013).

Pilkington, Ed (2012), 'Amanda Hocking, the writer who made millions by self-publishing online', *The Guardian*, www.guardian.co.uk/books/2012/jan/12/amanda-hocking-self-publishing (accessed 23 July 2013).

Rooney, Mick (2010), *To Self-Publish or Not to Self-Publish*, Leicester: Troubador.

Ross, Orna (2012), 'Is exploiting self-publishing authors to be the new publishing model?', ALLi, http://selfpublishingadvice.org/blog/is-exploiting-authors-to-be-the-new-publishing-model (accessed 23 July 2013).

The Independent Publishing Magazine (2013), 'Publisher Services Index', http://www.theindependentpublishingmagazine.com/p/publishing-ser.html (accessed 1 August 2013).

The Self Publishing Magazine, quarterly printed and digital magazine aimed at all self-publishing authors. www.selfpublishgmagazine.com

Williams, Charlotte (2011), 'Ed Victor sets up publishing imprint', www.thebookseller.com/news/ed-victor-sets-publishing-imprint.html (accessed 13 July 2013).

www.selfpublishingconference.org.uk The Self Publishing Conference is an annual event bringing self-publishers and influential people within the self-publishing industry together.

52

Literary Life: Prizes, Anthologies, Festivals, Reviewing, Grants

Thomas Shapcott

Prizes

In the world of contemporary literary culture there are many baits and inducements still, even though book culture is, as it always was, threatened by economic and other challenges. There are, for instance, the proliferation of literary prizes which range from the world-acclaimed (and profitable) Booker Prize, the Whitbread Prize, to the Pulitzer Prize (in the US), the Governor General's Prize (Canada) and the Miles Franklin Award (Australia) as well as a veritable host of other prizes and awards.

These represent pinnacles, and even runners-up in the very grand awards can proudly announce the fact on their next dust-jacket, or their CV. Such prizes represent the peak, or the ultimate goal, for aspiring authors. I have listed a handful, but in the English-speaking countries there are dozens more of almost equal prestige. Authors, publishers, even book-sellers, can find in such prizes the very real incentive to foster the promotion of winning (or even short-listed) books, and everyone gains.

The proliferation of literary awards accelerated towards the end of the twentieth century (the IMPAC Dublin literary prize – for a novel – only began in 1993, and it is the richest prize in money terms and, increasingly, in prestige terms). One of the consequences of this has been a certain sense of glut, so that it becomes increasingly difficult to gain media attention. Such awards, however, remain of great value to an author – and not only in cash terms (and in some countries, including Australia, the cash prize is, in effect, shared by the lucky author with the taxation department). Feature articles, 'profiles' and radio or television interviews suddenly become easier, or more frequent. Libraries show an interest (and in some countries Public Lending Right for books held in libraries can add effectively to an author's steady income). Many a book that might have been in danger of sinking into the morass of publishers' back-lists has been saved because of an award.

Winning an award, often enough, is sufficient to draw the attention of film-makers to a book. If film-makers take out an 'option' on a book for possible film or television adaptation, the amount of such option might be a token, and in 90 percent of cases it remains the only evidence of that gleam in the author's, or the film-maker's, eye. But to have one's novel turned into a film, or TV special, can well be the gold at the end of the rainbow. Authors, themselves, have many gruelling tales of their experiences with the eventual adaptation of their work into another medium, so be warned. Many authors advise 'Take the money and run.'

But even a commercially, or critically, unsuccessful adaptation to the screen can help an author to struggle on. I am reminded of a story told by the Australian Frank Moorhouse. His book *The Coca Cola Kid* (1985) was made into a movie by the renowned Serbian film director Dusan Makevejev. It flopped in cinemas, but has continued to have an ongoing life as a video, which has yielded Moorhouse a trickle of royalties ever since.

Libraries, and that new form of library, the video or DVD store, can provide small but often ongoing revenue sources for an author. Traditionally, royalties on book publica-tion have been the mainstay of a writer's income, and most writers who can negotiate an advance on their next book are in the strongest position.

Literary prizes may represent the pinnacle of an author's financial rewards and due acknowledgment of their literary achievement. There are many other smaller prizes and awards that the novice author would do well to investigate. These, like the major prizes, have proliferated in the last few decades. They range from modest competitions (for a poem, a story, sometimes even a novel, biography or non-fiction manuscript) and can be the first test of a writer's ability to match their work with that of other aspirants. Many now established writers gained their initial encouragement by winning quite small prizes for an individual poem, story, etc. And it is certainly a useful indication when submitting a manuscript to a book publisher to list such awards.

Some minor awards carry a substantial measure of prestige. When national newspapers, for instance, decide to enter this field, the winning work almost certainly will attract con-siderable interest. I am an Australian, therefore this brings to my mind examples from my own country. *The Age* newspaper in Melbourne has an annual short-story award, which is run in association with the Melbourne branch of International PEN, an internationally associated author's body. This short-story award has been the launching-pad for emerging writers. A fairly recent winner, Elliot Perlman, followed his Age-winning short story with a novel, *Three Dollars*, which has in 2005 been made into an Australian film. That initial award established his name as somebody to watch.

Writing is, in the end, a curiously competitive activity. You might, in the solitude of your room, face onto your imagination and a blank page, but the moment you submit your poem, your story, your article or your larger manuscript to an editor, you are entering the tide of quite frantic activity. An editor will assess any incoming submission with a thor-oughly attuned awareness of the total scene, whether that scene be the regional one of a small competition, a journal with a subscription list of only a few hundred, or something much larger – a national award, a major magazine, a large book publisher.

Entering a small competition can be a first step along the way. It is true, subjectivity comes into it: did the judge (did all the judges?) wake up with a hangover and a bad temper? Did the work you submitted cross some invisible barrier? (Too long, too short, too much bad language, too little vernacular, whatever?). Most, if not all, small literary prizes are submitted to the judging panel anonymously, names of authors removed. That, at least, helps avoid questions of bias. Many awards have more than one judge: another safeguard.

Not to win the award can be disheartening. I always advise my students: 'You can feel suicidal for twenty-four hours; after that you have to gird your loins and keep plugging on. Look at the work again: sometimes such a rebuff makes you see it in a fresh light.'

I also advise students never to take one rejection as The End. The literary world is crowded with stories of poems, stories, books that were initially turned back but later succeeded. In my own writing life, early, I had several poems which were rejected by editors but which, later, were accepted by other publishers and then subsequently were anthologised, not once, but several times. I learned the lesson.

Anthologies

This brings me to the important role anthologies can have in capturing the flavour or the essence of a culture. Again, the proliferation of anthologies has become an important publishing stratagem. The least useful of these are probably those anthologies which merely cannibalise from earlier anthologies. They take the easy way out, selecting already 'proven' poems or stories. Useful for keeping dribs and drabs of income coming in, if you are an already anthologised author, yes. But not helpful otherwise, at least from the writer's point of view.

Anthologies are, at best, ephemeral. *Best Poems of …*, or *Best Stories*, etc., are the obvious examples. These are often an annual production, which seeks to cull from a year's published output the 'pick of the crop'. The usual problems about who makes such a selection will arise. But, on the whole, such anthologies are useful in drawing attention to what is new, what is being written about, who is emerging. Book publishers and editors certainly pay attention.

Other anthologies might cover local or regional (or national) writing, and the most frequent of these do concentrate more on recent work even when they cover an historical perspective. This is because there is always a strong pressure to demonstrate that the past is not the only repository of good or relevant or 'characteristic' writing. Even when an anthologist sets a specific historical target, such as *Second World War Poets*, there is a certain pressure to uncover something new, or forgotten, or neglected, if only to show the anthologist's skill, or research.

Anthologies also cover themes: cats, animals, birds, seasons. And there are anthologies of love poems, anti-love poems, gay love poems, and why not hate poems? The newer author can often make some initial mark by getting into such an anthology.

How to do it? Quite often the prospective anthologist, or publisher, calls for submissions and there are many writers' organisations which publish newsletters listing this sort of information. For a writer, there is much to be gained from being part of a writers' union, or society. Not only for information concerning forthcoming anthologies, but also for news of competitions and awards, with closing dates and guidelines.

Modern technology has also spawned web-based magazines and sites where a writer can submit or place their work. Some of these have earned a legitimate credibility, while others remain largely unlooked at in cyberspace. Web technology, though, does offer a stimulating range of possibilities, especially for the emerging writer. Feedback and the opportunity for 'conversation' with like minds has also, with this technology, broken through the barriers of distance and time. No longer need a writer feel isolated completely in a garret, backyard shed or a corner of the kitchen table.

In 'publishing' on the web there can be some risks. Theft, or plagiarism, is one of them. 'There is no copyright in ideas', is an old maxim, and legal definition, but any author feels a certain proprietary guardianship of their own specific order of words and what those words indicate or illustrate. To see this lifted, and claimed by others, can be a galling experience.

Unfortunately, copyright laws are often expensive to uphold. The challenge to the very concept of copyright is at the heart of what all the astonishing developments in reprography (from the web to CD and DVD copying) are about, but it has to be borne in mind that it was the legal concept of a creator's copyright which has been instrumental in creating a world where such work can be not only recognised but financially rewarded. Mozart, we remember, was buried in a pauper's grave.

Festivals

Literary or Writers' Festivals have proliferated over the last few decades. The Edinburgh Festival, starting in 1947, was perhaps the first, though it was essentially a music festival. Nevertheless, it started something when writers began to be invited to participate. What was the great novelty in this was something that the post-war evolution of air travel helped bring about: authors from different countries participated; they met each other (friendships were started, enmities were sparked, the possibility of dialogue and exchange grew). From this beginning, literary festivals, often with visiting writers from distant places, evolved. Such festivals have proved that not only the sight, and voices, of writers onstage together might be like a gladiatorial contest, it can also be stimulating or diverting. Literary Festivals, essentially, are not for writers, they are for readers, and listeners. It has become a venue for readers of books to see and recognise and put flesh, as it were, upon the names of those whose books have entranced them. Or have repelled them. Or have raised their interest. In the world today, there are innumerable literary festivals and often with audiences in numbers which astonish the journalists, or the literary hacks. Probably the top such festivals at the moment would be the Toronto Harbourfront readings, commenced in 1980, the Rotterdam Poetry Festival, and the Writers' Week of the Adelaide Festival, in Australia. The Adelaide Writers' Week began inauspiciously enough in 1960 and is held every second year. Since the 1970s audience numbers have increased astonishingly. It is held in two large marquees under shady planetrees in parkland near the Adelaide Festival Hall. The event lasts for one week, and there is a book tent which has sold huge numbers of books by the visiting authors, to the delight of their publishers (and no doubt the authors themselves).

Attendances at each session almost invariably fill each tent and often there is an overflow, sitting on plastic chairs in the shade. Writers like Salman Rushdie, Peter Carey, David Malouf or Margaret Atwood have attracted up to two thousand people, who have listened attentively to every word, and have then rushed out to the book tent. This festival is perhaps unique, in that all sessions are free. Not only readers and writers crowd the area, but also literary agents, publishers and media representatives are always to be seen.

Such festivals are echoed in all the Australian capital cities, and many regional centres. Canada, England, Ireland and the US also host similar events. The modern author is always well advised to see if he or she can be invited onto 'the circuit', and, when invited, especially if internationally, a hefty stack of their own books for sale, on the spot, is always recommended.

Poets have long since learned that the best sale opportunities for their books are at point-of-contact: readings, seminars, conferences. Bookshops, with the exception of specialist bookshops, do not carry large stocks of poetry collections. The Canada Council many years ago instituted a series of author's tours through regional centres. A poet has to be pretty bad (or a very poor performer) not to be able to sell at least one or two copies at each reading. Short story writers can have a similar effect. This is the sort of undetected literary life of a writer, an underground base of activities which can have a slow cumulative impact. It can have an impact, certainly, upon the writer. There is nothing quite like airing your own work before an audience. Charles Dickens, long ago, learned how to hone his performances, and the excerpts from his novels, so as to achieve maximum effect. Many a contemporary writer has also gained useful experience into the *sound* of their own writing from public performance.

Festivals and public readings: they were once the province of the very famous or the very notorious. Charles Dickens, indeed, or Dylan Thomas. Nowadays they are increasingly the spotting ground for new talent, and for emerging writers. No literary festival these days could concentrate only on the 'big names'. Readers have been trained to expect the additional element: new writers, emerging talent. In the world of 'ten-minute celebrity' one of the essential components which aligns itself also to the cult of 'youth culture' is the demand for new voices, new faces, new experiences. In this sense, a festival like the Adelaide Writers' Week has an enviable record of 'talent spotting'. Many writers who were virtually unknown when they were invited to Adelaide, subsequently have become the big names in their generation of writers. Their Adelaide book sales have been, as it were, the harbinger of their later success.

It has been said that contemporary literary culture has become ghettoised: sales of 'literary novels' are declining, poetry collections are token, short stories have almost lost their place in the market. There are ironies in this, and explanations. The twentieth century saw the rise of powerful rivals to the book for a place in people's leisure time: first, radio, and then television, and then video, CD and DVD, not to mention the exciting liberation of personal travel, the jet plane and the computer. Books do remain the most efficient and effective medium for the communication of ideas and are an essential prompt to the imagination. They are portable, do not need cords, wires and electrical installation. They do not disappear into cyberspace at the flick of a foolish finger.

Even though you can get the *Encyclopaedia Britannica* on CD it still remains easier and more satisfying to be able to turn up an individual paper page. All the newspapers of the world may eventually be available on the web, but the physical interest in turning pages remains – as well as the strange delight of uncovering the unexpected, that article on the same page as the one you were seeking, that quaintly reverberant advertisement adjacent, with its laughably cheap prices. The printed word holds the past, and the future. Not even the image, for all its mystery and allure, quite unlocks the same door to the mind.

Literary culture has survived these new challenges. We have been seduced by sheer numbers to think of 'success' in terms of multitudes. But I think we should remember that the plays of Shakespeare played to audiences of only hundreds. It was many centuries before the printed texts of those plays became the stuff of massive print runs. The novels of Dickens (and of Marie Corelli) may have sold in their many thousands, but even in an age when there was only the print medium, I doubt that even something like Thackeray's *Vanity Fair* would have reached more than modest numbers, and a poet like Gerard Manley Hopkins, before his eventual apotheosis in the twentieth century, was scribbling for himself alone. Even T. S. Eliot's *The Waste Land* sold only a handful of copies at its first printing.

Reviewing

Perhaps what I am saying is, it is useful to get a perspective. In some ways, things move in cycles. A current craving for novelty advantages the new and the young (and perhaps the photogenic) but it also implies the dreaded assertion that 'you have passed your use-by date' to anything or anyone who has been 'around too long'. The cycle, though, does cause eventual re-evaluation of former work or achievements. Just as fashion is forced to re-cycle earlier modes and colours, shapes, sizes, so in the cultural world of books and the imagination, there is a constant sifting to see relevances and pre-echoes in the work of a generation of writers a couple of decades earlier. The re-discovery of many women writers, for instance, illustrates this; or the re-discovery of certain iconic figures by a newer generation (Rimbaud has been continuously re-discovered by waves of young people in America, Canada, Australia; Hart Crane seems on the point of another revival; no doubt Ginsberg will be re-discovered anew).

The important thing is, the literary novel is not dead; it is very much alive, but the world it competes in is a far different, and more difficult world than that which greeted its predecessors. As the IMPAC Dublin fiction prize illustrates, the competition is increasingly international: translation of contemporary fiction (and, to a lesser extent, poetry) has become very much a factor in the modern reader's mind. In the last month I have read new fiction by authors from Japan, Lebanon, Sweden, Spain and Italy, as well as work from the US, Canada, England and, of course, Australia. The English-language book world, when we include (as does the IMPAC Dublin award) translation, has become wonderfully full and varied.

Unfortunately, that also means that the available space, in this increasingly varied and competitive market, becomes, for the individual creator, alarmingly tight. For the incoming author, this does present a real problem.

It should be said, however, that still in many ways, the new author has it pretty good. Perhaps here I can again refer to an Australian example, because I believe it illustrates a wider trend over the period, from the 1950s to this first decade of the twenty-first century.

In 1960 a well-known Australian book reviewer published his assessment of six new collections of Australian verse. 'It is impossible', he said, 'that there can have been six books of poetry of any value published here in any one year'. Four of those six books were by poets who continue to have very high reputations indeed in Australian poetry, and of the other two, one was a light-hearted collection by a well-known wit, and the other was one of the last of the heartfelt Second World War gatherings, historically trenchant if not a notable addition to the genre. What was illustrated by that reviewer was the concept that there was a certain elite summit permitted only to a very few. What he did not understand was that a literary culture, to thrive, needs a rich and varied compost of activity. Australian poetry, in 1960, was about to launch itself into a couple of decades of fruitful achievement, an achievement that was to lead to an increasing number of translations, anthologies and overseas printing of the work of that upcoming generation of Australian poets, who include Peter Porter, Les Murray, John Tranter and David Malouf, among many others.

A similar dismissive attitude was, in the 1960s, being expressed about short stories and novels. Both of these, over the next few decades, also experienced international interest and publication. Regional cultures everywhere have benefited from what we might now call a post-colonial sensibility which has applied itself, not only to a new way of appraising recent and contemporary work, but also to ways of seeing earlier achievements.

One of the openings for a prospective or emerging author has traditionally been that of reviewing. Book reviews appear regularly in major (and minor) newspapers, in literary and current affairs journals, and in specifically literary magazines, as well as in radio and other media. In many countries, community radio affords a good outlet for review features, especially if they have topical or local interest.

Many authors have earned their bread and butter, especially between major projects, by writing reviews. This is not surprising. If you are, yourself, by your own writing, keeping abreast of contemporary trends and activity, editors quickly recognise that you might be able to offer an informed voice in assessing the most recent book of one of your peers, or (better, from your point of view) someone contemporary who is quite new to you. Certainly, I have encountered the work of some extremely interesting and challenging foreign writers (in translation) through being offered their novels to review. Your own specialty, as a writer, may be fiction, or poetry, but in reviewing editors quite often place a particular trust in you and your views, no matter what the genre. I know one internationally famous poet who instructed the major newspaper who approached him not to send him poetry, but non-fiction books of curious or quirky interest. His reviews were always full of fascinating insights, and he gained a world of new material, much of which eventually found its way, in various guises, into his own writing.

Apart from the mean capitalistic enterprise of doing book reviews, and the possible new discoveries you may make from reading material which otherwise would not have come your way, book reviews, so long as they carry your name as the reviewer, do no harm at all in keeping that name, as it were, in the public eye. For a novelist, or for a poet or short story writer, there can be extended periods between publication of one work and the next. As a book reviewer, you have a more than fair chance of keeping your name, at least modestly, in print. Of course, if you did a streaking act across the local playing field when some visiting Royal, or major politician, were present you would no doubt achieve rather more immediate media attention, though the cost might be disproportionate. Nevertheless, to have your name attached to a book review, or to regular reviews, might be, in the end, more valuable. In addition, the actual content, and quality, of your review, might be more likely to gain your subsequent published book, some measure of interest.

Many writers have begun their careers in journalism. If newer generations of writers seem to have emerged through university or creative writing courses, the disciplines of journalism – deadlines, word length, immediate impact – are still very useful for the apprentice writer. Freelance journalism has its appeal. The role of the 'public intellectual' is one that seems to be attracting increasing attention, and Opinion Pieces are featured in newspapers as a means of demonstrating a more committed approach to issues, particularly in this age of one-minute grabs on television and one paragraph fillers (under the colour images) on the main pages. Several authors I know have become regular contributors of such 'opinion pieces' and have subsequently published extended essays on controversial or topical subjects in journals and magazines. Their own writing, and publishing, careers have certainly been enhanced.

Grants

In contemporary literary culture there is perhaps one additional area which is worth discussing, at least in general terms. That is the literary grant.

In the world which developed in the latter twentieth century, the emergence and expansion of grants for writers, and in the creative arts, has been a notable feature. In Western countries, before this phenomenon evolved, patronage was private and limited, with perhaps the exception of a few grants for the aged and indigent. In the affluent period of the last third of the twentieth century the Arts Council of Great Britain, the Canada Council and the Australia Council might be seen as the exemplars of the new form of arts patronage. This was, essentially, public funding, even if the purse strings were at some remove from the assessment and granting process. The Soviet bloc had traditionally favoured creative artists, if at a great cost in terms of what they were supposed to produce to earn such patronage. The Scandinavian countries seem to have been influential in their forms of patronage, especially their funding of writers. The Canada Council began in the 1960s with a hearty annual funding base. In some ways this was understandable. Canada's national sense of identity was sorely pressed with the consciousness of their big brother just down below the border. The Canada Council instituted a wide-ranging series of grants and subsidies, for writers, for publishers, and for promotion of Canadian literature both at home and abroad.

In Australia the Australia Council expanded its patronage of writers and Australian literature in 1973, though its newly-formed Literature Board actually was successor to an earlier Commonwealth Literary Fund, dating from 1908 (and which had been formed initially to provide a few literary pensions). Funding for the Literature Board was nothing like that in the Canada Council, but it did enable the Board to begin a hugely influential series of grants for writers to 'buy time' in order to tackle 'new works' (and which was to lead to the much-acclaimed 'new Renaissance' in Australian fiction from 1980 on). Book subsidies, promotional grants and writers-in-residence schemes were also initiated.

In all these new patronage projects, and in those initiated in other English-speaking countries, the result over the succeeding decades, has been an undoubted increase in literary activity, and in awareness of that activity, both at home and abroad. In that sense, these schemes have been outstandingly successful.

For the contemporary writer, the emerging writer, these schemes, and the consolidation of these schemes over the decades, has led to what might be called a bureaucratic rigidification. One of the modern literary art forms is the writing of grant applications, to the particular arts body involved. These can vary from the relatively informal or ad hoc letter of request, accompanied by necessary back-up data or samples of writing, to complex printed page documents littered with boxes to tick, spaces to fill out and appendices to append, and beware of hidden traps.

Some people have made a profession as form fillers, and the range of funding agencies has proliferated. In my country, Australia, there is the Australia Council, which is the national arts funding agency; then all the Australian States have their own State Arts Funding agencies; in addition there are regional funding sources, corporate or privately sponsored arts funding agencies, and of course international sources of monies, if your project involves the wider perspective.

For the budding author, access to any of these money-cows is attractive and dispiriting. Competition is usually fierce – and in that sense, as in submitting a manuscript to an editor, the same advice is pertinent. Try, and try again. In both cases, a first submission is usually only, in effect, a calling card. As a young poet, I submitted prolifically for two years before I even received a note on my reject slip and was first published shortly after. In the case of the Literature Board, I happened to be a member of that first Board, but I did see many cases where a first application was turned down (almost certainly because of the high number of requests for funding) but then the same applicant applied in subsequent years, when their case was favourably received. In quite a number of these, this was because the assessors on the panel had at least noted the name, and the sense of promise in that earlier application).

Award of a grant is still a major incentive to a writer and does help buy time for their next project. Some writers, though, have discovered that once they do have that grant, the challenge of sitting down and actually writing the sustained work they applied for is too much. A few writers have ceased writing altogether. Four months, I have noted, seems the crisis time. If, after four months you still have not filled that first blank page, chances are you never will. Receipt of a writing grant, therefore, is a test as well as an accolade.

George Bernard Shaw once, famously, said, 'If you can't write, teach'.

Teachers of creative writing are increasingly in demand and it can be a living. I was a teacher in this field for eight years, but at least I wrote, also. I think I learned as much from the experience as did my pupils. Perhaps I should add, as a final point, that this is a growth area in the contemporary literature culture we find ourselves in. And we are, all of us, capable of learning.

53

The Writer as Teacher

Gareth Creer

Why do it?

OK, you're a writer and you have probably been taught how to make yourself a better writer, be it at university, as part of a Writer's Group, or simply by buying this book. You want to be a writer, not a teacher, but you're reading this chapter. Why?

Amis is at full throttle, spitting at his critics after our literary guardians have been giving him another battering. The great man is fighting back: 'Nobody sticks their hand up at the back of class when the teacher asks what they want to do when they grow up and says "Sir! Sir, I want to be a critic. I want to be a critic!"'

This is Amis reasserting the innate superiority of the writer over his critic, of somebody who does over somebody who interprets. The superiority of the writer over everybody. I had just been published for the first time when I nodded along to Amis's mantra in Sheffield's Waterstones. The novel I had written for the MA Writing at Sheffield Hallam had been snapped up by Transworld and I was on my way, following in the steps of the people who had taught me – all award-winning novelists who sold the secrets of their craft on the side.

One such novelist is Mo Hayder, now teaching Creative Writing at Bath Spa University. Mo is great at what she does, writing literary thrillers that poke away at the boundaries of the genre. Despite the critical acclaim and the sales, just writing is somehow not enough. Here's a taste of Mo on the subject of teaching and writing:

> I'm a rare thing indeed. A novelist not forced to rely on a supplementary income to support her writing. Privileged in that I don't need another job. So why do I regularly teach on the MA in Creative Writing at Bath Spa university?
>
> The answer varies according to my mood. I was a self-taught novelist and couldn't afford to attend a creative writing course until, paradoxically, I was already published. So could teaching be my peculiar form of voyeurism? The slightly sadistic pleasure of watching others go through the struggles I went through? Or maybe there's always been a latent teacher struggling inside me (I was certainly the bossiest girl in school). In less introspective times I convince myself I teach for the simple pleasure of watching burgeoning literary voices develop over the months. That I'm addicted to the nerdy buzz of analysing narrative mechanics. But if I'm honest I think I teach because I crave what all teachers crave, the holy grail of seeing a student beat the odds, push through myriad obstacles and land a publishing deal.

At least six writers with the talent to be published have passed through my classroom, and, although things may change over time, none of them has seen a publishing contract. Is it possible their talent alone wasn't sufficient? Is it possible that what they lacked was the most important ingredient: the drive and that rare species of insanity needed to succeed as a novelist? Or, more chilling, is it simply that I'm not a very good teacher? I can respond to most of these questions, except this last one. But then, maybe some things are better left unanswered.

Four years after I'd heard Amis in Sheffield I had two books under my belt and a fair share of good reviews, no more than my fair share of bad. But I was thinking about encroaching upon my writing time. I was thinking of teaching others how they might write better, and a vision of Amis came to me. Why teach it when you could be doing it?

Six years on and ten years after that night in Sheffield, I'm still writing, still teaching, still loving it all. I've taught in schools and in prisons; on other peoples' holidays and in bail hostels; in drug rehab clinics and in universities, and in my book there are plenty of reasons writers might consider teaching as well as doing.

Schoolkids and junkies, bohos and cons, students and housewives, none of them come visiting your desk. You don't see them in The Ivy or in the back of your cab home on the way home from a literary dinner. Any writer needs material. There has to be something to write about, something for your audience in what you're writing. There will always be plenty of ourselves in what we write and for some people there will always be too much of themselves to ever make it past being a diarist into being an entertainer. We all have to be the authors of stuff that *other people* want to read.

I've always thought of writing as like going to the well. We sit at our desks and we plumb. We send down the bucket into what we know and what we think: we delve into our experience and knowledge and embellish it by setting the imagination to work. What we know is a sum of the life we have led, the places we have been, the people we have loved and loathed; our disappointments and hopes, our unfulfilled desires and the hurdles we have overcome. Add to that all the articles and books we have read, the films and plays, the arguments we have won and lost. The key is to be 'out there'. This is what ensures that the well never runs dry.

Having to get up, get out, catch a bus or miss a bus; have an argument with your boss or get pissed off because somebody is swinging the lead – these are some of the thousands of things that keep us engaged with our audience. If you work as well as write (and as my friends who have proper jobs say, 'you might be good at what you do but don't call it work') then these thousand things rise up to meet you.

To go with their material a writer needs time, and teaching is one of the few jobs that gives you time – not as much as it did fifteen, twenty years ago, but enough. Teaching, as is the case with any career or series of jobs that you might choose to dovetail with your writing, also provides the writer with an element of certainty. Even a successful writer gets paid by the chunk. There are things that can even out your income and in the case of novelists, film option deals or foreign deals can provide much needed dollops of cash when you least expect it. Appearance fees and magazine articles are useful too, and for radio writers repeat fees can also bring a welcome return on work that might have been done, dusted and forgotten about months or years ago. However, very, very few writers can ever be absolutely certain that there is another advance coming from where the last one did.

The knowledge that some money is coming in every month helps keep the writer sane. More importantly, it can allow us to write the book we really want. We can afford to hold out, take risks. And this is the paradox – encroaching into your writing time can provide the writer with a more creative space within which to work.

There is another argument in favour of teaching which some writers proffer. I'm not so sure. Some say the writer's palette can be extended by teaching, their appreciation of the business of writing enriched by coaxing the next generation. Reading other people's work is stimulating, it keeps us engaged with the market, alerts us to where the next crop of stimuli is coming from. For me, this is a moot point and whilst I found my work with prison inmates really did energise my own writing, I find less of a connection with the body of work which I oversee and mark at university. It can distract, can appear as a white noise during those periods on the bus or in a café, idling in your armchair at home, when all you want is a blank page with nobody else's voice whispering, echoing. That said, there is much to be said for writing within such a creative and intellectual environment as a university.

Martyn Bedford is an acclaimed novelist and is Lecturer in Creative Writing and Director of the MA in Novel Writing at Manchester University. This is what he has to say about his life as a writer and teacher.

> I'd done a bit of creative writing teaching after my first couple of novels came out – a residency at Borders, some one-off workshops for libraries and literature festivals, and a residential stint on an Arvon course. Then I did a Q & A session with the creative writing students at the University of Manchester, where one of my books was on their reading list. As it happened, one of the two tutors handed in her notice that day and her colleague suggested I apply for the job.
>
> When I saw what the pay was relative to the number of hours' actual work, and how much free time it would still leave for my writing, I decided to go for it. I'd done an MA in Creative Writing at UEA in 1993–4 and had always liked the writing workshop environment – as a student and from the bits of tutoring I'd done – so I reckoned I'd enjoy the job. And the money from writing was just starting to ease off around then, so the extra income would come in handy.
>
> I still enjoy it – especially working with the students in the workshop, and in the development of their fiction. The university admin, I could do without. And, of course, there are times when I've spent a day critiquing other people's stuff when I really wanted to be writing my own. But that goes with the territory, and I try to compartmentalise the job as best I can to leave myself enough time (and enough creative energy) to make sure my writing doesn't suffer more than it has to. If anything, I've got better at making the most of the time I have to write.
>
> As a full-time novelist, which I was for five years, I used to fritter away a lot of the time and wasn't much more productive than I am now. Also, critiquing other writers' work has, I think, sharpened up my critical skills when it comes to editing and revising my own work-in-progress.

Are you up to it?

As well as being convinced of the merits of being a writer and teacher, you should also have an appetite for the task. You must believe that creative writing can be taught. The fact that you have bought or borrowed this book and have got this far suggests this is probably the case.

You will come across plenty of people (other academics or the guy across the hall who takes *The Daily Mail*) who don't see the point. What is the point? I believe that you can't necessarily make anybody a decent writer, but you can make everybody a better writer. And that includes ourselves. If you are thinking of becoming a teacher of creative writing, I'd ask you to think long and hard about what the point is. Come up with your own manifesto, carry it around with you, this will help you keep true to yourself.

The life of a jobbing teacher who writes is varied. To start with, you'll be in different environments with groups of differing ability; different ages and social backgrounds. As long as you can focus on the writing and stay attuned to the writer in all of us, you will be able to adapt what you know to what they need to know. But, what is your ethos?

As you travel around, teaching here and there, the chances are you will have no corporate objectives to serve, no mission statement to preach. What you need is your own hymn sheet. Like the writer needs their voice, the teacher needs an approach, a belief system.

Much like writing, the business of teaching writing requires the teacher to engage. Think of your learner as a reader and find a way to captivate them, spin them along on the back of the hundreds of reasons why you yourself write, construct a methodology for keeping them with you when you unlock the secrets of how you write, how you get better. And all the time, communicate that truth – that you too are constantly trying to improve. Your audiences will differ and the targets you set will also vary dramatically, but the essence of what you teach should come from the heart. If you are coaxing heroin addicts into using the pen and the page as a tool for rehabilitation you first have to articulate (to yourself and to them) the kind of refuge and the kind of signposts that writing offers you.

The most difficult thing about teaching writing is that as soon as someone invites you into their world and pays you for the privilege of hearing what you have to say, it becomes all about them. Not you. We writers, necessarily, wander through life thinking it is all about us. And when we are writing, it has to be. Teaching the stuff is different and not all of us will be able to make that switch.

Again, I ask you, what is the point?

How do you get to do it?

'How do you get to do what you do?'

It's a question I am asked by my undergraduate students as much as 'How d'you get published, then?' They can obviously see I enjoy the teaching and they can see it can complement, not distract from, the writing. So what do you say to someone who wants to teach creative writing? All of the above. That is, make yourself aware of the point and the pitfalls of doing it. Have a good reason. What then?

It's a bit like getting your equity card. You've got to have experience to get experience. Be as imaginative as you can in breaking that circle. Build your CV. And all the time . . . never stop writing. A creative-writing teacher who doesn't write is like a mechanic who doesn't drive, a chef who doesn't eat ...

Think you're good enough? Now you have to do anything and everything you can to break the circle: get used to speaking in public; join a writer's group; get into the habit of contributing to and chairing workshops. Apply for anything remotely connected to teaching creative writing. This will involve trawling the council's FE courses, getting on the mailing lists of the Arts council bulletins. You may have to create your own opportunities by writing to local schools and offering to take classes. National Book Day is one opportunity and check out local literary heroes as the focal point for a class. Find a point of connection between you and your learners. Talk to the local library services to see if they want a writer's group to be formed and overseen.

Almost by definition, there is little point in writing here about how to develop your initiative, how to fashion an opportunity from nothing. Simply, look to the groundswell of writers around you and find a way to give them what they need. And remember, sometimes you'll get paid, sometimes you won't.

In terms of getting into a more structured career as a teaching writer, some things do help.

First, formalise your credentials for being able to teach by enrolling on an MA course in the subject area. This doesn't just teach you how to write but it lets you see first-hand how the subject is taught. It will furnish you with exercises and approaches. It will help finesse your notion of what sort of teacher you want to be. It may put you off and, when you think about it, this might be the best lesson you ever learn. An MA in Writing can also start the process of getting connected.

Just like it is important to squeeze the last drop from every connection you have when trying to get published, the more people you know the better when it comes to teaching writing. You won't simply throw the mortar board and gown to one side and step up to the white board and OHP when you have finished an MA, but you may get to hear of work-shops that need managing in a nearby FE College. Or you may hear of somebody taking a sabbatical. Someone at your host institution might like your style and ask you to help out here and there. And when you create your own opportunities, the back-up of having an MA will be the proof that you actually do know what you say you know.

Make yourself aware of funding opportunities for writing projects. These may be projects that are up and running. Or they may be guidelines for independent projects to help a pre-scribed learner group. It may be a case of you identifying a need and starting from scratch in an effort to find the funds to run a community outreach project or a social exclusion initiative.

And don't forget to write. Getting your own work published is paramount for the writer as teacher. If you're not doing this then you carry the burden of proof as to whether you know enough to guide other people through the wilderness of being a writer. Also, your publishing track record is imperative if you want to forge a career in Higher Education. Universities are required to demonstrate research activity and for the Writer as Teacher, research activity means ISBN.

Take some time out now to do a short exercise. A friend has alerted you to a benefactor inviting applications to 'promote the use of writing as a means of improving the nation's cultural consciousness'. The funding application requires a fifty-word summary of your proposed project. If successful, you will be provided with a £15,000 per year budget for your three-year project.

Come up with three ideas. Use the following words and phrases as stimuli, if you wish, but come up with at least one totally original idea.

Magazine.   Storytelling.   Asylum-seekers.   Rehabilitation.   Reminiscence.   Hospitals.
After-school.   AA.   Probation.
Disability.   Homeless.   Job-enrichment.
Trains.   Illiteracy.   Redundancy.   Alzheimers   Funerals.   Parks.

Try not to cheat by going back to or looking at 'Writing as Therapy' or 'Writing in the Community'.

One way to do it

To put some flesh on these bones, I'll run through how I got into teaching and give a potted history of the various projects I have been involved in. It is an unremarkable journey but not untypical.

With my MA completed and the novel I wrote for my dissertation, *Skin and Bone*, with Transworld, I had just completed my second novel in a two-book deal. I found it a difficult process – writing for an audience I knew was there – and I had been writing full-time for five years since I gave up my 'proper job'. I was missing getting out of the house, lamenting the plight of a writer where you can go from one winter to the next toiling away at the keyboard without anybody saying 'well done' or 'thank you'. Don't under-estimate the importance of inconsequential affirmation.

Flicking through the Tuesday *Guardian*, I read an advert for Writers in Residence in Prisons and decided to apply. Within a couple of months I was driving down the motorway to a Young Offenders Institution to host writing workshops, run a magazine, and rage against the machinery of governors and prison officers. I felt alive. I felt wanted.

Through the network of connections within the arts council and regional literature development officers, I ran more and more workshops, gave more and more masterclasses. I was earning bits on the side and building my repertoire, learning how to pitch for different audiences and adapt when exercises that went well one week went horribly wrong the next. I was breaking the circle, gaining experience through experience. The miles were clocking up and my writing time was squeezed.

The next step for me was to get a part-time job on the creative writing programme at Liverpool John Moores University and now I was getting paid holidays in which to write but there was an administrative burden as well as an academic fog to blur the creative focus. Working in a university sounds ideal for a writer but it might not be for everybody. In any creative writing department, you'll be sucked into the forcefields of neighbours who write about other people doing it. If you listen hard you might hear the pulse and creak of sap rising in London Fields, somewhere between Ladbroke Grove and the Upper East Side.

Teaching writing at university can be extremely varied. I have taught undergraduates, MA students and supervised PhDs, and you soon have to become accustomed with the idea of progression. We cannot simply teach the same things on a joint honours BA programme as we would on a full time MA degree. At various levels you will find yourself introducing certain techniques or developing understanding or encouraging a synthesis to demonstrate understanding. If you want to teach as well as write you have to do more than simply let the best writing come out of the best students.

If you are serious about becoming a creative writing teacher within a formal teaching institution, I would urge you to think about what aspiring writers need at different levels of learning. Write off to all the courses you can think of for a copy of their prospectus or route handbook. Challenge what those courses are doing and how they are doing it. Think about how you would deliver a one- or two- or three-year course in the subject.

Aileen La Tourette runs the PhD programme in the Centre For Writing at Liverpool John Moores University and she also teaches on undergraduate and MA routes. This is what she says about that final level of academic progression:

> The purpose of higher degrees in writing has always seemed to me to be to get you writing and keep you writing with a degree of structure and supervision. It's hard to be your own critic, everyone knows. It's easy to waste time, even years. The typical MA will present you with a

series of critical and creative hoops to jump through, and will give the benefit of lengthy and considered professional feedback on your performance. It will also put you in a world where other people are writing, and bring you into contact with published writers as well as agents and editors.

A PhD is more reflective. It offers the opportunity to really think about your writing at a profound level and in the context of contemporary writers and contemporary critical theory. It allows you to take on a subject that requires research and also frees you to experiment with whatever form you choose. Creative Writing PhDs are very new, they are still being defined. It's an exciting area at the moment, with lots of discussion going on as to what they are, could or should be. The creative tension between the creative and critical components of the PhD is at the core of the discussion. The creative component is dominant but actually to study one's own creative process is exciting, scary – almost breaking a taboo; and hopefully enlightening.

Supervising a PhD student represents, I guess, one end of the spectrum of teaching creative writing. The other end is what has always lit my candle, though, and two years ago I established a project to work with ex-offenders, using writing as a way of trying to turn their lives around.

I am drawn to what some might say is the bottom of the pile and some might say that is where people have most to gain. As a writer it is easy to see that this is where the stakes are highest and it's where you're most likely to have your mind blown.

54

Making a Living as a Writer

Livi Michael

I wish she had some other means of support besides writing; I think it bad in its effect upon her writing, which must be pumped up instead of bubbling out. And very bad for her health, poor girl . . . I think Miss Bronte had hold of the true idea, when she said to me last summer, 'If I had to earn my living, I would go out as a governess again, much as I dislike the life; but I think one should only write out of the fulness of one's heart, spontaneously'.
(Gaskell, cited in Uglow 1993: 311–12)

I am so pulled hither and thither by circumstances. The calm, the coolness, the silent grass-growing mood in which a man ought always to compose, – that, I fear, can seldom be mine. Dollars damn me . . . what I feel most moved to write, that is banned – it will not pay . . . So the product is a final hash.
(Melville, cited in Olsen 1980: 7)

How bitterly did unreplying Pierre feel in his heart that to most of the great works of humanity, their authors had given not weeks and months, not years and years, but their wholly surrendered and dedicated lives.
(Melville, cited in Olsen 1980: 8)

In recent years there has been a significant growth in the number of people attempting to publish their writing. A massive expansion in creative-writing courses, the well-publicised large advances paid for certain books, and the ease with which writers can now publish their own work electronically, means that a greater proportion of people are hoping to write for a living. This applies more to the writing of fiction and drama than poetry, a field in which it is notoriously difficult to earn a living. The good news is that the number of books published is also increasing; data from Nielsen BookScan suggests that the number of books published in the UK has increased from 121,517 in 2001 to 133,224 in 2009 (Nielsen BookScan 2010).

There is a similar healthy increase in sales. According to an an article in *The Guardian*, in which Lloyd Shepherd also cites Nielsen Book Scan figures, in 2011, 229 million books were sold in the UK as compared to 162 million in 2001 (Shepherd 2011). But should these figures generate greater optimism in the aspiring writer? Or, in other words, do they translate into income?

What kinds of income come from writing?

Income which comes directly from writing books falls into two categories; advance and royalties. An advance is what it says it is – money offered to the writer that is set against sales of the published work. This may vary dramatically. Although it has been suggested that only one in five books earn out their advances, it seems that most writers are offered advances that reflect the likely earnings of their book (Pool 2000). Until the advance is earned out, no royalties (income from sales of the book) are received. This means that, if you are offered a £10,000 advance, and the royalty on each book is 50p, you will not receive money from royalties until more than 20,000 copies of the book have been sold. The royalty is usually a percentage of the price that the book is sold for in the shops – this may also vary from 2% to 17.5%. More famous authors can sometimes demand a higher rate of royalty.

Any advance offered is usually paid in three parts: at the time of commission (a work may be commissioned in advance of writing or when it is first submitted for publication), at the time of delivery (when it has been accepted as ready for publication according to the specifications of the editor) and at publication itself. The full process of publication may take more than two years.

Most professional writers have agents, and the agent's fee (usually 15%) is taken out of the advance, so that if your advance is £10,000, £1,500 of this will be paid to the agent, and VAT of 17.5% is payable on this commission in the UK but not in the US.

Then there is tax, of course. Recent changes in the UK tax law mean that authors do not have to declare money from an advance until the full advance has been paid, which may be an advantage if you earn considerably more in one year than the next.

In the UK, but not the US, authors also receive money from libraries. Once your book is published it can be registered with an organisation called Public Lending Rights (PLR) who collect and distribute monies from libraries to authors. This is usually a small amount – in 1999 only 38% of writers received more than £100 from library earnings. The average figure was £277 in 2012 and £275 in 2011 – so it is rising slowly, rather than dramatically. It rises with the number of works published, especially since libraries frequently stock works which are otherwise unavailable because they are out of print.

The Author's Licensing and Collecting Services (ALCS) collects and distributes money from the photocopying and reproducing of published works. Amounts tend to be smaller than those received from PLR, especially for fiction, though some educational works are created as photocopyable resources and generate income accordingly.

If you are lucky, then the book you have written will be translated into other media – for example, film, television, radio – or it may sell in other countries, and money will be paid for this, though again with the usual deductions to the agent, tax and so on. It is incontrovertibly true, however, that income from writing is unlikely to offer as much as a professional salary when broken down into yearly amounts.

How much do authors earn?

In the year 2000, a survey of author's incomes in the UK was conducted by the Society of Authors. One quarter of all members returned questionnaires about their gross incomes from writing. This was a total of 1,711 authors, and the results were printed in *The Author* magazine as follows:

46% earned under £5,000
15% earned £5,000–£10,000
14% earned £10,000–£20, 000
9% earned £20,000–£30,000
4% earned £30,000–£40,000
3% earned £40,000–£50,000
4% earned £50,000–£75,000
2% earned £75,000–£100,000
3% earned over £100,000
(Pool 2000: 60)

Of the respondents, 46% stated that writing was their main source of income, although most had other, supplementary, income and only 13.5%, or 230, claimed writing as their only source of income. Interestingly, 14 of these said that they earned under £5,000 a year!

What these figures do not show is whether or not the year in question was exceptional – it is quite possible to earn £75,000 in one year and two in the next, and vice versa. They do not show the uncertainty of income, and the fact that it can take money more than six months to filter through the system so that it is difficult to budget monthly, and they do not show whether those writers for whom writing was their main source of income were actually able to write what they wanted to write, or whether they had been forced to turn to other forms of writing purely for income.

But in simple terms, three quarters of Society members earned less than the national average wage (£20,919 in 2000) and two thirds earned less than half the national average wage. Twenty years previously, when a similar survey was undertaken, only about half the respondents earned under half the national average wage.

In the US, comparable surveys have been undertaken by the Department of Labor, and the National Writers Union, and the results have led one writer to suggest that 'if a nation can be judged by its treatment of writers, America could be prosecuted for economic crimes against its poets, authors and journalists' (DuVergne Smith 1995). The survey concluded that:

- Experienced writers work long hours, are highly educated, yet their median income from freelancing totals only $4,000 a year.
- While 61% of writers work full time, only 16% of freelance writers earn more than $30,000 a year.
- Over half of all writers must work outside the field of writing for cash.
- Writers' incomes fall far below those of their equally educated peers.
- The working week totals 52 hours for most writers who work in multiple fields and earn non-writing income.
- Compared to their male counterparts, female full-time writers earn comparable, or higher, writing incomes.
- Writers frequently cross genre lines, with an average of 4.6 writing fields – from advertising to poetry to non-fiction books – per person.

The Bureau of Labor Statistics concludes that it is necessary for most freelance writers to support themselves with income from other sources (US Department of Labor 2010).

In 2006 ALCS undertook the most wide-ranging study of author's incomes to date. It was conducted by the Centre for Intellectual Property Policy and Management (CIPPM) at

Bournemouth University, by Professor Martin Kretschmer and Professor Philip Hardwick. The aim was to produce a set of independently validated data about authors' earnings in the UK and in Germany and 25,000 questionnaires were sent out to members of ALCS and members of two professional bodies in Germany, the VS and the VDD. Responses were sufficient for a statistical survey to be made: 6.8% (UK) and 4.5% (Germany). The survey was able to take into account tax and insurance data held by government statistical offices, and respondents included teachers and academics. The conclusions were not encouraging: 'Benchmarking the results against the Society of Authors survey (2000) appears to indicate that the earnings of a typical writer are deteriorating in real terms' (ALCS 2013).

The survey made an interesting distinction between professional authors and main-income authors: professional authors devote more than 50% of their time to writing; main-income authors earn more than 50% of their income from writing. This suggests that people who devote more than 50% of their time to writing do not necessarily generate more than 50% of their income from writing. The survey concluded that there was 'significant inequality within the profession'. The top 10 % of authors earn more than 50% of their total income from writing; the bottom 50% earn less than 10% of their total income from writing. Most writers supplement their income from other sources. Only 20.3% of writers in the UK earn all their income from writing. This figure is slightly higher in Germany, a fact which is attributed to the higher cost of living in the UK (especially London), and also to the wider availability of grants in Germany.

The survey suggests that the first ten years of a writer's career is the hardest, when the median income generated is still only £5,000 a year. It also points out that female main-income authors earn 59% of their male counterparts. Among main-income authors, a 60/40 earnings bias occurs in favour of men.

The conclusion, unsurprisingly, is that 'writing is shown to be a very risky profession, with median earnings less than one quarter of the typical wage of a UK employee'.

What factors have affected income from writing?

The evidence suggests, then, that it is actually harder to earn a living from writing now than it used to be. But why?

In *How to Market Books*, Alison Baverstock comprehensively analyses the changes affecting the UK publishing industry since 1980, when 'much of publishing was still a cottage industry, characterised by individuals who ran eponymous publishing houses' (Baverstock 2000: 1). Today, large international companies such as Bertelsmann, Hachette and HarperCollins dominate the UK publishing scene, and of course Random House has recently merged with Penguin to create 'the biggest book publisher in the world'. UK publishing is no longer UK owned or dominated; judgements about what is being read in Britain may be made, and certainly funded, outside the UK, and it is increasingly difficult to earn income on books that are published solely in the UK. Also, the trend is to pursue commercial synergy – to develop a product that can simultaneously be made into film, book, cartoon, T-shirt, or even theme parks.

The Net Book Agreement (NBA) disappeared in 1995. Under the terms of this agreement, a book could not be sold to the retailer at a price lower than that fixed by its publisher, so the producer rather than the retailer fixed the price of the goods being sold, and incentives to purchase such as free offers, were relatively rare. In general, the demise of the agreement has greatly strengthened the hand of the larger publishers at the expense of the smaller ones, chain stores have flourished at the expense of independent bookshops, and wholesalers have grown hugely. There are more varied retail outlets, such as supermarkets and garden centres, which may demand huge discounts from publishers, and bookstores have diversified their stock so that books compete for retail space with videos and music. Popular bestsellers occupy a far greater shelf space than lesser-known titles, and throughout bookstores stock is more homogenised. More people are buying more books, but the variety is decreasing. 'Bookshops organise themselves around the bestseller', Penguin's managing director has said, and the difference between big and small titles is ever more extreme (Taylor 2002: 8).

The revolution of the Internet has generated several economic difficulties for the publishing world. Amazon is the largest online retailer and seller of books, but it demands huge discounts from publishers. The issue of royalties for ebooks has never been satisfactorily resolved, though there is some evidence to suggest that authors who publish their books online do rather better from sales than from advances.

What is the effect on the author?

- Unless they self-publish, or turn to the small presses, authors have little control over the marketing of their books, from the budget spent to the cover. Little, Brown's marketing director, Alison Lindsay, confirmed that 'We are now spending a greater proportion of the marketing budget on fewer titles' (Taylor 2002: 8).
- Authors have no control over book distribution. Bookshops are unlikely to be interested in the fact that you are a local author or in the self-published work – decisions as to which books are stocked and given prominence are generally taken centrally, not by individual bookshops.
- Decisions about the marketability of certain books, or writers, are based on orders from Amazon and the large retail establishments. Frequently the intermediaries (book buyers, etc.) do not have time to read the actual books.
- If large retail establishments such as supermarkets demand more than 65% discount from the publishers, then the royalties received by the author may be based on the net profits received by the publisher rather than on copies sold.
- Major booksellers order only enough copies of a book to last a couple of weeks before re-ordering, thus the shelf life of a book may be shortened.
- Changes in the publishing industry have meant an unusually rapid turnover of staff. It is not unusual to work with several editors in the course of producing a single work. More significantly, when a new senior editor is brought in, he or she may want to build his or her own list. Many authors have been quietly dropped from the lists of publishers with whom they previously had a stable, long-term relationship.
- Libraries, like bookshops, have had to diversify, transforming their role within the community. The amount spent by libraries on books varies significantly from one area to another, and is under the control of local councils, but the evidence suggests that each year the budget for books is reduced.

Overall, then, the trend is towards greater insecurity for the writer, who cannot depend on being 'nurtured' by any one publishing firm, or count on a wide distribution of their books to the reading public. The emphasis is less on the individual author than on the 'brand'. Large advances may be paid for a single work which fails to earn out the advance, and then gradually or rapidly, the author may be dropped from the publishing list. It is harder, therefore, to develop a long-term career, with a body of published work, even though, according to the survey on writer's incomes, an established body of work does still seem to be the way to earn money as a writer. This 'sits uneasily with the trend in some fiction houses to reduce the range of works published, focusing instead on a smaller number of potential big sellers' (Pool 2000: 60).

There is an increasing emphasis on the author being pro-active and participating directly in the marketing process: using social media, Twitter and Facebook, writing a blog. In *Marketing Your Book: An Author's Guide*, Alison Baverstock gives advice on using the media, giving effective interviews, developing a website, and promoting yourself by giving talks, lectures and workshops. People who consider themselves to be professional writers often diversify and use their skills in a variety of ways which supplement their main writing work, from reviewing to copywriting and proofreading, writing articles and short stories. There are also residencies, fellowships and grants offered by (amongst others) the Royal Literary Fund and the Society of Authors. These help writers through the inevitable 'lean patches' in their careers, but most supplementary activities are time-consuming and may detract from the work that the writer really wants to do. When the Society of Authors surveyed its members, some 39% agreed with the statement 'To bring in money, I need to undertake literary activities that are not otherwise attractive to me' (Pool 2000: 61). It is possible that some writers find these supplementary activities as demanding as the work they gave up in the first place.

Why give up the day job?

As yet there is no survey analysing the reasons why some writers decide to write full time. I have met writers who felt that it was a mistake, or at least a premature decision based on the advance they received for their first book. Despite available statistics, there still seems to be widespread ignorance about the reality of earning a living as a writer, and some writers still feel that once they are published they are on their way to fame, fortune and regular publication. Rather more become full-time writers because their partners are earning a steady income, and/or because they have no dependants. Others, like myself, make calculated decisions, aware that it may be a provisional and temporary state, but convinced that, if they never took the risk they would always regret it.

When I left my job as senior lecturer at a university, I was giving up a good deal of security. I had tenure and the department where I worked had always accorded creative writing full status within its undergraduate and postgraduate courses. Compared to some writers in the academy, therefore, I had a good deal. I knew about the risks, having taught seminars on the facts and figures of professional writing. Furthermore, I was a single parent, and on the surface my decision might have been seen as irresponsible. The full process of decision-making took about six months before I handed in my notice. I bore in mind the following factors:

- I had already published seven books and had two more awaiting publication, so I was not leaving in a burst of optimism after my first publishing deal. I was already fully acquainted with the insecurities of the publishing world.
- I had recently made the move into children's fiction, and my books for children were rather more popular than my books for adults.
- A number of children's writers I had met were doing regular workshops at schools and libraries, thus earning a decent supplementary income. These outlets seemed more available to writers of children's fiction than to writers of adult fiction.

- I was already receiving requests to appear at festivals and schools that I had to turn down because of my university job. It was becoming more and more difficult to commit fully to both professional fields.
- However demanding these supplementary activities might become, they would at least promote my name and sell my books, thus indirectly furthering my writing career.
- I had published in several areas of writing, including articles and short stories, and was prepared to keep up this 'portfolio' approach to my writing career.
- I was used to living on a 'shoestring' budget and was worried that if I became too accustomed to a good regular salary I might never take the risk of leaving.
- The chance to earn a living as a writer would only be there as long as I was actively publishing. In all likelihood a freelance career would not see me through to retirement and at some point I might have to get a different job, but I did not want to miss the opportunity by waiting another few years.

This was early in 2004. I maintained a career as a freelance writer for nine years. Despite occasionally missing the social nature of the academy, and enduring days when I felt totally blocked in my writing, insecure about the future and so on, I do not regret my decision. When I look back on my early work, I can see where the constant interruptions of family life and the pressures of an academic career took their toll. In other words, my writing seemed to improve once I was able to commit to it fully.

There were times, however, when I took on such a large number of professional engagements at schools or festivals that I could not commit to it fully. It is hard to turn down work as a freelance writer. Also, the unexpected happened; the next novel that I wanted to write was for adults, not children. At the same time, schools were cutting down their budgets for visiting writers, and I was not advertising myself because so much time was devoted to my new book. It was a risk to write it when I had not published any adult fiction for several years. And initially, predictably, I could not place.

This was in 2012, the year dominated by *Fifty Shades of Grey*, when most other books seemed to slip by unnoticed. And there were other alarming developments for the writer. Following a court case, Hachette took the decision to ask their authors to make changes to their manuscripts before offering a contract. The issue of rights reversion has become controversial. Many publishers are no longer willing to allow rights to out-of-print books to revert to the author in case they can make sales from ebooks or small print runs. In these and in other, subtly corrosive ways, it seems that the 'authority' and independence of the author is being undermined; that what is important is the survival of the publishing industry in an era when literature is no longer the dominant cultural medium.

The process of waiting to place my new novel changed my vision of what a writer is. My early dream of self-sufficiency as a writer now seemed to be a dream of dependency on an extremely unstable and unpredictable world. Accordingly, I took a permanent academic post at a different university. Now I can say, in all honesty, that I would rather be dependent on the academic world than on the world of publishing.

I was lucky. Shortly after taking the new job, my novel was accepted by Penguin, and I am currently writing the sequel. Once again I am in an environment sympathetic to writers, but where the mental energy required is similar to that used for writing. I attempt to not let teaching dominate my writing but, in order to do the job properly, it is necessary to engage creatively with the student.

I believe that most writers would recognise Melville's sentiments quoted at the start of this chapter. They want to commit fully to the writing process, they are in search of the 'silent, grass-growing mood' that the pressures of modern life rarely permit. They do not, however, want to turn into professional 'hacks', or for their writing to suffer in the process. Both Elizabeth Gaskell and Herman Melville were making their observations on professional writing in 1851. Since then the world has changed dramatically, though it does seem that the writer is still damned by dollars, euros, bahts etc. The ways in which individual writers negotiate this problem have also changed and are as infinitely varied as the writers themselves. But we do not seem to be any closer to a solution.

References

ALCS (Authors Licensing and Collecting Society) (2013), *What are Words Worth? Counting the cost of a writing career in the 21st century: a survey of 25,000 writers*, http://www.alcs.co.uk/CMSPages/GetFile.aspx?nodeguid=2004f4fa-54de-4aa3-9d4f-773e6aa112a1 (accessed 18 July 2013).

Baverstock, Alison (2000), *How to Market Books*, London: Kogan Page.

Baverstock, Alison (2001), *Marketing Your Book: An Author's Guide*, London: A & C Black.

DuVergne Smith, Nancy (1995), *The Freelance Writers' Lot: The NWU American Writers Survey Profiles*, New York: National Writers Union.

Federation of European Publishers (2012), 'European Book Publishing Statistics', http://www.sne.fr/img/pdf/Doc%20pour%20Flash%20et%20Lettre/European-book-publishing-stat2011.pdf (accessed 31 July 2013).

Griffin, Victoria (2001), 'Take the Lead', *The Author*, CXII:2, 59–60.

Nielsen BookScan (2010), press release, http://www.nielsenbookscan.co.uk/uploads/press/NielsenBook_BookProductionFigures3_Jan2010.pdf (accessed 11 September 2013).

Pool, Kate (2000), 'Love, Not Money', *The Author*, CXI:2, 58–66.

Olsen, Tillie (1980), *Silences*, London: Virago.

Shepherd, Lloyd (2011), 'The Death of Books Has Been Greatly Exaggerated', *The Guardian* (30 August 2011), http://www.theguardian.com/books/2011/aug/30/death-books-exaggerated (accessed 31 July 2013).

Taylor, Debbie, (2002), 'The Age of the Bestseller', *Mslexia*, 12, 7–10.

Uglow, Jenny (1993), *Elizabeth Gaskell*, London: Faber.

US Department of Labor (2010), 'Writers and Authors', http://www.bls.gov/ooh/media-and-communication/writers-and-authors.htm#tab-5 (accessed 1 October 2013).

Glossary

The glossary provides brief definitions of terms or acronyms which occur in *The Handbook* and which may be unfamiliar. Definitions are given within the context in which the terms appear, rather than attempting to provide a comprehensive, dictionary-style gloss. Names in brackets refer to chapters/authors in the book where there is some related discussion.

Academy A term broadly referring to institutions involved in teaching and research in Higher Education.

Alumni Graduates of Higher Education.

Analytical essay Sometimes required as part of a creative writing course, it is usually a critical essay analysing published or produced work. (Newman; McCracken)

Arvon Course (UK) Creative writing courses in the UK run by the Arvon Foundation.

Assessment pattern 'A list of the written, practical (if any), oral (if any) and online (if any) assignments you will be required to submit in order to graduate' (Newman).

Automatic writing A type of writing which strives to forego 'conscious intention' on the part of the writer, in an attempt to tap into either the subconscious or other voices, for example, as might be experienced whilst in an altered state of consciousness. (Kunin; Field)

Avant-garde In general this refers to the work of artists, writers, musicians etc. which is considered new and original, 'ahead' of, or at least 'outside', what is regarded mainstream or traditional at a particular time. It is also therefore sometimes used to describe 'experimental' work. (Kunin; Field)

AWP (US) Association of Writers and Writing Programs. The main body in the US representing the interests of writers in education. www.awpwriter.org

Beat sheet/Beat document (US/UK) A sheet used to identify the main dramatic points in a script. (Duncan)

Blog A contraction of 'web-log'. An individual (or small group) diary that is 'unmediated' and made available on the web and exists as an open forum inviting feedback, discussion and opinion. (Sheard; Treleaven)

'Calling card' Work which can be presented to an agent or producer which showcases a writer's ability and potential, although (particularly with script) itself is unlikely to be made. (Friedmann; Brodie)

Chatroom A means of students (and tutors) communicating with each other in a 'virtual' space, that is, via the Internet, designed to encourage debate and (sometimes) a forum for discussion of each other's work. (Treleaven)

Close reading This is an approach to the interpretation and understanding of literature developed in education in the UK which concentrates on the qualities 'inherent' within the writing itself, rather than a reliance on contextual knowledge, to inform appreciation or criticism. Its methods are similar to those of New Criticism in the US. (Ramey)

Collage At one time part of avant-garde experimentalism, historically the technique is an assemblage of different media, for example, newspaper cut-outs, bits of textile, etc., stuck together on a canvas. The 'cut-and-paste' method has moved across to other arts, including literature. (Kunin; Field)

Contact hours The actual amount of hours a student will be in a workshop, seminar or tutorial with the tutor, as opposed to 'self-directed' study, for instance, where the student works independently of the tutor.

Copyright Assignment of ownership to artistic work or similar. See specifically the chapter on 'Copyright', Humphrey with Penhaligan, and also chapters by Sheard, Wolff and Brodie.

Craft lecture (US) A lecture devoted to some aspect of the craft of writing.

Creative nonfiction Originating in the US, but now widespread, this is a type of writing typified by a literary approach to factual material. (Gutkind)

Critical commentary Sometimes students are asked to provide a critical analysis to accompany their creative writing submissions. The commentary itself is not usually graded but can inform the marker's opinion of the work. Also called 'Supplementary Discourse'. (Newman)

Curricula The learning, teaching and assessment that forms a programme or course.

Cut-up(s) Printed text is 'cut up' and then mixed and re-arranged to generate new and surprising material. See also 'fold-in'. (Kunin; Field)

Defamiliarisation Originating with a group of Russian artists, writers and critics, 'defamiliarisation' means making familiar objects or ideas appear 'strange' ('making strange' is another version) so that we see them in a new light and come to a different/improved understanding or perception of those objects or ideas.

Dirty Realism A style of North-American prose-writing dating from the 1970s and 1980s which uses a pared-down language in the manner of minimalism. Writers associated with it include Richard Ford, Raymond Carver and Tobias Wolff. Issue 8 of *Granta* magazine, 'Dirty Realism' (June 1983), is credited with bringing it to a wider audience.

EIS (UK) Enterprise Investment Scheme, a government tax-based incentive used to fund films (Friedmann.)

Experimental writing Writing that self-consciously operates outside mainstream or traditional literature and attempts to break those strictures, or writing that tries to do things that haven't been done before. (See specifically the chapters by Thalia Field and Aaron Kunin; also see Lauri Ramey's chapter, which argues that creative-writing courses often foreground as valuable to their programmes many of the elements of experimental writing – 'such as exploration, unpredictability, uncertainty of outcome, and innovation' – without naming it 'experimental'. See also Sampson, Sargent, Sheard, Bassnett.)

First-person narrative A piece of writing delivered in the 'first person', for example, 'I was born in the year 1632, in the city of York, of a good family' (Defoe, *Robinson Crusoe*). Usually regarded as offering a more intense perspective for the author and reader, but with the danger of being too narrow a viewpoint to sustain interest at length unless handled very carefully. (Chapters on prose writing. See also Smith, 'The Literary Agent [Novel]'.)

Flash Fiction Short prose-fiction narratives, generally of a thousand words or less. (Williams)

Fold-in A sheet of printed text is folded and then the artist reads across the resulting mismatch. In essence a less violent variant of the cut-up technique. (Kunin; Field)

Formative assessment Assessment that contributes to the development of the student's work: 'Formative assessment is not linked to a mark, and focuses on strengths and points for improvement' (Newman; compare 'Summative Assessment').

Forums 'Noticeboard-style text-based discussion sites, usually centred around a common interest'. (Treleaven; Sheard)

Free indirect discourse A style of narration which is technically third person but limited to the perspective or thoughts of one character, and is thus somewhere in-between first- and third person. (Dale)

Genre Literature is often subdivided according to 'genre', that is, certain types of literature are grouped together. The main generic divisions are into 'drama', 'prose' and 'poetry'. The term also exists (confusingly) to cover what are sometimes called 'sub-genres'. For example 'science fiction' and 'romance' are genres of writing, and are sometimes classed as 'genre fiction', which in turn may be further divided, for example, Robert Heinlein's 'Military SF'. (Rain; Crawford; Dale; Kiteley)

Genre Fiction Used to define a writing which has well-defined parameters, for example 'Science Fiction' and 'Fantasy' (see the chapter on 'Genre'). Sometimes used disparagingly to classify writing that is formulaic rather than original, as opposed to 'literary fiction'. (Crawford; Dale; Hubbard)

Hypertext Strictly speaking, texts which link to other texts. Most commonly found on the web, where words, phrases and documents are 'linked' to other words, phrases, websites and documents. 'HTML', the predominant 'code' which underpins web pages, stands for 'hyper-text mark-up language'. The term is also used sometimes to refer to the contemporary ('postmodern') understanding of the way writing functions in general: texts, rather than being 'unique', are regarded as part of a vast web of 'textuality', with each text connected to, and the result of, many other texts.

Iambic pentameter A line of verse containing five iambs. An iamb is a metrical 'foot' consisting of an unstressed syllable followed by a stressed syllable; for example, 'rĕgrét' (with the rhythm 'de dum') is iambic, where ˘ represents an unstressed syllable, and ´ a stressed one. 'Iambic pentameter' therefore signifies five iambs for a line and (historically) is undoubtedly the favoured metrical line in English poetry. This, from Pope's 'Eloisa to Abelard', will serve as an example: 'Back through the paths of pleasing sense I ran', which, using the notation suggested, would be:

Băck thróugh | thĕ páths | ŏf pléa | sĭng sénse | Ĭ rán

(See W. N. Herbert's chapter on 'Form in Poetry' for a much fuller explanation. See also Pattison.)

Internet The global interconnection of computer networks which shares and communicates electronic information. Information can be in the form of documents, emails, webcasts etc. It is distinct from 'the Web', with which it is sometimes mistakenly interchanged. The Web ('World Wide Web') refers specifically to the interconnection (via hyperlinks and URLs) of (html) documents.

Iowa Writers' Workshop (US) Usually recognised as the pioneer of creative-writing teaching in Higher Education. (Leahy, Cantrell and Swander)

ISBN International Standard Book Number. Sometimes regarded as a measure of status. (Sheard)

Language poetry A type of poetry associated with a wide range of North American poets, emergent in the late 1960s and early 1970s and still very influential. The tendency is for texts which focus on the technical resources of language at the expense of accessibility, and thus overtly require much 'input' from the reader to 'create' meaning, rather than finding meaning or the lyrical expression of emotion within the poem. Sometimes referred to as L=A=N=G=U=A=G=E poetry/poets, although strictly speaking this is the name of the journal associated with some of the poets which ran 1978–80. (Kunin; Field)

Lipogram A work written with a letter or group of letters missing. The most famous example is probably Georges Perec's novel *La Disparition* (1969), which omits the letter 'e', the commonest letter in English. (Kunin)

Literary fiction A term used to describe 'original writing', as opposed to 'genre fiction', and sometimes regarded as embodying higher aesthetic values and literary worth.

Low-residency Some courses are taught as 'low-residency', that is, much of the teaching is done via 'distance learning', using the Internet, email, telephone etc., with one or two weeks devoted to a meeting of all those on the programme, usually for an intense series of workshops.

MA Master of Arts. In the UK, postgraduate masters are Master of Arts. In the US the degree is an MFA, Master of Fine Arts. (Harper; Dawson)

Magic realism A style of writing, usually regarded as originating in South America, which treats fantastical material in a realist fashion. Magical realists include Borges, Marquez, and, in Europe, Kafka.

Major (US) A term designating the main subject taken by a student.

Man Booker (UK) Previously 'The Booker', a prize awarded annually for the best original English-language novel by a member of the Commonwealth or Republic of Ireland. There is now (since 2005) also the International Man Booker, for which any novelist in the world is eligible.

Memoir 'A story *from* a life', as distinct from autobiography, which attempts to cover the whole of a life. (Barrington)

MFA Master of Fine Arts. Title of the postgraduate degree in the US. (Harper; Dawson)

Microblog A short blog. (Treleaven)

Microfiction Another term for Flash Fiction. (Williams)

Modernism An umbrella term for a group of artists, writers and thinkers at the end of the nineteenth century/beginning of the twentieth, mainly concentrated in Europe but with significant American input. Although the term covers a wide range of artistic projects which might seem to have little in common, much of it is characterised by an attempt to break with what were then more traditional, 'realist' methods of representation. There is an increasing focus on the tools of representation rather than on what is being represented: Conrad uses 'time-shifts' to upset linearity, and 'unreliable narrators' to question methods of narration; Gertrude Stein dismantles and reconfigures grammatical structures and syntax. (Earnshaw)

Nanofiction Another term for Flash Fiction. (Williams)

Naturalism A style of writing mainly associated with French novelists like Zola which narrates using detailed 'concrete' description in a neutral, objective or scientific manner.

New Criticism An approach to literature developed in the US which placed an emphasis on qualities 'inherent' in the writing itself, rather than relying on biographical or other contextual information for interpretation. Its counterpart in the UK was Practical Criticism. (Ramey)

One-to-one tutorials This is where a student gets individual feedback on his or her work, as opposed to feedback in a workshop or seminar setting where there are other students present.

Oulipo *Ouvroir pour la littérature potentielle* (Workshop for Potential Literature). A French group, part of whose interest was in the application of rules for generating literature. (Kunin)

Pedagogy Relating to teaching and the principles of teaching.

Peer review In the context of creative-writing programmes, this usually refers to the critiquing of work by fellow students, such as happens in workshops.

PEN International PEN is the 'worldwide association of writers' which 'exists to promote friendship and intellectual co-operation among writers everywhere, to fight for freedom of expression and represent the conscience of world literature' (website). It exists as both an international literary organisation and a human-rights organisation. www.internationalpen.org.uk

Pitch A concise presentation of a project to a (hopefully) interested party, as in 'pitching a film' to a potential producer or funder.

Plagiarism Knowingly taking the work of others and passing it off as your own. (Newman for educational context; Kunin for 'creative' use of others' work; Humphrey, with Penhaligan, for infringement of copyright; Shapcott.)

Point of view The angle from which a story is told, for example, the child's point of view or a particular character, or first, second or third person. (Rogers; Dale; Kilian)

Portfolio This usually refers to the body of work that the student builds up throughout the degree – a collection of his or her best writing. A portfolio might also be required as part of the application when applying for entrance to a creative-writing MA or MFA.

Postmodernism Usually refers to a type of art which emerged in the late 1950s/early 1960s. In opposition to modernist art, which it saw as its immediate predecessor, it is nevertheless likewise an umbrella term for many different practices. However, characteristic of postmodern art and literature are: self-referentiality – works which refer to themselves or refer to their existence 'in the real world'; intertextuality – an embrace, through allusion and cannibilisation, of the idea that all texts are related to all other texts; a dismantling of the tools and techniques of art rather than 'hiding' them, for example, pointing out to the reader/viewer that they are reading a novel/watching film; an attack on received notions of 'self' and 'identity'; an attack on the notion of absolute Truth in favour of 'individual' or 'local' truths; relativism; a collapse of the high art/low art distinction.

Poststructuralism Related to, though not synonymous with, postmodernism. The term mainly refers to a body of critical and theoretical work which came to the fore in a number of different academic disciplines in the late 1950s/early 1960s. Structuralism was a belief that 'structures' underpin the world at all levels, so that in the field of anthropology rituals could be described in terms of binary oppositions ('the raw and the cooked'), meaning in language was a function of 'signifier' and 'signified', and poems could be read as sets of oppositions established by the texts. Poststructuralism 'undid' structures by questioning the terms of oppositions. For example, for the poststructuralist, the opposition male/female, rather than identifying two genders which can be defined according to natural, essential elements, are seen to be co-dependent ('male' cannot be defined without 'female'). The consequence of this is that all 'meaning', all 'truth', all 'identity' are only ever provisional and transient.

Print-on-Demand (POD) Technology which allows for books to be printed 'one at a time, as required, with no stock having to be printed in advance and then stored'. (Rowland)

QAA (England and Wales) Quality Assurance Agency for Higher Education. In England and Wales, the body that oversees standards in higher education. (Newman)

Residentials Creative-writing programmes taught as low-residency or distance learning often have a 'residential' element where students on the course meet together for a short amount of time (1–2 weeks), either at the Institution itself or a 'writer's retreat'.

Richard and Judy Show (UK) A popular daytime TV magazine programme in the UK (2001–9).

Romanticism An intellectual and aesthetic 'movement' in the second half of the eighteenth century, first half of the nineteenth, originating in Europe, and characterised by an interest in the self and emotion, often at the expense of what was regarded as the preceding orthodoxy of society and reason. The French Revolution was often seen as emblematic of, and a spur to, Romanticism.

Short-short story Another term for Flash Fiction. (Williams)

Slush pile When publishers receive material which they have not asked to see, that is, when they receive work which has not been commissioned but has been sent in speculatively, these novels, poetry, scripts are put on the 'slush pile'. The fate of submissions consigned to the slush pile is open to great debate and rumour, but it is usually accepted that it will be at the bottom of the list of things for publishers to look at, especially for established publishers or agents.

Social media 'Social media is the name given to internet websites which combine a high amount of user-generated content with the opportunity to make connections with other users'. (Treleaven; Baverstock)

Social networking Networking via social media. (Treleaven)

Sudden fiction Another term for Flash Fiction. (Williams)

Summative assessment Assessment used to determine the student's progress or achievement at the end of a course, and usually used to give a mark and/or grade.

Supplementary discourse See 'Critical commentary'.

Tenure When an academic post is made secure it is said to be 'tenured'. This is regarded as important in that such job security is seen to ensure academic freedom.

Third-person narrative A narrative which uses a perspective 'outside' of the characters and allows for the possibility of a more objective or neutral point of view, and can be seen as more flexible than first person since all necessary information can be provided without the constraints of only seeing things through one pair of eyes. The opening to Jane Austen's *Emma* is third person, although the tone is not quite neutral: 'Emma Woodhouse, handsome, clever, and rich, with a comfortable home and happy disposition, seemed to unite some of the best blessings of existence; and had lived nearly twenty-one years in the world with very little to distress or vex her'.

Twitter A popular site for microblogging. (Treleaven)

Voice A commonly-used term with two main meanings. (1) Students are often encouraged to 'find their voice', which tends to mean a writing-style which is unique to them. (2) Writing which involves creating 'characters' is often looking for the 'voice' which makes a character distinctive, usually through dialogue. (Rogers; Dale; Hubbard; Brown)

Web, The Shorthand for 'World Wide Web', the 'www' that often prefixes web-addresses.

This describes the connection of web pages to one another and is part of the Internet. (Sheard)

WordPress A popular site for blogging. (Treleaven)

Workshop The standard way of teaching creative writing is via workshops, which usually involves students offering their writing for critique from fellow students and a guiding tutor. (Newman; McCracken)

Writer's & Artists' Yearbook (UK) Published annually by A&C Black, this lists publishing houses, magazines, agents, and includes useful articles.

Useful Websites

AHRC (Arts and Humanities Research Council; UK) www.ahrc.ac.uk. The main funding body for students taking postgraduate degrees in the UK.

Arts Council (UK) 'Arts Council England is the national development agency for the arts in England, distributing public money from Government and the National Lottery'. Funds individual artists as well as art groups, projects and institutions. www.artscouncil.org.uk

Australia Council for the Arts 'The Australia Council is the Australian Government's arts funding and advisory body. It directly supports young, emerging and established artists, as well as new and established'. www.australiacouncil.gov.au

AWP (US) Association of Writers and Writing Programs. The main advocacy body in the US for writers in education. 'The mission of The Association of Writers & Writing Programs is to foster literary talent and achievement, to advance the art of writing as essential to a good education, and to serve the makers, teachers, students, and readers of contemporary writing'. www.awpwriter.org

Canada Council for the Arts Arts funding body in Canada. www.canadacouncil.ca

'Diversity' website Has an archive of radio broadcasts. www.suttonelms.org.uk

English Subject Centre (UK) Although it ceased to operate in 2011, its website is maintained by CCUE and has resources relating to the teaching of creative writing. www.english.heacademy.ac.uk

Film Genres www.filmsite.org/genres.html

Gradschools.com (US/World) Comprehensive listing of graduate programmes in the US; also has listing of postgraduate creative-writing courses outside the US. www.gradschools.com

NAWE (UK) 'The National Association of Writers in Education (NAWE) is the one organisation supporting the development of creative writing of all genres and in all educational and community settings throughout the UK'. www.nawe.co.uk

New Writing The International Journal for the Practice and Theory of Creative Writing. www.tandfonline.com/loi/rmnw#.Ul05G3fSnVW

PEN International A world organisation for writers devoted to intellectual and human-rights issues. www.pen-international.org.uk

Poetry Magazines (UK) Run by the Poetry Library in London. www.poetrymagazines.org.uk

Poetry Book Society (UK) 'Founded by T. S. Eliot in 1953, the Poetry Book Society (PBS) is an organisation devoted to developing and maintaining a readership for poetry in the UK'. www.poetrybooks.co.uk

The Poetry Society (UK) 'The Poetry Society is a membership-based and Arts Council England-funded registered charity, whose stated aims are to promote the study, use and enjoyment of poetry'. www.poetrysociety.org.uk

Poets and Writers (US) Main site for writers in the US. Publishes the *Poets and Writers Magazine*. www.pw.org

Scriptorama (US) A site providing hundreds of film scripts. www.script-o-rama.com

Scriptwriter Magazine www.scriptwritermagazine.com

TEXT (Australia) Electronic journal for the Australasian Association of Writing Programs (AAWP). www.textjournal.com.au

UK Council for Graduate Education www.ukcge.ac.uk

UK Film Council industry.bfi.org.uk

Writers Guild of America www.wga.org

Contributors

Judith Barrington's books include *Lifesaving: A Memoir* (2000), winner of the Lambda Book Award, and *Writing the Memoir: from Truth to Art* (2nd ed., 2002). In addition, she has published five collections of poetry and in 2013 won the Gregory O'Donoghue Poetry Prize at the International Spring Poetry Festival in Cork, Ireland. In 2012, she was visiting writer at Stanford University and has taught literary memoir on the faculty of the MFA Program at the University of Alaska, Anchorage, and at the Almassera in Spain. She grew up in Sussex and now lives in Oregon.

Susan Bassnett is Professor of Comparative Literature and Special Advisor for Translation Studies at the University of Warwick. Recent publications include *Translation Studies* (4th ed., 2013), *Translation* in the Routledge New Critical Idiom series (2013), *Reflections on Translation* (2011), *Ted Hughes* (2010) and, co-edited with Peter Bush, *The Translator as Writer* (2006). A collection of her poetry and translations, *Exchanging Lives* was published in 2002. In addition to her academic writing, Susan is also a journalist and poet and is a Fellow of the Royal Society of Literature.

Alison Baverstock is Course Leader for MA Publishing at Kingston University. A former publisher, she has researched and written widely about the industry and the role of the author and her most recent research has been into self-publishing. She is the author of many titles, including *Is There a Book in You?* (2006), *The Naked Author: A Guide to Self-publishing* (2011) and *Are Books Different?* (1993). In 2007 she was presented with the Pandora Award for services to the publishing industry. www.alisonbaverstock.com

Timothy Braun is an American writer and teacher living in Austin, Texas. You can learn more about him at timothybraun.com

Alan Brodie is Managing Director of Alan Brodie Representation Ltd, a literary agency specialising in writers working in theatre, radio, film and television and in playwrights' estates (www.alanbrodie.com). He is Chair of the Trustees of the Noel Coward Foundation and a Trustee of Chichester Festival Theatre. Alan served as co-chair of the Personal Managers' Association, the trade association for UK talent agencies across the UK, from 2004 to 2009.

Alan Brown writes for children across a wide age range. His books for younger children include the picture books *Never Lie on a Lion* and *Love-a-Duck*, and story books such as *A Dog of My Own* and *The Incredible Journey of Walter Rat*. Books for older children include *Sword and Sorcery* and *Michael and the Monkey King* (both now Kindle ebooks) and narrative non-fiction such as *Tolpuddle Boy*. *Turtle's Song* celebrates the life of a green turtle and gained awards in Australia. Alan works on creative writing with children and adults in writing groups, schools and libraries.

Mary Cantrell is an Associate Professor of English at Tulsa Community College. Her publications include 'Teaching and evaluation: why bother?' in *Power and Identity in the Creative Writing Classroom: The Authority Project* (2005). She has presented several papers at the Associated Writing Program's annual conference and has served as a fiction editor for *Nimrod* International Literary Journal for over fifteen years.

Gareth Creer is Head of Writing at Liverpool John Moores University and runs 'Free To Write', a project which works with inmates and ex-offenders. His novels, *Skin and Bone*, *Cradle To Grave* and *Big Sky* are published in English and in translation and he has also written for the *New Statesman*, *Sunday Times* and *Daily Telegraph*. His short fiction has been published widely and he is author, under another name, of the Staffe series of novels, published in nine languages.

John Dale is the author of six books including the best-selling *Huckstepp*, two crime novels and a memoir, *Wild Life*, an investigation into the fatal shooting of his grandfather in 1940s Tasmania. He has edited two anthologies, *Out West* and *Car Lovers*, and co-edited a third anthology, *Best on Ground*. His most recent novel, *Leaving Suzie Pye*, was translated into Turkish. He is Professor of Writing at the University of Technology Sydney.

Paul Dawson is the author of *Creative Writing and the New Humanities* (2005) and *The Return of the Omniscient Narrator: Authorship and Authority in Twenty-first Century Fiction* (2013). He has also published a collection of poems, *Imagining Winter* (2006), which won the national IP Picks Best Poetry Award in Australia. Paul is a Senior Lecturer in the School of the Arts and Media at the University of New South Wales.

Stephen V. Duncan is a Professor at Loyola Marymount University in Los Angeles, California. His credits include co-creator of the CBS–TV drama series *Tour of Duty*; writer-producer, ABC–TV drama series *A Man Called Hawk*; and co-writer of the TNT original movie *The Court-Martial of Jackie Robinson*. He is the author of *A Guide to Screenwriting Success: Writing for Film and Television* (2006) and *Genre Screenwriting: How to Write Popular Screenplays That Sell* (2008).

Steven Earnshaw is Professor of English Literature at Sheffield Hallam University. His publications include *Beginning Realism* (2010), *Existentialism* (2006), *The Pub in Literature* (2000) and *The Direction of Literary Theory* (1996). He was previously Head of English at Sheffield Hallam University and Course Leader of its MA Writing.

Thalia Field has published three books – *Point and Line* (2000), *Incarnate: Story Material* (2004) and *Bird Lovers, Backyard* (2010) – as well as a 'performance novel', *ULULU:*

Clown Shrapnel (2007) and a book-length essay, *A Prank of Georges* (2010, co-authored with Abigail Lang). Thalia is on the Literary Arts faculty at Brown University.

Julian Friedmann is Joint Managing Director of the Blake Friedmann Literary, Film & Television Agency. He is author of *How to Make Money Scriptwriting* (2nd ed., 2000), editor of the two-volume *Writing Long-running Television Series* and Editor of Europe's leading scriptwriting magazine, *ScriptWriter*. He designed and set up PILOTS to train writers and script editors in developing long-running television series for the EU MEDIA Programme and the MA in Television Scriptwriting at De Montfort University in Leicester. He teaches all over Europe.

Lee Gutkind is the author or editor of more than two dozen books of, and is founder and editor of, *Creative Nonfiction*, the first and largest literary magazine to publish non-fiction, exclusively. He is Distinguished Writer in Residence, at the Consortium Science, Policy & Outcomes and Professor in the Hugh Downs School of Human Communication at Arizona State University. Lee has pioneered the teaching of creative non-fiction, conducting workshops and presenting readings throughout the world. His most recent book is *You Can't Make This Stuff Up: The Complete Guide to Writing Creative Nonfiction – from Memoir to Literary Journalism and Everything in Between* (2012).

Graeme Harper is a Professor of Creative Writing and Dean of The Honors College at Oakland University, Michigan, and an honorary professor in the UK. His work includes *The Blackwell Companion to Creative Writing* (2013), *Inside Creative Writing* (2012), *On Creative Writing* (2010), and, as Brooke Biaz, *The Invention of Dying* (2013), *Moon Dance* (2010) and *Small Maps of the World* (2006). He is Editor of *New Writing: the International Journal for the Practice and Theory of Creative Writing*.

Mike Harris is a Senior Lecturer on the MA Writing at Sheffield Hallam University. He is a scriptwriter and theatre director who has written for stage, radio and television.

W. N. Herbert is Professor of Poetry and Creative Writing at Newcastle University. He has published seven volumes of poetry and four pamphlets and he is widely anthologised. He contributed the 'Writing Poetry' section to the Open University's *Creative Writing: A Workbook with Readings* (2006) and his collection, *Bad Shaman Blues* (2006), was a Poetry Book Society Recommendation.

Susan Hubbard's seven books include *The Society of S* (2007), *The Year of Disappearances* (2008) and *The Season of Risks* (2010). Her two short-fiction collections received national awards in the United States. She has served as Writer in Residence at several universities and artists' colonies. Her fiction has been translated and published in over fifteen countries. Susan is Professor of English at the University of Central Florida. www.susanhubbard.com

Shay A. Humphrey is a partner at Rider, Weiner & Frankel, PC in New Windsor, New York, with her practice focused on corporate and intellectual property law. She earned her undergraduate degree from Vassar College and her law degree from the University of Florida, College of Law. She has been an instructor for Pace University, teaching its Legal Aspects of Publishing course.

Crawford Kilian is a retired instructor who taught Communications at Capilano College, North Vancouver, for forty years. He has published twenty-one books, including eleven novels, and hundreds of articles. He is a contributing editor at *The Tyee*, an online magazine in Vancouver. His recent books include the Fourth Edition of *Writing for the Web* (2009) and Second Edition of *Writing Science Fiction and Fantasy* (2007).

Brian Kiteley teaches in the Creative Writing PhD program at the University of Denver. He has published three novels, *The River Gods* (2009), *Still Life with Insects* (1990), and *I Know Many Songs, but I Cannot Sing* (1996); and two books of fiction exercises, *The 3 A.M. Epiphany* (2005) and *The 4 A.M. Breakthrough* (2009).

Aaron Kunin is the author of two books of poems, *Folding Ruler Star* (2005) and *The Sore Throat and Other Poems* (2010). He is an Associate Professor of English at Pomona College in California.

Anna Leahy is the author of *Constituents of Matter* (2007), which won the Wick Poetry Prize. She edited *Power and Identity in the Creative Writing Classroom* (2005) and continues to publish widely in the areas of pedagogy and the profession. She has also published poetry and nonfiction and co-writes Lofty Ambitions blog. Anna teaches in the MFA and BFA programs at Chapman University, where she directs Tabula Poetica and is editor of *TAB: The Journal of Poetry & Poetics*.

Scott McCracken teaches English at Keele University. His is the author of *Masculinities, Modernist Fiction and the Urban Public Sphere* (2007) and co-editor of *The Cambridge Companion to Popular Fiction* (2012, with David Glover).

E. A. Markham (1939–2008) was a poet, short-story writer, dramatist and novelist. His publications included *A Rough Climate* (2002), which was short-listed for the T. S. Eliot Prize, and *Hinterland: Caribbean Poetry from the West Indies and Britain* (ed., 1989). He had a number of writing fellowships and was Professor Emeritus of Creative Writing, Sheffield Hallam University. In 1997 he was awarded the Certificate of Honour by the Government of Montserrat and in 2003 he was elected as a Fellow of the Royal Society of Literature.

Livi Michael is the author of six books for adults and eleven for children. Recent titles include *The Whispering Road* (2005) and *The Angel Stone* (2006). She has taught English and Creative Writing at Sheffield Hallam University, and currently teaches at Manchester Metropolitan University. For a number of years she was a freelance writer. Her books have won numerous awards.

John Milne trained as a painter at art school but has spent most of his working life as a writer. He is the author of nine novels, one work of non-fiction and over seventy hours of TV drama. As a novelist he won the John Llewellyn Rhys Prize, as a scriptwriter he has won a CWA Edgar and a Writer's Guild Award. He teaches Creative Writing at Sheffield Hallam University.

Mary Mount is Editorial Director at Viking/Penguin Books.

Brighde Mullins' plays include *The Bourgeois Pig* (2012), *Monkey in the Middle* (1999), *Those Who Can Do* (2007), *Topographical Eden* (1997), *Pathological Venus* (1995) and *Click* (2002). Her monologue *Somewhere Special (With You)* appears in *Monologues for Women by Women* (2005). Her plays have been produced in London, New York, San Francisco and Los Angeles. Her book of poems is *Water Stories* (2004). Awards include a Guggenheim, the Whiting Award, United States Artists and many others. She is Director of the Master of Professional Writing program (a multi-genre creative writing program) at the University of Southern California.

Linda Newbery's young adult novels *The Shell House* (2003) and *Sisterland* (2004) were both shortlisted for the Carnegie Medal, and *Set in Stone* was the Costa Children's Book of 2006. With Yvonne Coppard she is co-author of *Writing Children's Fiction: a Writers' and Artists' Companion* (2013) and she edits the teenage section of *Armadillo* on-line review magazine. In 2013 she published *Quarter Past Two on a Wednesday Afternoon*, her first novel for adults.

Jenny Newman is the author of two novels, *Going In* (1995) and *Life Class* (2000). She is the editor of *The Faber Book of Seductions* (1988) and co-editor of *The Writer's Workbook* (2004) and *Contemporary British and Irish Novelists* (2004). She has published widely on contemporary British and North American fiction, and on the teaching of creative writing, and her own short fiction has appeared in *The London Magazine*, *Riptide* and *Pen Pusher* and on BBC Radio 4.

Sean O'Brien's *Collected Poems* appeared in 2012. He is the author of seven collections of poetry, most recently *November* (2011). He has won the T.S. Eliot Prize, the Forward Prize (three times) and the E. M. Forster Award. His plays have been staged by the National Theatre and Live Theatre/RSC. His latest stage work is a verse translation of Tirso de Molina's *Don Gil of the Green Breeches* (2013). His short story collection *The Silence Room* appeared in 2008 and his novel *Afterlife* in 2009. He has translated Dante's *Inferno* (2006) and the poems of Corsino Fortes (2008). His critical writing includes *The Deregulated Muse* (1998) and *Journeys to the Interior: Ideas of England in Contemporary Poetry* (2012). *Train Songs*, an anthology of railway poems co-edited with Don Paterson, was published in 2013. Sean writes for *The Guardian*, *The Independent* and the *Times Literary Supplement* and is Professor of Poetry at Newcastle University.

Bonnie O'Neill has an MA in Film from San Francisco State University. She has written and consulted for feature films, TV, documentary and educational films and video. Bonnie is the producer and co-director of *Housewife in the Heart of Darkness* (2014). She teaches Film courses at Diablo Valley College and The Art Institute of California in San Francisco.

Pat Pattison is a Professor at Berklee College of Music, where he teaches Lyric Writing and Poetry. In addition to his four books, Pat has developed five online courses through berkleemusic.com and a songwriting MOOC through coursera.org. He has written over fifty articles for various magazines and blogs, and he continues to present songwriting clinics across the US, Canada, Australia, New Zealand, the UK and Europe. Several of his students have won Grammys, including John Mayer and Gillian Welch.

Lee Penhaligan is a Consultant Solicitor with Scott-Moncrieff & Associates Ltd (London) and Apex Law LLP (Kent) and specialises in all non-contentious media work, including advising, negotiating and drafting agreements for authors and other rights' owners. Lee qualified as a Solicitor in England and Wales in 1990 gaining First-Class Honours in her Solicitors' Final Examinations.

David Rain is an Australian writer who lives in London. His novels include *The Heat of the Sun* (2012), the story of Madame Butterfly's half-American child. As 'Tom Arden' he has published fantasy and science fiction including the five-volume *Orokon* sequence; he has also published poetry, short stories, columns and reviews, and taught literature and writing at the University of Adelaide, Queen's University of Belfast and the University of Brighton. He presently teaches at Middlesex University, London.

Lauri Ramey is Director of the Center for Contemporary Poetry and Poetics, and Professor of Creative Writing and English at California State University at Los Angeles. Her books include *Slave Songs and the Birth of African American Poetry* (2010), *The Heritage Series of Black Poetry* (2008), *Black British Writing* (2004, with R. Victoria Arana), *What I Say* (2010, with Aldon Lynn Nielsen) and *Every Goodbye Ain't Gone* (2006, with Aldon Lynn Nielsen). Her poetry has appeared in numerous journals including *nthposition*, *Poetrybay*, *Kansas Quarterly*, *NYCBigCityLit* and *Portland Review*.

Jane Rogers has written eight novels including *Mr Wroe's Virgins* (1991; dramatised as an award-winning BBC drama serial) and *Promised Lands* (1995; Writers Guild Best Fiction Award). *The Testament of Jessie Lamb* (2012) won the Arthur C. Clarke Award and has been translated into seven languages. Short story collection *Hitting Trees with Sticks* (2012) was shortlisted for the 2013 Edgehill Prize. Radio work includes original drama and adaptations. She is Professor of Writing at Sheffield Hallam University and Fellow of the Royal Society of Literature. www.janerogers.org

Jane Rowland is the editor of *The Self Publishing Magazine*, a quarterly print and digital magazine covering all aspects of self-publishing. She is the author of *Publishing and Printing Terminology for Self-Publishers* (2010) and the Marketing Director at Matador, working on behalf of self-publishing authors.

Fiona Sampson is Professor of Poetry at the University of Roehampton. She has published more than twenty books, including five collections of poetry, an edition of Shelley, and studies of contemporary British poetry and of music and poetics. Among her honours are the Newdigate Prize, a Cholmondeley award, various Poetry Book Society recommendations, Writer's Awards from the Arts Councils of England and Wales, and prizes in Macedonia and the US. She has been shortlisted twice for both the T. S. Eliot and Forward Prizes. Published in more than thirty languages, she is a Fellow of the Royal Society of Literature.

Linda Sargent works as a freelance writer/storyteller and publisher's reader. Published work includes *Paper Wings* (2010), fictional short stories for children and adults, and a non-fiction work, *Words and Wings: A Training Guide in Creative Reminiscence Work* (2002) commissioned by SEMLAC and Outreach and Partnerships, one of the guides in RESOURCE's Disability Portfolio.

Tom Shapcott is an Emeritus Professor who initiated the postgraduate Creative Writing course at the University of Adelaide from 1997 to 2005. He has written fifteen collections of poetry and six novels. He was director of the Australia Council's Literature Board for seven years, and Executive Director of the National Book Council (1992–7)

James Sheard is a poet with a long-standing interest in Net culture and practice. He has an MA Writing from Sheffield Hallam University. His pamphlet *Hotel Mastbosch* (2003) won the Ictus Prize and was PBS Pamphlet Choice for Winter 2003. His collection *Scattering Eva* (2005) was shortlisted for The Forward Prize for Best First Collection and his collection *Dammtor* (2010) was a Poetry Book Society Recommendation. He is Senior Lecturer for Creative Writing at Keele University.

David Smith is a partner at Annette Green Authors' Agency, established in 1998. An English graduate, he worked for several years as Distribution Manager for the Time Out Group before returning to college and retraining as a lawyer. His wife Annette Green founded their agency after leaving A. M. Heath, and David joined in 2000. They do not specialise, believing that the only criterion for judging a work of fiction or non-fiction should be its sheer quality.

Hazel Smith is a Research Professor in the Writing and Society Research Centre at the University of Western Sydney. She is author of several books, including *The Writing Experiment: Strategies for Innovative Creative Writing* (2005), and co-editor (with Roger T. Dean) of *Practice-led Research, Research-led Practice in the Creative Arts* (Edinburgh University Press, 2009). Hazel is also a poet, performer and new media artist. She has published three volumes of poetry including *The Erotics of Geography* (2008), a book and CD Rom; three CDs of performance work and numerous multimedia works.

Mary Swander is a Distinguished Professor at Iowa State University and is the Poet Laureate of Iowa. Her latest work is *Vang* (2013), a drama about recent immigrant farmers that is touring the United States and Europe. She has been teaching creative writing for thirty years throughout the US in schools, colleges and universities.

George Szirtes is a Reader in Creative Writing at the University of East Anglia. Poetry publications include *New and Collected Poems* (2008), *The Burning of the Books and Other Poems* (2009), *The Budapest File* (2000), *An English Apocalypse* (2001) and *Reel* (2004, winner of the T. S. Eliot Prize). He was trained as an artist and now works as poet, translator, editor, critic and teacher.

Lou Treleaven is a writer, artist and adult education teacher living in Bedfordshire. She blogs at www.loutreleaven.wordpress.com where she shares writing advice and opportunities. Her articles on the creative use of social media and backing up your work have been published by *Writing Magazine* and she enjoys writing scripts for her local drama group.

Chase Twichell's most recent book is *Horses Where the Answers Should Have Been: New & Selected Poems* (2010), which won both the Kingsley Tufts Award and the Balcones Poetry Prize. She is the author of six previous books, as well as the translator, with Tony K. Stewart, of *The Lover of God* (2003), and co-editor of *The Practice of Poetry: Writing Exercises from Poets who Teach* (1992).

Stephanie Vanderslice is Associate Professor in the Department of Writing and Speech at the University of Central Arkansas. Her most recent publications include essays in *Teaching Creative Writing* (2006, edited by Graeme Harper) and *Power and Identity in the Creative Writing Classroom* (2005), and she co-edited (with Kelly Ritter) *This is (not) Just to Say: Lore and Creative Writing Pedagogy* (2007). Stephanie also writes personal essays, fiction and children's fiction. She lives outside Little Rock, Arkansas with her husband and two sons.

Tony Williams's very short stories are collected in *All the Bananas I've Never Eaten: Tales of Love and Loneliness* (2012). His poetry collection *The Corner of Arundel Lane and Charles Street* (2009) was shortlisted for the Aldeburgh First Collection Prize, and *All the Rooms of Uncle's Head* (2011) was Poetry Book Society Pamphlet Choice. He teaches creative writing at Northumbria University.

Rebecca Wolff is the editor and publisher of *Fence*, a nonprofit literary journal published twice yearly since 1998, and Fence Books. For more about these publications visit www.fencemag.com and www.fencebooks.com. She is also the author of two books of poems, *Manderley* (2001) and *Figment* (2004). She lives with her family in the Hudson Valley of New York State.

Index

Page references in *italics* indicate a glossary term.